# The Pearson
# Custom Program for **CIS**

ITEC J264

Computer Applications in Business

University of South Carolina

**PEARSON**

**Senior Vice President, Editorial:** Patrick F. Boles
**Sponsoring Editors:** Ana Díaz-Caneja and David J. Maltby
**Development Editor:** Christina Martin
**Editorial Assistant:** Hannah Coker
**Operations Manager:** Eric M. Kenney
**Production Manager:** Jennifer Berry
**Art Director:** Renée Sartell
**Cover Designers:** Blair Brown and Kristen Kiley

*Cover Art:* Jerry Driendl/Getty Images, Inc.; Steve Bloom/Getty Images, Inc.; "Cheetah" courtesy of Marvin Mattelson/ Getty Images; "Tabs" courtesy of Andrey Prokhorov/iStockphoto; "Open Doors" courtesy of Spectral-Design/iStockphoto; "Compass" courtesy of Laurent Hamels/Getty Images; "Fortune Teller" courtesy of Ingvald Kaldhussaeter/iStockphoto; "Ladder of Success" courtesy of iStockphoto; "Global Communication in Blue" courtesy of iStockphoto.

This special edition published in cooperation with Pearson Learning Solutions.

Printed in the United States of America.

Please visit our website at *www.pearsonlearningsolutions.com.*

Attention bookstores: For permission to return any unsold stock, contact us at *pe-uscustomreturns@pearson.com.*

Pearson Learning Solutions, 501 Boylston Street, Suite 900, Boston, MA 02116
A Pearson Education Company
www.pearsoned.com

ISBN 10: 1-256-55904-0
ISBN 13: 978-1-256-55904-7

# Table of Contents

# Table of Contents

## 4. Reviewing Progress & Grades

    a. Grades

    b. Course Content Navigator

    c. Grades Area

    d. Viewing Submissions

## 5. Getting Help

    e. Tutor Service

    f. Student Product Support

    g. MyITLab Website

For more information, please visit **www.myitlab.com.**

Registering & Logging in

Navigating Your Course

Assignments & Tests

Reviewing Progress & Grades

Getting Help

# 1 | Registering and Logging In

Designed to help you succeed in your course, MyITLab provides you with a training and testing environment for Microsoft® Office applications, computer skills, and computer concepts.

## Registering for MyITLab

To access your MyITLab online course for the first time, you need to register and log in.

To register, you will need:

- A valid email address
- A Student Access Code
- A Course ID from your instructor
- Your school's ZIP code

To access MyITLab, go to **www.myitlab.com**.

> **Note:** Before using MyITLab on a personal computer, make sure your computer meets the system requirements. You can do this by running the **One-Step Installer & Launch** Tool; **click here** to access the tool. If you are using a computer in a lab at your school, the system will likely already meet all necessary requirements. For further information, **click here**.

- Click the **Student** button, under Register on the homepage.

Select "**Yes, I have an access code**" if you purchased your course materials and have the MyITLab Student Access Kit. If you do not have a Student Access Kit, select "**No, I need to buy access**" and you can purchase access online with a major credit card or pay pal account.

- After you make your selection, click **Next**.
- After reading the License and Privacy Agreement, click **I Accept** at the bottom right of the screen.

Registering &
Logging in

Navigating
Your Course

Assignments
& Tests

Reviewing
Progress & Grades

Getting Help

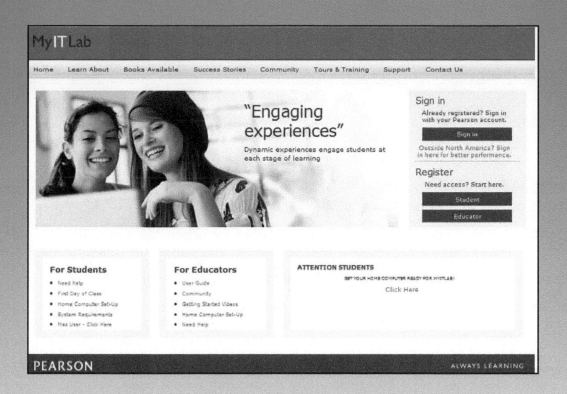

For more information, please visit **www.myitlab.com**.

On the Access Information Screen, you are asked whether you already have a Pearson Education Account. Select the option that applies to you:

- **Yes:** Select this option if you have previously registered for other Pearson online courses. If so, you may already have a login name and password. You can enter this information now.

- **No:** Select this option if you have never registered for a Pearson online course.

- **Not Sure:** Select this option if you aren't sure if you have a Pearson account. Enter your email address and click **Search**. If you have an account, your login information will be sent to your email address within a few moments. You can then change your selection to Yes, and enter your login name and password.

Once you have made your selection, you are ready to enter your access code. You can either type in your code or click **Switch to a single box for pasting your access code** to paste your code into the text box.

> **Note:** Make sure you enter your access code EXACTLY as it is written. Your accesscode will look like this example: PSPMIL-ABYSS-MAPLE-MEWED-CENTO-SIRES

Once you have entered your access code, click **Next** on the bottom right of the screen.

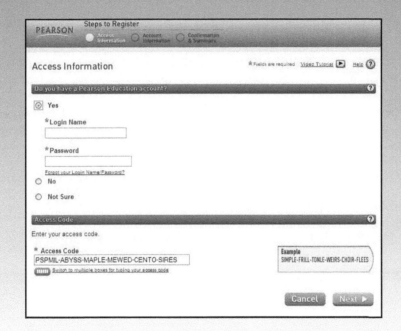

For more information, please visit **www.myitlab.com**.

Registering &
Logging in

Navigating
Your Course

Assignments
&Tests

Reviewing
Progress & Grades

Getting Help

If you have previously registered for a Pearson online course, your account information will automatically appear on the Account Information page. Otherwise, you will need to enter the information in the boxes. Be sure to use your full name and a valid email address.

In the School Location section, select United States from the School Country drop-down menu. Enter your school ZIP code, and then select your school from the drop-down list.

**Note:** If your school is not listed, make sure you entered the correct ZIP code for your school. If the ZIP code is correct, scroll to the bottom of the drop-down list, select Other, and enter your school name, city, and state.

In the next section of the page, you are asked to select a Security Question and Answer, in order to protect the privacy of your account.

- Once you are finished entering your information, click **Next** at the bottom right of the screen.

Your registration is now complete. Be sure to print this page for your records.

- Click on the **Print this Page** button at the top right of the screen.

**Note:** This information will also be emailed to you.

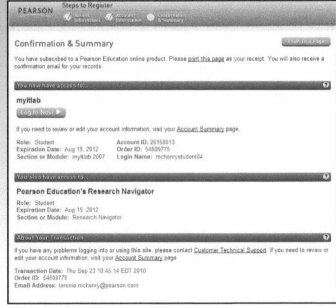

For more information, please visit **www.myitlab.com.**

## Home Computer Set-Up

The **NEW One-Step Installer and Launch Tool** will install all the necessary MyITLab files on your home machine, and make all important setting adjustments for you. It is a critical tool for your success in using MyITLab, as it is designed to make your experience with the product more simplistic.

The One-Step Tool will place an icon on your desktop that you will use for easy access to the MyITLab login page for the remainder of the term.

1. Click on the Home Computer Set-Up link found on the MyITLab homepage to download the One-Step Installer & Launch Tool.

2. When prompted, click **Run** to initiate the process (do not select 'Save').

3. Follow the prompts on the screen and complete each of the wizards to finish installing all necessary elements.

4. **Once complete, close ALL internet browser windows that you might have open.**

5. Locate the new Launch MyITLab icon now on your desktop. Double-click the icon and begin logging into MyITLab.

6. Please make sure all internet windows are closed and that you use the **Launch MyITLab** icon on your desktop **EVERY TIME** you login/access MyITLab for the rest of the term.
   (You do not need to access this One-Step Installer & Launch Tool download page anymore. Just use the icon on your desktop.) Ensuring a successful experience with MyITLab, the Launch MyITLab icon will perform the following actions:

   a. Empty your Temporary Internet Files.

   b. Set your screen resolution to the optimal setting for MyITLab (1024x768) and reset your screen resolution when Internet Explorer is closed.

   c. Launch Internet Explorer and take you to the MyITLab website.

**INTERNET EXPLORER 9 USERS:** When you click to download the One-Step Installer & Launch Tool you will receive a warning message in a new window. To continue with the installation, click the **Actions** button. On the next screen click **More Options** and then click **Run Anyway**. This process will NOT harm your computer.

*Should you experience difficulty in using the One-Step Installer & Launch Tool on your home machine, please contact Technical Support. You can also utilize the Basic Installation Wizard and Home Diagnostic Tool (found on the Home Computer Set-Up tab on the MyITLab Support tab) in addition to, or instead of the above tool.*

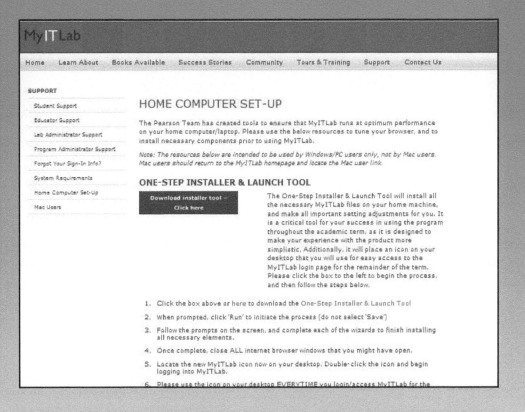

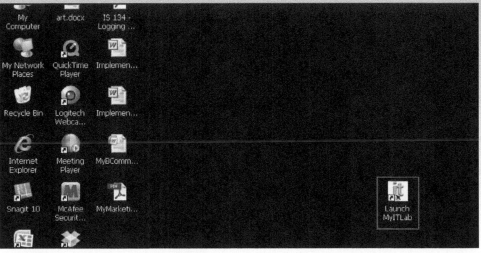

For more information, please visit **www.myitlab.com.**

**Mac Users**

You must have already registered for MyITLab before using the Mac solution. If you have not done so, please go to **www.myitlab.com** to register and establish your account. For further information, **click here**

After you have registered for MyITLab, click the Mac Users link under "For Students" on the MyITLab homepage.

The MyITLab Mac solution uses a remote desktop client to run MyITLab in a virtual Windows environment.

- **Step 1:** Install the MS RDC Application (ONE TIME ONLY).

- **Step 2:** Download & Launch the Remote Desktop [RDP] File.

- **Step 3:** Login to MyITLab via the virtual session.

**Click here** to watch our "How To" video: **Mac Video**

**Click here** to download step-by-step instructions: **Mac User Guide**

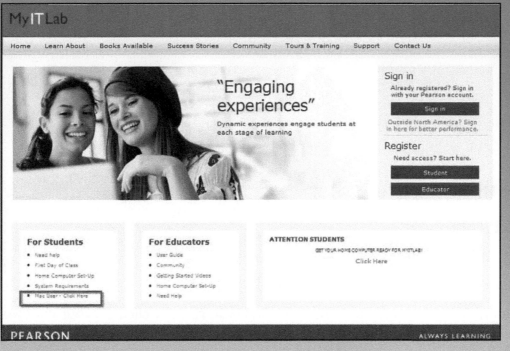

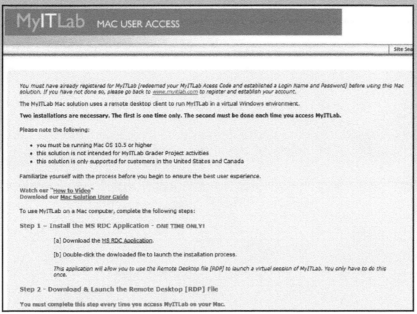

For more information, please visit **www.myitlab.com.**

**Logging into Your MyITLab Course**

Go to **www.myitlab.com**.

- Click the **Sign In** button on the right side of the page.

- Enter your Login Name and Password and then click **Login**.

You are now on the My Courses page. To enter your MyITLab course, click on your course.

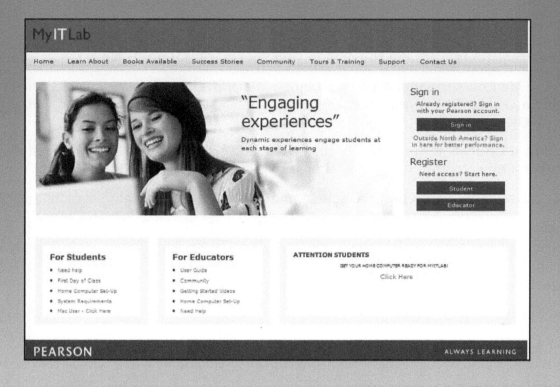

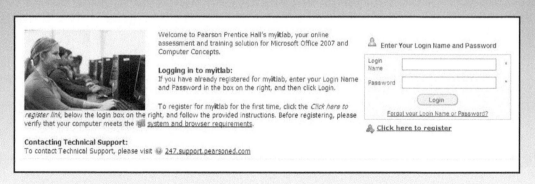

For more information, please visit **www.myitlab.com.**

**Enrolling into your MyITLab Course**

Now that you have registered, it's time to enroll in your course. Click **Log in Now** to log into MyITLab.

You are now on the My Courses page. A pop-up window will appear welcoming you and reminding you that you need a Course ID to enroll in your course. Check the "Do not display this message again" box and then click **OK**.

- Click **Enroll in a Course** in the center of the screen and type the Course ID provided by your instructor. (Your Course ID will look similar to this example: CRSABQW-123456.)

On the Confirm Course page, verify that the course and instructor are correct.

- Click **Submit**.

Verify that you are enrolled in the correct course.

- Click the **Confirm** button on the left side of the screen.

You now have access to your course.

- Click **Enter Course Now**.

> **Note:** If this is not the correct course, make sure you entered the Course ID correctly. If you are still having trouble, contact your instructor. (The Course ID will be in this format: CRSABWQ-123456.)

> **Note:** If you are working in your school computer lab, you can skip the next section. Click here to proceed.

Registering &
Logging in

Navigating
Your Course

Assignments
&Tests

Reviewing
Progress & Grades

Getting Help

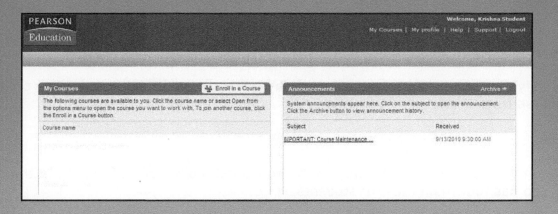

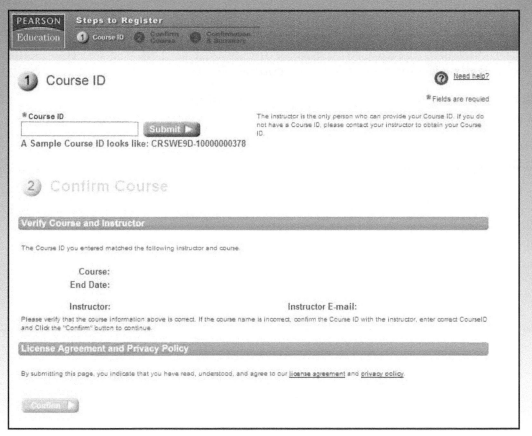

For more information, please visit **www.myitlab.com.**

# 2 | Navigating Your Course

After you log into MyITLab, the My Courses page displays. To enter your MyITLab course, click your MyITLab course from the list of course names.

## Using the Toolbar

To navigate through your course, use the tabs on the horizontal toolbar across the top of the course. By default, MyITLab has four main tabs for students:

1. The **Today's View** tool helps you organize and manage your course information all in one place. For further information, **click here**.

2. The **Course Content** tool allows you to access the content in your course. This is where you will find and work on all the assignments for your course. For further information, **click here**.

3. The **Grades** tool allows you to view your grades and assignment submissions and send a message to your instructor. For further information, **click here**.

4. The **Communicate** tool allows you to send messages to your instructor and view received email. For further information, **click here**.

**Note:** Your instructor may choose to rearrange the tabs and content of your MyITLab course. If you are not sure where to find your course materials, ask your instructor.

Registering & Logging in

Navigating Your Course

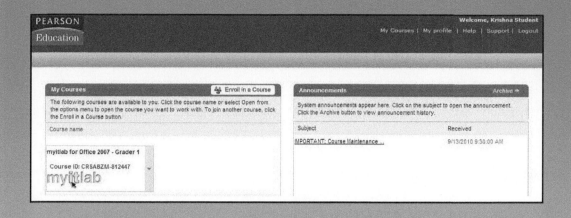

Assignments & Tests

Reviewing Progress & Grades

Gradebook

For more information, please visit **www.myitlab.com.**

## Using the Today's View Homepage

When you first enter your course, the Today's View tab appears. Today's View provides a single page where you can track, organize, and manage your assignments. It also displays any Welcome messages or Announcements added by your instructor.

Today's View includes two main areas: Notifications and Calendar.

### Notifications

The Notifications area on the left includes several sections—Welcome Message, Announcements, To Do, Alerts, and Performance:

a. **Welcome Message** displays greetings and introduces the course. Depending on how your instructor has set up the course, you may have no messages in this area (or this area may not appear in your course).

b. **Announcements** displays any announcements posted by your instructor. The number of announcements currently posted appears in parentheses next to the Announcements link in the left navigation bar of the Notifications area.

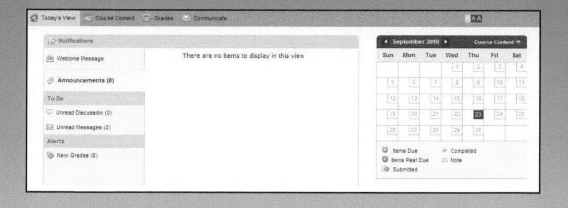

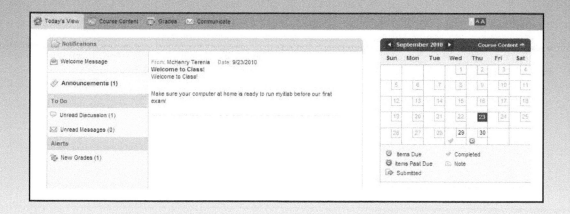

For more information, please visit **www.myitlab.com.**

c. **To Do** shows notifications of any Unread Discussions, Instructor Grading, or Unread Messages posted or sent by your instructor or other students. The number of instances of each notification appears in parentheses next to each link.

○ The Unread Discussions section displays a list of Discussion topics with unread posts.

○ The Instructor Grading section displays any activities graded by your instructor, such as Dropbox (file upload) activities.

○ The Unread Messages section lists unread mail messages. The first ten unread mails in your inbox will appear here.

d. **Alerts** shows any New Grades you have received.

○ The number of activities for which new grades have been posted appears in parentheses next to the New Grades link.

○ To view the details for each activity, click the **New Grades** link.

○ The activity name, along with the number of new grades posted for it, will appear. Each activity is listed with two options: View All Submissions and Send Message.

○ Clicking an activity name will open the Grades tab and display that activity in the Grades window.

○ You can also go to the Grades window by clicking the Go to Grades link.

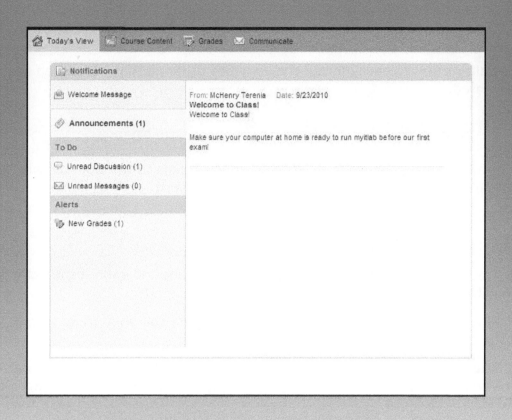

For more information, please visit **www.myitlab.com.**

## Calendar

The Course Calendar allows you to easily locate the activities or items that have been assigned to you, with due dates highlighted.

If you click a date in the calendar, the Course Content window opens to the Course Calendar, which lists any assignments for that day. To go directly to **Course Content**, click the Course Content link.

The Course Content tab will open to the View All Content tab.

The calendar displays the following icons:

- **Completed:** The date on which you complete an assignment and submit the activity are indicated with a checkmark icon.

- **Items Due:** When a due date is set for an activity, the date will be marked with a blue clock icon.

- **Items Past Due:** If an activity is not submitted on or before the due date, the date will be marked with a red clock icon. If your instructor accepts the submission of the activity after the due date, the icon is replaced.

- **Submitted:** This icon indicates the date on which you submit a completed activity.

- **Note:** Any note or information added for a date will be marked with the appropriate icon.

For more information, please visit **www.myitlab.com.**

## Accessing the Content and Activities for Your Course

The **Course Content** tab allows you to access the course content your instructor has made available to you for your course. Through this tab you can also keep track of scheduled activities and their due dates.

Course Content provides two different ways to view and access your assignments and content: View All Content and Course Calendar View.

Using an eText? Click Here

### View All Content

The **View All Content** tab lists the items available in your course. They may be available individually or in folders.

### Viewing the Status of an Activity or Item

The status of each item is displayed below the item name to the left of the Options menu. Items in your course may be in one of the following states:

**Not Viewed:** Indicates that you have not opened this activity.

**Viewed:** Indicates that you have opened the activity.

**Submitted:** Indicates you have completed the activity and submitted it for grading.

> **Note:** The submitted icon appears for activities that have at least one instructor graded question that has not yet been graded by your instructor.

**Submitted Late:** You have submitted an activity past the due date and your instructor has not accepted the submission.

**Passed:** You have met the requirements for a passing grade.

**Not Started:** Either you have not yet opened the activity or you have opened and closed it without submitting it. This status does not apply to activities that allow you to "Save for Later."

**Not Passed:** You have not met the requirements for a passing grade.

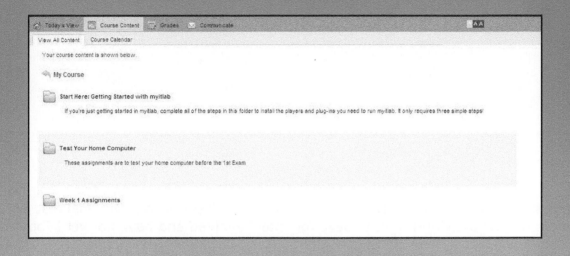

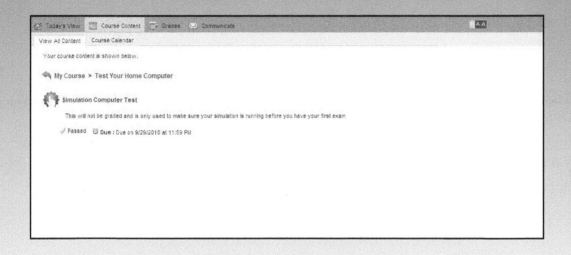

For more information, please visit **www.myitlab.com.**

**In Progress:** You have either started a Study Plan and not yet passed the final test or you have opened an activity that has "Save for Later" enabled and have not yet submitted it.

**Optional:** Your instructor recommends completing this activity but may not include it in your grade.

**Completed:** You have completed the activity or item.

**Assigned:** An activity or item has been assigned to you, but it has not been added to the calendar.

**Scheduled:** An activity or item has been set with a defined start date and end date; it will be available to you only during that time frame.

**Due:** A due date has been set for the submission of the activity or item, and you must submit the activity on or before the due date for a grade.

**Past Due:** You have not submitted the activity or item before the specified due date.

For information on accessing your assignments, **click here**.

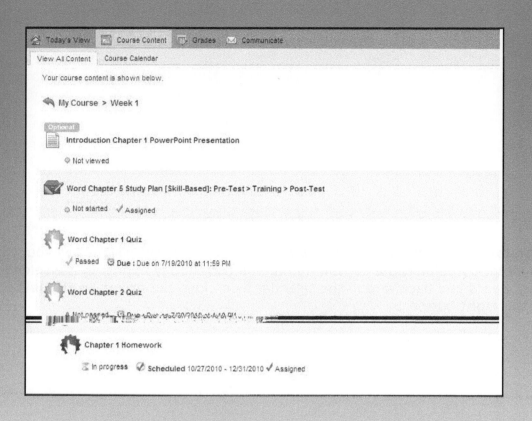

Registering & Logging in

Navigating Your Course

Assignments & Tests

Reviewing Progress & Grades

Getting Help

For more information, please visit **www.myitlab.com.**

**Course Calendar**

The **Course Calendar** allows you to easily locate the activities or items assigned to you, with a due date highlighted. By default, the current month and current day appear in the calendar. You can navigate forward and backward in the calendar by clicking the **arrow to the left** button or the **arrow to the right** button.

For further information, <u>click here</u>.

Registering &
Logging in

Navigating
Your Course

Assignments
&Tests

Reviewing
Progress & Grades

Getting Help

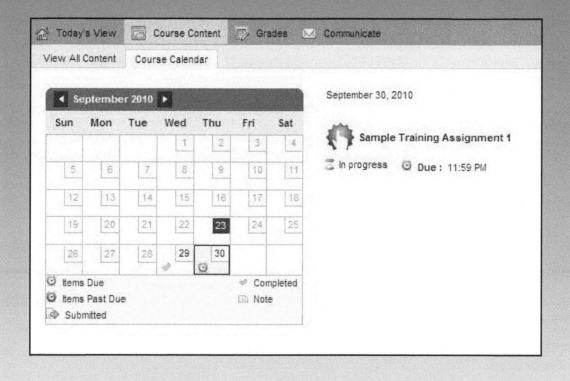

For more information, please visit **www.myitlab.com.**

# 3 | Assignments & Tests

From the Course Content tab you can access all of your assignments. To open an assignment or activity you can simply click on it or you can use the Options dropdown menu and click **Open**.

## Using the Options Menu for Activities

While completing your assignments in MyITLab, you will notice that each assignment has an Options menu. This menu differs according to the content or activity type.

To access the Options menu, hold your mouse over the assignment name and click the arrow that appears on the right side of the name.

Each item or assignment type (Folder, Activity, Discussion Topic, File, and Link) has the following two options: Open and Send message.

**Open:** Click Open to open the item or start the activity.

**Note:** If this is a discussion question, clicking **Open** will open a discussion window where you can read and submit a response to the discussion topic.

For some activities, a message screen will appear with information; click the Start button on this screen to start the activity.

**Send Message:** Click Send Message to open the Compose New Mail window, where you can send a new email message.

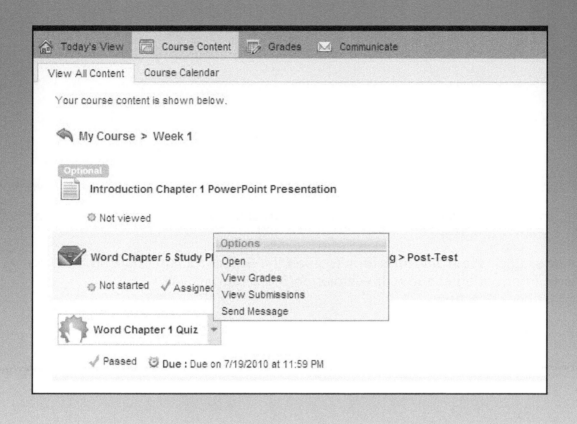

For more information, please visit **www.myitlab.com.**

Registering &
Logging in

Navigating
Your Course

Assignments
& Tests

Reviewing
Progress & Grades

Getting Help

For Activities (Exams, Training, Dropbox, and Grader Assignments) you also have the following options:

**View Grades:** Click **View Grades** to open the Grades tab and review the grades for that activity.
For further information, **click here**.

**View Submissions:** Click **View Submissions** to open the Student Submission/Study Guide window, which lists detailed information about your submission(s) for that activity.
For further information, **click here**.

**Note:** If your instructor has disabled the View Submissions feature, you will see a notice that indicates the feature is currently not available.

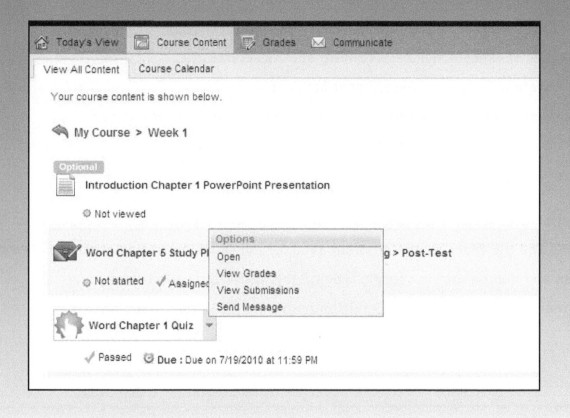

Registering &
Logging in

Navigating
Your Course

Assignments
&Tests

Reviewing
Progress & Grades

Getting Help

For more information, please visit **www.myitlab.com.**

## Completing and Submitting Your Assignments

MyITLab includes assignments in an Office simulation that are a direct match to the content in your textbook. Your assignments are divided into two types:

- **Project-Based:** You are working towards completing a finished project and must finish the questions in the order presented.

- **Skill-Based:** You can complete the questions in the order presented or you can click the **Question List** button and select the question you want to answer.

There are two types of Office activities: **Training** and **Assessment**.

To start and complete a Training or Assessment activity:

In your course, navigate to and click on the name of a training activity or exam.

Wait for the assignment to load. After the activity loads, you will see the simulated Windows desktop. On the bottom of the screen, you will see the MyITLab dashboard.

The blue horizontal bar at the top provides the following information:

1. An indication of whether the activity is a training activity or an exam.

2. Your name and the specific chapter information for the Office series you are using.

3. The name and number of the specific activity; this correlates to your text.

For more information, please visit **www.myitlab.com**.

For more information, please visit **www.myitlab.com.**

You are then provided with additional buttons you can click while working on your assignment:

- **Show me:** MyITLab will perform the tasks for you through an animation that includes audio; then you will complete the task yourself.

- **Hint:** Tells you what to do and directs you to the correct actions so you can perform the task yourself.

- **Question list:** You select the question you want to answer. As you finish each question, it will be grayed out. (This is available only for Skill-Based activities.)

- **Save file for later:** If your instructor has permitted it, you can save your work and return to the assignment later. This option is only available in Training assignments.

- **Time remaining:** If there is a time limit, the remaining time to complete the activity will appear here.

- **Questions remaining:** Counts down the number of questions you have left to complete.

- **Submit:** Use this button to submit your assignment for grading.

- **?:** This button will access the online help system.

### Project-Based Training Only

- **Show document:** You will see a miniature display of the completed document at the left and the "Steps to Create Document" at the right. This can give you an idea what your finished project will look like and how many steps remain.

To close this window, click the X in the upper-right corner.

### Exams Only

- There are no **Show Me** or **Hint** options in an exam.

- By default, you will not have an option to "Save for Later."

Registering &
Logging in

Navigating
Your Course

Assignments
&Tests

Reviewing
Progress & Grades

Getting Help

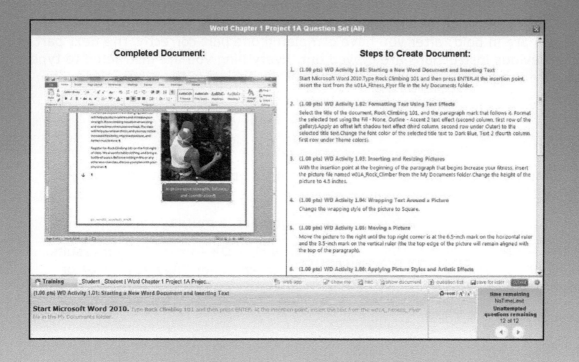

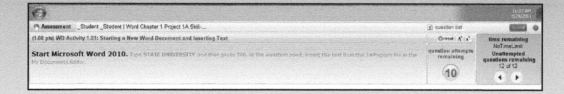

For more information, please visit **www.myitl**

Your instructions for a simulation assignment appear at the bottom portion of the dashboard. Current instructions are in bold; after you have completed one part correctly, the next part appears and the previous instructions are grayed out. Everything you are instructed to type will be blue; be sure to type the characters exactly as they appear in the instructions.

**Note:** If you are using MyITLab for Office 2007, everything you are instructed to type will appear in orange.

After you have completed everything correctly or have used up all the question attempts, MyITLab automatically moves you to the next question.

When you have completed all the questions in the assignment, a message appears

indicating that the assignment is complete. You may now click **OK** to submit your results. If you choose to exit the training prior to completion, you can either **Save for Later** or **Submit** the assignment.

- Click **OK** to submit.

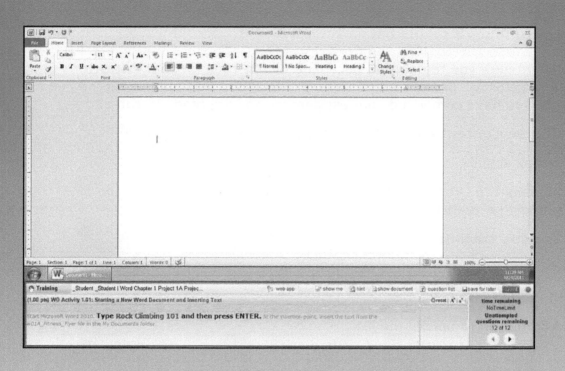

For more information, please visit **www.myitlab.com.**

## Submitting Your Dropbox Assignment

Dropbox activities require you to upload a document or other file for your instructor to grade. Your instructor will provide instructions for setting up and completing the assignment. Once you have completed your assignment and are ready to submit:

- Click the **Course Content** tab on the top navigation bar of your screen.

Locate your Dropbox activity.

- Click the name of the Dropbox activity (or click **Open** on the Options menu of the corresponding activity).
- Click the **Browse button**.

Locate the file on your computer. Select the file and then:

- Click **Open** in the Choose File box.
- Click the **Add** button to upload the file.

**Note:** If you want to remove a file, click the **Remove** button.

You can upload multiple files per question. When you are done uploading your assignment files:

- Click the **Finish: Submit for Grading** button.

You will receive a confirmation message indicating that your Dropbox assignment was submitted.

- Click **Return to Course Content** to return to the course.

**Note:** Dropbox assignments are manually graded by your instructor so you will not see a grade immediately.

Registering &
Logging in

Navigating
Your Course

Assignments
&Tests

Reviewing
Progress & Grades

Getting Help

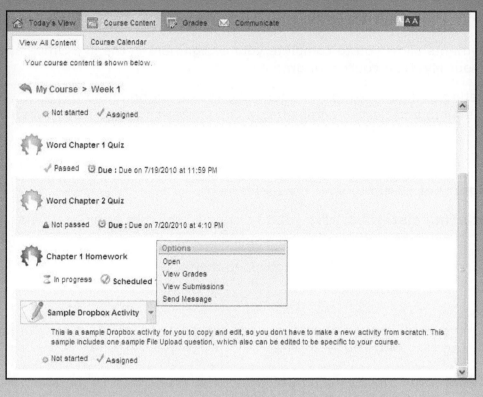

🏠 Today's View    🗂 Course Content    📋 Grades    ✉ Communicate      A A A

View All Content     Course Calendar

Your course content is shown below.

🔙 My Course > Week 1

   ◉ Not started    ✓ Assigned

Word Chapter 1 Quiz

   ✓ Passed    🕐 Due : Due on 7/19/2010 at 11:59 PM

Word Chapter 2 Quiz

   ⚠ Not passed    🕐 Due : Due on 7/20/2010 at 4:10 PM

Chapter 1 Homework

| Options |
| --- |
| Open |
| View Grades |
| View Submissions |
| Send Message |

   ⌛ In progress    ⊘ Scheduled

Sample Dropbox Activity

This is a sample Dropbox activity for you to copy and edit, so you don't have to make a new activity from scratch. This sample includes one sample File Upload question, which also can be edited to be specific to your course.

   ◉ Not started    ✓ Assigned

---

**Word Dropbox assignment**      FINISH: Submit for Grading ⇨

Browse for a file and click ADD button to upload it. You cannot upload Files of more than 4MB

Complete the project on page 89 of your textbook. Then upload your file for grading      (40points)

[     ] [ Browse... ]

[ Add ] [ Remove ]

FINISH: Submit for Grading ⇨

For more information, please visit **www.myitlab.com.**

## Submitting a MyITLab Grader Assignment

MyITLab Grader assignments allow you to complete your assignment in the live Office application and then upload it to your MyITLab course for grading.

Instructions for completing and submitting a Grader assignment can be found **here**.
This document contains hints and tips for completing a Grader assignment successfully.
Below is a set of basic instructions only.

First locate your Grader assignment (For information about accessing your assignment, **click here**.)

- Click on the **assignment name** to start the assignment.

**Step 1: Download Starting Materials:** asks you to download the files associated with this assignment.

- Click the **green arrow** next to each file to download the files.

**Note:** You may want to print the instruction sheet for convenience as you work the assignment. It will be the first file available for download. You can save it to your storage device or to a designated folder on your computer.

**Step 2: Work on Assignment:** requires you to complete the assignment in the appropriate Office software (Word, Excel®, Access® or PowerPoint®).

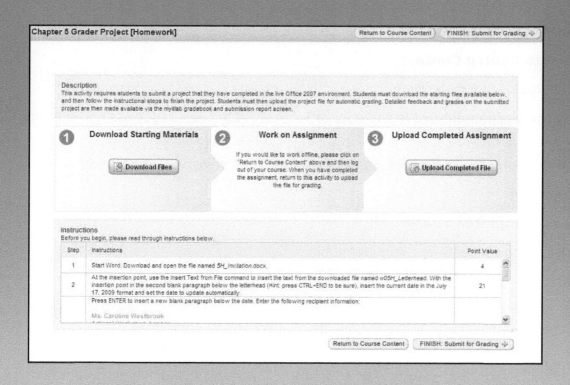

Chapter 5 Grader Project [Homework]          Return to Course Content     FINISH: Submit for Grading

**Description**
This activity requires students to submit a project that they have completed in the live Office 2007 environment. Students must download the starting files available below, and then follow the instructional steps to finish the project. Students must then upload the project file for automatic grading. Detailed feedback and grades on the submitted project are then made available via the myitlab gradebook and submission report screen.

**1  Download Starting Materials**

[ Download Files ]

**2  Work on Assignment**
If you would like to work offline, please click on "Return to Course Content" above and then log out of your course. When you have completed the assignment, return to this activity to upload the file for grading.

**3  Upload Completed Assignment**

[ Upload Completed File ]

**Instructions**
Before you begin, please read through instructions below.

| Step | Instructions | Point Value |
|------|-------------|-------------|
| 1 | Start Word. Download and open the file named *5H_Invitation.docx*. | 4 |
| 2 | At the insertion point, use the Insert Text from File command to insert the text from the downloaded file named *w05H_Letterhead*. With the insertion point in the second blank paragraph below the letterhead (Hint: press CTRL+END to be sure), insert the current date in the July 17, 2009 format and set the date to update automatically. | 21 |
| | Press ENTER to insert a new blank paragraph below the date. Enter the following recipient information:<br><br>Ms. Caroline Westbrook | |

Return to Course Content     FINISH: Submit for Grading

For more information, please visit **www.myitlab.com.**

45

You may now leave the Grader window in order to work on the assignment.

- Click **Return to Course Content**.

- Click **Yes** to close Grader.

After completing the assignment live in the application, return to the Grader assignment and go to Step 3.

**Step 3: Upload Completed Assignment: asks you to upload your completed**

assignment for grading.

- Click **Upload Completed File**.

Use the **Browse** button to locate the completed file.

- Click **Upload**.

At the top right, note the message reminding you to click **FINISH: Submit for Grading**. You will receive a confirmation message that the file has been successfully submitted.

**Note:** You must click **FINISH: Submit for Grading** for your assignment to be submitted.

The Grading Status indicates the assignment is being graded and the results will be available through View Submissions in your Course Content page.

- Click **Return to Course Content** to return to your course.

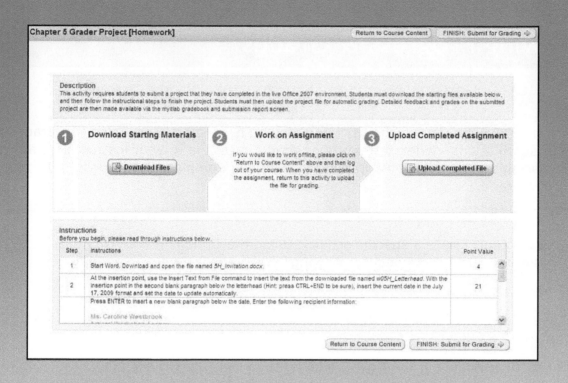

For more information, please visit **www.myitlab.com**.

# 4 Reviewing Progress & Grades

## Grades

MyITLab allows you to view grades for the assignments you have submitted. From the Grades tab, you can view your submissions, generate reports or send a message to your instructor. If an activity is not a gradable assignment, the activity status (for example, Completed, In Progress, Not attempted) displays instead of a grade.

You can access the Grades tool in four ways:

- Under Course Content, locate a specific activity. Using the Options menu, click **View Submissions**. This works best for viewing your grade for a single activity.

- Click the Grades tab in the toolbar.

- On the Today's View page, click the **New Grades** link in the left navigation bar of the Notifications area.

- Click the **Go to Grades** link in the New Grades area to view the Grades tab.

The Grades tool has two main areas:

- On the left side you will see the Course Content Navigator, which lists all the folders and activities in your course.

- On the right side is the Grades area with the list of graded activities.

## Course Content Navigator

The Course Content Navigator displays the folders and assignments available in your course. The folder structure is the same as the organization in your course.

To view the contents of a folder, click the folder name to open it.

By selecting a folder, you will change the Grades view to show the assignments in that folder.

Registering &
Logging in

Navigating
Your Course

Assignments
& Tests

Reviewing
Progress & Grades

Getting Help

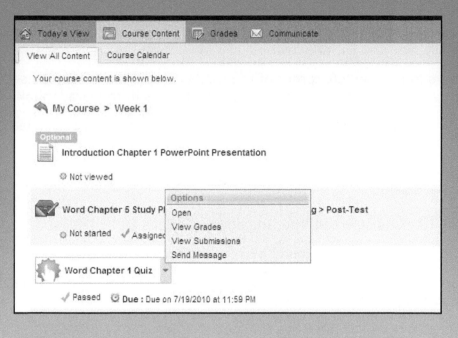

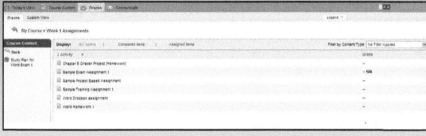

For more information, please visit **www.myitlab.com.**

## Grades Area

The Grades area includes a number of navigation and filtering options, including a Display option, a Filter by Content Type list, and the list of activities.

The Display option appears in the top left corner of the grades area. This option is used to display either all the items, only completed items or assigned items in the Gradebook.

- **Completed Items:** The Gradebook displays only those activities that have at least one submission.

**Note:** Completed items are selected by default.

- **All Items:** When All Items is selected, the Gradebook displays all activities.

- **Assigned Items:** These are items assigned by your instructor.

You can switch between views by clicking the link for each item at the top of the page. The currently selected option appears grayed out and cannot be clicked.

The Filter by Content List allows you to filter the Gradebook to show only grades for a particular activity type.

The Filter by Content Type list contains the following options:

- **No Filter Applied:** Displays all activity items.

- **Exam [Skill-Based]:** Displays only skill-based exams.

- **Exam [Project-Based]:** Displays only project-based (document-based) exams.

- **Training [Skill-Based]:** Displays only skill-based training.

To change the filter type, click the arrow next to Filter by Content Type and click on the filter you want.

For further information about filtering the Gradebook, click **help** within MyITLab.

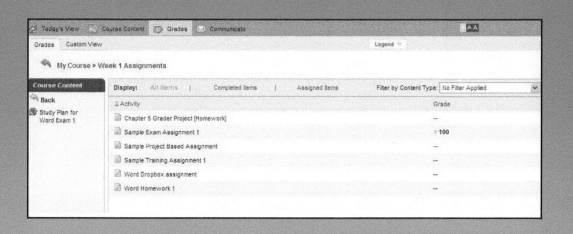

For more information, please visit **www.myitlab.com.**

In the Grades area, there are two column headers for each activity listed:

- **Activity:** Displays the name of the activity.

- **Grade:** Displays the grade obtained for the activity.

**Note:** If the graded activity has comments added by your instructor, you can click the icon that appears next to the grade to view your instructor's comments.

Each activity also has an Options menu specific to its type. Hover your mouse over the name of the activity until you see the arrow, then click on the arrow to see your menu options.

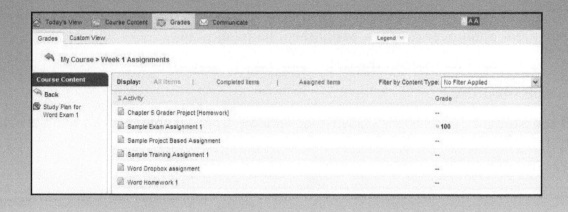

For more information, please visit **www.myitlab.com.**

## Viewing Submissions

MyITLab allows you to view your submissions for a particular activity and see exactly how our assignment was scored. In most cases, you can see the markups on your assignments.

> **Note:** Viewing submissions is a feature your instructor has the option to turn on or off for assignments.

To view your submission for a specific activity, locate your assignment under the Grades tab or in your Course Content tab. For further information, **click here**.

Locate your assignment and hover over the assignment name or grade.

- Click the arrow to the right to open the Options menu.

- Click **View Submissions**.

You are now on the Student Submission/Study Guide window. This window has two main areas: the Header and the Submission area.

- At the top right of the page, click **Show Info**.

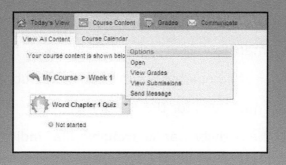

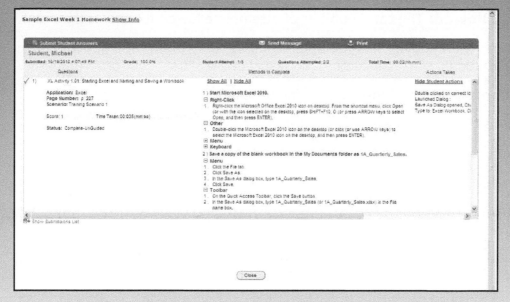

For more information, please visit **www.myitlab.com.**

This shows you the Header area for the page, where you will find the following:

- **Name:** The name of your assignment.

- **Total Submissions:** The number of completed submissions you submitted for the activity.

- **Questions:** The total number of questions for the assignment.

- **Available:** The dates on which the activity was/is available ("a" indicates the activity is always available).

- **Max. Attempts Allowed:** The total number of attempts allowed for the assignment.

- **Attempts Record:** If an activity has multiple attempts, only one grade appears in the Gradebook, as defined by your instructor: Highest, Lowest, First, Last or Average.

- **Max. Time to Complete:** The time allowed for completing the assignment.

The Submission area has its own header that contains:

- **Submitted:** The date and time you submitted your assignment.

- **Grade:** Your grade.

- **Student Attempt:** The attempt your activity is graded on. For example, it may be your first of three attempts allowed so you would see "1/3."

- **Questions Attempted:** The number of questions you attempted for the assignment. For example, you may have skipped one question in ten, so you would see "9/10."

- **Total Time:** The total time you took to complete the assignment.

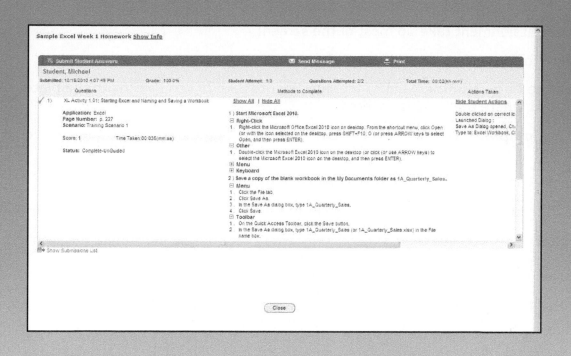

For more information, please visit **www.myitlab.com.**

The details in your assignment take up most of the screen:

- **Questions:** Provides information about the question.
  - ○ Click on the **Page Number**, below the question, to take to you directly to the place in the eText where that skill is covered.

- **Methods to Complete:** Gives detailed information regarding the ways the question could be completed:
  - ○ For the specific steps, click the **plus sign** before any method.
  - ○ To see the details for all methods, click **Show All**.

- **Action Taken:** Lets you see the correct and incorrect actions you performed for each question. These details are an excellent resource for understanding why you may not have received credit, or full credit, for a question.

- **Preview the Question in Player:** Lets you review the question within the MyITLab simulation for an immediate chance to retry incorrect questions.

**Note:** For objective assignments (multiple choice, true-false, fill-in-the-blank, and matching), you will not see all these columns. Instead you will see the question followed by the answer.

If your answer was correct, a ✓ icon appears; if incorrect, a ✗ icon appears.

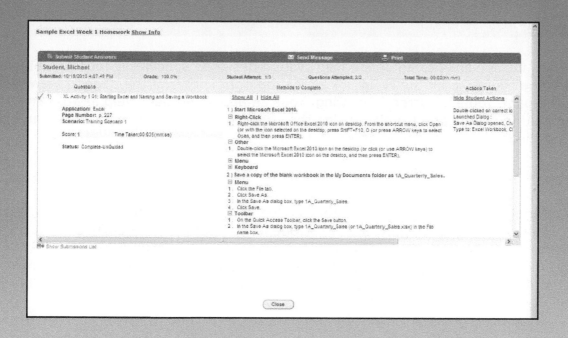

For more information, please visit **www.myitlab.com.**

# 5 | Getting Help

All MyITLab courses include links to an online help system designed specifically for MyITLab students. From any page in the course, click the **Help** link at the top right corner of the page to view interactive help specific to the page you are currently viewing. You can access Student Help at any time if you need guidance on completing exams and training, using the study plan, checking your grades, and more. Navigate by using the index or searching on key terms.

## Tutor Service

Pearson is now offering students access to a Tutor Service 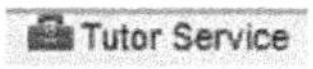 within MyITLab! The Pearson utor Service provides a convenient opportunity for students to interact with qualified instructors, 24/7, to receive valuable help with concepts and illustrations covered in their course. Your first Tutor Service session is offered FREE as part of your subscription to MyITLab and additional tutor sessions can be purchased any time! Access the Tutor Service through the Tutor Service button on the toolbar in the upper right hand corner of your MyITLab course.

## Student Product Support

If you need technical assistance or if you would like to ask a question or submit feedback about MyITLab, contact our Student Support team at:

**http://247.pearsoned.com**

From there, you can explore our online knowledge base, chat with a representative, and more. Student Support is available 24 hours a day, 7 days a week.

## MyITLab Website

For more information about getting started in MyITLab, additional help and user guides, and feature updates, visit our website at **www.myitlab.com**.

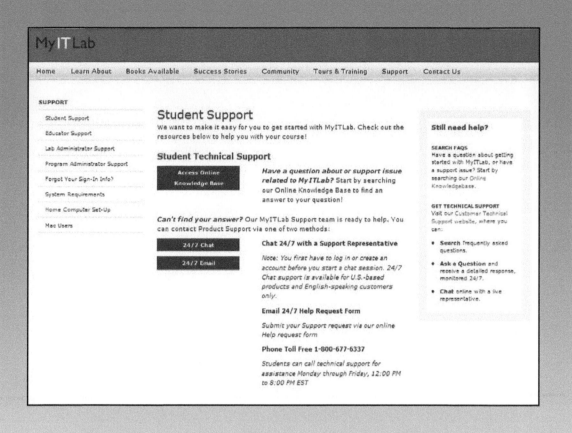

## Student Support

We want to make it easy for you to get started with MyITLab. Check out the resources below to help you with your course!

### Student Technical Support

**Access Online Knowledge Base**

*Have a question about or support issue related to MyITLab?* Start by searching our Online Knowledge Base to find an answer to your question!

*Can't find your answer?* Our MyITLab Support team is ready to help. You can contact Product Support via one of two methods:

**24/7 Chat**

**24/7 Email**

**Chat 24/7 with a Support Representative**

*Note: You first have to log in or create an account before you start a chat session. 24/7 Chat support is available for U.S.-based products and English-speaking customers only.*

**Email 24/7 Help Request Form**

*Submit your Support request via our online Help request form*

**Phone Toll Free 1-800-677-6337**

*Students can call technical support for assistance Monday through Friday, 12:00 PM to 8:00 PM EST*

### Still need help?

**SEARCH FAQS**
Have a question about getting started with MyITLab, or have a support issue? Start by searching our Online Knowledgebase.

**GET TECHNICAL SUPPORT**
Visit our Customer Technical Support website, where you can:

* **Search** frequently asked questions.
* **Ask a Question** and receive a detailed response, monitored 24/7.
* **Chat** online with a live representative.

For more information, please visit **www.myitlab.com.**

61

## EXCEL

# INTRODUCTION TO EXCEL

## What Is a Spreadsheet?

Watch the
**Set-up
Video**
for this
Case Study!

## CASE STUDY | OK Office Systems

You are an assistant manager at OK Office Systems (OKOS) in Oklahoma City. OKOS sells a wide range of computer systems, peripherals, and furniture for small- and medium-sized organizations in the metropolitan area. To compete against large, global big-box office supply stores, OKOS provides competitive pricing by ordering directly from local manufacturers rather than dealing with distributors.

The manager asked you to help prepare a markup, discount, and profit analysis for selected items on sale. The manager has been keeping these data in a ledger, but you will develop a spreadsheet to perform the necessary calculations. Although your experience with Microsoft Office Excel 2010 may be limited, you are excited to apply your knowledge and skills to your newly assigned responsibility.

When you get to the Hands-On Exercises, you will create and format the analytical spreadsheet to practice the skills you learn in this chapter.

## OBJECTIVES | AFTER YOU READ THIS CHAPTER, YOU WILL BE ABLE TO:

1. Plan for effective workbook and worksheet design
2. Explore the Excel window
3. Enter and edit cell data
4. Use symbols and the order of precedence
5. Use Auto Fill
6. Display cell formulas

7. Manage worksheets
8. Manage columns and rows
9. Select, move, copy, and paste
10. Apply alignment and font options
11. Apply number formats
12. Select page setup options
13. Print a worksheet

From Excel Chapter 1 of *Exploring Microsoft Office 2010 Volume 1*, First Edition, Robert T. Grauer, Mary Anne Poatsy, Keith Mulbery, Michelle Hulett, Cynthia Krebs, Keith Mast. Copyright © 2011 by Pearson Education, Inc. Published by Pearson Prentice Hall, Inc. All rights reserved.

# Introduction to Spreadsheets

The ability to organize, calculate, and evaluate quantitative data is one of the most important skills needed today for personal, as well as managerial, decision making. In your personal life, you track expenses for your household budget, maintain a savings plan, and determine what amount you can afford for a house or car payment. Retail managers create and analyze their organizations' annual budgets, sales projections, and inventory records. Charitable organizations track the donations they receive, the distribution of those donations, and overhead expenditures. Scientists track the results of their experiments and perform statistical analysis to draw conclusions and recommendations.

> The ability to organize, calculate, and evaluate quantitative data is one of the most important skills needed today.

Regardless of what type of quantitative analysis you need to do, you can use a spreadsheet to help you maintain data and perform calculations. A *spreadsheet* is an electronic file that contains a grid of columns and rows used to organize related data and to display results of calculations, enabling interpretation of quantitative data for decision making. A *spreadsheet program* is a computer application, such as Microsoft Excel, that you use to create and modify electronic spreadsheets.

> A **spreadsheet** is an electronic file that contains a grid of columns and rows containing related data.
>
> A **spreadsheet program** is a computer application used to create and modify spreadsheets.

Performing calculations using a calculator and then entering the results into a ledger can lead to inaccurate values. If an input value is incorrect or needs to be updated, you have to recalculate the results manually, which is time-consuming and can lead to inaccuracies. An electronic spreadsheet makes data-entry changes easy. If the formulas are correctly constructed, the results recalculate automatically and accurately, saving time and reducing room for error. The left side of Figure 1 shows the original spreadsheet with the $450 cost, 75% markup rate, and calculated retail price. The right side shows the updated spreadsheet with a $500 cost, 65.5% markup, and automatically updated retail price.

| Original Spreadsheet Values and Results | | | | | Modified Spreadsheet Values and Results | | | |
|---|---|---|---|---|---|---|---|---|
| Product | Cost | Markup Rate | Retail Price | | Product | Cost | Markup Rate | Retail Price |
| Electronics: | | | | | Electronics: | | | |
| Computer System | $400.00 | 50.00% | $600.00 | | Computer System | $400.00 | 50.00% | $600.00 |
| 28" Monitor | $195.00 | 83.50% | $357.83 | | 28" Monitor | $195.00 | 83.50% | $357.83 |
| Color Laser Printer | $450.00 | 75.00% | $787.50 | | Color Laser Printer | $500.00 | 65.50% | $827.50 |

**FIGURE 1** Original and Modified Values ➤

*Changed values* · *Automatically updated retail price* · *Original calculated retail price* · *Original values*

In this section, you will learn how to design workbooks and worksheets. In addition, you will explore the Excel window and learn the name of each window element. Then, you will enter text, values, dates, and formulas in a worksheet.

# Planning for Effective Workbook and Worksheet Design

Microsoft Excel is the most popular spreadsheet program used today. In Excel, a *worksheet* is a single spreadsheet that typically contains descriptive labels, numeric values, formulas, functions, and graphical representations of data. A *workbook* is a collection of one or more related worksheets contained within a single file. By default, new workbooks contain three worksheets. Storing multiple worksheets within one workbook helps organize related data together in one file and enables you to perform calculations among the worksheets within the workbook. For example, you can create a budget workbook of 13 worksheets, one for each month to store your personal income and expenses and a final worksheet to calculate totals across the entire year.

> A **worksheet** is a spreadsheet that contains formulas, functions, values, text, and visual aids.
>
> A **workbook** is a file containing related worksheets.

You should plan the structure before you start entering data into a worksheet. Using the OKOS case study as an example, the steps to design the workbook and a worksheet include the following:

1. **State the purpose of the worksheet.** The purpose of the OKOS worksheet is to provide data, including a profit margin, on selected products on sale.

An **input area** is a range of cells containing values for variables used in formulas.

An **output area** is a range of cells containing results based on manipulating the variables.

2. **Decide what input values are needed.** Create an ***input area***, a range of cells to enter values for your variables or assumptions. Clearly label an input area so that users know where to change values. For the OKOS worksheet, list the product names, the costs OKOS pays the manufacturers, the markup rates, and the proposed discount rates for the sale. Enter these data in individual cells to enable changes if needed.

3. **Decide what outputs are needed to achieve the purpose of the worksheet.** Create an ***output area***, a range of cells that contains the results of manipulating values in the input area. As the OKOS assistant manager, you need to calculate the retail price (i.e., the selling price to your customers), the sale price, and the profit margin. As you plan your formulas, avoid constants (raw numbers); instead, use references to cells containing numbers.

4. **Assign the worksheet inputs and results into columns and rows, and consider labeling.** Typically, descriptive labels appear in the first column to represent each row of data. For the OKOS worksheet, enter the product names in the first column. Labels at the top of each column represent individual columns of data, such as cost, markup rate, and selling price.

5. **Enter the labels, values, and formulas in Excel.** Change the input values to test that your formulas produce correct results. If necessary, correct any errors in the formulas to produce correct results regardless of the input values. For the OKOS worksheet, change some of the original costs and markup rates to ensure the calculated retail price, selling price, and profit margin percentage results update correctly.

6. **Format the numerical values in the worksheet.** Align decimal points in columns of numbers. In the OKOS worksheet, use Accounting Number Format and the Percent Style to format the numerical data. Adjust the number of decimal places as needed.

7. **Format the descriptive titles and labels attractively but so as not to distract your audience from the purpose of the worksheet.** Include a descriptive title and label for each column. Add bold to headings, increase the font size for readability, and use color to draw attention to important values or trends. In the OKOS worksheet, you will center the main title over all the columns and apply a larger font size to it.

8. **Document the worksheet as thoroughly as possible.** Include the current date, your name as the author of the worksheet, assumptions, and purpose of the worksheet.

9. **Save the completed workbook.** Preview and prepare printouts for distribution in meetings, or send an electronic copy of the workbook to those who need it.

Figure 2 shows the completed worksheet in Excel.

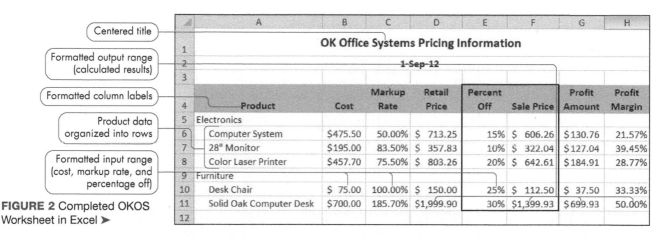

**FIGURE 2** Completed OKOS Worksheet in Excel ➤

# Exploring the Excel Window

By now, you should be familiar with the standard interface of Microsoft Office applications: the Quick Access Toolbar, title bar, control buttons, Ribbon, Home tab, the Backstage view, and scroll bars. The Excel window includes screen elements that are similar to other Office applications and items that are unique to Excel. Figure 3 identifies elements specific to the Excel window, and Table 1 lists and describes the Excel window elements.

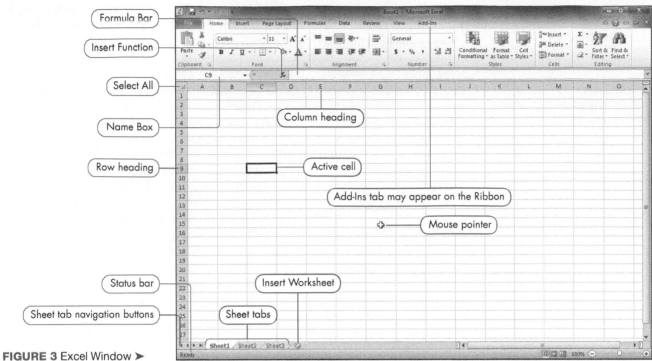

**FIGURE 3** Excel Window ➤

---

You may see an Add-Ins tab on the Ribbon. This tab indicates that additional functionality, such as an updated Office feature or an Office-compatible program, has been added to your system. Add-Ins are designed to increase your productivity.

---

**TABLE 1 Excel Elements**

| Element | Description |
|---------|-------------|
| **Name Box** | The ***Name Box*** is an identifier that displays the address of the cell currently used in the worksheet. You can use the Name Box to go to a cell, assign a name to one or more cells, or select a function. |
| ☒ **Cancel** | Cancel appears to the right of the Name Box when you enter or edit data. Click Cancel to cancel the data entry or edit and revert back to the previous data in the cell, if any. Cancel disappears after you click it. |
| ☑ **Enter** | Enter appears to the right of the Name Box when you enter or edit data. Click Enter to accept data typed in the active cell and keep the current cell active. The Enter check mark disappears after you enter the data. |
| *fx* **Insert Function** | Click to display the Insert Function dialog box, which enables you to search for and select a function to insert into the active cell. |
| **Formula Bar** | The ***Formula Bar***, the area that appears below the Ribbon and to the right of Insert Function, shows the contents of the active cell. You can enter or edit cell contents here or directly in the active cell. Drag the bottom border of the Formula Bar down to increase the space of the Formula Bar to display large amounts of data or a long formula contained in the active cell. |
| **Select All** | The square at the intersection of the row and column headings in the top-left corner of the worksheet. Click it to select everything contained in the active worksheet. |

The **Name Box** identifies the address of the current cell.

The **Formula Bar** displays the content (text, value, date, or formula) in the active cell.

| TABLE 1 | (Continued) |
|---|---|
| Element | Description |
| Column headings | The letters above the columns, such as A, B, C, and so on. |
| Row headings | The numbers to the left of the rows are row headings, such as 1, 2, 3, and so on. |
| Sheet tabs | *Sheet tabs*, located at the bottom-left corner of the Excel window, show the names of the worksheets contained in the workbook. Three sheet tabs, initially named Sheet1, Sheet2, and Sheet3, are included when you start a new Excel workbook. You can rename sheets with more meaningful names. To display the contents of a particular worksheet, click its sheet tab. |
| Sheet Tab Navigation buttons | If your workbook contains several worksheets, Excel may not show all the sheet tabs at the same time. Use the buttons to display the first, previous, next, or last worksheet. |
| Status bar | Located at the bottom of the Excel window, below the sheet tabs and above the Windows taskbar, the status bar displays information about a selected command or operation in progress. For example, it displays *Select destination and press ENTER or choose Paste* after you use the Copy command. |

## Identify Columns, Rows, and Cells

A worksheet contains columns and rows, with each column and row assigned a heading. Columns are assigned alphabetic headings from columns A to Z, continuing from AA to AZ, and then from BA to BZ until XFD, which is the last of the possible 16,384 columns. Rows have numeric headings ranging from 1 to 1,048,576 (the maximum number of rows available).

A **cell** is the intersection of a column and row.

A **cell address** identifies a cell by a column letter and a row number.

The intersection of a column and row is a *cell*; a total of over 17 billion cells are available in a worksheet. Each cell has a unique *cell address*, identified by first its column letter and then its row number. For example, the cell at the intersection of column A and row 9 is cell A9. Cell references are useful when referencing data in formulas, or in navigation.

## Navigate In and Among Worksheets

The **active cell** is the current cell, indicated by a dark border.

The *active cell* is the current cell. Excel displays a dark border around the active cell in the worksheet window, and the cell address of the active cell appears in the Name Box. The contents of the active cell, or the formula used to calculate the results of the active cell, appear in the Formula Bar. You can change the active cell by using the mouse to click in a different cell. If you work in a large worksheet, you may not be able to see the entire contents in one screen; use the vertical and horizontal scroll bars to display another area of the worksheet, and then click in the desired cell to make it the active cell.

To navigate to a new cell, click it, or use the arrow keys on the keyboard. When you press Enter, the next cell down in the same column becomes the active cell. Table 2 lists the keyboard methods for navigating within a worksheet. The Go To command is helpful for navigating to a cell that is not visible onscreen.

| TABLE 2 Keystrokes and Actions | |
|---|---|
| Keystroke | Used to |
| ↑ | Move up one cell in the same column. |
| ↓ | Move down one cell in the same column. |
| ← | Move left one cell in the same row. |
| → | Move right one cell in the same row. |
| Tab | Move right one cell in the same row. |

*(Continued)*

A **sheet tab** displays the name of a worksheet within a workbook.

| TABLE 2 (Continued) | |
|---|---|
| Keystroke | Used to |
| Page Up | Move the active cell up one screen. |
| Page Down | Move the active cell down one screen. |
| Home | Move the active cell to column A of current row. |
| Ctrl+Home | Make cell A1 the active cell. |
| Ctrl+End | Make the rightmost, lowermost active corner of the worksheet—the intersection of the last column and row that contains data—the active cell. Does not move to cell XFD1048576 unless that cell contains data. |
| F5 or Ctrl+G | Display the Go To dialog box to enter any cell address. |

To display the contents of another worksheet within the workbook, click the sheet tab at the bottom of the workbook window. The active sheet tab has a white background color. After you click a sheet tab, you can then navigate within that worksheet.

# Entering and Editing Cell Data

The four types of data that you can enter in a cell in an Excel worksheet are text; values; dates; and formulas, including functions. Figure 4 shows examples of text, values, dates, and formula results.

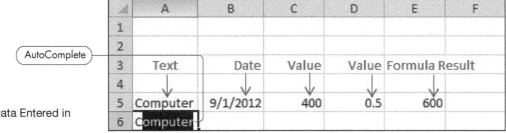

**FIGURE 4** Data Entered in Cells ➤

## Enter Text

**Text** includes letters, numbers, symbols, and spaces.

*Text* is any combination of letters, numbers, symbols, and spaces not used in calculations. Excel treats phone numbers, such as 555-1234, and social security numbers, such as 123-45-6789, as text entries. You enter text for a worksheet title to describe the contents of the worksheet, as row and column labels to describe data, and as cell data. Text aligns at the left cell margin by default. To enter text in a cell, do the following:

- Make sure the cell is active where you want to enter text.
- Enter the text.
- ✓ Press Enter, press an arrow key on the keyboard, or click Enter—the check mark between the Name Box and the Formula Bar. If you want to enter data without making another cell the active cell, click Enter instead of pressing Enter.

> **TIP** Line Break in a Cell
>
> If you have a long text label that does not fit well in a cell, you can insert a line break to display the text label on multiple lines within the cell. To insert a line break while you are typing a label, press Alt+Enter where you want to start the next line of text within the cell.

## Enter Values

A **value** is a number that represents a quantity or an amount.

*Values* are numbers that represent a quantity or a measurable amount. Excel usually distinguishes between text and value data based on what you enter. The primary difference between text and value entries is that value entries can be the basis of calculations, whereas text cannot. Values align at the right cell margin by default. After entering values, you can align decimal places and add identifying characters, such as $ or %.

## Enter Dates

You can enter dates and times in a variety of formats in cells, such as 9/15/2012; 9/15/12; September 15, 2012; or 15-Sep-12. You can also enter times, such as 1:30 PM or 13:30. You should enter a static date to document when you create or modify a workbook or to document the specific point in time when the data were accurate, such as on a balance sheet or income statement. Dates are values, so they align at the right cell margin.

Excel displays dates differently from the way it stores dates. For example, the displayed date 9/15/2012 represents the fifteenth day in September in the year 2012. Excel stores dates as serial numbers starting at 1 with January 1, 1900, so 9/15/2012 is stored as 41167 so that you can create formulas to calculate how many days exist between two dates.

## Enter Formulas

A **formula** is a combination of cell references, operators, values, and/or functions used to perform a calculation.

*Formulas* are the combination of cell references, arithmetic operations, values, and/or functions used in a calculation. For Excel to recognize a formula, you must start the formula with an equal sign (=). Because Excel requires that formulas start with =, it treats phone numbers, such as (405) 555-1234, as text, not values. In Figure 4, cell E5 contains the formula =C5*D5+C5. The result of the formula (600) displays in the cell.

## Edit and Clear Cell Contents

You can edit a cell's contents by doing one of the following:

- Click the cell, click in the Formula Bar, make the changes, and then click Enter on the left side of the Formula Bar.
- Double-click the cell, make changes in the cell, and then press Enter.
- Click the cell, press F2, make changes in the cell, and then press Enter.

You can clear a cell's contents by doing one of the following:

- Click the cell, and then press Delete.
- Click the cell, click Clear in the Editing group on the Home tab, and then select Clear Contents.

# 1 Introduction to Spreadsheets

As the assistant manager of OKOS, you need to create a worksheet that shows the cost (the amount OKOS pays its suppliers), the markup percentage (the amount by which the cost is increased), and the retail selling price. In addition, you need to list the discount percentage (such as 25% off) for each product, the sale price, and the profit margin percentage. Most of the cells in the worksheet will contain formulas. You have already planned the design as indicated in the steps listed earlier in this chapter.

**Skills covered:** Enter Text • Enter Unformatted Values • Enter a Date and Clear Cell Contents

---

## STEP 1 ⟩ ENTER TEXT

Now that you have planned your worksheet, you are ready to enter labels for the title, row labels, and column labels. Refer to Figure 5 as you complete Step 1.

| | A | B | C | D | E | F | G | H |
|---|---|---|---|---|---|---|---|---|
| 1 | OK Office Systems Pricing Information | | | | | | | |
| 2 | 1-Sep-12 | | | | | | | |
| 3 | | | | | | | | |
| 4 | Product | Cost | Markup Ra | Retail Pric | Percent O | Sale Price | Profit Margin | |
| 5 | Computer System | | | | | | | |
| 6 | Color Laser Printer | | | | | | | |
| 7 | Filing Cabinet | | | | | | | |
| 8 | Desk Chair | | | | | | | |
| 9 | Solid Oak Computer Desk | | | | | | | |
| 10 | 28" Monitor | | | | | | | |
| 11 | | | | | | | | |
| 12 | | | | | | | | |

**FIGURE 5** Text Entries ➤

FYI

a. Start Excel. Save the new workbook as **e01h1markup_LastnameFirstname**.

   When you save files, use your last and first names. For example, as the Excel author, I would save my workbook as e01h1markup_MulberyKeith.

b. Type **OK Office Systems Pricing Information** in **cell A1**, and then press **Enter**.

   When you press Enter, the next cell down—cell A2 in this case—becomes the active cell. The text does not completely fit in cell A1, and some of the text appears in cells B1, C1, and D1. If you make cell B1, C1, or D1 the active cell, the Formula Bar is empty, indicating that nothing is stored in those cells. If you were to type data in cell B1, that text would appear in cell B1, and although the contents of cell A1 would appear cut off, cell A1 still would contain the entire text.

c. Click **cell A4**, type **Product**, and then press **Enter**.

d. Continue typing the rest of the text in **cells A5** through **A10** as shown in Figure 5. Note that text appears to flow into column B.

   When you start typing *Co* in cell A6, AutoComplete displays a ScreenTip suggesting a previous text entry starting with *Co—Computer System*—but keep typing to enter *Color Laser Printer* instead. You just entered the product labels to describe the data on each row.

e. Click **cell B4** to make it the active cell. Type **Cost** and press **Tab**.

   Instead of pressing Enter to move down column B, you pressed Tab to make the cell to the right the active cell.

f.  Type the following text in the respective cells, pressing **Tab** after typing each column heading:

- **Markup Rate** in **cell C4**
- **Retail Price** in **cell D4**
- **Percent Off** in **cell E4**
- **Sale Price** in **cell F4**
- **Profit Margin** in **cell G4**

Notice that the text looks cut off when you enter data in the cell to the right. Do not worry about this now. You will adjust column widths and formatting later in this chapter.

> **TROUBLESHOOTING:** If you notice a typographical error, click in the cell containing the error, and then retype the label. Or press F2 to edit the cell contents, move the insertion point using the arrow keys, press Backspace or Delete to delete the incorrect characters, type the correct characters, and then press Enter. If you type a label in an incorrect cell, click the cell, and then press Delete.

 **FYI**

g.  Save the changes you made to the workbook.

You should develop a habit of saving periodically. That way if your system unexpectedly shuts down, you won't lose everything you worked on.

## STEP 2 ▶ ENTER UNFORMATTED VALUES

Now that you have entered the descriptive labels, you need to enter the cost, markup rate, and percent off for each product. Refer to Figure 6 as you complete Step 2.

| ◢ | A | B | C | D | E | F | G | H |
|---|---|---|---|---|---|---|---|---|
| 1 | OK Office Systems Pricing Information | | | | | | | |
| 2 | 1-Sep-12 | | | | | | | |
| 3 | | | | | | | | |
| 4 | Product | Cost | Markup Ra | Retail Pric | Percent O | Sale Price | Profit Margin | |
| 5 | Computer | 400 | 0.5 | | 0.15 | | | |
| 6 | Color Lase | 457.7 | 0.75 | | 0.2 | | | |
| 7 | Filing Cab | 68.75 | 0.905 | | 0.1 | | | |
| 8 | Desk Chai | 75 | 1 | | 0.25 | | | |
| 9 | Solid Oak | 700 | 1.857 | | 0.3 | | | |
| 10 | 28" Monit | 195 | 0.835 | | 0.1 | | | |
| 11 | | | | | | | | |
| 12 | | | | | | | | |

**FIGURE 6** Unformatted Values ▶

a.  Click **cell B5** to make it the active cell.

You are ready to enter the amount each product cost your company.

b.  Type **400** and press **Enter**.

c.  Type the remaining costs in **cells B6** through **B10** as shown in Figure 6.

>  **TIP** Numeric Keypad
>
> To improve your productivity, you should use the numeric keypad on the right side of your keyboard if your keyboard contains a numeric keypad. If you use a laptop, you can purchase a separate numeric keypad device to use. It is much faster to type values and use Enter on the number keypad rather than using the numbers on the keyboard. Make sure Num Lock is active before using the keypad to enter values.

☑ **d.** Click **cell C5**, type **0.5**, and then press **Enter**.

You entered the markup rate as a decimal instead of a percentage. You will apply Percent Style later, but now you can concentrate on data entry. When you enter decimal values less than zero, you can type the period and value without typing the zero first, such as *.5*. Excel will automatically add the zero. You can also enter percentages as 50%, but the approach this textbook takes is to enter raw data without typing formatting such as % and then to use number formatting options through Excel to display formatting symbols.

**e.** Type the remaining markup rates in **cells C6** through **C10** as shown in Figure 6.

**f.** Click **cell E5**, type **0.15**, and then press **Enter**.

You entered the markdown or percent off sale value as a decimal.

**g.** Type the remaining markdown rates in **cells E6** through **E10** as shown in Figure 6, and then save the changes to the workbook.

**ENTER A DATE AND CLEAR CELL CONTENTS**

As you review the worksheet, you realize you need to provide a date to indicate when the sale starts. Refer to Figure 7 as you complete Step 3.

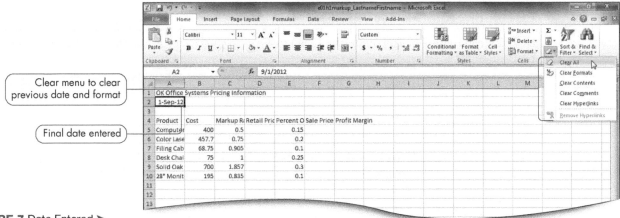

**FIGURE 7** Date Entered ➤

**a.** Click **cell A2**, type **9/1/12**, and then press **Enter**.

The date aligns on the right cell margin by default. Note that Excel displays *9/1/2012* instead of *9/1/12* as you entered.

**b.** Click **cell A2**. Click **Clear** in the Editing group on the Home tab, and then select **Clear All**.

The Clear All command clears both cell contents and formatting in the selected cell(s).

**c.** Type **September 1, 2012** in **cell A2**, and then press **Enter**.

When you enter a date in the format *September 1, 2012*, Excel displays the date in the customer number format: *1-Sep-12*. However, you can select a date number format in the Format Cells dialog box.

**d.** Save the workbook. Keep the workbook onscreen if you plan to continue with Hands-On Exercise 2. If not, close the workbook and exit Excel.

# Mathematics and Formulas

Formulas transform otherwise static numbers into meaningful results that can update as values change. For example, a payroll manager can build formulas to calculate the gross pay, deductions, and net pay for an organization's employees, or a doctoral student can create formulas to perform various statistical calculations to interpret his or her research data.

> Formulas transform otherwise static numbers into meaningful results.

You can use formulas to help you analyze how results will change as the input data change. You can change the value of your assumptions or inputs and explore the results quickly and accurately. For example, if the interest rate changes from 4% to 5%, how would that affect your monthly payment? Analyzing different input values in Excel is easy after you build formulas. Simply change an input value and observe the change in the formula results.

In this section, you will learn how to use mathematical operations in Excel formulas. You will refresh your memory of mathematical order of precedence and how to construct formulas using cell addresses so that when a value of an input cell changes, the result of the formula changes without you having to modify the formula.

## Using Symbols and the Order of Precedence

The four mathematical operations—addition, subtraction, multiplication, and division—are the basis of mathematical calculations. Table 3 lists the common arithmetic operators and their symbols.

| TABLE 3  Arithmetic Operators and Symbols | | |
|---|---|---|
| Operation | Common Symbol | Symbol in Excel |
| Addition | + | + |
| Subtraction | - | - |
| Multiplication | X | * |
| Division | ÷ | / |
| Exponentiation | ^ | ^ |

## Enter Cell References in Formulas

Start a formula by typing the equal sign (=), followed by the arithmetic expression. Do not include a space before or after the arithmetic operator. To add the contents of cells A2 and A3, enter =A2+A3 or =A3+A2. Excel uses the value stored in cell A2 (10) and adds it to the value stored in cell A3 (2). The result—12—appears in the cell instead of the formula itself. You can see the formula of the active cell by looking at the Formula Bar. Figure 8 shows a worksheet containing data and results of formulas. The figure also displays the actual formulas used to generate the calculated results.

| | A | B | C | D |
|---|---|---|---|---|
| 1 | Contents | | Description | Results |
| 2 | 10 | | First input value | 10 |
| 3 | 2 | | Second input value | 2 |
| 4 | =A2+A3 | | Sum of 10 and 2 | 12 |
| 5 | =A2-A3 | | Difference between 10 and 2 | 8 |
| 6 | =A2*A3 | | Product of 10 and 2 | 20 |
| 7 | =A2/A3 | | Results of dividing 10 by 2 | 5 |
| 8 | =A2^A3 | | Results of 10 to the 2nd power | 100 |

Input values → (A2, A3)

Output (formula results) →

**FIGURE 8** Formula Results ➤

If you type A2+A3 without the equal sign, Excel does not recognize that you entered a formula and stores the data as text.

You should use cell addresses instead of values as references in formulas where possible. You may include values in an input area—such as dates, salary, or costs—that you will need to reference in formulas. Referencing these cells in your formulas, instead of typing the value of the cell to which you are referring, keeps your formulas accurate if the values change. If you change the value of cell A2 to 5, the result of =A2+A3 displays 7 in cell A4. If you had typed actual values in the formula, =10+2, you would have to edit the formula each time a value changes. Always design worksheets in such a way as to be able to change input values without having to modify your formulas if an input value changes later.

> **TIP** Constants in Formulas
>
> Use cell references instead of actual values in formulas, unless the value is a constant. For example, to calculate the reciprocal of a percentage stored in cell B4, type =1-B4. The constant, 1, represents 100%, a value that never changes, although the percentage in cell B4 might change.

## Control the Results with the Order of Precedence

Recall the basic rules of performing calculations from a high school or college math class. What is calculated first in the expression =A1+A2*A3? Remember that multiplication is performed before addition, so the value in cell A2 is multiplied by the value in cell A3. Excel then adds the product to the value in cell A1.

The order of precedence (also called order of operations) is a rule that controls the sequence in which arithmetic operations are performed, which affects the results of the calculation. Excel performs mathematical calculations left to right in this order: **P**arentheses, **E**xponentiation, **M**ultiplication or **D**ivision, and finally **A**ddition or **S**ubtraction. Some people remember the order of precedence with the phrase **P**lease **E**xcuse **M**y **D**ear **A**unt **S**ally. Therefore, if you want to add the values in A1 and A2 and *then* multiply the sum by the value in cell A3, you need to enclose the addition operation in parentheses =(A1+A2)*A3 since anything in parentheses is calculated first. Without parentheses, multiplication has a higher order of precedence than addition and will be calculated first. Figure 9 shows formulas, formula explanations, and formula results based on the order of precedence. The result in cell A12 displays only five digits to the right of the decimal point.

The **order of precedence** controls the sequence in which Excel performs arithmetic operations.

| | A | B | C | D |
|---|---|---|---|---|
| 1 | 10 | | | |
| 2 | 5 | | | |
| 3 | 2 | | | |
| 4 | 4 | | | |
| 5 | | | | |
| 6 | Result | | Formula | Explanation |
| 7 | 20 | | =A1+A2*A3 | 5 x 2 = 10. The product 10 is then added to 10 stored in cell A1. |
| 8 | 30 | | =(A1+A2)*A3 | 10 + 5 = 15. The sum of 15 is then multiplied by 2 stored in cell A3. |
| 9 | 24 | | =A1+A2*A3+A4 | 5 x 2 = 10. 10 + 10 + 4 = 24. |
| 10 | 90 | | =(A1+A2)*(A3+A4) | 10 + 5 = 15; 2+4 = 6. 15 x 6 = 90. |
| 11 | 10 | | =A1/A2+A3*A4 | 10 / 5 = 2; 2 x 4 = 8; 2 + 8 = 10. |
| 12 | 5.71429 | | =A1/(A2+A3)*A4 | 5 + 2 = 7. 10 / 7 = 1.428571429. 1.42857149 * 4 = 5.714285714 |

**FIGURE 9** Formula Results Based on Order of Precedence ➤

# Using Auto Fill

Auto Fill enables you to copy the contents of a cell or cell range or to continue a sequence by dragging the fill handle over an adjacent cell or range of cells.

The **fill handle** is a small black square at the bottom-right corner of a cell.

*Auto Fill* enables you to copy the contents of a cell or a range of cells by dragging the ***fill handle*** (a small black square appearing in the bottom-right corner of a cell) over an adjacent cell or range of cells. To use Auto Fill, do the following:

1. Click the cell with the content you want to copy to make it the active cell.
2. Position the pointer over the bottom-right corner of the cell until it changes to the fill pointer (a thin black plus sign).
3. Drag the fill handle to repeat the content in other cells.

**Copying Formulas with Auto Fill.** After you enter a formula in a cell, you can duplicate the formula down a column or across a row without retyping it by using Auto Fill. Excel adapts each copied formula based on the type of cell references in the original formula.

**Completing Sequences with Auto Fill.** You can also use Auto Fill to complete a sequence. For example, if you enter *January* in a cell, you can use Auto Fill to enter the rest of the months in adjacent cells. Other sequences you can complete are quarters (Qtr 1, etc.), weekdays, and weekday abbreviations, by typing the first item and using Auto Fill to complete the other entries. For numeric values, however, you must specify the first two values in sequence. For example, if you want to fill in 5, 10, 15, and so on, you must enter the first two values in two cells, select the two cells, and then use Auto Fill so that Excel knows to increment by 5. Figure 10 shows the results of filling in months, abbreviated months, quarters, weekdays, abbreviated weekdays, and increments of 5.

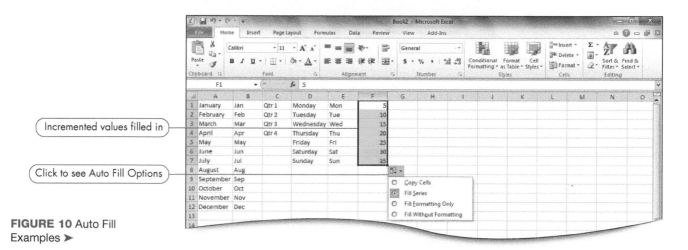

Incremented values filled in

Click to see Auto Fill Options

**FIGURE 10** Auto Fill Examples ➤

Immediately after you use Auto Fill, Excel displays the Auto Fill Options button in the bottom-right corner of the filled data (see Figure 10). Click the button to display four options: Copy Cells, Fill Series, Fill Formatting Only, or Fill Without Formatting.

**TIP** Fill Handle

To copy a formula down a column, double-click the fill handle. Excel will copy the formula in the active cell for each row of data to calculate in your worksheet. Cell addresses change automatically during the Auto Fill process. For example, if the original formula is =A1+B1 and you copy the formula down one cell, the copied formula is =A2+B2.

# Displaying Cell Formulas

When you enter a formula, Excel shows the result of the formula in the cell (see the top half of Figure 11); however, you might want to display the formulas instead of the calculated results in the cells (see the bottom half of Figure 11). The quickest way to display cell formulas is to press Ctrl and the grave accent (`) key, sometimes referred to as the tilde key, in the top-left corner of the keyboard, below Esc. You can also click Show Formulas in the Formula Auditing group on the Formulas tab to show and hide formulas. This is a toggle feature; do the same step to redisplay formula results.

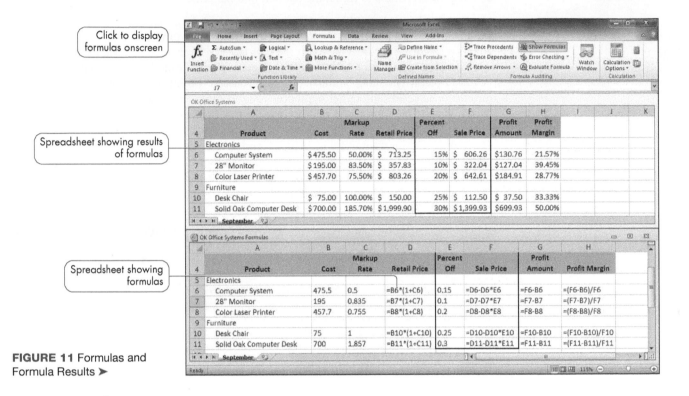

**FIGURE 11** Formulas and Formula Results ➤

# HANDS-ON EXERCISES

## 2 Mathematics and Formulas

In Hands-On Exercise 1, you created the basic worksheet for OKOS by entering text, values, and a date for items on sale this week. Now you need to insert formulas to calculate the missing results—specifically, the retail (before sale) value, sale price, and profit margin. You will use cell addresses in your formulas, so when you change a referenced value, the formula results will update automatically.

**Skills covered:** Enter the Retail Price Formula • Enter the Sale Price Formula • Enter the Profit Margin Formula • Copy Formulas with Auto Fill • Change Values and Display Formulas

---

### STEP 1 ▶ ENTER THE RETAIL PRICE FORMULA

The first formula you need to create is one to calculate the retail price. The retail price is the price you originally charge. It is based on a percentage of the original cost so that you earn a profit. Refer to Figure 12 as you complete Step 1.

Formula displayed in Formula Bar

Blue border and blue cell reference

Green border and green cell reference

| SUM | × ✓ fx | =B5*(1+C5) |

| | A | B | C | D | E | F | G | H |
|---|---|---|---|---|---|---|---|---|
| 1 | OK Office Systems Pricing Information | | | | | | | |
| 2 | 1-Sep-12 | | | | | | | |
| 3 | | | | | | | | |
| 4 | Product | Cost | Markup Ra | Retail Pric | Percent O | Sale Price | Profit Margin | |
| 5 | Computer | 400 | 0.5 | =B5*(1+C5) | | | | |
| 6 | Color Lase | 457.7 | 0.75 | | 0.2 | | | |
| 7 | Filing Cab | 68.75 | 0.905 | | 0.1 | | | |
| 8 | Desk Chai | 75 | 1 | | 0.25 | | | |
| 9 | Solid Oak | 700 | 1.857 | | 0.3 | | | |
| 10 | 28" Monit | 195 | 0.835 | | 0.1 | | | |
| 11 | | | | | | | | |
| 12 | | | | | | | | |

**FIGURE 12** Retail Formula ➤

a. Open the *e01h1markup_LastnameFirstname* workbook if you closed it after the last Hands-On Exercise, and then save it as **e01h2markup_LastnameFirstname**, changing *h1* to *h2*.

> TROUBLESHOOTING: If you make any major mistakes in this exercise, you can close the file, open *e01h1markup_LastnameFirstname* again, and then start this exercise over.

b. Click **cell D5**, the cell where you will enter the formula to calculate the retail selling price of the first item.

c. Type **=B5*(1+C5)** and view the formula and the colored cell borders on the screen.

As you type or edit a formula, each cell address in the formula displays in a specific color, and while you type or edit the formula, the cells referenced in the formula have a temporarily colored border. For example, in the formula =B5*(1+C5), B5 appears in blue, and C5 appears in green. Cell B5 has a temporarily blue border and cell C5 has a temporarily green border to help you identify cells as you construct your formulas (see Figure 12).

**d.** Click **Enter** to the left of the Formula Bar and view the formula.

The result of the formula, 600, appears in cell D5, and the formula displays in the Formula Bar. This formula first adds 1 (the decimal equivalent of 100%) to 0.5 (the value stored in cell C5). Excel multiplies that sum of 1.5 by 400 (the value stored in cell B5). The theory behind this formula is that the retail price is 150% of the original cost.

> **TIP** Alternative Formula
>
> An alternative formula also calculates the correct retail price: =B5*C5+B5 or =B5+B5*C5. In this formula, 400 (cell B5) is multiplied by 0.5 (cell C5); that result (200) represents the dollar value of the markup. Excel adds the value 200 to the original cost of 400 to obtain 600, the retail price. You were instructed to enter =B5*(1+C5) to demonstrate the order of precedence.

> **TROUBLESHOOTING:** If the result is not correct, click the cell and look at the formula in the Formula Bar. Click in the Formula Bar, edit the formula to match the formula shown in step 1c, and then click Enter. Make sure you start the formula with an equal sign.

**e.** Save the workbook with the new formula.

## STEP 2 ▷ ENTER THE SALE PRICE FORMULA

Now that you calculated the retail price, you want to calculate a sale price. This week, the computer is on sale for 15% off the retail price. Refer to Figure 13 as you complete Step 2.

| | F5 | | | $f_x$ | =D5-D5*E5 | | | |
|---|---|---|---|---|---|---|---|---|
| | A | B | C | D | E | F | G | H |
| 1 | OK Office Systems Pricing Information | | | | | | | |
| 2 | 1-Sep-12 | | | | | | | |
| 3 | | | | | | | | |
| 4 | Product | Cost | Markup Ra | Retail Pric | Percent O | Sale Price | Profit Margin | |
| 5 | Computer | 400 | 0.5 | 600 | 0.15 | 510 | | |
| 6 | Color Lase | 457.7 | 0.75 | | 0.2 | | | |
| 7 | Filing Cab | 68.75 | 0.905 | | 0.1 | | | |
| 8 | Desk Chai | 75 | 1 | | 0.25 | | | |
| 9 | Solid Oak | 700 | 1.857 | | 0.3 | | | |
| 10 | 28" Monit | 195 | 0.835 | | 0.1 | | | |
| 11 | | | | | | | | |
| 12 | | | | | | | | |

**FIGURE 13** Sale Price Formula ➤

**a.** Click **cell F5**, the cell where you will enter the formula to calculate the sale price.

**b.** Type **=D5-D5*E5** and notice the color-coding in the cell addresses. Press **Ctrl+Enter** to keep the current cell the active cell.

The result is 510. Looking at the formula, you might think D5-D5 equals zero; remember that because of the order of precedence rules, multiplication is calculated before subtraction. The product of 600 (cell D5) and 0.15 (cell E5) equals 90, which is then subtracted from 600 (cell D5), so the sale price is 510. If it helps to understand the formula better, add parentheses: =D5-(D5*E5).

c. View the Formula Bar, and then save the workbook with the new formula.

The Formula Bar displays the formula you entered.

## STEP 3 ENTER THE PROFIT MARGIN FORMULA

After calculating the sale price, you want to know the profit margin you earn. You paid $400 for the
computer and will sell it for $510. The profit is $110, which gives you a profit margin of 21.57%. Refer
to Figure 14 as you complete Step 3.

| G5 | | | | $f_x$ | =(F5-B5)/F5 | | | |
|---|---|---|---|---|---|---|---|---|
| ⊿ | A | B | C | D | E | F | G | H |
| 1 | OK Office Systems Pricing Information | | | | | | | |
| 2 | 1-Sep-12 | | | | | | | |
| 3 | | | | | | | | |
| 4 | Product | Cost | Markup R; | Retail Pric | Percent O | Sale Price | Profit Margin | |
| 5 | Computer | 400 | 0.5 | 600 | 0.15 | 510 | 0.215686 | |
| 6 | Color Lase | 457.7 | 0.75 | | 0.2 | | | |
| 7 | Filing Cab | 68.75 | 0.905 | | 0.1 | | | |
| 8 | Desk Chai | 75 | 1 | | 0.25 | | | |
| 9 | Solid Oak | 700 | 1.857 | | 0.3 | | | |
| 10 | 28" Monit | 195 | 0.835 | | 0.1 | | | |
| 11 | | | | | | | | |
| 12 | | | | | | | | |

**FIGURE 14** Profit Margin
Formula ➤

a. Click **cell G5**, the cell where you will enter the formula to calculate the profit margin.

The profit margin is the profit (difference in sales price and cost) percentage of the sale
price. This amount represents the amount to cover operating expenses and tax, which are
not covered in this analysis.

b. Type **=(F5-B5)/F5** and notice the color-coding in the cell addresses. Press **Ctrl+Enter**.

The formula must first calculate the profit, which is the difference between the sale price
(510) and the original cost (400). The difference (110) is then divided by the sale price (510)
to determine the profit margin of 0.215686 or 21.6%.

> **TROUBLESHOOTING:** If you type a backslash (\) instead of a forward slash (/), Excel will display
> an error message box. Make sure you type / as the division operator.

c. Look at the Formula Bar, and then save the workbook with the new formula.

The Formula Bar displays the formula you entered.

After double-checking the accuracy of your calculations for the first product, you are ready to copy the formulas down the columns to calculate the retail price, sale price, and profit margin for the other products. Refer to Figure 15 as you complete Step 4.

Cell references adjust in copied formula

Auto Fill Options

| | G6 | | | $f_x$ | =(F6-B6)/F6 | | | |
|---|---|---|---|---|---|---|---|---|
| | A | B | C | D | E | F | G | H |
| 1 | OK Office Systems Pricing Information | | | | | | | |
| 2 | 1-Sep-12 | | | | | | | |
| 3 | | | | | | | | |
| 4 | Product | Cost | Markup Ra | Retail Pric | Percent O | Sale Price | Profit Margin | |
| 5 | Computer | 400 | 0.5 | 600 | 0.15 | 510 | 0.215686 | |
| 6 | Color Lase | 457.7 | 0.75 | 800.975 | 0.2 | 640.78 | 0.285714 | |
| 7 | Filing Cab | 68.75 | 0.905 | 130.9688 | 0.1 | 117.8719 | 0.41674 | |
| 8 | Desk Chai | 75 | 1 | 150 | 0.25 | 112.5 | 0.333333 | |
| 9 | Solid Oak | 700 | 1.857 | 1999.9 | 0.3 | 1399.93 | 0.499975 | |
| 10 | 28" Monit | 195 | 0.835 | 357.825 | 0.1 | 322.0425 | 0.39449 | |
| 11 | | | | | | | | |
| 12 | | | | | | | | |

FIGURE 15 Auto Fill ➤

a. Click **cell D5**, the cell containing the formula to calculate the retail price for the first item.

b. Position the mouse pointer on the fill handle in the bottom-right corner of **cell D5**. When the pointer changes from a white plus sign to a thin black plus sign, double-click the **fill handle**.

Excel's Auto Fill feature copies the retail price formula for the remaining products in your worksheet. Excel detects when to stop copying the formula when it encounters a blank row, such as in row 11.

c. Click **cell D6**, the cell containing the first copied retail price formula, and look at the Formula Bar.

The original formula was =B5*(1+C5). The copied formula in cell D6 is =B6*(1+C6). Excel adjusts the cell addresses in the formula as it copies the formula down a column so that the results are based on each row's data rather than using the original formula's cell addresses for other products.

d. Select the **range F5:G5**. Double-click the **fill handle** in the bottom-right corner of **cell G5**.

Auto Fill copies the selected formulas down their respective columns. Notice Auto Fill Options down and to the right of the cell G10 fill handle, indicating you could select different fill options if you want.

e. Click **cell F6**, the cell containing the first copied sale price formula, and view the Formula Bar.

The original formula was =D5-D5*E5. The copied formula in cell F6 is =D6-D6*E6.

f. Click **cell G6**, the cell containing the first copied profit margin formula, and look at the Formula Bar. Save the changes to your workbook.

The original formula was =(F5-B5)/F5. The copied formula in cell G6 is =(F6-B6)/F6.

You want to see how the prices and profit margins are affected when you change some of the original values. For example, the supplier might notify you that the cost to you will increase. In addition, you want to see the formulas displayed in the cells temporarily. Refer to Figures 16 and 17 as you complete Step 5.

*Updated formula results*

*Changed values*

| | E8 | ▼ | | fx | 0.25 | | | |
|---|---|---|---|---|---|---|---|---|
| | A | B | C | D | E | F | G | H |
| 1 | OK Office Systems Pricing Information | | | | | | | |
| 2 | 1-Sep-12 | | | | | | | |
| 3 | | | | | | | | |
| 4 | Product | Cost | Markup Ra | Retail Pric | Percent O | Sale Price | Profit Margin | |
| 5 | Computer | 475.5 | 0.5 | 713.25 | 0.15 | 606.2625 | 0.215686 | |
| 6 | Color Lase | 457.7 | 0.755 | 803.2635 | 0.2 | 642.6108 | 0.287749 | |
| 7 | Filing Cab | 68.75 | 0.905 | 130.9688 | 0.05 | 124.4203 | 0.447437 | |
| 8 | Desk Chai | 75 | 1 | 150 | 0.25 | 112.5 | 0.333333 | |
| 9 | Solid Oak | 700 | 1.857 | 1999.9 | 0.3 | 1399.93 | 0.499975 | |
| 10 | 28" Monit | 195 | 0.835 | 357.825 | 0.1 | 322.0425 | 0.39449 | |
| 11 | | | | | | | | |
| 12 | | | | | | | | |

**FIGURE 16** Results of Changed Values ➤

a. Click **cell B5**, type **475.5**, and then press **Enter**.

The results of the retail price, sale price, and profit margin formulas change based on the new cost.

b. Click **cell C6**, type **0.755**, and then press **Enter**.

The results of the retail price, sale price, and profit margin formulas change based on the new markup rate.

c. Click **cell E7**, type **0.05**, and then press **Enter**.

The results of the sale price and profit margin formulas change based on the new markdown rate. Note that the retail price did not change since that formula is not based on the markdown rate.

d. Press **Ctrl+`** (the grave accent mark).

The workbook now displays the formulas rather than the formula results (see Figure 17). This is helpful when you want to review several formulas at one time.

*Date appears as a serial number*

*Values appear left-aligned*

*Formulas display instead of results*

| | E8 | ▼ | | fx | 0.25 | | |
|---|---|---|---|---|---|---|---|
| | A | B | C | D | E | F | G |
| 1 | OK Office Systems P | | | | | | |
| 2 | 41153 | | | | | | |
| 3 | | | | | | | |
| 4 | Product | Cost | Markup Rate | Retail Price | Percent Off | Sale Price | Profit Margin |
| 5 | Computer System | 475.5 | 0.5 | =B5*(1+C5) | 0.15 | =D5-D5*E5 | =(F5-B5)/F5 |
| 6 | Color Laser Printer | 457.7 | 0.755 | =B6*(1+C6) | 0.2 | =D6-D6*E6 | =(F6-B6)/F6 |
| 7 | Filing Cabinet | 68.75 | 0.905 | =B7*(1+C7) | 0.05 | =D7-D7*E7 | =(F7-B7)/F7 |
| 8 | Desk Chair | 75 | 1 | =B8*(1+C8) | 0.25 | =D8-D8*E8 | =(F8-B8)/F8 |
| 9 | Solid Oak Computer | 700 | 1.857 | =B9*(1+C9) | 0.3 | =D9-D9*E9 | =(F9-B9)/F9 |
| 10 | 28" Monitor | 195 | 0.835 | =B10*(1+C10) | 0.1 | =D10-D10*E10 | =(F10-B10)/F10 |
| 11 | | | | | | | |
| 12 | | | | | | | |

**FIGURE 17** Formulas in Cells ➤

e. Press **Ctrl+`** (the grave accent mark).

The workbook now displays the formula results in the cells again.

f. Save the workbook. Keep the workbook onscreen if you plan to continue with Hands-On Exercise 3. If not, close the workbook and exit Excel.

# Workbook and Worksheet Management

When you start a new blank workbook in Excel, the workbook contains three worksheets named Sheet1, Sheet2, and Sheet3. The text, values, dates, and formulas you enter into the individual sheets are saved under the one workbook file name. Having multiple worksheets in one workbook is helpful to keep related items together. For example, you might want one worksheet for each month to track your monthly income and expenses for one year. When tax time rolls around, you have all your data stored in one workbook file.

Although you should plan the worksheet and workbook before you start entering data, you might need to add, delete, or rename worksheets. Furthermore, within a worksheet you may want to insert a new row to accommodate new data, delete a column that you no longer need, adjust the size of columns and rows, or move or copy data to other locations.

In this section, you will learn how to manage workbooks by renaming, inserting, and deleting worksheets. You will also learn how to make changes to worksheet columns and rows, such as inserting, deleting, and adjusting sizes. Finally, you will learn how to move and copy data within a worksheet.

## Managing Worksheets

Creating a multiple-worksheet workbook takes some planning and maintenance. Worksheet tab names should reflect the contents of the respective worksheets. In addition, you can insert, copy, move, and delete worksheets within the workbook. You can even apply background color to the worksheet tabs so that they stand out onscreen. Figure 18 shows a workbook in which the sheet tabs have been renamed, colors have been applied to worksheet tabs, and a worksheet tab has been right-clicked so that the shortcut menu appears.

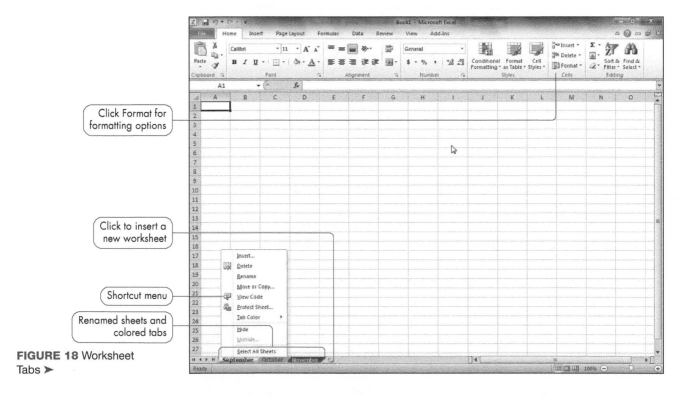

**FIGURE 18** Worksheet Tabs ➤

## Rename Worksheets

The default worksheet names—Sheet1, Sheet2, and Sheet3—are vague; they do not describe the contents of each worksheet. You should rename the worksheet tabs to reflect the sheet contents so that you, and anyone with whom you share your workbook, will be able to find data. For example, if your budget workbook contains monthly worksheets, name the worksheets *September*, *October*, etc. A teacher who uses a workbook to store a grade book for several classes should name each worksheet by class name or number, such as *MIS 1000* and *MIS 3430*. Although you can have spaces in worksheet names, you should keep worksheet names relatively short. The longer the worksheet names, the fewer sheet tabs you will see at the bottom of the workbook window without scrolling.

To rename a worksheet, do one of the following:

- Double-click a sheet tab, type the new name, and then press Enter.
- Click Format in the Cells group on the Home tab (see Figure 18), select Rename Sheet (see Figure 19), type the new sheet name, and then press Enter.
- Right-click the sheet tab, select Rename from the shortcut menu (see Figure 18), type the new sheet name, and then press Enter.

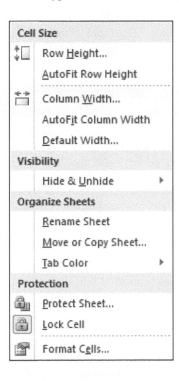

**FIGURE 19** Format Menu ➤

## Change Worksheet Tab Color

The active worksheet tab is white, whereas the default color of the tabs depends on the Windows color scheme. When you use multiple worksheets, you might want to apply a different color to each worksheet tab to make the tab stand out or to emphasize the difference between sheets. For example, you might apply red to the September tab, green to the October tab, and dark blue to the November tab.

To change the color of a worksheet tab, do one of the following:

- Click Format in the Cells group on the Home tab (see Figure 18), point to Tab Color (see Figure 19), and then click a color on the Tab Color palette.
- Right-click the sheet tab, point to Tab Color on the shortcut menu (see Figure 18), and then click a color on the Tab Color palette.

## Insert, Delete, Move, and Copy Worksheets

Sometimes you need more worksheets in the workbook than the three default sheets. For example, you might create a workbook that contains 12 worksheets—a worksheet for each month of the year. Each new worksheet you insert starts with a default name, such as Sheet4, numbered consecutively after the last Sheet#. After inserting worksheets, you can rename them to be more descriptive. You can delete extra worksheets from your workbook to keep it streamlined.

To insert a new worksheet, do one of the following:

- Click Insert Worksheet to the right of the last worksheet tab.
- Click the Insert arrow—either to the right or below Insert—in the Cells group on the Home tab, and then select Insert Sheet.
- Right-click any sheet tab, select Insert from the shortcut menu (see Figure 18), click Worksheet in the Insert dialog box, and then click OK.
- Press Shift+F11.

To delete a worksheet in a workbook, do one of the following:

- Click the Delete arrow—either to the right or below Delete—in the Cells group on the Home tab, and then select Delete Sheet.
- Right-click any sheet tab, and select Delete from the shortcut menu (see Figure 18).

**TIP   Ribbon Commands with Arrows**

Some commands, such as Insert in the Cells group, contain two parts: the main command and an arrow. The arrow may be below or to the right of the command, depending on the command, window size, or screen resolution. Instructions in the Exploring Series use the command name to instruct you to click the main command to perform the default action, such as "Click Insert in the Cells group" or "Click Delete in the Cells group." Instructions include the word *arrow* when you need to select an additional option, such as "Click the Insert arrow in the Cells group" or "Click the Delete arrow in the Cells group."

After inserting and deleting worksheets, you can arrange the worksheet tabs in a different sequence, especially if the newly inserted worksheets do not fall within a logical sequence.

To move a worksheet, do one of the following:

- Drag a worksheet tab to the desired location. As you drag a sheet tab, the pointer resembles a piece of paper. A down-pointing triangle appears between sheet tabs to indicate where the sheet will be moved when you release the mouse button.
- Click Format in the Cells group on the Home tab (see Figure 18) or right-click the sheet tab you want to move, and select Move or Copy to see the Move or Copy dialog box (see Figure 20). Select the workbook if you want to move the sheet to another workbook. In the *Before sheet* list, select the worksheet on whose left side you want the moved worksheet to be located, and then click OK. For example, assume the October worksheet was selected before displaying the dialog box. You then select November so that the October sheet moves before (or to the left) of November.

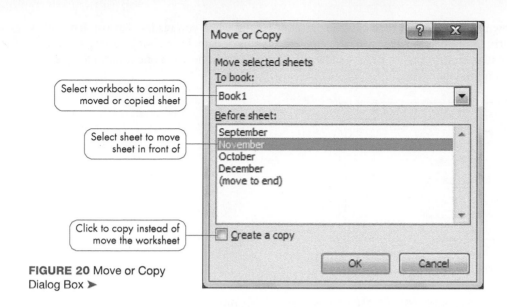

Select workbook to contain moved or copied sheet

Select sheet to move sheet in front of

Click to copy instead of move the worksheet

**FIGURE 20** Move or Copy Dialog Box ➤

The process for copying a worksheet is similar to moving a sheet. To copy a worksheet, press and hold Ctrl as you drag the worksheet tab. Alternatively, display the Move or Copy dialog box, select the options (see Figure 20), click the *Create a copy* check box, and then click OK.

# Managing Columns and Rows

As you enter and edit worksheet data, you can adjust the row and column structure. You can add rows and columns to accommodate new data, or you can delete data you no longer need. Adjusting the height and width of columns and rows can present the data better.

## Insert Cells, Columns, and Rows

After you construct a worksheet, you might need to insert cells, columns, or rows to accommodate new data. For example, you might need to insert a new column to perform calculations or a new row to list a new product. When you insert cells, rows, and columns, cell addresses in formulas adjust automatically.

To insert a new column or row, do one of the following:

- Click in the column or row for which you want to insert a new column to the left or a new row above, respectively. Click the Insert arrow in the Cells group on the Home tab, and then select Insert Sheet Columns or Insert Sheet Rows.
- Right-click the column letter or row number for which you want to insert a new column to the left or a new row above, respectively, and select Insert from the shortcut menu.

Excel inserts new columns to the *left* of the current column and new rows *above* the current row. If the current column is column C and you insert a new column, the new column becomes column C, and the original column C data are now in column D. Likewise, if the current row is 5 and you insert a new row, the new row is row 5, and the original row 5 data are now in row 6.

You can insert a single cell in a particular row or column. To insert a cell, click in the cell where you want the new cell, click the Insert arrow in the Cells group on the Home tab, and then select Insert Cells. Select an option from the Insert dialog box (see Figure 21) to position the new cell, and then click OK. Alternatively, click Insert in the Cells group. The default action of clicking Insert is to insert a cell at the current location, which moves existing data down in that column only. Inserting a cell is helpful when you realize that you left out an entry in one column after you have entered columns of data. Instead of inserting a new row for all columns, you just want to move the existing content down in one column to enter the missing value.

**FIGURE 21** Insert Dialog Box ➤

## Delete Cells, Columns, and Rows

If you no longer need a cell, column, or row, you can delete it. In these situations, you are deleting the entire cell, column, or row, not just the contents of the cell to leave empty cells. As with inserting new cells, any affected formulas adjust the cell references automatically. To delete a column or row, do one of the following:

- Click the column or row heading for the column or row you want to delete. Click Delete in the Cells group on the Home tab.
- Click in any cell within the column or row you want to delete. Click the Delete arrow in the Cells group on the Home tab, and then select Delete Sheet Columns or Delete Sheet Rows, respectively.
- Right-click the column letter or row number for the column or row you want to delete, and then select Delete from the shortcut menu.

To delete a cell or cells, select the cell(s), click the Delete arrow in the Cells group, and then select Delete Cells to display the Delete dialog box (see Figure 22). Click the appropriate option to shift cells left or up, and then click OK. Alternatively, click Delete in the Cells group. The default action of clicking Delete is to delete the active cell, which moves existing data up in that column only.

**FIGURE 22** Delete Dialog Box ➤

## Adjust Column Width

**Column width** is the horizontal measurement of a column.

After you enter data in a column, you often need to adjust the **column width**—the number of characters that can fit horizontally using the default font or the number of horizontal pixels—to show the contents of cells. For example, in the worksheet you created in Hands-On Exercises 1 and 2, the labels in column A displayed into column B when those adjacent cells were empty. However, after you typed values in column B, the labels in column A appeared truncated, or cut off. You will need to widen column A to show the full name of all of your products. Numbers appear as a series of pound signs (######) when the cell is too narrow to display the complete value, and text appears to be truncated.

To widen a column to accommodate the longest label or value in a column, do one of the following:

- Position the pointer on the vertical border between the current column heading and the next column heading. When the pointer displays as a two-headed arrow, double-click the border. For example, if column B is too narrow to display the content in that column, double-click the border between the column B and C headings.
- Click Format in the Cells group on the Home tab (see Figure 18), and then select AutoFit Column Width (see Figure 19).

You can drag the vertical border to the left to decrease the column width or to the right to increase the column width. As you drag the vertical border, Excel displays a ScreenTip specifying the width (see Figure 23). Excel column widths range from 0 to 255 characters. The final way to change column width is to click Format in the Cells group on the Home tab (see Figure 18), select Column Width (see Figure 19), type a value in the Column width box in the Column Width dialog box, and then click OK.

ScreenTip displaying column width

Mouse pointer as you drag the border between column headings

Current column width

Column width when you release the mouse button

| | A | B | C | D | E | F | G | H |
|---|---|---|---|---|---|---|---|---|
| | E8 | Width: 11.86 (88 pixels) | $f_x$ | 0.25 | | | | |
| 1 | OK Office Systems Pricing Information | | | | | | | |
| 2 | 1-Sep-12 | | | | | | | |
| 3 | | | | | | | | |
| 4 | Product | Cost | Markup Ra | Retail Pric | Percent O | Sale Price | Profit Margin | |
| 5 | Computer | 475.5 | 0.5 | 713.25 | 0.15 | 606.2625 | 0.215686 | |
| 6 | Color Lase | 457.7 | 0.755 | 803.2635 | 0.2 | 642.6108 | 0.287749 | |
| 7 | Filing Cab | 68.75 | 0.905 | 130.9688 | 0.05 | 124.4203 | 0.447437 | |
| 8 | Desk Chai | 75 | 1 | 150 | 0.25 | 112.5 | 0.333333 | |
| 9 | Solid Oak | 700 | 1.857 | 1999.9 | 0.3 | 1399.93 | 0.499975 | |
| 10 | 28" Monit | 195 | 0.835 | 357.825 | 0.1 | 322.0425 | 0.39449 | |
| 11 | | | | | | | | |
| 12 | | | | | | | | |

FIGURE 23 Changing Column Width ➤

## Adjust Row Height

**Row height** is the vertical measurement of a row.

When you increase the font size of cell contents, Excel automatically increases the *row height*—the vertical measurement of the row. However, if you insert a line break to create multiple lines of text in a cell, Excel might not increase the row height. You can adjust the row height in a way similar to how you change column width by double-clicking the border between row numbers or by selecting Row Height or AutoFit Row Height from the Format menu (see Figure 19). In Excel, row height is a value between 0 and 409 based on point size (abbreviated as *pt*). Whether you are measuring font sizes or row heights, one point size is equal to 1/72 of an inch. Your row height should be taller than your font size. For example, with an 11 pt font size, the default row height is 15.

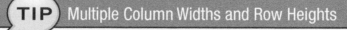

**TIP** Multiple Column Widths and Row Heights

You can set the size for more than one column or row at a time to make the selected columns or rows the same size. Drag across the column or row headings for the area you want to format, and then set the size using any method.

## Hide and Unhide Columns and Rows

If your worksheet contains confidential information, such as social security numbers or salary information, you might need to hide some columns and/or rows before you print a copy for public distribution. When you hide a column or a row, Excel prevents that column or row from displaying or printing. However, the column or row is not deleted. If you hide column B, you will see columns A and C side by side. If you hide row 9, you will see rows 8 and 10 together. Figure 24 shows that column B and row 9 are hidden. Excel displays a thicker border between column headings (such as between A and C), indicating one or more columns are hidden, and between row headings (such as between 8 and 10), indicating one or more rows are hidden.

Column B hidden (thicker border)

Row 9 hidden (thicker border)

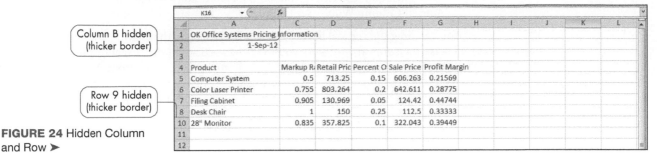

**FIGURE 24** Hidden Column and Row ➤

To hide a column or row, do one of the following:

- Click in the column or row you want to hide, click Format in the Cells group on the Home tab (see Figure 18), point to Hide & Unhide (see Figure 19), and then select Hide Columns or Hide Rows, depending on what you want to hide.
- Right-click the column or row heading(s) you want to hide, and then select Hide.

You can hide multiple columns and rows at the same time. To select adjacent columns (such as columns B through E) or adjacent rows (such as rows 2 through 4), drag across the adjacent column or row headings. To hide nonadjacent columns or rows, press and hold down Ctrl while you click the column or row headings. After selecting multiple columns or rows, use any acceptable method to hide the selected columns or rows.

To unhide a column or row, select the columns or rows on both sides of the hidden column or row. For example, if column B is hidden, drag across column letters A and C. Then do one of the following:

- Click Format in the Cells group on the Home tab (see Figure 18), point to Hide & Unhide (see Figure 19), and then select Unhide Columns or Unhide Rows, depending on what you want to display again.
- Right-click the column(s) or row(s) you want to hide, and then select Unhide.

> **TIP** Unhiding Column A, Row 1, and All Hidden Rows/Columns
>
> Unhiding column A or row 1 is different because you cannot select the row or column on either side. To unhide column A or row 1, type A1 in the Name Box, and then press Enter. Click Format in the Cells group on the Home tab, point to Hide & Unhide, and then select Unhide Columns or Unhide Rows to display column A or row 1, respectively. If you want to unhide all columns and rows, click Select All, and then use the Hide & Unhide submenu.

# Selecting, Moving, Copying, and Pasting

The basic tasks of selecting, cutting, copying, and pasting data are somewhat different when working in Excel.

## Select a Range

A **range** is a rectangular group of cells.

A **nonadjacent range** contains multiple ranges of cells.

A *range* refers to a group of adjacent or contiguous cells. A range may be as small as a single cell or as large as the entire worksheet. It may consist of a row or part of a row, a column or part of a column, or multiple rows or columns, but will always be a rectangular shape, as you must select the same number of cells in each row or column for the entire range. A range is specified by indicating the top-left and bottom-right cells in the selection. For example, in Figure 25, the date is a single-cell range in cell A2, the Color Laser Printer data are stored in the range A6:G6, the cost values are stored in the range B5:B10, and the sales prices and profit margins are stored in range F5:G10. A *nonadjacent range* contains multiple ranges, such as C5:C10 and E5:E10. At times, you need to select nonadjacent ranges so that you can apply the same formatting at the same time, such as formatting the nonadjacent range C5:C10 and E5:E10 with Percent Style.

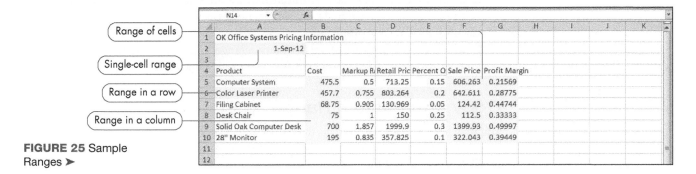

**FIGURE 25** Sample Ranges ➤

Table 4 lists methods you can use to select ranges, including nonadjacent ranges.

| TABLE 4 Selecting Ranges | |
| --- | --- |
| **To Select:** | **Do This:** |
| **A Range** | Click the first cell and drag until you select the entire range. Alternatively, click the first cell in the range, press and hold down Shift, and then click the last cell in the range. |
| **An Entire Column** | Click the column heading. |
| **An Entire Row** | Click the row heading. |
| **Current Range Containing Data** | Click in the range of data and then press Ctrl+A. |
| **All Cells in a Worksheet** | Click Select All, or press Ctrl+A twice. |
| **Nonadjacent Range** | Select the first range, press and hold down Ctrl, and then select additional range(s). |

A border appears around a selected range. Any command you execute will affect the entire range. The range remains selected until you select another range or click in any cell in the worksheet.

**TIP** Name Box

You can use the Name Box to select a range by clicking in the Name Box, typing a range address such as B15:D25, and then pressing Enter.

## Move a Range to Another Location

You can move cell contents from one range to another. For example, you might need to move an input area from the right side of the worksheet to above the output range. When you move a range containing text and values, the text and values do not change. However, any formulas that refer to cells in that range will update to reflect the new cell addresses. To move a range, do the following:

1. Select the range.
2. Use the Cut command to copy the range to the Clipboard. Excel outlines the range you cut with a moving dashed border. Unlike cutting data in other Office applications, the data you cut in Excel remain in their locations until you paste them elsewhere. After you use Cut, the status bar displays *Select destination and press ENTER or choose Paste*.
3. Make sure the destination range—the range where you want to move the data—has enough empty cells. If any cells within the destination range contain data, Excel overwrites that data when you use the Paste command.
4. Click in the top-left corner of the destination range, and then use the Paste command to insert the cut cells and remove them from the original location.

## Copy and Paste a Range

You may need to copy cell contents from one range to another. For example, you might copy your January budget to another worksheet to use as a model for creating your February budget. When you copy a range, the original data remain in their original locations. Cell references in copied formulas adjust based on their relative locations to the original data. To copy a range, do the following:

1. Select the range.
2. Use the Copy command to copy the contents of the selected range to the Clipboard. Excel outlines the range you copied with a moving dashed border. After you use Copy, the status bar displays *Select destination and press ENTER or choose Paste*.
3. Make sure the destination range—the range where you want to copy the data—has enough empty cells. If any cells within the destination range contain data, Excel overwrites that data when you use the Paste command.
4. Click in the top-left corner of the destination range where you want the duplicate data, and then use the Paste command. The original selected range remains selected with a moving dashed border around it.
5. Press Esc to deselect the range. Figure 26 shows a selected range and a copy of the range.

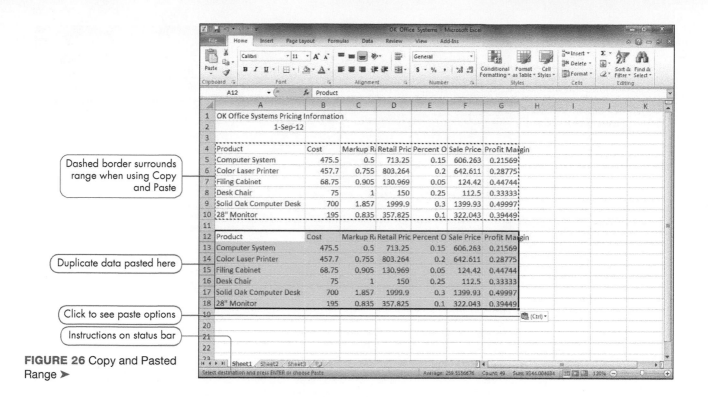

Dashed border surrounds range when using Copy and Paste

Duplicate data pasted here

Click to see paste options

Instructions on status bar

**FIGURE 26** Copy and Pasted Range ➤

**TIP** Copy as Picture

Instead of clicking Copy, if you click the Copy arrow in the Clipboard group, you can select Copy (the default option) or Copy as Picture. When you select Copy as Picture, you copy an *image* of the selected data. You can then paste the image elsewhere in the workbook or in a Word document or PowerPoint presentation. However, when you copy the data as an image, you cannot edit individual cell data when you paste the image.

**TIP** Paste Options Button

When you copy or paste data, Excel displays Paste Options in the bottom-right corner of the pasted data (see Figure 26). Click Paste Options to see different results for the pasted data.

## Use Paste Special

Sometimes you might want to paste data in a different format than they are in in the Clipboard. For example, you might want to copy a range containing formulas and cell references, and paste the range as values in another workbook that does not have the referenced cells. If you want to copy data from Excel and paste them into a Word document, you can paste the Excel data as a worksheet object, as unformatted text, or in another format. To paste data from the Clipboard into a different format, click the Paste arrow in the Clipboard group, and hover over a command to see a ScreenTip and a preview of how the pasted data will look. In Figure 27, the preview shows that a particular paste option will maintain formulas and number formatting; however, it will not maintain the text formatting, such as font color and centered text. After previewing different paste options, click the one you want in order to apply it.

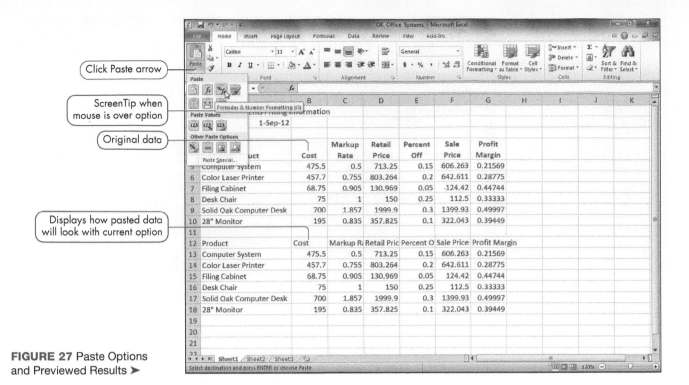

**Click Paste arrow**

**ScreenTip when mouse is over option**

**Original data**

**Displays how pasted data will look with current option**

**FIGURE 27** Paste Options and Previewed Results ➤

For more specific paste options, click the Paste arrow, and then select Paste Special to display the Paste Special dialog box (see Figure 28). This dialog box contains more options than the Paste menu. Click the desired option, and then click OK.

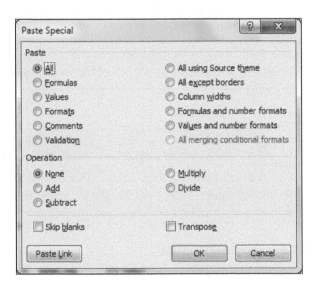

**FIGURE 28** Paste Special Dialog Box ➤

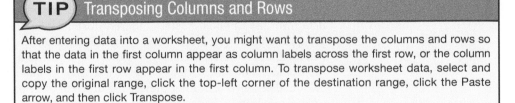

**TIP** Transposing Columns and Rows

After entering data into a worksheet, you might want to transpose the columns and rows so that the data in the first column appear as column labels across the first row, or the column labels in the first row appear in the first column. To transpose worksheet data, select and copy the original range, click the top-left corner of the destination range, click the Paste arrow, and then click Transpose.

Introduction to Excel

# HANDS-ON EXERCISES

## 3 Workbook and Worksheet Management

After reviewing the OKOS worksheet, you decide to rename the worksheet that contains the data and delete the other sheets. In addition, you decide to move the 28" Monitor data to display below the Computer System row and insert a column to calculate the amount of markup. You also need to adjust column widths to display data.

**Skills covered:** Manage Worksheets • Delete a Row • Insert a Column and Three Rows • Move a Row • Adjust Column Width and Row Height • Hide and Unhide Columns

---

**STEP 1** ▶ **MANAGE WORKSHEETS**

You want to rename Sheet1 to describe the worksheet contents and add a color to the sheet tab. In addition, you want to delete the blank worksheets. Refer to Figure 29 as you complete Step 1.

**FIGURE 29** Worksheets Managed ➤

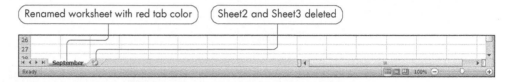

Renamed worksheet with red tab color     Sheet2 and Sheet3 deleted

a. Open the *e01h2markup_LastnameFirstname* workbook if you closed it after the last Hands-On Exercise, and save it as **e01h3markup_LastnameFirstname**, changing *h2* to *h3*.

b. Double-click the **Sheet1 sheet tab**, type **September**, and then press **Enter**.

   You just renamed Sheet1 as September.

c. Right-click the **September sheet tab**, point to **Tab Color**, and then click **Red** in the Standard Colors section.

   The worksheet tab color is red.

d. Click the **Sheet2 sheet tab**, click the **Delete arrow** in the Cells group on the Home tab, and then select **Delete Sheet**.

   You deleted the Sheet2 worksheet from the workbook.

> **TROUBLESHOOTING:** Delete in the Cells group, like some other commands in Excel, contains two parts: the main command icon and an arrow. Click the main command icon when instructed to click Delete to perform the default action. Click the arrow when instructed to click the Delete arrow for additional command options.

> **TROUBLESHOOTING:** Notice that Undo is unavailable on the Quick Access Toolbar. You can't undo deleting a worksheet. It is deleted!

e. Right-click the **Sheet3 sheet tab**, and then select **Delete** to delete the sheet. Save the workbook.

---

**STEP 2** ▶ **DELETE A ROW**

You just realized that you do not have enough filing cabinets in stock to offer on sale, so you need to delete the Filing Cabinet row. Refer to Figure 30 as you complete Step 2.

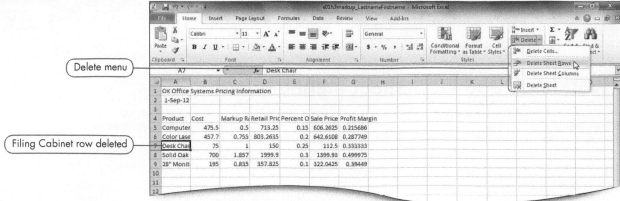

**FIGURE 30** Row Deleted ➤

a. Click **cell A7** (or any cell on row 7), the row that contains data for the Filing Cabinet.

b. Click the **Delete arrow** in the Cells group.

c. Select **Delete Sheet Rows**, and then save the workbook.

The Filing Cabinet row is deleted, and the remaining rows move up one row.

> **TROUBLESHOOTING:** If you accidentally delete the wrong row or accidentally select Delete Sheet Columns instead of Delete Sheet Rows, click Undo on the Quick Access Toolbar to restore the deleted row or column.

## STEP 3 ▶ INSERT A COLUMN AND THREE ROWS

You decide that you need a column to display the amount of profit. Because profit is a dollar amount, you want to keep the profit column close to another column of dollar amounts. Therefore, you will insert the profit column before the profit margin (percentage) column. You also want to insert new rows for product information and category names. Refer to Figure 31 as you complete Step 3.

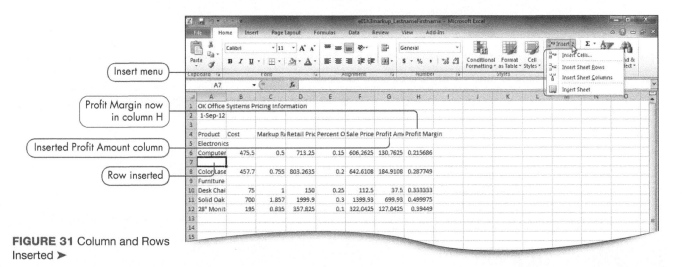

**FIGURE 31** Column and Rows Inserted ➤

a. Click **cell G5** (or any cell in column G), the column containing the Profit Margin.

You want to insert a column between the Sale Price and Profit Margin columns so that you can calculate the profit amount in dollars.

b. Click the **Insert arrow** in the Cells group, and then select **Insert Sheet Columns**.

You inserted a new, blank column G. The data in the original column G are now in column H.

c. Click **cell G4**, type **Profit Amount**, and then press **Enter**.

d. Make sure the active cell is **cell G5**. Type **=F5-B5** and then click **Enter** to the left of the Formula Bar. Double-click the **fill handle** to copy the formula down the column.

You calculated the profit amount by subtracting the original cost from the sale price. Although steps e and f below illustrate one way to insert a row, you can use other methods presented in this chapter.

e. Right-click the **row 5 heading**, the row containing the Computer System data.

Excel displays a shortcut menu consisting of commands you can perform.

f. Select **Insert** from the shortcut menu.

You inserted a new blank row 5, which is selected. The original rows of data move down a row each.

g. Click **cell A5**. Type **Electronics** and then press **Enter**.

You entered the category name Electronics above the list of electronic products.

h. Right-click the **row 8 heading**, the row containing the Desk Chair data, and then select **Insert** from the shortcut menu.

i. Click **cell A8**. Type **Furniture** and then press **Enter**.

You entered the category name Furniture above the list of furniture products. Now you want to insert a blank row after the Computer System row so that you can move the 28" Monitor data to the new row.

j. Insert a row between Computer System and Color Laser Printer. Click **cell A7**, and then save the workbook.

## STEP 4 ▶ MOVE A ROW

You want to move the 28" Monitor product to be immediately after the Computer System product. You previously inserted a blank row. Now you need to move the monitor row to this empty row. Refer to Figure 32 as you complete Step 4.

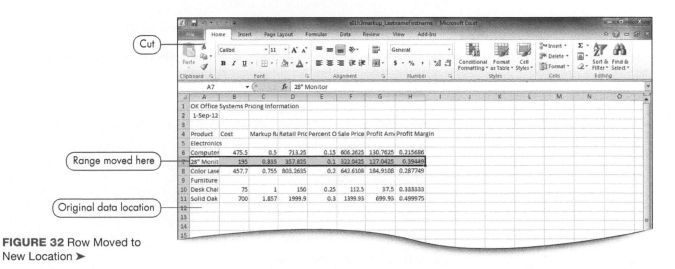

**FIGURE 32** Row Moved to New Location ➤

a. Click **cell A12**, and then drag to select the **range A12:H12**.

You selected the range of cells containing the 28" Monitor data.

b. Cut the selected range.

A moving dashed border outlines the selected range. The status bar displays the message *Select destination and press ENTER or choose Paste.*

c. Click **cell A7**, the new blank row you inserted in step 3j.

This is the first cell in the destination range.

d. Paste the data that you cut, and then save the workbook.

The 28" Monitor data are now located on row 7.

> **TROUBLESHOOTING:** If you cut and paste a row without inserting a new row first, Excel will overwrite the original row of data, which is why you inserted a new row in step 3.

## STEP 5 ▶ ADJUST COLUMN WIDTH AND ROW HEIGHT

As you review your worksheet, you notice that the labels in column A appear cut off. You need to increase the width of that column to display the entire product names. In addition, you want to make row 1 taller. Refer to Figure 33 as you complete Step 5.

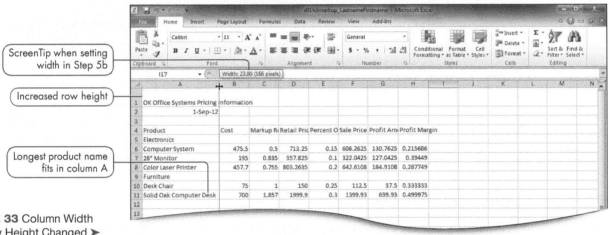

**FIGURE 33** Column Width and Row Height Changed ▶

a. Position the pointer between the column A and B headings. When the pointer looks like a double-headed arrow, double-click the **border**.

When you double-click the border between two columns, Excel adjusts the width of the column on the left side of the border to fit the contents of that column. In this case, Excel increased the width of column A. However, it is based on the title in cell A1, which will eventually span over all columns. Therefore, you want to decrease the column to avoid so much empty space in column A.

b. Position the pointer between the column A and B headings again. Drag the border to the left until the ScreenTip displays **Width: 23.00 (166 pixels)**. Release the mouse button.

You decreased the column width to 23 for column A. The longest product name is visible. You won't adjust the other column widths until after you apply formats to the column headings in Hands-On Exercise 4.

c. Click **cell A1**. Click **Format** in the Cells group, and then select **Row Height** to display the Row Height dialog box.

d. Type **30** in the **Row height box**, and then click **OK**. Save the workbook.

You doubled the height of the first row.

Introduction to Excel

96

## STEP 6 ▸ HIDE AND UNHIDE COLUMNS

To focus on the dollar amounts, you decide to hide the markup rate, discount rate, and profit margin columns. Refer to Figure 34 as you complete Step 6.

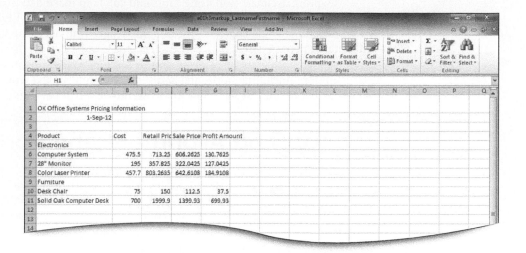

**FIGURE 34** Hidden Columns ➤

a. Click the **column C heading**, the column containing the Markup Rate values.

b. Press and hold down **Ctrl** as you click the **column E heading** and the **column H heading**.

   Holding down Ctrl enables you to select nonadjacent ranges. You want to hide the rate columns temporarily.

c. Click **Format** in the Cells group, point to **Hide & Unhide**, and then select **Hide Columns**.

   Excel hides the selected columns. You see a gap in column heading letters, indicating columns are hidden (see Figure 34).

d. Drag to select the **column G and I headings**.

   You want to unhide column H, so you must select the columns on both sides of the hidden column.

e. Click **Format** in the Cells group, point to **Hide & Unhide**, and then select **Unhide Columns**.

   Column H, which contains the Profit Margin values, is no longer hidden. You will keep the other columns hidden to save the workbook as evidence that you know how to hide columns. You will unhide the remaining columns in the next Hands-On Exercise.

f. Save the workbook. Keep the workbook onscreen if you plan to continue with Hands-On Exercise 4. If not, close the workbook, and exit Excel.

# Formatting

After entering data and formulas, you should format the worksheet to achieve a professional appearance. A professionally formatted worksheet—through adding appropriate symbols, aligning decimals, and using fonts and colors to make data stand out—makes finding and analyzing data easy. You apply different formats to accentuate meaningful details or to draw attention to specific ranges in the worksheet.

> Different formats accentuate meaningful details or draw attention to specific ranges.

In this section, you will learn to apply different alignment options, including horizontal and vertical alignment, text wrapping, and indent options. In addition, you will learn how to format different types of values.

## Applying Alignment and Font Options

Alignment refers to how data are positioned in cells. By now, you know that text aligns at the left cell margin, and dates and values align at the right cell margin. You can change the alignment of cell contents to improve the appearance of data within the cells. The Alignment group (see Figure 35) on the Home tab contains several features to help you align and format data.

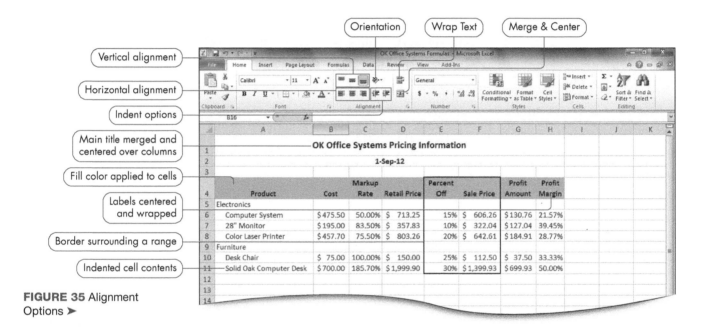

**FIGURE 35** Alignment Options ➤

## Change Horizontal and Vertical Cell Alignment

**Horizontal alignment** positions data between the left and right cell margins.

**Vertical alignment** positions data between the top and bottom cell margins.

You can align data horizontally or vertically. *Horizontal alignment* specifies the position of data between the left and right cell margins, and *vertical alignment* specifies the position of data between the top and bottom cell margins. Bottom Align is the default vertical alignment, as indicated by the orange background of Bottom Align on the Ribbon. After adjusting row height, you might need to change the vertical alignment to position data better in conjunction with data in adjacent cells. To change alignments, click the desired horizontal and/or vertical alignment setting in the Alignment group on the Home tab.

## Merge and Center Labels

You may want to place a title at the top of a worksheet and center it over the columns of data in the worksheet. You can center main titles over all columns in the worksheet, and you can center category titles over groups of related columns. To create a title, enter the text in the far left cell of the range. Select the range of cells across which you want to center the title, and then click Merge & Center in the Alignment group on the Home tab. Any data in the merge area are lost, except what is in the far left cell in the range. Excel merges the selected cells together into one cell, and the merged cell address is that of the original cell on the left. The data are centered between the left and right sides of the merged cell. In Figure 35, the title *OK Office Systems Pricing Information* is merged and centered over the data columns.

If you merge too many cells and want to split the merged cell back into its original multiple cells, click the merged cell, and then click Merge & Center. Unmerging places the data in the top-left cell.

## Increase and Decrease Indent

To offset labels, you can indent text within a cell. Accountants often indent the word Totals in financial statements so that it stands out from a list of items above the total row. Indenting helps others see the hierarchical structure of your spreadsheet data. To indent the contents of a cell, click Increase Indent in the Alignment group on the Home tab. The more you click Increase Indent, the more text is indented in the active cell. To decrease the indent, click Decrease Indent in the Alignment group. Figure 35 shows an example of an indented label.

## Wrap Text

**Wrap text** enables a label to appear on multiple lines within the current cell.

Sometimes you have to maintain specific column widths, but the data do not fit entirely. You can use *wrap text* to make data appear on multiple lines by adjusting the row height to fit the cell contents within the column width. When you click Wrap Text in the Alignment group, Excel wraps the text on two or more lines within the cell. This alignment option is helpful when the column headings are wider than the values contained in the column. In the next Hands-On Exercise, you will apply the Wrap Text option for the column headings so that you can see the text without widening the columns. Figure 35 shows an example of wrapped text.

## Apply Borders and Fill Color

A **border** is a line that surrounds a cell or a range.

You can apply a border or fill color to accentuate data in a worksheet. A ***border*** is a line that surrounds a cell or a range of cells. You can use borders to offset particular data from the rest of the data on the worksheet. To apply a border, select the cell or range that you want to have a border, click the Borders arrow in the Font group, and then select the desired border type. To remove a border, select No Border from the Borders menu.

**Fill color** is the background color appearing behind data in a cell.

To add some color to your worksheet to add emphasis to data or headers, you can apply a fill color. ***Fill color*** is a background color that displays behind the data. You should choose a fill color that contrasts with the font color. For example, if the font color is Black, you might want to choose Yellow fill color. If the font color is White, you might want to apply Blue or Dark Blue fill color. To apply a fill color, select the cell or range that you want to have a fill color, click the Fill Color arrow on the Home tab, and then select the color choice from the Fill Color palette. If you want to remove a fill color, select No Fill from the bottom of the palette.

For additional border and fill color options, display the Format Cells dialog box. Click the Border tab to select border options, including the border line style and color. Click the Fill tab to set the background color, fill effects, and patterns. Figure 35 shows examples of cells containing a border and fill color.

# Applying Number Formats

Values appear in General format (i.e., no special formatting) when you enter data. You should apply number formats based on the type of values in a cell, such as applying either the Accounting or Currency number format to monetary values. Changing the number format changes the way the number displays in a cell, but the format does not change the number's value. If, for example, you entered 123.456 into a cell and format the cell with Currency number type, the value shows as $123.46 onscreen, but the actual value 123.456 is used for calculations. When you apply a number format, you can specify the number of decimal places to display onscreen.

## Select an Appropriate Number Format

The default number format is General, which displays values as you originally enter them. General does not align decimal points in a column or include symbols, such as dollar signs, percent signs, or commas. Table 5 lists and describes the primary number formats in Excel.

| TABLE 5 Number Formats | |
| --- | --- |
| **Format Style** | **Display** |
| General | A number as it was originally entered. Numbers are shown as integers (e.g., 12345), decimal fractions (e.g., 1234.5), or in scientific notation (e.g., 1.23E+10) if the number exceeds 11 digits. |
| Number | A number with or without the 1000 separator (e.g., a comma) and with any number of decimal places. Negative numbers can be displayed with parentheses and/or red. |
| Currency | A number with the 1,000 separator and an optional dollar sign (which is placed immediately to the left of the number). Negative values are preceded by a minus sign or are displayed with parentheses or in red. Two decimal places display by default. |
| Accounting | A number with the 1,000 separator, an optional dollar sign (at the left border of the cell, vertically aligned within a column), negative values in parentheses, and zero values as hyphens. Two decimal places display by default. |
| Date | The date in different ways, such as March 14, 2012; 3/14/12; or 14-Mar-12. |
| Time | The time in different formats, such as 10:50 PM or 22:50 (24-hour time). |

*(Continued)*

| TABLE 5 (Continued) | |
|---|---|
| Format Style | Display |
| Percentage | The value as it would be multiplied by 100 (for display purpose), with the percent sign. The default number of decimal places is zero if you click Percent Style in the Number group or two decimal places if you use the Format Cells dialog box. However, you should typically increase the number of decimal points to show greater accuracy. |
| Fraction | A number as a fraction; appropriate when no exact decimal equivalent exists. A fraction is entered into a cell as a formula such as =1/3. If the cell is not formatted as a fraction, you will see the results of the formula. |
| Scientific | A number as a decimal fraction followed by a whole number exponent of 10; for example, the number 12345 would appear as 1.23E+04. The exponent, +04 in the example, is the number of places the decimal point is moved to the left (or right if the exponent is negative). Very small numbers have negative exponents. |
| Text | The data left-aligned; is useful for numerical values that have leading zeros and should be treated as text, such as ZIP codes or phone numbers. Apply Text format before typing a leading zero so that the zero displays in the cell. |
| Special | A number with editing characters, such as hyphens in a Social Security number. |
| Custom | Predefined customized number formats or special symbols to create your own customized number format. |

The Number group on the Home tab contains commands for applying Accounting Number Format, Percent Style, and Comma Style numbering formats. You can click the Accounting Number Format arrow and select other denominations, such as English pounds or euros. For other number formats, click the Number Format arrow and select the numbering format you want to use. For more specific numbering formats than those provided, select More Number Formats from the Number Format menu or click the Number Dialog Box Launcher to open the Format Cells dialog box with the Number tab options readily available. Figure 36 shows different number formats applied to values. The first six values are displayed with two decimal places.

| | A | B | C |
|---|---|---|---|
| 1 | General | 1234.56 | |
| 2 | Number | 1234.56 | |
| 3 | Currency | $1,234.56 | |
| 4 | Accounting | $          1,234.56 | |
| 5 | Comma | 1,234.56 | |
| 6 | Percent | 12.34% | |
| 7 | Short Date | 3/1/2012 | |
| 8 | Long Date | Thursday, March 01, 2012 | |

FIGURE 36 Number Formats ➤

## Increase and Decrease Decimal Places

After applying a number format, you may need to adjust the number of decimal places that display. For example, if you have an entire column of monetary values formatted in Accounting Number Format, Excel displays two decimal places by default. If the entire column of values contains whole dollar values and no cents, displaying .00 down the column looks cluttered. You can decrease the number of decimal places to show whole numbers only.

To change the number of decimal places displayed, click Increase Decimal in the Number group on the Home tab to display more decimal places for greater precision or Decrease Decimal to display fewer or no decimal places.

# HANDS-ON EXERCISES

## 4 Formatting

In the first three Hands-On Exercises, you entered data about products on sale, created formulas to calculate markup and profit, and inserted new rows and columns to accommodate additional data. You are ready to format the worksheet. Specifically, you need to center the title, align text, format values, and apply other formatting to enhance the readability of the worksheet.

**Skills covered:** Merge and Center the Title • Wrap and Align Text • Apply Number Formats and Decimal Places • Apply Borders and Fill Color • Indent Cell Contents

---

### STEP 1 ▶ MERGE AND CENTER THE TITLE

To make the title stand out, you want to center it over all the data columns. You will use the Merge & Center command to merge cells together and center the title at the same time. Refer to Figure 37 as you complete Step 1.

|  | A | B | C | D | E | F | G | H | I |
|---|---|---|---|---|---|---|---|---|---|
| 1 | OK Office Systems Pricing Information | | | | | | | | |
| 2 | 1-Sep-12 | | | | | | | | |
| 3 | | | | | | | | | |
| 4 | Product | Cost | Markup Ra | Retail Pric | Percent O | Sale Price | Profit Am | Profit Margin | |
| 5 | Electronics | | | | | | | | |
| 6 | Computer System | 475.5 | 0.5 | 713.25 | 0.15 | 606.2625 | 130.7625 | 0.215686 | |
| 7 | 28" Monitor | 195 | 0.835 | 357.825 | 0.1 | 322.0425 | 127.0425 | 0.39449 | |
| 8 | Color Laser Printer | 457.7 | 0.755 | 803.2635 | 0.2 | 642.6108 | 184.9108 | 0.287749 | |
| 9 | Furniture | | | | | | | | |
| 10 | Desk Chair | 75 | 1 | 150 | 0.25 | 112.5 | 37.5 | 0.333333 | |
| 11 | Solid Oak Computer Desk | 700 | 1.857 | 1999.9 | 0.3 | 1399.93 | 699.93 | 0.499975 | |
| 12 | | | | | | | | | |
| 13 | | | | | | | | | |

**FIGURE 37** Formatted Title ➤

a. Open the *e01h3markup_LastnameFirstname* workbook if you closed it after the last Hands-On Exercise, and save it as **e01h4markup_LastnameFirstname**, changing *h3* to *h4*.

b. Select the **column B, D, and F headings**. Unhide columns C and E as you learned in Hands-On Exercise 3.

c. Select the **range A1:H1**.

  You want to center the title over all columns of data.

d. Click **Merge & Center** in the Alignment group.

  Excel merges cells in the range A1:H1 into one cell and centers the title horizontally within the merged cell, which is cell A1.

> **TROUBLESHOOTING:** If you merge too many or not enough cells, you can unmerge the cells and start again. To unmerge cells, click in the merged cell. The Merge & Center command has an orange border when the active cell is merged. Click Merge & Center to unmerge the cell. Then select the correct range to merge and use Merge & Center again.

e. Bold the title, and then select **14 pt** size.

f. Select the **range A2:H2**. Merge and center the date, and then bold it.

g. Save the workbook.

Introduction to Excel

**WRAP AND ALIGN TEXT**

You will wrap the text in the column headings to avoid columns that are too wide for the data, but which will display the entire text of the column headings. In addition, you will horizontally center column headings between the left and right cell margins. Refer to Figure 38 as you complete Step 2.

Middle Align applied →

Text wrapped, centered, and bold →

| | A | B | C | D | E | F | G | H | I |
|---|---|---|---|---|---|---|---|---|---|
| 1 | OK Office Systems Pricing Information | | | | | | | | |
| 2 | 1-Sep-12 | | | | | | | | |
| 3 | | | | | | | | | |
| 4 | Product | Cost | Markup Rate | Retail Price | Percent Off | Sale Price | Profit Amount | Profit Margin | |
| 5 | Electronics | | | | | | | | |
| 6 | Computer System | 475.5 | 0.5 | 713.25 | 0.15 | 606.2625 | 130.7625 | 0.215686 | |
| 7 | 28" Monitor | 195 | 0.835 | 357.825 | 0.1 | 322.0425 | 127.0425 | 0.39449 | |
| 8 | Color Laser Printer | 457.7 | 0.755 | 803.2635 | 0.2 | 642.6108 | 184.9108 | 0.287749 | |
| 9 | Furniture | | | | | | | | |
| 10 | Desk Chair | 75 | 1 | 150 | 0.25 | 112.5 | 37.5 | 0.333333 | |
| 11 | Solid Oak Computer Desk | 700 | 1.857 | 1999.9 | 0.3 | 1399.93 | 699.93 | 0.499975 | |
| 12 | | | | | | | | | |

**FIGURE 38** Formatted Column Headings ➤

a. Select the **range A4:H4**.

You selected the multiple-word column headings.

b. Click **Wrap Text** in the Alignment group.

The column headings are now visible on two lines within each cell.

c. Click **Center** in the Alignment group. Bold the selected column headings.

The column headings are centered horizontally between the left and right edges of each cell.

d. Click **cell A1**, which contains the title.

e. Click **Middle Align** in the Alignment group. Save the workbook.

Middle Align vertically centers data between the top and bottom edges of the cell.

**APPLY NUMBER FORMATS AND DECIMAL PLACES**

You need to format the values to increase readability and look more professional. You will apply number formats and adjust the number of decimal points displayed. Refer to Figure 39 as you complete Step 3.

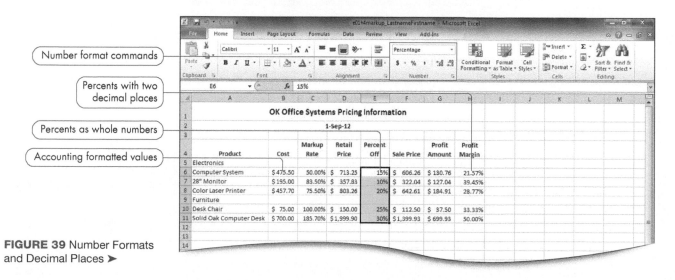

Number format commands

Percents with two decimal places

Percents as whole numbers

Accounting formatted values

**FIGURE 39** Number Formats and Decimal Places ➤

a. Select the **range B6:B11**, and then click **Accounting Number Format** in the Number group.

You formatted the selected range with Accounting Number Format. The dollar signs align on the left cell margins and the decimals align.

b. Select the **range D6:D11**. Press and hold down **Ctrl** as you select the **range F6:G11**.

Since you want to format nonadjacent ranges with the same formats, you hold down Ctrl.

c. Click **Accounting Number Format** in the Number group.

You formatted the selected nonadjacent ranges with the Accounting Number Format.

d. Select the **range C6:C11**, and then click **Percent Style** in the Number group.

You formatted the values in the selected ranges with Percent Style, showing whole numbers only.

e. Click **Increase Decimal** in the Number group twice.

You increased the decimal places to avoid misleading your readers by displaying the values as whole percentages.

f. Use Format Painter to copy the formats of the selected range to values in columns E and H.

g. Select the **range E6:E11**, and then click **Decrease Decimal** twice in the Number group. Save the workbook.

Since this range contained whole percentages, you do not need to show the decimal places.

## STEP 4 ▶ APPLY BORDERS AND FILL COLOR

You want to apply a light purple fill color to highlight the column headings. In addition, you want to emphasize the percent off and sale prices. You will do this by applying a border around that range. Refer to Figure 40 as you complete Step 4.

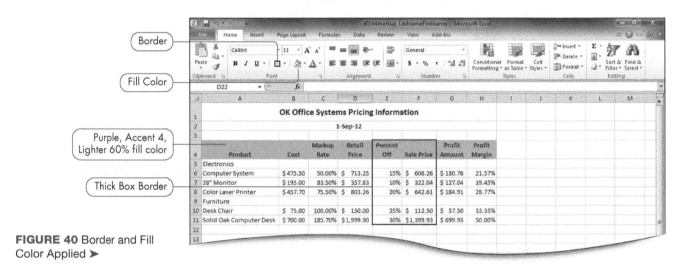

**FIGURE 40** Border and Fill Color Applied ➤

a. Select the **range A4:H4**.

b. Click the **Fill Color arrow** in the Font group.

c. Click **Purple, Accent 4, Lighter 60%** in the *Theme Colors* section. It is the third color down in the third column from the right.

You applied a fill color to the selected cells to draw attention to these cells.

d. Select the **range E4:F11**.

e. Click the **Border arrow** in the Font group, and then select **Thick Box Border**.

You applied a border around the selected cells.

f. Click in an empty cell below the columns of data to deselect the cells. Save the workbook.

## INDENT CELL CONTENTS

As you review the first column, you notice that the category names, Electronics and Furniture, don't stand out. You decide to indent the labels within each category to show which products are in each category. Refer to Figure 41 as you complete Step 5.

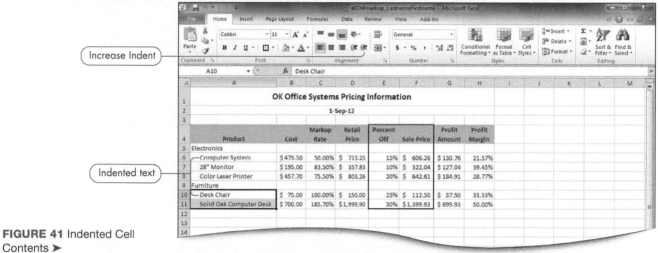

**FIGURE 41** Indented Cell Contents ➤

a. Select the **range A6:A8**, the cells containing electronic products.

b. Click **Increase Indent** in the Alignment group twice.

The three selected product names are indented below the Electronics heading.

c. Select the **range A10:A11**, the cells containing furniture products, and then click **Increase Indent** twice.

The two selected product names are indented below the Furniture heading. Notice that the product names appear cut off.

d. Increase the **column A** width to **26.00**.

e. Save the workbook. Keep the workbook onscreen if you plan to continue with Hands-On Exercise 5. If not, close the workbook, and exit Excel.

# Page Setup and Printing

Although you might distribute workbooks electronically as e-mail attachments or you might upload workbooks to a corporation server, you should prepare the worksheets in the workbook for printing. You should prepare worksheets in case you need to print them or in case others who receive an electronic copy of your workbook need to print the worksheets. The Page Layout tab provides options for controlling the printed worksheet (see Figure 42).

Page Setup
Dialog Box Launcher

**FIGURE 42** Page Layout Tab ➤

In this section, you will select options on the Page Layout tab. Specifically, you will use the Page Setup, Scale to Fit, and Sheet Options groups. After selecting page setup options, you are ready to print your worksheet.

## Selecting Page Setup Options

The Page Setup group on the Page Layout tab contains options to set the margins, select orientation, specify page size, select the print area, and apply other options. The Scale to Fit group contains options for adjusting the scaling of the spreadsheet on the printed page. When possible, use the commands in these groups to apply page settings. Table 6 lists and describes the commands in the Page Setup group.

| TABLE 6 Page Setup Commands | |
|---|---|
| **Command** | **Description** |
| **Margins** | Displays a menu to select predefined margin settings. The default margins are 0.75" top and bottom and 0.7" left and right. You will often change these margin settings to balance the worksheet data better on the printed page. If you need different margins, select Custom Margins. |
| **Orientation** | Displays orientation options. The default page orientation is portrait, which is appropriate for worksheets that contain more rows than columns. Select landscape orientation when worksheets contain more columns than can fit in portrait orientation. For example, the OKOS worksheet might appear better balanced in landscape orientation because it has eight columns. |
| **Size** | Displays a list of standard paper sizes. The default size is 8.5" by 11". If you have a different paper size, such as legal paper, select it from the list. |
| **Print Area** | Displays a list to set or clear the print area. When you have very large worksheets, you might want to print only a portion of that worksheet. To do so, select the range you want to print, click Print Area in the Page Setup group, and select Set Print Area. When you use the Print commands, only the range you specified will be printed. To clear the print area, click Print Area, and select Clear Print Area. |
| **Breaks** | Displays a list to insert or remove page breaks. |
| **Background** | Enables you to select an image to appear as the background behind the worksheet data when viewed onscreen (backgrounds do not appear when the worksheet is printed). |
| **Print Titles** | Enables you to select column headings and row labels to repeat on multiple-page printouts. |

## Specify Page Options

To apply several page setup options at once or to access options not found on the Ribbon, click the Page Setup Dialog Box Launcher. The Page Setup dialog box organizes options into four tabs: Page, Margins, Header/Footer, and Sheet. All tabs contain Print and Print Preview buttons. Figure 43 shows the Page tab.

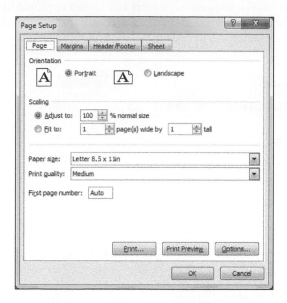

FIGURE 43 Page Setup Dialog Box Page Tab ➤

The Page tab contains options to select the orientation and paper size. In addition, it contains scaling options that are similar to the options in the Scale to Fit group on the Page Layout tab. You use scaling options to increase or decrease the size of characters on a printed page, similar to using a zoom setting on a photocopy machine. You can also use the Fit to option to force the data to print on a specified number of pages.

## Specify Margins Options

The Margins tab (see Figure 44) contains options for setting the specific margins. In addition, it contains options to center the worksheet data horizontally or vertically on the page. To balance worksheet data equally between the left and right margins, Excel users often center the page horizontally.

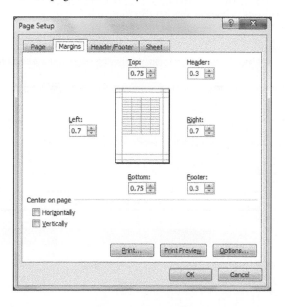

FIGURE 44 Page Setup Dialog Box Margins Tab ➤

## Create Headers and Footers

The Header/Footer tab (see Figure 45) lets you create a header and/or footer that appear at the top and/or bottom of every printed page. Click the arrows to choose from several preformatted entries, or alternatively, you can click Custom Header or Custom Footer, insert text and other objects, and then click the appropriate formatting button to customize your headers and footers. You can use headers and footers to provide additional information about the worksheet. You can include your name, the date the worksheet was prepared, and page numbers, for example.

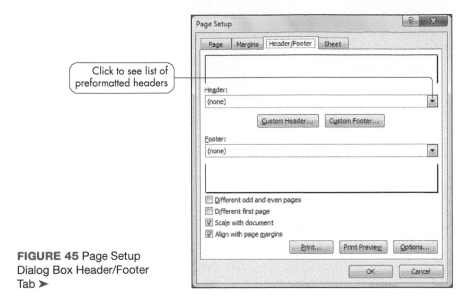

Click to see list of preformatted headers

**FIGURE 45** Page Setup Dialog Box Header/Footer Tab ➤

Instead of creating headers and footers using the Page Setup dialog box, you can click the Insert tab and click Header & Footer in the Text group. Excel displays the worksheet in Page Layout view with the insertion point in the center area of the header. If you click the View tab and then click Page Layout, you see an area that displays *Click to add header* at the top of the worksheet. You can click inside the left, center, or right section of a header or footer. When you do, Excel displays the Header & Footer Tools Design contextual tab (see Figure 46). You can enter text or insert data from the Header & Footer Elements group on the tab. To get back to Normal view, click any cell in the worksheet, and then click Normal in the Workbook Views group on the View tab.

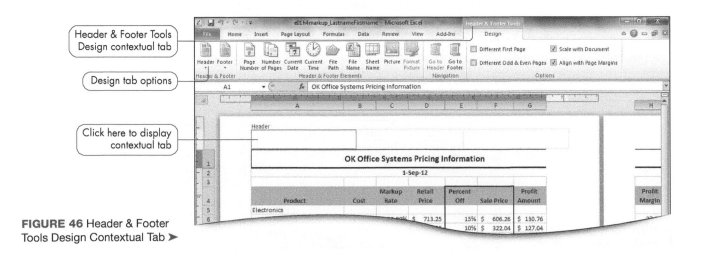

Header & Footer Tools Design contextual tab

Design tab options

Click here to display contextual tab

**FIGURE 46** Header & Footer Tools Design Contextual Tab ➤

## Select Sheet Options

The Sheet tab (see Figure 47) contains options for setting the print area, print titles, print options, and page order. Some of these options are also located in the Sheet Options group on the Page Layout tab on the Ribbon. By default, Excel displays gridlines onscreen to show you each cell's margins, but the gridlines do not print unless you specifically select the Gridlines check box in the Page Setup dialog box or the Print Gridlines check box in the Sheet Options group on the Page Layout tab. In addition, Excel displays row (1, 2, 3, etc.) and column (A, B, C, etc.) headings onscreen. However, these headings do not print unless you click the Row and column headings check box in the Page Setup dialog box or click the Print Headings check box in the Sheet Options group on the Page Layout tab.

**FIGURE 47** Page Setup Dialog Box Sheet Tab ➤

**TIP** Printing Gridlines and Headings

For most worksheets, you do not need to print gridlines and row/column headings. However, when you want to display and print cell formulas instead of formula results, you might want to print the gridlines and row/column headings. Doing so will help you analyze your formulas. The gridlines help you see the cell boundaries, and the headings help you know what data are in each cell. At times, you might want to display gridlines to separate data on a regular printout to increase readability.

# Printing a Worksheet

Before printing a worksheet, you should click the File tab and then select Print. The Backstage view displays print options and displays the worksheet in print preview mode.

> The Backstage view helps you see in advance if the data are balanced on the page.

This mode helps you see in advance if the data are balanced on the page or if data will print on multiple pages. The bottom of the Backstage view indicates how many total pages will print. If the settings are correct, you can specify the print options. If you do not like how the worksheet will print, click the Page Layout tab so that you can adjust margins, scaling, column widths, and so on until the worksheet data appear the way you want them to print.

# HANDS-ON EXERCISES

## 5 Page Setup and Printing

You are ready to complete the OKOS worksheet. Before printing the worksheet for your supervisor, you want to make sure the data will appear professional when printed. You will adjust some page setup options to put the finishing touches on the worksheet.

**Skills covered:** Set Page Orientation • Set Margin Options • Create a Header • Print Preview and Print • Adjust Scaling and Set Sheet Options

### STEP 1 ▶ SET PAGE ORIENTATION

Because the worksheet has several columns, you decide to print it in landscape orientation.

    **a.** Open the *e01h4markup_LastnameFirstname* workbook if you closed it after the last Hands-On Exercise, and save it as **e01h5markup_LastnameFirstname**, changing *h4* to *h5*.

    **b.** Click the **Page Layout tab**.

    **c.** Click **Orientation** in the Page Setup group.

    **d.** Select **Landscape** from the list. Save the workbook.

    If you print the worksheet, the data will print in landscape orientation.

### STEP 2 ▶ SET MARGIN OPTIONS

You want to set a 1" top margin and center the data between the left and right margins.

    **a.** Click **Margins** in the Page Setup group on the Page Layout tab.

    As you review the list of options, you notice the list does not contain an option to center the worksheet data horizontally.

    **b.** Select **Custom Margins**.

    The Page Setup dialog box opens with the Margins tab options displayed.

    **c.** Click the **Top spin box** to display *1*.

    You set a 1" top margin. You don't need to change the left and right margins since you will center the worksheet data horizontally between the original margins.

    **d.** Click the **Horizontally check box** in the *Center on page* section, and then click **OK**. Save the workbook.

    The worksheet data will be centered between the left and right margins.

### STEP 3 ▶ CREATE A HEADER

To document the worksheet, you want to include your name, the current date, and the worksheet tab name in a header. Refer to Figure 48 as you complete Step 3.

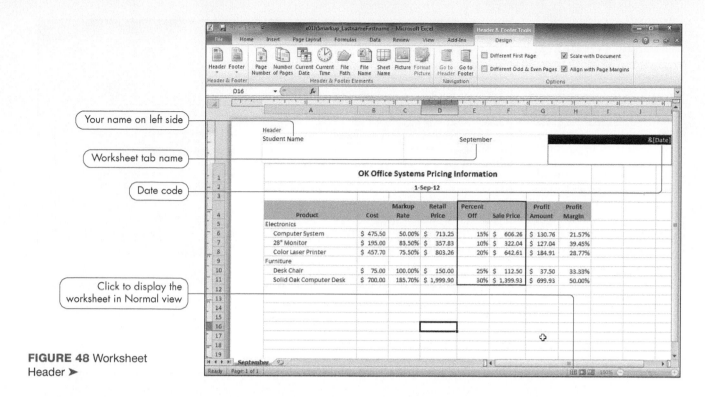

Your name on left side

Worksheet tab name

Date code

Click to display the
worksheet in Normal view

**FIGURE 48** Worksheet
Header ➤

a. Click the **Insert tab**, and then click **Header & Footer** in the Text group.

Excel displays the Header & Footer Tools Design tab, and the worksheet displays in Page
Layout view. The insertion point blinks inside the center section of the Header.

b. Click in the left section of the header, and then type your name.

c. Click in the center section of the header, and then click **Sheet Name** in the Header & Footer
Elements group on the Design tab.

Excel inserts the code &[Tab]. This code displays the name of the worksheet. If you change
the worksheet tab name, the header will reflect the new sheet name.

d. Click in the right section of the header, and then click **Current Date** in the Header & Footer
Elements group on the Design tab.

Excel inserts the code &[Date]. This code displays the current date based on the computer
clock when you print the worksheet. If you want a specific date to appear regardless of the
date you open or print the worksheet, you would have to type that date manually. When you
click in a different header section, the codes, such as &[Tab], display the actual tab name
instead of the code.

e. Click in any cell in the worksheet, click **Normal** on the status bar, and then save the workbook.

## STEP 4 ▶ PRINT PREVIEW AND PRINT

Before printing the worksheet, you should print preview it. Doing so helps you detect margin problems
and other issues, such as a single row or column of data flowing onto a new page. Refer to Figure 49 as
you complete Step 4.

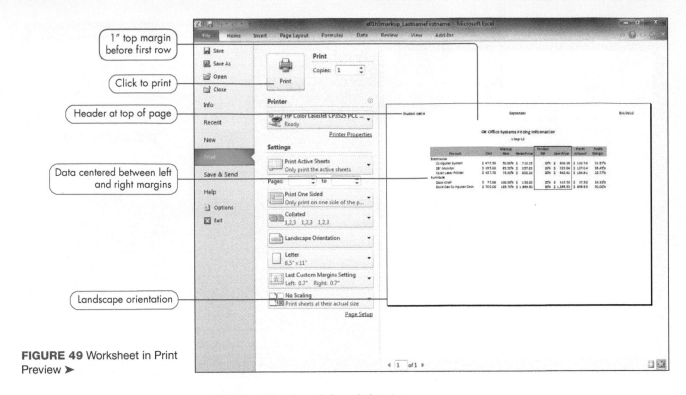

**1" top margin before first row**

**Click to print**

**Header at top of page**

**Data centered between left and right margins**

**Landscape orientation**

**FIGURE 49** Worksheet in Print Preview ➤

a. Click the **File tab**, and then click **Print**.

The Backstage view displays print options and a preview of the worksheet.

b. Verify the Printer name displays the printer that you want to use to print your worksheet.

c. Click **Print** to print the worksheet, and then save the workbook.

Check your printed worksheet to make sure the data are formatted correctly. After you click Print, the Home tab is displayed. If you decide not to print at this time, you need to click the Home tab yourself.

## STEP 5 ▸ ADJUST SCALING AND SET SHEET OPTIONS

You want to print a copy of the worksheet formulas to check the logic of the formulas. You need to display the formulas, select options to print gridlines and headings, and then decrease the scaling so that the data print on one page. Refer to Figure 50 as you complete Step 5.

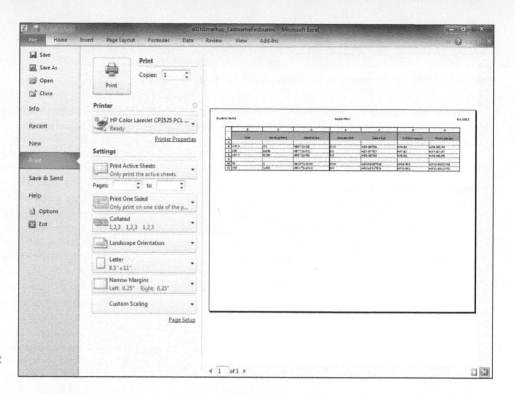

**FIGURE 50** Worksheet in Print Preview ➤

a. Press **Ctrl+`** to display cell formulas.

b. Click the **Page Layout tab**. Click the **Print Gridlines check box**, and then click the **Print Headings check box** in the Sheet Options group.

Since you want to print cell formulas, it is helpful to display the gridlines and row and column headings on that printout.

c. Click the **File tab**, and then click **Print**.

The bottom of the Backstage view displays 1 of 2, indicating the worksheet no longer prints on one page.

d. Click **Next Page** (the right triangle at the bottom of the Backstage view), and then click the **Page Layout tab**.

e. Click **Margins** in the Page Setup group, and then select **Narrow**.

f. Select the **range B4:H11**, click **Print Area** in the Page Setup group, and then select **Set Print Area**.

g. Click the **Scale spin box** in the Scale to Fit group on the Page Layout tab until it displays **90%**.

The dotted line indicating the page break now appears on the right side of the last column, indicating that the worksheet data will print on one page. If you want to verify that the worksheet will print on one page, display it in print preview.

h. Print the worksheet. Save and close the *e01h5markup_LastnameFirstname* workbook and submit the worksheet based on your instructor's directions.

Check your printed worksheet to make sure the data are formatted correctly.

# CHAPTER OBJECTIVES REVIEW

After reading this chapter, you have accomplished the following objectives:

1. **Plan for effective workbook and worksheet design.** Planning before entering data helps ensure better worksheet design. Planning involves stating the purpose, identifying input values, determining outputs, and deciding what data to add into columns and rows.

2. **Explore the Excel window.** Excel shares many common elements with other Office programs, but also includes unique elements. The Name Box identifies the location of the active cell, indicated first by column letter and then by row number, for example, A10. The Formula Bar displays the contents of the current cell. Select All enables users to select all items in the worksheet. Column and row headings identify column letters and row numbers. Sheet tabs provide different worksheets within the workbook. Navigation buttons enable users to navigate among worksheet tabs.

3. **Enter and edit cell data.** You can enter text, values, dates, and formulas in cells. Text aligns on the left cell margin, and values and dates align on the right cell margin. Values represent quantities that can be used in calculations. Dates may be entered in a variety of formats. You can edit or clear the contents of cells.

4. **Use symbols and order of precedence.** The basic arithmetic symbols are +, −, *, /, and ^ in Excel. The order of operations is the sequence in which mathematical operations is performed: parentheses, exponents, multiplication, division, addition, and subtraction. Formulas start with an equal sign, should include cell references containing values, and should not contain raw values except constants.

5. **Use Auto Fill.** To copy a formula down a column or across a row, double-click or drag the fill handle. You can use Auto Fill to copy formulas, number patterns, names of months, weekdays, etc.

6. **Display cell formulas.** By default, the results of formulas appear in cells instead of the actual formulas. You can display formulas within the cells to help troubleshoot formulas by pressing Ctrl+`.

7. **Manage worksheets.** The default worksheet tab names are Sheet1, Sheet2, and Sheet3. You can rename the worksheet tabs to be more meaningful, delete extra worksheets, insert new worksheets, and apply colors to worksheet tabs. In addition, you can move worksheets or copy worksheets.

8. **Manage columns and rows.** Although you should plan a worksheet before creating it, you can insert new columns and rows or delete columns and rows that you no longer need. You can also increase or decrease the height or width of rows and columns to display data better. Hiding rows and columns protects confidential data from being displayed or printed.

9. **Select, move, copy, and paste.** A range may be a single cell or a rectangular block of cells. After selecting a range, you can cut it to move it to another range or copy it to another location in the worksheet. You should ensure the designation range contains enough empty cells to accommodate the data you cut or copied to avoid overwriting existing data. The Paste Special option enables you to specify how the data are pasted into the worksheet.

10. **Apply alignment and font options.** You can apply horizontal and vertical alignment to format data in cells or use Merge & Center to combine cells and center titles over columns of data. To indicate hierarchy of data or to offset a label you can increase or decrease how much the data are indented in a cell. Use the Wrap Text option to present text on multiple lines in order to avoid having extra-wide columns. You can further improve readability of worksheets by adding appropriate borders around important ranges or applying fill colors to cells.

11. **Apply number formats.** The default number format is General, which does not apply any particular format to values. Apply appropriate formats to values to present the data with the correct symbols and decimal alignment. For example, Accounting is a common number format for monetary values. Other popular number formats include Percentage and Date. After applying a number format, you can increase or decrease the number of decimal points displayed.

12. **Select page setup options.** The Page Layout tab on the Ribbon contains options for setting margins, selecting orientation, specifying page size, selecting the print area, and applying other settings. In addition, you can display the Page Setup dialog box to specify these and other settings to control how data will print. You can insert a header or footer to display documentation, such as your name, date, time, and worksheet tab name.

13. **Print a worksheet.** Before printing a worksheet, you should display a preview in the Backstage view to ensure the data will print correctly. The Backstage view helps you see if margins are correct or if isolated rows or columns will print on separate pages. After making appropriate adjustments, you can print the worksheet.

# KEY TERMS

| | | |
|---|---|---|
| Active cell | Formula Bar | Sheet tab |
| Auto Fill | Horizontal alignment | Spreadsheet |
| Border | Input area | Spreadsheet program |
| Cell | Name Box | Text |
| Cell address | Nonadjacent range | Value |
| Column width | Order of precedence | Vertical alignment |
| Fill color | Output area | Workbook |
| Fill handle | Range | Worksheet |
| Formula | Row height | Wrap text |

1. What is the first step in planning an effective worksheet?

    (a) Enter labels, values, and formulas.
    (b) State the purpose of the worksheet.
    (c) Identify the input and output areas.
    (d) Decide how to format the worksheet data.

2. What Excel interface item is not displayed until you start typing or editing data in a cell?

    (a) Insert Function
    (b) Name Box
    (c) Formula Bar
    (d) Enter

3. Given the formula =B1*B2+B3/B4^2 where B1 contains 3, B2 contains 4, B3 contains 32, and B4 contains 4, what is the result?

    (a) 14
    (b) 121
    (c) 76
    (d) 9216

4. Why would you press Ctrl+` in Excel?

    (a) To display the print options
    (b) To undo a mistake you made
    (c) To display cell formulas
    (d) To enable the AutoComplete feature

5. Which of the following is a nonadjacent range?

    (a) C15:D30
    (b) L15:L65
    (c) A1:Z99
    (d) A1:A10, D1:D10

6. If you want to balance a title over several columns, what do you do?

    (a) Enter the data in the cell that is about midway across the spreadsheet.
    (b) Merge and center the data over all columns.
    (c) Use the Increase Indent command until the title looks balanced.
    (d) Click Center to center the title horizontally over several columns.

7. Which of the following characteristics is not applicable to the Accounting Number Format?

    (a) Dollar sign immediately on the left side of the value
    (b) Commas to separate thousands
    (c) Two decimal places
    (d) Zero values displayed as hyphens

8. If you want to see a preview of how a worksheet will appear on a hard copy, what do you do?

    (a) Change the Zoom to 100%.
    (b) Click the Page Layout tab, and then click the Print check box in the Sheet Options group.
    (c) Click the File tab, and then click Print.
    (d) Click the Page Setup Dialog Box Launcher.

9. Assume that the data on a worksheet consume a whole printed page and a couple of columns on a second page. You can do all of the following except what to force the data to print all on one page?

    (a) Decrease the Scale value.
    (b) Increase the left and right margins.
    (c) Decrease column widths if possible.
    (d) Select a smaller range as the print area.

10. What should you do if you see a column of pound signs (###) instead of values or results of formulas?

    (a) Increase the zoom percentage.
    (b) Delete the column.
    (c) Adjust the row height.
    (d) Increase the column width.

## 1 Mathematics Review

After a nice summer break, you want to brush up on your math skills. Since you are learning Excel, you decide to test your logic by creating formulas in Excel. Your first step is to plan the spreadsheet design. After having read this chapter, you realize that you should avoid values in formulas most of the time. Therefore, you will create an input area that contains values you will use in your formulas. To test your knowledge of formulas, you need to create an output area that will contain a variety of formulas using cell references from the input area. You need to include a formatted title, the date prepared, and your name. After creating and verifying formula results, you plan to change the input values and observe changes in the formula results. After verifying the results, you will copy the data to Sheet2, display cell formulas, and apply page layout options. This exercise follows the same set of skills as used in Hands-On Exercises 1, 2, 3, and 5 in the chapter. Refer to Figure 51 as you complete this exercise.

| | A | B | C | D | E |
|---|---|---|---|---|---|
| 1 | **Excel Formulas and Order of Precedence** | | | | |
| 2 | Date Created: | 9/1/2012 | | Student Name | |
| 3 | | | | | |
| 4 | **Input Area:** | | | **Output Area:** | |
| 5 | First Value | 1 | | Sum of 1st and 2nd values | 3 |
| 6 | Second Value | 2 | | Difference between 4th and 1st values | 3 |
| 7 | Third Value | 3 | | Product of 2nd and 3rd values | 6 |
| 8 | Fourth Value | 4 | | Quotient of 3rd and 1st values | 3 |
| 9 | | | | 2nd value to the power of 3rd value | 8 |
| 10 | | | | 1st value added to product of 2nd and 4th values and difference between sum and 3rd value | 6 |
| 11 | | | | Product of sum of 1st and 2nd and difference between 4th and 3rd values | 3 |
| 12 | | | | Product of 1st and 2nd added to product of 3rd and 4th values | 14 |
| 13 | | | | | |

**FIGURE 51** Formula Practice ➤

a. Start Excel. If Excel is already open, click the **File tab**, select **New**, and then click **Create** to display a blank workbook. Save the workbook as **e01p1math_LastnameFirstname**.

b. Type **Excel Formulas and Order of Precedence** in **cell A1**, and then press **Enter**.

c. Type the labels in **cells A2** through **A8** as shown in Figure 51, type the current date in **cell B2** in the format shown, and then type the values shown in **cells B5:B8**. Column A labels will appear cut off after you enter values in column B, and the column B values will be right-aligned at this point.

d. Type your name in **cell D2**, and then type the labels in **cells D4:D12** as shown in Figure 51. Column D labels will overlap into columns E through L at this point.

e. Adjust the column widths by doing the following:
   - Click in any cell in column A, and then click **Format** in the Cells group.
   - Select **Column Width**, type **12.5** in the **Column width box**, and then click **OK**.
   - Use the instructions in the first two bullets above to set a **35.5** width for **column D**.
   - Use the instructions in the first two bullets above to set a **11.43** width for **column B**.

f. Format the title:
   - Select the **range A1:E1**.
   - Click **Merge & Center** in the Alignment group.
   - Bold the title and apply **14 pt** size.

g. Apply the following font and alignment formats:
- Bold **cells A4** and **D4.**
- Select the **range B5:B8**, and then click **Center** in the Alignment group.
- Select the **range D10:D12**, and then click **Wrap Text** in the Alignment group.

h. Enter the following formulas in **column E:**
- Click **cell E5.** Type **=B5+B6** and press **Enter.** Excel adds the value stored in cell B5 (1) to the value stored in cell B6 (2). The result (3) appears in cell E5, as described in cell D5. You can check your results with the results shown in Figure 51.
- Enter appropriate formulas in **cells E6:E8**, pressing **Enter** after entering each formula. Subtract to calculate a difference, multiply to calculate a product, and divide to calculate a quotient.
- Type **=B6^B7** in **cell E9**, and then press **Enter.** Estimate the answer: $2*2*2 = 8$.
- Enter **=B5+B6\*B8-B7** in **cell E10**, and then press **Enter.** Estimate the answer: $2*4=8$; $1+8 = 9$; $9-3 = 6$. Multiplication occurs first, followed by addition, and finally subtraction.
- Enter **=(B5+B6)\*(B8-B7)** in **cell E11**, and then press **Enter.** Estimate the answer: $1+2 = 3$; $4-3 = 1$; $3*1 = 3$. Notice that this formula is almost identical to the previous formula; however, the parentheses affect the order of operations. Calculations in parentheses occur before the multiplication.
- Enter **=B5\*B6+B7\*B8** in **cell E12**, and then press **Enter.** Estimate the answer: $1*2 = 2$; $3*4 = 12$; $2+12 = 14$.

i. Edit a formula and the input values:
- Click **cell E12**, and then click in the **Formula Bar** to edit the formula. Add parentheses as shown: **=(B5\*B6)+(B7\*B8)**, and then click **Enter** to the left side of the Formula Bar. The answer is still 14. The parentheses do not affect order of precedence since multiplication occurred before the addition. The parentheses help improve the readability of the formula.
- Click **cell B5**, type **2**, and then press **Enter.** Type **4**, press **Enter**, type **6**, press **Enter**, type **8**, and then press **Enter.**
- Double-check the results of the formulas using a calculator or your head. The new results in cells E5:E12 should be 6, 6, 24, 3, 4096, 28, 12, and 56, respectively.

j. Double-click the **Sheet1 tab**, type **Results**, and then press **Enter.** Right-click the **Results tab**, select **Move or Copy**, click (**move to end**) in the *Before sheet* section, click the **Create a copy check box**, and then click **OK.** Double-click the **Results (2) tab**, type **Formulas**, and then press **Enter.** Right-click the **Sheet2 tab**, and then select **Delete.** Delete the Sheet3 tab.

k. Make sure the Formulas worksheet tab is active, click the **Page Layout tab**, and then do the following:
- Click **Orientation** in the Page Setup group, and then select **Landscape.**
- Click the **Print Gridlines check box**, and then click the **Print Headings check box** in the Sheet Options group.

l. Click the **Formulas tab**, and then click **Show Formulas** in the Formula Auditing group. Double-click between the column A and column B headings to adjust the column A width. Double-click between the column B and column C headings to adjust the column B width. Set **24.0** width for **column D.**

m. Click the **File tab**, and then click **Print.** Verify that the worksheet will print on one page. Click the **File tab** again to close the Backstage view.

n. Save and close the workbook, and submit the worksheet based on your instructor's directions.

## 2 Calendar Formatting

You want to create a calendar for October. The calendar will enable you to practice alignment settings, including center, merge and center, and indents. In addition, you will need to adjust column widths and increase row height to create cells large enough to enter important information, such as birthdays, in your calendar. You will use Auto Fill to complete the days of the week and the days within each week. To improve the appearance of the calendar, you will add fill colors, font colors, borders, and clip art. This exercise follows the same set of skills as used in Hands-On Exercises 1–5 in the chapter. Refer to Figure 52 as you complete this exercise.

**FIGURE 52** October Calendar Page ➤

a. Click the **File tab**, select **New**, and then click **Create** to display a blank workbook. Save the workbook as **e01p2october_LastnameFirstname**.

b. Type **October** in **cell A1**, and then click **Enter** on the left side of the Formula Bar.

c. Format the title:
   • Select the **range A1:G1**, and then click **Merge & Center** in the Alignment group.
   • Apply **48 pt** size.
   • Click the **Fill Color arrow**, and then click **Orange, Accent 6** on the top row of the *Theme Colors* section of the color palette.

d. Complete the days of the week:
   • Type **Sunday** in **cell A2**, and then click **Enter** on the left side of the Formula Bar.
   • Drag the fill handle in **cell A2** across the row through **cell G2** to use Auto Fill to complete the rest of the weekdays.
   • Click the **Fill Color arrow**, and then select **Orange, Accent 6, Lighter 80%**. Click the **Font Color arrow**, and then click **Orange, Accent 6**. Apply bold and **14 pt** size. Click **Middle Align**, and then click **Center** in the Alignment group.

e. Complete the days of the month:
   • Type **1** in **cell B3**, press **Tab**, type **2** in **cell C3**, and then click **Enter** on the left side of the Formula Bar.
   • Select the **range B3:C3**. Drag the fill handle in **cell C3** across the row through **cell G3** to use Auto Fill to complete the rest of the days for the first week.
   • Type **7** in **cell A4**, press **Tab**, type **8** in **cell B4**, and then click **Enter** on the left side of the Formula Bar. Use the fill handle to complete the days for the second week.
   • Type **14** in **cell A5**, press **Tab**, type **15** in **cell B5**, and then click **Enter** on the left side of the Formula Bar. Use the fill handle to complete the days for the third week.
   • Use the fill handle to complete the days of the month (up to 31).

f. Format the columns and rows:
   • Select **columns A:G**. Click **Format** in the Cells group, select **Column Width**, type **16** in the **Column width box**, and then click **OK**.
   • Select **row 2**. Click **Format** in the Cells group, select **Row Height**, type **54**, and then click **OK**.
   • Select **rows 3:7**. Set an **80** row height.
   • Select the **range A2:G7**. Click the **Borders arrow** in the Font group, and then select **All Borders**.
   • Select the **range A3:G7**. Click **Top Align** and **Align Text Left** in the Alignment group. Click **Increase Indent**. Bold the numbers and apply **12 pt** size.

Introduction to Excel

118

g. Insert and size images:
 • Display the Clip Art task pane. Search for and insert the Halloween image in the **October 31 cell**. Size the image to fit within the cell.
 • Search for and insert an image of Columbus in the **October 15 cell**. Size the image to fit within the cell.

h. Double-click **Sheet1**, type **October**, and then press **Enter**. Right-click **Sheet2**, and then select **Delete**. Delete Sheet3.

i. Click the **Page Layout tab**. Click **Orientation** in the Page Setup group, and then select **Landscape**.

j. Click the **Insert tab**, and then click **Header & Footer** in the Text group. Click in the left side of the header, and then type your name. Click in the center of the header, and then click **Sheet Name** in the Header & Footer Elements group on the Design tab. Click in the right side of the header, and then click **File Name** in the Header & Footer Elements group on the Design tab. Click in any cell in the workbook, and then click **Normal** on the status bar.

k. Save and close the workbook, and submit based on your instructor's directions.

## 3 Elementary School Attendance

As the principal of Wellsville Elementary School, you have to prepare periodic reports about student attendance. You decided to create a spreadsheet in Excel to store data by each grade level for a particular day. You will complete your spreadsheet by entering formulas to calculate the percentages of students who were present and absent each day. You also want to format the spreadsheet to present the data effectively. This exercise follows the same set of skills as used in Hands-On Exercises 1–5 in the chapter. Refer to Figure 53 as you complete this exercise.

|   | A | B | C | D | E | F |
|---|---|---|---|---|---|---|
| 1 | **Wellsville Elementary** | | | | | |
| 2 | Monday, April 30, 2012 | | | | | |
| 3 | | | | | | |
| 4 | **Grade Level** | Total Students | Number Present | Attendance Rate | Absence Rate | |
| 5 | Pre-K | 15 | 10 | 66.67% | 33.33% | |
| 6 | Kindergarten | 35 | 30 | 85.71% | 14.29% | |
| 7 | First Grade | 50 | 41 | 82.00% | 18.00% | |
| 8 | Second Grade | 45 | 44 | 97.78% | 2.22% | |
| 9 | Third Grade | 47 | 46 | 97.87% | 2.13% | |
| 10 | Fourth Grade | 38 | 38 | 100.00% | 0.00% | |
| 11 | Fifth Grade | 42 | 40 | 95.24% | 4.76% | |
| 12 | | | | | | |

**FIGURE 53** Attendance Report ➤

a. Open the *e01p3attend* workbook and save it as **e01p3attend_LastnameFirstname** so that you can return to the original workbook if necessary.

b. Adjust alignments by doing the following from the Alignment group on the Home tab:
 • Select the **range A1:F1**, and then click **Merge & Center** in the Alignment group to center the title over the data columns. Merge and center the date in the second row over the data columns.
 • Select the **range A4:F4**. Click **Wrap Text**, and then click **Center** in the Alignment group to center and word-wrap the column headings.

c. Click **cell D4**. Click the **Delete arrow** in the Cells group, and then select **Delete Sheet Columns** to delete the empty column D.

d. Move the Pre-K row above the Kindergarten row by doing the following:
- Right-click the **row 5 heading**, and then select **Insert** from the shortcut menu to insert a new row.
- Select the **range A12:E12**. Cut the selected range, click **cell A5**, and then paste.

e. Select the **range A5:E11**. Click **Format** in the Cells group, and then select **Row Height**. Type **24** and click **OK** to increase the row height.

f. Calculate the percentages of students who were present and absent today by doing the following:
- Click **cell D5**. Type **=C5/B5** and press **Tab** to enter the formula and make **cell E5** the active cell. This formula divides the number of students present by the total number of students in Pre-K.
- Type **=(B5-C5)/B5** and click **Enter** on the left side of the Formula Bar to enter the formula and keep **cell E5** as the active cell. This formula must first calculate the number of students who were absent by subtracting the number of students present from the total number of students in Pre-K. The difference is divided by the total number of students to determine the percentage of students absent.
- Select the **range D5:E5**. Click **Percent Style** in the Number group, and then click **Increase Decimal** twice in the Number group. With both cells still selected, double-click the fill handle in the bottom-right corner of **cell E5** to copy the formulas down the columns.
- Click the **Formulas tab**, and then click **Show Formulas** in the Formula Auditing group to display cell formulas. Review the formulas, and then click **Show Formulas** to display formula results again.

g. Press **Ctrl+Home** to make **cell A1** the active cell. Spell-check the worksheet and make necessary changes.

h. Click the **Page Layout tab**. Click **Margins** in the Page Setup group, select **Custom Margins**, click the **Horizontally check box**, and then click **OK**.

i. Click the **Insert tab**. Click **Header & Footer** in the Text group. Click in the left side of the header, and then type your name. Press **Tab**, and then click **Current Date** in the Header & Footer Elements group. Press **Tab**, and then click **File Name** in the Header & Footer Elements group. Click **cell A1**, and then click **Normal** on the status bar.

j. Save and close the workbook, and submit based on your instructor's directions.

# MID-LEVEL EXERCISES

## 1 Fuel Efficiency

Your summer vacation involved traveling through several states to visit relatives and to view the scenic attractions. While traveling, you kept a travel log of mileage and gasoline purchases. Now that the vacation is over, you want to determine the fuel efficiency of your automobile. The partially completed worksheet includes the beginning mileage for the vacation trips and the amount of fuel purchased.

a. Open the *e01m1fuel* workbook and save the workbook as **e01m1fuel_LastnameFirstname** so that you can return to the original workbook if necessary.

b. Insert a new column between columns B and C, and then type **Miles Driven** as the column heading.

c. Select the range of beginning miles in **cells A5:A12**. Copy the selected range to duplicate the values in **cells B4:B11** to ensure that the ending mileage for one trip is identical to the beginning mileage for the next trip.

d. Create the formula to calculate the miles driven for the first trip. Copy the formula down the **Miles Driven column**.

e. Create the formula to calculate the miles per gallon for the first trip. Copy the formula down the **Miles Per Gallon column**.

f. Merge and center the title over the data columns. Apply bold, **16 pt** size, and **Blue, Accent 1** font color.

g. Format the column headings: bold, centered, wrap text, and **Blue, Accent 1, Lighter 80% fill color**.

h. Apply **Comma Style** to the values in the Beginning and Ending columns, and then display these values as whole numbers. Display the values in the Miles Per Gallon column with two decimal places.

i. Delete Sheet2 and Sheet3. Rename *Sheet1* as **Mileage**.

j. Set these page settings: 2" top margin, centered horizontally, **125%** scaling.

k. Insert a header with your name on the left side, the sheet name code in the center, and the file name code on the right side.

l. Save and close the workbook, and submit based on your instructor's directions.

## 2 Guest House Rental Rates

You manage a beach guest house in Ft. Lauderdale. The guest house contains three types of rental units. You set prices based on peak and off-peak times of the year. You want to calculate the maximum daily revenue for each rental type, assuming all units of each type are rented. In addition, you want to calculate the discount rate for off-peak rental times. After calculating the revenue and discount rate, you want to improve the appearance of the worksheet by applying font, alignment, and number formats. Refer to Figure 54 as you complete this exercise.

| | A | B | C | D | E | F | G |
|---|---|---|---|---|---|---|---|
| 1 | | | Beachfront Guest House | | | | |
| 2 | | | Effective May 1, 2012 | | | | |
| 3 | | | | | | | |
| 4 | | | Peak Rentals | | Off-Peak Rentals | | |
| 5 | Rental Type | No. Units | Per Day | Maximum Revenue | Per Day | Maximum Revenue | Discount Rate |
| 6 | Studio Apartment | 6 | $149.95 | $ 899.70 | $112.50 | $ 675.00 | 25.0% |
| 7 | 1 Bedroom Suite | 4 | $250.45 | $ 1,001.80 | $174.00 | $ 696.00 | 30.5% |
| 8 | 2 Bedroom Suite | 2 | $450.00 | $ 900.00 | $247.55 | $ 495.10 | 45.0% |

**FIGURE 54** Beachfront Guest House Rental Summary ➤

a. Open the *e01m2rentals* workbook and save the workbook as **e01m2rentals_LastnameFirstname** so that you can return to the original workbook if necessary.
b. Create and copy the following formulas:
   - Calculate the Peak Rentals Maximum Revenue based on the number of units and the rental price per day.
   - Calculate the Off-Peak Rentals Maximum Revenue based on the number of units and the rental price per day.
   - Calculate the discount rate for the Off-Peak rental price per day. For example, using the peak and off-peak per day values, the studio apartment rents for 75% of its peak rental rate. However, you need to calculate and display the off-peak discount rate, which is 25%.
c. Format the monetary values with **Accounting Number Format**. Format the discount rate in **Percent Style** with one decimal place.
d. Format the headings on row 4:
   - Merge and center *Peak Rentals* over the two columns of peak rental data. Apply bold, **Dark Red fill color** and **White, Background 1 font color**.
   - Merge and center *Off-Peak Rentals* over the three columns of off-peak rental data. Apply bold, **Blue fill color**, and **White, Background 1 font color**.
e. Center, bold, and wrap the headings on row 5.
f. Apply **Red**, **Accent 2**, **Lighter 80% fill color** to the **range C5:D8**. Apply **Blue**, **Accent 1**, **Lighter 80% fill color** to the **range E5:G8**.
g. Set **1″** top, bottom, left, and right margins. Center the data horizontally on the page.
h. Insert a header with your name on the left side, the sheet name code in the center, and the file name code on the right side.
i. Insert a new worksheet, and then name it **Formulas**. Copy the data from the Rental Rates worksheet to the Formulas worksheet. On the Formulas worksheet, select **landscape orientation** and the options to print gridlines and headings. Display cell formulas and adjust column widths so that the data will fit on one page. Insert a header with the same specifications that you did for the Rental Rates worksheet.
j. Save and close the workbook, and submit based on your instructor's directions.

## 3  Real Estate Sales Report

You own a small real estate company in Enid, Oklahoma. You want to analyze sales for selected properties. Your assistant prepared a spreadsheet with some of the data from the files. You need to calculate the number of days that the houses were on the market and their sales percentage of the list price. In one situation, the house was involved in a bidding war between two families that really wanted the house. Therefore, the sale price exceeded the list price.

a. Open the *e01m3sales* workbook and save the workbook as **e01m3sales_LastnameFirstname** so that you can return to the original workbook if necessary.
b. Delete the row that has incomplete sales data. The owners took their house off the market.
c. Calculate the number of days each house was on the market. Copy the formula down that column.
d. Calculate the sale price percentage of the list price. The second house was listed for $500,250, but it sold for only $400,125. Therefore, the sale percentage of the list price is 79.99%. Format the percentages with two decimal places.
e. Format prices with **Accounting Number Format** with zero decimal places.
f. Wrap the headings on row 4.
g. Insert a new column between the Date Sold and List Price columns. Move the Days on Market column to the new location. Then delete the empty column B.
h. Edit the list date of the 41 Chestnut Circle house to be **4/20/2012**. Edit the list price of the house on Amsterdam Drive to be **$355,000**.
i. Select the **property rows**, and then set a **20** row height. Adjust column widths as necessary.
j. Select **landscape orientation**, and then set the scaling to **130%**. Center the data horizontally and vertically on the page.
k. Insert a header with your name, the current date code, and the current time code.
l. Save and close the workbook, and submit based on your instructor's directions.

You manage a publishing company that publishes and sells books to bookstores in Austin. Your assistant prepared a standard six-month royalty statement for one author. You need to insert formulas, format the worksheets, and then prepare royalty statements for other authors.

## Enter Data into the Worksheet

You need to enter and format a title, enter the date indicating the end of the statement period, and then delete a blank column. You also need to insert a row for the standard discount rate row, a percentage that you discount the books from the retail price to sell to the bookstores.

a. Open the *e01c1royal* workbook and save it as **e01c1royal_LastnameFirstname**.

b. Type **Royalty Statement** in **cell A1**. Merge and center the title over the four data columns. Select **16 pt** size, and apply **Purple font color**.

c. Type **6/30/2012** in **cell B3**, and then left-align the date.

d. Delete the blank column between the Hardback and Paperback columns.

e. Insert a new row between *Retail Price* and *Price to Bookstore*. Enter **Standard Discount Rate**, **0.55**, and **0.5**. Format the two values as **Percent Style**.

## Calculate Values

You need to insert formulas to perform necessary calculations.

a. Enter the **Percent Returned formula** in the Hardback column. The percent returned indicates the percentage of books sold but returned to the publisher.

b. Enter the **Price to Bookstore formula**. This is the price at which you sell the books to the bookstore and is based on the retail price and the standard discount. For example, if a book has a $10 retail price and a 55% discount, you sell the book for $4.50.

c. Enter the **Net Retail Sales formula**. The net retail sales is the revenue from the net units sold at the retail price. Gross units sold minus the returned units equals net units sold.

d. Enter the **Royalty to Author formula**. Royalties are based on net retail sales and the applicable royalty rate.

e. Enter the **Royalty per Book formula**. This amount is the author's earnings on every book sold but not returned.

f. Copy the formulas to the Paperback column.

## Format the Values

You are ready to format the values to improve the readability.

a. Apply **Comma Style** with zero decimal places to the quantities in the *Units Sold* section.

b. Apply **Percent Style** with one decimal place to the Units Sold values, **Percent Style** with zero decimal places to the Pricing values, and **Percent Style** with two decimal places to the Royalty Information values.

c. Apply **Accounting Number Format** to all monetary values.

## Format the Worksheet

You want to improve the appearance of the rest of the worksheet.

a. Select the **Hardback** and **Paperback labels**. Apply bold, right-alignment, and **Purple font color**.

b. Select the **Units Sold section heading**. Apply bold and **Purple, Accent 4, Lighter 40% fill color**.

c. Use **Format Painter** to apply the formats from the Units Sold label to the Pricing and Royalty Information labels.

d. Select the individual labels within each section (e.g., *Gross Units Sold*) and indent the labels twice. Widen column A as needed.

e. Select the **range A7:C10** (the *Units Sold* section), and then apply the **Outside Borders border style**. Apply the same border style to the *Pricing* and *Royalty Information* sections.

## Manage the Workbook

You want to duplicate the royalty statement worksheet to use as a model to prepare a royalty statement for another author. You will apply page setup options and insert a header on both worksheets.

a. Insert a new worksheet on the right side of the Jacobs worksheet. Rename the worksheet as **Lopez**.

b. Change the Jacobs sheet tab to **Red**. Change the Lopez sheet tab to **Dark Blue**.

c. Copy Jacobs' data to the Lopez worksheet.

d. Make these changes on the Lopez worksheet: **Lopez** (author), **5000** (hardback gross units), **15000** (paperback gross units), **400** (hardback returns), **175** (paperback returns), **19.95** (hardback retail price), and **7.95** (paperback retail price).

e. Click the **Jacobs sheet tab**, and then press and hold down **Ctrl** as you click the **Lopez sheet tab** to select both worksheets. Select the margin setting to center the data horizontally on the page. Insert a header with your name on the left side, the sheet name code in the center, and the file name code on the right side.

f. Change back to Normal view. Right-click the **Jacobs sheet name**, and then select **Ungroup Sheets**.

## Display Formulas and Print the Workbook

You want to print the formatted Jacobs worksheet to display the calculated results. To provide evidence of the formulas, you want to display and print cell formulas in the Lopez worksheet.

a. Display the cell formulas for the Lopez worksheet.

b. Select options to print the gridlines and headings.

c. Adjust the column widths so that the formula printout will print on one page.

d. Submit either a hard copy of both worksheets or an electronic copy of the workbook to your professor as instructed. Close the workbook.

# BEYOND THE CLASSROOM

### Server's Tip Distribution

GENERAL CASE

You are a server at a restaurant in Seattle. When you get tips, you calculate the percentage of the subtotal to determine your performance based on the tip. You must tip the bartender 15% of the drink amount and the server assistant 12% of your total tip amount. You started to design a spreadsheet to enter data for one shift. Open *e01b1tips* and save it as **e01b1tips_LastnameFirstname**. Now you need to insert columns for the bartender and assistant tip rates, perform calculations, and format the data. After entering the formulas, use Auto Fill to copy the formulas down the respective columns. Include a notes section that explains the tipping rates for the bartender and server assistant. Decide where to place this information. Add and format a descriptive title, date, and time of shift. To format the data, apply concepts learned in the chapter: font, borders, fill color, alignment, wrap text, and number formats. Select appropriate options on the Page Layout tab. Copy the data to Sheet2, display cell formulas, print gridlines, print headings, set the print area to the column headings and data, and adjust the column widths. Include a footer with appropriate data for the two worksheets. Manage the workbook by deleting extra worksheets, renaming the two worksheets that contain data, and adding worksheet tab colors to both sheets. Save and close the workbook, and submit based on your instructor's directions.

### Credit Card Rebate

RESEARCH CASE

You recently found out the personal-use Costco TrueEarnings® American Express credit card earns annual rebates on all purchases, whether at Costco or other places. You want to see how much rebate you would have received had you used this credit card for purchases in the past year. Use the Internet to research the percentage rebates for different categories. Plan the design of the spreadsheet. Enter the categories, rebate percentages, amount of money you spent in each category, and a formula to calculate the amount of rebate. Use the Excel Help feature to learn how to add several cells using a function instead of adding cells individually and how to apply a Double Accounting underline. Then insert the appropriate function to total your categorical purchases and rebate amounts. Apply appropriate formatting and page setup options as discussed in this chapter for readability. Underline the last monetary values for the last data row, and apply the Double Accounting underline style to the totals. Insert a header with imperative documentation. Save the workbook as **e01b2rebate_LastnameFirstname**. Save and close the workbook, and submit based on your instructor's directions.

### Housing Estimates

DISASTER RECOVERY

One of your friends is starting a house construction business. Your friend developed an Excel workbook to prepare a cost estimate for a potential client. However, the workbook contains several errors. You offer to review the workbook, identify the errors, and correct them. Open *e01b3house* and save it as **e01b3house_LastnameFirstname**. Research how to insert comments in cells. As you identify the errors, insert comments in the respective cells to explain the errors. Correct the errors. Insert your name on the left side of the header. The other header and page setup options are already set. Save and close the workbook, and submit based on your instructor's directions.

EXCEL

# FORMULAS AND FUNCTIONS

## Performing Quantitative Analysis

Watch the Set-up Video for this Case Study!

### CASE STUDY | Denver Mortgage Company

You are an assistant to Erica Matheson, a mortgage broker at the Denver Mortgage Company. Erica spends her days reviewing mortgage rates and trends, meeting with potential clients, and preparing paperwork. She relies on your expertise in using Excel to help you analyze mortgage data.

Today, Erica provided you with a spreadsheet containing data for five mortgages. She asked you to perform some basic calculations so that she can check the output provided by her system. She needs you to calculate the amount financed, the periodic interest rate, the total number of payment periods, monthly payments, and other details for each mortgage. In addition, you will perform some basic statistics, such as totals and averages. After you complete these tasks, Erica wants you to create a separate worksheet with additional input data to automate calculations for future loans.

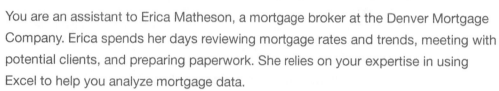

### OBJECTIVES AFTER YOU READ THIS CHAPTER, YOU WILL BE ABLE TO:

1. Use semi-selection to create a formula
2. Use relative, absolute, and mixed cell references in formulas
3. Avoid circular references
4. Insert a function
5. Total values with the SUM function
6. Insert basic statistical functions
7. Use date functions
8. Determine results with the IF function
9. Use lookup functions
10. Calculate payments with the PMT function
11. Create and maintain range names
12. Use range names in formulas

# Formula Basics

By increasing your understanding of formulas, you can build robust spreadsheets that perform a variety of calculations for quantitative analysis. Your ability to build sophisticated spreadsheets and to interpret the results increases your value to any organization. By now, you should be able to build simple formulas using cell references and mathematical operators and using the order of precedence to control the sequence of calculations in formulas.

> Your ability to build sophisticated spreadsheets and to interpret the results increases your value to any organization.

In this section, you will use the semi-selection method to create formulas. In addition, you will create formulas in which cell addresses change or remain fixed when you copy them. Finally, you will learn how to identify and prevent circular references in formulas.

## Using Semi-Selection to Create a Formula

You have learned how to create formulas by typing the cell references (for example, =A1+A2) to create a formula. To decrease typing time and ensure accuracy, you can use *semi-selection*, a process of selecting a cell or range of cells for entering cell references as you create formulas. Semi-selection is often called *pointing* because you use the mouse pointer to select cells as you build the formula. To use the semi-selection technique to create a formula, do the following:

**Semi-selection** (or pointing) is the process of using the mouse pointer to select cells while building a formula.

1. Click the cell where you want to create the formula.
2. Type an equal sign (=) to start a formula.
3. Click the cell or drag to select the cell range that contains the value(s) to use in the formula. A moving marquee appears around the cell or range you select, and Excel displays the cell or range reference in the formula.
4. Type a mathematical operator.
5. Continue clicking cells, selecting ranges, and typing operators to finish the formula. Use the scroll bars if the cell is in a remote location in the worksheet, or click a worksheet tab to see a cell in another worksheet.
6. Press Enter to complete the formula.

## Using Relative, Absolute, and Mixed Cell References in Formulas

When you copy a formula, Excel either adjusts or preserves the cell references in the copied formulas based on how the cell references appear in the original formula. Excel uses three different ways to reference a cell in a formula: relative, absolute, and mixed. Figure 1 shows a worksheet containing various cell references in formulas. When you create an original formula that you will copy to other cells, ask yourself the following: Do the cell references need to adjust for the copied formulas, or should the cell references always refer to the same cell location, regardless where the copied formula is located?

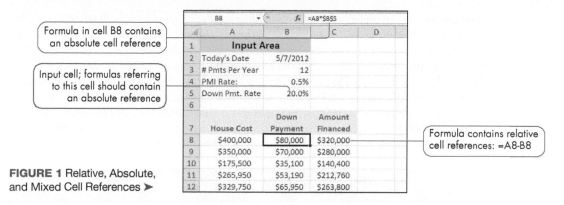

**FIGURE 1** Relative, Absolute, and Mixed Cell References ➤

## Use a Relative Cell Reference

A **relative cell reference** indicates a cell's relative location from the cell containing the formula; the cell reference changes when the formula is copied.

A *relative cell reference* indicates a cell's relative location, such as two rows up and one column to the left, from the cell containing the formula. When you copy a formula containing a relative cell reference, the cell references in the copied formula change relative to the position of the copied formula. Regardless of where you copy the formula, the cell references in the copied formula maintain the same relative distance from the copied formula cell, as the cell references relative location to the original formula cell.

In Figure 1, the formulas in column C contain relative cell references. When you copy the original formula =A8-B8 from cell C8 down to cell C9, the copied formula changes to =A9-B9. Because you copy the formula down the column to cell C12, the column letters in the formula stay the same, but the row numbers change, down one row number at a time. Relative references are indicated by using the cell address. Using relative cell addresses to calculate the amount financed ensures that each borrower's down payment is subtracted from his or her respective house cost.

## Use an Absolute Cell Reference

An **absolute cell reference** indicates a cell's specific location; the cell reference does not change when you copy the formula.

An *absolute cell reference* provides a permanent reference to a specific cell. When you copy a formula containing an absolute cell reference, the cell reference in the copied formula does not change, regardless of where you copy the formula. An absolute cell reference appears with a dollar sign before both the column letter and row number, such as $B$5.

Figure 1 illustrates an effective use of an input area, a range in a worksheet that contains values that you can change. You build formulas using absolute references to the cells in the input area. By using cell references from an input area, you can change the value in the input area and the formulas that refer to those cells update automatically. If an input value changes (e.g., the down payment rate changes from 20% to 25%), enter the new input value in only one cell (e.g., B5), and Excel recalculates the amount of recommended down payment for all the formulas.

In Figure 1, the formulas in column B calculate down payments based on the house costs in column A and on the required down payment percentage, which is stored in cell B5. The formula uses an absolute cell reference to cell B5, which currently contains the value 20%. Cell B8 contains the formula to calculate the first borrower's down payment: =A8*$B$5. A8 is a relative address that changes as you copy the formula down the column so that the down payment is based on each borrower's respective house cost (A8 becomes A9 on the 9th row, A10 on the 10th row, etc.). $B$5 is an absolute cell reference to the cell B5, which currently contains 20%. The absolute cell reference $B$5 prevents the cell reference to B5 from changing when you copy the formula to calculate the recommended down payment for the other borrowers.

## Use a Mixed Cell Reference

A **mixed cell reference** contains both an absolute and a relative cell reference in a formula; the absolute part does not change but the relative part does when you copy the formula.

A *mixed cell reference* combines an absolute cell reference with a relative cell reference. When you copy a formula containing a mixed cell reference, either the column letter or the row number that has the absolute reference remains fixed while the other part of the cell reference that is relative changes in the copied formula. $B5 and B$5 are examples of mixed cell references. In the reference $B5, the column B is absolute, and the row number is relative; when you copy the formula, the column letter, B, does not change, but the row number will change. In the reference B$5, the column letter, B, changes, but the row number, 5, does not change. To create a mixed reference, type the dollar sign to the left of the part of the cell reference you want to be absolute.

In the example shown in Figure 1, you could change the formula in cell B8 to be =A8*B$5. Because you are copying down the same column, only the row reference 5 must be absolute; the column letter stays the same. In situations where you can use either absolute or mixed references, consider using mixed references to shorten the length of the formula.

> **TIP** The F4 Key
>
> The F4 key toggles through relative, absolute, and mixed references. Click a cell reference within a formula on the Formula Bar, and then press F4 to change it. For example, click in B5 in the formula =A8*B5. Press F4, and the relative cell reference (B5) changes to an absolute cell reference ($B$5). Press F4 again, and $B$5 becomes a mixed reference (B$5); press F4 again, and it becomes another mixed reference ($B5). Press F4 a fourth time, and the cell reference returns to the original relative reference (B5).

# Avoiding Circular References

A **circular reference** occurs when a formula directly or indirectly refers to itself.

If a formula contains a direct or an indirect reference to the cell containing the formula, a *circular reference* exists. For example, assume you enter the formula =A8-C8 in cell C8. Because the formula is in cell C8, using the cell address C8 within the formula creates a circular reference. Circular references usually cause inaccurate results, and Excel displays a warning message when you enter a formula containing a circular reference or when you open an Excel workbook that contains an existing circular reference (see Figure 2). Click Help to display the *Remove or allow a circular reference* Help topic, or click OK to accept the circular reference. The status bar indicates the location of a circular reference until it has been resolved.

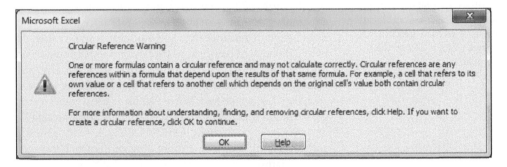

**FIGURE 2** Circular Reference Warning ➤

If the circular reference warning appears when creating a formula, use Help to activate formula auditing tools to help you identify what is causing the circular reference.

> **TIP** Green Triangles
>
> Excel displays a green triangle in the top-left corner of a cell if it detects a potential error in a formula. Click the cell to see the Trace Error button (yellow diamond with exclamation mark). When you click Trace Error, Excel displays information about the potential error and how to correct it. In some cases, Excel may anticipate an inconsistent formula or the omission of adjacent cells in a formula. For example, if you add a column of values for the year 2012, the error message indicates that you did not include the year itself. However, the year is merely a label and should not be included; therefore, you would ignore that error message.

Formulas and Functions

# 1 Formula Basics

Erica prepared a workbook containing data for five mortgages financed with the Denver Mortgage Company. The data include house cost, down payment, mortgage rate, number of years to pay off the mortgage, and the financing date for each mortgage.

**Skills covered:** Use Semi-Selection to Create a Formula • Copy a Formula with a Relative Cell Reference • Enter a Formula with an Absolute Cell Reference • Enter a Formula with a Mixed Cell Reference • Create and Correct a Circular Reference

## STEP 1 ▶ USE SEMI-SELECTION TO CREATE A FORMULA

Your first step is to calculate the amount financed by each borrower by creating a formula that calculates the difference between the cost of the house and the down payment. You decide to use the semi-selection technique. Refer to Figure 3 as you complete Step 1.

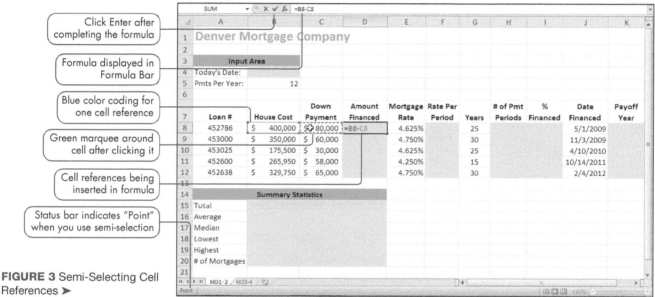

Click Enter after completing the formula

Formula displayed in Formula Bar

Blue color coding for one cell reference

Green marquee around cell after clicking it

Cell references being inserted in formula

Status bar indicates "Point" when you use semi-selection

**FIGURE 3** Semi-Selecting Cell References ▶

a. Open *e02h1loans* and save it as **e02h1loans_LastnameFirstname**.

> **TROUBLESHOOTING:** If you make any major mistakes in this exercise, you can close the file, open *e02h1loans* again, and then start this exercise over.

The workbook contains two worksheets: HO1-2 (for Hands-On Exercises 1 and 2) and HO3-4 (for Hands-On Exercises 3 and 4). You will enter formulas in the shaded cells.

b. Click the **HO1-2 worksheet tab**, and then click **cell D8**.

This is where you will create a formula to calculate the first borrower's amount financed.

c. Type = and click **cell B8**, the cell containing the first borrower's house cost.

You type an equal sign to start the formula, and then you click the first cell containing a value you want to use in the formula. A blue marquee appears around cell B8, and the B8 cell reference appears to the right of the equal sign in the formula.

d. Type - and click **cell C8**, the cell containing the down payment by the first borrower.

A green marquee appears around cell C8, and the C8 cell reference appears to the right of the subtraction sign in the formula (see Figure 3).

> **TROUBLESHOOTING:** If you click the wrong cell, click the correct cell to change the cell reference in the formula. If you realize the mistake after typing an arithmetic operator or after entering the formula, you must edit the formula to change the cell reference.

e. Click **Enter** to the left of the Formula Bar to complete the formula. Save the workbook.

The first borrower financed (i.e., borrowed) $320,000, the difference between the cost ($400,000) and the down payment ($80,000).

## STEP 2 ▶ COPY A FORMULA WITH A RELATIVE CELL REFERENCE

After verifying the results of the amount financed by the first borrower, you are ready to copy the formula. Before copying the formula, determine if the cell references should be relative or absolute. For this formula, you want cell references to change for each row. For each borrower, you want to base the amount financed on his or her own data, so you decide to keep the relative cell references in the formula. Refer to Figure 4 as you complete Step 2.

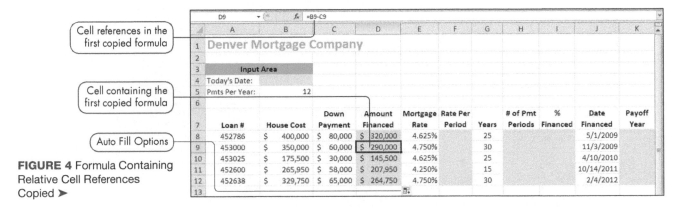

Cell references in the first copied formula

Cell containing the first copied formula

Auto Fill Options

**FIGURE 4** Formula Containing Relative Cell References Copied ▶

a. Make sure that **cell D8** is the active cell but does not have a blinking insertion point.

b. Double-click the **cell D8 fill handle**.

You copied the formula down the Amount Financed column for each mortgage row.

> **TIP** Auto Fill Options
>
> The Auto Fill Options button appears in the bottom-right corner of the copied formulas. If you click it, you can see that the default is Copy Cells. If you want to copy only formatting, click Fill Formatting Only. If you want to copy data only, click Fill Without Formatting.

c. Click **cell D9**, and then view the formula in the Formula Bar.

The formula in cell D8 is =B8-C8. The formula pasted in cell D9 is =B9-C9. Because the original formula contained relative cell references, when you copy the formula down a column, the row numbers for the cell references change. Each result represents the amount financed for that particular borrower.

d. Press ⬇ and look at the cell references in the Formula Bar to see how the references change for each formula you copied. Save the workbook with the new formula you created.

**STEP 3** **ENTER A FORMULA WITH AN ABSOLUTE CELL REFERENCE**

Column E contains the annual percentage rate (APR) for each mortgage. Because the borrowers will make monthly payments, you need to calculate the monthly interest rate by dividing the APR by 12 (the number of payments in one year) for each borrower. Refer to Figure 5 as you complete Step 3.

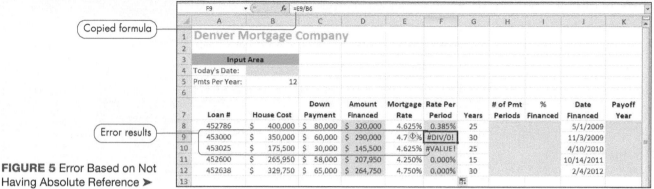

Copied formula

Error results

**FIGURE 5** Error Based on Not Having Absolute Reference ➤

a. Click **cell F8**.

You need to create a formula to calculate the monthly interest rate for the first borrower.

b. Type = and click **cell E8**, the cell containing the first fixed mortgage rate.

c. Type / and click **cell B5**, the cell containing the value 12.

Typically, you should avoid typing values directly in formulas. Although the number of months in one year will always be 12, you use a cell reference so that the company could change the payment period to bimonthly (24 payments per year) or quarterly (four payments per year) without adjusting the formula.

d. Click **Enter** to the left of the Formula Bar, double-click the **cell F8 fill handle**, click **cell F9**, and then view the results (see Figure 5).

An error icon displays to the left of cell F9, cell F9 displays #DIV/0!, and cell F10 displays #VALUE!. The original formula was =E8/B5. Because you copied the formula =E8/B5 down the column, the first copied formula is =E9/B6, and the second copied formula is =E10/B7. Although you want the mortgage rate cell reference (E8) to change (E9, E10, etc.) from row to row, you do not want the divisor to change. You need all formulas to divide by the value stored in cell B5, so you will edit the formula to make B5 an absolute reference.

> **TIP** Error Icons
>
> You can position the mouse pointer over the error icon to see a tip indicating what is wrong, such as *The formula or function used is dividing by zero or empty cells*. You can click the icon to see a menu of options to learn more about the error and how to correct it.

e. Undo the Auto Fill process. Click within or to the right of **B5** in the Formula Bar.

f. Press **F4**, and then click **Enter** to the left of the Formula Bar.

Excel changes the cell reference from B5 to $B$5, making it absolute.

g. Copy the formula down the Rate Per Period column. Click **cell F9**, and then view the formula in the Formula Bar. Save the workbook with the new formula you created.

The formula in cell F9 is =E9/$B$5. The reference to E9 is relative and B5 is absolute.

ENTER A FORMULA WITH A MIXED CELL REFERENCE

The next formula you need to enter will calculate the total number of payment periods for each loan. Refer to Figure 6 as you complete Step 4.

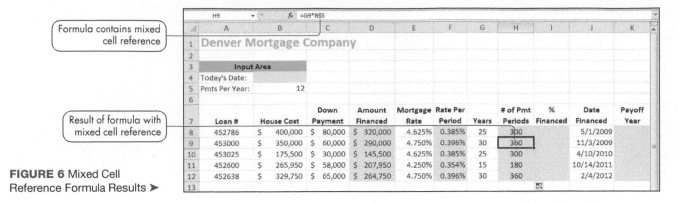

Formula contains mixed cell reference

Result of formula with mixed cell reference

**FIGURE 6** Mixed Cell Reference Formula Results ➤

a. Click **cell H8**.

b. Type = and click **cell G8**, the cell containing *25*, the number of years to pay off the loan for the first borrower.

   You need to multiply the number of years (25) by the number of payment periods in one year (12) using cell references.

c. Type * and click **cell B5**.

   You want B5 to be absolute so that the cell reference remains B5 when you copy the formula.

d. Press **F4** to make the cell reference absolute, and then click **Enter** to the left of the Formula Bar.

   The product of 25 years and 12 months is 300.

e. Copy the formula down the # of Pmt Periods column.

   The first copied formula is =G9*$B$5, and the result is 360. You want to see what happens if you change the absolute reference to a mixed reference and then copy the formula again. Because you are copying down a column, the column letter B can be relative since it will not change either way, but the row number 5 must be absolute.

f. Undo the copied formulas. Click **cell H8**, and then click within the **$B$5 cell reference** in the Formula Bar. Press **F4** to change the cell reference to a mixed cell reference, B$5. Press **Ctrl+Enter**, and then copy the formula down the # of Pmt Periods column. Click **cell H9**. Save the workbook with the new formula you created.

   The first copied formula is =G9*B$5, and the result is still 360. In this situation, using either an absolute reference or a mixed reference provides the same results.

CREATE AND CORRECT A CIRCULAR REFERENCE

Erica wants to know what percentage of the house cost each borrower will finance. As you create the formula, you enter a circular reference. After studying the results, you correct the circular error and plan future formulas that avoid this problem. Refer to Figure 7 as you complete Step 5.

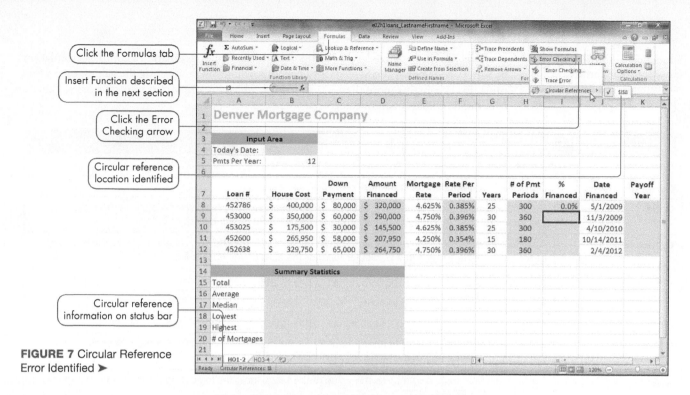

Click the Formulas tab

Insert Function described in the next section

Click the Error Checking arrow

Circular reference location identified

Circular reference information on status bar

**FIGURE 7** Circular Reference Error Identified ➤

a. Click **cell I8**, type **=I8/B8**, and then press **Enter**.

The Circular Reference Warning message box appears.

b. Read the description of the error, and then click **Help**.

A Help window opens, displaying information about circular references.

c. Read the Help topic information, and then close the Help window.

Notice that the left side of the status bar displays *Circular References: I8*. You will follow the advice given in the Help window to fix it.

d. Click the **Formulas tab**, click the **Error Checking arrow** in the Formula Auditing group, and then point to **Circular References**.

The Circular References menu displays a list of cells containing circular references.

e. Select **$I$8** from the list to make it the active cell.

Because the formula is stored in cell I8, the formula cannot refer to the cell itself. You need to divide the value in the Amount Financed column by the value in the House Cost column.

f. Edit the formula to be **=D8/B8**. Copy the formula down the % Financed column.

The first borrower financed 80% of the cost of the house: $320,000 financed divided by $400,000 cost.

g. Save the workbook. Keep the workbook onscreen if you plan to continue with Hands-On Exercise 2. If not, close the workbook and exit Excel.

# Function Basics

A **function** is a predefined formula that performs a calculation.

An Excel *function* is a predefined computation that simplifies creating a complex calculation by using dialog boxes and ScreenTips to prompt you through selecting the values for the formula. Excel contains more than 325 functions, which are organized into categories. Table 1 lists and describes function categories.

| TABLE 1 Function Categories and Descriptions | |
|---|---|
| **Category** | **Description** |
| **Compatibility** | Contains functions compatible with Excel 2007 and earlier. |
| **Cube** | Returns values based on data in a cube, such as validating membership in a club, returning a member's ranking, and displaying aggregated values from the club data set. |
| **Database** | Analyzes records stored in a database format in Excel and returns key values, such as the number of records, average value in a particular field, or the sum of values in a field. |
| **Date & Time** | Provides methods for manipulating date and time values. |
| **Engineering** | Calculates values commonly used by engineers, such as value conversions. |
| **Financial** | Performs financial calculations, such as payments, rates, present value, and future value. |
| **Information** | Provides information about the contents of a cell, typically displaying TRUE if the cell contains a particular data type such as a value. |
| **Logical** | Performs logical tests and returns the value of the tests. Includes logical operators for combined tests, such as AND, OR, and NOT. |
| **Lookup & Reference** | Looks up values, creates links to cells, or provides references to cells in a worksheet. |
| **Math & Trig** | Performs standard math and trigonometry calculations. |
| **Statistical** | Performs common statistical calculations, such as averages and standard deviations. |
| **Text** | Manipulates text strings, such as combining text or converting text to lowercase. |

**Syntax** is a set of rules that govern the structure and components for properly entering a function.

An **argument** is an input, such as a cell reference or value, needed to complete a function.

When using functions, you must adhere to correct *syntax*, the rules that dictate the structure and components required to perform the necessary calculations. The basic syntax of a function requires a function to start with an equal sign, to contain the function name, and to specify its arguments. The function name describes the purpose of the function. For example, the function name SUM indicates that the function sums or adds values. A function's *arguments* specify the inputs—such as cells or values—that are required to complete the operation. Arguments are enclosed in parentheses, with the opening parenthesis immediately following the function name. Some functions, such as TODAY, do not require arguments; however, you must include the parentheses with nothing inside them. In some cases, a function requires multiple arguments separated by commas.

In this section, you will learn how to insert common functions using the keyboard and the Insert Function and Function Arguments dialog boxes.

## Inserting a Function

**Formula AutoComplete** displays a list of functions and defined names as you enter a function.

To insert a function by typing, first type an equal sign, and then begin typing the function name. *Formula AutoComplete* displays a list of functions and defined names that match letters as you type a formula. For example, if you type =SU, Formula AutoComplete displays a list of functions and names that start with *SU* (see Figure 8). You can double-click the function name from the list or continue typing the function name. You can even scroll through the list to see the ScreenTip describing the function.

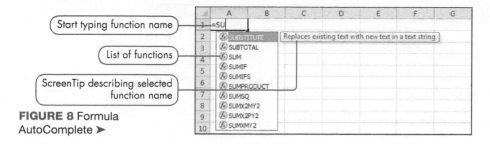

Start typing function name

List of functions

ScreenTip describing selected
function name

**FIGURE 8** Formula
AutoComplete ➤

A **function ScreenTip** is a small
pop-up description that displays
the arguments for a function as
you enter it.

After you type the function name and opening parenthesis, Excel displays the *function ScreenTip*, a small pop-up description that displays the function's arguments. The argument you are currently entering is bold in the function ScreenTip (see Figure 9). Square brackets indicate optional arguments. For example, the SUM function requires the number1 argument, but the number2 argument is optional. Click the argument name in the function ScreenTip to select the actual argument in the cell.

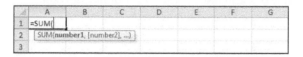

**FIGURE 9** Function
ScreenTip ➤

You can also use the Insert Function dialog box to search for a function, select a function category, and select a function from the list (see Figure 10). The dialog box is helpful if you want to browse a list of functions, especially if you are not sure of the function you need and want to see descriptions. To display the Insert Function dialog box, click Insert Function, which looks like *fx*, between the Name Box and the Formula Bar, or click Insert Function in the Function Library group on the Formulas tab. From within the dialog box, select a function category, such as Most Recently Used, and then select a function to display the syntax and a brief description of that function. Click *Help on this function* to display specific information about the selected function.

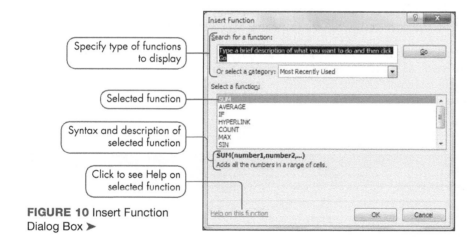

Specify type of functions
to display

Selected function

Syntax and description of
selected function

Click to see Help on
selected function

**FIGURE 10** Insert Function
Dialog Box ➤

When you find the function you want, click OK. The Function Arguments dialog box opens so that you can enter the arguments for that specific function (see Figure 11). Bold arguments are required; argument names that are not bold are optional. The function can operate without the optional argument, which is used when you need additional specifications to calculate a result. Type the cell references in the argument boxes, or click a collapse button to the right side of an argument box to select the cell or range of cells in the worksheet to designate as that argument. The value or results of a formula contained in the argument cell displays on the right side of the argument box. If the argument is not valid, Excel displays an error description on the right side of the argument box.

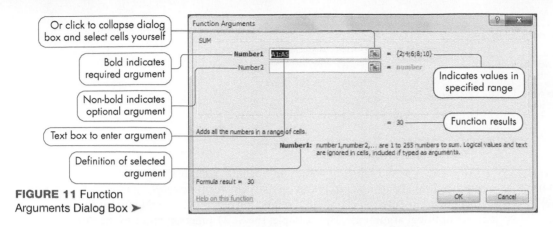

Or click to collapse dialog box and select cells yourself

Bold indicates required argument

Non-bold indicates optional argument

Text box to enter argument

Definition of selected argument

Indicates values in specified range

Function results

**FIGURE 11** Function Arguments Dialog Box ➤

The bottom of the Function Arguments dialog box displays a description of the function and a description of the argument containing the insertion point. As you enter arguments, the dialog box also displays the results of the function.

> **TIP** #NAME?
>
> If you enter a function, and #NAME? appears in the cell, you might have mistyped the function name. To avoid this problem, select the function name from the Formula AutoComplete list as you type the function name, or use the Insert Function dialog box. You can also type the function name in all lowercase letters. If you enter a function name correctly, Excel converts the name to all capital letters when you press Enter, indicating that you spelled the function name correctly.

## Totaling Values with the SUM Function

The **SUM function** calculates the total of values contained in two or more cells.

One of the most commonly used functions is the *SUM function*, which totals values in two or more cells and then displays the result in the cell containing the function. This function is more efficient to create when you need to add the values contained in three or more cells. For example, to add the contents of cells A2 through A14, you could enter =A2+A3+A4+A5+A6+A7+A8+A9+A10+A11+A12+A13+A14, which is time-consuming and increases the probability of entering an inaccurate cell reference, such as entering a cell reference twice or accidentally leaving out a cell reference. Instead, you could use the SUM function:

=SUM(number 1, [number 2], . . .)

> **TIP** Function Syntax
>
> In this book, the function syntax lines are highlighted. Arguments enclosed by brackets [ ] are optional. However, you do not actually type the brackets in the functions. The other arguments are required.

The SUM function contains one required argument—number1—that represents a range of cells to add. The number2 optional argument is used when you want to sum nonadjacent cells or ranges, such as =SUM(A2:A14,F2:F14).

To insert the SUM function, type =SUM(A2:A14). A2:A14 represents the range containing the values to sum. You can also use semi-selection to select the range of cells. Because the SUM function is the most commonly used function, it is available on the Ribbon: Click Sum in the Editing group on the Home tab, or click AutoSum in the Function Library group on the Formulas tab. Figure 12 shows the result of using the SUM function to total scores (898).

Formulas and Functions

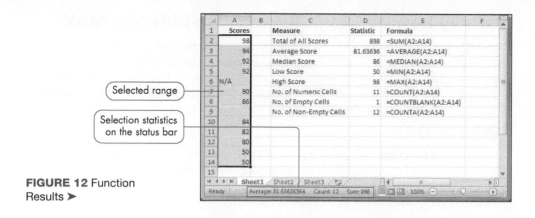

**FIGURE 12** Function Results ➤

**TIP** Avoiding Functions for Basic Formulas

Do not use a function for a basic mathematical expression. For example, although =SUM(B4/C4) produces the same result as =B4/C4, the SUM function is not needed to perform the basic arithmetic division. Use the most appropriate, clear-cut formula, =B4/C4.

# Inserting Basic Statistical Functions

Excel includes commonly used statistical functions that you can use to calculate how much you spend on average per month on DVD rentals, what your highest electric bill is to control spending, and what your lowest test score is so you know what score you need to earn on your final exam to achieve the grade you desire. You can also use statistical functions to create or monitor your budget.

If you click AutoSum, Excel inserts the SUM function. However, if you click the AutoSum arrow in the Editing group on the Home tab, Excel displays a list of basic functions to select: Sum, Average, Count Numbers, Max, and Min. If you want to insert another function, select More Functions from the list.

## Find Central Tendency with the AVERAGE and MEDIAN Functions

The **AVERAGE function** calculates the arithmetic mean, or average, of values in a range.

People often describe data based on central tendency, which means that values tend to cluster around a central value. Excel provides two functions to calculate central tendency: AVERAGE and MEDIAN. The *AVERAGE function* calculates the arithmetic mean, or average, for the values in a range of cells. You can use this function to calculate the class average on a biology test, or the average number of points scored per game by a basketball player. In Figure 12, =AVERAGE(A2:A14) returns 81.63636 as the average test score.

=AVERAGE(number 1,[number2], . . .)

The **MEDIAN function** identifies the midpoint value in a set of values.

The *MEDIAN function* finds the midpoint value, which is the value that one half of the population is above or below. The median is particularly useful because extreme values often influence arithmetic mean calculated by the AVERAGE function. In Figure 12, the two extreme test scores of 50 distort the average. The rest of the test scores range from 80 to 98. The median for test scores is 86, which indicates that half the test scores are above 86 and half the test scores are below 86. This statistic is more reflective of the data set than the average is.

=MEDIAN(number 1,[number 2], . . .)

## Identify Low and High Values with MIN and MAX

The **MIN function** displays the lowest value in a range.

The *MIN function* analyzes an argument list to determine the lowest value, such as the lowest score on a test. Manually inspecting a range of values to identify the lowest value is inefficient, especially in large spreadsheets. If you change values in the range, the MIN function will identify the new lowest value and display it in the cell containing the MIN function. In Figure 12, =MIN(A2:A14) identifies that 50 is the lowest test score.

=MIN(number 1,[number 2],...)

The **MAX function** identifies the highest value in a range.

The *MAX function* analyzes an argument list to determine the highest value, such as the highest score on a test. Like the MIN function, when the values in the range change, the MAX function will display the new highest value within the range of cells. In Figure 12, =MAX(A2:A14) identifies 98 as the highest test score.

=MAX(number 1,[number 2],...)

 **TIP** Nonadjacent Ranges

You can use multiple ranges as arguments, such as finding the largest number within two nonadjacent (nonconsecutive) ranges. For example, you can find the highest test score where some scores are stored in cells A2:A14, and others are stored in cells K2:K14. Separate each range with a comma in the argument list, so that the formula is =MAX(A2:A14,K2:K14).

## Identify the Total Number with COUNT Functions

The **COUNT function** tallies the number of cells in a range that contain values.

Excel provides three basic count functions: COUNT, COUNTBLANK and COUNTA to count the cells in a range that meet a particular criterion. The *COUNT function* tallies the number of cells in a range that contain values you can use in calculations, such as numerical and date data, but excludes blank cells or text entries from the tally. In Figure 12, the selected range spans 13 cells; however, the COUNT function returns 11, the number of cells that contain numerical data. It does not count the cell containing the text *N/A* or the blank cell.

The **COUNTBLANK function** tallies the number of blank cells in a range.

The **COUNTA function** tallies the number of cells in a range that are not empty.

The *COUNTBLANK function* tallies the number of cells in a range that are blank. In Figure 12, the COUNTBLANK function identifies that one cell in the range A2:A14 is blank. The *COUNTA function* tallies the number of cells in a range that are not blank, that is, cells that contain data whether a value, text, or a formula. In Figure 12, =COUNTA(A2:A14) returns 12, indicating the range A2:A14 contains 12 cells that contain some form of data. It does not count the blank cell.

=COUNT(number 1,[number 2],...)

=COUNTBLANK(number 1,[number 2],...)

=COUNTA(number 1,[number 2],...)

 **TIP** Average, Count, and Sum

When you select a range of cells containing values, by default Excel displays the average, count, and sum of those values on the status bar (see Figure 12). You can customize the status bar to show other selection statistics, such as the minimum and maximum values for a selected range. To display or hide particular selection statistics, right-click the status bar, and then select the statistic.

## Use Other Math and Statistical Functions

In addition to the functions you have learned in this chapter, Excel provides over 100 other math and statistical functions. Table 2 lists and describes some of these functions that you might find helpful in your business, education, and general statistics courses.

TABLE 2  Math and Statistical Functions

| Function Syntax | Description |
|---|---|
| =ABS(number) | Displays the absolute (i.e., positive) value of a number. |
| =FREQUENCY(data_array,bins_array) | Counts how often values appear in a given range. |
| =INT(number) | Rounds a value number down to the nearest whole number. |
| =MODE.SNGL(number1,[number2],…) | Displays the most frequently occurring value in a list. |
| =PI() | Returns the value of *pi* that is accurate up to 15 digits. |
| =PRODUCT(number1,[number2],…) | Multiplies all values within the argument list. |
| =RANDBETWEEN(bottom,top) | Generates a random number between two numbers you specify. |
| =RANK.AVG(number,ref,[order]) | Identifies a value's rank within a list of values; returns an average rank for identical values. |
| =RANK.EQ(number,ref,[order]) | Identifies a value's rank within a list of values; the top rank is identified for all identical values. |
| =ROUND(number,num_digits) | Rounds a value to a specific number of digits. Rounds numbers of 5 and greater up and those less than 5 down. |
| =SUMPRODUCT(array1,[array2],[array3],…) | Finds the result of multiplying values in one range by the related values in another column and then adding those products. |
| =TRIMMEAN(array,percent) | Returns the arithmetic average of the internal values in a range by excluding a specified percentage of values at the upper and lower values in the data set. This function helps reduce the effect outliers (i.e., extreme values) have on the arithmetic mean. |
| =TRUNC(number,[num_digits]) | Returns the integer equivalent of a number by truncating or removing the decimal or fractional part of the number. For example, =TRUNC(45.5) returns 45. |

> **TIP  ROUND vs. Decrease Decimal Points**
>
> When you click Decrease Decimal in the Number group to display fewer or no digits after a decimal point, Excel still stores the original value's decimal places so that those digits can be used in calculations. The ROUND function changes the stored value to its rounded state.

# Using Date Functions

Because Excel treats dates as serial numbers, you can perform calculations using dates. For example, assume today is January 1, 2012, and you graduate on May 12, 2012. To determine how many days until graduation, subtract today's date from the graduation date. Excel uses the serial numbers for these dates (40909 and 41041) to calculate the difference of 132 days.

You can use date and time functions to calculate when employees are eligible for certain benefits, how many days it takes to complete a project, or if an account is 30, 60, or more days past due. The Reference table on the next page lists several popular date/time functions.

## Insert the TODAY Function

The **TODAY function** displays the current date.

The *TODAY function* displays the current date in a cell. Excel updates the function results when you open or print the workbook. The function is expressed as =TODAY(). The TODAY() function does not require arguments, but you must include the parentheses for the function to work. If you omit the parentheses, Excel displays #NAME? in the cell with a green triangle in the top-left corner of the cell. When you click the cell, an error icon appears that you can click for more information.

## Insert the NOW Function

The **NOW function** displays the current date and time.

The *NOW function* uses the computer's clock to display the current date and time you last opened the workbook, so the value will change every time the workbook is opened. Like the TODAY function, the NOW function does not require arguments, but you must include the parentheses. Omitting the parentheses creates a #NAME? error.

> **TIP** Update the Date and Time
>
> Both the TODAY and NOW functions display the date/time the workbook was last opened or last calculated. These functions do not continuously update the date and time while the workbook is open. To update the date and time, press F9 or click the Formulas tab, and then click Calculate now in the Calculation group.

# REFERENCE  Date/Time Functions

| Function Syntax | Description | Example | Example Results |
|---|---|---|---|
| =TODAY() | Displays today's date: month, day, year. | =TODAY() | 5/12/2012 |
| =NOW() | Displays today's date and current military time. | =NOW() | 5/12/2012 14:32 |
| =DATE(year,month,day) | Returns the serial number for a date. | =DATE(2012,1,1) | 40909 or 1/1/2012 |
| =EDATE(start_date,months) | Displays the serial number of a date a specified number of months in the future or past. | =EDATE(DATE(2012, 1,1),6) | 41091 |
| =DAY(serial_number) | Displays the day within a month for a serial number (e.g., 41196 represents 10/14/2012). Entering 41196 as the DAY function argument returns 14 as the 14th day of the month. | =DAY(41196) | 14 |
| =EOMONTH(start_date, months) | Identifies the last day of a month a specified number of months from a serial number representing a date (e.g., 40915 represents 1/7/2012, 3 months is 4/7/2012, the last day of April is April 30, which is serial number 41029). | =EOMONTH(40915,3) | 41029 |
| =MONTH(serial_number) | Returns the month (1 to 12) for a serial number. | =MONTH(40945) | 2 |
| =NETWORKDAYS(start_ date,end_date,[holidays]) | Calculates the number of work days (excluding weekends and specified holidays) between two dates. | =NETWORKDAYS(40 915,41091,F9:F10) | 124 |
| =WEEKDAY(serial_number, [return_type]) | Identifies the weekday (1 to 7) for a serial number. | =WEEKDAY(40915,1) | 7 |
| =WORKDAY(start_date, days,[holidays]) | Calculates a serial number of a date a specified number of days before or after a particular date, excluding specified holidays. | =WORKDAY(41029, 25,E9:E11) | 41065 |
| =YEAR(serial_number) | Identifies the year for a serial number. | =YEAR(41029) | 2012 |
| =YEARFRAC(start_date, end_date,[basis]) | Calculates the fraction of a year between two dates based on the number of whole days. | =YEARFRAC(40915, 41091) | 0.483333333 |

# HANDS-ON EXERCISES

## 2 Function Basics

The Denver Mortgage Company's worksheet contains an area in which you must enter summary statistics. In addition, you need to include today's date and identify what year each mortgage will be paid off.

**Skills covered:** Use the SUM Function • Use the AVERAGE Function • Use the MEDIAN Function • Use the MIN, MAX, and COUNT Functions • Use the TODAY and YEAR Functions

### STEP 1 ▶ USE THE SUM FUNCTION

The first summary statistic you need to calculate is the total value of the houses bought by the borrowers. You will use the SUM function. Refer to Figure 13 as you complete Step 1.

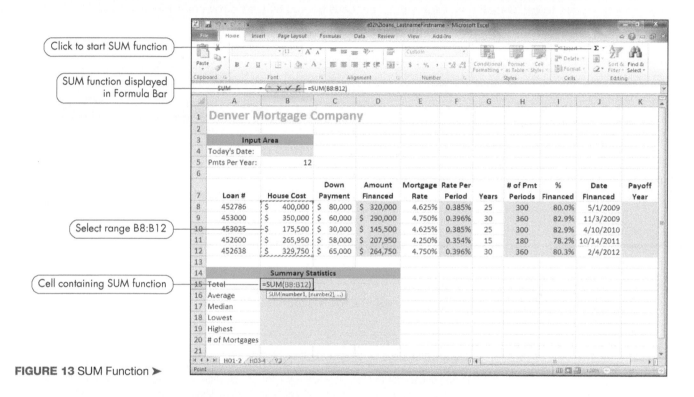

**FIGURE 13** SUM Function ➤

a. Open *e02h1loans_LastnameFirstname* if you closed it at the end of Hands-On Exercise 1. Save the workbook with the new name **e02h2loans_LastnameFirstname**, changing *h1* to *h2*.

b. Click the **Home tab**, if needed, and then click **cell B15**, the cell where you will enter a formula for the total house cost.

c. Click **AutoSum** in the Editing group.

> **TROUBLESHOOTING:** Click the main part of the AutoSum command. If you click the AutoSum arrow, then select Sum.

Excel anticipates the range of cells containing values you want to sum based on where you enter the formula—in this case, A8:D14. This is not the correct range, so you must enter the correct range.

**d.** Select the **range B8:B12**, the cells containing house costs.

As you use the semi-selection process, Excel enters the range in the SUM function.

> **TROUBLESHOOTING:** If you accidentally entered the function without changing the arguments, you can repeat steps b–d, or you can edit the arguments in the Formula Bar by deleting the default range, typing B8:B12 between the parentheses, and then pressing Enter.

**e.** Click **Enter** to the left of the Formula Bar, and then save the workbook.

Cell B15 contains the function = SUM(B8:B12), and the result is $1,521,200.

---

**STEP 2** **USE THE AVERAGE FUNCTION**

Before copying the functions to calculate the total down payments and amounts financed, you want to calculate the average value of houses bought by the borrowers. Refer to Figure 14 as you complete Step 2.

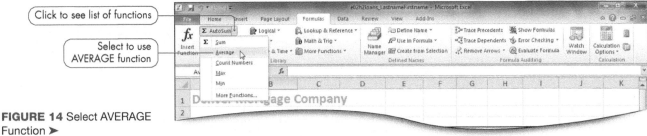

**FIGURE 14** Select AVERAGE Function ➤

**a.** Click the **Formulas tab**, and then click **cell B16**, the cell where you will display the average cost of the houses.

**b.** Click the **AutoSum arrow** in the Function Library group, and then select **Average**.

Excel anticipates cell B15, which is the total cost of the houses. You need to change the range.

> **TROUBLESHOOTING:** AutoSum, like some other commands in Excel, contains two parts: the main command icon and an arrow. Click the main command icon when instructed to click AutoSum to perform the default action. Click the arrow when instructed to click AutoSum arrow for additional options. If you accidentally clicked AutoSum instead of the arrow, press Esc to cancel the SUM function from being completed, and then try step b again.

**c.** Select the **range B8:B12**, the cells containing the house costs.

The function is =AVERAGE(B8:B12).

**d.** Press **Enter** to complete the function and make **cell B17** the active cell, and then save the workbook.

The average house cost is $304,240.

## STEP 3 ▸ USE THE MEDIAN FUNCTION

You realize that extreme values may distort the average. Therefore, you decide to identify the median value of houses bought to compare it to the average. Refer to Figure 15 as you complete Step 3.

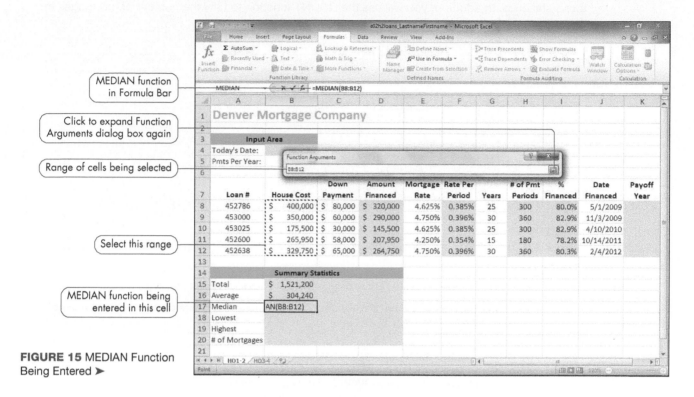

**FIGURE 15** MEDIAN Function Being Entered ➤

Labels on figure:
- MEDIAN function in Formula Bar
- Click to expand Function Arguments dialog box again
- Range of cells being selected
- Select this range
- MEDIAN function being entered in this cell

**a.** Make sure **cell B17** is the active cell. Click **Insert Function** to the left of the Formula Bar or in the Function Library group.

The Insert Function dialog box opens. Use this dialog box to select the MEDIAN function since it is not available on the Ribbon.

**b.** Type **median** in the **Search for a function box**, and then click **Go**.

Excel displays a list of possible functions in the *Select a function* list. The MEDIAN function is selected at the top of the list; the bottom of the dialog box displays the syntax and the description.

**c.** Read the MEDIAN function's description, and then click **OK**.

The Function Arguments dialog box opens. It contains one required argument, Number1, representing a range of cells containing values. It has an optional argument, Number2, which you can use if you have nonadjacent ranges that contain values.

**d.** Click the **collapse button** to the right of the Number1 box.

You collapsed the Function Arguments dialog box so that you can select the range.

**e.** Select the **range B8:B12**, and then click the **expand button** in the Function Arguments dialog box.

The Function Arguments dialog box expands again.

**f.** Click **OK** to accept the function arguments and close the dialog box. Save the workbook.

Half of the houses purchased cost over the median, $329,750, and half of the houses cost less than this value. Notice the difference between the median and the average: The average is lower because it is affected by the lowest-costing house, $175,500.

Erica wants to know the least and most expensive houses so that she can analyze typical customers of the Denver Mortgage Company. You will use the MIN and MAX functions to obtain these statistics. In addition, you will use the COUNT function to tally the number of mortgages in the sample. Refer to Figure 16 as you complete Step 4.

| | Loan # | House Cost | Down Payment | Amount Financed | Mortgage Rate | Rate Per Period | Years | # of Pmt Periods | % Financed | Date Financed | Payoff Year |
|---|---|---|---|---|---|---|---|---|---|---|---|
| 7 | | | | | | | | | | | |
| 8 | 452786 | $ 400,000 | $ 80,000 | $ 320,000 | 4.625% | 0.385% | 25 | 300 | 80.0% | 5/1/2009 | |
| 9 | 453000 | $ 425,000 | $ 60,000 | $ 365,000 | 4.750% | 0.396% | 30 | 360 | 85.9% | 11/3/2009 | |
| 10 | 453025 | $ 175,500 | $ 30,000 | $ 145,500 | 4.625% | 0.385% | 25 | 300 | 82.9% | 4/10/2010 | |
| 11 | 452600 | $ 265,950 | $ 58,000 | $ 207,950 | 4.250% | 0.354% | 15 | 180 | 78.2% | 10/14/2011 | |
| 12 | 452638 | $ 329,750 | $ 65,000 | $ 264,750 | 4.750% | 0.396% | 30 | 360 | 80.3% | 2/4/2012 | |
| 13 | | | | | | | | | | | |
| 14 | | Summary Statistics | | | | | | | | | |
| 15 | Total | $ 1,596,200 | $ 293,000 | $1,303,200 | | | | | | | |
| 16 | Average | $ 319,240 | $ 58,600 | $ 260,640 | | | | | | | |
| 17 | Median | $ 329,750 | $ 60,000 | $ 264,750 | | | | | | | |
| 18 | Lowest | $ 175,500 | $ 30,000 | $ 145,500 | | | | | | | |
| 19 | Highest | $ 425,000 | $ 80,000 | $ 365,000 | | | | | | | |
| 20 | # of Mortgages | 5 | 5 | 5 | | | | | | | |
| 21 | | | | | | | | | | | |

HO1-2  HO3-4

Ready          120%

**FIGURE 16** MIN, MAX, and COUNT Function Results ▶

a. Click **cell B18**, the cell to display the cost of the lowest-costing house.

b. Click the **AutoSum arrow** in the Function Library group, select **Min**, select the **range B8:B12**, and then press **Enter**.

   The MIN function identifies that the lowest-costing house is $175,500.

c. Click **cell B19**, if needed. Click the **AutoSum arrow** in the Function Library group, select **Max**, select the **range B8:B12**, and then press **Enter**.

   The MAX function identifies that the highest-costing house is $400,000.

d. Click **cell B20**, if needed. Type =**COUNT(B8:B12)** and press **Enter**.

   As you type the letter *C*, Formula AutoComplete suggests functions starting with *C*. As you continue typing, the list of functions narrows. After you type the beginning parenthesis, Excel displays the function ScreenTip, indicating the arguments for the function. The range B8:B12 contains five cells.

e. Select the **range B15:B20**.

   You want to select the range of original statistics to copy the cells all at one time to the next two columns.

f. Drag the fill handle to the right by two columns to copy the functions. Click **cell D20**.

   Because you used relative cell references in the functions, the range changes from =COUNT(B8:B12) to =COUNT(D8:D12).

g. Change the value in **cell B9** to **425000**. Save the workbook.

   The results of several formulas and functions change, including the total, average, and max house costs.

You have two date functions to enter to complete the first worksheet. Refer to Figure 17 as you complete Step 5.

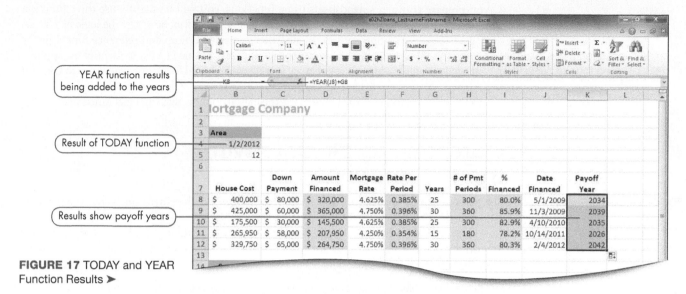

YEAR function results being added to the years

Result of TODAY function

Results show payoff years

**FIGURE 17** TODAY and YEAR Function Results ▶

a. Click **cell B4**, the cell to contain the current date.

b. Click **Date & Time** in the Function Library group, select **TODAY** to display the Function Arguments dialog box, and then click **OK** to close the dialog box.

Excel inserts the current date in Short Date format, such as 1/2/2012, based on the computer system's date. The Function Arguments dialog box opens, although no arguments are necessary for this function.

c. Click **cell K8**, click **Date & Time** in the Function Library group, scroll through the list, and then select **YEAR**.

The Function Arguments dialog box opens so that you can enter the argument, a serial number for a date.

d. Click **cell J8** to enter it in the **Serial_number box**. Click **OK**.

The function returns 2009, the year the first mortgage was taken out. However, you want the year the mortgage will be paid off. The YEAR function returns the year from a date. You need to add the years to the result of the function to calculate the year that the borrower will pay off the mortgage.

e. Press **F2** to edit the formula stored in cell K8. With the insertion point on the right side of the closing parenthesis, type **+G8**, and then press **Ctrl+Enter**.

Pressing Ctrl+Enter is the alternative to clicking Enter by the Formula Bar. It keeps the current cell as the active cell. The results show a date: 7/26/1905. You need to apply the Number format to display the year.

f. Click the **Home tab**, click the **Number Format arrow** in the Number group, and then select **Number**. Decrease the number of decimal points to show the value as a whole number.

You applied the Number format instead of the Comma format because although the Comma format is correct for quantities, such as 2,034 units, it is not appropriate for the year 2034.

g. Copy the formula down the column.

h. Save the workbook. Keep the workbook onscreen if you plan to continue with Hands-On Exercise 3. If not, close the workbook and exit Excel.

# Logical, Lookup, and Financial Functions

As you prepare complex spreadsheets using functions, you will frequently use three function categories: logical, lookup and reference, and finance. Logical functions test the logic of a situation and return a particular result. Lookup and reference functions are useful when you need to look up a value in a list to identify the applicable value. Financial functions are useful to anyone who plans to take out a loan or invest money.

> Financial functions are useful to anyone who plans to take out a loan or invest money.

In this section, you will learn how to use the logical, lookup, and financial functions.

## Determining Results with the IF Function

The **IF function** evaluates a condition and returns one value if the condition is true and a different value if the condition is false.

The most common logical function is the *IF function*, which returns one value when a condition is met or is true and returns another value when the condition is not met or is false. For example, a company gives a $500 bonus to employees who meet their quarterly goals, but no bonus to employees who did not meet their goals. The IF function enables you to make decisions based on worksheet data.

=IF(logical_test,value_if_true,value_if_false)

The IF function has three arguments: (1) a condition that is tested to determine if it is either true or false, (2) the resulting value if the condition is true, and (3) the resulting value if the condition is false.

Figure 18 lists several sample IF functions, how they are evaluated, and their results.

|  | A | B | C |
|---|---|---|---|
| 1 | **Input Values** | | |
| 2 | $1,000 | | |
| 3 | $2,000 | | |
| 4 | 10% | | |
| 5 | 5% | | |
| 6 | $250 | | |
| 7 | | | |
| 8 | | | |
| 9 | IF Function | Evaluation | Result |
| 10 | =IF(A2=A3,A4,A5) | 1000 is equal to 2000: FALSE | 5% |
| 11 | =IF(A2<A3,A4,A5) | 1000 is less than 2000: TRUE | 10% |
| 12 | =IF(A2<A3,A5*A2,MAX(A3*A4,A6)) | 1000 is less than 2000: TRUE | $50 |
| 13 | =IF(A2<>A3,"Not Equal","Equal") | 1000 and 2000 are not equal: TRUE | Not Equal |
| 14 | =IF(A2*A4=A3*A5,A6,0) | 100 (A2*A4) is equal to 100 (A3*A5): TRUE | $250 |

**FIGURE 18** Sample IF Functions ➤

## Design the Logical Test

The **logical test** is an expression that evaluates to true or false.

The first argument for the IF function is the logical test. The *logical test* is a formula that contains either a value or an expression that evaluates to true or false. The logical expression is typically a binary expression, meaning that it requires a comparison between at least two variables, such as the values stored in cells A2 and A3. Table 3 lists and describes the logical operators to make the comparison in the logical test.

In Figure 18, the first logical test in cell A10 is A2=A3. The logical test compares the values in cells A2 and A3 to see if they are equal. The logical test in cell A14 is A2*A4=A3*A5. The value stored in cell A2 (1,000) is multiplied by the value in cell A4 (10%). The result (100) is then compared to the product of cell A3 (2,000) and cell A5 (5%), which is also 100. Note that the logical test can compare two cell references, or it can perform calculations and then compare the results of those calculations.

| TABLE 3 | Logical Operators |
|---------|-------------------|
| **Operator** | **Description** |
| = | Equal to |
| <> | Not equal to |
| < | Less than |
| > | Greater than |
| <= | Less than or equal to |
| >= | Greater than or equal to |

 **TIP** Using Text in Formulas

You can use text within a formula. For example, to perform a logical test to see if the contents of a cell match text, the logical test would be: B5="Yes". When you compare text, you must surround the text with quotation marks.

## Design the Value_If_True and Value_If_False Arguments

The second and third arguments of an IF function are value_if_true and value_if_false. When Excel evaluates the logical test, the result is either true or false. If the logical test evaluates to true, the value_if_true argument executes. If the logical test evaluates to false, the value_if_false argument executes. Only one of the last two arguments is executed; both arguments cannot be executed, since the logical test is either true or false but not both.

The value_if_true and value_if_false arguments can contain text, cell references, formulas, or constants (not recommended). In Figure 18, the value_if_true argument in cell A10 is A4, and the value_if_false argument is A5. Since the logical test (A2=A3) is false, the value_if_false argument is executed, and the result displays the same value that is stored in cell A5, which is 5%. In cell A13, the value_if_true argument is "Not Equal", and the value_if_false argument is "Equal". Since the logical test (A2<>A3) is true, the value_if_true argument is executed, and the result displays the text *Not Equal* in the cell containing the function. If you want the result of the function to be blank if a condition is met or not met, type "" (beginning and ending quotation marks).

## Nest Basic Functions as Arguments

A **nested function** is a function that contains another function embedded inside one or more of its arguments.

A *nested function* occurs when one function is embedded as an argument within another function. For example, within the function in cell A12 in Figure 18, the MAX function is nested in the value_if_false argument of the IF function. Nesting functions enables you to create more complex formulas to handle a variety of situations. In this situation, if the logical test evaluates to false, the value_if_false argument of MAX(A3*A4,A6) would execute. Excel would find the product of A3 and A4 and return the higher of that value (200) or the contents of cell A6 (250). You can even nest functions as part of the logical test or value_if_true argument.

In addition to nesting functions within the IF function, you can nest functions within other functions, such as =SUM(MIN(A1:A5),D10:D15). The nested MIN function identifies the lowest value in the range A1:A5 and adds that value to those stored in the range D10:D15.

# Using Lookup Functions

You can use lookup and reference functions to look up values to perform calculations or display results. For example, when you order merchandise on a Web site, the Web server looks up the shipping costs based on weight and distance, or at the end of a semester, your professor uses your numerical average, such as 88%, to look up the letter grade to assign, such as B+.

## Create the Lookup Table

A **lookup table** is a range that contains data for the basis of the lookup and data to be retrieved.

Before you insert lookup functions, you need to create a lookup table. A ***lookup table*** is a range containing a table of values or text that can be retrieved. The table should contain at least two rows and two columns, not including headings. It is important to plan the table so that it conforms to the way in which Excel can utilize the data in it.

Excel cannot interpret the structure of Table 4. To look up a value in a range (such as the range 80–89), you must arrange data from the lowest to the highest value and include only the lowest value in the range (such as 80) instead of the complete range. If the values you look up are *exact* values, you can arrange the first column in any logical order. The lowest value for a category or in a series is the ***breakpoint***. The first column contains the breakpoints—such as 60, 70, 80, and 90—or the lowest values to achieve a particular grade. The lookup table contains one or more additional columns of related data to retrieve. Table 5 shows how to construct the lookup table in Excel.

The **breakpoint** is the lowest value for a specific category or series in a lookup table.

| TABLE 4 | Grading Scale |
|---|---|
| **Range** | **Grade** |
| 90–100 | A |
| 80–89 | B |
| 70–79 | C |
| 60–69 | D |
| Below 60 | F |

| TABLE 5 | Grades Lookup Table |
|---|---|
| **Range** | **Grade** |
| 0 | F |
| 60 | D |
| 70 | C |
| 80 | B |
| 90 | A |

## Understand the VLOOKUP Function Syntax

The **VLOOKUP function** looks up a value in a vertical lookup table and returns a related result from the lookup table.

The ***VLOOKUP function*** accepts a value, looks the value up in a vertical lookup table, and returns a result. Use VLOOKUP to search for exact matches or for the nearest value that is less than or equal to the search value, such as assigning a B grade for an 87% class average. The VLOOKUP function has the following three required arguments and one optional argument: (1) lookup_value, (2) table_array, (3) col_index_number, and (4) range_lookup.

=VLOOKUP(lookup_value,table_array,col_index_number,[range_lookup])

Figure 19 shows a partial grade book that contains a vertical lookup table, as well as the final scores and letter grades. The function in cell F3 is =VLOOKUP(E3,$A$3:$B$7,2).

| | F3 | | | $f_x$ | =VLOOKUP(E3,$A$3:$B$7,2) | | |
|---|---|---|---|---|---|---|---|
| | A | B | C | D | E | F | G |
| 1 | Grading Scale | | | Partial Gradebook | | | |
| 2 | Breakpoint | Grade | | Names | Final Score | Letter Grade | |
| 3 | 0 | F | | Abbott | 85 | B | |
| 4 | 60 | D | | Carter | 69 | D | |
| 5 | 70 | C | | Hon | 90 | A | |
| 6 | 80 | B | | Jackson | 74 | C | |
| 7 | 90 | A | | Miller | 80 | B | |
| 8 | | | | Nelsen | 78 | C | |

**FIGURE 19** VLOOKUP Function for Grade Book ➤

The **lookup value** is a reference to a cell containing a value to look up.

The **table array** is a range containing a lookup table.

The **column index number** is the argument in a VLOOKUP function that identifies which lookup table column from which to return a value.

The *lookup value* is the cell reference of the cell that contains the value to look up. The lookup value for the first student is cell E3, which contains 85. The *table array* is the range that contains the lookup table: $A$3:$B$7. The table array range must be absolute and cannot include column labels for the lookup table. The *column index number* is the column number in the lookup table that contains the return values. In this example, the column index number is 2.

 **TIP** Using Values in Formulas

You know to avoid values in formulas because values might change. However, notice that the value 2 is the col_index_number argument of the VLOOKUP function. The value 2 refers to a particular column within the lookup table and is an acceptable use of a number within a formula.

## Understand How Excel Processes the Lookup

The VLOOKUP function identifies the value stored in the lookup value argument and then searches the first column of the lookup table until it finds an exact match (if possible). If Excel finds an exact match, it returns the value stored in the column designated by the column index number on that same row. If the table contains breakpoints for ranges rather than exact matches, Excel identifies the correct range based on comparing the lookup value to the breakpoints in the first column. If the lookup value is larger than the breakpoint, it looks to the next breakpoint to see if the lookup value is larger than that breakpoint also. When Excel detects that the lookup value is not greater than the next breakpoint, it stays on that row. It then uses the column index number to identify the column containing the value to return for the lookup value. Because Excel goes sequentially through the breakpoints, it is mandatory that the breakpoints are arranged from the lowest value to the highest value for ranges.

For example, the VLOOKUP function to assign letter grades works like this: Excel identifies the lookup value (85 stored in cell E3) and compares it to the values in the first column of the lookup table (stored in cells A3:B7). It tries to find an exact match for the value 85; however, the table contains breakpoints rather than every conceivable numeric average. Because the lookup table is arranged from the lowest to the highest breakpoints, Excel detects that 85 is greater than the 80 breakpoint but is not greater than the 90 breakpoint. Therefore, it stays on the 80 row. Excel then looks at the column index number of 2 and returns the letter grade of B, which is located in the second column of the lookup table. The returned grade of B is then stored in cell F3, which contains the VLOOKUP function.

Instead of looking up values in a range, you can look up a value for an exact match using the optional range_lookup argument in the VLOOKUP function. By default, the range_lookup is set implicitly to TRUE, which is appropriate to look up values in a range. However, to look up an exact match, you must specify FALSE in the range_lookup argument. For example, if you are looking up product numbers, you must find an exact match to display the price. The function would look like this: =VLOOKUP(D15,$A$1:$B$50,2,FALSE). The VLOOKUP function returns a value for the first lookup value that matches the first column of the lookup table. If no exact match is found, the function returns #N/A.

## Use the HLOOKUP Function

You can design your lookup table horizontally, so that the first row contains the values for the basis of the lookup or the breakpoints, and additional rows contain data to be retrieved. With a horizontal lookup table, you must use the *HLOOKUP function*. Table 6 shows how the grading scale would look as a horizontal lookup table.

The **HLOOKUP function** looks up a value in a horizontal lookup table where the first row contains the values to compare with the lookup value.

| TABLE 6 | Horizontal Lookup Table | | | |
|---|---|---|---|---|
| 0 | 60 | 70 | 80 | 90 |
| F | D | C | B | A |

Logical, Lookup, and Financial Functions • Excel 2010

The syntax is almost the same as the syntax for the VLOOKUP function, except the third argument is row_index_number instead of col_index_number.

=HLOOKUP(lookup_value,table_array,row_index_number,[range_lookup])

# Calculating Payments with the PMT Function

Excel contains several financial functions to help you perform calculations with monetary values. If you take out a loan to purchase a car, you need to know the monthly payment, which depends on the price of the car, the down payment, and the terms of the loan, in order to determine if you can afford the car. The decision is made easier by developing the worksheet in Figure 20 and then by changing the various input values as indicated.

| | B9 | | $f_x$ | =PMT(B6,B8,-B3) | |
|---|---|---|---|---|---|
| | A | B | C | D | |
| 1 | Purchase Price | $25,999.00 | | | |
| 2 | Down Payment | $ 5,000.00 | | | |
| 3 | Amount to Finance | $20,999.00 | | | |
| 4 | Payments per Year | 12 | | | |
| 5 | Interest Rate (APR) | 5.250% | | | |
| 6 | Periodic Rate (Monthly) | 0.438% | | | |
| 7 | Term (Years) | 5 | | | |
| 8 | No. of Payment Periods | 60 | | | |
| 9 | Monthly Payment | $ 398.69 | | | |
| 10 | | | | | |

**FIGURE 20** Car Loan Worksheet ➤

Creating a loan model helps you evaluate your options. You realize that the purchase of a $25,999 car is prohibitive because the monthly payment is almost $398.69. Purchasing a less expensive car, coming up with a substantial down payment, taking out a longer term loan, or finding a better interest rate can decrease your monthly payments.

The *PMT function* calculates payments for a loan with a fixed amount at a fixed periodic rate for a fixed time period. The PMT function uses up to five arguments, three of which are required and two of which are optional: (1) rate, (2) nper, (3) pv, (4) fv, and (5) type.

The **PMT function** calculates the periodic payment for a loan with a fixed interest rate and fixed term.

=PMT(rate,nper,pv,[fv],[type])

The *rate* is the periodic interest rate, the interest rate per payment period. If the annual percentage rate (APR) is 12% and you make monthly payments, the periodic rate is 1% (12%/12 months). With the same APR and quarterly payments, the periodic rate is 3% (12%/4 quarters). Divide the APR by the number of payment periods in one year. However, instead of dividing the APR by 12 within the PMT function, calculate the periodic interest rate in cell B6 in Figure 20 and use that calculated rate in the PMT function.

The **rate** is the periodic interest rate, such as a monthly interest rate.

The *nper* is the total number of payment periods. The term of a loan is usually stated in years; however, you make several payments per year. For monthly payments, you make 12 payments per year. To calculate the nper, multiply the number of years by the number of payments in one year. Instead of calculating the number of payment periods in the PMT function, calculate the number of payment periods in cell B8 and use that calculated value in the PMT function.

The **nper** is the number of total payment periods.

The *pv* is the present value of the loan. The result of the PMT function is a negative value because it represents your debt. However, you can display the result as a positive value by typing a minus sign in front of the present value cell reference in the PMT function.

The **pv** is the present value of the loan.

## 3 Logical, Lookup, and Financial Functions

Erica wants you to complete a similar model that she might use for future mortgage data analysis. As you study the model, you realize you need to incorporate logical, lookup, and financial functions.

**Skills covered:** Use the VLOOKUP Function • Use the PMT Function • Use the IF Function

---

### STEP 1 ▶ USE THE VLOOKUP FUNCTION

Rates vary based on the number of years to pay off the loan. Erica created a lookup table for three common mortgage years, and she entered the current APR. The lookup table will provide efficiency later when the rates change. You will use the VLOOKUP function to display the correct rate for each customer based on the number of years of the respective loans. Refer to Figure 21 as you complete Step 1.

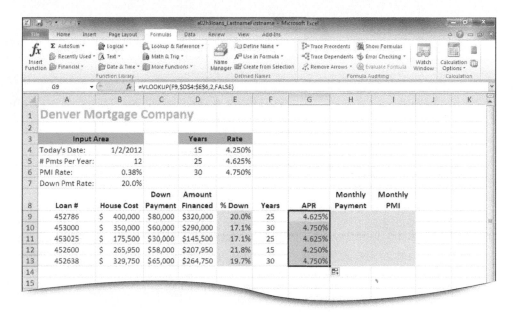

**FIGURE 21** VLOOKUP Function ➤

a. Open *e02h2loans_LastnameFirstname* if you closed it at the end of Hands-On Exercise 2. Save the workbook with the new name **e02h3loans_LastnameFirstname**, changing *h2* to *h3*.

b. Click the **HO3-4 worksheet tab** to display the worksheet containing the data to complete. Click **cell G9**, the cell that will store the APR for the first customer.

c. Click the **Formulas tab**, click **Lookup & Reference** in the Function Library group, and then select **VLOOKUP**.

   The Function Arguments dialog box opens. You need to enter the three required and one optional argument.

d. Click **F9** to enter F9 in the **Lookup_value box**.

   Cell F9 contains the value you need to look up from the table: 25 years.

> **TROUBLESHOOTING:** If you cannot see the cell you need to use in an argument, click the Function Arguments dialog box title bar, and drag the dialog box on the screen until you can see and click the cell you need for the argument.

e. Press **Tab**, and then select the **range D4:E6** in the **Table_array box**.

This is the range that contains that data for the lookup table. The Years values in the table are arranged in ascending order (from lowest to highest). Do not select the column headings for the range. Anticipate what will happen if you copy the formula down the column. What do you need to do to ensure that the cell references always point to the exact location of the table? If your answer is to make the table array cell references absolute, then you answered correctly.

f. Press **F4** to make the range references absolute.

The Table_array box now contains $D$4:$E$6.

g. Press **Tab**, and then type **2** in the **Col_index_num box**.

The second column of the lookup table contains the APRs that you want to return and display in the cells containing the formulas.

h. Press **Tab**, and then type **False** in the **Range_lookup box**.

You want the formula to display an error if an incorrect number of years has been entered. To ensure an exact match to look up in the table, you enter *False* in the optional argument.

i. Click **OK**.

The VLOOKUP function looks up the first person's years (25), finds an exact match in the first column of the lookup table, and then returns the corresponding APR, which is 4.625%.

j. Copy the formula down the column, and then save the workbook.

Spot check the results to make sure the function returned the correct APR based on the number of years.

---

**STEP 2**  **USE THE PMT FUNCTION**

The worksheet now has all the necessary data for you to calculate the monthly payment for each loan: the APR, the number of years for the loan, the number of payment periods in one year, and the initial loan amount. You will use the PMT function to calculate the monthly payment, which includes paying back the principal amount with interest. This calculation does not include escrow amounts, such as property taxes or insurance. Refer to Figure 22 as you complete Step 2.

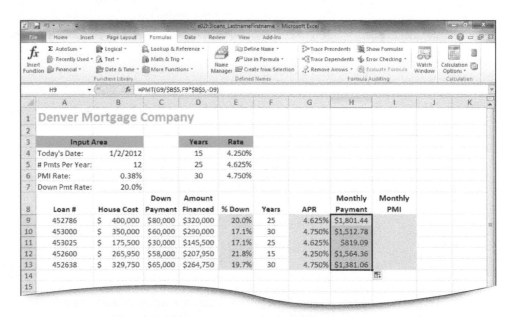

**FIGURE 22** PMT Function ➤

a. Click **cell H9**, the cell that will store the payment for the first customer.

b. Click **Financial** in the Function Library group, scroll through the list, and then select **PMT**.

> **TROUBLESHOOTING:** Make sure you select PMT, not PPMT. The PPMT function calculates the principal portion of a particular monthly payment, not the total monthly payment itself.

The Function Arguments dialog box opens. You need to enter the three required arguments.

c. Type **G9/B5** in the **Rate box**.

Before going on to the next argument, think about what will happen if you copy the formula. The argument will be G10/B6 for the next customer. Are those cell references correct? G10 does contain the APR for the next customer, but B6 does not contain the correct number of payments in one year. Therefore, you need to make B5 an absolute cell reference because the number of payments per year does not vary.

d. Press **F4** to make the reference absolute.

e. Press **Tab**, and then type **F9*$B$5** in the **Nper box**.

You calculate the nper by multiplying the number of years by the number of payments in one year. Again, you must make B5 an absolute cell reference so that it does not change when you copy the formula down the column.

f. Press **Tab**, and then type **-D9** in the **Pv box**.

The bottom of the dialog box indicates that the monthly payment is 1801.444075 or $1,801.44.

> **TROUBLESHOOTING:** If the payment displays as a negative value, you probably forgot to type the minus sign in front of the D9 reference in the Pv box. Edit the function, and type the minus sign in the correct place.

g. Click **OK**. Copy the formula down the column, and then save the workbook.

## STEP 3 ▶ USE THE IF FUNCTION

Lenders often want borrowers to have a 20% down payment. If borrowers do not put in 20% of the cost of the house as a down payment, they pay a private mortgage insurance (PMI) fee. PMI serves to protect lenders from absorbing loss if the borrower defaults on the loan, and it enables borrowers with less cash to secure a loan. The PMI fee is about 0.38% of the amount financed. Some borrowers have to pay PMI for a few months or years until the balance owed is less than 80% of the appraised value. The worksheet contains the necessary values input area. You need to use the IF function to determine which borrowers must pay PMI and how much they will pay. Refer to Figure 23 as you complete Step 3.

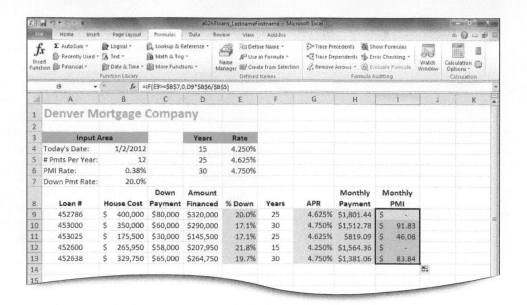

**FIGURE 23** IF Function ➤

a. Click **cell I9**, the cell that will store the PMI, if any, for the first customer.

b. Click **Logical** in the Function Library group, and then select **IF**.

The Function Arguments dialog box opens. You need to enter the three arguments.

c. Type **E9>=$B$7** in the **Logical_test box**.

The logical test compares the down payment percentage to see if the customer's down payment is at least 20%, the threshold stored in B7, of the amount financed. The customer's percentage cell reference needs to be relative so that it will change when you copy it down the column; however, cell B7 must be absolute because it contains the threshold value.

d. Press **Tab**, and then type **0** in the **Value_if_true box**.

If the customer makes a down payment that is at least 20% of the purchase price, the customer does not pay PMI. The first customer paid 20% of the purchase price, so he or she does not have to pay PMI.

e. Press **Tab**, and then type **D9*$B$6/$B$5** in the **Value_if_false box**.

If the logical test is false, the customer must pay PMI, which is calculated by dividing the yearly PMI (0.38%) by 12 and multiplying the result by the amount financed.

f. Click **OK**, and then copy the formula down the column.

The second, third, and fifth customers must pay PMI because their respective down payments were less than 20% of the purchase price.

> **TROUBLESHOOTING:** If the results are not as you expected, check the logical operators. People often mistype < and > or forget to type = for >= situations. Correct any errors in the original formula, and then copy the formula again.

g. Save the workbook. Keep the workbook onscreen if you plan to continue with Hands-On Exercise 4. If not, close the workbook and exit Excel.

# Range Names

A **range name** is a word or string of characters that represents one or more cells.

To simplify entering ranges in formulas, you can use range names. A ***range name*** is a word or string of characters assigned to one or more cells. Think of range names in this way: Your college identifies you by your student ID; however, your professors call you by an easy-to-remember name, such as Micah or Kristin. Similarly, instead of using cell addresses, you can use descriptive range names in formulas. Going back to the VLOOKUP example shown in Figure 19, you can assign the range name *Grades* to cells A3:B7 and then modify the VLOOKUP function to be =VLOOKUP(E3,Grades,2), using the range name *Grades* in the formula. Another benefit of using range names is that they are absolute references, which helps ensure accuracy in your calculations.

In this section, you will work with range names. First, you will learn how to create and maintain range names. Then you will learn how to use a range name in a formula.

## Creating and Maintaining Range Names

Before you can use a range name in a formula, you must first create the name. Each range name within a workbook must be unique. For example, you can't assign the name *COST* to ranges on several worksheets or on the same sheet.

After you create a range name, you might need to change its name or change the range of cells. If you no longer need a range name, you can delete it. You can also insert a list of range names and their respective cell ranges for reference.

### Create a Range Name

A range name can contain up to 255 characters, but it must begin with a letter or an underscore. You can use a combination of upper- or lowercase letters, numbers, periods, and underscores throughout the range name. A range name cannot include spaces or special characters. You should create range names that describe the range of cells being named, but names cannot be identical to the cell contents. Keep the range names relatively short to make them easier to use in formulas. Table 7 lists acceptable and unacceptable range names.

| TABLE 7 | Range Names |
| --- | --- |
| **Name** | **Description** |
| Grades | Acceptable range name |
| COL | Acceptable abbreviation for cost-of-living |
| Tax_Rate | Acceptable name with underscore |
| Commission Rate | Unacceptable name; can't use spaces in names |
| Discount Rate % | Unacceptable name; can't use special symbols and spaces |
| 2009_Rate | Unacceptable name; can't start with a number |
| Rate_2012 | Acceptable name with underscore and numbers |

To create a range name, select the range of cells you want to name, and do one of the following:

- Click in the Name Box, type the range name, and then press Enter.
- Click the Formulas tab, click Define Name in the Defined Names group to open the New Name dialog box (see Figure 24), type the range name in the Name box, and then click OK.
- Click the Formulas tab, click Name Manager in the Defined Names group to open the Name Manager dialog box, click New, type the range name in the Name box, click OK, and then click Close.

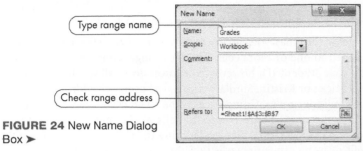

**FIGURE 24** New Name Dialog Box ➤

You can create several range names at the same time if your worksheet already includes ranges with values and descriptive labels. To do this, select the range of cells containing the labels that you want to become names and the cells that contain the values to name, click Create from Selection in the Defined Named group on the Formulas tab, and then select an option in the Create Names from Selection dialog box (see Figure 25).

**FIGURE 25** Create Names from Selection Dialog Box ➤

## Edit or Delete a Range Name

You can use the Name Manager dialog box to edit existing range names, delete range names, and create new range names. To open the Name Manager dialog box shown in Figure 26, click Name Manager in the Defined Names group on the Formulas tab. To edit a range or range name, click the range name in the list, and then click Edit. In the Edit Name dialog box, make your edits, and then click OK.

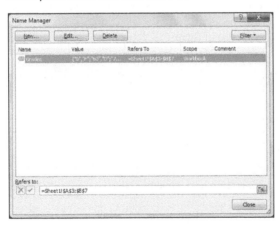

**FIGURE 26** Name Manager Dialog Box ➤

To delete a range name, open the Name Manager dialog box, select the name you want to delete, click Delete, and then click OK in the confirmation message box.

If you change a range name, any formulas that use the range name reflect the new name automatically. For example, if a formula contains =cost*rate and you change the name rate to tax_rate, Excel updates the formula to be =cost*tax_rate. If you delete a range name and a formula depends on that range name, Excel displays #NAME?—indicating an Invalid Name Error.

## Insert a Table of Range Names

Documentation is an important part of good spreadsheet design. People often document workbooks with date or time stamps that indicate the last date of revision, notes describing how to use a workbook, and so on. One way to document a workbook is to insert a list of

Formulas and Functions

range names in a worksheet. To insert a list of range names, click *Use in Formula* in the Defined Names group on the Formulas tab, and then select Paste Names. The Paste Name dialog box opens (see Figure 27), listing all range names in the current workbook. Click Paste List to insert a list of range names in alphabetical order. The first column contains a list of range names, and the second column contains the worksheet names and range locations.

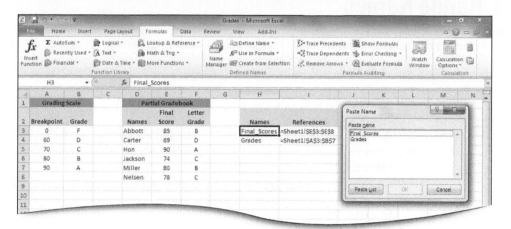

**FIGURE 27** Paste Name Dialog Box and List of Range Names ➤

**TIP** List of Range Names

When you paste range names, the list will overwrite any existing data in a worksheet, so consider pasting the list in a separate worksheet. If you add, edit, or delete range names, the list does not update automatically. To keep the list current, you would need to paste the list again.

# Using Range Names in Formulas

You can use range names in formulas instead of cell references. For example, if cell C15 contains a purchase amount, and cell C5 contains the sales tax rate, instead of typing =C15*C5, you can type the range names in the formula, such as =purchase*tax_rate. When you type a formula, Formula AutoComplete displays a list of range names, as well as functions, that start with the letters as you type (see Figure 28). Double-click the range name to insert it in the formula.

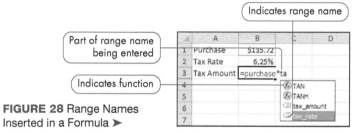

**FIGURE 28** Range Names Inserted in a Formula ➤

Another benefit of using range names is that if you have to copy the formula, you do not have to make the cell reference absolute in the formula. Furthermore, if you share your workbook with others, range names in formulas help others understand what values are used in the calculations.

**TIP** Go to a Range Name

Use the Go To dialog box to go to the top-left cell in a range specified by a range name.

## 4 Range Names

You decide to simplify the VLOOKUP function by using a range name for the lookup table instead of the actual cell references. After creating a range name, you will modify some range names Erica created, and then create a list of range names.

**Skills covered:** Create a Range Name • Edit and Delete Range Names • Use a Range Name in a Formula • Insert a List of Range Names

### STEP 1 ▶ CREATE A RANGE NAME

You want to assign a range name to the lookup table of years and APRs. Refer to Figure 29 as you complete Step 1.

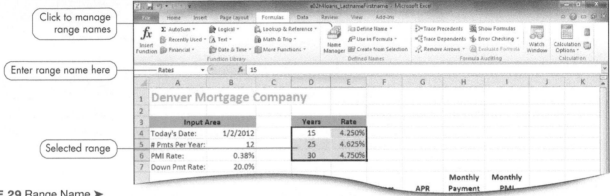

**FIGURE 29** Range Name ➤

a. Open *e02h3loans_LastnameFirstname* if you closed it at the end of Hands-On Exercise 3. Save the workbook with the new name **e02h4loans_LastnameFirstname**, changing *h3* to *h4*.

b. Make sure the **HO3-4 worksheet tab** is active. Select **range D4:E6** (the lookup table).

c. Type **Rates** in the **Name Box**, and then press **Enter**. Save the workbook.

### STEP 2 ▶ EDIT AND DELETE RANGE NAMES

You noticed that Erica added some range names. You will open the Name Manager dialog box to view and make changes to the range names. Refer to Figure 30 as you complete Step 2.

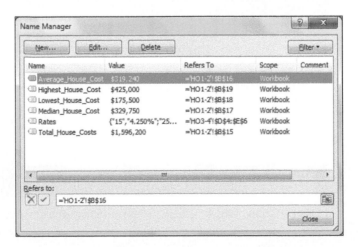

**FIGURE 30** Updated Range Names ➤

a. Click **Name Manager** in the Defined Names group.

The Name Manager dialog box opens. The first name is *Avg_Cost*. You want to rename it to have a naming structure consistent with the other Cost names, such as Total_House_Costs.

b. Select **Avg_Cost**, and then click **Edit** to open the Edit Name dialog box.

c. Type **Average_House_Cost** in the **Name box**, and then click **OK**.

d. Select **Title** in the Name Manager dialog box.

This range name applies to a cell containing text, which does not need a name as it cannot be used in calculations. You decide to delete the range name.

e. Click **Delete**, read the warning message box, and then click **OK** to confirm the deletion of the Title range name.

f. Click **Close**, and then save the workbook.

## STEP 3 ▶ USE A RANGE NAME IN A FORMULA

You will the VLOOKUP function by replacing the existing Table_array argument with the range name. This will help Erica interpret the VLOOKUP function. Refer to Figure 31 as you complete Step 3.

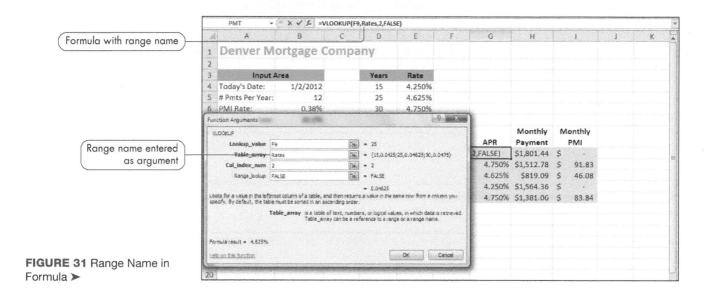

**FIGURE 31** Range Name in Formula ➤

a. Click **cell G9**, the cell containing the VLOOKUP function.

b. Click **Insert Function** between the Name Box and the Formula Bar to open the Function Arguments dialog box.

The Table_array argument contains $D$4:$E$6, the absolute reference to the lookup table.

c. Select **$D$4:$E$6** in the **Table_array box**, type **Rates**, and then click **OK**.

The new function is =VLOOKUP(F9,Rates,2,FALSE).

d. Copy the updated formula down the column, and then save the workbook.

The results are the same as they were when you used the absolute cell references. However, the formulas are shorter and easier to read with the range names.

Before submitting the completed workbook to Erica, you want to create a documentation worksheet that lists all of the range names in the workbook. Refer to Figure 32 as you complete Step 4.

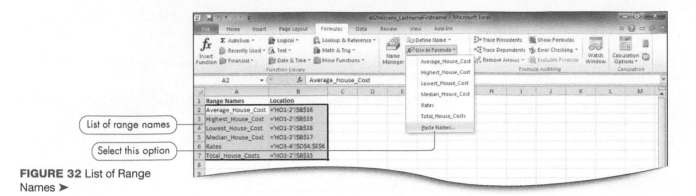

**List of range names**

**Select this option**

**FIGURE 32** List of Range Names ➤

a. Click **Insert Worksheet** to the right of the worksheet tabs, and then double-click the default sheet name, **Sheet1**. Type **Range Names** and press **Enter**.

You inserted and renamed the new worksheet to reflect the data you will add to it.

b. Type **Range Names** in **cell A1**, and then type **Location** in **cell B1**. Bold these headings.

These column headings will appear above the list of range names.

c. Click **cell A2**, click **Use in Formula** in the Defined Names group on the Formulas tab, and then select **Paste Names**.

The Paste Name dialog box opens, displaying all of the range names in the workbook.

d. Click **Paste List**.

Excel pastes an alphabetical list of range names starting in cell A2. The second column displays the locations of the range names.

e. Increase the widths of columns A and B to fit the data.

f. Save and close the workbook, and submit based on your instructor's directions.

After reading this chapter, you have accomplished the following objectives:

1. **Use semi-selection to create a formula.** Semi-selection is a pointing process where you click or drag to select cells to add cell references to a formula.

2. **Use relative, absolute, and mixed cell references in formulas.** Cell references within formulas are relative, absolute, or mixed. A relative reference indicates a cell's location relative to the formula cell. When you copy the formula, the relative cell reference changes. An absolute reference is a permanent pointer to a particular cell, indicated with dollar signs before the column letter and row number, such as $B$5. When you copy the formula, the absolute cell reference does not change. A mixed reference contains part absolute and part relative reference, such as $B5 or B$5. Depending on the type of relative reference, either the column or row reference changes while the other remains constant when you copy the formula.

3. **Avoid circular references.** A circular reference occurs when a formula refers to the cell containing the formula. The status bar indicates the location of a circular reference. You should correct circular references to prevent inaccurate results.

4. **Insert a function.** A function is a predefined formula that performs a calculation. It contains the function name and arguments. Formula AutoComplete, function ScreenTips, and the Insert Function dialog box help you select and create functions. The Function Arguments dialog box guides you through entering requirements for each argument.

5. **Total values with the SUM function.** The SUM function calculates the total of a range of values. The syntax is =SUM(number1,[number2],…) where the arguments are cell references to one or more ranges.

6. **Insert basic statistical functions.** The AVERAGE function calculates the arithmetic mean of values in a range. The MEDIAN function identifies the midpoint value in a set of values. The MIN function identifies the lowest value in a range, whereas the MAX function identifies the highest value in a range. The COUNT function tallies the number of cells in a range, whereas the COUNTBLANK function tallies the number of blank cells in a range. Excel contains other math and statistical functions, such as FREQUENCY and MODE.

7. **Use date functions.** The TODAY function displays the current date, and the NOW function displays the current date and time. Other date functions identify a particular day of the week, identify the number of net working days between two dates, and display a serial number representing a date.

8. **Determine results with the IF function.** The IF function is a logical function that evaluates a logical test using logical operators, such as <, >, and =, and returns one value if the condition is true and another value if the condition is false. The value_if_true and value_if_false arguments can contain cell references, text, or calculations. You can nest or embed other functions inside one or more of the arguments of an IF function to create more complex formulas.

9. **Use lookup functions.** The VLOOKUP function looks up a value for a particular record, compares it to a lookup table, and returns a result in another column of the lookup table. Design the lookup table using exact values or the breakpoints for ranges. If an exact match is required, the optional fourth argument should be FALSE; otherwise, the fourth argument can remain empty. The HLOOKUP function looks up values by row (horizontally) rather than by column (vertically).

10. **Calculate payments with the PMT function.** The PMT function calculates periodic payments for a loan with a fixed interest rate and a fixed term. The PMT function requires the periodic interest rate, the total number of payment periods, and the original value of the loan. You can use the PMT function to calculate monthly car or mortgage payments.

11. **Create and maintain range names.** A range name is a descriptive name that corresponds with one or more cells. A range name may contain letters, numbers, and underscores, but must start with either a letter or an underscore. The quick way to create a range name is to select the range, type the name in the Name Box, and then press Enter. Use the Name Manager dialog box to edit, create, or delete range names. You can insert a list of range names on a worksheet.

12. **Use range names in formulas.** You can use range names in formulas instead of cell references. Range names are absolute and can make your formula easier to interpret by using a descriptive name for the value(s) contained in a cell or range.

# KEY TERMS

| | | | |
|---|---|---|---|
| Absolute cell reference | Formula AutoComplete | MEDIAN function | Range name |
| Argument | Function | MIN function | Rate |
| AVERAGE function | Function ScreenTip | Mixed cell reference | Relative cell reference |
| Breakpoint | HLOOKUP function | Nested function | Semi-selection |
| Circular reference | IF function | NOW function | SUM function |
| Column index number | Logical test | Nper | Syntax |
| COUNT function | Lookup table | PMT function | Table array |
| COUNTA function | Lookup value | Pointing | TODAY function |
| COUNTBLANK function | MAX function | Pv | VLOOKUP function |

# MULTIPLE CHOICE

1. If cell D15 contains the formula =$C$5*D15, what is the D15 in the formula?

   (a) Mixed reference
   (b) Absolute reference
   (c) Circular reference
   (d) Range name

2. What function would most appropriately accomplish the same thing as =(B5+C5+D5+E5+F5)/5?

   (a) =SUM(B5:F5)/5
   (b) =AVERAGE(B5:F5)
   (c) =MEDIAN(B5:F5)
   (d) =COUNT(B5:F5)

3. When you type a function, what appears after you type the opening parenthesis?

   (a) Function ScreenTip
   (b) Formula AutoComplete
   (c) Insert Function dialog box
   (d) Function Arguments dialog box

4. A formula containing the entry =$B3 is copied to a cell one column to the right and two rows down. How will the entry appear in its new location?

   (a) =$B3
   (b) =B3
   (c) =$C5
   (d) =$B5

5. Cell B10 contains a date, such as 1/1/2012. Which formula will determine how many days are between that date and the current date, given that the cell containing the formula is formatted with Number Format?

   (a) =TODAY()
   (b) =CURRENT()-B10
   (c) =TODAY()-B10
   (d) =TODAY()+NOW()

6. Given that cells A1, A2, and A3 contain values 2, 3, and 10, respectively, and B6, C6, and D6 contain values 10, 20, and 30, respectively, what value will be returned by the function =IF(B6>A3,C6*A1,D6*A2)?

   (a) 10
   (b) 40
   (c) 60
   (d) 90

7. Given the function =VLOOKUP(C6,D12:F18,3), the entries in:

   (a) Range D12:D18 are in ascending order.
   (b) Range D12:D18 are in descending order.
   (c) The third column of the lookup table must be text only.
   (d) Range D12:D18 contain multiple values in each cell.

8. The function =PMT(C5,C7,-C3) is stored in cell C15. What must be stored in cell C7?

   (a) APR
   (b) Periodic interest rate
   (c) Loan amount
   (d) Number of payment periods

9. Which of the following is not an appropriate use of the SUM function?

   (a) =SUM(D15-C15)
   (b) =SUM(F1:G10)
   (c) =SUM(A8:A15,D8:D15)
   (d) =SUM(B3:B45)

10. Which of the following is not an acceptable range name?

   (a) FICA
   (b) Test_Weight
   (c) Goal for 2012
   (d) Target_2012

## 1 Blue Skies Airlines

You are an analyst for Blue Skies Airlines, a regional airline headquartered in Kansas City. Blue Skies has up to 10 departures a day from the Kansas City Airport. Your assistant developed a template for you to store daily flight data about the number of passengers per flight. Each regional aircraft can hold up to 70 passengers. You need to calculate the occupancy rate, which is the percent of each flight that is occupied. In addition, you need daily statistics, such as total number of passengers, averages, least full flights, and so forth, so that decisions can be made for future flight departures out of Kansas City. You also want to calculate weekly statistics per flight number. This exercise follows the same set of skills as used in Hands-On Exercises 1 and 2 in the chapter. Refer to Figure 33 as you complete this exercise.

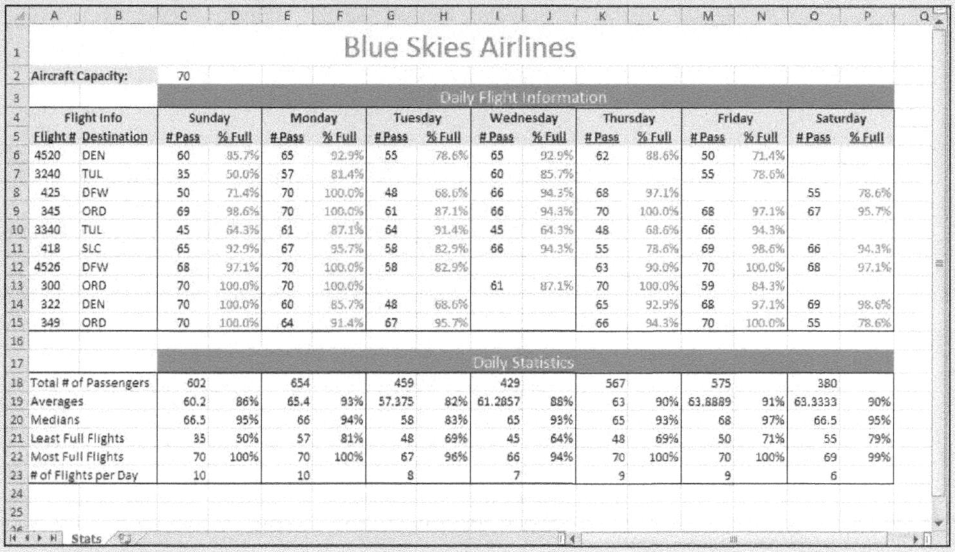

Blue Skies Airlines

Aircraft Capacity: 70

Daily Flight Information

| Flight Info | | Sunday | | Monday | | Tuesday | | Wednesday | | Thursday | | Friday | | Saturday | |
|---|---|---|---|---|---|---|---|---|---|---|---|---|---|---|---|
| Flight # | Destination | # Pass | % Full | # Pass | % Full | # Pass | % Full | # Pass | % Full | # Pass | % Full | # Pass | % Full | # Pass | % Full |
| 4520 | DEN | 60 | 85.7% | 65 | 92.9% | 55 | 78.6% | 65 | 92.9% | 62 | 88.6% | 50 | 71.4% | | |
| 3240 | TUL | 35 | 50.0% | 57 | 81.4% | | | 60 | 85.7% | | | 55 | 78.6% | | |
| 425 | DFW | 50 | 71.4% | 70 | 100.0% | 48 | 68.6% | 66 | 94.3% | 68 | 97.1% | | | 55 | 78.6% |
| 345 | ORD | 69 | 98.6% | 70 | 100.0% | 61 | 87.1% | 66 | 94.3% | 70 | 100.0% | 68 | 97.1% | 67 | 95.7% |
| 3340 | TUL | 45 | 64.3% | 61 | 87.1% | 64 | 91.4% | 45 | 64.3% | 48 | 68.6% | 66 | 94.3% | | |
| 418 | SLC | 65 | 92.9% | 67 | 95.7% | 58 | 82.9% | 66 | 94.3% | 55 | 78.6% | 69 | 98.6% | 66 | 94.3% |
| 4526 | DFW | 68 | 97.1% | 70 | 100.0% | 58 | 82.9% | | | 63 | 90.0% | 70 | 100.0% | 68 | 97.1% |
| 300 | ORD | 70 | 100.0% | 70 | 100.0% | | | 61 | 87.1% | 70 | 100.0% | 59 | 84.3% | | |
| 322 | DEN | 70 | 100.0% | 60 | 85.7% | 48 | 68.6% | | | 65 | 92.9% | 68 | 97.1% | 69 | 98.6% |
| 349 | ORD | 70 | 100.0% | 64 | 91.4% | 67 | 95.7% | | | 66 | 94.3% | 70 | 100.0% | 55 | 78.6% |

Daily Statistics

| | | | | | | | | | | | | | | | |
|---|---|---|---|---|---|---|---|---|---|---|---|---|---|---|---|
| Total # of Passengers | | 602 | | 654 | | 459 | | 429 | | 567 | | 575 | | 380 | |
| Averages | | 60.2 | 86% | 65.4 | 93% | 57.375 | 82% | 61.2857 | 88% | 63 | 90% | 63.8889 | 91% | 63.3333 | 90% |
| Medians | | 66.5 | 95% | 66 | 94% | 58 | 83% | 65 | 93% | 65 | 93% | 68 | 97% | 66.5 | 95% |
| Least Full Flights | | 35 | 50% | 57 | 81% | 48 | 69% | 45 | 64% | 48 | 69% | 50 | 71% | 55 | 79% |
| Most Full Flights | | 70 | 100% | 70 | 100% | 67 | 96% | 66 | 94% | 70 | 100% | 70 | 100% | 69 | 99% |
| # of Flights per Day | | 10 | | 10 | | 8 | | 7 | | 9 | | 9 | | 6 | |

Stats

**FIGURE 33** Blue Skies Airlines ➤

a. Open *e02p1flights* and save it as **e02p1flights_LastnameFirstname.**

b. Click **cell D6**, the cell to display the occupancy percent for Flight 4520 on Sunday, and do the following:
   - Type = and click **cell C6**. Type / and click **cell C2.**
   - Press **F4** to make cell C2 absolute.
   - Click **Enter** to the left of the Formula Bar. The occupancy rate of Flight 4520 is 85.7%.
   - Double-click the **cell D6 fill handle** to copy the formula down the column.

c. Click **cell D7** and notice that the bottom border disappears from cell D15. When you copy a formula, Excel also copies the original cell's format. The cell containing the original formula did not have a bottom border, so when you copied the formula down the column, Excel formatted it to match the original cell with no border. To reapply the border, click **cell D15**, click the **Border arrow** in the Font group on the Home tab, and then select **Bottom Border.**

d. Select the **range D6:D15**, copy it to the Clipboard, and paste it starting in **cell F6**. Notice the formula in cell F6 changes to = E6/$C$2. The first cell reference changes from C6 to E6, maintaining its relative location from the pasted formula. $C$2 remains absolute so that the number of passengers per flight is always divided by the value stored in cell C2. The copied range is still in the Clipboard. Paste the formula into the remaining % Full columns (columns H, J, L, N, and P). Press **Esc** to turn off the marquee around the original copied range.

e. Clean up the data by deleting *0.0%* in cells, such as H7. The 0.0% is misleading as it implies the flight was empty; however, some flights do not operate on all days. Check your worksheet against the *Daily Flight Information* section in Figure 33.

f.  Calculate the total number of passengers per day by doing the following:
- Click **cell C18**.
- Click **AutoSum** in the Editing group.
- Select the **range C6:C15**, and then press **Enter**.

g.  Calculate the average number of passengers per day by doing the following:
- Click **cell C19**.
- Click the **AutoSum arrow** in the Editing group, and then select **Average**.
- Select the **range C6:C15**, and then click **Enter** to the left of the Formula Bar.

h.  Calculate the median number of passengers per day by doing the following:
- Click **cell C20**.
- Click **Insert Function** to the left of the Formula Bar, type **median** in the **Search for a function box**, and then click **Go**.
- Click **MEDIAN** in the **Select a function box**, and then click **OK**.
- Select the **range C6:C15** to enter it in the **Number1 box**, and then click **OK**.

i.  Calculate the least number of passengers on a daily flight by doing the following:
- Click **cell C21**.
- Click the **AutoSum arrow** in the Editing group, and then select **Min**.
- Select the **range C6:C15**, and then press **Enter**.

j.  Calculate the most passengers on a daily flight by doing the following:
- Click **cell C22**.
- Click the **AutoSum arrow** in the Editing group, and then select **Max**.
- Select the **range C6:C15**, and then press **Enter**.

k.  Calculate the number of flights for Sunday by doing the following:
- Click **cell C23**.
- Click the **AutoSum arrow** in the Editing group, and then select **Count Numbers**.
- Select the **range C6:C15**, and then press **Enter**.

l.  Calculate the average, median, least, and full percentages in **cells D19:D22**. Format the values with Percent Style with zero decimal places. Do not copy the formulas from column C to column D, as that will change the borders. You won't insert a SUM function in cell D18 because it does not make sense to total the occupancy rate percentage column. Select **cells C18:D23**, copy the range, and then paste in these cells: **E18, G18, I18, K18, M18, and O18**. Press **Esc** after pasting.

m. Create a footer with your name on the left side, the date code in the center, and the file name code on the right side.

n.  Save and close the workbook, and submit based on your instructor's directions.

## 2  Central Nevada College Salaries

You work in the Human Resources Department at Central Nevada College. You are preparing a spreadsheet model to calculate bonuses based on performance ratings, where ratings between 1 and 1.9 do not receive bonuses, ratings between 2 and 2.9 earn $100 bonuses, ratings between 3 and 3.9 earn $250 bonuses, ratings between 4 and 4.9 earn $500 bonuses, and ratings of 5 or higher earn $1,000 bonuses. In addition, you need to calculate annual raises based on years employed. Employees who have worked five or more years earn a 3.25% raise; employees who have not worked at least five years earn a 2% raise. The partially completed worksheet does not yet contain range names. This exercise follows the same set of skills as used in Hands-On Exercises 1, 2, 3, and 4 in the chapter. Refer to Figure 34 as you complete this exercise.

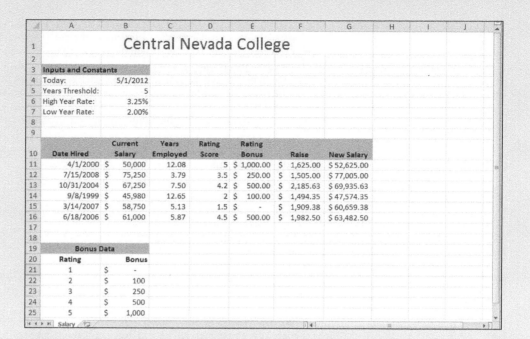

| | A | B | C | D | E | F | G | H | I | J |
|---|---|---|---|---|---|---|---|---|---|---|
| 1 | | | Central Nevada College | | | | | | | |
| 2 | | | | | | | | | | |
| 3 | Inputs and Constants | | | | | | | | | |
| 4 | Today: | 5/1/2012 | | | | | | | | |
| 5 | Years Threshold: | 5 | | | | | | | | |
| 6 | High Year Rate: | 3.25% | | | | | | | | |
| 7 | Low Year Rate: | 2.00% | | | | | | | | |
| 8 | | | | | | | | | | |
| 9 | | | | | | | | | | |
| 10 | Date Hired | Current Salary | Years Employed | Rating Score | Rating Bonus | Raise | New Salary | | | |
| 11 | 4/1/2000 | $ 50,000 | 12.08 | 5 | $ 1,000.00 | $ 1,625.00 | $ 52,625.00 | | | |
| 12 | 7/15/2008 | $ 75,250 | 3.79 | 3.5 | $ 250.00 | $ 1,505.00 | $ 77,005.00 | | | |
| 13 | 10/31/2004 | $ 67,250 | 7.50 | 4.2 | $ 500.00 | $ 2,185.63 | $ 69,935.63 | | | |
| 14 | 9/8/1999 | $ 45,980 | 12.65 | 2 | $ 100.00 | $ 1,494.35 | $ 47,574.35 | | | |
| 15 | 3/14/2007 | $ 58,750 | 5.13 | 1.5 | $ - | $ 1,909.38 | $ 60,659.38 | | | |
| 16 | 6/18/2006 | $ 61,000 | 5.87 | 4.5 | $ 500.00 | $ 1,982.50 | $ 63,482.50 | | | |
| 17 | | | | | | | | | | |
| 18 | | | | | | | | | | |
| 19 | Bonus Data | | | | | | | | | |
| 20 | Rating | | Bonus | | | | | | | |
| 21 | 1 | $ - | | | | | | | | |
| 22 | 2 | $ 100 | | | | | | | | |
| 23 | 3 | $ 250 | | | | | | | | |
| 24 | 4 | $ 500 | | | | | | | | |
| 25 | 5 | $ 1,000 | | | | | | | | |

Salary

**FIGURE 34** Central Nevada College Salaries ➤

a. Open *e02p2salary* and save it as **e02p2salary_LastnameFirstname**.

b. Click **cell B4**, click the **Formulas tab**, click **Date & Time** in the Function Library, select **TODAY**, and then click **OK** to enter today's date in the cell.

c. Enter a formula to calculate the number of years employed by doing the following:
   - Click **cell C11**.
   - Click **Date & Time** in the Function Library group, scroll through the list, and then select **YEARFRAC**.
   - Click **cell A11** to enter the cell reference in the **Start_date box**.
   - Press **Tab**, and then click **cell B4** to enter the cell reference in the **End_date box**.
   - Ask yourself if the cell references should be relative or absolute. You should answer *relative* for **cell A11** so that it will change as you copy it for the other employees. You should answer *absolute* or *mixed* for **cell B4** so that it always refers to the cell containing the TODAY function as you copy the formula.
   - Press **F4** to make **cell B4** absolute, and then click **OK**. (Although you could have used the formula =($B$4-A11)/365 to calculate the number of years, the YEARFRAC function provides better accuracy since it accounts for leap years and the divisor 365 does not.
   - Double-click the **cell C11 fill handle** to copy the YEARFRAC function down the Years Employed column. Your results will differ based on the date contained in cell B4.

d. Enter the breakpoint and bonus data for the lookup table by doing the following:
   - Click **cell A21**, type **1**, and then press **Ctrl+Enter**.
   - Click the **Home tab**, click **Fill** in the Editing group, and then select **Series**. Click **Columns** in the *Series in* section, leave the Step value at **1**, type **5** in the **Stop value box**, and then click **OK**.
   - Click **cell B21**. Enter **0, 100, 250, 500**, and **1000** down the column. The cells have been previously formatted with Accounting Number Format with zero decimal places.
   - Select **range A21:B25**, click in the **Name Box**, type **Bonus**, and then press **Enter** to name the range.

e. Enter the bonus based on rating by doing the following:
   - Click **cell E11**, and then click the **Formulas tab**.
   - Click **Lookup & Reference** in the Function Library group, and then select **VLOOKUP**.
   - Click **cell D11** to enter the cell reference in the **Lookup_value box**.
   - Press **Tab**, and then type **Bonus** to enter the range name for the lookup table in the **Table_array box**.
   - Press **Tab**, type **2** to represent the second column in the lookup table, and then click **OK**.
   - Double-click the **cell E11 fill handle** to copy the formula down the Rating Bonus column.

f. Enter the raise based on years employed by doing the following:
   - Click **cell F11**.
   - Click **Logical** in the Function Library group, and then select **IF**.

- Click **cell C11**, type **>=** and then click **cell B5**. Press **F4** to enter C11>=$B$5 to compare the years employed to the absolute reference of the five-year threshold in the **Logical_test box**.
- Press **Tab**, click **cell B11**, type * and then click **cell B6**. Press **F4** to enter B11*$B$6 to calculate a 3.25% raise for employees who worked five years or more in the **Value_if_true box**.
- Press **Tab**, click **cell B11**, type * and then click **cell B7**. Press **F4** to enter B11*$B$7 to calculate a 2% raise for employees who worked less than five years in the **Value_if_false box**. Click **OK**.
- Double-click the **cell F11 fill handle** to copy the formula down the Raise column.

g. Click **cell G11**. Type **=B11+E11+F11** to add the current salary, the bonus, and the raise to calculate the new salary. Press **Ctrl+Enter** to keep **cell G11** the active cell, and then double-click the **cell G11 fill handle** to copy the formula down the column.

h. Create a footer with your name on the left side, the date code in the center, and the file name code on the right side.

i. Save and close the workbook, and submit based on your instructor's directions.

## 3  Client Mortgage Calculator

You are an agent with Koyle Real Estate in Bowling Green, Ohio. Customers often ask you what their monthly mortgage payments will be. You decide to develop an Excel template you can use to enter the house cost, current APR, yearly property tax, and estimated yearly property insurance. Borrowers who want the lowest interest rates make a 20% down payment. You will assign range names and use them in the formulas. This exercise follows the same set of skills as used in Hands-On Exercises 2, 3, and 4 in the chapter. Refer to Figure 35 as you complete this exercise.

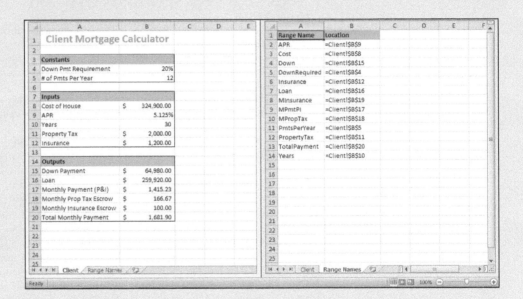

**FIGURE 35** Client Mortgage Calculator ➤

a. Open *e02p3client* and save it as **e02p3client_LastnameFirstname**.

b. Create a range name for the down payment requirement by doing the following: Click **cell B4**, click in the **Name Box**, type **DownRequired**, and then press **Enter**. The number of payments per year value has already been assigned the range name PmtsPerYear.

DISCOVER

c. Name the input values by doing the following:
- Select **range A8:B12**.
- Click the **Formulas tab**, and then click **Create from Selection** in the Defined Names group.
- Make sure *Left column* is selected, and then click **OK**.
- Click each input value cell in **range B8:B12** and look at the newly created names in the Name Box.

d. Edit the range names by doing the following:
- Click **Name Manager** in the Defined Names group.
- Click **Cost_of_House**, click **Edit**, type **Cost**, and then click **OK.**
- Change *Property_Tax* to **PropertyTax.**
- Click **CONSTANTS** in the list, click **Delete**, and then click **OK** to delete it.
- Close the Name Manager.

e. Name the output values using the Create from Selection method you used in step c. Then edit the range names using the same approach you used in step d.
- Change *Down_Payment* to **Down.**
- Change *Monthly_Payment__P_I* to **MPmtPI.**
- Change *Monthly_Property_Tax_Escrow* to **MPropTax.**
- Change *Monthly_Insurance_Escrow* to **MInsurance.**
- Change *Total_Monthly_Payment* to **TotalPayment.**

f. Enter the first two formulas with range names in the Outputs area by doing the following:
- Click **cell B15.** Type **=Cost*down** and double-click **DownRequired** from the **Formula AutoComplete list.** If the list does not appear, type the entire name **DownRequired.** Then press **Enter** to enter the formula =Cost*DownRequired.
- Click **cell B16.** Type **=cost-down** and press **Enter.**

g. Enter the PMT function to calculate the monthly payment of principal and interest by doing the following:
- Click **cell B17.** Click **Financial** in the Function Library group, scroll down, and then select **PMT.**
- Click **cell B9**, type **/** and then click **cell B5** to enter APR/PmtsPerYear in the **Rate box.**
- Press **Tab**, click **cell B10**, type **\*** and then click **cell B5** to enter Years*PmtsPerYear in the **Nper box.**
- Press **Tab**, type **-loan** in the **Pv box**, and then click **OK.**

h. Enter the monthly property tax formula by doing the following:
- Click **cell B18.** Type **=** to start the formula.
- Click **Use in Formula** in the Defined Names group, and select **PropertyTax.**
- Type **/** and click **Use in Formula** in the Defined Names group. Select **PmtsPerYear**, and then press **Enter.**

i. Adapt step h to enter the formula =Insurance/PmtsPerYear in **cell B19.**

j. Enter **=SUM(B17:B19)** in **cell B20.**

k. Select **range B15:B20**, and then apply **Accounting Number Format.**

l. Click the **Range Names worksheet tab**, click **cell A2**, click the **Formulas tab**, click **Use in Formula** in the Defined Names group, select **Paste Names**, and then click **Paste List** to paste an alphabetical list of range names in the worksheet. Adjust the column widths.

m. Create a footer with your name on the left side, the date code in the center, and the file name code on the right side for both worksheets.

n. Save and close the workbook, and submit based on your instructor's directions.

## 1 Sunrise Credit Union Weekly Payroll

As manager of the Sunrise Credit Union, you are responsible for managing the weekly payroll. Your assistant developed a partial worksheet, but you need to enter the formulas to calculate the regular pay, overtime pay, gross pay, taxable pay, withholding tax, FICA, and net pay. In addition, you want to total pay columns and calculate some basic statistics. As you construct formulas, make sure you use absolute and relative cell references correctly in formulas and avoid circular references.

a. Open the *e02m1payroll* workbook and save it as **e02m1payroll_LastnameFirstname**.

b. Study the worksheet structure, and then read the business rules in the Notes section.

c. Use IF functions to calculate the regular pay and overtime pay based on a regular 40-hour workweek. Pay overtime only for overtime hours. Calculate the gross pay based on the regular and overtime pay. Abram's regular pay is $398. With eight overtime hours, Abram's overtime pay is $119.40.

d. Create a formula to calculate the taxable pay. With two dependents, Abram's taxable pay is $417.40.

e. Use the appropriate function to identify and calculate the federal withholding tax. With a taxable pay of $417.40, Abram's tax rate is 25%, and the withholding tax is $104.35.

f. Calculate FICA based on gross pay and the FICA rate, and then calculate the net pay.

g. Calculate the total regular pay, overtime pay, gross pay, taxable pay, withholding tax, FICA, and net pay.

h. Copy all formulas down their respective columns.

i. Apply **Accounting Number Format** to the **range C5:C16**. Apply **Accounting Number Format** to the first row of monetary data and to the total row. Apply **Comma Style** to the monetary values for the other employees. Underline the last employee's monetary values, and then use the Format Cells dialog box to apply **Double Accounting Underline** for the totals.

j. Insert appropriate functions to calculate the average, highest, and lowest values in the Summary Statistics area of the worksheet.

 k. At your instructor's discretion, use Help to learn about the FREQUENCY function. The Help feature contains sample data for you to copy and practice in a new worksheet to learn about this function. You can close the practice worksheet containing the Help data without saving it. You want to determine the number (frequency) of employees who worked less than 20 hours, between 20 and 29 hours, between 30 and 40 hours, and over 40 hours. **Cells J28:J31** list the ranges. You need to translate this range into correct values for the Bin column in **cells I28:I30** and then enter the FREQUENCY function in **cells K28:K31**. The function should identify one employee who worked between 0 and 19 hours and six employees who worked more than 40 hours.

l. Apply other page setup formats as needed.

m. Insert a footer with your name on the left side, the date code in the center, and the file name code on the right side.

n. Save and close the workbook, and submit based on your instructor's directions.

## 2 First Bank of Missouri

As a loan officer at First Bank of Missouri, you track house loans. You started a spreadsheet that contains client names, the selling price of houses, and the term of the loans. You are ready to calculate the interest rate, which is based on the term. In addition, you need to calculate the required down payment, the amount to be financed, and the monthly payment for each customer. To keep your formulas easy to read, you will create and use range names. Finally, you need to calculate some basic statistics.

a. Open the *e02m2bank* workbook and save it as **e02m2bank_LastnameFirstname**.

b. Enter a function to display the current date in **cell G3**.

c. Assign appropriate range names to the number of payments per year value and to the lookup table.

d. Use range names when possible in formulas, and avoid creating circular references.

e. Use an appropriate function to display the interest rate for the first customer.

f. Use an appropriate lookup function to calculate the amount of the down payment for the first customer. The down payment is based on the term and the selling price. The first customer's amount is $68,975.

g. Calculate the amount to be financed for the first customer.

h. Calculate the monthly payment for the first customer using range names and cell references. The first customer's monthly payment is $1,142.65.

i. Copy the formulas down their respective columns. Format interest rates with **Percent Style** with two decimal places. Format monetary values with **Accounting Number Format** with two decimal places.

j. Calculate the number of loans and other summary statistics. Format the statistics as needed.

k. Create a section, complete with column headings, for the range names. Place this area below the lookup table.

l. Insert a footer with your name on the left side, the sheet name code in the center, and the file name code on the right side.

m. Save and close the workbook, and submit based on your instructor's directions.

## 3  Professor's Grade Book

You are a teaching assistant for Dr. Denise Gerber, who teaches an introductory C# programming class at your college. One of your routine tasks is to enter assignment and test grades into the grade book. Now that the semester is almost over, you need to create formulas to calculate category averages, the overall weighted average, and the letter grade for each student. In addition, Dr. Gerber wants to see general statistics, such as average, median, low, and high for each graded assignment and test, as well as category averages and total averages. Furthermore, you need to create the grading scale on the documentation worksheet and use it to display the appropriate letter grade for each student.

a. Open the *e02m3grades* workbook and save it as **e02m3grades_LastnameFirstname**.

b. Use breakpoints to enter the grading scale in the correct structure on the Documentation worksheet, and then name the grading scale range **Grades**. The grading scale is as follows:

| | |
|---|---|
| 95+ | A |
| 90–94.9 | A– |
| 87–89.9 | B+ |
| 83–86.9 | B |
| 80–82.9 | B– |
| 77–79.9 | C+ |
| 73–76.9 | C |
| 70–72.9 | C– |
| 67–69.9 | D+ |
| 63–66.9 | D |
| 60–62.9 | D– |
| 0–59.9 | F |

c. Calculate the total lab points earned for the first student in **cell T8** in the Grades worksheet. The first student earned 93 lab points.

d. Calculate the average of the two midterm tests for the first student in **cell W8**. The student's midterm test average is 87.

e.  Calculate the assignment average for the first student in cell I8. The formula should drop the lowest score before calculating the average. Hint: You need to use a combination of three functions: SUM, MIN, and COUNT. The first student's assignment average is 94.2 after dropping the lowest assignment score.

f.  Calculate the weighted total points based on the four category points (assignment average, lab points, midterm average, and final exam) and their respective weights (stored in the range B40:B43) in cell Y8. Use relative and absolute cell references as needed in the formula. The first student's total weighted score is 90.

g.  Use the appropriate function to calculate the letter grade equivalent in **cell Z8**. Use the range name in the function. The first student's letter grade is A–.

h.  Copy the formulas down their respective columns for the other students.

i.  Name the passing score threshold in **cell B5** with the range name **Passing**. Display a message in the last grade book column based on the student's semester performance. If a student earned a final score of 70 or higher, display *Enroll in CS 202*. Otherwise, display *RETAKE CS 101*.

j.  Calculate the average, median, low, and high scores for each assignment, lab, test, category average, and total score. Display individual averages with no decimal places; display category and final score averages with one decimal place. Display other statistics with no decimal places.

k.  Insert a list of range names in the designated area in the Documentation worksheet. Complete the documentation by inserting your name, today's date, and a purpose statement in the designated areas.

DISCOVER

l.  At your instructor's discretion, add a column to display each student's rank in the class. Use Help to learn how to insert the RANK function.

m.  Select page setup options as needed to print the Grades worksheet on one page.

n.  Insert a footer with your name on the left side, the sheet name code in the center, and the file name code on the right side of each worksheet.

o.  Save and close the workbook, and submit based on your instructor's directions.

You are a sales representative at the local fitness center, Buff and Tuff Gym. Your manager expects each representative to track weekly new membership data, so you created a spreadsheet to store data. Membership costs are based on membership type. Clients can rent a locker for an additional annual fee. You are required to collect a down payment based on membership type, determine the balance, and then calculate the monthly payment based on a standard interest rate. In addition, you need to calculate general statistics to summarize for your manager. Spot-check results to make sure you created formulas and functions correctly.

## Perform Preliminary Work

You need to open the starting workbook you created, acknowledge the existing circular reference error, and assign a range name to the membership lookup table. You will correct the circular reference error later.

a. Open the *e02c1gym* workbook, click **Help**, read about circular references, close the Help window that appears, and save the workbook as **e02c1gym_LastnameFirstname**.

b. Assign the name **Membership** to the **range A18:C20**.

c. Insert a function to display the current date in **cell B2**.

## Calculate Cost, Annual Total, and Total Due

You are ready to calculate the basic annual membership cost and the total annual cost. The basic annual membership is determined based on each client's membership type, using the lookup table.

a. Insert a function in **cell C5** to display the basic annual membership cost for the first client.

b. Use a function to calculate the annual total amount, which is the sum of the basic cost and locker fees for those who rent a locker. The Locker column displays *Yes* for clients who rent a locker and *No* for those who don't.

c. Calculate the total amount due for the first client based on the annual total and the number of years in the contract.

d. Copy the three formulas down their respective columns.

## Determine the Down Payment and Balance

You need to collect a down payment based on the type of membership for each new client. Then you must determine how much each client owes.

a. Insert the function to display the amount of down payment for the first client.

b. Find and correct the circular reference for the balance. The balance is the difference between the total due and the down payment.

c. Copy the two formulas for the rest of the clients.

## Calculate the Monthly Payment

Clients pay the remainder by making monthly payments. Monthly payments are based on the number of years specified in the client's contract and a standard interest rate.

a. Insert the function to calculate the first client's monthly payment, using appropriate relative and absolute cell references.

b. Copy the formula down the column.

c. Edit the formula by changing the appropriate cell reference to a mixed cell reference. Copy the formula down.

## Finalize the Workbook

You need to perform some basic statistical calculations and finalize the workbook with formatting and page setup options.

a. Calculate totals on row 14.

b. Insert the appropriate functions in the *Summary Statistics* section of the worksheet: **cells H18:H22**. Format the payments with **Accounting Number Format**, and format the number of new members appropriately.

c. Format the other column headings on rows 4 and 17 to match the fill color in the **range E17:H17**. Wrap text for the column headings.

d. Format the monetary values for Andrews and the total row with **Accounting Number Format**. Use zero decimal places for whole amounts, and display two decimal places for the monthly payment. Apply **Comma Style** to the internal monetary values. Underline the values before the totals, and then apply **Double Accounting Underline** (found in the Format Cells dialog box) for the totals.

e. Set **0.3"** left and right margins, and then ensure the page prints on only one page.

f. Insert a footer with your name on the left side, the date code in the center, and the file name code on the right side.

g. Save and close the workbook, and submit based on your instructor's directions.

# BEYOND THE CLASSROOM

## Blue Skies Airlines

**GENERAL CASE**

In Practice Exercise 1, you worked with the Blue Skies Airlines' daily flight statistics. If you did not complete that exercise, review the introductory paragraph, steps, and Figure 33. Open *e02b1blue* and save it as **e02b1blue_LastnameFirstName**. It is inefficient to delete 0.0% when a flight does not exist for a particular day, so you will create a formula that enters an empty text string if the number column contains a hyphen (-) using the IF function to evaluate if the # Pass column does not contain a hyphen. The value_if_true argument should calculate the occupancy percentage. The value_if_false argument should enter an empty text string, indicated by "". Copy the function to other days' % Full columns. Calculate the average daily percentage full for Flight 4520 in the Weekly Statistics area of the worksheet. Note that you need to use nonadjacent cell addresses in the function. Include empty % Full cells so that you can copy the formula down for the other flights. The empty cells do not affect the results. The average daily occupancy rate for Flight 4520 is 85.0%. Calculate the low and high daily occupancy rates. For Flight 4520, the lowest occupancy rate is 71.4%, and the highest occupancy rate is 92.9%. Insert a function to count the number of days each flight was made. Reapply the bottom border to the statistics area, if needed. Change the scaling so that the worksheet fits on one page. Include a footer with your name on the left side, the date code in the center, and the file name code on the right side. Save and close the workbook, and submit based on your instructor's directions.

## Mall Lease Rates

**RESEARCH CASE**

As general manager of a shopping mall, you developed a spreadsheet to list current tenant data. Open *e02b2mall*, and save it as **e02b2mall_LastnameFirstname**. You need to calculate the expiration date, price per square foot, annual rent, and monthly rent for each tenant. Use Help to research how you can construct a nested DATE function that will display the expiration date. The function should add the number of years for the lease but should subtract one day. For example, a five-year lease that started on January 1, 2010, expires on December 31, 2014, not on January 1, 2015. Assign three range names: the lookup table and the two constants. The price per square foot is based on two things: length of the lease and the number of square feet. If a tenant's space is less than the threshold, the tenant's price per square footage is based on the regular price. If a tenant's space is at least 3,000 square feet, the tenant's price is based on the adjusted square footage price. Use Help or search the Internet to learn how to nest the VLOOKUP within the IF function. You will need two nested functions. Use range names in the functions. Calculate the annual rent, which is the product of the square footage and price per square footage per tenant. Then calculate the monthly rent. Avoid circular references in your formulas. Format values appropriately. Include a footer with your name on the left side, the date code in the center, and the file name code on the right side. Save and close the workbook, and submit based on your instructor's directions.

## Park City Condo Rental

**DISASTER RECOVERY**

You and some friends are planning a Labor Day vacation to Park City, Utah. You have secured a four-day condominium that costs $1,200. Some people will stay all four days; others will stay part of the weekend. One of your friends constructed a worksheet to help calculate each person's cost of the rental. The people who stay Thursday night will split the nightly cost evenly. To keep the costs down, everyone agreed to pay $30 per night per person for Friday, Saturday, and/or Sunday nights. Depending on the number of people who stay each night, the group may owe more money. Kyle, Ian, Isaac, and Daryl agreed to split the difference in the total rental cost and the amount the group members paid. Open *e02b3parkcity*, address the circular reference error message that appears, and save the workbook as **e02b3parkcity_LastnameFirstname**. Review the worksheet structure, including the assumptions and calculation notes at the bottom of the worksheet. Check the formulas and functions, making necessary corrections. With the existing data, the number of people staying each night is 5, 7, 10, and 10, respectively. The total paid given the above assumptions is $1,110, giving a difference of $90 to be divided evenly among the first four people. Kyle's share should be $172.50. In the cells containing errors, insert comments to describe the error, and then fix the formulas. Verify the accuracy of formulas by entering an IF function in cell I1 to ensure the totals match. Nick, James, and Body inform you they can't stay Sunday night, and Rob wants to stay Friday night. Change the input accordingly. The updated total paid is now $1,200, and the difference is $150. Include a footer with your name on the left side, the date code in the center, and the file name code on the right side. Save and close the workbook, and submit based on your instructor's directions.

# EXCEL
# CHARTS
## Depicting Data Visually

## CASE STUDY | Hort University Majors

You are an assistant in the Institutional Research Department for Hort University, a prestigious university on the East Coast. You help conduct research using the university's information systems to provide statistics on the student population, alumni, and more. Your department stores an abundance of data to provide needed results upon request.

Dr. Alisha Musto, your boss, asked that you analyze the number of majors by the six colleges: Arts, Business, Education, Humanities & Social Science, Science & Health, and Technology & Computing. In addition, Dr. Musto wants you to include the undeclared majors in your analysis. You created an Excel worksheet with the data, but you want to create a series of charts that will help Dr. Musto analyze the enrollment data.

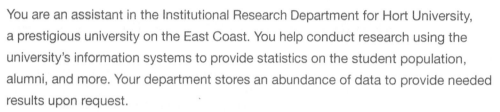

## OBJECTIVES   AFTER YOU READ THIS CHAPTER, YOU WILL BE ABLE TO:

1. Decide which chart type to create
2. Create a chart
3. Change the chart type
4. Change the data source and structure
5. Apply a chart layout and a chart style
6. Move a chart

7. Print charts
8. Insert and customize a sparkline
9. Select and format chart elements
10. Customize chart labels
11. Format the axes and gridlines
12. Add a trendline

From Excel Chapter 3 of *Exploring Microsoft Office 2010 Volume 1*, First Edition, Robert T. Grauer, Mary Anne Poatsy, Keith Mulbery, Michelle Hulett, Cynthia Krebs, Keith Mast. Copyright © 2011 by Pearson Education, Inc. Published by Pearson Prentice Hall, Inc. All rights reserved.

# Chart Basics

The expression "a picture is worth a thousand words" means that a visual can be a more effective way to communicate or interpret data than words or numbers. Storing, organizing, and performing calculations on quantitative data, such as in the spreadsheets you have created, are important, but you must also be able to analyze the data to determine what they mean. A *chart* is a visual representation of numerical data that compares data and helps reveal trends or patterns to help people make informed decisions. An effective chart depicts data in a clear, easy-to-interpret manner and contains enough data to be useful but not too much that the data overwhelm people.

> An effective chart depicts data in a clear, easy-to-interpret manner....

A **chart** is a visual representation of numerical data.

In this section, you will learn chart terminology and how to choose the best chart type, such as pie or line, to fit your needs. You will select the range of cells containing the numerical values and labels from which to create the chart, choose the chart type, insert the chart, and designate the chart's location.

# Deciding Which Chart Type to Create

Before creating a chart, study the data you want to represent visually. Look at the structure of the worksheet—the column labels, the row labels, the quantitative data, and the calculated values. Decide what you want to convey to your audience: Does the worksheet hold a single set of data, such as average snowfall at one ski resort, or multiple sets of data, such as average snowfall at several ski resorts? Do you want to depict data for one specific time period or over several time periods, such as several years or decades? Based on the data on which you want to focus, you decide which type of chart best represents that data. With Excel, you can create a variety of types of charts. The four most common chart types are column, bar, line, and pie.

You should organize the worksheet data before creating a chart by ensuring that the values in columns and rows are on the same value system (such as dollars or units) in order to make comparisons, that labels are descriptive, and that no blank rows or columns exist in the primary dataset. Figure 1 shows a worksheet containing the number of students who have declared a major within each college at Hort University. These data will be used to illustrate several chart types. Each cell containing a value is a *data point*. For example, the value 1,330 is a data point for the Arts data in the 2012 column. A group of related data points that appear in row(s) or column(s) in the worksheet create a *data series*. For example, the values 950, 1,000, 1,325, and 1,330 comprise the Arts data series. Textual information, such as column and row labels (college names, months, years, product names, etc.), is used to create *category labels* in charts.

A **data point** is a numeric value that describes a single value on a chart.

A **data series** is a group of related data points.

A **category label** is text that describes a collection of data points in a chart.

| | A | B | C | D | E | F |
|---|---|---|---|---|---|---|
| 1 | **Hort University** | | | | | |
| 2 | Number of Majors by College | | | | | |
| 3 | | | | | | |
| 4 | | 2009 | 2010 | 2011 | 2012 | Average |
| 5 | Arts | 950 | 1,000 | 1,325 | 1,330 | 1,151 |
| 6 | Business | 3,975 | 3,650 | 3,775 | 4,000 | 3,850 |
| 7 | Education | 1,500 | 1,425 | 1,435 | 1,400 | 1,440 |
| 8 | Humanities & Social Science | 2,300 | 2,250 | 2,500 | 3,500 | 2,638 |
| 9 | Science & Health | 1,895 | 1,650 | 1,700 | 1,800 | 1,761 |
| 10 | Technology & Computing | 4,500 | 4,325 | 4,400 | 4,800 | 4,506 |
| 11 | Undeclared | 5,200 | 5,500 | 5,000 | 4,700 | 5,100 |
| 12 | Totals by Year | 20,320 | 19,800 | 20,135 | 21,530 | 20,446 |
| 13 | | | | | | |

**FIGURE 1** Sample Dataset ➤

Charts

174

# Create a Column Chart

A **column chart** displays data comparisons vertically in columns.

The **chart area** contains the entire chart and all of its elements.

The **plot area** contains a graphical representation of values in a data series.

The **X-axis** is a horizontal line that borders the plot area to provide a frame of reference for measurement.

The **Y-axis** is a vertical line that borders the plot area to provide a frame of reference for measurement.

The **category axis** provides descriptive group names for subdividing the data series.

The **value axis** displays incremental values to identify the values of the data series.

A *column chart* displays data vertically in columns. You use column charts to compare values across different categories, such as comparing revenue among different cities or comparing quarterly revenue in one year. Column charts are most effective when they are limited to small numbers of categories—generally seven or fewer. If more categories exist, the columns appear too close together, making it difficult to read the labels.

Before you create a chart, you need to know the names of the different chart elements. The *chart area* contains the entire chart and all of its elements, including the plot area, titles, legend, and labels. The *plot area* is the region containing the graphical representation of the values in the data series. Two axes form a border around the plot area. The *X-axis* is a horizontal border that provides a frame of reference for measuring data horizontally. The *Y-axis* is a vertical border that provides a frame of reference for measuring data vertically. Excel refers to the axes as the category axis and value axis. The *category axis* displays descriptive group names or labels, such as college names or cities, to identify data. The *value axis* displays incremental numbers to identify approximate values, such as dollars or units, of data points in the chart. In a column chart, the category axis is the X-axis, and the value axis is the Y-axis.

The column chart in Figure 2 compares the number of majors by college for only one year using the data from the worksheet in Figure 1. In Figure 2, the college labels stored in the first column—the range A5:A11—form the horizontal category axis, and the data points representing the number of majors in 2012 in the range E5:E11 form the vertical value axis. The height of each column represents the value of the individual data points: The larger the value, the taller the column. For example, Business has a taller column than the Arts and Education columns, indicating that more students major in Business than Arts or Education.

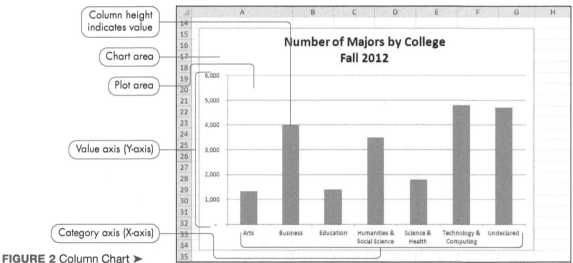

**FIGURE 2** Column Chart ➤

A **single data series** compares values for one set of data.

A **multiple data series** compares two or more sets of data in one chart.

A **clustered column chart** groups or clusters similar data in columns to compare values across categories.

Figure 2 shows a column chart representing a *single data series*—data for only Fall 2012. However, you might want to create a column chart that contains multiple data series. A *multiple data series* chart compares two or more sets of data, such as the number of majors by college for four years. After you select the chart category, such as Column or Line, select a chart subtype. Within each chart category, Excel provides many variations or subtypes, such as clustered, stacked, and 100% stacked.

A *clustered column chart* compares groups or clusters of columns set side-by-side for easy comparison. The clustered column chart facilitates quick comparisons across data series, and it is effective for comparing several data points among categories. Figure 3 shows a clustered column chart created from the data in Figure 1. By default, the row titles appear on the category axis, and the yearly data series appear as columns with the value axis showing incremental numbers. Excel assigns a different color to each yearly data series and

A **legend** is a key that identifies the color, gradient, picture, texture, or pattern fill assigned to each data series in a chart.

includes a legend. A ***legend*** is a key that identifies the color, gradient, picture, texture, or pattern assigned to each data series in a chart. For example, the 2012 data appear in purple. This chart clusters yearly data series for each college, enabling you to compare yearly trends for each major.

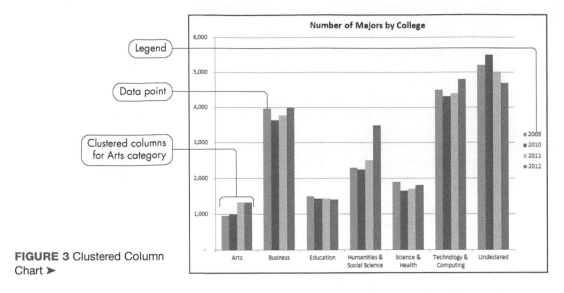

**FIGURE 3** Clustered Column Chart ➤

Figure 4 shows another clustered column chart in which the categories and data series are reversed. The years appear on the category axis, and the colleges appear as color-coded data series and in the legend. This chart gives a different perspective from that in Figure 3 in that it helps your audience understand the differences in majors per year rather than focusing on each major separately for several years.

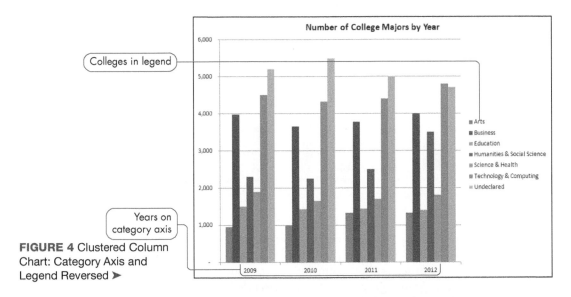

**FIGURE 4** Clustered Column Chart: Category Axis and Legend Reversed ➤

A **stacked column chart** places stacks of data in segments on top of each other in one column, with each category in the data series represented by a different color.

A ***stacked column chart*** shows the relationship of individual data points to the whole category. Unlike a clustered column chart that displays several columns (one for each data series) for a category (such as Arts), a stacked column chart displays only one column for each category. Each category within the stacked column is color-coded for one data series. Use the stacked column chart when you want to compare total values across categories, as well as to display the individual category values. Figure 5 shows a stacked column chart in which a single column represents each categorical year, and each column stacks color-coded data-point segments representing the different colleges. The stacked column chart enables you to determine the total number of majors for each year. The height of each color-coded data point enables you to identify the relative contribution of each college to the total number of yearly majors. A disadvantage of the stacked column chart is that the segments within each column do not start at the same point, making it more difficult to compare individual segment values across categories.

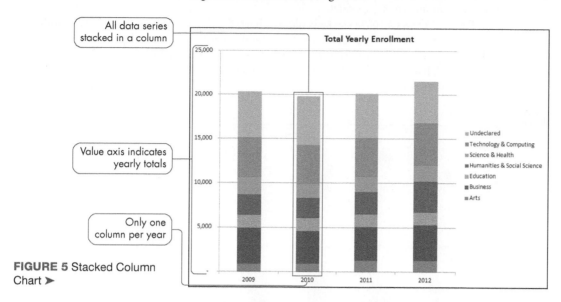

All data series stacked in a column

Value axis indicates yearly totals

Only one column per year

**FIGURE 5** Stacked Column Chart ➤

When you create a stacked column chart, you must ensure data are *additive*, meaning that each column represents a sum of the data for each segment. Figure 5 correctly uses years as the category axis and the colleges as data series. Within each year, Excel adds the number of majors by college, and the columns display the sum of the majors. For example, the total number of majors in 2012 is over 20,000. Figure 6 shows an incorrectly constructed stacked column chart because the yearly number of majors by college is *not* additive. It is incorrect to state that the university has 15,000 total business majors for four years. Be careful when constructing stacked column charts to ensure that they lead to logical interpretation of data.

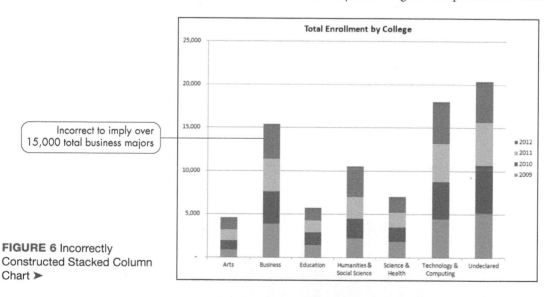

Incorrect to imply over 15,000 total business majors

**FIGURE 6** Incorrectly Constructed Stacked Column Chart ➤

A **100% stacked column chart** places (stacks) data in one column per category, with each column having the same height of 100%.

A ***100% stacked column chart*** compares the percentage each data point contributes to the total for each category. Similar to the stacked column chart, the 100% stacked column chart displays only one column per category. The value axis displays percentages rather than values, and all columns are the same height: 100%. Excel converts each data point value into a percentage of the total for each category. Use this type of chart when you are more interested in comparing relative percentage contributions across categories rather than actual values across categories. For example, a regional manager for a department store realizes that not every store is the same size and that the different stores have different sales volumes. Instead of comparing sales by department for each store, you might want to display percentage of sales by department to facilitate comparisons of percentage contributions for each department within its own store's sales.

Figure 7 shows a 100% stacked column chart. Excel computes the total 2012 enrollment (21,530 in our example), calculates the enrollment percentage by college, and displays each column segment in proportion to its computed percentage. The Arts College had 1,330 majors, which accounts for 6% of the total number of majors, where the total enrollment for any given year is 100%.

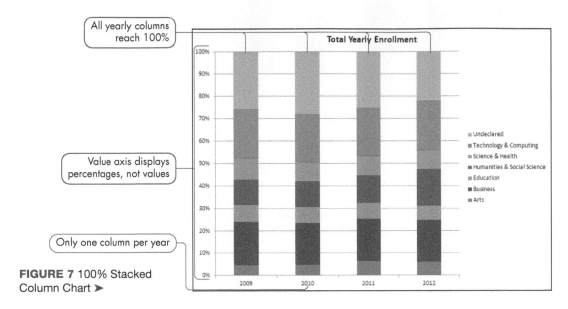

**FIGURE 7** 100% Stacked
Column Chart ➤

A **3-D chart** adds a third dimension to each data series, creating a distorted perspective of the data.

Excel enables you to create special-effects charts, such as 3-D, cylinder, pyramid, or cone charts. A **3-D chart** adds a third dimension to each data series. Although the 3-D clustered column chart in Figure 8 might look exciting, the third dimension does not plot another value. It is a superficial enhancement that might distort the charted data. In 3-D column charts, some columns might appear taller or shorter than they actually are because of the angle of the 3-D effect, or some columns might be hidden by taller columns in front of them. Therefore, avoid the temptation to create 3-D charts.

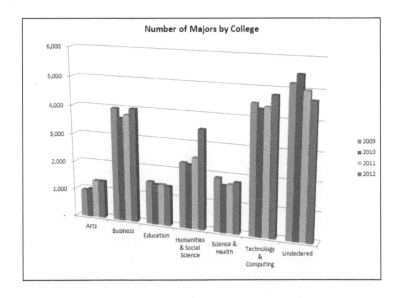

**FIGURE 8** 3-D Clustered
Column Chart ➤

Charts

## Create a Bar Chart

A **bar chart** compares values across categories using horizontal bars.

A *bar chart* compares values across categories using horizontal bars. In a bar chart, the horizontal axis displays values, and the vertical axis displays categories (see Figure 9). A bar chart conveys the same type of information as a column chart; however, a bar chart is preferable when category names are long, such as *Humanities & Social Science*. A bar chart enables category names to appear in an easy-to-read format, whereas a column chart might display category names at an awkward angle or smaller font size. Like column charts, bar charts have several subtypes, such as clustered, stacked, 100% stacked, 3-D, cylinder, cone, or pyramid subtypes.

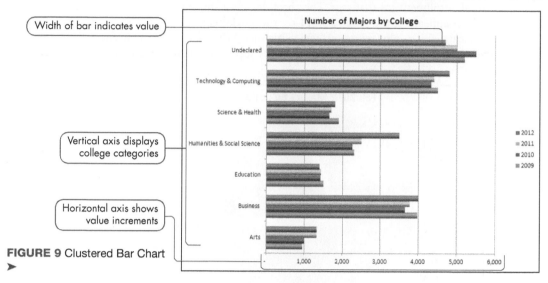

Width of bar indicates value

Vertical axis displays college categories

Horizontal axis shows value increments

**FIGURE 9** Clustered Bar Chart ➤

## Create a Line Chart

A **line chart** uses a line to connect data points in order to show trends over a period of time.

A *line chart* displays lines connecting data points to show trends over equal time periods, such as months, quarters, years, or decades. With multiple data series, Excel displays each data series with a different line color. The category axis (X-axis) represents time, such as ten-year increments, whereas the value axis (Y-axis) represents the value, such as a monetary value or quantity. A line chart enables a user to easily spot trends in the data since the line continues to the next data point. The line, stacked, and 100% stacked line charts do not have specific indicators for each data point. To show each data point, select Line with Markers, Stacked Line with Markers, or 100% Stacked Line with Markers. Figure 10 shows a line chart indicating the number of majors by college over time, making it easy to see the enrollment trends. For example, the Arts enrollment spiked in 2010 while enrollments in other colleges decreased that year.

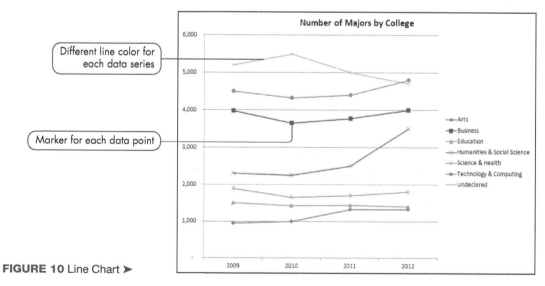

Different line color for each data series

Marker for each data point

**FIGURE 10** Line Chart ➤

Chart Basics • Excel 2010

179

## Create a Pie Chart

A **pie chart** shows each data point in proportion to the whole data series as a slice in a circular pie.

A *pie chart* shows each data point as a proportion to the whole data series. The pie chart displays as a circle or "pie," where the entire pie represents the total value of the data series. Each slice represents a single data point. The larger the slice, the larger percentage that data point contributes to the whole. Use a pie chart when you want to convey percentage or market share. Unlike column, bar, and line charts, pie charts represent a single data series only.

The pie chart in Figure 11 divides the pie representing total Fall 2012 enrollment into seven slices, one for each college. The size of each slice is proportional to the percentage of total enrollment for that year. The chart depicts a single data series (Fall 2012 enrollment), which appears in the range E5:E11 on the worksheet in Figure 1. Excel creates a legend to indicate which color represents which pie slice. When you create a pie chart, limit it to about seven slices. Pie charts with too many slices appear too busy to interpret.

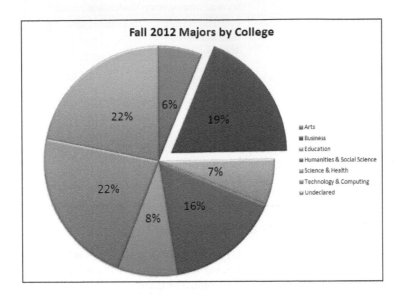

**FIGURE 11** Pie Chart ➤

Similar to the way it creates a 100% stacked column chart, Excel creates a pie chart by computing the total 2012 enrollment (21,530 in our example), calculating the enrollment percentage by college and drawing each slice of the pie in proportion to its computed percentage. The Business College had 4,000 majors, which accounts for 19% of the total number of majors. You can focus a person's attention on a particular slice by separating one or more slices from the rest of the chart in an *exploded pie chart*, as shown in Figure 11. Additional pie subtypes include pie of pie, bar of pie, and 3-D pie charts.

An **exploded pie chart** separates one or more pie slices from the rest of the pie chart.

## Create Other Chart Types

Excel enables you to create seven other basic chart types: area, X Y (scatter), stock, surface, doughnut, bubble, and radar. Each chart type has many chart subtypes available.

An **area chart** emphasizes magnitude of changes over time by filling in the space between lines with a color.

An *area chart* is similar to a line chart in that it shows trends over time. Like the line chart, the area chart uses continuous lines to connect data points. The difference between a line chart and an area chart is that the area chart displays colors between the lines. People sometimes view area charts as making the data series more distinguishable because of the filled-in colors. Figure 12 shows a stacked area chart representing yearly enrollments by college. The shaded areas provide a more dramatic effect than a line chart.

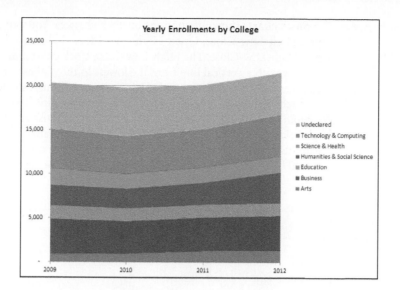

**FIGURE 12** Stacked Area Chart ➤

> **TIP** Hidden Data
>
> When creating an area chart, be careful which subtype you select. For some subtypes such as a 3-D area chart, the chart might hide smaller data values behind data series with larger values. If this happens, you can change subtypes or apply a transparency fill to see any hidden data values.

An **X Y (scatter) chart** shows a relationship between two variables.

An **X Y (scatter) chart** shows a relationship between two variables using their X and Y coordinates. Excel plots one variable on the horizontal X-axis and the other variable on the vertical Y-axis. Scatter charts are often used to represent data in educational, scientific, and medical experiments. A scatter chart is essentially the plotted values without any connecting line. A scatter chart helps you determine if a relationship exists between two different sets of numerical data. For example, you can plot the number of minutes students view a computer-based training (CBT) module and their test scores to see if a relationship exists between the two variables (see Figure 13).

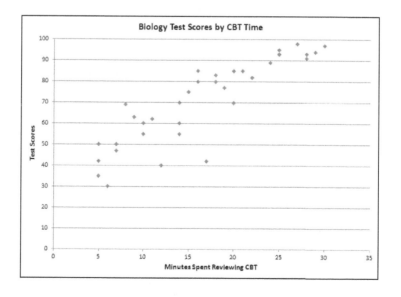

**FIGURE 13** Scatter (X Y) Chart ➤

A **stock chart** shows the high, low, and close prices for individual stocks over time.

**Stock charts** show fluctuations in stock changes. You can select one of four stock subtypes: High-Low-Close, Open-High-Low-Close, Volume-High-Low-Close, and Volume-Open-High-Low-Close. The High-Low-Close stock chart marks a stock's trading range on a given day with a vertical line from the lowest to the highest stock prices. Horizontal bars or rectangles mark the opening and closing prices. Although stock charts may have some other uses, such as showing a range of temperatures over time, they usually show stock prices. To create an Open-High-Low-Close stock chart, you must arrange data with Opening Price, High Price, Low Price, and Closing Price as column labels in that sequence. If you want to create other variations of stock charts, you must arrange data in a structured sequence required by Excel. Figure 14 shows three days of stock prices for a particular stock.

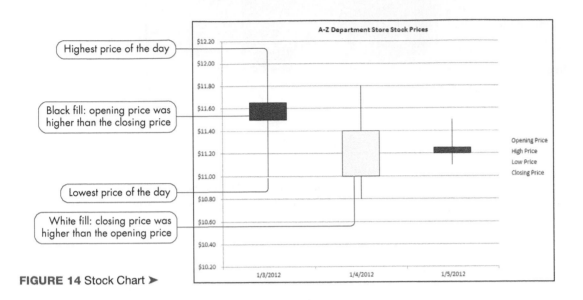

**FIGURE 14** Stock Chart ➤

The stock chart legend may not explain the chart clearly. However, you can still identify prices. The rectangle represents the difference in the opening and closing prices. If the rectangle has a white fill, the closing price is higher than the opening price. If the rectangle has a black fill, the opening price is higher than the closing price. In Figure 14, the opening price was $11.65, and the closing price was $11.50 on January 3. A line below the rectangle indicates that the lowest trading price is lower than the opening and closing prices. In Figure 14, the lowest price was $11.00 on January 3. A line above the rectangle indicates the highest trading price is higher than the opening and closing prices. In Figure 14, the highest price was $12.00 on January 3. If no line exists below the rectangle, the lowest price equals either the opening or closing price, and if no line exists above the rectangle, the highest price equals either the opening or closing price.

A **surface chart** displays trends using two dimensions on a continuous curve.

The **surface chart** is similar to a line chart; however, it represents numeric data and numeric categories. This chart type takes on some of the same characteristics as a topographic map of hills and valleys (see Figure 15). Excel fills in all data points with colors. Surface charts are not as common as other chart types because they require more data points and often confuse people.

Charts

182

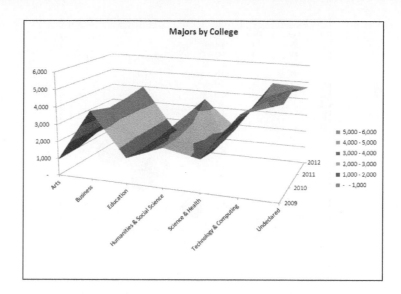

**FIGURE 15** Surface
Chart ➤

A **doughnut chart** displays
values as percentages of the
whole but may contain more
than one data series.

The **doughnut chart** is similar to a pie chart in that it shows the relationship of parts to
a whole, but the doughnut chart can display more than one series of data, and it has a hole in
the middle. Like a clustered or stacked column chart, a doughnut chart plots multiple data
series. Each ring represents a data series, with the outer ring receiving the most emphasis.
Although the doughnut chart is able to display multiple data series, people often have difficulty interpreting it. Figure 16 illustrates the 2011 and 2012 data series, with the 2012 data
series on the outer ring. The chart shows each college as a segment of each ring of the doughnut. The larger the segment, the larger the value.

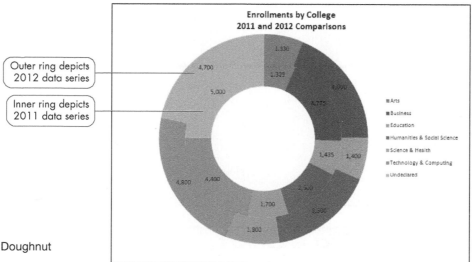

**FIGURE 16** Doughnut
Chart ➤

A **bubble chart** shows
relationships among three values
by using bubbles.

The **bubble chart** is similar to a scatter chart, but it uses round bubbles instead of data
points to represent a third dimension. Similar to the scatter chart, the bubble chart does not
contain a category axis. The horizontal and vertical axes are both value axes. The third value
determines the size of the bubble where the larger the value, the larger the bubble. People
often use bubble charts to depict financial data. In Figure 17, age, years at the company, and
salaries are compared. When creating a bubble chart, do not select the column headings, as
they might distort the data.

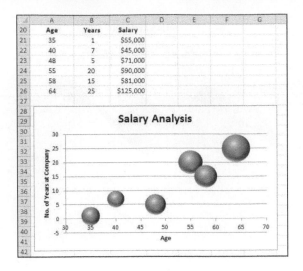

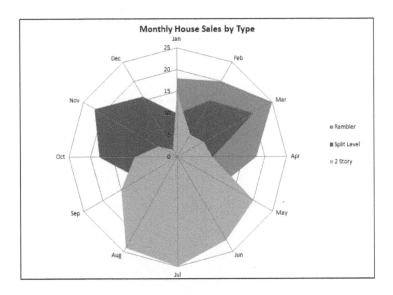

**FIGURE 17** Bubble Chart ➤

A **radar chart** compares aggregate values of three or more variables represented on axes starting from the same point.

The final chart type is the ***radar chart***, which uses each category as a spoke radiating from the center point to the outer edges of the chart. Each spoke represents each data series, and lines connect the data points between spokes, similar to a spider web. You can create a radar chart to compare aggregate values for several data series. Figure 18 shows a radar chart comparing monthly house sales by house type (rambler, split level, 2 story). The house type categories appear in different colors, while the months appear on the outer edges of the chart.

**FIGURE 18** Radar Chart ➤

# Creating a Chart

Creating a chart involves selecting the data source and choosing the chart type. After you insert a chart, you will position and size it.

## Select the Data Source

Identify the chart data range by selecting the data series, any descriptive labels you need to construct the category labels, and the series labels you need to create the legend. Edit the row and column labels if they are not clear and concise. Table 1 describes what you should select for various charts. If the labels and data series are not stored in adjacent cells, press and hold Ctrl while selecting the nonadjacent ranges. Using Figure 1 as a guide, you would select the range A4:E11 to create a clustered column chart with multiple data series. To create the pie

Charts

chart in Figure 11, select the range A5:A11, and then press and hold Ctrl while you select the range E5:E11. If your worksheet has titles and subtitles, you should not select them. Doing so would add unnecessary text to the legend.

| TABLE 1 Data Selection for Charts | | |
|---|---|---|
| **Chart Type** | **What to Select** | **Figure 1 Example** |
| **Column, Bar, Line, Area, Doughnut** | Row labels (such as colleges), column labels (such as years), and one or more data series | A4:E11 |
| **Pie** | Row labels (such as colleges) and only one data series (such as 2012), but not column headings | A5:A11,E5:E11 |
| **Bubble** | Three different data series (such as age, years, and salary) | A21:C26 (in Figure 17) |
| **X Y (Scatter)** | Two related numeric datasets (such as minutes studying and test scores) | * |

*Figure 1 does not contain data conducive to an X Y (scatter) chart.

> **TIP** Total Rows and Columns
>
> Make sure that each data series uses the same scale. For example, don't include aggregates, such as totals or averages, along with individual data points. Doing so would distort the plotted data. Compare the clustered column chart in Figure 3 to Figure 19. In Figure 19, the chart's design is incorrect because it mixes individual data points with the totals and yearly averages.

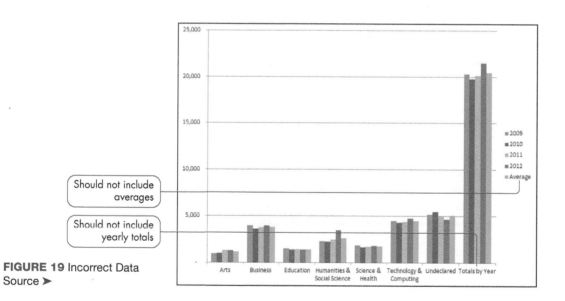

**FIGURE 19** Incorrect Data Source ➤

## Select the Chart Type

After you select the range of cells that you want to be the source for the chart, you need to select the chart type. To insert a chart for the selected range, click the Insert tab, and then do one of the following:

- Click the chart type (such as Column) in the Charts group, and then click a chart subtype (such as Clustered Column) from the chart gallery.

- Click the Charts Dialog Box Launcher to display the Insert Chart dialog box (see Figure 20), select a chart type on the left side, select a chart subtype, and then click OK.

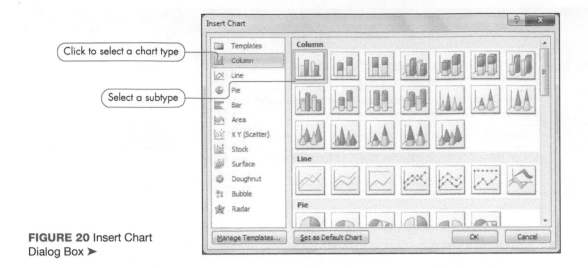

Click to select a chart type

Select a subtype

**FIGURE 20** Insert Chart Dialog Box ➤

A **chart sheet** contains a single chart and no spreadsheet data.

Excel inserts the chart as an embedded object on the current worksheet. You can leave the chart on the same worksheet as the worksheet data used to create the chart, or you can place the chart in a separate worksheet, called a **chart sheet**. A chart sheet contains a single chart only; you cannot enter data and formulas on a chart sheet. If you leave the chart in the same worksheet (see Figure 17), you can print the data and chart on the same page. If you want to print or view a full-sized chart, you can move the chart to its own chart sheet.

## Position and Size the Chart

When you first create a chart, Excel inserts the chart in the worksheet, often to the right side of, but sometimes on top of and covering up, the data area. To move the chart to a new location, position the mouse pointer over the chart area. When you see the Chart Area ScreenTip and the mouse pointer includes the white arrowhead and a four-headed arrow (see Figure 21), drag the chart to the desired location.

A **sizing handle,** indicated by faint dots on the outside border of a selected chart, enables you to adjust the size of the chart.

To change the size of a chart, select the chart if necessary. Position the mouse pointer on the outer edge of the chart where you see three or four faint dots. These dots are called *sizing handles.* When the mouse pointer changes to a two-headed arrow, drag the border to adjust the chart's height or width. Drag a corner sizing handle to increase or decrease the height and width of the chart at the same time. Press and hold down Shift as you drag a corner sizing handle to change the height and width proportionately. You can also change the chart size by clicking the Format tab and changing the height and width values in the Size group (see Figure 21).

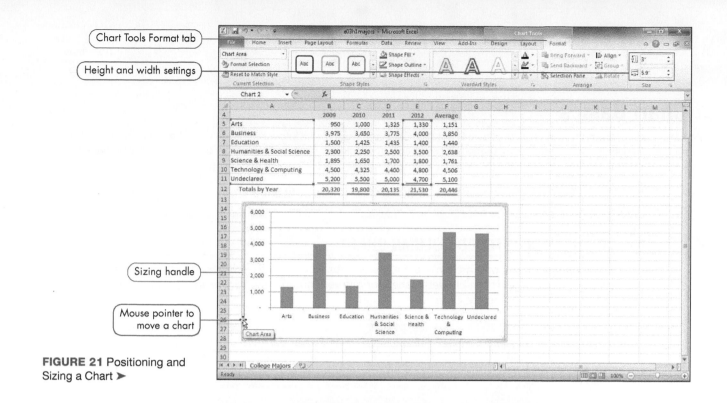

Chart Tools Format tab

Height and width settings

Sizing handle

Mouse pointer to move a chart

**FIGURE 21** Positioning and Sizing a Chart ➤

**TIP** Chart Tools Contextual Tab

When you select a chart, Excel displays the Chart Tools contextual tab, containing the Design, Layout, and Format tabs. You can use the commands on these tabs to modify the chart.

## 1 Chart Basics

Yesterday, you gathered the enrollment data for Hort University and organized it into a structured worksheet that contains the number of majors for the last four years, organized by college. You included yearly totals and the average number of majors. Now you are ready to transform the data into visually appealing charts.

**Skills covered:** Create a Clustered Column Chart • Change the Chart Position and Size • Create a Pie Chart • Explode a Pie Slice • Change Worksheet Data

---

### STEP 1 ▶ CREATE A CLUSTERED COLUMN CHART

Dr. Musto wants to compare large amounts of data. You know that the clustered column chart is effective at depicting multiple data series for different categories, so you will create one first. Refer to Figure 22 as you complete Step 1.

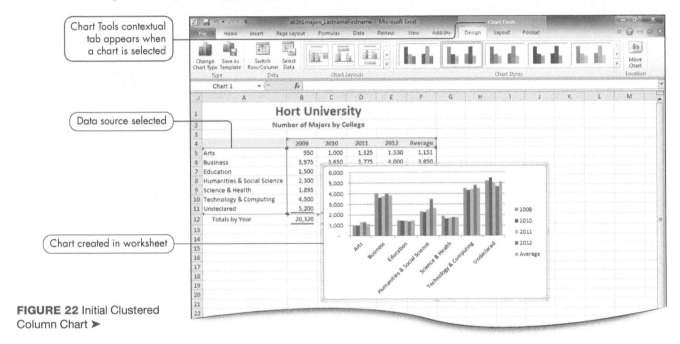

**FIGURE 22** Initial Clustered Column Chart ➤

a. Open *e03h1majors* and save it as **e03h1majors_LastnameFirstname**.

> **TROUBLESHOOTING:** If you make any major mistakes in this exercise, you can close the file, open *e03h1majors* again, and then start this exercise over.

b. Select the **range A4:F11**.

You included the average column in your selection. Although you should not mix individual values and aggregates such as averages in the same chart, we will do this now and later show you how you can modify the data source after you create the chart.

c. Click the **Insert tab**, and then click **Column** in the Charts group.

The Column gallery opens, displaying the different column subtypes you can create.

d. Click **Clustered Column** in the *2-D Column* section of the gallery. Save the workbook.

Excel inserts the clustered column chart in the worksheet.

Charts

## CHANGE THE CHART POSITION AND SIZE

Excel inserts the chart next to the worksheet data. You want to reposition the chart and then adjust the size so that the college category labels do not display at an angle to make the chart readable for Dr. Musto. Refer to Figure 23 as you complete Step 2.

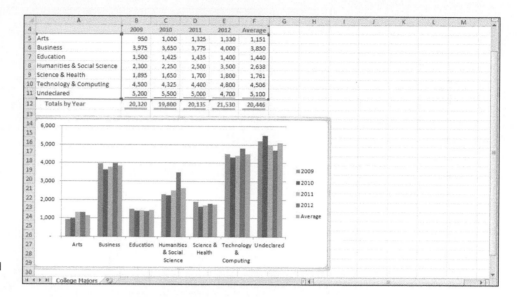

**FIGURE 23** Repositioned and Resized Chart ➤

a. Position the mouse pointer over the empty area of the chart area.

The mouse pointer includes a four-headed arrow with the regular white arrowhead, and the Chart Area ScreenTip displays.

> **TROUBLESHOOTING:** Make sure you see the Chart Area ScreenTip as you perform step b. If you move the mouse pointer to another chart element—such as the legend—you will move or size that element instead of moving the entire chart.

b. Drag the chart so that the top-left corner of the chart appears in **cell A14**.

You positioned the chart below the worksheet data.

c. Drag the bottom-right sizing handle down and to the right to **cell H29**. Save the workbook.

You increased both the height and the width at the same time. The college labels on the category axis no longer appear at an angle. You will leave the clustered column chart in its current state for the moment while you create another chart.

> **TIP** The F11 Key
>
> Pressing F11 is a fast way to create a column chart in a new chart sheet. Select the worksheet data source, and then press F11 to create the chart.

Dr. Musto has also asked you to create a chart showing the percentage of majors for the current year. You know that pie charts are excellent for illustrating percentages and proportions. Refer to Figure 24 as you complete Step 3.

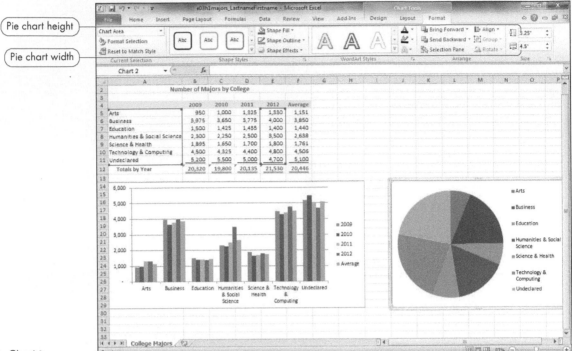

**FIGURE 24** Pie Chart ➤

a. Select the **range A5:A11**, which contains the college category labels.

b. Press and hold **Ctrl** as you select the **range E5:E11**, which contains the 2012 values.

   Remember that you have to press and hold Ctrl to select nonadjacent ranges.

---

**TIP  Parallel Ranges**

Nonadjacent ranges should be parallel so that the legend will correctly reflect the data series. This means that each range should contain the same number of related cells. For example, A5:A11 and E5:E11 are parallel ranges in which E5:E11 contains values that relate to range A5:A11.

---

c. Click the **Insert tab**, click **Pie** in the Charts group, and then select **Pie** in the 2-D Pie group on the gallery.

   Excel inserts a pie chart in the worksheet. The pie chart may overlap part of the worksheet data and the clustered column chart.

d. Drag the chart so that the top-left corner appears in **cell J14**.

---

**TROUBLESHOOTING:** Make sure that you see the Chart Area ScreenTip before you start dragging. Otherwise, you might accidentally drag a chart element, such as the legend or plot area. If you accidentally move the legend or plot area, press Ctrl+Z to undo the move.

---

Charts

**e.** Click the **Format tab**.

**f.** Type **3.25** in the **Shape Height box** in the Size group, and then press **Enter**.

You increased the chart height to 3.25".

**g.** Type **4.5** in the **Shape Width box** in the Size group, and then press **Enter**. Save the workbook.

Compare the size of your pie chart to the one shown in Figure 24. The zoom in the figure was decreased to display a broader view of the two charts together.

**EXPLODE A PIE SLICE**

Dr. Musto is concerned about the number of undeclared majors. You decide to explode the Undeclared pie slice to draw attention to it. Refer to Figure 25 as you complete Step 4.

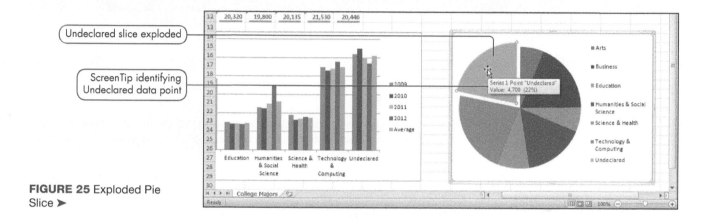

**FIGURE 25** Exploded Pie Slice ➤

**a.** Make sure the pie chart is still selected.

**b.** Click any slice of the chart.

Excel selects all pie slices, as indicated by circular selection handles at the corner of each slice and in the center of the pie.

**c.** Click the **Undeclared slice**, the light blue slice in the top-left corner of the chart.

The Undeclared slice is the only selected slice.

> **TROUBLESHOOTING:** If you double-click the chart instead of clicking a single data point, the Format Data Point dialog box appears. If this happens, click Close in the dialog box, and then click the individual pie slice to select that slice only.

**d.** Drag the **Undeclared slice** away from the pie a little bit. Save the workbook.

You exploded the pie slice by separating it from the rest of the pie.

**CHANGE WORKSHEET DATA**

While you have been preparing two charts, some updated data came into the Institutional Research Department office. You need to update the worksheet data to update the charts. Refer to Figure 26 as you complete Step 5.

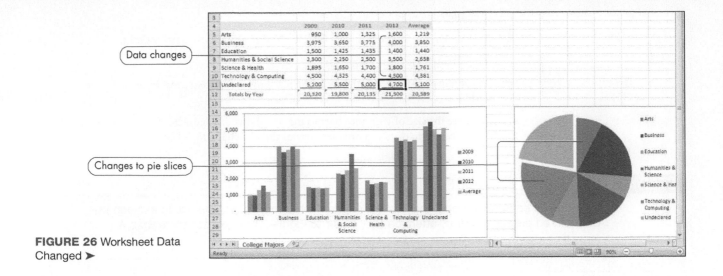

FIGURE 26 Worksheet Data
Changed ➤

a. Click **cell E5**, the cell containing *1,330*—the number of students majoring in the College of Arts in 2012.

b. Type **1600** and press **Enter**.

   Notice that the total changes in cell E12, the average yearly number of Arts majors changes in cell F5, the total average students changes in cell F12, and the two charts are adjusted to reflect the new value.

c. Click **cell E10**, the cell containing *4,800*—the number of students majoring in the College of Technology and Computing.

d. Type **4300** and press **Enter**.

   Compare the updated charts to those shown in Figures 25 and 26. Notice the changes in the worksheet and the chart. With a smaller value, the Technology & Computing slice is smaller, while the other slices represent proportionally higher percentages of the total majors for 2012.

e. Save the workbook. Keep the workbook onscreen if you plan to continue with Hands-On Exercise 2. If not, close the workbook and exit Excel.

Charts

# Chart Design

When you select a chart, Excel displays the Chart Tools contextual tab. That tab contains three specific tabs: Design, Layout, and Format. You used the Format tab to set the chart height and width in the first Hands-On Exercise. The Chart Tools Design contextual tab contains options to modify the overall chart design. You can change the chart type, modify the data source, select a chart layout, select a chart style, and move the chart. Figure 27 shows the Design tab.

**FIGURE 27** Design Tab ➤

The Design tab provides commands for specifying the structure of a chart. Specifically, you can change the chart type and change the data source to build the chart. In addition, you can specify a chart layout that controls which chart elements display and where, select a chart style, and move the chart to a different location.

In this section, you will learn about the Design tab options and how to make changes to a chart's design. In addition, you will learn how to insert and format sparkline charts.

## Changing the Chart Type

After you create a chart, you might want to change how the data are depicted by using other chart types. For example, you might want to change a line chart to a surface chart to see the dramatic effect of the fill colors or change a stacked column chart to a 100% stacked column chart to compare the segment percentages within their respective categories. To change the chart type, do the following:

1. Select the chart.
2. Click the Design tab.
3. Click Change Chart Type in the Type group to open the Change Chart Type dialog box.
4. Select the desired chart type, and then click OK.

---

**TIP** Saving a Chart as a Template

Companies often require a similar look for charts used in presentations. After you spend time customizing a chart to your company's specifications, you can save it as a template to create additional charts. To save a chart as a template, select the chart, click the Design tab, and then click Save as Template in the Type group. The Save Chart Template dialog box opens, in which you can select the template location and type a template name. Click Save in the dialog box to save the template. To use a chart template that you have created, click Templates in the Insert Chart dialog box, select the desired chart template, and then click OK.

---

# Changing the Data Source and Structure

By default, Excel displays the row labels in the first column (such as the college names in Figure 1) on the category axis and the column labels (such as years) as the data series and in the legend. You can reverse how the chart presents the data—for example, place the column labels (e.g., years) on the category axis and the row labels (e.g., colleges) as data series and in the legend. To reverse the data series, click Switch Row/Column in the Data group. Figure 28 shows two chart versions of the same data. The chart on the left shows the row labels (months) on the category axis and the housing types as data series and in the legend. The chart on the right reverses the category axis and data series. The first chart compares house types for each month, and the second chart compares the number of sales of each house type throughout the year.

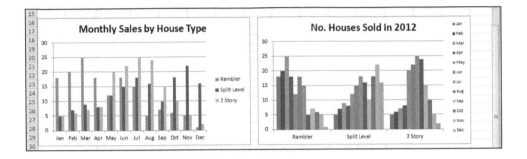

**FIGURE 28** Original Chart and Reversed Row/Column Chart ➤

After creating a chart, you might notice extraneous data caused by selecting too many cells for the data source, or you might want to add to or delete data from the chart by clicking Select Data in the Data group to open the Select Data Source dialog box (see Figure 29). Select the desired range in the worksheet to modify the data source, or adjust the legend and horizontal axis within the dialog box.

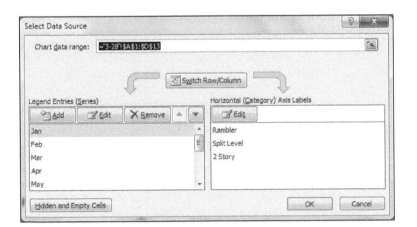

**FIGURE 29** Select Data Source Dialog Box ➤

# Applying a Chart Layout and a Chart Style

The Chart Layouts group enables you to apply predefined layouts to a chart. A chart layout determines which chart elements appear in the chart area and how they are positioned within the chart area. Chart layouts are useful when you are first learning about charts and chart elements or to create consistently laid out charts. As you learn more about charting, you may want to customize your charts by using the commands on the Layout tab.

The Chart Styles group contains predefined styles that control the color of the chart area, plot area, and data series. Styles also affect the look of the data series, such as flat, 3-D, or beveled. Figure 30 shows the Chart Styles gallery. When choosing a chart style, make sure the style complements the chart data and is easy to read. Also, consider whether you will display the chart onscreen in a presentation or print the chart. If you will display the chart in a presentation, select a style with a black background. If you plan to print the chart, select a chart style with a white background to avoid wasting toner printing a background. If you print with a black and white printer, use the first column of black and gray styles.

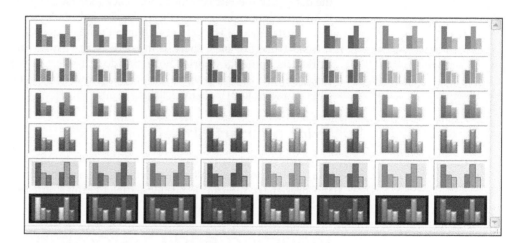

**FIGURE 30** Chart Styles Gallery ➤

# Moving a Chart

By default, Excel creates charts on the same worksheet as the original dataset, but you can move the chart to its own chart sheet in the workbook. To move a chart to another sheet or a new sheet, do the following:

1. Select the chart to display the Chart Tools contextual tab.
2. Click the Design tab.
3. Click Move Chart in the Location group to open the Move Chart dialog box (see Figure 31).
4. Click *New sheet* to move the chart to its own sheet, or click *Object in*, click the *Object in* arrow, select the worksheet to which you want to move the chart, and then click OK.

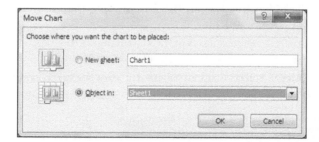

**FIGURE 31** Move Chart Dialog Box ➤

---

**TIP** Chart Sheet Name

The default chart sheet name is Chart1, Chart2, etc. You can rename the sheet before you click OK in the Move Chart dialog box or by double-clicking the chart sheet tab, typing a new name, and then pressing Enter.

---

Chart Design • Excel 2010

# Printing Charts

Just like for printing any worksheet data, preview the chart in the Backstage view before you print to check margins, spacing, and page breaks to ensure a balanced printout.

## Print an Embedded Chart

If you embedded a chart on the same sheet as the data source, you need to decide if you want to print the data only, the data *and* the chart, or the chart only. To print the data only, select the data, click the File tab, click Print, click the first arrow in the Settings section and select Print Selection, and then click Print. To print only the chart, select the chart, and then display the Backstage view. The default setting is Print Selected Chart, and clicking Print will print the chart as a full-page chart. If the data and chart are on the same worksheet, print the worksheet contents to print both, but do not select either the chart or the data before displaying the Backstage view. The preview shows you what will print. Make sure it displays what you want to print before clicking Print.

## Print a Chart Sheet

If you moved the chart to a chart sheet, the chart is the only item on that worksheet. When you display the print options, the default is Print Active Sheets, and the chart will print as a full-page chart. You can change the setting to Print Entire Workbook.

# Inserting and Customizing a Sparkline

*A **sparkline** is a miniature chart contained in a single cell.*

Excel 2010 enables you to create miniature charts called sparklines. A ***sparkline*** is a small line, column, or win/loss chart contained in a single cell. The purpose of a sparkline is to present a condensed, simple, succinct visual illustration of data. Unlike a regular chart, a sparkline does not include a chart title or axes labels. Inserting sparklines next to data helps your audience understand data quickly without having to look at a full-scale chart.

*A sparkline presents a condensed, simple, succinct visual illustration of data.*

## Create a Sparkline

Before creating a sparkline, identify what data you want to depict and where you want to place it. To create a sparkline, do the following:

1. Click the Insert tab.
2. Click Line, Column, or Win/Loss in the Sparklines group. The Create Sparklines dialog box opens (see Figure 32).
3. Type the cell references in the Data Range box, or click the collapse button (if necessary), select the range, and then click the expand button.
4. Enter or select the range where you want the sparkline to appear in the Location Range box, and then click OK. The default cell location is the active cell unless you change it.

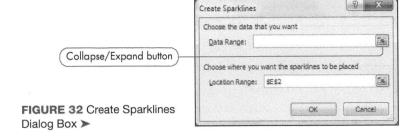

**FIGURE 32** Create Sparklines Dialog Box ➤

Charts

## Apply Design Characteristics to a Sparkline

After you insert a sparkline, the Sparkline Tools Design contextual tab displays, with options to customize the sparkline. Click Edit Data in the Sparkline group to change the data source or sparkline location and indicate how empty cells appear, such as gaps or zeros. You can also change the sparkline type to Line, Column, or Win/Loss in the Type group.

The Show group enables you to display points within the sparkline. For example, click the Markers check box to display markers for all data points on the sparkline, or click High Point to display a marker for the high point, such as for the highest sales or highest price per gallon of gasoline for a time period. The Style group enables you to change the sparkline style, similar to how you can apply different chart styles to charts. Click Sparkline Color to change the color of the sparkline. Click Marker Color, point to a marker type—such as High Point—and then click the color for that marker. Make sure the marker color contrasts with the sparkline color. Figure 33 shows a blue sparkline to indicate trends for the yearly students. The High Point marker is red.

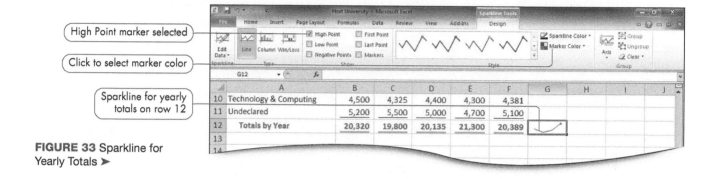

**FIGURE 33** Sparkline for Yearly Totals ➤

> **TIP** Clear Sparklines
>
> To clear the sparklines, select the cells containing sparklines, click the Clear arrow in the Group group on the Sparkline Tools Design tab, and then select either Clear Selected Sparklines or Clear Selected Sparkline Groups.

# HANDS-ON EXERCISES

## 2 Chart Design

You have studied the Design tab and decide to change some design elements on your two charts. You will move the pie chart to a chart sheet so that Dr. Musto can focus on the chart. You will use other options on the Design tab to modify the charts.

**Skills covered:** Move a Chart • Apply a Chart Style and Chart Layout • Change the Data • Change the Chart Type • Insert a Sparkline • Print a Chart

---

### STEP 1 ▶ MOVE A CHART

Your first task is to move the pie chart to its own sheet so that the worksheet data and the clustered column chart do not distract Dr. Musto. Refer to Figure 34 as you complete Step 1.

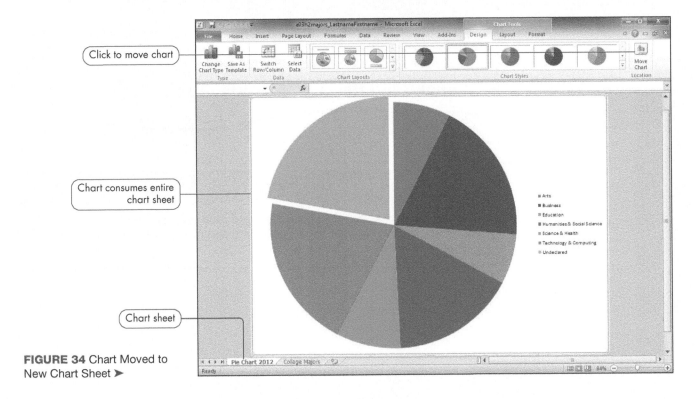

**FIGURE 34** Chart Moved to New Chart Sheet ➤

a. Open *e03h1majors_LastnameFirstname* if you closed it at the end of Hands-On Exercise 1. Save the workbook with the new name **e03h2majors_LastnameFirstname**, changing *h1* to *h2*.

b. Click the outside border of the pie chart to select it.

c. Click the **Design tab**, and then click **Move Chart** in the Location group.

   The Move Chart dialog box opens so that you can specify a new or existing sheet to which to move the chart.

d. Click **New sheet**, type **Pie Chart 2012**, and then click **OK**. Save the workbook.

   Excel moves the pie chart out of the original worksheet, creates a new sheet named Pie Chart 2012, and inserts the chart on that sheet.

Charts

The pie chart looks a little flat, but you know that changing it to a 3-D pie chart could distort the data. A better solution is to apply an interesting chart style. In addition, you apply a layout to change the location of chart elements. Refer to Figure 35 as you complete Step 2.

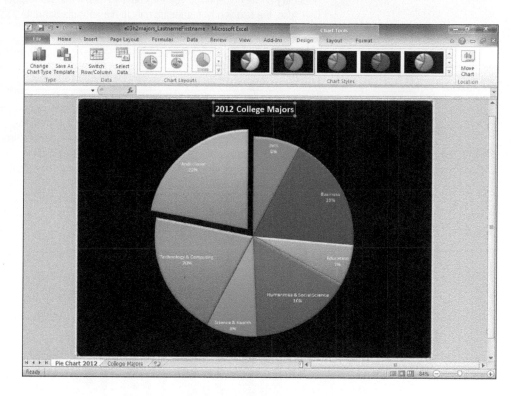

**FIGURE 35** Chart Style Applied ➤

a. Click the **More button** in the Chart Styles group.

> **TROUBLESHOOTING:** More looks like a horizontal line with a down-pointing triangle.

Excel displays the Chart Styles gallery.

b. Click **Style 42**, the second style from the left on the last row of the gallery.

When you position the mouse pointer over a gallery option, Excel displays a ScreenTip with the style name. When you click Style 42, Excel closes the Chart Styles gallery and applies Style 42 to the chart.

c. Click **Layout 1** in the Chart Layouts group. Save the workbook.

Excel adds a Chart Title placeholder, removes the legend, and inserts the category labels and the respective percentages within the pie slices.

---

**TIP** Pie Chart Labels

The Layout 1 chart layout displays the category names and related percentages on the respective pie slices and removes the legend. This layout is helpful when a pie chart has more than four slices so that you do not have to match pie slice colors with the legend.

---

**d.** Click the **Chart Title placeholder**, type **2012 College Majors**, and then press **Enter**. Save the workbook.

> **TROUBLESHOOTING:** If you click inside the Chart Title placeholder instead of just the outer boundary of the placeholder, you may have to delete the placeholder text before typing the new title. Also, the text you type appears only in the Formula Bar until you press Enter. Then it appears in the chart title.

**STEP 3** **CHANGE THE DATA**

You realize that the clustered column chart contains aggregated data (averages) along with the other data series. You need to remove the extra data before showing the chart to Dr. Musto. In addition, you notice that Excel placed the years in the legend and the colleges on the X-axis. Dr. Musto wants to be able to compare all majors for each year (that is, all majors for 2009, then all majors for 2010, and so on) instead of the change in Arts majors throughout the years. Refer to Figure 36 as you complete Step 3.

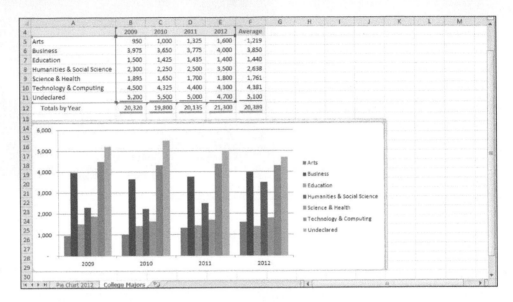

**FIGURE 36** Adjusted Data for Chart ➤

**a.** Click the **College Majors worksheet tab** to display the worksheet data and clustered column chart.

**b.** Click the clustered column chart to select it, and then click the **Design tab**, if necessary.

**c.** Click **Select Data** in the Data group.

The Select Data Source dialog box opens, and Excel selects the original data source in the worksheet.

**d.** Click **Average** in the **Legend Entries (Series) list**.

You need to remove the aggregated data.

**e.** Click **Remove**, and then click **OK**.

**f.** Click **Switch Row/Column** in the Data group.

Excel reverses the data series and category labels so that the years are category labels and the college data are data series and in the legend.

**g.** Drag the middle-right sizing handle to the right to the end of column J to widen the chart area. Save the workbook.

After reversing the rows and columns, the columns look tall and thin. You widened the chart area to make the columns appear better proportioned.

**CHANGE THE CHART TYPE**

Dr. Musto likes what you have done so far, but she would like the column chart to indicate total number of majors per year. You will change the chart to a stacked column chart. Refer to Figure 37 as you complete Step 4.

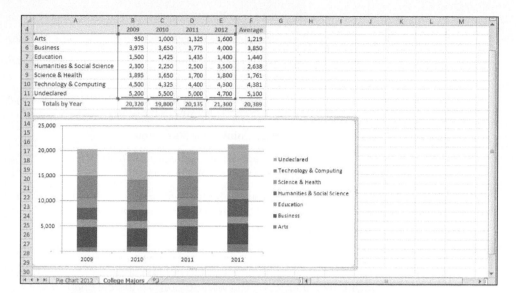

**FIGURE 37** Stacked Column Chart ➤

a. Click the **Design tab**, if necessary, and then click **Change Chart Type** in the Type group.

The Change Chart Type dialog box opens. The left side displays the main chart types, and the right side contains a gallery of subtypes for each main type.

b. Click **Stacked Column** in the *Column subtype* section, and then click **OK**.

You converted the chart from a clustered column chart to a stacked column chart. The stacked column chart displays the total number of majors per year. Each yearly column contains segments representing each college. Now that you changed the chart to a stacked column chart, the columns look too short and wide.

c. Decrease the chart width so that the right edge ends at the end of column I. Save the workbook.

**STEP 5** **INSERT A SPARKLINE**

You want to insert sparklines to show the enrollment trends for majors in each college at Hort University. After inserting the sparklines, you will display high points to stand out for Dr. Musto and other administrators who want a quick visual of the trends. Refer to Figure 38 as you complete Step 5.

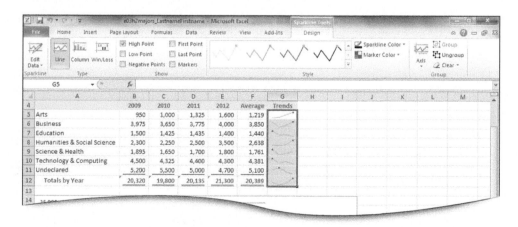

**FIGURE 38** Sparklines Inserted to Show Trends ➤

**FYI**

a. Type **Trends** in **cell G4**, use **Format Painter** to apply the styles from **cell F4** to **cell G4**, and then click **cell G5**.

   You entered a heading in the column above where you will insert the sparklines.

b. Click the **Insert tab**, and then click **Line** in the Sparklines group.

c. Select the **range B5:E12** to enter it in the **Data Range box**.

d. Press **Tab**, select the **range G5:G12** to enter it in the **Location Range box**, and then click **OK**.

   Excel inserts sparklines in range G5:G12. Each sparkline depicts data for its row. The sparklines are still selected, and the Sparkline Tools Design contextual tab displays.

e. Click the **More button** in the Style group, and then click **Sparkline Style Colorful #4**, the fourth style on the last row of the gallery.

f. Click **High Point** in the Show group.

   A marker appears for the high point of each data series for each Trendline. You want to change the marker color to stand out.

g. Click **Marker Color** in the Style group, point to **High Point**, and then click **Red** in the *Standard Colors* section. Save the workbook.

## STEP 6 ▶ PRINT A CHART

Dr. Musto wants you to print the stacked column chart and the worksheet data for her as a reference for a meeting this afternoon. You want to preview the pie chart to see how it would look when printed as a full page.

a. Click **cell A4** to deselect the sparklines.

   To print both the chart and the worksheet data, you must deselect the chart.

b. Click the **File tab**, and then click **Print**.

   The Backstage view shows a preview that the worksheet data and the chart will print on one page.

c. Click **Print** if you or your instructor wants a printout.

d. Click the **Pie Chart 2012 worksheet tab**, click the **File tab**, click **Print** to preview the printout to ensure it would print on one page, and then click the **Home tab** to go back to the chart window.

e. Save the workbook. Keep the workbook onscreen if you plan to continue with Hands-On Exercise 3. If not, close the workbook and exit Excel.

Charts

# Chart Layout

The Chart Tools Layout tab (see Figure 39) enables you to enhance your charts by selecting specific chart elements, inserting objects, displaying or removing chart elements, customizing the axes, formatting the background, and including analysis. When adding visual elements to a chart, make sure these elements enhance the effectiveness of the chart instead of overpowering it.

> When adding visual elements to a chart, make sure these elements enhance the effectiveness of the chart instead of overpowering it.

**FIGURE 39** Chart Tools Layout Tab ➤

In this section, you will learn how to modify a chart by adjusting individual chart elements, such as the chart title and data labels. In addition, you will learn how to format chart elements, including applying fill colors to a data series.

## Selecting and Formatting Chart Elements

A chart includes several elements—the chart area, the plot area, data series, the horizontal axis, the vertical axis, and the legend—each of which you can customize. When you position the mouse pointer over the chart, Excel displays a ScreenTip with the name of that chart element. To select a chart element, click it when you see the ScreenTip, or click the Chart Elements arrow in the Current Selection group, and then select the element from the list.

After you select a chart element, you can format it and change its settings. You can apply font settings, such as increasing the font size, from the Font group on the Home tab. You can format the values by applying a number style or by changing the number of decimal places on the value axis using the options in the Number group on the Home tab.

You can apply multiple settings at once using a Format dialog box, such as Format Data Series. To format the selected chart element, click Format Selection in the Current Selection group, or right-click the chart element, and then select Format *element* to display the appropriate dialog box (see Figure 40).

**FIGURE 40** Format Data Series Dialog Box ➤

Chart Layout • Excel 2010

203

The left side of the dialog box lists major categories, such as Fill and Border Color. When you click a category, the right side of the dialog box displays specific options to customize the chart element. For example, when you select the Fill category, the right side displays fill options. When you click a specific option in the right side, such as *Picture or texture fill*, the dialog box displays additional fill options. You can use the Fill options to change the fill color of one or more data series. Avoid making a chart look busy with too many different colors. If you are changing the fill color of a chart area or plot area, make sure the color you select provides enough contrast with the other chart elements.

To format the plot area, click Plot Area in the Background group. Select None to remove any current plot area colors, select Show Plot Area to display the plot area, or select More Plot Area Options to open the Format Plot Area dialog box so that you can apply a fill color to the plot area, similar to selecting fill colors in the Format Data Series dialog box shown in Figure 40.

> **TIP** Use Images or Textures
>
> For less formal presentations, you might want to use images or a texture to fill the data series, chart area, or plot area instead of a solid fill color. To use an image or a texture, click *Picture or texture fill* in the Format Data Series dialog box. Click File or Clip Art in the *Insert from* section, and then insert an image file or search the Microsoft Web site to insert an image. Use the Stack option to avoid distorting the image. To add a texture, click Texture, and then select a textured background. Figure 41 shows a stacked image as the first data series fill, a texture fill for the second data series, and a gradient fill for the plot area. Generally, do not mix images and textures; in addition to illustrating different fill options, this figure also shows how adding too many features creates a distracting chart.

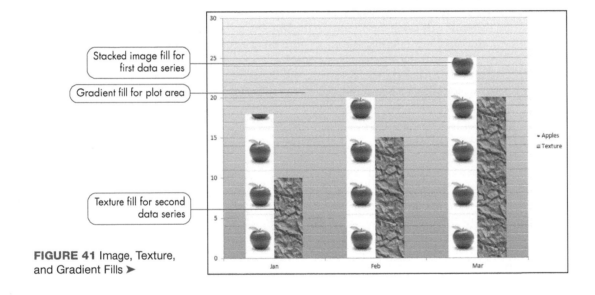

**FIGURE 41** Image, Texture, and Gradient Fills ➤

Charts

# Customizing Chart Labels

You should include appropriate labels to describe chart elements. Figure 42 identifies basic chart labels.

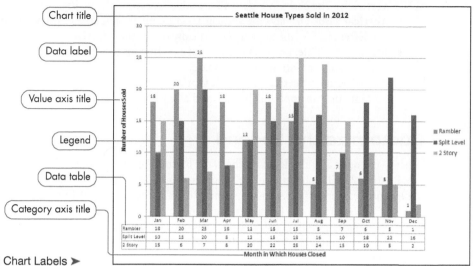

Chart title
Data label
Value axis title
Legend
Data table
Category axis title

**FIGURE 42** Chart Labels ➤

## Insert and Format the Chart Title

A **chart title** is a label that describes the chart.

A *chart title* is the label that describes the entire chart. Chart titles should reflect the purpose of the chart. For example, *Houses Sold* would be too generic for the chart in Figure 42. *Seattle House Types Sold in 2012* indicates the where (Seattle), the what (House Types Sold), and the when (2012).

Excel does not include a chart title by default. Some chart layouts in the Chart Layouts group on the Design tab include a placeholder so that you can enter a title for the current chart. To add, remove, or change the position of a chart title, click Chart Title in the Labels group on the Layout tab, and then select one of the following options:

- **None.** Removes a chart title from the current chart.
- **Centered Overlay Title.** Centers the chart title horizontally without resizing the chart; the title appears over the top of the chart.
- **Above Chart.** Centers the title above the chart (see Figure 42), decreasing the chart size to make room for the chart title.
- **More Title Options.** Opens the Format Chart Title dialog box so that you can apply fill, border, and alignment settings.

## Position and Format the Axis Titles

An **axis title** is a label that describes either the category axis or the value axis.

*Axis titles* are labels that describe the category and value axes. If the names on the category axis are not self-explanatory, you can add a label to describe it. The value axis often needs further explanation, such as *In Millions of Dollars* to describe the unit of measurement. To display category axis title options, click Axis Titles in the Labels group, point to Primary Horizontal Axis Title, and then select one of the following:

- **None.** Removes the horizontal axis title from the current chart.
- **Title Below Axis.** Displays the horizontal axis title below the category axis.
- **More Primary Horizontal Axis Title Options.** Opens the Format Axis Title dialog box so that you can apply fill, border, and alignment settings.

To display the value axis title options, click Axis Titles in the Labels group, point to Primary Vertical Axis Title, and then select one of the following:

- **None.** Removes the value axis title from the current chart.
- **Rotated Title.** Displays the value axis title on the left side of the value axis, rotated vertically. The chart in Figure 42 uses the Rotated Title setting.
- **Vertical Title.** Displays the vertical axis title on the left side of the value axis, with the letters in the title appearing vertically down the left edge.
- **Horizontal Title.** Displays the vertical axis title on the left side of the value axis; the title consumes more horizontal space.
- **More Primary Vertical Axis Title Options.** Opens the Format Axis Title dialog box so that you can apply fill, border, and alignment settings.

## Customize the Legend

When you create a multiple series chart, the legend appears on the right side of the plot area (see Figure 42). Click Legend in the Labels group on the Layout tab to change the location of the legend or overlay the legend on either the left or right side of the plot area. Select More Legend Options from the Legend menu to open the Format Legend dialog box so that you can apply a background fill color, display a border around the legend, select a border color or line style, and apply a shadow effect. Remove the legend if it duplicates data found elsewhere in the chart.

## Insert and Format Data Labels

A **data label** is the value or name of a data point.

*Data labels* are descriptive labels that show the exact value of the data points on the value axis. The chart in Figure 42 displays data labels for the Rambler data series. Only add data labels when they are necessary for a specific data series; adding data labels for every data point will clutter the chart.

When you select a data label, Excel selects all data labels in that data series. To format the labels, click Format Selection in the Current Selection group, or right-click and select Format Data Labels to open the Format Data Labels dialog box (see Figure 43).

**FIGURE 43** Format Data Labels Dialog Box ➤

The Format Data Labels dialog box enables you to specify what to display as the label. The default Label Contains setting displays values, but you can display additional data such as the category name. Displaying additional data can clutter the chart. You can also specify the position of the label, such as Center or Outside End. If the numeric data labels are not formatted, click Number on the left side of the dialog box, and then apply number formats.

> **TIP** Pie Chart Data Labels
>
> When you first create a pie chart, Excel generates a legend to identify the category labels for the different slice colors, but it does not display data labels. You can display values, percentages, and even category labels on or next to each slice. Pie charts often include percentage data labels. If you also include category labels, hide the legend to avoid duplicating elements.

## Include and Format a Data Table

A data table is a grid that contains the data source values and labels. If you embed a chart on the same worksheet as the data source, you do not need to include a data table. Only add a data table with a chart to a chart sheet if you need the audience to know the exact values.

To display a data table, click Data Table in the Labels group, and then select Show Data Table. Figure 42 shows a data table at the bottom of the chart area. To see the color-coding along with the category labels, select Show Data Table with Legend Keys, which enables you to omit the legend.

# Formatting the Axes and Gridlines

Based on the data source values and structure, Excel determines the starting, incremental, and stopping values that display on the value axis when you create the chart. You might want to adjust the value axis. For example, when working with large values such as 4,567,890, the value axis displays increments, such as 4,000,000 and 5,000,000. You can simplify the value axis by displaying values in millions, so that the values on the axis are 4 and 5 with the word *Millions* placed by the value axis to indicate the units. Figure 44 shows two charts—one with original intervals and one in millions.

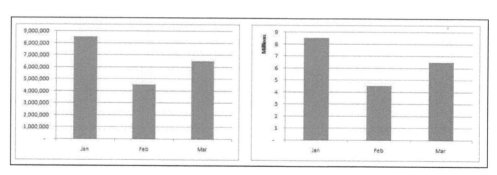

**FIGURE 44** Value Axis Scaling ➤

To change the number representation, click Axes in the Axes group, and then point to Primary Vertical Axis. Next, select how you want to represent the value axis: Show Default Axis, Show Axis in Thousands, Show Axis in Millions, Show Axis in Billions, or Show Axis in Log Scale. Select More Primary Vertical Axis Options to open the Format Axis dialog box so that you can customize the value axis values.

Although less commonly used, the Primary Horizontal Axis menu enables you to display the axis from left to right (the default), right to left with the value axis on the right side of the chart and the categories in reverse order on the category axis, or without a category axis. Select More Primary Horizontal Axis Options to customize the horizontal axis.

A **gridline** is a horizontal or vertical line that extends from the horizontal or vertical axis through the plot area.

**Gridlines** are horizontal or vertical lines that span across the chart to help people identify the values plotted by the visual elements, such as a column. Excel displays horizontal gridlines for column, line, scatter, stock, surface, and bubble charts and vertical gridlines for bar charts. If you do not want to display gridlines in a chart, click Gridlines in the Axes group, point to either Primary Horizontal Gridlines or Primary Vertical Gridlines, and then select None. To add more gridlines, select Minor Gridlines or Major & Minor Gridlines.

## Adding a Trendline

A **trendline** is a line used to depict trends and forecast future data.

Charts help reveal trends, patterns, and other tendencies that are difficult to identify by looking at values in a worksheet. A **trendline** is a line that depicts trends or helps forecast future data. Trendlines are commonly used in prediction, such as to determine the future trends of sales, or the success rate of a new prescription drug. You can use trendlines in unstacked column, bar, line, stock, scatter, and bubble charts. To add a trendline, click Trendline in the Analysis group, and then select the type you want: Linear Trendline, Exponential Trendline, Linear Forecast Trendline, or Two Period Moving Average. Figure 45 shows two linear forecast trendlines, one applied to the Business data series and one applied to the Undeclared data series. Notice that this trendline provides a forecast (prediction) for two additional time periods—2013 and 2014—although the years are not depicted on the X-axis. Excel analyzes the plotted data to forecast values for the next two time periods when you select the Linear Forecast Trendline. If you apply Linear Trendline only, Excel displays the trendline for the data but does not forecast data points for the future.

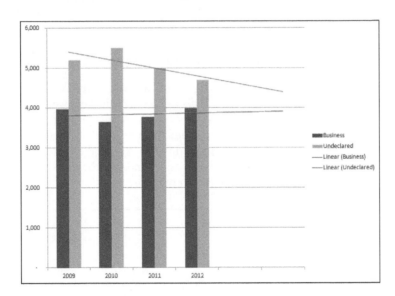

**FIGURE 45** Trendlines ➤

# HANDS-ON EXERCISES

myitlab
HOE3 Training

## 3 Chart Layout

You want to enhance the column chart by using some options on the Layout tab to add the final touches needed before you give the charts to Dr. Musto to review.

**Skills covered:** Add a Chart Title • Add and Format Axis Titles • Add Data Labels • Apply Fill Colors • Insert a Trendline

---

### STEP 1 ADD A CHART TITLE

When you applied a chart layout to the pie chart, Excel displayed a placeholder for the chart title. However, you need to add a chart title for the column chart. You also want to copy the chart and modify it so that you can provide two different perspectives for Dr. Musto. Refer to Figure 46 as you complete Step 1.

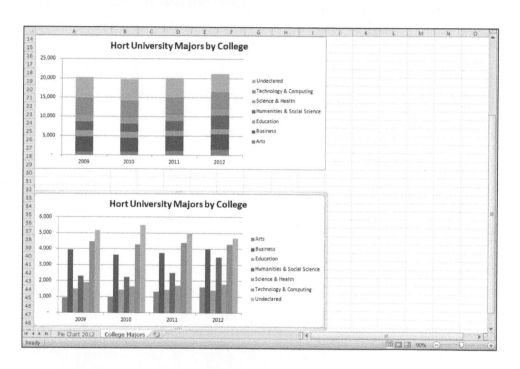

**FIGURE 46** Charts with Titles ➤

a. Open *e03h2majors_LastnameFirstname* if you closed it at the end of Hands-On Exercise 2. Save the workbook with the new name **e03h3majors_LastnameFirstname**, changing *h2* to *h3*.

b. Click the stacked column chart to select it.

c. Click the **Layout tab**, click **Chart Title** in the Labels group, and then select **Above Chart**.

Excel displays the Chart Title placeholder, and the plot area decreases to make room for the chart title.

d. Type **Hort University Majors by College** and press **Enter**.

e. Click the **Chart Elements arrow** in the Current Selection group, and then select **Chart Area**.

You selected the entire chart area so that you can copy it.

f. Press **Ctrl+C**, click **cell A33**, and then press **Ctrl+V** to paste the top-left corner of the chart here. Change the second chart to a **Clustered Column chart**. Save the workbook.

Hands-On Exercises • Excel 2010

209

**ADD AND FORMAT AXIS TITLES**

You decide to add an axis title to the value axis to clarify the values in the clustered column chart. For the stacked column chart, you want to change the value axis increments. Refer to Figure 47 as you complete Step 2.

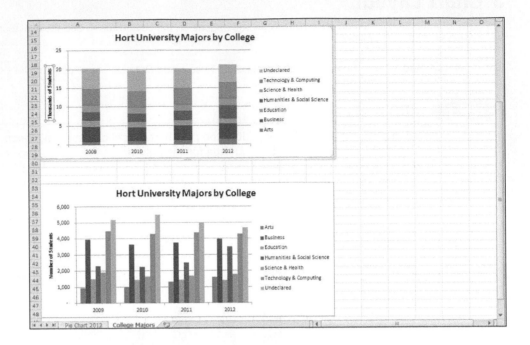

**FIGURE 47** Axis Titles and Values Changed ➤

a. Make sure the clustered column chart is selected, and then use the scroll bars if necessary to view the entire chart.

b. Click the **Layout tab**, click **Axis Titles** in the Labels group, point to **Primary Vertical Axis Title**, and then select **Rotated Title**.

Excel inserts the Axis Title placeholder on the left side of the value axis.

c. Type **Number of Students** and press **Enter**.

The text you typed replaces the placeholder text after you press Enter.

d. Select the stacked column chart, click the **Layout tab** (if necessary), click **Axes** in the Axes group, point to **Primary Vertical Axis**, and then select **Show Axis in Thousands**.

Excel changes the value axis values to thousands and includes the label *Thousands* to the left side of the value axis.

e. Click **Thousands** to select it, type **Thousands of Students**, and then press **Enter**.

f. Drag the **Thousands of Students label** down to appear vertically centered with the value axis increments. Save the workbook.

**STEP 3** **ADD DATA LABELS**

Dr. Musto wants you to emphasize the Undeclared majors data series by adding data labels for that data series. You will have to be careful to add data labels for only the Undeclared data series, as adding data labels for all data series would clutter the chart. Refer to Figure 48 as you complete Step 3.

Charts

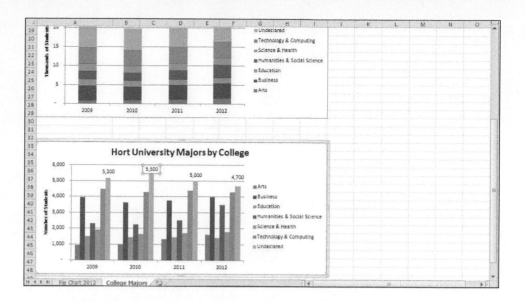

**FIGURE 48** Data Labels for One Data Series ➤

a. Select the clustered column chart, click the **Chart Elements arrow** in the Current Selection group, and then select **Series "Undeclared"**.

Excel selects all of the Undeclared (light blue) columns in the chart.

b. Click **Data Labels** in the Labels group, and then select **Outside End**.

You added data labels to the selected Undeclared data series.

> **TROUBLESHOOTING:** If data labels appear for all columns, use the Undo feature. Make sure you select only the Undeclared data series columns, and then add data labels again.

c. Look at the data labels to see if they are on gridlines.

The 4,700 and 5,500 data labels are on gridlines.

d. Click the **4,700 data label** twice, pausing between clicks.

Only the 4,700 data label should be selected.

> **TROUBLESHOOTING:** If you double-click a data label instead of pausing between individual clicks, the Format Data Labels dialog box appears. If this happens, click Close in the dialog box, and then repeat step d, pausing longer between clicks.

e. Click the outer edge of the **4,700 data label border**, and then drag the label up a little so that it is off the gridline.

f. Select the **5,500 data label**, and then drag it below the top gridline. Save the workbook.

## STEP 4 ▶ APPLY FILL COLORS

Dr. Musto wants the Business data series color to stand out, so you will apply a brighter red fill to that series. In addition, you want to apply a gradient color to the plot area so that the chart stands out from the rest of the page. Refer to Figure 49 as you complete Step 4.

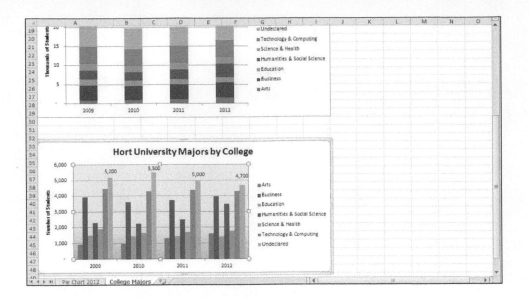

FIGURE 49 Chart with
Different Fill Colors ➤

a. Make sure the clustered column chart is still selected, click the **Chart Elements arrow** in the Current Selection group, and then select **Series "Business"** or click one of the **Business columns**.

The Business data series columns are selected.

b. Click **Format Selection** in the Current Selection group.

The Format Data Series dialog box opens so that you can format the Business data series.

c. Click **Fill** on the left side of the dialog box, and then click **Solid fill**.

The dialog box displays additional fill options.

d. Click **Color**, click **Red** in the *Standard Colors* section of the gallery, and then click **Close**.

The Business data series appears in red.

e. Click **Plot Area** in the Background group, and then select **More Plot Area Options**.

The Format Plot Area dialog box opens.

f. Click **Gradient fill**, click **Preset colors**, click **Parchment** (using the ScreenTips to help you find the correct preset color), and then click **Close**.

Be careful when selecting plot area colors to ensure that the data series columns, bars, or lines still stand out. Print a sample on a color printer to help make the decision.

## STEP 5 ▸ INSERT A TRENDLINE

Identifying trends is important when planning college budgets. Colleges with growing enrollments need additional funding to support more students. It looks like the numbers of humanities and social science majors are increasing, but you want to add a trendline to verify your analysis. Refer to Figure 50 as you complete Step 5.

Charts

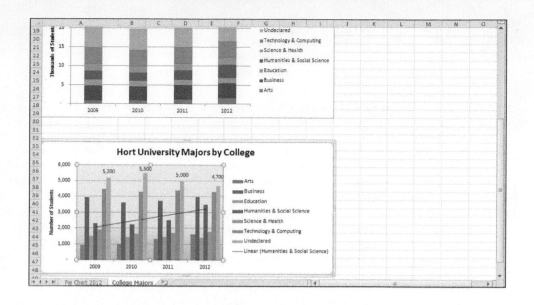

**FIGURE 50** Trendline ➤

a. Make sure the clustered column chart is still selected.

b. Click **Trendline** in the Analysis group, and then select **Linear Trendline**.

The Add Trendline dialog box opens so that you can select which data series you want to use for the trendline.

c. Click **Humanities & Social Science**, and then click **OK**.

Excel adds a trendline based on the data series you specified. The trend is a steady increase in the number of majors in this discipline.

d. Save and close the workbook, and submit based on your instructor's directions.

After reading this chapter, you have accomplished the following objectives:

1. **Decide which chart type to create.** Choose a chart type that will present the data in a way that communicates the message effectively to your audience. Column charts compare categorical data, bar charts compare categorical data horizontally, line charts illustrate trends over time, and pie charts show proportions to the whole. Variations of each major chart type are called *subtypes*.

2. **Create a chart.** The first step in creating a chart is to identify and select the range of cells that will be used as the data source. Be careful to select similar data series to avoid distorting the chart. After selecting the data source, click the desired chart type on the Insert tab. Excel inserts charts on the same worksheet as the data. You can move the chart and adjust the size of the chart area. When you create a chart or select an existing chart, Excel displays the Chart Tools contextual tab with three tabs: Design, Layout, and Format.

3. **Change the chart type.** You can change a chart to a different chart type if you believe a different chart type will represent the data better.

4. **Change the data source and structure.** You can add or remove data from the data source to change the data in the chart. The Select Data Source dialog box enables you to modify the ranges used for the data series. Excel usually places the first column of data as the category axis and the first row of data as the legend, but you can switch the row and column layout. The Design tab contains options for changing the data source and structure.

5. **Apply a chart layout and a chart style.** You can apply a chart layout to control what chart elements are included and where they are positioned within the chart area. You can apply a chart style, which determines formatting, such as the background color and the data series color. The Design tab contains options for selecting the chart layout and chart style.

6. **Move a chart.** You can position a chart on the same worksheet as the data source, or you can move the chart to its own sheet. The Move Chart dialog box enables you to select a new sheet and name the new chart sheet at the same time. The chart sheet will then contain a full-sized chart and no data. You can also move a chart to an existing worksheet. When you do this, the chart is an embedded object on that sheet, and the sheet may contain other data.

7. **Print charts.** You can print a chart with or without its corresponding data source. To print a chart with its data series, the chart needs to be on the same worksheet as the data source. To ensure both the data and the chart print, make sure the chart is not selected. If the chart is on its own sheet or if you select the chart on a worksheet containing other data, the chart will print as a full-sized chart.

8. **Insert and customize a sparkline.** A sparkline is a miniature chart in one cell representing a single data series. It gives a quick visual of the data to aid in comprehension. You can customize sparklines by changing the data source, location, and style. In addition, you can display markers, such as High Point, and change the line or marker color.

9. **Select and format chart elements.** Because each chart element is an individual object in the chart area, you can select and format each element separately. The Format dialog boxes enable you to apply fill colors, select border colors, and apply other settings. For the value axis, you can format values and specify the number of decimal places to display. For basic formatting, such as font color, use the options in the Font group on the Home tab.

10. **Customize chart labels.** The Labels group on the Layout tab enables you to add or remove chart elements: chart title, axis titles, legend, data labels, and a data table. The chart title should clearly describe the data and purpose of the chart. Include axis titles when you need to clarify the values on the value axis or the categories on the category axis. Customize the legend when you want to change its position within the chart area or hide the legend. Display data labels to provide exact values for data points in one or more data series; however, be careful the data labels do not overlap. If a chart is contained on a chart sheet, you might want to show the data table that contains the values used from the data source.

11. **Format the axes and gridlines.** The Axes group on the Layout tab enables you to control the horizontal and vertical axes. You can select the minimum, maximum, and increments on the value axis, and you can display both major and minor gridlines to help your audience read across the plot area.

12. **Add a trendline.** A trendline is a line that depicts trends. Trendlines are used to help make predictions or forecasts based on the current dataset. Excel enables you to select different types of trendlines based on the type of statistical analysis you want to perform.

# KEY TERMS

100% stacked column chart
3-D chart
Area chart
Axis title
Bar chart
Bubble chart
Category axis
Category label
Chart
Chart area
Chart sheet
Chart title
Clustered column chart

Column chart
Data label
Data point
Data series
Doughnut chart
Exploded pie chart
Gridline
Legend
Line chart
Multiple data series
Pie chart
Plot area
Radar chart

Single data series
Sizing handle
Sparkline
Stacked column chart
Stock chart
Surface chart
Trendline
Value axis
X Y (scatter) chart
X-axis
Y-axis

1. Which type of chart is the **least** appropriate for depicting yearly rainfall totals for five cities for four years?

    (a) Pie chart

    (b) Line chart

    (c) Column chart

    (d) Bar chart

2. What is the typical sequence for creating a chart?

    (a) Select the chart type, select the data source, and then size and position the chart.

    (b) Select the data source, size the chart, select the chart type, and then position the chart.

    (c) Select the data source, select the chart type, and then size and position the chart.

    (d) Click the cell to contain the chart, select the chart type, and then select the data source.

3. Which of the following applies to a sparkline?

    (a) Chart title

    (b) Single-cell chart

    (c) Legend

    (d) Multiple data series

4. If you want to show exact values for a data series in a bar chart, what chart element should you display?

    (a) Chart title

    (b) Legend

    (c) Value axis title

    (d) Data labels

5. The value axis currently shows increments such as 50,000 and 100,000. What do you select to display increments of 50 and 100?

    (a) More Primary Vertical Axis Title Options

    (b) Show Axis in Thousands

    (c) Show Axis in Millions

    (d) Show Right to Left Axis

6. You want to create a single chart that shows each of five divisions' proportion of yearly sales for each year for five years. Which type of chart can accommodate your needs?

    (a) Pie chart

    (b) Surface chart

    (c) Clustered bar chart

    (d) 100% stacked column chart

7. Currently, a column chart shows values on the value axis, years on the category axis, and state names in the legend. What should you do if you want to organize data with the states on the category axis and the years shown in the legend?

    (a) Change the chart type to a clustered column chart.

    (b) Click Switch Row/Column in the Data group on the Design tab.

    (c) Click Layout 2 in the Chart Layouts group on the Design tab, and then apply a different chart style.

    (d) Click Legend in the Labels group on the Layout tab, and then select Show Legend at Bottom.

8. Which tab contains commands to apply a predefined chart layout that controls what elements are included, where, and their color scheme?

    (a) Design

    (b) Layout

    (c) Format

    (d) Page Layout

9. A chart and its related data source are located on the same worksheet. What is the default Print option if the chart is selected prior to displaying the Backstage view?

    (a) Print Entire Workbook

    (b) Print Selection

    (c) Print Selected Chart

    (d) Print Active Sheets

10. Which of the following is *not* a way to display the Format Data Series dialog box for the Arts data series in a column chart?

    (a) Press and hold Shift as you click each Arts column.

    (b) Click an Arts column, and then click Format Selection in the Current Selection group on the Layout tab.

    (c) Right-click an Arts column, and then select Format Data Series.

    (d) Click the Chart Elements arrow in the Current Selection group, select the Arts data series, and then click Format Selection in the Current Selection group on the Layout tab.

Your cousin, Rita Dansie, wants to analyze her family's utility expenses for 2012. She wants to save money during months when utility expenses are lower so that her family will have money budgeted for months when the total utility expenses are higher. She gave you her files for the electric, gas, and water bills for the year 2012. You created a worksheet that lists the individual expenses per month, along with yearly totals per utility type and monthly totals. You will create some charts to depict the data. This exercise follows the same set of skills as used in Hands-On Exercises 1 and 2 in the chapter. Refer to Figure 51 as you complete this exercise.

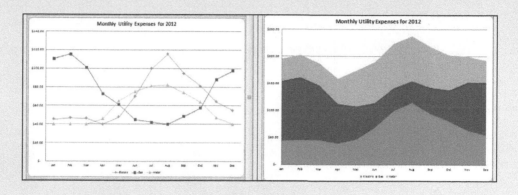

**FIGURE 51** Dansie Family Utility Expenses ➤

a. Open *e03p1utilities* and save it as **e03p1utilities_LastnameFirstname**.

b. Select the **range A4:E17**, and then click the **Insert tab**.

c. Click **Column** in the Charts group, and then select **Clustered Column**. After creating the chart, you realize you need to adjust the data source because you included the monthly and yearly totals.

d. Click the **Design tab**, if necessary. Click **Select Data** in the Data group to open the Select Data Source dialog box, and then do the following:
   - Click **Monthly Totals** in the **Legend Entries (Series) list**, and then click **Remove**.
   - Click in the **Chart data range box**, and then change *17* to **16** at the end of the range.
   - Click **OK** to finalize removing the monthly and yearly totals from the chart.

e. Position the mouse pointer over the chart area. When you see the Chart Area ScreenTip, drag the chart so that the top-left edge of the chart is in **cell A19**.

f. Click the **Format tab**. Click in the **Shape Width box** in the Size group, type **6**, and then press **Enter**.

g. Click the **Design tab**, and then click **Layout 3** in the Chart Layouts group.

h. Click the **Chart Title placeholder**, type **Monthly Utility Expenses for 2012**, and then press **Enter**.

i. Click the **More button** in the Chart Styles group, and then click **Style 26** (second style, fourth row).

j. Click the clustered column chart, use the **Copy command**, and then paste a copy of the chart in **cell A36**. With the second chart selected, do the following:
   - Click the **Design tab**, click **Change Chart Type** in the Type group, select **Line with Markers** in the *Line* section, and then click **OK**.
   - Click the **More button** in the Chart Styles group, and then click **Style 2** (second style, first row).
   - Copy the selected chart, and then paste it in **cell A52**.

k. Make sure the third chart is selected, and then do the following:
   - Click the **Design tab**, if necessary, click **Change Chart Type** in the Type group, select **Area** on the left side, click **Stacked Area**, and then click **OK**.
   - Click **Move Chart** in the Location group, click **New sheet**, type **Area Chart**, and then click **OK**.

l. Click the **Expenses worksheet tab**, scroll up to see the line chart, and then select the line chart. Click the **Design tab**, if necessary, click **Move Chart** in the Location group, click **New sheet**, type **Line Chart**, and then click **OK**.

m. Create a footer with your name on the left side, the sheet name code in the center, and the file name code on the right side on the worksheet and on the two chart sheets.

n. Click the **File tab**, and then click **Print**. Look at the preview window for each worksheet. Print all three worksheets for your reference, based on your instructor's directions.

o. Save and close the workbook, and submit based on your instructor's directions.

## 2 U.S. Population Estimates

You work for a major corporation headquartered in Chicago. One of your responsibilities is to analyze population statistics to identify geographic regions in which you can increase your market presence. You often visit the U.S. Census Bureau's Web site to download and analyze the data. You need to create a chart to present at a meeting tomorrow morning. This exercise follows the same set of skills as used in Hands-On Exercises 1, 2, and 3 in the chapter. Refer to Figure 52 as you complete this exercise.

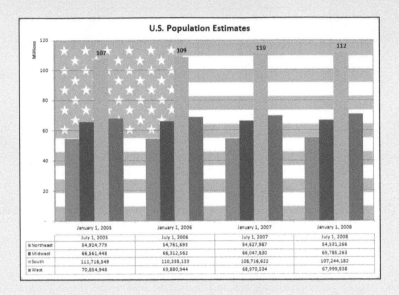

**FIGURE 52** U.S. Population Estimates ➤

a. Open *e03p2uspop* and save it as **e03p2uspop_LastnameFirstname**.

b. Select the **range A3:E7**, click the **Insert tab**, click **Column** in the Charts group, and then click **Clustered Column** in the *2-D Column* section.

c. Click **Move Chart** in the Location group on the Design tab. Click **New sheet**, type **Column Chart**, and then click **OK**.

d. Click the **Layout tab**, and then add a chart title by doing the following:
   • Click **Chart Title** in the Labels group, and then select **Above Chart**.
   • Type **U.S. Population Estimates** and press **Enter**.

e. Add data labels by doing the following:
   • Click the **Chart Elements arrow** in the Current Selection group, and then select **Series "South"**.
   • Click **Data Labels** in the Labels group, and then select **Outside End**.
   • Click the data labels to select them, apply **bold**, and then apply a **12-pt font** size.

f. Click the **Layout tab**, if necessary, click **Data Table** in the Labels group, and then select **Show Data Table with Legend Keys**.

g. Click **Legend** in the Labels group, and then select **None**.

h. Click **Axes** in the Axes group, point to **Primary Vertical Axis**, and then select **Show Axis in Millions**.

i. Click **Plot Area** in the Background group, and then select **More Plot Area Options**. Do the following in the Format Plot Area dialog box:
   • Click **Picture or texture fill**.
   • Click **Clip Art**, then in the Select Picture dialog box, search for and insert a picture of the **U.S. flag**.

Charts

218

- Select the image, and then click **OK**.
- Drag the **Transparency slider** to **70%**, and then click **Close**.

j. Click the **Population worksheet tab**, click **cell B9**, and create sparklines by doing the following:
- Click the **Insert tab**, and click **Column** in the Sparklines group.
- Select the **range B4:B7** to enter the range in the **Data Range box**.
- Ensure **$B$9** appears in the **Location Range box**, and then click **OK**.
- Increase the row height of row 9 to **42.00**.

k. Adapt step j to create sparklines in the **range C9:E9**.

l. Create a footer with your name on the left side, the sheet name code in the center, and the file name code on the right side of both worksheets.

m. Save and close the workbook, and submit based on your instructor's directions.

## 3 Gas Prices in Boston

You are interested in moving to Boston, but you want to know about the city's gasoline prices. You downloaded data from a government site, but it is overwhelming to detect trends when you have over 200 weekly data points. You create a chart to help you interpret the data. This exercise follows the same set of skills as used in Hands-On Exercises 1, 2, and 3 in the chapter. Refer to Figure 53 as you complete this exercise.

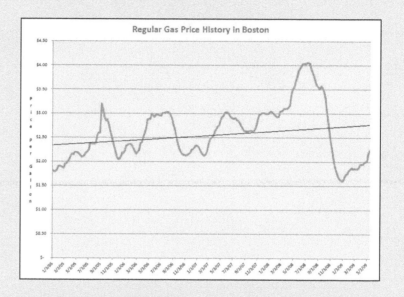

**FIGURE 53** Boston Gas Prices ➤

a. Open *e03p3boston* and save it as **e03p3boston_LastnameFirstname**.

b. Select **cells A6:B235**, click the **Insert tab**, click **Line** in the Charts group, and then click **Line** in the *2-D Line* section. Excel creates the chart and displays the Chart Tools Design tab.

c. Click **Move Chart** in the Location group, click **New sheet**, type **Line Chart**, and then click **OK**.

d. Click the **Layout tab**, click **Legend** in the Labels group, and then select **None** to remove the legend.

e. Click the chart title to select it, type **Regular Gas Price History in Boston**, and then press **Enter**.

f. Click **Axis Titles** in the Labels group, point to **Primary Vertical Axis Title**, select **Vertical Title**, type **Price per Gallon**, and then press **Enter**.

g. Click **Axes** in the Axes group, point to **Primary Vertical Axis**, and then select **More Primary Vertical Axis Options**. Do the following in the Format Axis dialog box:
- Make sure that **Axis Options** is selected on the left side of the Format Axis dialog box, click the **Display units arrow**, and then select **Hundreds**.
- Click **Number** on the left side of the dialog box, click **Accounting** in the **Category list**, and then click **Close**.

h. Click the **Hundreds label**, and then press **Delete**. You converted the cents per gallon to dollars and cents per gallon.

i. Click **Axes** in the Axes group, point to **Primary Horizontal Axis**, and then select **More Primary Horizontal Axis Options**. Click **Number** on the left side of the Format Axis dialog box, click **Date** in the **Category list** if necessary, select **3/14/01** in the **Type list**, and then click **Close**.

j. Use the Home tab to change the category axis, value axis, and value axis labels to **9-pt** size. Apply the **Orange, Accent 6, Darker 25% font color** to the chart title.

k. Click the **Design tab**, click the **More button** in the Chart styles group, and then click **Style 40** (first style on the right side of the fifth row).

l. Click the **Layout tab**, click **Trendline**, and then select **Exponential Trendline**.

m. Create a footer with your name on the left side, the sheet name code in the center, and the file name code on the right side.

n. Click the **File tab**, click **Print**, and then look at the preview. Print the chart sheet if instructed.

o. Save and close the workbook, and submit based on your instructor's directions.

Charts

## 1  Car Ratings

You work for an independent automobile rating company that provides statistics to consumers. A group of testers recently evaluated four 2012 mid-sized passenger car models and provided the data to you in a worksheet. You need to transform the data into meaningful charts that you will include on your company's Web site. Refer to Figure 54 as you complete this exercise.

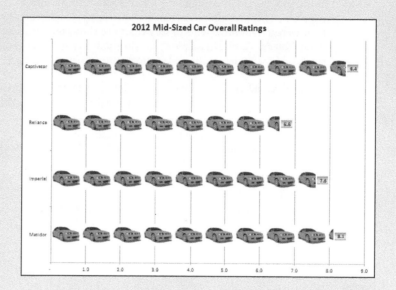

**FIGURE 54** Automobile Ratings Chart ➤

**DISCOVER**

a. Open *e03m1autos* and save it as **e03m1autos_LastnameFirstname**.

b. Insert a column sparkline individually for each car model and for the overall category ratings in column H. Include all ratings, including the average. Apply a different style to each sparkline. Change the row height to **20** for rows containing sparklines.

c. Select the **range A3:F8**, and then create a stacked column chart. You realize that the data in this chart is not cumulative and that you included the overall ratings by category. You also notice that the chart is located to the side of the data. Make the following changes:
   • Change the chart to a clustered column chart.
   • Remove the overall category from the data source.
   • Position the chart starting in **cell A11**, and then increase the chart width through **cell G27**.

d. Make the following design changes:
   • Select **Layout 1** as the chart layout style.
   • Edit the chart title to be **2012 Mid-Sized Car Ratings by Category**.
   • Apply the **Red, Accent 2, Darker 25% font color** to the chart title.
   • Apply the **Style 12 chart style**.

e. Create another chart on a new chart sheet:
   • Select the **range A4:A7**, press and hold **Ctrl**, and then select the **range G4:G7**—the models and the overall ratings.
   • Create a clustered bar chart.
   • Move the chart to its own sheet named **Overall Ratings**.

f. Make the following changes to the bar chart (see Figure 54):
   • Remove the legend.
   • Add the title **2012 Mid-Sized Car Overall Ratings** above the chart.
   • Apply the **Style 2 chart style**, if necessary.
   • Add data labels in the Outside End position, and then bold the data labels. Apply the **Fog gradient fill color** to the data labels.
   • Select the data series, and then apply a picture fill, searching for clip art of a blue automobile. Select the option to stack the images instead of stretching one image per data marker.

g. Insert a footer with your name on the left side, the sheet name code in the center, and the file name code on the right side on all worksheets.

h. Adjust the page setup option to fit the worksheet to one page with 0.5" left and right margins. Print the worksheet that contains the data and the clustered column chart per your instructor's directions.

i. Save and close the workbook, and submit based on your instructor's directions.

## 2  Grade Analysis

You are a teaching assistant for Dr. Monica Unice's introductory psychology class. You have maintained her grade book all semester, entering three test scores for each student and calculating the final average. Dr. Unice wants to see a chart that shows the percentage of students who earn each letter grade. You decide to create a pie chart. She wants to see if a correlation exists between attendance and students' final grades, so you will create a scatter chart.

a. Open *e03m2psych* and save it as **e03m2psych_LastnameFirstname**.

b. Create a pie chart from the Final Grade Distribution data located below the student data, and then move the pie chart to its own sheet named **Grades Pie**.

c. Customize the pie chart with these specifications:
   • **Layout 1 chart layout** with the title **PSY 2030 Final Grade Distribution - Fall 2012**
   • F grade slice exploded
   • **20-pt** size for the data labels, with a center label position, and gradient fill
   • Border: no line

d. Apply these standard fill colors to the respective data points:
   • A: Blue
   • B: Green
   • C: Orange
   • D: Purple
   • F: Red

e. Create a Scatter with only Markers chart using the attendance record and final averages from the Grades worksheet, and then move the scatter chart to its own sheet. Name the sheet **Attend Grades**.

f. Apply these label settings to the scatter chart:
   • Legend: none
   • Chart title above chart: **Attendance - Final Average Relationship**
   • X-axis title: **Percentage of Attendance**
   • Y-axis rotated title: **Student Final Averages**

g. Use Help to learn how to apply the following axis settings:
   • Y-axis: 40 starting point, 100 maximum score, 10 point increments, and a number format with zero decimal places
   • X-axis: 40 starting point, automatic increments, automatic maximum

h. Add the **Parchment gradient fill** to the plot area.

i. Insert a linear trendline.

j. Center the worksheet horizontally between the left and right margins on the Grades worksheet.

k. Insert a footer with your name on the left side, the sheet name code in the center, and the file name code on the right side for all three worksheets.

l. Save and close the workbook, and submit based on your instructor's directions.

You are an assistant manager at Premiere Movie Source, an online company that enables customers to download movies for a fee. You are required to track movie download sales by genre. You gathered the data for September 2012 and organized it in an Excel workbook. You are ready to create charts to help represent the data so that you can make a presentation to your manager later this week.

## Change Data Source, Position, and Size

You already created a clustered column chart, but you selected too many cells for the data source. You need to open the workbook and adjust the data source for the chart. In addition, you want to position and size the chart.

a. Open the *e03c1movies* workbook and save it as **e03c1movies_LastnameFirstname**.

b. Remove the Category Totals from the legend, and then adjust the data range to exclude the weekly totals.

c. Position and size the chart to fill the **range A18:L37**.

d. Change the row and column orientation so that the weeks appear in the category axis and the genres appear in the legend.

## Add Chart Labels

You want to add a chart title and a value axis title and change the legend's position.

a. Add a chart title above the chart.

b. Enter the text **September 2012 Downloads by Genre**.

c. Add a rotated value axis title.

d. Enter the text **Number of Downloads**.

e. Move the legend to the top of the chart, and then drag the bottom of the chart area down to cover row 40.

## Format Chart Elements

You are ready to apply the finishing touches to the clustered column chart. You will adjust the font size of the category axis and display additional gridlines to make it easier to identify values for the data series. You will add and adjust data labels to the Drama data series. Finally, you will add a linear trendline to the chart to visualize trends.

a. Format the category axis with **12-pt size**.

b. Display major and minor horizontal gridlines.

c. Select the **Drama data series**, and then add data labels in the Outside End position.

d. Add a **Yellow fill color** to the data labels.

e. Add a linear trendline to the Drama data series.

## Insert and Format Sparklines

You want to show weekly trends for each genre by inserting sparklines in the column to the right of Category Totals.

a. Insert a **Line sparkline** for the weekly (but not category totals) data for Action & Adventure in **cell G5**.

b. Copy the sparkline down the column.

c. Format the sparklines by applying **Sparkline Style Dark #6**, display the high point, and format the high point marker in **Red**.

## Create Another Chart

You want to create a chart that will show the monthly volume of downloads by genre. You decide to create a bar chart with genre labels along the left side of the chart.

a. Select the genres and weekly totals. Create a clustered bar chart.

b. Move the chart to its own sheet, and then name the sheet **Bar Chart**.

c. Change the chart type to a stacked bar chart.

d. Add a chart title above the chart, and then enter **Sept 2012 Total Monthly Downloads by Genre**.

## Format the Bar Chart

You want to enhance the appearance of the chart by applying a chart style and adjusting the axis values.

a. Apply the **Style 31 chart style** to the bar chart.

b. Display the value axis in units of thousands.

c. Display the category axis names in reverse order using the Format Axis dialog box.

d. Apply the **Layout 3 layout style** to the chart.

## Printing the Charts

You want to print the bar chart on its own page, but you want to print the clustered column chart with the original data. To ensure the worksheet data and chart print on the same page, you need to adjust the page setup options.

a. Create a footer on each worksheet with your name, the sheet name code, and the file name code.

b. Apply landscape orientation for the original worksheet.

c. Set 0.2" left, right, top, and bottom margins for the original worksheet.

d. Select the option that makes the worksheet print on only one page.

e. Print both worksheets.

f. Save and close the workbook, and submit based on your instructor's directions.

# BEYOND THE CLASSROOM

## Widget Company Stock Prices

GENERAL CASE

You want to track your investment in Widget Company. Open *e03b1stock* and save it as **e03b1stock_LastnameFirstname**. Create the appropriate stock chart based on the existing sequence of data, keeping in mind that data must be in a specific structure to create the chart. Move the chart to a new chart sheet, and name the sheet **Stock Chart**. Apply the Style 37 chart style, remove the legend, and display the data table. Add a centered overlay title that describes the chart. Select the chart title; apply a solid fill using Olive Green, Accent 3, Darker 50%; and apply White, Background 1 font color. Add a linear trendline for the closing price. Create a footer with your name, the sheet name code, and file name code. Save and close the workbook, and submit based on your instructor's directions.

## Box Office Movie Data

RESEARCH CASE

As a contributing writer for an entertainment magazine, you have been asked to gather data on box office opening revenue for movies released in the theaters this month. Conduct some online research to identify six newly released movies, their release dates, and the revenue generated. Start a new workbook. Organize the data from the lowest-grossing movie to the highest-grossing movie. Apply appropriate formatting, and include a main and secondary title for the worksheet. Save the workbook as **e03b2boxoffice_LastnameFirstname**. Use the data to create a bar chart on a separate worksheet, showing the movie names on the vertical axis and revenue on the horizontal axis. Assign names to the worksheet tabs, and delete the extra worksheets. Format the value axis in millions, and apply Accounting or Currency format, if needed. Insert a chart title that describes the data. Apply a different chart style. Use Help to research how to insert text boxes. Insert a text box for the first bar containing the release date. Position the text box on top of the bar, and select a contrasting font color. Copy the text box for the remaining movie bars, and edit each text box to display the respective release dates. Create a footer with your name, the sheet name code, and the file name code. Print a copy of the chart for your records. Save and close the workbook, and submit based on your instructor's directions.

## Harper County Houses Sold

DISASTER RECOVERY

You want to analyze the number of houses sold by type (e.g., rambler, two-story, etc.) in each quarter during 2012. Your intern created an initial chart, but it contains a lot of problems. Open *e03b3houses* and save it as **e03b3houses_LastnameFirstname**. Identify the errors and poor design. List the errors and your corrections in a two-column format below the chart. Then correct problems in the chart. Create a footer with your name, the sheet name code, and the file name code. Adjust the margins and scaling to print the worksheet data, including the error list, and chart on one page. Save and close the workbook, and submit based on your instructor's directions.

Charts

224

# EXCEL
# DATASETS AND TABLES
## Managing Large Volumes of Data

Watch the Set-up Video for this Case Study!

## CASE STUDY | The Spa Experts

Shortly after graduating from college, you and your best friend, Ryan Paap, started a business selling spas and hot tubs. Business has been good, and your expansive showroom and wide selection appeal to a variety of customers. You and Ryan maintain a large inventory to attract the impulse buyer and currently have agreements with three manufacturers: Serenity Spas, The Original Hot Tub, and Port-a-Spa. Each manufacturer offers spas and hot tubs that appeal to different segments of the market, from affordable to exorbitant.

The business has grown rapidly, and you need to analyze the sales data in order to increase future profits. For example, which vendor generates the most sales? Who is the leading salesperson? Do most customers purchase or finance? Are sales promotions necessary to promote business, or will customers pay the full price?

You created a worksheet that has sales data for the current month. Each transaction appears on a separate row and contains the transaction number, date, sales representatives' first and last names, the spa manufacturer, payment type (financed or paid in full), transaction (standard or promotion), and the amount of the sale. You are ready to start analyzing the data in Excel.

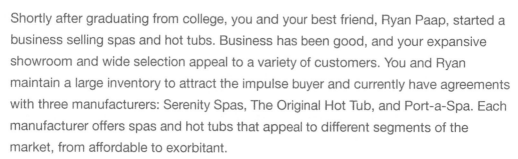

## OBJECTIVES   AFTER YOU READ THIS CHAPTER, YOU WILL BE ABLE TO:

1. Freeze rows and columns
2. Print large datasets
3. Understand table design
4. Create a table
5. Apply a table style
6. Sort data

7. Filter data
8. Use structured references and a total row
9. Apply conditional formatting
10. Create a new rule
11. Sort and filter using conditional formatting

# Large Datasets

So far you have worked with worksheets that contain small datasets, a collection of structured, related data in columns and rows. In reality, you will probably work with large datasets consisting of hundreds or thousands of rows and columns of data. When you work with small datasets, you can usually view most or all of the data without scrolling. When you work with large datasets, column and row labels scroll offscreen when you scroll through the worksheet. Large, widescreen monitors set at high resolutions display more data onscreen; however, you may not be able to view the entire dataset. You might want to keep some data always in view, even as you scroll throughout the dataset. Figure 1 shows the Spa Experts' January sales transactions. Because it contains a lot of transactions, the entire dataset is not visible. You could decrease the zoom level; however, doing so decreases the text size onscreen, making it hard to read the data.

> Working with large datasets is challenging because column and row labels scroll offscreen....

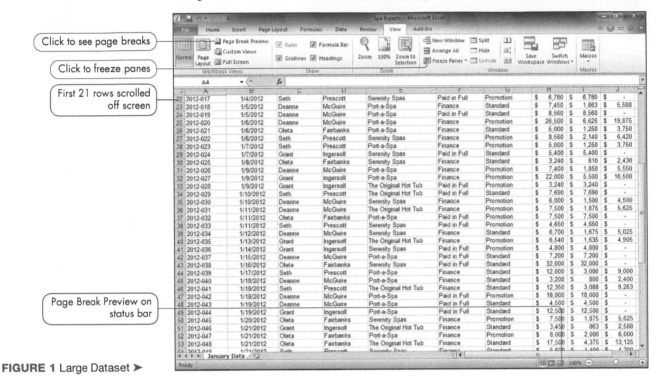

Click to see page breaks

Click to freeze panes

First 21 rows scrolled off screen

Page Break Preview on status bar

**FIGURE 1** Large Dataset ➤

In order to view other columns, use the horizontal scroll bar to view one or more columns to the right. When the active cell is in the last visible column (cell J1, for example), pressing → displays one or two more columns on the right. Clicking the down arrow in the vertical scroll bar or pressing ↓ when the active cell is in the bottom visible row moves the screen down one row. As you scroll down and to the right, the rows and columns that were originally visible are no longer visible.

In this section, you will learn how to freeze panes and print large worksheets. In particular, you will learn how to keep labels onscreen as you scroll and how to adjust settings that control how large worksheets print.

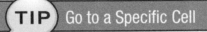

**TIP** Go to a Specific Cell

You can navigate through a large worksheet by using the Go To command. Click Find & Select in the Editing group on the Home tab and select Go To (or press F5 or Ctrl+G) to display the Go To dialog box, enter the cell address in the Reference box, and then press Enter to go to the cell. You can also click in the Name Box, type the cell reference, and then press Enter.

# Freezing Rows and Columns

When you scroll to parts of a dataset not initially visible, some rows and columns disappear from view. When the row and column labels scroll off the screen, you may not remember what each column represents. You can keep labels onscreen by freezing them. *Freezing* is the process of keeping rows and/or columns visible onscreen at all times even when you scroll through a large dataset. To freeze labels from scrolling offscreen, click the View tab, click Freeze Panes in the Window group, and then select a freeze option. Table 1 describes the three freeze options.

**Freezing** keeps rows and/or columns visible as you scroll through a worksheet.

| TABLE 1 | Freeze Options |
|---|---|
| **Option** | **Description** |
| **Freeze Panes** | Keeps both rows and columns above and to the left of the active cell visible as you scroll through a worksheet. |
| **Freeze Top Row** | Keeps only the top row visible as you scroll through a worksheet. |
| **Freeze First Column** | Keeps only the first column visible as you scroll through a worksheet. |

To freeze one or more rows and columns, use the Freeze Panes option. Before selecting this option, make the active cell one row below and one column to the right of the rows and columns you want to freeze. For example, to freeze the first five rows and the first two columns, make cell C6 the active cell before clicking a Freeze Panes option. As Figure 2 shows, Excel displays a horizontal line below the last frozen row (row 5) and a vertical line to the right of the last frozen column (column B). As you scroll down, the unfrozen rows, such as rows 6–14, disappear. As you scroll to the right, the unfrozen columns, such as columns C and D, disappear.

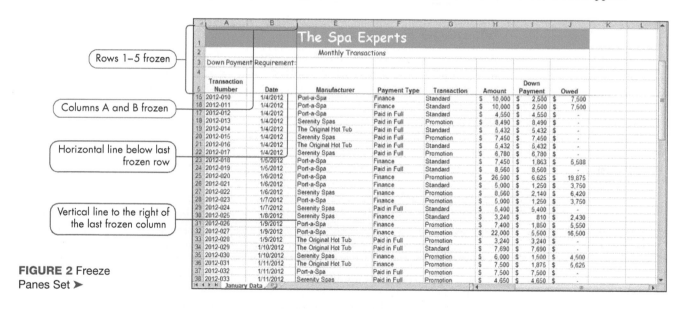

Rows 1–5 frozen

Columns A and B frozen

Horizontal line below last frozen row

Vertical line to the right of the last frozen column

**FIGURE 2** Freeze Panes Set ➤

To unlock the rows and columns from remaining onscreen as you scroll, click Freeze Panes in the Window group, and then select Unfreeze Panes, which only appears on the menu when you have frozen rows and/or columns. After you unfreeze the panes, the Unfreeze Panes option disappears, and the Freeze Panes option appears on the menu again.

When you freeze panes and press Ctrl+Home, the first unfrozen cell is the active cell instead of cell A1. For example, with columns A and B and rows 1–5 frozen in Figure 2, pressing Ctrl+Home makes cell C6 the active cell. If you need to edit a cell in the frozen area, click the particular cell to make it active, and then edit the data.

# Printing Large Datasets

Printing all or parts of a large dataset presents special challenges. For a large dataset, some columns and rows may print on several pages. Analyzing the data for individual printed pages is difficult when each page does not contain column and row labels. To prevent wasting paper, always preview large datasets in the Backstage view before printing data. Doing so enables you to adjust page settings until you are satisfied with how the data will print.

The Page Layout tab (see Figure 3) contains many options to help you prepare large datasets to print. Previously, you changed the page orientation, set different margins, and adjusted the scaling. In addition, you can manage page breaks, set the print area, and print titles.

Click to set the print area

Click to insert a page break

Click to print titles (labels) on each printed page

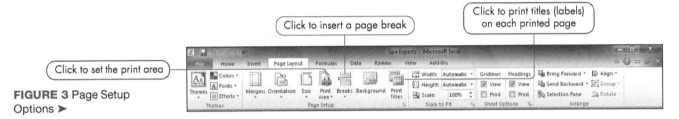

**FIGURE 3** Page Setup Options ➤

## Manage Page Breaks

A **page break** indicates where data starts on a new printed page.

Based on the paper size, orientation, margins, and other settings, Excel identifies how much data can print on a page. Then it displays a *page break*, indicating where data will start on another printed page. To identify where these automatic page breaks will occur, click Page Break Preview on the status bar or in the Workbook Views group on the Views tab. If the Welcome to Page Break Preview message box appears, click OK. Excel displays watermarks, such as *Page 1*, indicating the area that will print on a specific page. Blue dashed lines indicate where the automatic page breaks occur, and solid blue lines indicate manual page breaks.

If the automatic page breaks occur in undesirable locations, you can adjust the page breaks. For example, if you have a worksheet listing sales data by date, the automatic page break might occur within a group of rows for one date, such as between two rows of data for 1/21/2012. To make all rows for that date appear together, insert a page break above the first data row for that date. To do this, drag a page break line to the desired location. You can also set a manual break at a specific location by doing the following:

1. Click the cell that you want to be the first row and column on a new printed page. If you want cell A50 to start a new page, click cell A50. If you click cell D50, you create a page for columns A through C, and then column D starts a new page.
2. Click the Page Layout tab.
3. Click Breaks in the Page Setup group, and then select Insert Page Break. Excel displays a solid blue line in Page Break Preview or a dashed line in Normal view to indicate the manual page breaks you set in the worksheet. Figure 4 shows a worksheet with both automatic and manual page breaks.

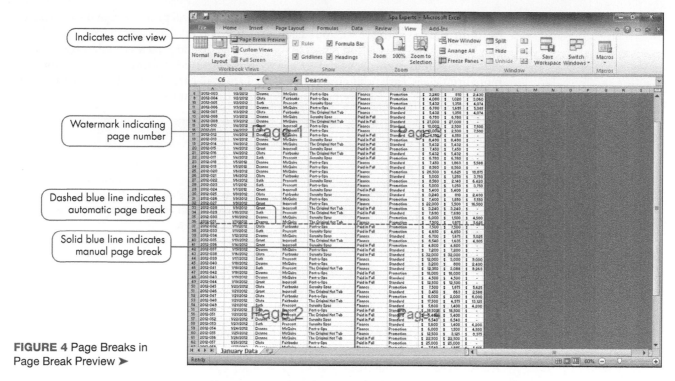

Indicates active view

Watermark indicating page number

Dashed blue line indicates automatic page break

Solid blue line indicates manual page break

**FIGURE 4** Page Breaks in Page Break Preview ➤

To remove a manual page break, click the cell below a horizontal page break or the cell to the right of a vertical page break, click Breaks in the Page Setup group, and then select Remove Page Break. To reset all page breaks back to the automatic page breaks, click Breaks in the Page Setup group, and then select Reset All Page Breaks.

## Set and Clear a Print Area

A **print area** defines the range of data to print.

The default settings send an entire dataset on the active worksheet to the printer. However, you might want to print only part of the worksheet data. For example, you might want to print an input area only or transactions that occurred on a particular date. You can set the *print area*, which is the range of cells that will print. To print part of a worksheet, do the following:

1. Select the range you want to print.
2. Click the Page Layout tab, and then click Print Area in the Page Setup group.
3. Select Set Print Area. Excel displays solid blue lines in Page Break Preview or thin black dashed lines around the print area in Normal view or Page Layout view (see Figure 5).

Click to set print area

Dotted lines indicate boundaries of print area

**FIGURE 5** Print Area ➤

When you use the Print command, only the print area will print. In Page Break Preview, the print area has a white background and solid blue border; the rest of the worksheet has a gray background. You can add ranges to the print area. To add print areas, select the range of cells you want to print, click Print Area, and then select Add to Print Area. When you add more print areas, each print area will print on a separate page. To clear the print area, click Print Area in the Page Setup group, and then select Clear Print Area.

---

**TIP** Print a Selection

Another way to print part of a worksheet is to select the range you want to print. Click the File tab, and then click Print to see the print options and the worksheet in print preview. Click the first arrow in the *Settings* section, and then select Print Selection. Selecting the Print Selection option is a quick way to print a selected range. If you want to always print the same range, select the range in the worksheet, and set it as a print area.

---

## Print Titles

When you print large worksheets, make sure every column and row contains descriptive labels on each page. Having the column and row labels print on only the first page does not help your audience identify data on subsequent pages. When you click Print Titles in the Page Setup group on the Page Layout tab, Excel opens the Page Setup dialog box. The Sheet tab within the dialog box is active so that you can select which row(s) and/or column(s) to repeat on each printout (see Figure 6).

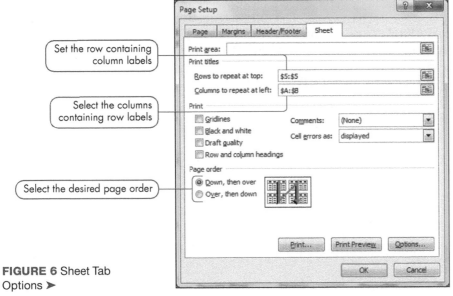

**FIGURE 6** Sheet Tab Options ➤

In the Spa Experts dataset, not all of the rows will print on the same page as the column labels. To print the column labels at the top of each printout, select the range in the *Rows to repeat at top* box. For example, row 5 contains column labels, such as Manufacturer. If your worksheet has more columns that can print on a page, you might want to display the row labels. To print the row headings on the left side of each printout, select the range in the *Columns to repeat at left* box. For example, columns A and B contain the transaction numbers and dates.

## Control Print Page Order

**Print order** is the sequence in which pages print.

**Print order** is the sequence in which the pages are printed. By default, the pages print in this order: top-left section, bottom-left section, top-right section, and bottom-right section. However, you might want to print the entire top portion of the worksheet before printing the bottom portion.

To change the print order, click the Page Setup Dialog Box Launcher in the Page Setup group, click the Sheet tab, and then click either *Down, then over* or *Over, then down* (see Figure 6).

Datasets and Tables

# HANDS-ON EXERCISES

## 1 Large Datasets

You want to review the large dataset you created that shows the January transactions for your business, Spa Experts. You want to view the data and adjust some page setup options so that you can print necessary headings on each printed page.

**Skills covered:** Freeze and Unfreeze Panes • Display and Change Page Breaks • Set and Clear a Print Area • Print Worksheet Titles • Change the Page Order

### STEP 1 ▶ FREEZE AND UNFREEZE PANES

Before setting up the dataset to print, you want to view the data onscreen. The dataset contains more rows than will display onscreen at the same time. You decide to freeze the headings to stay onscreen as you scroll through the transactions. Refer to Figure 7 as you complete Step 1.

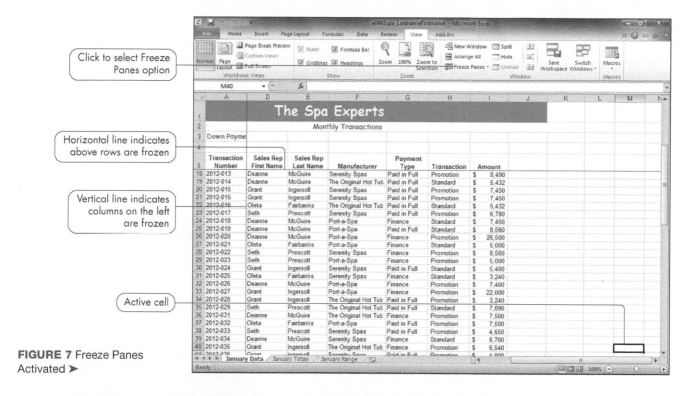

**FIGURE 7** Freeze Panes Activated ▶

a. Open *e04h1spa* and save it as **e04h1spa_LastnameFirstname**.

> **TROUBLESHOOTING:** If you make any major mistakes in this exercise, you can close the file, open *e04h1spa* again, and then start this exercise over.

The workbook contains three worksheets: January Data (to complete tasks in Hands-On Exercises 1, 2, and 3), January Totals (to complete tasks in Hands-On Exercise 3), and January Range (to complete tasks in Hands-On Exercise 4).

b. Click the **View tab**, click **Freeze Panes** in the Window group, and then select **Freeze Top Row**.

A black horizontal line appears between rows 1 and 2.

c. Press **Page Down** to scroll down through the worksheet.

As rows scroll off the top of the Excel window, the first row remains frozen onscreen. The title by itself is not helpful; you need to freeze the column headings as well.

d. Click **Freeze Panes** in the Window group.

Notice that the first option is now Unfreeze Panes.

e. Select **Unfreeze Panes**.

The top row is no longer frozen.

f. Click **cell B6**, the cell below the row and one column to the right of what you want to freeze. Click **Freeze Panes** in the Window group, and then select **Freeze Panes**.

Excel displays a vertical line between columns A and B, indicating that column A is frozen, and a horizontal line between rows 5 and 6, indicating the first five rows are frozen.

g. Press **Ctrl+G**, type **M40** in the **Reference box** of the Go To dialog box, and then click **OK** to make **cell M40** the active cell. Save the workbook.

Notice that rows 6 through 17 are not visible, and columns B and C are not visible since they scrolled off the screen.

> **TROUBLESHOOTING:** Your screen may differ from what Figure 7 shows due to different Windows resolution settings. If necessary, continue scrolling right and down until you see columns and rows scrolling offscreen while column A and the first five rows remain onscreen.

## STEP 2 ▶ DISPLAY AND CHANGE PAGE BREAKS

You plan to print the dataset so that you and your business partner Ryan can discuss the transactions in your weekly meeting. You know that large datasets do not fit on one printed page, so you want to see where the automatic page breaks will be. Refer to Figure 8 as you complete Step 2.

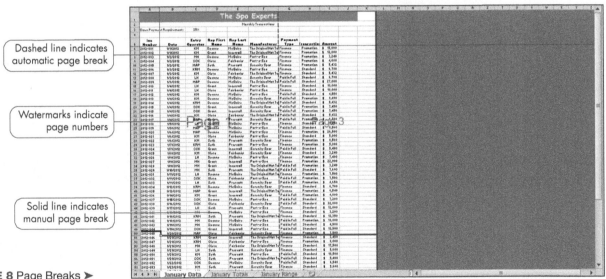

Dashed line indicates automatic page break

Watermarks indicate page numbers

Solid line indicates manual page break

**FIGURE 8** Page Breaks ➤

a. Press **Ctrl+Home** to jump to **cell B6**, the first cell in the unfrozen area. Click the **View tab** if necessary, and then click **Page Break Preview** in the Workbook Views group or on the status bar.

> **TROUBLESHOOTING:** If the Welcome to Page Break Preview message box opens instructing you how to adjust page breaks, click OK.

**b.** Drag the **Zoom slider** to the left until the zoom is **50%**.

Excel displays blue dashed lines to indicate the page breaks. The horizontal page break is between rows 51 and 52. You want to make sure all transactions for a particular day do not span between printed pages, so you need to move the page break up to keep all 1/21/2012 transactions together.

**c.** Click **cell A51**, the cell to start the top of the second page.

**d.** Click the **Page Layout tab**, click **Breaks** in the Page Setup group, and then select **Insert Page Break**. Save the workbook.

You inserted a page break between rows 50 and 51 so that the 1/21/2012 transactions will be on one page.

> **TROUBLESHOOTING:** If Excel displays a solid line between columns and removes the automatic vertical page break, you selected the wrong cell before inserting a page break. Excel inserts page breaks above and to the left of the active cell. If the page breaks are in the wrong place, click Undo on the Quick Access Toolbar and complete steps c and d again.

> **TIP** Using the Pointer to Move Page Breaks
>
> Instead of clicking Breaks in the Page Setup group, you can use the mouse pointer to adjust a page break. Position the pointer on the page break line to see the two-headed arrow. Drag the page break line to move it where you want the page break to occur.

## STEP 3 ▶ SET AND CLEAR A PRINT AREA

You want to focus on the first five days of transactions. To avoid printing more data than you need, you can set the print area to only that data. Refer to Figure 9 as you complete Step 3.

White/blue background with yellow border indicates print area

Gray background indicates non-printing area

**FIGURE 9** Print Area Set ➤

**a.** Change the zoom back to **100%**. Scroll up to see the first row of January data. Select the **range D5:I25**, the range of data for the first five days of the month.

b. Click the **Page Layout tab**, if necessary, click **Print Area** in the Page Setup group, and then select **Set Print Area**.

Excel displays the print area with a solid yellow border. The rest of the worksheet displays with a gray background, as shown in Figure 9.

c. Click the **Page Setup Dialog Box Launcher** in the Page Setup group. Use the dialog box to create a footer with your name on the left side, the sheet name code in the center, and the file name code on the right side.

d. Click the **File tab**, and then click **Print** to verify that only the print area will print. Click the **File tab** to close the Backstage view.

e. Click **Print Area** in the Page Setup group, and then select **Clear Print Area**. Save the workbook.

## STEP 4 ▶ PRINT WORKSHEET TITLES

When you looked at the entire dataset in Page Break Preview, you noticed it would print on four pages. Only the first page will print both row and column headings. Page 2 will print the remaining row headings, page 3 will print the remaining column headings, and page 4 will not print either heading. You want to make sure the column and row headings print on all pages. To do this, you will print titles. Refer to Figure 10 as you complete Step 4.

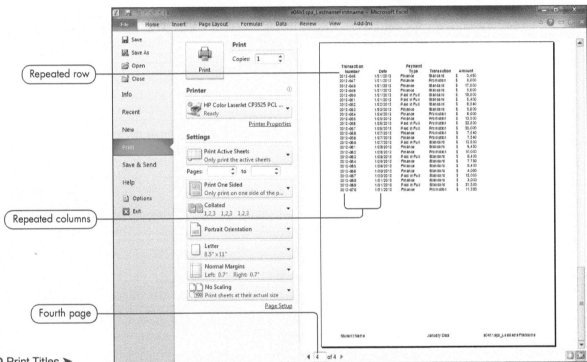

**FIGURE 10** Print Titles ➤

a. Click **Print Titles** in the Page Setup group.

The Page Setup dialog box opens, displaying the Sheet tab.

b. Click the **Rows to repeat at top collapse button** to collapse the dialog box.

c. Click the **row 5 heading**, and then click the **expand button** to expand the Page Setup dialog box again.

You selected the fifth row, which contains the headings that identify content in the columns.

d. Click in the **Columns to repeat at left box**, type **A:B**, and then click **Print Preview**.

You should verify the page breaks and titles in Print Preview.

Datasets and Tables

234

**e.** Click **Next Page** at the bottom of the Backstage view. Look at the second page to see the column headings for the last 11 days of transactions. Click **Next Page** twice to see the third and fourth pages.

Figure 10 shows a preview of the fourth page. The fifth row—the descriptive column headings—appears at the top of the page, and the first two columns of row headings (Transaction Number and Date) appear on all pages now.

**f.** Click the **Page Layout tab** to close the Backstage view. Save the workbook.

---

**STEP 5** ▶ **CHANGE THE PAGE ORDER**

Although all four pages will print with titles, you want to print all columns for the first half of the monthly transactions rather than printing the first few columns of all transactions and then printing the last columns for all transactions. Refer to Figure 11 as you complete Step 5.

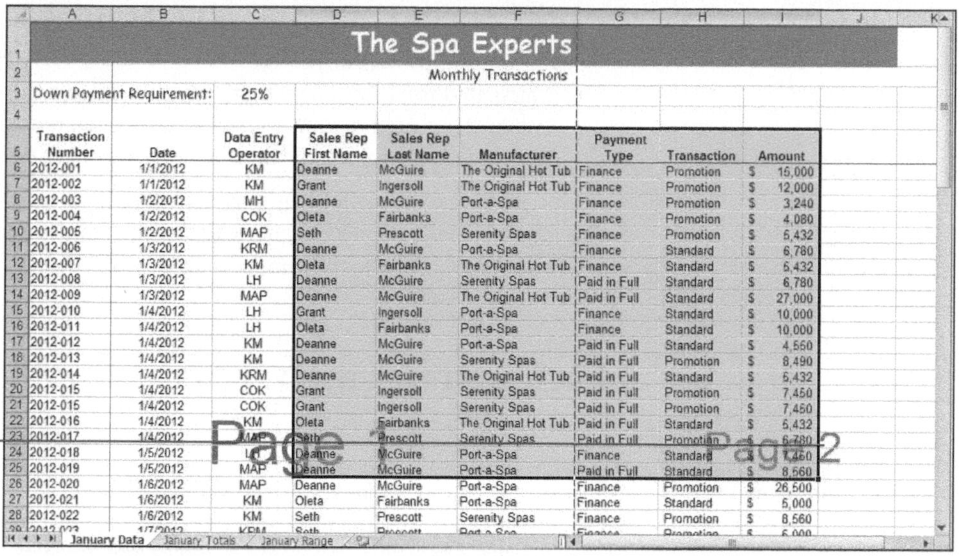

**FIGURE 11** Different Page Order ➤

**a.** Click the **Page Layout tab**, if necessary, and then click the **Page Setup Dialog Box Launcher** in the Page Setup group.

**b.** Click the **Sheet tab** in the Page Setup dialog box.

**c.** Click **Over, then down**.

The preview shows that the pages print left to right and then back down left to right, in a Z manner.

**d.** Click **OK**.

Notice the Page 2 watermark appears on the right side of Page 1 rather than below it.

**e.** Save the workbook. Keep the workbook onscreen if you plan to continue with Hands-On Exercise 2. If not, close the workbook and exit Excel.

# Excel Tables

All organizations maintain lists of data. Businesses maintain inventory lists, educational institutions maintain lists of students and faculty, and governmental entities maintain lists of contracts. Although more complicated related data should be stored in a database management program, such as Access, you can maintain structured lists in Excel tables. A *table* is a structured range that contains related data organized in such a way as to facilitate data management and analysis. Although you can manage and analyze a range of data, a table provides many advantages over a range of data:

All organizations maintain lists of data.

A **table** is an area in the worksheet that contains rows and columns of related data formatted to enable data management and analysis.

- Column headings that remain onscreen during scrolling without having to use Freeze Panes
- Filter lists for efficient sorting and filtering
- Predefined table styles to format table rows and columns with complementary fill colors
- Ability to create and edit calculated columns where the formulas copy down the columns automatically
- Calculated total row enabling the user to choose from a variety of functions
- Use of structured references instead of cell references in formulas
- Ability to export the table data to a SharePoint list

In this section, you will learn table terminology and rules for structuring data. You will create a table from existing data, manage records and fields, and remove duplicates. Then, you will apply a table style to format the table.

## Understanding Table Design

A **field** is an individual piece of data, such as a last name.

An Excel table is like a database table: it provides a structured organization of data in columns and rows. Each column represents a *field*, which is an individual piece of data, such as last names or quantities sold. You should create fields with the least amount of data. For example, instead of a Name field, separate data into First Name and Last Name fields. Instead of one large address field, separate addresses into Street Address, City, State, and ZIP Code fields. Storing data into the smallest units possible enables you to manipulate the data in a variety of ways for output.

A **record** is a complete set of data for an entity.

Each row in an Excel table represents a *record*, which is a collection of data about one entity, such as data for one person. For example, your record in your professor's grade book contains specific data about you, such as your name, ID, test scores, etc. The professor maintains a record of similar data for each student in the class. In an Excel table, each cell represents one piece of data (in the respective field columns) for a particular record.

Often, people create tables from existing worksheet data. For example, a data-entry operator for the Spa Experts might enter data in a worksheet instead of creating a table first. Just as you spend time planning a worksheet, you should plan the structure for a table. Think about who will use the table, what types of reports you need to produce, and what types of searches might be done. The more thorough your planning process, the fewer changes you will have to make to the table after you create it. To help plan your table, follow these guidelines:

- Enter field names on the top row.
- Keep field names relatively short, descriptive, and unique. No two field names should be identical.
- Format the field names so that they stand out from the data.
- Enter data for each record on a row below the field names.
- Do not leave blank rows between records or between the field names and the first record.
- Delete any blank columns between fields in the dataset.

- Make sure each record has something unique about it, such as a transaction number or ID.
- Insert at least one blank row and one blank column between the table and other data, such as the main titles, input area, or other tables. When possible, place separate tables on separate worksheets.

## Creating a Table

When your worksheet data are structured correctly, you can easily create a table. To create a table from existing data, do the following:

1. Click within the existing range of data.
2. Click the Insert tab, and then click Table in the Tables group. As Figure 12 shows, the Create Table dialog box opens, prompting you to enter the range of data. If Excel does not correctly predict the range, select the range for the *Where is the data for your table?* box. If the existing range contains column headings, select the *My table has headers* check box.
3. Click OK to create the table.

FIGURE 12 Create Table Dialog Box ➤

The Table Tools Design tab appears. Excel applies the default Table Style Medium 9 banded rows to your table, and each cell in the header row has filter arrows (see Figure 13). Excel assigns a name to each table, such as Table1. You can change the table name by clicking in the Table Name box in the Properties group, typing a new name using the same rules you applied when assigning range names, and then pressing Enter.

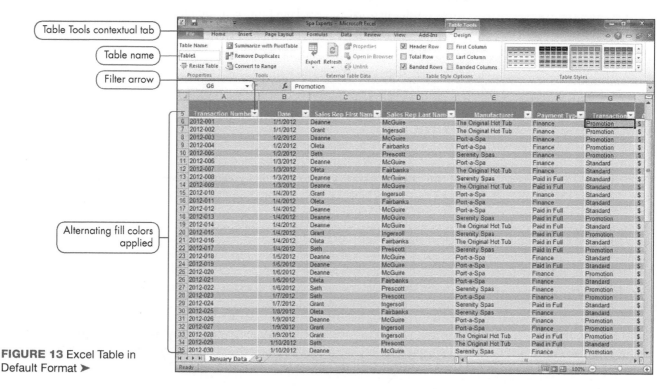

FIGURE 13 Excel Table in Default Format ➤

If you do not have existing data, you can create a table structure, and then add data to it later. Select an empty range, and then follow the above steps to create the range for the table. The default table style is Table Style Medium 2, and the default column headings are Column1, Column2, and so on. Click the column heading and type a descriptive label to replace the temporary heading. Excel applies table formatting to the empty rows. You are then ready to add data for each row in the empty table.

> **TIP** Converting a Table to a Range
>
> Tables provide an abundance of advantages to regular ranges. You might want to convert a table back to a range of data to accomplish other tasks. To convert a table back to a range, click within the table range, click the Table Tools Design tab, click Convert to Range in the Tools group, and then click Yes in the message box asking, *Do you want to convert the table to a normal range?*

## Add, Edit, and Delete Records

After you create a table, you will need to maintain it, such as by adding new records. For example, you might need to add a new client or employee record, or add a new item to an inventory table or transaction table. To add a record to your table, do the following:

1. Click a cell in the record below where you want the new record inserted. If you want to add a new record below the last record, click the row containing the last record.
2. Click the Home tab, and then click the Insert arrow in the Cells group.
3. Select Insert Table Rows Above to insert a row above the current row, or select Insert Table Row Below if the current row is the last one and you want a row below it.

Sometimes, you need to change data for a record. For example, when a client moves, you need to change the client's address and phone number. You edit data in a table the same way you edit data in a regular worksheet cell.

Finally, you can delete records. For example, if you maintain an inventory of artwork in your house and sell a piece of art, delete that record from the table. To delete a record from the table:

1. Click a cell in the record that you want to delete.
2. Click the Home tab, and then click the Delete arrow in the Cells group.
3. Select Delete Table Rows.

## Add and Delete Fields

Even if you carefully plan the fields for a table, you might decide to add new fields. For example, you might want to add a field for the customer names to the Spa Experts transaction table. To insert a field:

1. Click in any data cell (but not the cell containing the field name) in a field that will be to the right of the new field. For example, to insert a new field between the fields in columns A and B, click any cell in column B.
2. Click the Home tab, and then click the Insert arrow in the Cells group.
3. Select Insert Table Columns to the Left.

You can also delete a field if you no longer need any data for that particular field. Although deleting records and fields is easy, you must make sure not to delete data erroneously. If you accidentally delete data, click Undo immediately. To delete a field, do the following:

1. Click a cell in the field that you want to delete.
2. Click the Delete arrow in the Cells group on the Home tab.
3. Select Delete Table Columns.

## Remove Duplicate Rows

You might accidentally enter duplicate records in a table, which can give false results when totaling or performing other calculations on the dataset. For a small table, you might be able to detect duplicate records by scanning the data. For large tables, it is more difficult to identify duplicate records by simply scanning the table with the eye. To remove duplicate records, do the following:

1. Click within the table, and then click the Design tab.
2. Click Remove Duplicates in the Tools group to display the Remove Duplicates dialog box (see Figure 14).
3. Click Select All to set the criteria to find a duplicate for every field in the record, and then click OK. If you select individual columns, Excel looks for duplicates in that one column only, and deletes all but one record that contains that data. For example, if you delete duplicate records where the manufacturer is Serenity Spas, only one transaction would remain. The other customers' transactions that contain Serenity Spas would be deleted. Excel will display a message box informing you how many duplicate rows it removed.

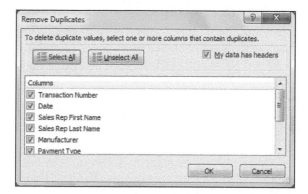

**FIGURE 14** Remove
Duplicates Dialog Box ➤

# Applying a Table Style

Formatting tables can make them more attractive and easier to read, and can emphasize data. The Design tab provides a variety of formatting options for tables. Excel applies a table style when you create a table. *Table styles* control the fill color of the header row (the row containing field names) and rows of records. In addition, table styles specify bold and border lines. You can change the table style to a color scheme that complements your organization's color scheme or to emphasize data in the table. Click the More button to see the Table Styles gallery (see Figure 15). To see how a table style will format your table using Live Preview, position the pointer over a style in the Table Styles gallery. After you identify a style you want, click it to apply it to the table.

A **table style** controls the fill color of the header row, columns, and records in a table.

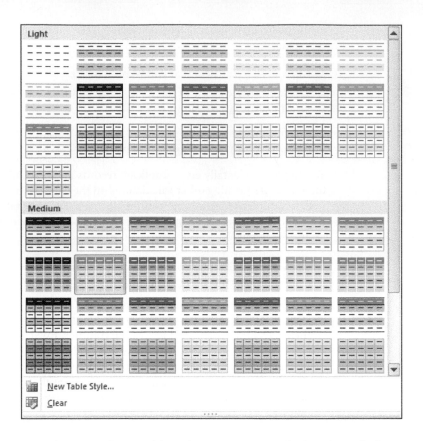

**FIGURE 15** Table Styles Gallery ➤

After you select a table style, you can control what the style formats. The Table Style Options group contains check boxes to select specific format actions in a table. Table 2 lists the options and the effect of each check box. Whatever formatting and formatting effects you choose to use, avoid overformatting the table. It is not good to apply so many formatting effects that the message you want to present with the data is obscured or lost.

| TABLE 2 Table Style Options | |
|---|---|
| **Check Box** | **Action** |
| **Header Row** | Displays the header row (field names) when checked; removes field names when not checked. Header Row formatting takes priority over column formats. |
| **Total Row** | Displays a total row when selected. Total Row formatting takes priority over column formats. |
| **First Column** | Applies a different format to the first column so that the row headings stand out. First Column formatting takes priority over Banded Rows formatting. |
| **Last Column** | Applies a different format to the last column so that the last column of data stands out; effective for aggregated data, such as grand totals, per row. Last Column formatting takes priority over Banded Rows formatting. |
| **Banded Rows** | Displays alternate fill colors for even and odd rows to help distinguish records. |
| **Banded Columns** | Displays alternate fill colors for even and odd columns to help distinguish fields. |

## 2 Excel Tables

Now that you understand Excel tables, you need to convert the January transactions data from basic worksheet data to a table. As you review the table, you will adjust its structure by deleting an unnecessary field and adding two missing fields. Then, you will focus on the transaction records by adding a missing record and removing a duplicate record. Finally, you will enhance the table appearance by selecting a table style.

**Skills covered:** Create a Table • Delete and Add Fields • Add a Record • Remove Duplicate Rows • Apply a Table Style

### STEP 1 ▶ CREATE A TABLE

Although the Spa Experts' January transaction data are organized in an Excel worksheet, you know that you will have additional functionality if you convert the range to a table. Refer to Figure 16 as you complete Step 1.

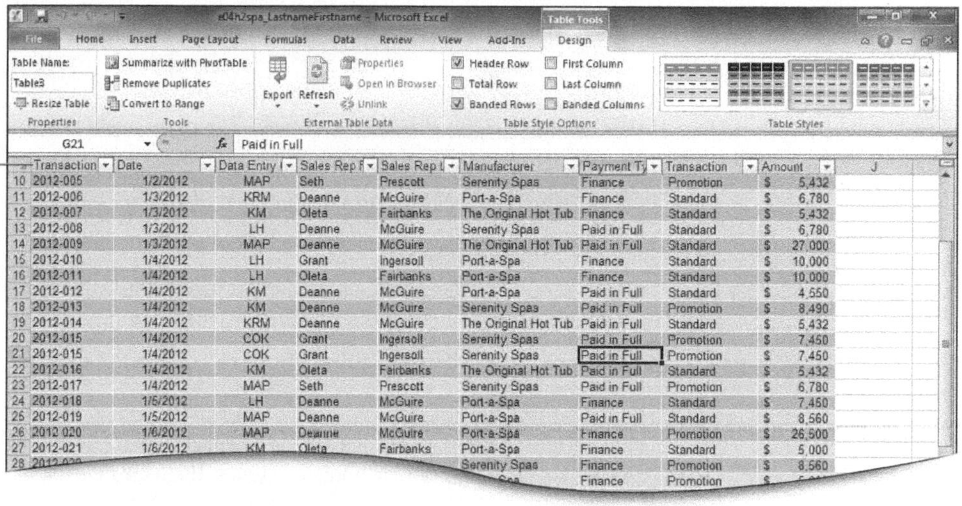

**FIGURE 16** Range Converted to a Table ➤

> Table column headings replace lettered column headings

a. Open *e04h1spa_LastnameFirstname* if you closed it at the end of Hands-On Exercise 1, and then save it as **e04h2spa_LastnameFirstname**, changing *h1* to *h2*.

b. Click **Normal** on the status bar, and then click the **Insert tab**.

c. Click in any cell within the transactional data. Click **Table** in the Tables group.

The Create Table dialog box opens. The Where is the data for your table? box displays =$A$5:$I$75. You need to keep the *My table has headers* check box selected so that the headings on the fifth row become the field names for the table.

d. Click **OK**, and then click **cell A5**.

Excel creates a table from the specified range and displays the Table Tools Design tab, filter arrows, and alternating fill colors for every other record. The columns widen to fit the field names, although the wrap text option is still applied to those cells.

e. Set **12.00 column widths** to these fields: Transaction Number, Data Entry Operator, Sales Rep First Name, Sales Rep Last Name, and Payment Type.

f. Unfreeze the panes, and then scroll through the table. Save the workbook.

With a regular range of data, column headings scroll off the top of the screen if you don't freeze panes. When you scroll within a table, the table column headings remain onscreen by moving up to where the Excel column (letter) headings usually display (see Figure 16).

DELETE AND ADD FIELDS

The original range included the Data Entry Operator's initials. You decide that you no longer need this column, so you will delete it. In addition, you want to add a field to display down payment amounts in the future. Refer to Figure 17 as you complete Step 2.

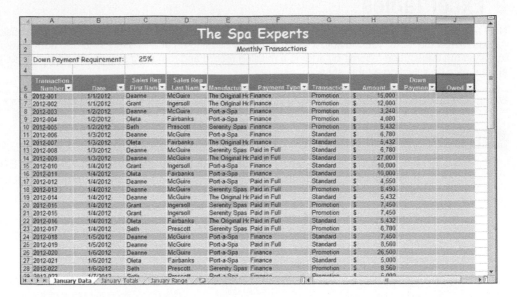

**FIGURE 17** Field Name Changes ➤

a. Click **cell C6** or any cell containing a value in the Data Entry Operator column.

You need to make a cell active in the field that you want to remove.

b. Click the **Home tab**, click the **Delete arrow** in the Cells group, and then select **Delete Table Columns**.

Excel deletes the Data Entry Operator column. Notice that the 25% remains in cell C3.

> **TROUBLESHOOTING:** If the 25% is deleted in cell C3, you probably selected Delete Sheet Columns instead of Delete Table Columns. Undo the deletion, and then repeat step b.

c. Click **cell I5**, the first blank cell on the right side of the field names.

d. Type **Down Payment** and press **Ctrl+Enter**.

Excel extends the table formatting to column I automatically. A filter arrow appears for the newly created field name, and alternating fill colors appear in the rows below the field name.

e. Click **Wrap Text** in the Alignment group.

f. Click **cell J5**, type **Owed**, and then press **Ctrl+Enter** to keep cell J5 active. Click **Center** in the Alignment group. Save the workbook.

ADD A RECORD

As you review the January transaction table, you notice that transaction 2012-030 is missing. After finding the paper invoice, you are ready to add a record with the missing transaction data. Refer to Figure 18 as you complete Step 3.

Datasets and Tables

242

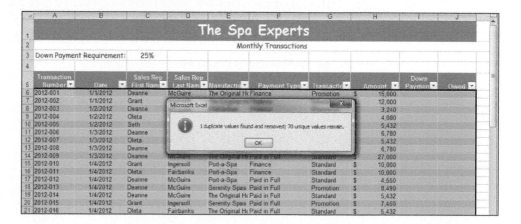

| | Transaction ▼ | Date ▼ | Sales Rep F ▼ | Sales Rep L ▼ | Manufactur ▼ | Payment Type ▼ | Transaction ▼ | Amount ▼ | Down Paym ▼ | Owed ▼ |
|---|---|---|---|---|---|---|---|---|---|---|
| 7 | 2012-002 | 1/1/2012 | Grant | Ingersoll | The Original Hc | Finance | Promotion | $ 12,000 | | |
| 8 | 2012-003 | 1/2/2012 | Deanne | McGuire | Port-a-Spa | Finance | Promotion | $ 3,240 | | |
| 9 | 2012-004 | 1/2/2012 | Oleta | Fairbanks | Port-a-Spa | Finance | Promotion | $ 4,080 | | |
| 10 | 2012-005 | 1/2/2012 | Seth | Prescott | Serenity Spas | Finance | Promotion | $ 5,432 | | |
| 11 | 2012-006 | 1/3/2012 | Deanne | McGuire | Port-a-Spa | Finance | Standard | $ 6,780 | | |
| 12 | 2012-007 | 1/3/2012 | Oleta | Fairbanks | The Original Hc | Finance | Standard | $ 5,432 | | |
| 13 | 2012-008 | 1/3/2012 | Deanne | McGuire | Serenity Spas | Paid in Full | Standard | $ 6,780 | | |
| 14 | 2012-009 | 1/3/2012 | Deanne | McGuire | The Original Hc | Paid in Full | Standard | $ 27,000 | | |
| 15 | 2012-010 | 1/4/2012 | Grant | Ingersoll | Port-a-Spa | Finance | Standard | $ 10,000 | | |
| 16 | 2012-011 | 1/4/2012 | Oleta | Fairbanks | Port-a-Spa | Finance | Standard | $ 10,000 | | |
| 17 | 2012-012 | 1/4/2012 | Deanne | McGuire | Port-a-Spa | Paid in Full | Standard | $ 4,550 | | |
| 18 | 2012-013 | 1/4/2012 | Deanne | McGuire | Serenity Spas | Paid in Full | Promotion | $ 8,490 | | |
| 19 | 2012-014 | 1/4/2012 | Deanne | McGuire | The Original Hc | Paid in Full | Standard | $ 5,432 | | |
| 20 | 2012-015 | 1/4/2012 | Grant | Ingersoll | Serenity Spas | Paid in Full | Promotion | $ 7,450 | | |
| 21 | 2012-015 | 1/4/2012 | Grant | Ingersoll | Serenity Spas | Paid in Full | Promotion | $ 7,450 | | |
| 22 | 2012-016 | 1/4/2012 | Oleta | Fairbanks | The Original Hc | Paid in Full | Standard | $ 5,432 | | |
| 23 | 2012-017 | 1/4/2012 | Seth | Prescott | Serenity Spas | Paid in Full | Promotion | $ 6,780 | | |
| 24 | 2012-018 | 1/5/2012 | Deanne | McGuire | Port-a-Spa | Finance | Standard | $ 7,450 | | |
| 25 | 2012-019 | 1/5/2012 | Deanne | McGuire | Port-a-Spa | Paid in Full | Standard | $ 8,560 | | |
| 26 | 2012-020 | 1/6/2012 | Deanne | McGuire | Port-a-Spa | Finance | Promotion | $ 26,500 | | |
| 27 | 2012-021 | 1/6/2012 | Oleta | Fairbanks | Port-a-Spa | Finance | Standard | $ 5,000 | | |
| 28 | 2012-022 | 1/6/2012 | Seth | Prescott | Serenity Spas | Finance | Promotion | $ 8,560 | | |
| 29 | 2012-023 | 1/7/2012 | Seth | Prescott | Port-a-Spa | Finance | Promotion | $ 5,000 | | |
| 30 | 2012-024 | 1/7/2012 | Grant | Ingersoll | Serenity Spas | Paid in Full | Standard | $ 5,400 | | |
| 31 | 2012-025 | 1/8/2012 | Oleta | Fairbanks | Serenity Spas | Finance | Standard | $ 3,240 | | |
| 32 | 2012-026 | 1/9/2012 | Deanne | McGuire | Port-a-Spa | Finance | Promotion | $ 7,400 | | |
| 33 | 2012-027 | 1/9/2012 | Grant | Ingersoll | Port-a-Spa | Finance | Promotion | $ 22,000 | | |
| 34 | 2012-028 | 1/9/2012 | Grant | Ingersoll | The Original Hc | Paid in Full | Promotion | $ 3,240 | | |
| 35 | 2012-029 | 1/10/2012 | Seth | Prescott | The Original Hc | Paid in Full | Standard | $ 7,690 | | |
| 36 | 2012-030 | 1/10/2012 | Deanne | McGuire | Serenity Spas | Finance | Promotion | $ 6,000 | | |
| 37 | 2012-031 | 1/11/2012 | Deanne | McGuire | The Original Hc | Finance | Promotion | $ 7,500 | | |
| 38 | 2012-032 | 1/11/2012 | Oleta | Fairbanks | Port-a-Spa | Finance | Promotion | $ 7,500 | | |

**Duplicate rows** (rows 20–21)

**Record added** (rows 35–36)

**FIGURE 18** Missing Record Added ➤

January Data / January Totals / January Range

a. Click **cell A36** or any cell within the table range on row 36.

You need to make a cell active on the row in which you want to insert the new table row.

b. Click the **Home tab**, click the **Insert arrow** in the Cells group, and then select **Insert Table Rows Above**.

Excel inserts a new table row on row 36. The rest of the records move down by one row.

c. Enter the following data in the respective fields on the newly created row. AutoComplete will help you enter the names, manufacturer, payment type, and transaction text. Then save the workbook.

- Transaction Number: **2012-030**
- Date: **1/10/2012**
- Sales Rep First Name: **Deanne**
- Sales Rep Last Name: **McGuire**

- Manufacturer: **Serenity Spas**
- Payment Type: **Finance**
- Transaction: **Promotion**
- Amount: **6000**

**STEP 4** ▶ **REMOVE DUPLICATE ROWS**

As you continue checking the transaction records, you think the table contains some duplicate records. To avoid having to look at the entire table row-by-row, you want to have Excel find and remove the duplicate rows for you. Refer to Figure 19 as you complete Step 4.

| | A | B | C | D | E | F | G | H | I | J |
|---|---|---|---|---|---|---|---|---|---|---|
| 1 | | | | **The Spa Experts** | | | | | | |
| 2 | | | | Monthly Transactions | | | | | | |
| 3 | Down Payment Requirement: | 25% | | | | | | | | |
| 4 | | | | | | | | | | |
| 5 | Transaction Number | Date | Sales Rep First Name | Sales Rep Last Name | Manufactu | Payment Type | Transactio | Amount | Down Payment | Owed |
| 6 | 2012-001 | 1/1/2012 | Deanne | McGuire | The Original Hc | Finance | Promotion | $ 15,000 | | |
| 7 | 2012-002 | 1/1/2012 | Grant | | | | | 12,000 | | |
| 8 | 2012-003 | 1/2/2012 | Deanne | | | | | 3,240 | | |
| 9 | 2012-004 | 1/2/2012 | Oleta | | | | | 4,080 | | |
| 10 | 2012-005 | 1/2/2012 | Seth | | | | | 5,432 | | |
| 11 | 2012-006 | 1/3/2012 | Deanne | | | | | 6,780 | | |
| 12 | 2012-007 | 1/3/2012 | Oleta | | | | | 5,432 | | |
| 13 | 2012-008 | 1/3/2012 | Deanne | | | | | 6,780 | | |
| 14 | 2012-009 | 1/3/2012 | | McGuire | The Original Hc | Paid in Full | Standard | 27,000 | | |
| 15 | 2012-010 | 1/4/2012 | Grant | Ingersoll | Port-a-Spa | Finance | Standard | $ 10,000 | | |
| 16 | 2012-011 | 1/4/2012 | Oleta | Fairbanks | Port-a-Spa | Finance | Standard | $ 10,000 | | |
| 17 | 2012-012 | 1/4/2012 | Deanne | McGuire | Port-a-Spa | Paid in Full | Standard | $ 4,550 | | |
| 18 | 2012-013 | 1/4/2012 | Deanne | McGuire | Serenity Spas | Paid in Full | Promotion | $ 8,490 | | |
| 19 | 2012-014 | 1/4/2012 | Deanne | McGuire | The Original Hc | Paid in Full | Standard | $ 5,432 | | |
| 20 | 2012-015 | 1/4/2012 | Grant | Ingersoll | Serenity Spas | Paid in Full | Promotion | $ 7,450 | | |
| 21 | 2012-016 | 1/4/2012 | Oleta | Fairbanks | The Original Hc | Paid in Full | Standard | $ 5,432 | | |

Microsoft Excel

1 duplicate values found and removed; 70 unique values remain.

OK

**FIGURE 19** Duplicate Record Removed ➤

a. Scroll to see rows 20 and 21. Click the **Design tab**.

  The records on rows 20 and 21 are identical. You need to remove one row.

b. Click **Remove Duplicates** in the Tools group.

  The Remove Duplicates dialog box opens.

c. Click **Select All**, if necessary, to select all table columns.

d. Click the **My data has headers check box**, if necessary, and then click **OK**.

  Excel displays a message box indicating the number of duplicate records found and removed. The message box also specifies how many unique records remain.

e. Click **OK** in the message box. Save the workbook.

STEP 5 **APPLY A TABLE STYLE**

Now that you have modified fields and records, you want to apply a table style to format the table. Refer to Figure 20 as you complete Step 5.

**FIGURE 20** Table Style Applied ➤

a. Click the **More button** in the Table Styles group to display the Table Styles gallery.

b. Position the mouse pointer over the fourth style on the second row in the *Light* section.

  Live Preview shows the table with the Table Style Light 10 style but does not apply it.

c. Click **Table Style Medium 6**, the sixth style on the first row in the *Medium* section.

  Excel formats the table with the Table Style Medium 6 format.

d. Click in the **Name Box**, type **A1**, and press **Enter** to go to **cell A1**, the title. Click the **Home tab**, click the **Fill Color arrow** in the Font group, and then click **Aqua, Accent 5**.

  You applied a fill color for the title to match the fill color of the field names.

e. Widen column E to **18.14**.

f. Save the workbook. Keep the workbook onscreen if you plan to continue with Hands-On Exercise 3. If not, close the workbook and exit Excel.

# Table Manipulation and Aggregation

When you convert data to a table, you have a variety of options to manipulate that data, in addition to managing fields and records and applying predefined table styles. You can arrange data in different sequences, display only particular records instead of the entire dataset, and aggregate data. Although Excel provides many advantages for using tables over a range, you might need to convert a table back to a range to perform a few tasks that are not available for tables.

> You can add more meaning to tables by aggregating data.

In this section, you will learn how to sort records by text, numbers, and dates in a table. In addition, you will learn how to filter data based on conditions you set. You will create structured formulas to perform calculations, and add a total row.

## Sorting Data

Table data are easier to understand and work with if you organize the data. In Figure 1, the data are arranged by transaction number. You might want to organize the table by showing sales by sales associate, or to display all financed spas together, followed by all paid-in-full spas. *Sorting* arranges records by the value of one or more fields within a table.

> **Sorting** arranges records in a table by the value in field(s) within a table.

### Sort One Column

You can sort data by one or more columns. To sort by only one column, you can use any of the following methods for either a range of data or a table:

- Click Sort & Filter in the Editing group on the Home tab.
- Click Sort A to Z, Sort Z to A, or Sort in the Sort & Filter group on the Data tab.
- Right-click the field to sort, point to Sort from the shortcut menu, and select the type of sort you want.

When you format data as a table, the field names appear in a header row, which contains sort and filter arrows. Click the arrow for the column you want to sort and select the type of sort you want. Table 3 lists sort options by data type.

| TABLE 3 | Sort Options | |
|---|---|---|
| **Data Type** | **Options** | **Explanation** |
| **Text** | Sort A to Z | Arranges data in alphabetical order. |
| | Sort Z to A | Arranges data in reverse alphabetical order. |
| **Dates** | Sort Oldest to Newest | Displays data in chronological order, from oldest to newest. |
| | Sort Newest to Oldest | Displays data in reverse chronological order, from newest to oldest. |
| **Values** | Sort Smallest to Largest | Arranges values from the smallest value to the largest value. |
| | Sort Largest to Smallest | Arranges values from the largest value to the smallest value. |

### Use the Sort Dialog Box to Sort Multiple Columns

At times sorting by only one field yields several records that have the same information—for example the same last name or the same manufacturer. Sales representative names and manufacturer names appear several times. A single sort field does not uniquely identify a record. You might need both last name and first name to identify an individual. Using multiple level sorts allows differentiation among records with the same data in the first (primary) sort level. For example, you might want to sort by sales rep names, manufacturer, and then by price. Excel enables you to sort data on 64 different levels. To perform a multiple level sort:

1. Click in any cell in the table.
2. Click Sort in the Sort & Filter group on the Data tab to display the Sort dialog box.
3. Select the primary sort level by clicking the *Sort by* arrow and selecting the column to sort by, and then clicking the Order arrow and selecting the sort order from the list.
4. Click Add Level, select the second sort level by clicking the *Then by* arrow and selecting the column to sort by, clicking the Order arrow, and then selecting the sort order from the list.
5. Continue to click Add Level and add sort levels until you have entered all sort levels. See Figure 21. Click OK.

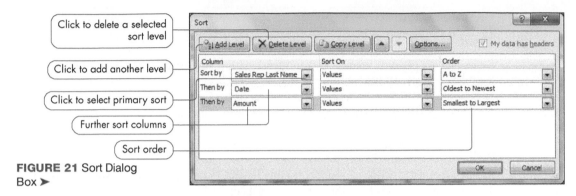

**FIGURE 21** Sort Dialog Box ➤

## Create a Custom Sort

Excel arranges data in defined sequences, such as alphabetical order. For example, weekdays are sorted alphabetically: Friday, Monday, Saturday, Sunday, Thursday, Tuesday, and Wednesday. However, you might want to create a custom sort sequence. For example, you can create a custom sort to arrange weekdays in order from Sunday to Saturday.

To create a custom sort sequence, click Sort in the Sort & Filter group on the Data tab. Click the Order arrow, and then select Custom List to display the Custom Lists dialog box (see Figure 22). Select an existing sort sequence in the *Custom lists* box, or select NEW LIST, click Add, and then type the entries in the desired sort sequence in the *List entries* box, pressing Enter between entries. Click Add, and then click OK.

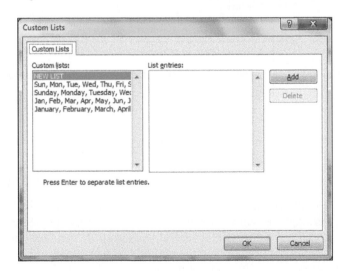

**FIGURE 22** Custom Lists Dialog Box ➤

# Filtering Data

**Filtering** is the process of displaying only records that meet specific conditions.

You might want to show only particular records. *Filtering* is the process of specifying conditions to display only those records that meet certain conditions. For example, you might want to filter the data to show transactions for only Oleta Fairbanks. To filter records by a particular field, click the column's filter arrow. The list displays each unique label, value, or date contained in the column. Deselect the (Select All) check box, and then click the check box for each value you want to include in the filtered results.

Often you will need to apply more than one filter to display the needed records. You can filter more than one column. Each additional filter is based on the current filtered data and further reduces a data subset. To apply multiple filters, click each column's filter arrow, and select the values to include in the filtered data results.

> **TIP** Copying Before Filtering Data
>
> Often, you need to show different filters applied to the same dataset. You can copy the data to another worksheet, and then filter the copied data to preserve the original dataset.

## Apply Text Filters

When you apply a filter to a text column, the filter menu displays each unique text item. You can select one or more text items from the list. For example, select Fairbanks to show only records for this salesperson. To display records for both Fairbanks and Prescott, deselect the (Select All) check mark, and then click the Fairbanks and Prescott check boxes. You can also select Text Filters to see a submenu of additional options, such as *Begins With*, to select all records where the name begins with the letter G, for example.

Figure 23 shows the Last Name filter menu with two names selected. Excel displays records for these two reps only. The records for the other sales reps are hidden but not deleted. The filter arrow displays a filter icon, indicating which column is filtered. Excel displays the row numbers in blue, indicating that you applied a filter. The missing row numbers indicate hidden rows of data. When you remove the filter, all the records display again.

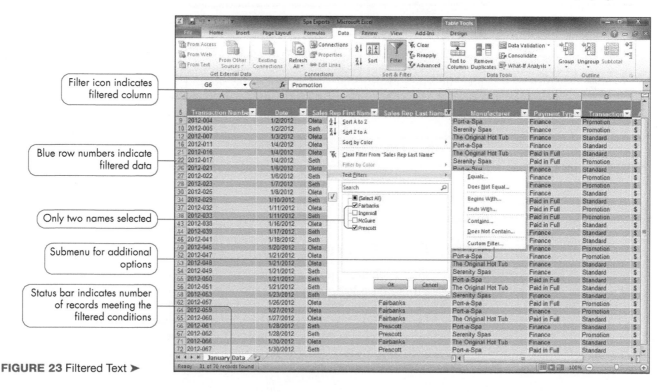

**FIGURE 23** Filtered Text ➤

Callouts on figure:
- Filter icon indicates filtered column
- Blue row numbers indicate filtered data
- Only two names selected
- Submenu for additional options
- Status bar indicates number of records meeting the filtered conditions

Table Manipulation and Aggregation • Excel 2010

247

## TIP Filter Arrows

Before you filter a table, the Filter command in the Sort & Filter group on the Data tab is orange, indicating the filter arrows are displayed. Click Filter to toggle the filter arrows on and off. To filter a range of data instead of a table, activate the filter arrows by clicking Filter.

## Apply Number Filters

When you filter a column of numbers, you can select specific numbers. You might want to filter numbers by a range, such as numbers greater than $5,000 or numbers between $4,000 and $5,000. The submenu enables you to set a variety of number filters. In Figure 24, the amounts are filtered to show only those that are above the average amount. In this situation, Excel calculates the average amount as $9,577. Only records above that amount display.

If the field contains a large number of unique entries, you can click in the Search box, and then type a value, text label, or date. Doing so narrows the visible list so that you do not have to scroll through the entire list. For example, if you enter $7, the list will display only values that start with $7.

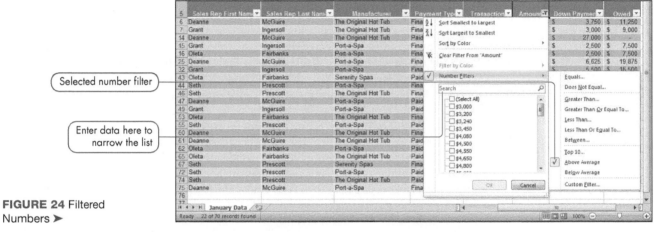

**FIGURE 24** Filtered Numbers ➤

The Top 10 option enables you to specify the top records. Although the option name is Top 10, you can specify the number or percentage of records to display. For example, you can filter the list to display only the top five or the bottom 7%. Figure 25 shows the Top 10 AutoFilter dialog box. Click the first arrow to select either Top or Bottom, click the spin arrows to indicate a value, and then click the last arrow to select either Items or Percent.

**FIGURE 25** Top 10 AutoFilter Dialog Box ➤

## Apply Date Filters

When you filter a column of dates, you can select specific dates or a date range, such as dates after 1/15/2012 or dates between 1/1/2012 and 1/7/2012. The submenu enables you to set a variety of date filters. In Figure 26, the dates are filtered to show only those that are after 1/15/2012. For more specific date options, point to Date Filters, point to All Dates in the Period, and then select a period, such as Quarter 2 or October.

Datasets and Tables

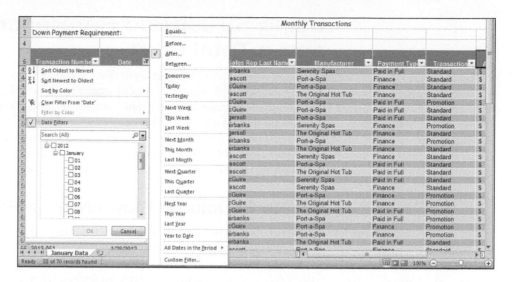

FIGURE 26 Filtered Dates ➤

## Apply a Custom Filter

If you select options such as *Greater Than* or *Before*, Excel displays the Custom AutoFilter dialog box (see Figure 27). You can also select Custom Filter from the menu to display this dialog box, which is designed for more complex filtering requirements.

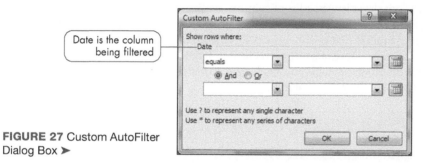

Date is the column being filtered

FIGURE 27 Custom AutoFilter Dialog Box ➤

The dialog box indicates the column being filtered, such as Date. To set the filters, click the arrows to select the comparison type, such as equals or contains. Click the arrow on the right to select a specific text, value, or date entry, or type the data yourself. For ranges of dates or values, click And, and then specify the comparison operator and value or date for the next condition row. For text, click Or. For example, if you want both Kansas and Kentucky, you must select Or because one data entry contains either Kansas or Kentucky but not both at the same time.

You can use wildcards to represent characters. For example, to select all states starting with New, type New * in the second box. The asterisk (*) represents any number of characters. If you want a wildcard for only a single character, type the question mark (?).

## Clear Filters

After reviewing the filtered data, you can remove the filters to see the entire dataset again. To remove only one filter and keep the other filters, click the filter arrow for the column from which you wish to clear the filter, and then select Clear Filter From. Excel then removes that column's filter and displays records previously hidden by that filter. To remove all filters, click Filter in the Sort & Filter group on the Data tab, or click Sort & Filter in the Editing group on the Home tab and select Filter. Excel clears all filters and displays all records in the dataset.

# Using Structured References and a Total Row

Excel aids you in quantitative analysis. Your value to an organization increases with your ability to create sophisticated formulas, aggregate data in a meaningful way, and interpret those results. Although you can create complex formulas that you understand, you should strive to create formulas that other people can understand. Creating easy-to-read formulas helps you present self-documenting formulas that require less explanation on your part. When you create formulas for tables, you can use built-in functionality (such as structured references and a total row) that assists you in building understandable formulas.

## Create Structured References in Formulas

Your experience in building formulas involves using cell references, such as =SUM(B1:B15) or =H6*$B$3, or range names, such as grades in =VLOOKUP(E5,grades,2). You can use cell references and range names in formulas to perform calculations in a table, as well as another type of reference for formulas in tables: structured references. A ***structured reference*** is a tag or use of a table element, such as a column heading, as a reference in a formula. Structured references in formulas clearly indicate what type of data is used in the calculations.

A structured reference requires brackets around column headings or field names, such as =[Amount]-[Down Payment]. The use of column headings without row references in a structured formula is called an *unqualified reference*. While creating a formula by typing, Formula AutoComplete displays a list of column headings after you type the equal sign and the opening bracket (see Figure 28). Type or double-click the name from the list, and then type the closing bracket. Excel displays a colored border around the column being referenced. When you enter a formula using structured references, Excel copies the formula down the rest of the column in the table automatically, compared to typing references in formulas and copying the formula down a column.

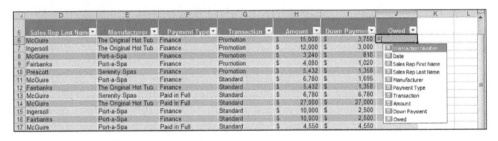

**FIGURE 28** Structured Reference Creation ➤

You can still use the semi-selection process to create a formula. If you use the pointing process to enter a formula in a table, Excel builds a formula like this: =[@Amount]-[@Down Payment], where the @ indicates the current row. If you use the semi-selection process to create a formula outside the table, the formula includes the table name and row as well, such as =Table1[@Amount]-Table1[@Down Payment]. Table1 is the name of the table, and Amount and Down Payment are column headings. This structured formula that includes references, such as table numbers, is called a *fully qualified reference*. When you build formulas *within* a table, you can use either unqualified or fully qualified structured references. If you need to use table data in a formula *outside* the table boundaries, you must use fully qualified structured references.

> **TIP** Complex Structured References
>
> You can create structured reference tags to other elements, such as headers and totals. The more you know how to incorporate structured references, the more powerful your tables are to you. Look up *structured references* in Help for detailed explanations and examples of more complex use of structured references.

A **structured reference** is a tag or use of a table element as a reference in a formula.

# Create a Total Row

Aggregating data provides more meaningful quantitative interpretation than individual values at times. For regular ranges of data, you use basic statistical functions, such as SUM, AVERAGE, MIN, and MAX, to provide meaning for a dataset. An Excel table provides the advantage of being able to display a total row automatically without creating the aggregate function yourself. A *total row* appears below the last row of records in an Excel table and enables you to display summary statistics, such as a sum of values displayed in a column. To display and use the total row:

> A **total row** appears as the last row of a table to display summary statistics, such as a sum.

1. Click the Design tab.
2. Click Total Row in the Table Style Options group. Excel displays the total row below the last record in the table. Excel displays *Total* in the first column of the total row. Excel either sums or counts data for the last column, depending on the type of data stored in that column. If the last column consists of values, Excel sums the values. If the last column is text, Excel counts the number of records.
3. Click a cell in the total row, and then click that cell's total row arrow and select the function results, such as Average, that you desire. To add a total to another column, click in the empty cell for that column in the total row, and then click the arrow to select the desired function. Select None to remove the function.

Figure 29 shows the active total row with totals applied to the Amount and Down Payment columns. A list of functions displays to change the function for the last column.

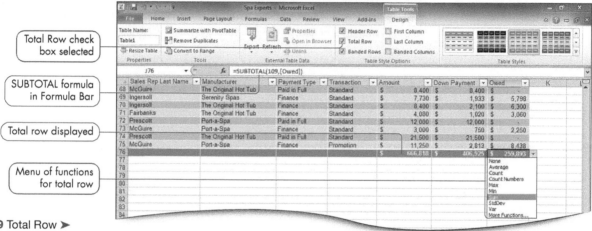

**FIGURE 29** Total Row ➤

=SUBTOTAL(function_num,ref1,...

> The **SUBTOTAL function** calculates an aggregate for values in a range or database.

The SUBTOTAL function calculates results on the total row. The **SUBTOTAL** *function* calculates an aggregate value, such as totals, for values in a range or database. The function for the total row looks like this: =SUBTOTAL(109,[Owed]). The function_num argument is a number that represents a function (see Table 4). The number 109 represents the SUM function. The ref1 argument indicates the range of values to calculate. In this case, [Owed] represents the Owed field. A benefit of the SUBTOTAL function is that it subtotals data for filtered records, so you have an accurate total for the visible records.

| TABLE 4 | SUBTOTAL Function Numbers | |
|---|---|---|
| Function | Database Number | Table Number |
| AVERAGE | 1 | 101 |
| COUNT | 2 | 102 |
| COUNTA | 3 | 103 |
| MAX | 4 | 104 |
| MIN | 5 | 105 |
| PRODUCT | 6 | 106 |
| STDEV | 7 | 107 |
| STDEVP | 8 | 108 |
| SUM | 9 | 109 |
| VAR | 10 | 110 |
| VARP | 11 | 111 |

**TIP** Filtering Data and Subtotals

If you filter the data and display the total row, the SUBTOTAL function's 109 argument ensures that only the displayed data are summed; data for hidden rows are not calculated in the aggregate function.

# HANDS-ON EXERCISES

## 3 Table Manipulation and Aggregation

You want to start analyzing the January transactions for Spa Experts by sorting and filtering data in a variety of ways to help you understand the transactions better. In addition, you need to calculate the required down payment amount and how much customers owe for their spas. Finally, you will convert the table back to a range.

**Skills covered:** Sort Individual Columns • Use the Sort Dialog Box • Apply Text Filters • Apply a Number Filter • Apply a Date Filter • Create Structured References • Add a Total Row • Convert a Table to a Range

---

### STEP 1 ▶ SORT INDIVIDUAL COLUMNS

First, you want to compare the number of transactions by sales rep, so you will sort the data by the Last Name field. After reviewing the transactions by sales reps, you want to see what manufacturer's spas are sold most often. Refer to Figure 30 as you complete Step 1.

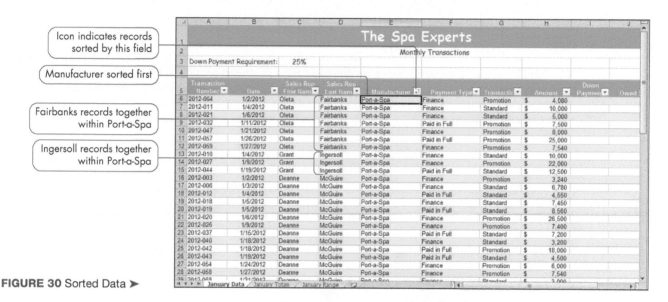

**FIGURE 30** Sorted Data ➤

a. Open *e04h2spa_LastnameFirstname* if you closed it at the end of Hands-On Exercise 2. Save the workbook with the new name **e04h3spa_LastnameFirstname**, changing *h2* to *h3*.

b. Click the **Sales Rep Last Name filter arrow**, and then select **Sort A to Z**.

Excel arranges the records in alphabetical order by last name. All transactions completed by Fairbanks display first. Within each sales rep, records appear in their original sequence by transaction number. Without actually counting the records, which sales rep appears to have the most sales? According to the sorted list, McGuire sold the most spas in January. The up arrow icon on the Last Name filter arrow indicates records are sorted in alphabetical order by that column.

> **TIP** Name Sorts
>
> Always check the table to determine how many levels of sorting you need to apply. If your table contains several people with the same last name but different first names, you would first sort by the Last Name field, and then sort by First Name field individually. All the people with the last name Fairbanks would be grouped together and then further sorted by first name, such as Amanda and then Bradley. To ensure that Excel sorts in the sequence you desire, use the Sort dialog box instead of sorting columns individually.

c. Click the **Manufacturer filter arrow**, and then select **Sort A to Z**.

Excel arranges the records in alphabetical order by manufacturer. Port-a-Spa displays first. Within the Port-a-Spa group, the records are further sorted by the previous sort: last name. Fairbanks appears before Ingersoll. The up arrow icon within the Manufacturer filter arrow indicates that records are sorted in alphabetical order by this column (see Figure 30).

d. Click the **Transaction Number filter arrow**, and then select **Sort A to Z**. Save the workbook.

Excel arranges the records back in their original sequence—by transaction number.

---

**STEP 2** ▶ **USE THE SORT DIALOG BOX**

You want to review the transactions by payment type (financed or paid in full). Within each payment type, you want to further compare the transaction type (promotion or standard). Finally, you want to compare costs within the sorted records by displaying the highest costs first. You will use the Sort dialog box to perform a three-level sort. Refer to Figure 31 as you complete Step 2.

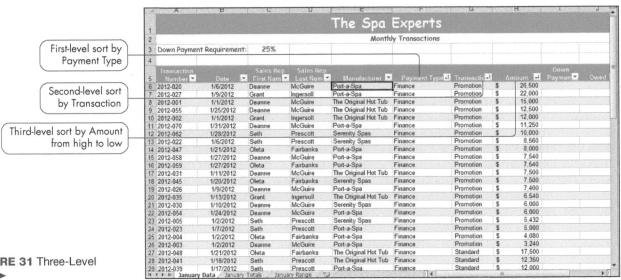

**FIGURE 31** Three-Level Sort ▶

a. Click inside the table. Click the **Data tab**.

Both the Data and Home tabs contain commands to open the Sort dialog box.

b. Click **Sort** in the Sort & Filter group.

The Sort dialog box opens. You start by specifying the column for the primary sort. In this case, you want to sort the records first by the Payment Type column.

c. Click the **Sort by arrow**, and then select **Payment Type**.

The default Sort On is Values, and the default Order is A to Z.

d. Click **Add Level**.

The Sort dialog box adds the *Then by* row, which adds a secondary sort.

e. Click the **Then by arrow**, and then select **Transaction**.

Excel will first sort the records by the Payment Type. Within each Payment Type, Excel will further sort records by Transaction.

f. Click **Add Level** to add another *Then by* row. Click the second **Then by arrow**, and then select **Amount**.

g. Click the **Order arrow** for the Amount sort, and then select **Largest to Smallest**.

Within the Payment Type and Transaction sorts, this will arrange the records with the largest amount first in descending order to the smallest amount.

h. Click **OK** and scroll through the records. Save the workbook.

Figure 31 shows the sorted records. Most customers finance their spas instead of paying for their spas in full. For the financed spas, about half were promotional sales and half were standard sales. For those spas paid in full, a majority of the transactions were standard sales, indicating that people with money don't necessarily wait for a promotional sale to buy their spas.

## STEP 3 ▶ APPLY TEXT FILTERS

Now that you know McGuire had the most transactions, you want to focus on her sales for January. In particular, you want to filter the table to show only her records. You notice that she sells more Port-a-Spas and The Original Hot Tub than the Serenity Spas, so you will filter out the Serenity Spa sales. Refer to Figure 32 as you complete Step 3.

| Transaction Number | Date | Sales Rep First Name | Sales Rep Last Name | Manufacturer | Payment Type | Transaction | Amount | Down Payment | Owed |
|---|---|---|---|---|---|---|---|---|---|
| 2012-020 | 1/6/2012 | Deanne | McGuire | Port-a-Spa | Finance | Promotion | $ 26,500 | | |
| 2012-001 | 1/1/2012 | Deanne | McGuire | The Original Hot Tub | Finance | Promotion | $ 15,000 | | |
| 2012-055 | 1/25/2012 | Deanne | McGuire | The Original Hot Tub | Finance | Promotion | $ 12,500 | | |
| 2012-070 | 1/31/2012 | Deanne | McGuire | Port-a-Spa | Finance | Promotion | $ 11,250 | | |
| 2012-058 | 1/27/2012 | Deanne | McGuire | Port-a-Spa | Finance | Promotion | $ 7,540 | | |
| 2012-031 | 1/11/2012 | Deanne | McGuire | The Original Hot Tub | Finance | Promotion | $ 7,500 | | |
| 2012-026 | 1/9/2012 | Deanne | McGuire | Port-a-Spa | Finance | Promotion | $ 7,400 | | |
| 2012-054 | 1/24/2012 | Deanne | McGuire | Port-a-Spa | Finance | Promotion | $ 6,000 | | |
| 2012-003 | 1/2/2012 | Deanne | McGuire | Port-a-Spa | Finance | Promotion | $ 3,240 | | |
| 2012-018 | 1/5/2012 | Deanne | McGuire | Port-a-Spa | Finance | Standard | $ 7,450 | | |
| 2012-006 | 1/3/2012 | Deanne | McGuire | Port-a-Spa | Finance | Standard | $ 6,780 | | |
| 2012-040 | 1/18/2012 | Deanne | McGuire | Port-a-Spa | Finance | Standard | $ 3,200 | | |
| 2012-068 | 1/31/2012 | Deanne | McGuire | Port-a-Spa | Finance | Standard | $ 3,000 | | |
| 2012-056 | 1/26/2012 | Deanne | McGuire | The Original Hot Tub | Paid in Full | Promotion | $ 22,500 | | |
| 2012-042 | 1/18/2012 | Deanne | McGuire | Port-a-Spa | Paid in Full | Promotion | $ 18,000 | | |
| 2012-009 | 1/3/2012 | Deanne | McGuire | The Original Hot Tub | Paid in Full | Standard | $ 27,000 | | |
| 2012-019 | 1/5/2012 | Deanne | McGuire | Port-a-Spa | Paid in Full | Standard | $ 8,560 | | |
| 2012-063 | 1/28/2012 | Deanne | McGuire | The Original Hot Tub | Paid in Full | Standard | $ 8,400 | | |
| 2012-037 | 1/15/2012 | Deanne | McGuire | Port-a-Spa | Paid in Full | Standard | $ 7,200 | | |
| 2012-014 | 1/4/2012 | Deanne | McGuire | The Original Hot Tub | Paid in Full | Standard | $ 5,432 | | |
| 2012-012 | 1/4/2012 | Deanne | McGuire | Port-a-Spa | Paid in Full | Standard | $ 4,550 | | |
| 2012-043 | 1/19/2012 | Deanne | McGuire | Port-a-Spa | Paid in Full | Standard | $ 4,500 | | |

January Data / January Totals / January Range

Ready    22 of 70 records found

**FIGURE 32** McGuire Sales for Two Manufacturers ▶

a. Click the **Sales Rep Last Name filter arrow**.

The (Select All) check box is selected.

b. Click the **(Select All) check box** to deselect all last names.

c. Click the **McGuire check box**, and then click **OK**.

The status bar indicates that 27 out of 70 records meet the filtering condition. The Last Name filter arrow includes a funnel icon, indicating that this column is filtered.

d. Click the **Manufacturer filter arrow**.

e. Click the **Serenity Spas check box** to deselect this manufacturer, and then click **OK**. Save the workbook.

You filtered out the Serenity Spas brand that McGuire sold. The remaining 22 records show McGuire's sales for the Port-a-Spas and The Original Hot Tub brands sold. The Manufacturer filter arrow includes a funnel icon, indicating that this column is also filtered.

## STEP 4 ▶ APPLY A NUMBER FILTER

You now want to focus on the amount of sales for McGuire. In particular, you are interested in how much gross revenue she generated for spas that cost at least $10,000 or more. Refer to Figure 33 as you complete Step 4.

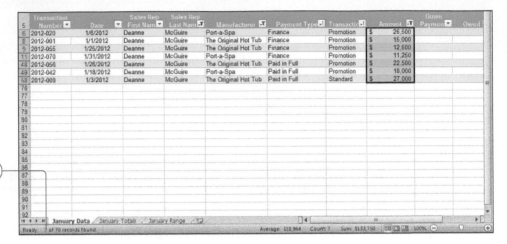

Number of filtered records

**FIGURE 33** Filtered to Amounts Greater Than or Equal To $10,000 ➤

a. Select the **range H6:H75** of the filtered list, and then view the status bar.

The average transaction amount is $10,159 with 22 transactions (i.e., 22 filtered records). McGuire's total January sales are $223,502. You will use this total to see how much of the $223,502 sales generated are for higher-priced models she sold.

b. Click the **Amount filter arrow**.

c. Point to **Number Filters**, and then select **Greater Than Or Equal To**.

The Custom AutoFilter dialog box opens. The default comparison is *is greater than or equal to*, although you could change it if needed.

d. Type **10000** in the box to the right of *is greater than or equal to*, and then click **OK**. Save the workbook.

When typing numbers, you can type raw numbers such as 10000 or formatted numbers such as $10,000. Out of the original 27 spas McGuire sold, she sold only 7 of the Port-a-Spas and The Original Hot Tub brands that cost $10,000 or more. Out of the $223,502 total sales for those two brands, McGuire sold $132,750 in the higher-priced models costing $10,000 or more.

> **TROUBLESHOOTING:** If no records display or if too many records display, you might have entered 100000 or 1000. Repeat steps b–d.

Datasets and Tables

APPLY A DATE FILTER

Finally, you want to study McGuire's sales records for the week of January 22. You will add a date filter to identify those sales records. Refer to Figure 34 as you complete Step 5.

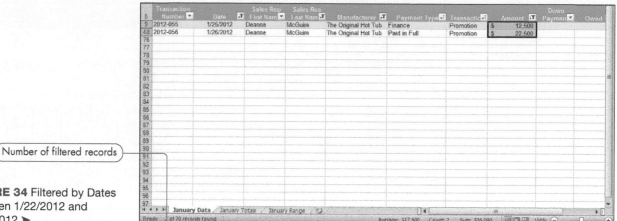

Number of filtered records

**FIGURE 34** Filtered by Dates Between 1/22/2012 and 1/28/2012 ➤

a. Click the **Date filter arrow**.

b. Point to **Date Filters**, and then select **Between**.

The Custom AutoFilter dialog box opens. The default comparisons are *is after or equal to* and *is before or equal to*, ready for you to enter the date specifications.

c. Type **1/22/2012** in the box on the right side of *is after or equal to*.

You specified the starting date of the range of dates to include. You will keep the *And* option selected.

d. Type **1/28/2012** in the box on the right side of *is before or equal to*. Click **OK**. Save the workbook.

McGuire had only two sales during that week, totaling $35,000.

---

**STEP 6** CREATE STRUCTURED REFERENCES

To continue reviewing the January transactions, you need to calculate the required down payment for customers who financed their spas. The required down payment is located above the table data so that you can change that value if needed later. In addition, you need to calculate how much customers owe on their spas if they did not pay in full. You will use structured formulas to perform these calculations. Refer to Figure 35 as you complete Step 6.

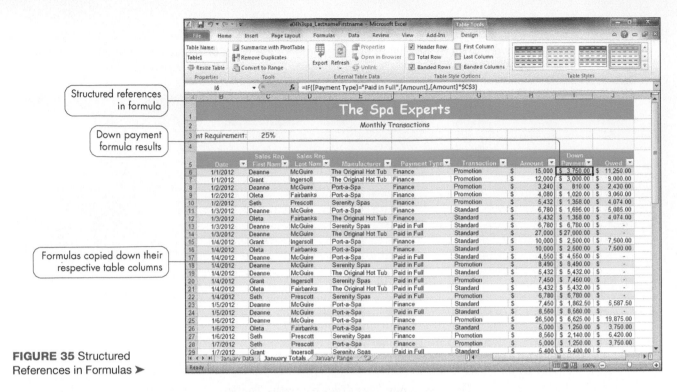

Structured references in formula

Down payment formula results

Formulas copied down their respective table columns

**FIGURE 35** Structured References in Formulas ➤

**a.** Click the **January Totals worksheet tab**.

To preserve the integrity of the sorting and filtering in case your instructor wants to verify your work, you will continue with an identical table on another worksheet.

**b.** Click in the **Name Box**, type **I6**, and then press **Enter** to go to **cell I6**. Click **Insert Function** on the Formula Bar to open the Insert Function dialog box, select **IF** in the **Select a function list**, and then click **OK**.

**c.** Type **[Payment Type]="Paid in Full"** in the **Logical_test box**.

The logical test evaluates whether a customer paid in full, indicated in the Payment Type column. Remember to type the brackets around the column heading.

**d.** Type **[Amount]** in the **Value_if_true box**.

If a customer pays in full, their down payment is the full amount.

**e.** Type **[Amount]*$C$3** in the **Value_if_false box**.

If a customer does not pay in full, they must pay a required down payment. You use [Amount] to refer to the Amount column in the table. You must enclose the column heading in brackets. The amount of the spa is multiplied by the absolute reference to C3, the cell containing the required down payment percentage. You make this cell reference absolute so that it does not change when Excel copies the formula down the Down Payment column. Figure 35 shows the formula in the formula bar.

**f.** Click **OK** to enter the formula (see Figure 35).

Because you are entering formulas in a table, Excel copies the formula down the column automatically. The first customer must finance $3,750 (25% of $15,000). The columns in the current worksheet have been formatted as Accounting Number Format for you.

> **TROUBLESHOOTING:** If the results seem incorrect, check your function. Errors will result if you do not enclose the field names in brackets, if you have misspelled a field name, if you omit the quotation marks around *Paid in Full*, and so on. Correct any errors.

Datasets and Tables

g. Click **cell J6.** Type the formula =[**Amount**]-[**Down Payment**] and press **Enter**. Save the workbook.

The formula calculates how much customers owe if they finance their hot tubs. Excel copies the formula down the column.

## STEP 7  ADD A TOTAL ROW

The table is almost complete, but you want to see the monthly totals for the Amount, Down Payment, and Owed columns. Instead of entering SUM functions yourself, you will add a total row. Refer to Figure 36 as you complete Step 7.

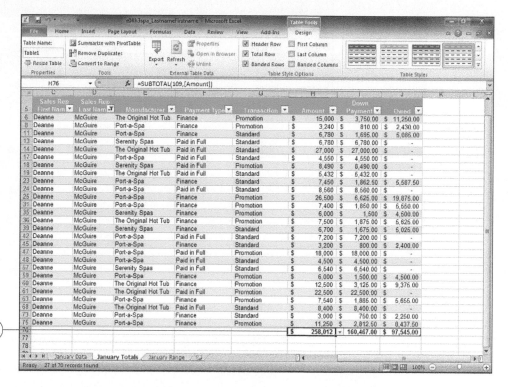

Totals added

**FIGURE 36** Totals for Filtered Table ➤

a. Click the **Design tab,** and then click **Total Row** in the Table Style Options group.

Excel displays the total row after the last record. It sums the last column of values automatically. The total amount customers owe is $259,893.00.

b. Click the **Down Payment cell** in row 76, click the **total arrow,** and then select **Sum.** Increase the Down Payment column width as needed.

You added a total to the Down Payment column. The total amount of down payment collected is $406,925.00. The formula appears as =SUBTOTAL(109,[Down Payment]) in the Formula Bar.

c. Click the **Amount cell** in row 76, click the **total arrow,** and then select **Sum.**

You added a total to the Amount column. The total amount of spa sales is $666,818. The formula appears as =SUBTOTAL(109,[Amount]) in the Formula Bar.

d. Filter by McGuire again. Save the workbook.

Notice that the total row values change to display the totals for only the filtered records.

Hands-On Exercises • Excel 2010

Your last task for now is to convert a copy of the table to a range again so that you can apply other formats. Refer to Figure 37 as you complete Step 8.

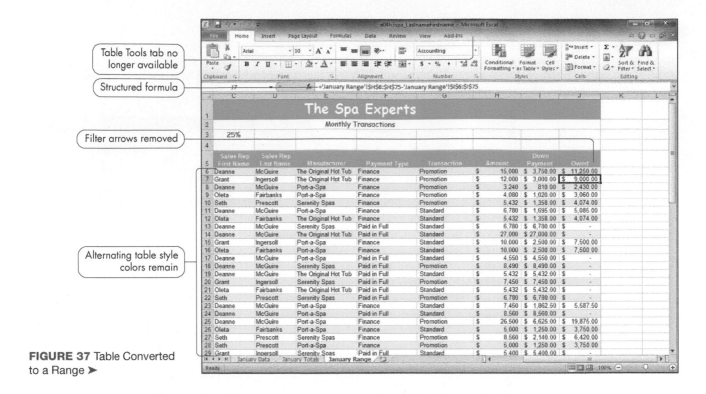

**FIGURE 37** Table Converted to a Range ▶

a. Click the **January Range worksheet tab**.

To preserve the integrity of the sorting and filtering in case your instructor wants to verify your work, you will continue with an identical table on another worksheet.

b. Click within the table, and then click the **Design tab**, if necessary.

c. Click **Convert to Range** in the Tools group.

Excel displays a message box asking if you want to convert the table to a range.

d. Click **Yes**.

Excel converts the table to a range. The filter arrows disappear, and the Table Tools no longer display. The range is still formatted using the table style you applied. The structured formula =[Amount]-[Down Payment] changes (see Figure 37).

e. Double-click the border between the column I and J headers to increase the width of column I so that the down payment total displays on the last row.

f. Save the workbook. Keep the workbook onscreen if you plan to continue with Hands-On Exercise 4. If not, close the workbook and exit Excel.

# Conditional Formatting

You use table styles, or a variety of font, alignment, and number formats on the Home tab, to format a worksheet. You can also apply special formatting to cells that contain particular values or text using conditional formatting. ***Conditional formatting*** applies special formatting to highlight or emphasize cells that meet specific conditions. For example, a sales manager might want to highlight cells containing the top 10 sales amounts, or a professor might want to highlight test scores that fall below the average. You can also apply conditional formatting to point out data for a specific date or duplicate values in a range.

In this section, you will learn about the five conditional formatting categories and how to apply conditional formatting to a range of values based on a condition you set.

## Applying Conditional Formatting

Conditional formatting helps you and your audience understand a dataset better because it adds a visual element to the cells. The term is called *conditional* because the formatting occurs when a condition is met. This is similar logic to the IF function you have used. Remember with an IF function, you create a logical test that is evaluated. If the logical or conditional test is true, the function produces one result. If the logical or conditional test is false, the function produces another result. With conditional formatting, if the condition is true, Excel formats the cell automatically based on that condition. If the condition is false, Excel does not format the cell. If you change a value in a conditionally formatted cell, Excel examines the new value to see if it should apply the conditional format. Table 5 lists and describes a number of different conditional formats that you can apply.

> Conditional formatting helps you and your audience understand a dataset better because it adds a visual element to the cells.

| TABLE 5   Conditional Formatting Options | |
|---|---|
| **Conditional Formatting** | **Description** |
| **Highlight Cells Rules** | Highlights cells with a fill color, font color, or border (such as Light Red Fill with Dark Red Text) if values are greater than, less than, between two values, equal to a value, or duplicate values; text that contains particular characters; or dates when a date meets a particular condition, such as *In the last 7 days*. |
| **Top/Bottom Rules** | Formats cells with values in the top 10 items, top 10%, bottom 10 items, bottom 10%, values, above average, or below average. You can change the exact values to format the top or bottom items or percentages, such as top 5 or bottom 15%. |
| **Data Bars** | Applies a gradient or solid fill bar in which the width of the bar represents the current cell's value compared to other cells' values. |
| **Color Scales** | Formats different cells with different colors, assigning one color to the lowest group of values and another color to the highest group of values, with gradient colors to other values. |
| **Icon Sets** | Inserts an icon from an icon palette in each cell to indicate values compared to each other. |

To apply a conditional format, select the cells for which you want to apply a conditional format, click the Home tab, click Conditional Formatting in the Styles group, and select the conditional formatting category you want to apply.

## Apply the Highlight Cells Rules

The Highlight Cells Rules category enables you to apply a highlight to cells that meet a condition, such as a value greater than a particular value. This option contains predefined combinations of fill colors, font colors, and/or borders. This category is useful because it helps you identify and format automatically values of interest. For example, a weather tracker who developed a worksheet containing the temperatures for each day of a month might want to apply a conditional format to cells that contain temperatures between 70 and 75 degrees. To apply this conditional formatting, she would select Highlight Cells Rules, and then select Between. In the Between dialog box (see Figure 38), the weather tracker would type 70 in the *Format cells that are BETWEEN* box and 75 in the *and* box, select the type of conditional formatting, such as *Light Red Fill with Dark Red Text*, and then click OK to apply the formats.

Figure 39 shows two columns of data that contain conditional formats. The Manufacturer column contains a conditional format to highlight text with a Light Red Fill with Dark Red Text for cells that contain *Serenity Spas*, and the Amount column contains a conditional format to highlight with Red Border values between $10,000 and $20,000.

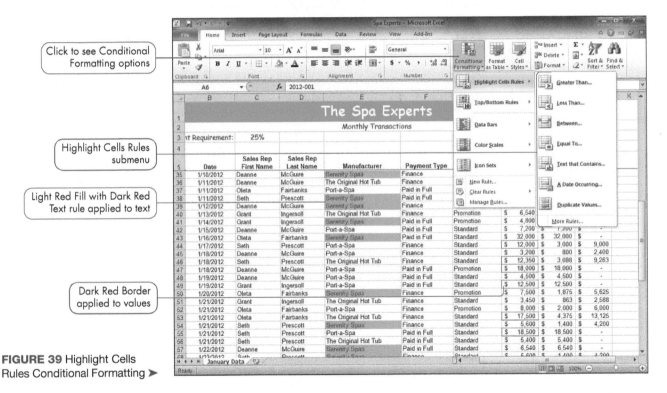

**FIGURE 39** Highlight Cells Rules Conditional Formatting ➤

## Specify Top/Bottom Rules

You may not know the exact values to format conditionally. You might be interested in identifying the top five sales to reward the sales associates, or want to identify the bottom 15% of automobile dealers so that you can close underperforming locations. The Top/Bottom Rules category enables you to specify the top or bottom number or percentage in a selected range. In addition, the Top/Bottom Rules category enables you to identify values that are above or below the average value in that range. In Figure 40, the selected range is conditionally formatted to highlight the top three amounts. Although the menu option is Top 10 Items, you can specify the exact number of items to highlight.

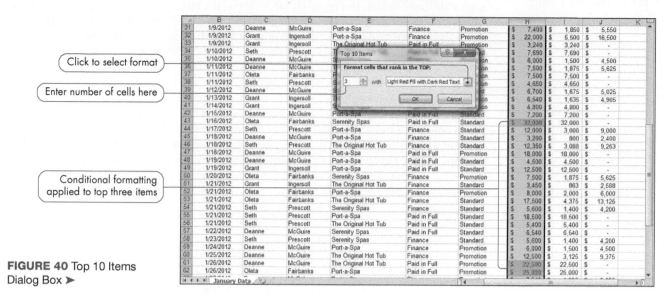

FIGURE 40 Top 10 Items Dialog Box ➤

## Display Data Bars, Color Scales, and Icon Sets

A **data bar** is a horizontal gradient or solid fill indicating the cell's relative value compared to other selected cells.

*Data bars* help you visualize the value of a cell relative to other cells, as shown in Figure 41. The width of the gradient or solid data bar represents the value in a cell, with a wider bar representing a higher value and a shorter bar a lower value. Use data bar conditional formatting when identifying high and low values. Excel locates the largest value and displays the widest data bar in that cell. Excel then finds the smallest value and displays the smallest data bar in that cell. Excel sizes the data bars for the remaining cells based on their relative values. If you change the values in your worksheet, Excel automatically updates the widths of the data bars. Data bars are more effective with wider columns than narrow columns. Figure 41 shows data bar conditional formatting applied to the Amount column. The widest data bar displays in the cell containing the largest amount of $27,000, and the smallest data bar appears in the cells containing the smallest value of $3,240. The data bar widths of other cells help you see the value differences. Excel uses the same color for each data bar, but each bar differs in size based on the value in the respective cells.

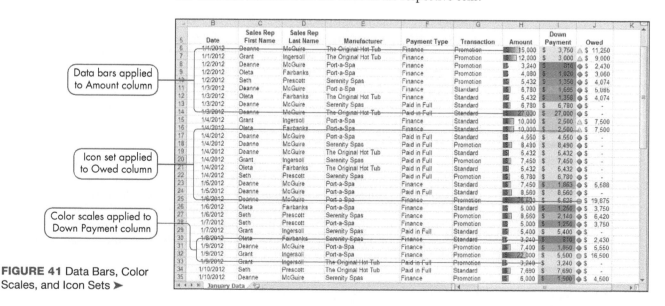

FIGURE 41 Data Bars, Color Scales, and Icon Sets ➤

A **color scale** is a conditional format that displays a particular color based on the relative value of the cell contents to other selected cells.

*Color scales* format cells with different colors based on the relative value of a cell compared to other selected cells. You can apply a two- or three-color scale. This scale assists in comparing a range of cells using gradations of those colors. The shade of the color represents higher or lower values. In Figure 41, for example, the red color scales display for the lowest values, the green color displays for the highest values, and gradients of yellow and orange represent the middle range of values in the Down Payment column. Use color scales to understand variation in the data to identify trends, for example to view good stock returns and weak stock returns.

An **icon set** is a conditional format that displays an icon representing a value in the top third, quarter, or fifth based on values in the selected range.

*Icon sets* are little symbols or signs that display in cells to classify data into three, four, or five categories, based on the values in the selected range. Excel determines categories of value ranges and assigns an icon to each range. In Figure 41, a three-icon set was applied to the Owed column. Excel divided the range of values between the lowest value $0 and the highest value of $19,875 into thirds. The red diamond icon displays for the cells containing values in the lowest third ($0 to $6,625), the yellow triangle icon displays for cells containing the values in the middle third ($6,626 to $12,150), and the green circle icon displays for cells containing values in the top third ($13,251 to $19,875). This helps you identify the spas with the most financing. Most spa purchases fall into the lowest third.

> ### TIP Don't Overdo It!
>
> Although conditional formatting helps identify trends, you should use this feature wisely. Apply conditional formatting when you want to emphasize important data. When you decide to apply conditional formatting, think about which category is best to highlight the data. Sometimes simple highlighting will suffice when you want to point out data meeting a particular condition; other times, you might want to apply data bars to point out relative differences among values. Finally, don't apply conditional formatting to too many columns.

## Clear Rules

To clear conditional formatting from the entire worksheet, click Conditional Formatting in the Styles group on the Home tab, point to Clear Rules, and select Clear Rules from Entire Sheet. To remove conditional formatting from a range of cells, select cells. Then click Conditional Formatting, point to Clear Rules, and then select Clear Rules from Selected Cells.

# Creating a New Rule

The default conditional formatting categories provide a variety of options. Excel also enables you to create your own rules to specify different fill colors, borders, or other formatting if you don't want the default settings. Excel provides three ways to create a new rule:

- Click Conditional Formatting in the Cell Styles group, and then select New Rule.
- Click Conditional Formatting in the Cell Styles group, select Manage Rules to open the Conditional Formatting Rules Manager dialog box, and then click New Rule.
- Click Conditional Formatting in the Cell Styles group, select a rule category such as Highlight Cells Rules, and then select More Rules.

The New Formatting Rule dialog box opens (see Figure 42) so that you can define your new conditional formatting rule. First, select a rule type, such as *Format all cells based on their values*. The *Edit the Rule Description* section changes, based on the rule type you select. With the default rule type selected, you can specify the format style (2-Color Scale, 3-Color Scale, Data Bar, or Icon Sets). You can then specify the minimum and maximum values, the fill colors for color sets or data bars or the icons for icon sets. After you edit the rule description, click OK to save your new conditional format.

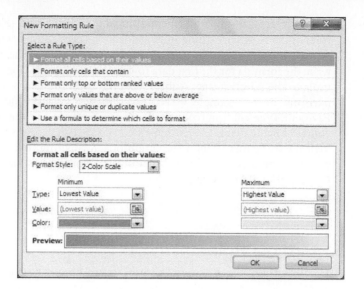

**FIGURE 42** New Formatting Rule Dialog Box ➤

If you select any rule type except the *Format all cells based on their values* rule, the dialog box contains a Format button. When you click Format, the Format Cells dialog box opens so that you can specify number, font, border, and fill formats to apply to your rule.

> **TIP  Format Only Cells That Contain**
>
> This option provides a wide array of things you can format: values, text, dates, blanks, no blanks, errors, or no errors. Formatting blanks is helpful to see where you are missing data, and formatting cells containing errors helps you find those errors quickly.

## Use Formulas in Conditional Formatting

Excel provides a vast number of conditional formatting options. If you need to create a complex conditional formatting rule, you can select a rule that uses a formula to format cells. For example, you might want to format amounts of financed spas *and* amounts that are $10,000 or more. Figure 43 shows the Edit Formatting Rule dialog box and the corresponding conditional formatting applied to cells.

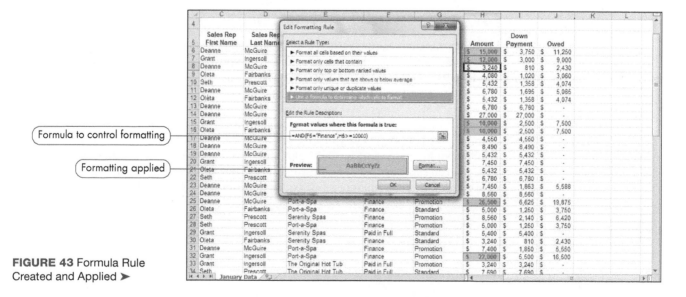

**FIGURE 43** Formula Rule Created and Applied ➤

To create a formula-based conditional formatting rule, select the data and create a new rule. In the New Formatting Rule dialog box, select *Use a formula to determine which cells to format*, and then type the formula in the *Format values where this formula is true* box. You write the formula for the first data row, such as F6 and H6. Excel then applies the general formula to the selected range, substituting the appropriate cell reference as it makes the comparisons. In this example, =AND(F6="Finance",H6>=10000) requires that the text in the Payment Type column (column F) contain Finance and the Amount column (column H) contain a value that is greater than or equal to $10,000. The AND function requires that both logical tests be met to apply the conditional formatting. Two logical tests are required; however, you can include additional logical tests. Note that *all* logical tests must be true to apply the conditional formatting.

= AND(logical1,logical2,... )

## Manage Rules

To edit or delete conditional formatting rules you create, click Conditional Formatting in the Styles group, and then select Manage Rules. The Conditional Formatting Rules Manager dialog box opens (see Figure 44). Click the *Show formatting rules for* arrow and select from current selection, the entire worksheet, or a specific table. Then select the rule, and then click Edit Rule or Delete Rule.

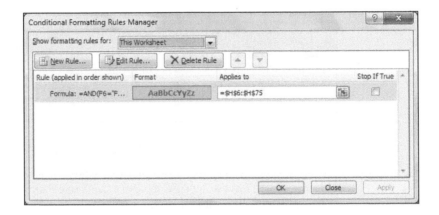

**FIGURE 44** Conditional Formatting Rules Manager Dialog Box ➤

# Sorting and Filtering Using Conditional Formatting

Earlier in this chapter, you learned how to sort and filter to change the order of fields or the records displayed. Now that you know how to apply conditional formatting, you can sort and filter by conditional formatting as well.

For example, if you applied the Highlight Cells Rules, Top/Bottom Rules, or Color Scales conditional formatting, you can sort the column by color so that all cells containing the highlight appear first or last. To do this, display the filter arrows, click the arrow for the conditionally formatted column you wish to sort, point to Sort by Color, and then click the fill color or No Fill in the Sort by Cell Color area. If you applied the Data Bars conditional format, you can't sort by data bars, but you can sort by values, which will arrange the data bars in ascending or descending order. If you applied the Icon Sets conditional formatting, you can filter by icon.

# HANDS-ON EXERCISES

## 4 Conditional Formatting

Your business partner, Ryan, wants to review the transactions with you. He is interested in Fairbanks' sales record and the five highest spa amounts. In addition, he wants to compare the down payment amounts visually. Finally, he wants to analyze the amounts owed for sales completed by Prescott.

**Skills covered:** Highlight Cells Rules • Specify Top/Bottom Rules • Display Data Bars • Create a New Rule • Filter by Rule

---

> **STEP 1** ### HIGHLIGHT CELLS RULES

You want to identify Fairbanks' spa sales for January without filtering the data. You will apply a conditional format to apply a fill and font color so that cells containing her last name stand out. Refer to Figure 45 as you complete Step 1.

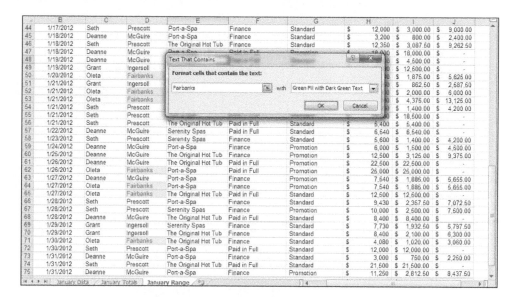

**FIGURE 45** Text Formatted with Highlight Text Rules ➤

a. Open *e04h3spa_LastnameFirstname* if you closed it at the end of Hands-On Exercise 3. Save the workbook with the new name **e04h4spa_LastnameFirstname**, changing *h3* to *h4*.

b. Select **row headings 6 through 75** in the January Range worksheet. Click the **Home tab**, if necessary, click the **Fill Color arrow**, and then select **No Fill**.

   You removed the previous table style with banded rows. This will avoid having too many fill colors when you apply conditional formatting rules.

c. Select the **range D6:D75**, which is the column containing the sales representatives' last names.

d. Click **Conditional Formatting** in the Styles group, point to **Highlight Cells Rules**, and then select **Text that Contains**.

   The Text That Contains dialog box opens.

e. Type **Fairbanks** in the box, click the **with arrow**, and then select **Green Fill with Dark Green Text**. Click **OK**. Deselect the range, and then save the workbook.

   Excel formats only cells that contain Fairbanks with the fill and font color.

**STEP 2** ▶ **SPECIFY TOP/BOTTOM RULES**

Ryan is now interested in identifying the highest five spa sales in January. Instead of sorting the records, you will use the Top/Bottom Rules conditional formatting. Refer to Figure 46 as you complete Step 2.

**FIGURE 46** Top 5 Amounts Conditionally Formatted ▶

a. Select the **range H6:H75**, the range containing the amounts.

b. Click **Conditional Formatting** in the Styles group, point to **Top/Bottom Rules**, and then select **Top 10 Items**.

   The Top 10 Items dialog box opens.

c. Click the **spin arrow** to display 5, click the **with arrow**, and then select **Light Red Fill**. Click **OK**.

d. Scroll through the worksheet to see the top five amounts (three of which are shown in Figure 46). Save the workbook.

**STEP 3** ▶ **DISPLAY DATA BARS**

Now Ryan wants to compare all of the down payments. Data bars would add a nice visual element as Ryan compares down payment amounts. Refer to Figure 47 as you complete Step 3.

| | B | C | D | E | F | G | H | I | J |
|---|---|---|---|---|---|---|---|---|---|
| 44 | 1/17/2012 | Seth | Prescott | Port-a-Spa | Finance | Standard | $ 12,000 | $ 3,000.00 | $ 9,000.00 |
| 45 | 1/18/2012 | Deanne | McGuire | Port-a-Spa | Finance | Standard | $ 3,200 | $ 800.00 | $ 2,400.00 |
| 46 | 1/18/2012 | Seth | Prescott | The Original Hot Tub | Finance | Standard | $ 12,350 | $ 3,087.50 | $ 9,262.50 |
| 47 | 1/18/2012 | Deanne | McGuire | Port-a-Spa | Paid in Full | Promotion | $ 18,000 | $ 18,000.00 | $ - |
| 48 | 1/19/2012 | Deanne | McGuire | Port-a-Spa | Paid in Full | Standard | $ 4,500 | $ 4,500.00 | $ - |
| 49 | 1/19/2012 | Grant | Ingersoll | Port-a-Spa | Paid in Full | Standard | $ 12,500 | $ 12,500.00 | $ - |
| 50 | 1/20/2012 | Oleta | Fairbanks | Serenity Spas | Finance | Promotion | $ 7,500 | $ 1,875.00 | $ 5,625.00 |
| 51 | 1/21/2012 | Grant | Ingersoll | The Original Hot Tub | Finance | Standard | $ 3,450 | $ 862.50 | $ 2,587.50 |
| 52 | 1/21/2012 | Oleta | Fairbanks | Port-a-Spa | Finance | Promotion | $ 8,000 | $ 2,000.00 | $ 6,000.00 |
| 53 | 1/21/2012 | Oleta | Fairbanks | The Original Hot Tub | Finance | Standard | $ 17,500 | $ 4,375.00 | $ 13,125.00 |
| 54 | 1/21/2012 | Seth | Prescott | Serenity Spas | Finance | Standard | $ 5,600 | $ 1,400.00 | $ 4,200.00 |
| 55 | 1/21/2012 | Seth | Prescott | Port-a-Spa | Paid in Full | Standard | $ 18,500 | $ 18,500.00 | $ - |
| 56 | 1/21/2012 | Seth | Prescott | The Original Hot Tub | Finance | Standard | $ 5,400 | $ 5,400.00 | $ - |
| 57 | 1/22/2012 | Deanne | McGuire | Serenity Spas | Paid in Full | Standard | $ 6,540 | $ 6,540.00 | $ - |
| 58 | 1/23/2012 | Seth | Prescott | Serenity Spas | Finance | Standard | $ 5,600 | $ 1,400.00 | $ 4,200.00 |
| 59 | 1/24/2012 | Deanne | McGuire | Port-a-Spa | Finance | Promotion | $ 6,000 | $ 1,500.00 | $ 4,500.00 |
| 60 | 1/25/2012 | Deanne | McGuire | The Original Hot Tub | Finance | Promotion | $ 12,500 | $ 3,125.00 | $ 9,375.00 |
| 61 | 1/26/2012 | Deanne | McGuire | The Original Hot Tub | Paid in Full | Promotion | $ 22,500 | $ 22,500.00 | $ - |
| 62 | 1/26/2012 | Oleta | Fairbanks | Port-a-Spa | Paid in Full | Promotion | $ 25,000 | $ 25,000.00 | $ - |
| 63 | 1/27/2012 | Deanne | McGuire | Port-a-Spa | Finance | Promotion | $ 7,540 | $ 1,885.00 | $ 5,655.00 |
| 64 | 1/27/2012 | Oleta | Fairbanks | Port-a-Spa | Finance | Promotion | $ 7,540 | $ 1,885.00 | $ 5,655.00 |
| 65 | 1/27/2012 | Oleta | Fairbanks | The Original Hot Tub | Finance | Standard | $ 12,500 | $ 12,500.00 | $ - |
| 66 | 1/28/2012 | Seth | Prescott | Port-a-Spa | Finance | Standard | $ 9,430 | $ 2,357.50 | $ 7,072.50 |
| 67 | 1/28/2012 | Seth | Prescott | Serenity Spas | Finance | Promotion | $ 10,000 | $ 2,500.00 | $ 7,500.00 |
| 68 | 1/28/2012 | Deanne | McGuire | The Original Hot Tub | Paid in Full | Standard | $ 8,400 | $ 8,400.00 | $ - |
| 69 | 1/29/2012 | Grant | Ingersoll | Serenity Spas | Finance | Standard | $ 7,730 | $ 1,932.50 | $ 5,797.50 |
| 70 | 1/29/2012 | Grant | Ingersoll | The Original Hot Tub | Finance | Standard | $ 8,400 | $ 2,100.00 | $ 6,300.00 |
| 71 | 1/30/2012 | Oleta | Fairbanks | The Original Hot Tub | Finance | Standard | $ 4,080 | $ 1,020.00 | $ 3,060.00 |
| 72 | 1/30/2012 | Seth | Prescott | Port-a-Spa | Paid in Full | Standard | $ 12,000 | $ 12,000.00 | $ - |
| 73 | 1/31/2012 | Deanne | McGuire | Port-a-Spa | Finance | Standard | $ 3,000 | $ 750.00 | $ 2,250.00 |
| 74 | 1/31/2012 | Seth | Prescott | The Original Hot Tub | Finance | Standard | $ 21,500 | $ 21,500.00 | $ - |
| 75 | 1/31/2012 | Deanne | McGuire | Port-a-Spa | Finance | Promotion | $ 11,250 | $ 2,812.50 | $ 8,437.50 |

**FIGURE 47** Data Bars Conditional Formatting ➤

a. Select the **range I6:I75**, which contains the down payment amounts.

b. Click **Conditional Formatting** in the Styles group, point to **Data Bars**, and then select **Purple Data Bar** in the *Gradient Fill* section. Scroll through the list, and then save the workbook.

Excel displays data bars in each cell. The larger bar widths help Ryan identify quickly the largest down payments. However, the largest down payments are identical to the original amounts when the customers pay in full. This result illustrates that you should not accept the results at face value. Doing so would provide you with an inaccurate analysis.

## STEP 4 ▷ CREATE A NEW RULE

Ryan's next request is to analyze the amounts owed by Prescott's customers. In particular, he wants to know how many customers owe more than $5,000. To do this, you realize you need to create a custom rule that evaluates both the Sales Rep Last Name column and the Owed column. Refer to Figure 48 as you complete Step 4.

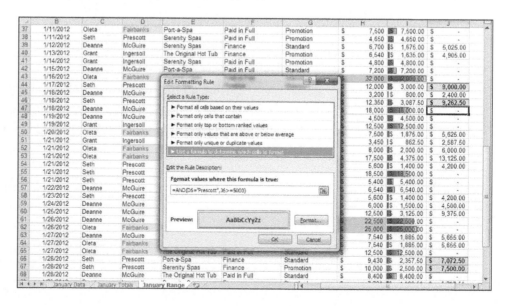

**FIGURE 48** Custom Rule Created ➤

a. Select the **range J6:J75**, which contains the amounts owed.

b. Click **Conditional Formatting** in the Styles group, and then select **New Rule**.

The New Formatting Rule dialog box opens.

c. Select **Use a formula to determine which cells to format**.

d. Type **=AND(D6="Prescott",J6>=5000)** in the **Format values where this formula is true box**.

Because you are comparing the contents of cell D6 to text, you must enclose the text within quotation marks.

e. Click **Format** to open the Format Cells dialog box.

f. Click the **Font tab**, if necessary, and then click **Bold** in the **Font style list**. Click the **Border tab**, click the **Color arrow**, select **Purple**, and then click **Outline**. Click the **Fill tab**, click the **lightest purple background color** (the eighth color on the first row below the first horizontal line), and then click **OK**. Look at Figure 48 to compare your new rule.

The figure shows the Edit Formatting Rule dialog box, but the options are similar to the New Formatting Rule dialog box.

g. Click **OK** in New Formatting Rule dialog box, and then scroll through the list to see which amounts owed are greater than $5,000 for Prescott only. Save the workbook.

**STEP 5 ▷ FILTER BY RULE**

Ryan commented that it is difficult to see which of Prescott's transactions were greater than $5,000 without scrolling. To help Ryan review the Owed column where you applied a formula-based conditional format, you will filter that column by the fill color. Refer to Figure 49 as you complete Step 5.

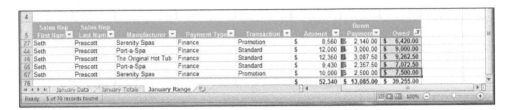

**FIGURE 49** Owed Column Filtered by Fill Color ➤

a. Deselect the range by clicking inside the dataset. Click **Sort & Filter** in the Editing group, and then select **Filter**.

Filter arrows display for the column headings.

b. Click the **Owed filter arrow**, point to **Filter by Color**, and then select the **light purple fill color**.

Excel filters the range to display records where the fill color is lavender. Now it is easy to see that Prescott sold five spas where the customers owe more than $5,000.

c. Save and close the workbook, and submit based on your instructor's directions.

# CHAPTER OBJECTIVES REVIEW

After reading this chapter, you have accomplished the following objectives:

1. **Freeze rows and columns.** To prevent labels from scrolling offscreen, freeze rows or columns. The Freeze Panes setting freezes the row(s) above and the column(s) to the left of the active cell. When you scroll, those rows and columns remain onscreen so that you know what type of data is in each row or column. You can use Unfreeze Panes to clear the frozen rows and columns.

2. **Print large datasets.** Display the data in Page Break Preview to see the automatic page breaks. Dashed blue lines indicate automatic page breaks. You can insert manual page breaks, indicated by solid blue lines. If you do not want to print an entire worksheet, select a range and set a print area. Dotted lines surround the print area onscreen. When a dataset will print on several pages, you can control the sequence in which the pages will print.

3. **Understand table design.** A table is a structured range that contains related data. Tables have several benefits over regular ranges, such as keeping headings onscreen as you scroll. Each table column is a field. The column headings, called *field names*, appear on the first row of a table. Each row is a complete set of data for one record. You should plan a table. For example, create unique field names on the first row of the table, and enter data immediately below the field names, avoiding blank rows.

4. **Create a table.** You can create a table from existing structured data. Excel applies the Table Style Medium 9 format and assigns a default name, such as Table1, to the table. When the active cell is within a table, the Table Tools display with the Design tab. You can insert and delete table rows and columns and remove duplicate records in your table.

5. **Apply a table style.** Table styles control the fill color of the header row and records within the table. To further customize the formatting, click options, such as First Column or Total Row in the Table Style Options group.

6. **Sort data.** The data in a table are often easier to understand and work with if they are in some meaningful order. Sorting arranges records in a table by the value of one or more fields within the table. You can sort text in alphabetical or reverse alphabetical order, values from smallest to largest or largest to smallest, and dates from oldest to newest or newest to oldest. To sort a single field, click the filter arrow and select the sort method from the list. To sort multiple fields, open the Sort

dialog box and add column levels and sort orders. You can create a custom sort for unique data.

7. **Filter data.** Filtering is the process of specifying conditions for displaying records in a table. Only records that meet those conditions display; the other records are hidden until you clear the filters. You can apply text, value, and date filters based on the data in a particular field.

8. **Use structured references and a total row.** A structured reference uses field names instead of cell references, such as =[Amount]-[Down Payment]. Field names must appear in brackets within the formula. When you press Enter, Excel copies the formula down the column. You can display a total row after the last record. Excel sums the values in the last column automatically or counts the number of text entries. You can add totals to other columns, and you can select a different function, such as Average.

9. **Apply conditional formatting.** Conditional formatting applies special formatting to cells that contain values that meet set conditions. The five major conditional formatting categories are Highlight Cells Rules, Top/Bottom Rules, Data Bars, Color Scales, and Icon Sets. Data bars display horizontal bars that compare values within the selected range. The larger the value, the wider the horizontal bar. Color scales indicate values that occur within particular ranges. Icon sets display icons representing a number's relative value compared to other numbers in the range. When you no longer need conditional formatting, you can clear it for the selected range or entire worksheet.

10. **Create a new rule.** You can create conditional format rules. The New Formatting Rule dialog box enables you to select a rule type. Based on the type you select, the *Edit the Rule Description* section changes to provide specific options for defining your rule. You can create rules based on formulas to set conditions based on content in multiple columns. Use the Conditional Formatting Rules Manager dialog box to edit and delete rules.

11. **Sort and filter using conditional formatting.** After you apply conditional formatting, you can sort or filter a column based on its formats. Use Sort by Color to select a sort sequence, or select Filter by Color to filter out records that do not meet the color condition you specify.

# KEY TERMS

| | | |
|---|---|---|
| Color scale | Icon set | Structured reference |
| Conditional formatting | Page break | SUBTOTAL function |
| Data bar | Print area | Table |
| Field | Print order | Table style |
| Filtering | Record | Total row |
| Freezing | Sorting | |

1. You have a large dataset that will print on several pages. You want to ensure that related records print on the same page with column and row labels visible and that confidential information is not printed. You should apply all of the following page setup options except which one to accomplish this?

    (a) Set a print area.
    (b) Print titles.
    (c) Adjust page breaks.
    (d) Change the print page order.

2. You are working with a large worksheet. Your row headings are in column A. Which command(s) should be used to see the row headings and the distant information in columns X, Y, and Z?

    (a) Freeze Panes command
    (b) Hide Rows command
    (c) New Window command and cascade the windows
    (d) Split Rows command

3. Which statement is not a recommended guideline for planning a table in Excel?

    (a) Avoid naming two fields with the same name.
    (b) Ensure no blank columns separate data columns within the table.
    (c) Leave one blank row between records in the table.
    (d) Include field names on the first row of the table.

4. You have a list of all the employees in your organization. The list contains employee name, office, title, and salary. You want to list all employees in each office branch. The branches should be listed alphabetically, with the employee earning the highest salary listed first in each office. Which is true of your sort order?

    (a) Branch office is the primary sort and should be in A to Z order.
    (b) Salary is the primary sort and should be from highest to lowest.
    (c) Salary is the primary sort and should be from lowest to highest.
    (d) Branch office is the primary sort and should be in Z to A order.

5. You suspect a table has several identical records. What should you do?

    (a) Do nothing; a logical reason probably exists to keep identical records.
    (b) Use the Remove Duplicates command.
    (c) Look at each row yourself, and manually delete duplicate records.
    (d) Find the duplicate records and change some of the data to be different.

6. Which check box in the Table Style Options group enables you to apply different formatting to the records in a table?

    (a) Header Row
    (b) Banded Rows
    (c) Banded Columns
    (d) Total Row

7. Which date filter option enables you to specify criteria for selecting a range of dates, such as between 3/15/2012 and 7/15/2012?

    (a) Equals
    (b) Before
    (c) All Dates in the Period
    (d) Between

8. You want to display a total row that identifies the oldest date in a field in your table. What function do you select from the list?

    (a) Max
    (b) Sum
    (c) Min
    (d) Count

9. What type of conditional formatting displays horizontal colors in which the width of the bar indicates relative size compared to other values in the selected range?

    (a) Color Scales
    (b) Icon Sets
    (c) Data Bars
    (d) Sparklines

10. When you select the _____ rule type, the New Formatting Rule dialog box does not show the Format button.

    (a) Format all cells based on their values
    (b) Format only cells that contain
    (c) Use a formula to determine which cells to format
    (d) Format only unique or duplicate values

## 1 Fiesta® Collection

Your Aunt Laura has been collecting Fiesta dinnerware, a popular brand from The Homer Laughlin China Company, since it was reintroduced in 1986. Her collection has grown, and she enlisted you to help her maintain a list. So far, you and Aunt Laura have entered data by color, item number, and item. In addition, you researched current replacement costs from Homer Laughlin's Web site (www.fiestafactorydirect.com); Replacements, Ltd. (www.replacements.com); and eBay (www.ebay.com). Now you need to apply techniques to manage the list, convert it to a table, and then apply table features. This exercise follows the same set of skills as used in Hands-On Exercises 1, 2, and 3 in the chapter. Refer to Figure 50 as you complete this exercise.

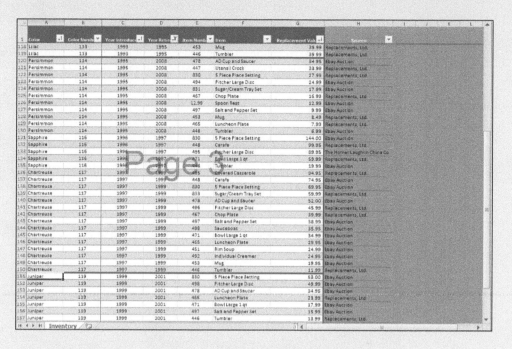

**FIGURE 50** Fiesta® Collection ➤

a. Open *e04p1fiesta* and save it as **e04p1fiesta_LastnameFirstname**.

b. Click **cell C2**, click the **View tab**, click **Freeze Panes** in the Window group, and then select **Freeze Panes**.

c. Press **Ctrl+End** to go to the last data cell. Note that the frozen rows and column headings remain onscreen. Press **Ctrl+Home** to go back to **cell C2**.

d. Click the **Insert tab**, click **Table** in the Tables group, and then click **OK** in the Create Table dialog box.

e. Click the **More button** in the Table Styles group, and then click **Table Style Medium 3**.

f. Click **Remove Duplicates** in the Tools group, click **Select All** to ensure all columns are selected, and then click **OK**. Click **OK** in the message box that informs you that 12 duplicate values were found and removed.

g. Click within the table. Click the **Data tab**, and then click **Sort** in the Sort & Filter group. Do the following in the Sort dialog box:
   - Click the **Sort by arrow**, and then select **Year Introduced**.
   - Click **Add Level**, click the **Then by arrow**, and then select **Color**.
   - Click **Add Level**, click the **Then by arrow**, select **Replacement Value**, click the **Order arrow**, and then select **Largest to Smallest**. Click **OK**.

h. Click the **Year Retired filter arrow**, deselect the **(Blanks) check box**, and then click **OK** to filter out current colors and display only retired colors.

i.  Click the **Design tab**, and then click **Total Row** in the Table Style Options group. Scroll down to the total row on row 316, click the **Source total cell** (which contains a count), click the **Source total arrow**, and then select **None**. Click **cell G6**, the Replacement Value total cell, click the **Replacement Value total arrow**, and then select **Sum**.

j.  Prepare the worksheet in case your Aunt Laura wants a printout by doing the following:
    - Click the **Page Layout tab**, click **Orientation** in the Page Setup group, and then select **Landscape**.
    - Click **Print Titles**, click the **Rows to repeat at top collapse button**, click the **row 1 header**, and then click the **expand button**. Click **OK**.
    - Select **cells A1:G316**. Click **Print Area**, and then select **Set Print Area**.
    - Click the **View tab**, and then click **Page Break Preview**. If the message box appears, click **OK**.

k.  Click **cell A89**, click the **Page Layout tab**, click **Breaks** in the Page Setup group, and then select **Insert Page Break** to insert a page break so that the Periwinkle Blue item on row 89 appears after the page break, along with the other Periwinkle Blue items.

l.  Adapt step k to insert a page break before **cell A120** to move Persimmon to the top of a page. Insert another page break before **cell A151** to move Juniper to the top of a page.

m.  Create a footer with your name on the left side, the date code in the center, and the file name code on the right side.

n.  Save and close the workbook, and submit based on your instructor's directions.

## 2 Salary Data

As the Human Resources Manager, you maintain employee salary data. You exported data from the corporate database into an Excel workbook. You want to convert the data to a table. You will use structured references to calculate raises and new salaries. Finally, you want to display a total row to show the total salaries. This exercise follows the same set of skills as used in Hands-On Exercises 1, 2, and 3 in the chapter. Refer to Figure 51 as you complete this exercise.

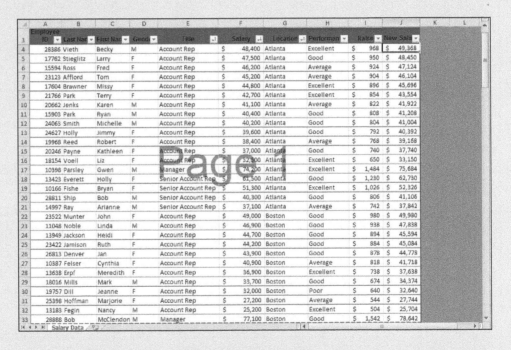

**FIGURE 51** Salary Data ➤

a.  Open *e04p2salary* and save it as **e04p2salary_LastnameFirstname**.

b.  Click in the dataset. Click the **Insert tab**, click **Table** in the Tables group, and then click **OK**.

c.  Click the **More button** in the Table Styles group, and then click **Table Style Light 10**.

d.  Click the **Data tab**, click **Sort** in the Sort & Filter group, and then do the following in the Sort dialog box:
    - Click the **Sort by arrow**, and then select **Location**.
    - Click **Add Level**, click the **Then by arrow**, and then select **Title**.

Datasets and Tables

- Click **Add Level**, click the **Then by arrow**, select **Salary**, click the **Order arrow**, and then select **Largest to Smallest**. Then click **OK**.

e. Click **cell I3**, type **Raise**, and then press **Tab**. Type **New Salary** in **cell J3**, and then press **Enter**.

f. Click **cell I4**, type =[ and then double-click **Salary** from the list. Type ]*$I$1 and press **Enter**.

g. Click **cell J4**, type =[Salary]+[Raise], and then press **Enter**.

h. Format the last two columns with **Accounting Number Format** with no decimal places.

i. Click the **Design tab**, and then click **Total Row** in the Table Style Options group. Scroll to the bottom of the table, click the **Raise total cell** on row 159, click the **Raise total row arrow**, and then select **Sum**. Click the **Salary total cell** on row 159, click the **Salary total row arrow**, and then select **Sum**.

j. Prepare the worksheet to be printed by doing the following:
   - Click the **Page Layout tab**, and then set **landscape orientation**. Adjust column widths so that the data fits on one page, wrap text, and center align field names.
   - Click **Print Titles**, click the **Rows to repeat at top collapse button**, click **row 3**, click the **expand button**, and then click **OK**.
   - Click the **View tab**, and then click **Page Break Preview**. If a message box appears, click **OK**.

k. Drag the second page break to be between rows 58 and 59. Move the third page break to be between rows 81 and 82. Move the fourth page break to be between rows 110 and 111. Move the last page break to be between rows 139 and 140.

l. Create a footer with your name on the left side, the date code in the center, and the file name code on the right side.

m. Save and close the workbook, and submit based on your instructor's directions.

## 3  Dentist Association Donation List

The Midwest Regional Dentist Association is planning its annual meeting in Lincoln, Nebraska, this spring. Several members donated items for door prizes at the closing general session. You need to organize the list of donations and format it to highlight particular data for your supervisor, who is on the conference board of directors. This exercise follows the same set of skills as used in Hands-On Exercises 2, 3, and 4 in the chapter. Refer to Figure 52 as you complete this exercise.

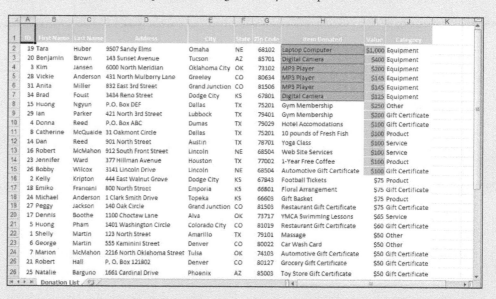

**FIGURE 52** Donation List ➤

a. Open *e04p3donate* and save it as **e04p3donate_LastnameFirstname**.

b. Click the **Design tab**, click **Remove Duplicates** in the Tools group, and then click **OK**. Click **OK** in the message box that tells you that Excel removed three duplicate records.

c. Click **Convert to Range** in the Tools group, and then click **Yes** in the message box.

d. Select the **range A2:J35**, click the **Home tab**, click the **Fill Color arrow** in the Font group, and then select **No Fill** to remove the table fill colors.

e. Select the **range I2:I35**. Click **Conditional Formatting** in the Styles group, point to **Highlight Cells Rules**, and then select **Greater Than**. Type **99** in the **Format cells that are GREATER THAN box**, and then click **OK**.

f. Select **cells H2:H35**. Create a custom conditional format by doing the following:
   - Click **Conditional Formatting** in the Styles group, and then select **New Rule**.
   - Click **Use a formula to determine which cells to format**.
   - Type =**(J2="Equipment")** in the **Format values where this formula is true box**. The basic condition is testing to see if the contents of cell J2 equal the word *Equipment*. You type *Equipment* in quotation marks since you are comparing text instead of a value.
   - Click **Format**, click the **Fill tab** if necessary, and then click **Red, Accent 2, Lighter 60%** (sixth background color on the second row below the first horizontal line).
   - Click the **Border tab**, click the **Color arrow**, click **Dark Red**, and then click **Outline**.
   - Click **OK** in each dialog box.

g. Click anywhere in the table to deselect the range. Click **Sort & Filter** in the Editing group, and then select **Custom Sort**. The dialog box may contain existing sort conditions for the State and City fields, which you will replace. Set the following sort conditions:
   - Click the **Sort by arrow**, and then select **Item Donated**. Click the **Sort On arrow**, and then select **Cell Color**. Click the **Order arrow**, and then select the **RGB(242, 220, 219)** or **RGB(230, 184, 183) fill color**. The fill color displays for the Order.
   - Click the **Then by arrow**, and then select **Value**. Click the **Order arrow**, and then select **Largest to Smallest**.
   - Click **OK**.

h. Select **landscape orientation**, set appropriate margins, and adjust column widths so that all the data will print on one page. Do not decrease the scaling.

i. Create a footer with your name on the left side, the sheet name code in the center, and the file name code on the right side.

j. Save and close the workbook, and submit based on your instructor's directions.

Datasets and Tables

276

## 1 University Band Member List

You are the assistant to the band director at Mountain State University. The secretary created a list of band members, which you need to prepare to print. In addition, you want to convert the data to a table, manipulate the data, and meet with the band director to discuss the roster and ensure you have ample coverage of all instruments, chair position, and classification. For example, if 75% of flute players are 2nd chair, you might want to reassign some flute players to 1st or 3rd chair. Or if all of your baritone players are seniors, you might need to recruit some freshmen baritone players.

a. Open *e04m1band* and save it as **e04m1band_LastnameFirstname**.
b. Freeze the panes so that the column headings and the student IDs, last names, and first names do not scroll offscreen.
**DISCOVER** c. Convert the data to a table, and then name the table **BandRoster**.
d. Apply **Table Style Medium 7** to the table. Use Format Painter to copy the heading formats to the Solo Rating heading, if needed.
**DISCOVER** e. Sort the table by Instrument, then Chair, and then Class. Create a custom sort order for Class so that it appears in this sequence: Senior, Junior, Sophomore, and Freshman.
f. Remove duplicate records from the table. Excel should find and remove two duplicate records.
g. Add a total row to determine the average scholarship amount per student. Remove any other totals that appear. Change the row heading in **cell A75** to **Average**.
h. Copy the Band Members worksheet, and then place the copied worksheet to the right of the original worksheet. Rename the duplicate worksheet **Filtered Seniors**.
i. Filter the copied table to show only seniors who are 1st or 2nd chair and were awarded a scholarship of at least $4,750 or more. The status bar indicates 10 of 73 records found.
j. Adjust orientation, column widths, margins, row height, and wrap text so that the filtered data will fit on one page.
k. Display the Band Members worksheet in Page Break Preview.
   • Select **landscape orientation**. Adjust the page breaks so that the Instrument column will print on the same pages as the Chair, Class, and Scholarship columns.
   • Repeat the column headings and student ID, last name, and first name on printouts. Adjust the widths of the last five columns as needed, and increase the height of the first row. Do not change the margins or orientation.
   • Set the print range to print all columns and rows except the Solo Rating column.
   • Change the print page order to print horizontally and then down.
l. Create a footer with your name on the left side, the sheet name code in the center, and the file name code on the right side of each worksheet.
m. Check the Band Members worksheet in Print Preview to ensure that it can print on six pages.
n. Save and close the workbook, and submit based on your instructor's directions.

## 2 Credit Card Expenses

You started recording every credit card transaction so that you can analyze your monthly expenses. You used an Excel worksheet to track dates, places, categories, and amounts. Because you are a consultant who travels periodically, you also have business expenses. You included a column to indicate the business-related transactions. You are now ready to analyze the data. Refer to Figure 53 as you complete this exercise.

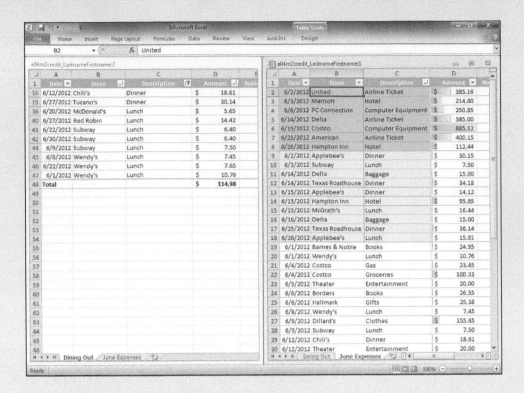

**FIGURE 53** Credit Card Analysis ➤

a. Open *e04m2credit* and save it as **e04m2credit_LastnameFirstname**.

b. Make sure the Dining Out worksheet is active. Convert the data to a table, and then apply **Table Style Light 11**.

c. Sort the table by the description in alphabetical order, sort the store in alphabetical order, and then sort by amount from smallest to largest in that sequence.

d. Filter the records to show personal (i.e., non-business) lunches and dinner expenses. Add a total row to sum the amounts but do not include other totals.

e. Click the **June Expenses worksheet tab**, and then apply the **Green Data Bar** in the *Gradient Fill* section setting to the Amount column.

f. Create a conditional formatting rule with these specifications:

DISCOVER

- Applies to the **range A2:C47**.
- Uses a formula to determine which cells to format based on amounts of $100 or more *and* that are classified as business expenses. Because this conditional formatting applies to several columns (A, B, and C), you must use mixed cell references in the formula.
- Formats data with a **Medium Green fill color** and a **Green line border** using the **Outline preset border style**.

g. Create a conditional formatting rule with these specifications:

DISCOVER

- Applies to the **range A2:C47**.
- Uses a formula to determine which cells to format based on amounts less than $100 *and* that are classified as business expenses. Because this conditional formatting applies to several columns (A, B, and C), you must use mixed cell references in the formula.
- Formats data with a **Light Green fill color** and a **Green line border** using the **Outline preset border style**.

DISCOVER

h. Create a custom color sort for the Description column with these specifications:
- Sorts on cell color.
- Displays the **Medium Green fill color** on Top as the primary sort.
- Displays the **Light Green fill color** on Top as the secondary sort.

i. Create a footer with your name on the left side, the sheet name code in the center, and the file name code on the right side on each worksheet.

j. Save and close the workbook, and submit based on your instructor's directions.

You work for a gallery that is an authorized Greenwich Workshop fine art dealer (www. greenwichworkshop.com). Customers in your area are especially fond of James C. Christensen's art. Although customers can visit the Web site to see images and details about his work, they have requested a list of all his artwork. Your assistant prepared a list of artwork: art, type, edition size, release date, and issue price. In addition, you included a column to identify what pieces are sold out at the publisher, indicating the rare, hard-to-obtain artwork that is available on the secondary market. You now want to convert the data to a table so that you can provide information to your customers.

a. Open *e04m3fineart* and save it as **e04m3fineart_LastnameFirstname**.

b. Convert the data to a table, and then apply **Table Style Medium 5**.

c. Add a row (below the The Yellow Rose record) for this missing piece of art: **The Yellow Rose, Masterwork Canvas Edition**, **50** edition size, **May 2009** release date, **$895** issue price. Enter **Yes** to indicate the piece is sold out.

d. Sort the table by type in alphabetical order and then by release date from newest to oldest.

e. Add a total row that shows the largest edition size and the most expensive issue price. Delete the Total label in **cell A173**. Add a descriptive label in **cell C173** to reflect the content on the total row.

**DISCOVER**

f. Create a custom conditional format for the Issue Price column with these specifications:
   - 4 Traffic Lights icon set (Black, Red, Yellow, Green)
   - Red icon when the number is greater than 1000
   - Yellow icon when the number is less than or equal to 1000 and greater than 500
   - Green icon when the number is less than or equal to 500 and greater than 250
   - Black icon when the number is less than or equal to 250.

g. Filter the table by the Green Traffic Light conditional formatting icon.

h. Set the print area to print the **range C1:H173**, select the **first row to repeat at the top of each printout**, set **1"** top and bottom margins, set **0.3"** left and right margins, and then select **landscape orientation**.

i. Wrap text and horizontally center column labels, and then adjust column widths and row heights as needed.

j. Adjust the page break so that at least five Limited Edition Canvas records print on the second page.

k. Create a footer with your name on the left side, the sheet name code in the center, and the file name code on the right side.

l. Save and close the workbook, and submit based on your instructor's directions.

You just got an internship at Mountain View Realty, a real estate firm that focuses on the North Utah County area. The previous intern developed a spreadsheet listing houses listed and sold during the past several months. She included addresses, location, list price, selling price, listing date, and date sold. You need to convert the data to a table and manipulate the table. You will manage the large worksheet, prepare the worksheet for printing, sort and filter the table, include calculations, and format the table.

## Prepare the Large Worksheet as a Table

You need to freeze the panes so that labels remain onscreen. You also want to convert the data to a table so that you can apply table options.

a. Open the *e04c1houses* workbook and save it as **e04c1houses_LastnameFirstname**.

b. Freeze the first row on the Sales Data worksheet.

c. Convert the data to a table, and then apply the **Table Style Medium 17**.

d. Remove duplicate records.

## Add Calculated Fields and a Total Row

The office manager asked you to insert a column to display the percent of list price. The formula finds the sale price percentage of the list price. For example, if a house was listed at $100,000 and sells for $75,000, the percentage of list price is 75%. In some cases, the percentage is more than 100%. This happens when a bidding war occurs, and buyers increase their offers, which results in the seller getting more than the list price.

a. Insert a new field to the right of the Selling Price field. Name the new field **Percent of List Price**.

b. Create a formula with structured references to calculate the percent of the list price.

c. Format the column with **Percent Style** with one decimal place.

d. Insert a new field to the right of the Sale Date field. Name the new field **Days on Market**.

e. Create a formula with structured references to calculate the number of days on the market. If the result displays in a date format, apply the **General number format** to the average.

f. Add a total row to display the average percent of list price and average number of days on market. Format the average number of days on market as a whole number. Use an appropriate label for the total row.

## Sort and Print the Table

To help the office manager compare house sales by city, you will sort the data. Then, you will prepare the large table to print.

a. Sort the table by city in alphabetical order, and add a second level to sort by days on market with the houses on the market the longest at the top within each city.

b. Adjust column widths so that the data is one page across (three pages total), and then wrap the column headings as needed.

c. Repeat the column headings on all pages.

d. Display the table in Page Break Preview.

e. Change page breaks so that city data does not span between pages, and then change back to Normal view.

f. Add a footer with your name on the left side, the sheet name code in the center, and the file name code on the right side.

## Copy and Filter the Data

The office manager needs to focus on houses that took longer than 30 days to sell within 3 cities. To keep the original data intact for the agents, you will copy the table data to a new sheet and use that sheet to display the filtered data.

a. Copy the Sales Data worksheet, and then place the duplicate worksheet to the right of the original worksheet tab. Convert the table to a range of data, and delete the average row.

b. Rename the duplicate worksheet **Filtered Data**.

c. Display the filter arrows for the data.

d. Filter the data to display the cities of *Alpine*, *Cedar Hills*, and *Eagle Mountain*.

e. Filter the data to display records for houses that were on the market 30 days or more.

## Apply Conditional Formatting

To highlight housing sales to illustrate trends, you will apply conditional formatting. Since data are sorted by city, you will use an icon set to color-code the number of days on market. You will also apply a data bar conditional formatting to the sale prices to help the office manager visualize the difference among the sales.

a. Apply the **3 Arrows (Colored) icon set** to the days on market values.

b. Apply the **Light Blue Data Bar conditional formatting** in the *Gradient Fill* section to the selling prices.

c. Create a new conditional format that applies **Yellow fill** and **bold font** to values that contain 95% or higher for the Percent of List Price column.

d. Edit the conditional format you created so that it formats values 98% or higher.

## Finalize the Workbook

You are ready to finalize the workbook by adding a footer to the new worksheet and saving the final workbook.

a. Add a footer with your name on the left side, the sheet name code in the center, and the file name code on the right side.

b. Remove all page breaks in the Filtered Data worksheet.

c. Select **landscape orientation**, and then set appropriate margins so that the data will print on one page.

d. Save and close the workbook, and submit based on your instructor's directions.

## Doctor Search

**GENERAL CASE**

You just moved to Florida with your family and are searching for doctors who can meet your family's medical needs. You obtained a list of more than 150 board-certified physicians from the state licensing agency. Open *e04b1doctors* and save it as **e04b1doctors_LastnameFirstname**. Freeze the panes to keep the column labels and IDs from scrolling offscreen. Convert the data to a table, and apply an appropriate table style. Filter the table to show only those who practice Cardiology, Pediatrics, and Internal Medicine and who are accepting new patients in Fort Lauderdale. Sort the filtered records by specialty, last name, and then first name. Set a print area to include all columns except the ID and New Patient columns. Apply a conditional format for dates after 1/1/2008 with a custom format of an Orange fill and a White font. Create a footer with your name, the sheet name code, and the file name code. Save and close the workbook, and submit based on your instructor's directions.

## Automobile Car Comparisons

**RESEARCH CASE**

You want to research various car models. Choose a category, such as sedan. Use the Internet to research at least 40 new vehicles. Start a new workbook and save it as **e04b2cars_LastnameFirstname**. Create an input area for a down payment of $5,000, APR, number of payment periods, and number of payments per year (12). Create a source area to list the URL of the Web site you used and the date you retrieved the information. Design the worksheet to list the make, model, year, transmission (automatic or manual), cylinders, liters, horsepower (HP), city miles per gallon (MPG), highway MPG, and manufacturer's suggested retail price. If you can't find the mpg for a particular vehicle, leave those cells blank. Format columns appropriately. Find information for at least five different makes. Include a few similar models, such as a Nissan Altima 2.5 and a Nissan Altima 3.5. Use the base prices. Freeze panes as necessary. Convert the data to a table and apply a table style of your choice. Sort by transmission, then by HP with the largest first, then by make, and finally by model. Add a new calculated column and use structured references to calculate the estimated monthly payment given the input cells. Add a total row to calculate the average HP, MPG, MSRP, and monthly payment. Apply a conditional format to apply a custom fill and font color for the five most expensive vehicles in the sorted list. Apply an icon set to the highway MPG values. On another worksheet, answer these questions: (1) What are the averages? (2) What are the averages for only automatic transmissions with V6 engines? (3) Which vehicle(s) had the highest highway MPG of all the vehicles? and (4) What is the mpg? Filter the Hwy MPG column by one icon color. Prepare both worksheets to print using appropriate page setup options. Create a footer with your name, the sheet name code, and the file name code. Save and close the workbook, and submit based on your instructor's directions.

## U.S. Population

**DISASTER RECOVERY**

A colleague at an advertising firm downloaded U.S. population information from the government Web site. In the process of creating tables, he made some errors and needs your help. Open *e04b3populate* and save it as **e04b3populate_LastnameFirstname**. As you find the errors, document them on the Errors worksheet and make the corrections. Your documentation should include these columns: Error Number, Location, Problem, and Solution. Both tables in the U.S. Population worksheet should show grand total populations per year. The state table should be sorted by region and then by state. Your colleague wants to emphasize the top 15% state populations for the most recent year in the state table. The last column should show percentage changes from year to year, such as 0.6%. Your colleague wants to print only the state data. Select the sorted data population for one region at a time to compare to the regional totals in the first table to cross-check the totals. For example, when you select the July 1, 2008, Midwest values in the second table, the status bar should display the same value as shown for the Midwest July 1, 2008, values in the first table. Create a footer with your name, the sheet name code, and the file name code. Save and close the workbook, and submit based on your instructor's directions.

EXCEL

# SUBTOTALS, PIVOTTABLES, AND PIVOTCHARTS

## Summarizing and Analyzing Data

Watch the Set-up Video for this Case Study!

## CASE STUDY | Ivory Halls Publishing Company

You are the new Vice President of the Sociology Division at Ivory Halls Publishing Company. The sociology domain has many disciplines, such as introductory sociology, family, research, gender issues, and more. Ivory Halls publishes several textbooks in each discipline to appeal to a vast array of university professors and students.

   One of your first tasks in your new position is to analyze sales for all books published in the Sociology Division. Your assistant prepared a list of books, their disciplines, and other pertinent data. The current list is not easy to analyze. You need to organize the data so that you can study the sales trends by discipline and area. The list contains current editions of all sociology textbooks. Some books are brand new—in their first edition—while other books are in their 10th edition. All of the books on the list have publication dates between 2009 and 2012.

## OBJECTIVES AFTER YOU READ THIS CHAPTER, YOU WILL BE ABLE TO:

1. Group and ungroup data
2. Subtotal data
3. Create a PivotTable
4. Change the values field
5. Modify a PivotTable
6. Sort, filter, and slice a PivotTable
7. Create a calculated field
8. Format a PivotTable
9. Create a PivotChart

From Excel Chapter 5 of *Exploring Microsoft Office 2010 Excel Comprehensive*, First Edition, Robert T. Grauer, Mary Anne Poatsy, Keith Mulbery. Copyright © 2011 by Pearson Education, Inc. Published by Pearson Prentice Hall, Inc. All rights reserved.

# Outlines and Subtotals

As you continue using large worksheets, you are probably developing an appreciation for functionality that enables you to manage the data and quickly provide answers to imperative questions. Data alone are meaningless; data translated into meaningful information increases your knowledge so that you can make well-informed decisions.

> ... meaningful information increases your knowledge so that you can make well-informed decisions.

Excel offers many tools to help you manage large amounts of data and translate the data into useful information. Previously, you used tools such as sorting, filtering, conditional formatting, tables, and charts. These tools help translate raw data into information so that you can identify trends, patterns, and anomalies in a dataset. Now you are ready to explore other functionalities that help you consolidate large amounts of data to help focus your attention on particular aspects of the dataset.

In this section, you will learn how to group data to create an outline, collapse and expand groups within the outline, and ungroup data to return data to its original state. In addition, you will learn how to insert subtotals for categories.

## Grouping and Ungrouping Data

When datasets are large, containing many categories and subcategories for detailed transactions, people often use multilayered data. For example, the primary category for the Sociology Division of Ivory Halls is Discipline, such as Aging/Death and Criminal Justice. Each discipline is subdivided into areas such as Deviance and Juvenile Delinquency. Because the magnitude of data in the worksheet could potentially occupy several hundreds or thousands of rows, you need to be able to organize the data. At the simplest level, you can perform a multi-level sort, sorting by discipline, then area, and finally by book title.

For a more structured approach to working with the dataset, you can create an outline. An *outline* is a hierarchical structure of data. You have probably created formal outlines when preparing a research paper for a class. Figure 1 shows a partial outline of topics for this chapter. Roman numerals indicate section titles, letters indicate objective headings, and lowercase Roman numerals indicate third-level headings.

An **outline** is a hierarchical structure of data.

---

I.      **Outlines and Subtotals**
     a.   Grouping and Ungrouping Data
     b.   Subtotaling Data
II.     **PivotTable Basics**
     a.   Creating a PivotTable
         i.   Add Fields for Row Labels and Values
        ii.   Add Fields for Column Labels
     b.   Changing the Values Field
     c.   Modifying a PivotTable
         i.   Add and Remove Fields
        ii.   Rearrange Fields in a PivotTable
       iii.   Refresh a PivotTable

---

**FIGURE 1** Formal Outline ➤

You can create structured outlines in Excel. To create an effective outline, you must ensure the data have a hierarchical structure. If your data are contained in a regular range instead of a table, you can attempt to create an automatic outline. To do this, click the Data tab, click the Group arrow in the Outline group, and select Auto Outline. If data are structured correctly, Excel creates the outline. If Excel cannot create the outline, it displays the message box *Cannot create an outline*. Excel will not create an outline or group data if the dataset does not contain a formula or an aggregate function such as SUM or SUBTOTAL.

**Grouping** is a process of joining related rows or columns of related data.

For more control in creating an outline, you can create your own groups. *Grouping* is the process of joining related rows or columns of related data together into a single entity. After you create groups in the dataset, you can collapse or expand groups to view selected areas of interest to analyze the data. Grouping enables you to hide raw data while you focus on key calculated results. In the sociology textbook example, you might only want to see overall discipline or area totals. In Figure 2, Excel grouped the data by columns and rows. Because the Units Sold and Unit Price columns are grouped, you can collapse this detail and focus on the Gross Sales for each book or group of books. A nested row grouping is applied to the data: first by discipline (Family, Introductory, and Social Psychology) and then subdivided by area (such as Family Interaction). The expanded Family Interaction and Marriage and Family areas show the details and their summary total rows, as well as the Family discipline total. The collapsed areas within the Introductory and Social Psychology disciplines show only the discipline total.

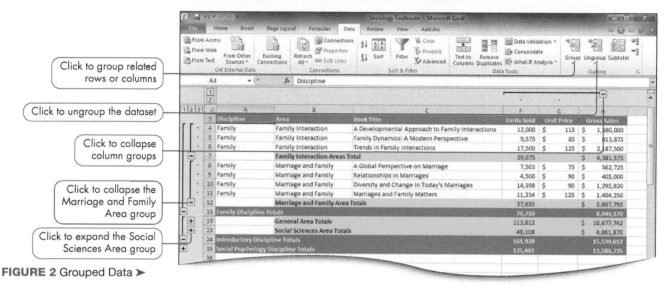

Click to group related rows or columns

Click to ungroup the dataset

Click to collapse column groups

Click to collapse the Marriage and Family Area group

Click to expand the Social Sciences Area group

**FIGURE 2** Grouped Data ➤

To group data, do the following:

1. Select the rows or columns you want to group. For column groups, you often select columns containing details but not aggregate columns, such as totals or averages.
2. Click the Data tab.
3. Click Group in the Outline group. If the Group dialog box opens, choose the option to group by columns or rows, and then click OK.

Excel displays a margin area of collapse and expand buttons (see Figure 2). If you grouped columns, the margin area appears above the columns. If you grouped rows, the margin area appears to the left of the first column. To collapse or hide a group, click the collapse button (−). The button changes to an expand button (+) so that you can expand the group later to see the details again. Although you could hide columns and rows, collapsing an outline hides multiple rows or columns at the same time.

If you no longer want the data outlined, remove the groups. To remove the groups, select all grouped columns or rows, and then click Ungroup in the Outline group.

## Subtotaling Data

Creating groupings by row can be time consuming because you have to enter formula rows by group. Instead of inserting temporary subtotal rows, use the Subtotal dialog box to create an automatic outline by rows *and* insert subtotals at the same time. You can use the Subtotal dialog box with ranges of data, but not with tables. Before using the Subtotal feature, you must sort the data based on a categorical column with duplicate values, such as the Area column. To create an automatic outline with subtotals, do the following:

1. Sort the data on a primary category, such as Area. **NOTE: If the data are not sorted by a major category, the subtotaled results will not be correct.**
2. Organize data in a range of cells, not a table. If you have a table, convert it to a range first.
3. Click in the range of data, and then click the Data tab.
4. Click Subtotal in the Outline group to open the Subtotal dialog box (see Figure 3).
5. Click the *At each change in* arrow, and then select the column by which the data are sorted. **NOTE: You must select the column by which you sorted data in Step 1.**
6. Click the *Use function* arrow, and then select the function you want to apply based on the data. For example, you can sum or average the units sold, but you cannot sum the unit prices because the unit prices are not additive.
7. Select the appropriate column heading check boxes in the *Add subtotal to* list for each field you want to total. You can use all functions for columns that contain numeric data. For text columns, you can only count the number of rows within the group.
8. Select any other check boxes you want to use, and then click OK.

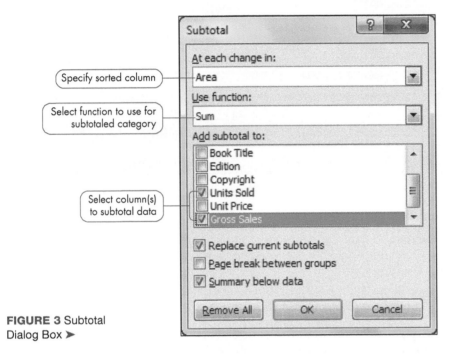

**FIGURE 3** Subtotal Dialog Box ➤

Excel inserts a subtotal row into the dataset when the value of a designated field, such as Area, changes from one row to the next. In Figure 4, Excel added the subtotal labels, such as Family Interaction Total, the total units sold (39,075), and the total gross sales ($4,381,375). Excel uses the SUBTOTAL function to calculate the subtotals using the function you select. For example, the first argument in the function (9) sums the values in the range specified in the second argument. If you want to find the average gross sales, the function would be =SUBTOTAL(1,H4:H6), where 1 represents an average. Subtotals display for each area, and a grand total appears at the bottom of the dataset. Table 1 explains the outline buttons that appear on the left side of the data.

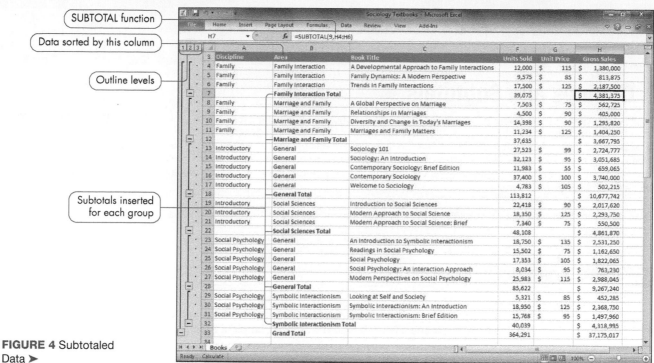

**FIGURE 4** Subtotaled Data ➤

Labels around Figure 4:
- SUBTOTAL function
- Data sorted by this column
- Outline levels
- Subtotals inserted for each group

| TABLE 1 | Outline Buttons |
|---------|-----------------|
| **Area** | **Description** |
| 1 | Collapse outline to display grand total only |
| 2 | Display subtotals by category and the grand total |
| 3 | Display the entire list |
| + | Expand an outline group to see its details |
| − | Collapse an outline group to see its category name only |

Figure 5 shows two collapsed versions of the expanded subtotaled data shown in Figure 4. In Figure 5, the first dataset is collapsed to the grand total only, and the second dataset is collapsed to show area subtotals and the grand total.

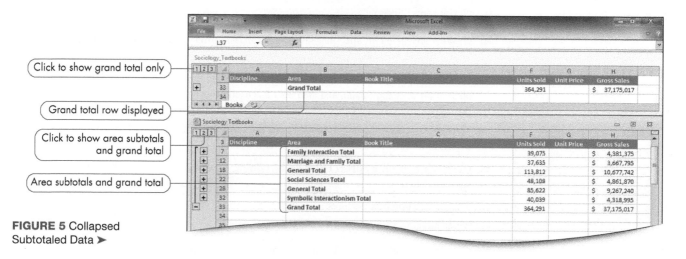

**FIGURE 5** Collapsed Subtotaled Data ➤

Labels around Figure 5:
- Click to show grand total only
- Grand total row displayed
- Click to show area subtotals and grand total
- Area subtotals and grand total

## 1 Outlines and Subtotals

As VP of the Sociology Division at Ivory Halls, you want to conduct a preliminary analysis of your current textbook offerings. You will organize the data and include area subtotals. Each textbook falls within a general discipline, and each discipline is divided into several areas. Details for each textbook include the title, current edition, and copyright year. The company tracks units sold, unit prices, and gross sales by two major types of sales: (1) wholesale sales to bookstores and (2) retail sales to individual consumers. Your assistant applied Freeze Panes to keep the column headings in row 4 and the disciplines and areas in columns A and B visible regardless of where you scroll.

**Skills covered:** Sort the Data • Subtotal the Data • Add a Second Subtotal • Collapse and Expand the Subtotals • Outline and Collapse Data

---

### STEP 1 ▸ SORT THE DATA

Before you can start analyzing the data, you must first organize it in some meaningful way. After studying the data for a few minutes, you decide to organize the data by sorting the dataset by discipline, then by area, and finally by book title. Refer to Figure 6 as you complete Step 1.

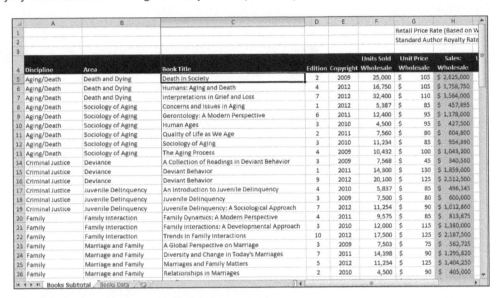

**FIGURE 6** Sorted Data ➤

a. Open *e05h1sociology*, and then save it as **e05h1sociology_LastnameFirstname**.

> **TROUBLESHOOTING:** If you make any major mistakes in this exercise, you can close the file, open *e05h1sociology* again, and then start this exercise over.

The workbook contains two worksheets: Books Subtotal for Hands-On Exercise 1 and Books Data for Hands-On Exercises 2–4.

b. Click **cell C10**, click **Sort & Filter** in the Editing group on the Home tab, and then select **Custom Sort**.

The Sort dialog box displays.

c. Click the **Sort by arrow**, and then select **Discipline**.

d. Click **Add Level**, click the **Then by arrow**, and then select **Area**.

e. Click **Add Level**, click the second **Then by arrow**, and then select **Book Title**. Click **OK**. Save the workbook.

Excel sorts the list by discipline in alphabetical order. Within each discipline, Excel sorts the list further by area. Within each area, Excel sorts the list by book title. The data are organized by discipline categories, so that you can apply subtotals to each discipline category.

Now that you sorted the list of sociology textbooks by discipline, you can use the Subtotal dialog box to insert subtotals for each discipline. You want to see the totals for the wholesale sales, retail sales, and combined book sales. Refer to Figure 7 as you complete Step 2.

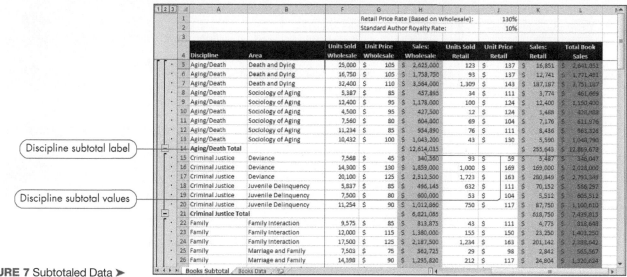

Discipline subtotal label

Discipline subtotal values

**FIGURE 7** Subtotaled Data ➤

a. Click the **Data tab**, and then click **Subtotal** in the Outline group.

The Subtotal dialog box opens. The default *At each change in* is the Discipline column, and the default *Use function* is Sum. These settings are correct.

b. Click the **Sales: Wholesale check box** in the *Add subtotal to* section.

c. Click the **Sales: Retail check box** in the *Add subtotal to* section.

Excel selected the last column—Total Book Sales—automatically. You selected the other two sales columns to total. You will leave the *Replace current subtotals* and *Summary below data* check boxes selected.

d. Click **OK**. Scroll to the right to see the subtotals, and then widen any columns as needed to see the subtotal values. Save the workbook.

Excel inserts subtotal rows after each discipline category. The subtotal rows include labels and subtotals for the wholesale sales, retail sales, and book sales columns.

> **TROUBLESHOOTING:** If your subtotals do not match the totals in Figure 7, check to see that you sorted the data correctly in Step 1. If you did not sort the data correctly, close the workbook, open the original data file again, and then follow Steps 1 and 2 again.

## STEP 3 ▶ ADD A SECOND SUBTOTAL

Displaying subtotals by discipline helps you compare sales data better; however, you want to add another level to see subtotals for each area within each discipline. To insert two levels of subtotals, you must subtotal the primary category first (Discipline) and then add a subtotal to the second category (Area). As you use the Subtotal dialog box, you want to keep the original subtotals intact. Refer to Figure 8 as you complete Step 3.

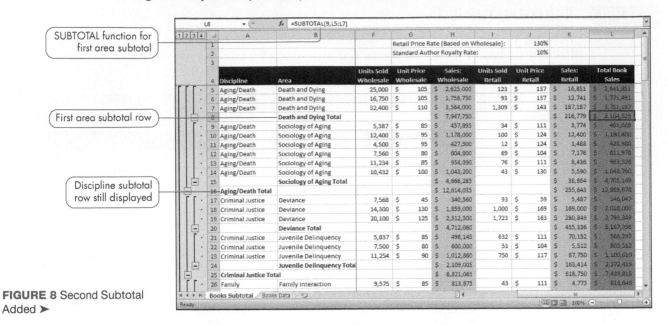

**FIGURE 8** Second Subtotal Added ➤

a. Click within the list, if necessary, and then click **Subtotal** in the Outline group.

The Subtotal dialog box opens.

b. Click the **At each change in arrow**, and then select **Area**.

The *Use function* is still Sum, and Excel remembers the last columns you selected in the *Add subtotal to* section—Sales: Wholesale, Sales: Retail, and Total Book Sales.

c. Click the **Replace current subtotals check box** to deselect it.

To keep the original subtotaled data by discipline, you must deselect this check box.

d. Click **OK**, and then click **cell L8**. Save the workbook.

Excel inserts subtotal rows after each area group. The Formula Bar displays =SUBTOTAL (9,L5:L7). Your data now have discipline subtotals and area subtotals within each discipline.

> **TROUBLESHOOTING:** If you subtotal the area first and then subtotal by discipline, Excel adds several discipline subtotals, which repeat the area subtotals. That is why you must subtotal by the primary category first, and then subtotal by the subdivision category.

## STEP 4 ▶ COLLAPSE AND EXPAND THE SUBTOTALS

You want to compare wholesale, retail, and book sales among the disciplines and then among areas within a discipline. Refer to Figure 9 as you complete Step 4.

Subtotals, PivotTables, and PivotCharts

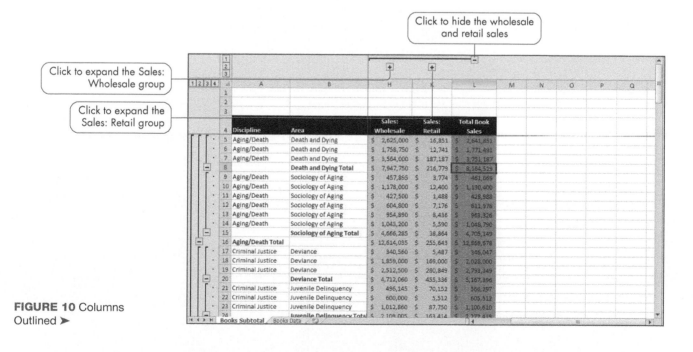

Click to collapse to grand totals

Click to display grand totals and discipline subtotals

| | Discipline | Area | Units Sold Wholesale | Unit Price Wholesale | Sales: Wholesale | Units Sold Retail | Unit Price Retail | Sales: Retail | Total Book Sales |
|---|---|---|---|---|---|---|---|---|---|
| 1 | | | | | Retail Price Rate (Based on Wholesale): | | | 130% | |
| 2 | | | | | Standard Author Royalty Rate: | | | 10% | |
| 16 | Aging/Death Total | | | | $ 12,614,035 | | | $ 255,643 | $ 12,869,678 |
| 25 | Criminal Justice Total | | | | $ 6,821,065 | | | $ 618,750 | $ 7,439,815 |
| 35 | Family Total | | | | $ 8,049,170 | | | $ 441,967 | $ 8,491,137 |
| 52 | Introductory Total | | | | $ 17,221,537 | | | $ 654,714 | $ 17,876,251 |
| 60 | Miscellaneous Total | | | | $ 3,179,795 | | | $ 247,268 | $ 3,427,063 |
| 78 | Race/Class/Gender Total | | | | $ 22,072,575 | | | $ 919,953 | $ 22,992,528 |
| 97 | Research/Stats Total | | | | $ 21,273,970 | | | $ 817,731 | $ 22,091,701 |
| 112 | Social Problems Total | | | | $ 10,615,950 | | | $ 135,277 | $ 10,751,227 |
| 123 | Social Psychology Total | | | | $ 13,586,235 | | | $ 708,009 | $ 14,294,244 |
| 124 | Grand Total | | | | $ 115,434,332 | | | $ 4,799,312 | $ 120,233,644 |

**FIGURE 9** Collapsed Subtotals List ➤

a. Click the **1** in the top-left outline area (to the left of the column headings).

   You collapsed the outline to show the grand totals only.

b. Click the **2** in the top-left outline area.

   See Figure 9. You expanded the outline to show the grand totals and the discipline subtotals. Which two disciplines had the highest wholesale and retail sales? Which discipline had the lowest total sales?

c. Click the **3** in the top-left outline area.

   You expanded the outline to show the grand totals, the discipline subtotals, and the area subtotals. Within the Introductory discipline, which area had the lowest sales? How do wholesale and retail sales compare? Are they proportionally the same within each area?

d. Click the **4** in the top-left outline area. Save the workbook.

   You expanded the outline to show all details again. If you had not added the second subtotal, the outline would have had three levels instead of four.

## STEP 5 ▸ OUTLINE AND COLLAPSE DATA

You want to see the values without scrolling or hiding columns. You will apply an outline to the columns so that you can collapse or expand the units sold and unit prices columns. Refer to Figure 10 as you complete Step 5.

Click to hide the wholesale and retail sales

Click to expand the Sales: Wholesale group

Click to expand the Sales: Retail group

| | Discipline | Area | Sales: Wholesale | Sales: Retail | Total Book Sales |
|---|---|---|---|---|---|
| 5 | Aging/Death | Death and Dying | $ 2,625,000 | $ 16,851 | $ 2,641,851 |
| 6 | Aging/Death | Death and Dying | $ 1,758,750 | $ 12,741 | $ 1,771,491 |
| 7 | Aging/Death | Death and Dying | $ 3,564,000 | $ 187,187 | $ 3,751,187 |
| 8 | | Death and Dying Total | $ 7,947,750 | $ 216,779 | $ 8,164,529 |
| 9 | Aging/Death | Sociology of Aging | $ 457,895 | $ 3,774 | $ 461,669 |
| 10 | Aging/Death | Sociology of Aging | $ 1,178,000 | $ 12,400 | $ 1,190,400 |
| 11 | Aging/Death | Sociology of Aging | $ 427,500 | $ 1,488 | $ 428,988 |
| 12 | Aging/Death | Sociology of Aging | $ 604,800 | $ 7,176 | $ 611,976 |
| 13 | Aging/Death | Sociology of Aging | $ 954,890 | $ 8,436 | $ 963,326 |
| 14 | Aging/Death | Sociology of Aging | $ 1,043,200 | $ 5,590 | $ 1,048,790 |
| 15 | | Sociology of Aging Total | $ 4,666,285 | $ 38,864 | $ 4,705,149 |
| 16 | Aging/Death Total | | $ 12,614,035 | $ 255,643 | $ 12,869,678 |
| 17 | Criminal Justice | Deviance | $ 340,560 | $ 5,487 | $ 346,047 |
| 18 | Criminal Justice | Deviance | $ 1,859,000 | $ 169,000 | $ 2,028,000 |
| 19 | Criminal Justice | Deviance | $ 2,512,500 | $ 280,849 | $ 2,793,349 |
| 20 | | Deviance Total | $ 4,712,060 | $ 455,336 | $ 5,167,396 |
| 21 | Criminal Justice | Juvenile Delinquency | $ 496,145 | $ 70,152 | $ 566,297 |
| 22 | Criminal Justice | Juvenile Delinquency | $ 600,000 | $ 5,512 | $ 605,512 |
| 23 | Criminal Justice | Juvenile Delinquency | $ 1,012,860 | $ 87,750 | $ 1,100,610 |
| 24 | | Juvenile Delinquency Total | $ 2,109,005 | $ 163,414 | $ 2,272,419 |

**FIGURE 10** Columns Outlined ➤

**a.** Click the **Group arrow** in the Outline group on the Data tab.

You want to see if Excel can create a column outline for you so that you do not have to select columns and group them individually.

**b.** Select **Auto Outline**.

Excel displays the message box *Modify existing outline?* because it recognized that an existing outline exists—the row subtotals outline.

**c.** Click **OK**.

Excel maintains the outlined subtotals and adds column subtotals for you. Horizontal lines and collapse buttons appear above the columns. The formula in column H is =F5*G5, so Excel creates an outline for these columns. The formula in column K is =I5*J5, so Excel creates an outline for these columns. It also creates a hierarchical outline of columns F through K since the formula in column L sums the values in columns H and K.

**d.** Click the **collapse (-) button** above **column L**.

You collapsed columns F through K so that you can see disciplines, areas, and total sales by title.

**e.** Click the **expand (+) button** above **column L**.

You expanded the outline to show columns F through K again.

**f.** Click the **collapse (-) button** above **column H**.

You collapsed the outline to hide columns F and G so you can focus on the wholesale sales without seeing the units sold or unit price columns to distract you.

**g.** Click the **collapse (-) button** above **column K**.

You collapsed the outline to hide columns I and J so you can focus on the retail sales without seeing the units sold or unit price columns to distract you.

**h.** Save the workbook. Keep the workbook onscreen if you plan to continue with Hands-On Exercise 2. If not, close the workbook and exit Excel.

# PivotTable Basics

Analyzing large amounts of data is important for making solid decisions. With the improvements in technology, more and more data are being collected and stored. Entering data is the easy part; retrieving data in a structured, meaningful way is more challenging. People rely on data mining experts to help with the retrieval process. ***Data mining*** is the process of analyzing large volumes of data, using advanced statistical techniques, and identifying trends and patterns in the data. Managers use data mining techniques to address a variety of questions, such as the following:

- What snack foods do customers purchase most when purchasing Pepsi products?
- What age group from what geographic region downloads the most top 10 songs from iTunes?
- What hotel chain and rental car combinations are most popular among Delta Air Lines passengers flying into Cincinnati?

What age group from what geographic region downloads the most top 10 songs from iTunes?

Questions similar to those above help organizations prepare their marketing plans to capitalize on consumer spending patterns. The more you know about your customer demographics, the better you can focus your strategic plans to increase your market share.

You can sort, filter, apply conditional formatting, and use subtotals to address some questions, but applying these different tools in various combinations to answer your questions or to identify the trends and patterns may be time consuming. You can use PivotTables in both Excel and Access to help you with data mining. A ***PivotTable*** is a powerful, interactive data mining feature that enables you to summarize and analyze large amounts of data. An advantage of using a PivotTable is that you can group data into one or more categories and perform a variety of calculations without altering the original data source. The most important benefit of a PivotTable is that it is dynamic. You can easily and quickly *pivot*, or rearrange, the data to see them from different angles, such as expanding or collapsing details, organizing and grouping data differently, and switching row and column categories. Viewing the PivotTable from different perspectives helps you more easily identify trends and patterns among the variables in the data that might not be obvious from looking at the data from only one angle.

In this section, you will learn how to create a PivotTable by organizing data into columns and rows to aggregate data.

## Creating a PivotTable

Before you create a PivotTable, ensure the data source is well structured. Applying the rules for good table design is a start: use meaningful column headings, ensure data accuracy, and avoid blank rows and columns in the dataset. To consolidate and aggregate data, at least one column must have duplicate values, such as the same city, state, or department name for several records in one field. You then use these columns of duplicate values to create categories for organizing and summarizing data. Another column must have numeric values to produce quantitative summaries, such as averages or sums. Figure 11 shows a structured list of some sociology books and a resulting PivotTable.

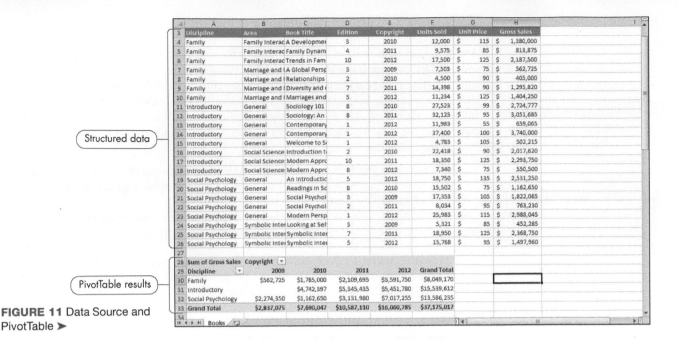

Structured data

PivotTable results

**FIGURE 11** Data Source and PivotTable ➤

| | A | B | C | D | E | F | G | H |
|---|---|---|---|---|---|---|---|---|
| 3 | Discipline | Area | Book Title | Edition | Copyright | Units Sold | Unit Price | Gross Sales |
| 4 | Family | Family Interac | A Developmer | 3 | 2010 | 12,000 | $ 115 | $ 1,380,000 |
| 5 | Family | Family Interac | Family Dynam | 4 | 2011 | 9,575 | $ 85 | $ 813,875 |
| 6 | Family | Family Interac | Trends in Fam | 10 | 2012 | 17,500 | $ 125 | $ 2,187,500 |
| 7 | Family | Marriage and I | A Global Persr | 3 | 2009 | 7,503 | $ 75 | $ 562,725 |
| 8 | Family | Marriage and I | Relationships | 2 | 2010 | 4,500 | $ 90 | $ 405,000 |
| 9 | Family | Marriage and I | Diversity and ( | 7 | 2011 | 14,398 | $ 90 | $ 1,295,820 |
| 10 | Family | Marriage and I | Marriages and | 5 | 2012 | 11,234 | $ 125 | $ 1,404,250 |
| 11 | Introductory | General | Sociology 101 | 8 | 2010 | 27,523 | $ 99 | $ 2,724,777 |
| 12 | Introductory | General | Sociology: An | 8 | 2011 | 32,123 | $ 95 | $ 3,051,685 |
| 13 | Introductory | General | Contemporary | 1 | 2012 | 11,983 | $ 55 | $ 659,065 |
| 14 | Introductory | General | Contemporary | 1 | 2012 | 37,400 | $ 100 | $ 3,740,000 |
| 15 | Introductory | General | Welcome to Sr | 1 | 2012 | 4,783 | $ 105 | $ 502,215 |
| 16 | Introductory | Social Science | Introduction tr | 2 | 2010 | 22,418 | $ 90 | $ 2,017,620 |
| 17 | Introductory | Social Science | Modern Apprc | 10 | 2011 | 18,350 | $ 125 | $ 2,293,750 |
| 18 | Introductory | Social Science | Modern Apprc | 8 | 2012 | 7,340 | $ 75 | $ 550,500 |
| 19 | Social Psychology | General | An Introductic | 5 | 2012 | 18,750 | $ 135 | $ 2,531,250 |
| 20 | Social Psychology | General | Readings in Sc | 8 | 2010 | 15,502 | $ 75 | $ 1,162,650 |
| 21 | Social Psychology | General | Social Psychol | 3 | 2009 | 17,353 | $ 105 | $ 1,822,065 |
| 22 | Social Psychology | General | Social Psychol | 2 | 2011 | 8,034 | $ 95 | $ 763,230 |
| 23 | Social Psychology | General | Modern Persp | 1 | 2012 | 25,983 | $ 115 | $ 2,988,045 |
| 24 | Social Psychology | Symbolic Inter | Looking at Sel | 3 | 2009 | 5,321 | $ 85 | $ 452,285 |
| 25 | Social Psychology | Symbolic Inter | Symbolic Inter | 7 | 2011 | 18,950 | $ 125 | $ 2,368,750 |
| 26 | Social Psychology | Symbolic Inter | Symbolic Inter | 5 | 2012 | 15,768 | $ 95 | $ 1,497,960 |
| 27 | | | | | | | | |
| 28 | Sum of Gross Sales | Copyright ▼ | | | | | | |
| 29 | Discipline ▼ | 2009 | 2010 | 2011 | 2012 | Grand Total | | |
| 30 | Family | $562,725 | $1,785,000 | $2,109,695 | $3,591,750 | $8,049,170 | | |
| 31 | Introductory | | $4,742,397 | $5,345,435 | $5,451,780 | $15,539,612 | | |
| 32 | Social Psychology | $2,274,350 | $1,162,650 | $3,131,980 | $7,017,255 | $13,586,235 | | |
| 33 | Grand Total | $2,837,075 | $7,690,047 | $10,587,110 | $16,060,785 | $37,175,017 | | |
| 34 | | | | | | | | |

Books

**TIP** PivotTable or Subtotals?

At first glance, you might think PivotTables are similar to subtotals because they both produce similar subtotals, but a PivotTable is more robust. You have more flexibility in designing the PivotTable than you have when using the Subtotal dialog box. If you need complex subtotals cross-referenced by two or more categories with filtering and other specifications, create a PivotTable. The PivotTable does not modify your original dataset by adding subtotals.

To create a PivotTable, do the following:

1. Click inside the dataset (the range of cells or table).

2. Click the Insert tab, and then click Insert PivotTable in the Tables group to open the Create PivotTable dialog box.

3. Specify the dataset by entering the range, if necessary, in the Table/Range box. If you selected a cell in a range or table, the range of cells or table name reference shows in the Table/Range box (see Figure 12).

4. Decide where you want to place the PivotTable. Click New Worksheet to create the PivotTable on a new worksheet, or click Existing Worksheet and enter the starting cell location for a particular worksheet to create the PivotTable on an existing worksheet. It is beneficial to create a PivotTable on a new worksheet to separate the PivotTable from the dataset. Doing so can prevent problems of accidentally inserting or deleting rows or columns in the table that also affect the PivotTable.

5. Click OK.

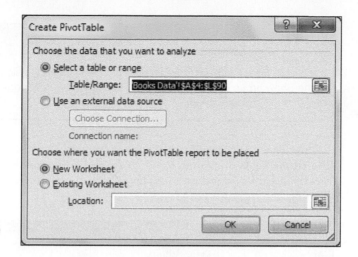

**FIGURE 12** Create PivotTable
Dialog Box ➤

**FIGURE 12** Create PivotTable
Dialog Box ➤

An empty PivotTable appears on the left side of the worksheet, and the PivotTable Field List appears on the right side of the screen so that you can add fields, create a layout, and customize the PivotTable (see Figure 13). While you are working on a PivotTable, the PivotTable Tools Options and Design contextual tabs appear. These tabs enable you to manipulate, customize, and format the PivotTable. If you click outside the PivotTable area, the PivotTable Tools and the PivotTable Field List disappear. Click within the PivotTable to display the PivotTable Field List and the PivotTable Tools with the Options and Design tabs again.

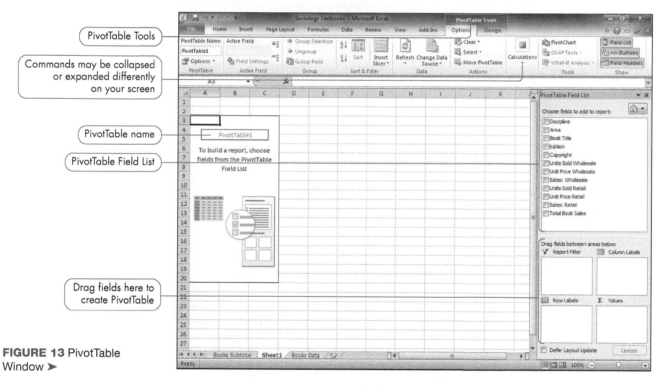

**FIGURE 13** PivotTable
Window ➤

As Figure 13 shows, the default PivotTable name is PivotTable1, where each PivotTable has its own number. You can assign a name to each PivotTable similar to how you assign names to tables. Click in the PivotTable Name box in the PivotTable group, type a new name, and then press Enter. Depending on your screen resolution, some groups (such as Calculations in Figure 13) on the Options tab may be collapsed. If the PivotTable group is collapsed, click the PivotTable arrow to display the PivotTable group commands, and then click in the PivotTable Name box to change the name of the PivotTable.

> **TIP** PivotTable Field List
>
> If the PivotTable Field List does not appear when you click inside a PivotTable, click Field List in the Show group on the Options tab. This command is a toggle, so you can click it to show or hide the PivotTable Field List.

The PivotTable Field List contains two sections. The *Choose fields to add to report* section lists all the fields or column headings from the original data source. Use the *Drag fields between areas below* section to arrange fields in one of the four PivotTable areas. Table 2 describes the areas of a PivotTable.

**TABLE 2 Areas of a PivotTable**

| Area | Description |
| --- | --- |
| **Values** | Displays summary statistics, such as totals or averages. |
| **Row Labels** | Organizes and groups data into categories on the left side of the PivotTable. Each group name occupies a single row. |
| **Column Labels** | Subdivides data into one or more additional categories to add depth to the PivotTable. |
| **Report Filter** | Filters the aggregated data to display results based on particular conditions you set. |

## Add Fields for Row Labels and Values

To start building your PivotTable, decide how you want to organize the consolidated data. Select a text field that you want to use to organize data into categories. The field you select should contain duplicate text, such as the same state for several records. For example, you might want to organize data by discipline, so you add the Discipline field to the Row Labels area box. To add this field as a row label, do one of the following:

- Click the field's check box in the *Choose fields to add to report* section. Excel adds the field to a PivotTable area based on the type of data stored in the field. If the field contains text, Excel usually places that field in the Row Labels area.
- Drag the field from the *Choose fields to add to report* section, and then drop it in the Row Labels area.
- Right-click the field name in the *Choose fields to add to report* section, and then select Add to Row Labels.

Excel displays the discipline row labels in alphabetical order down the left side of the PivotTable. Each discipline, such as Family, is listed only one time as a row label, regardless of how many times each label appears in the original dataset.

After designating the row labels, decide which field of values you want to summarize. Typically, you aggregate numerical data, such as quantities, monetary values, or percentages. For example, you might want to display the total sales of books sold within each discipline. To add a field for the value aggregate, do one of the following:

- Click the field's check box in the *Choose fields to add to report* section. For the first numeric field you select, Excel makes it the value aggregate, such as Sum of Sales.
- Drag the field from the *Choose fields to add to report* section, and then drop it in the Values area.
- Right-click the field name in the *Choose fields to add to report* section, and then select Add to Values.

Excel sums the values for each group listed in the Row Labels area. For example, the total sales for the Family discipline are $8,491,137. If you drag a text field, such as Book Title, instead of a numerical field to the Values area, Excel counts the number of records for each group listed in the Row Labels area. In this case, Excel counts seven books in the Family discipline.

## Add Fields for Column Labels

Although you can create subdivisions of data by adding more fields to the Row Labels area, you might want to arrange the subdivision categories in columns. Doing so minimizes the redundancy of duplicating subdivision row labels and helps consolidate the data even further. To subdivide data into columns, drag a field from the *Choose fields to add to report* section, and then drop it in the Column Labels area. Excel updates the aggregated values by the combination of row and column categories.

Figure 14 shows a PivotTable that uses the Discipline field as row labels, the Sum of Total Book Sales field as the values, and Copyright field as the column labels. Each discipline label and each copyright year label appears only once in the PivotTable. This added level of detail enables you to see the total sales for each discipline based on its copyright year. The PivotTable includes grand totals for each discipline and grand totals for each year.

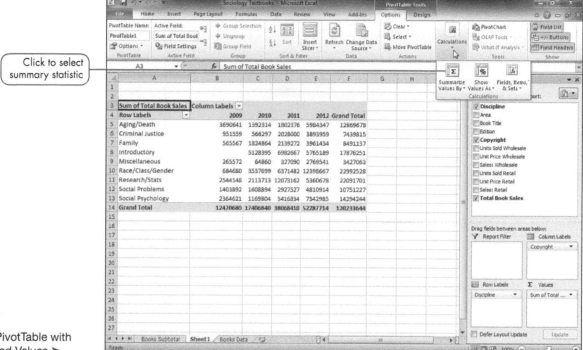

**FIGURE 14** PivotTable with Row Labels and Values ➤

## Changing the Values Field

Although Excel uses the SUM function as the default summary statistic, you can select a different function to evaluate the values. For example, you might want to calculate the average, lowest, or highest value within each group, or identify the lowest sales for each discipline/copyright year combination to see if the older books have decreased sales. In addition to changing the summary statistic, you might want to change the column heading that appears above the summary statistics in the PivotTable. By default, words indicate the summary statistic function applied, such as *Sum of Total Sales by Book* or *Average of Total Sales by*

*Book*, depending on the summary statistic applied to the values. Finally, you might need to format the aggregated values. To modify any of these value settings, do the following:

1. Click a value in the appropriate field in the PivotTable, and then click Field Settings in the Active Field group on the Options tab. Alternatively, click the field's arrow in the Values area, and then select Value Field Settings. The Value Field Settings dialog box displays (see Figure 15).

2. Type the name you want to appear as the column heading in the Custom Name box. For example, you might want the heading to appear as Total Sales instead of Sum of Total Book Sales.

3. Select the summary statistical function you want to use to summarize the values in the *Summarize value field by* list.

4. Click Number Format to open an abbreviated version of the Format Cells dialog box. Select a number type, such as Accounting, in the Category list; select other settings, such as number of decimal places in the *Decimal places* spin arrow; and then click OK.

5. Click OK in the Value Field Settings dialog box.

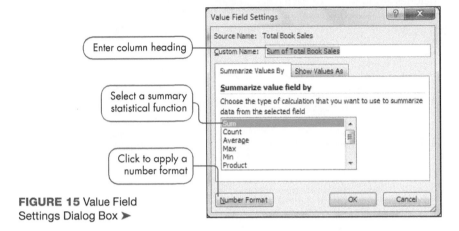

**FIGURE 15** Value Field Settings Dialog Box ➤

Another way to change the summary statistic is to click Summarize Values By in the Calculations group on the PivotTable Tools Options tab. Depending on your screen resolution, the commands in the Calculations group might not be visible. If the group is collapsed, click the Calculations arrow to display the commands in that group, and then click Summarize Values By. You can select Sum, Count, Average, Max, Min, and Product, or select More Options to display the Value Field Settings dialog box for additional options.

> **TIP  Multiple Summary Statistics**
>
> You can display more than one function for the same field. For example, you might want to show *both* the total book sales and the average book sales. To display multiple summary statistics, drag another copy of the same field to the Values area. Then you can set each column's value settings separately.

## Modifying a PivotTable

Although you plan how you group the data into rows and columns, you might want to modify the PivotTable to see the data from a different perspective. For example, you might want to switch the row and column orientation similar to how you can switch the category axis and data series within a column chart. In addition, you might want to add or remove fields from the PivotTable.

## Add and Remove Fields

You can create more depth to a PivotTable by adding more fields to the Row Labels and Column Labels areas in the PivotTable Field List. This enables you to build PivotTables with more sophisticated groups and subgroups. To add a field as a subdivision of an existing row label, drag the second field and drop it below the existing field name in the Row Labels area. Excel still lists each original row label only once, but it lists duplicates of the subcategories, if applicable, for each main category (see Figure 16). If you want to add a main row label as a higher-level grouping than the original row label, drop the second field name *above* the existing row label. Be careful when adding subcategories because the number of rows increases. Only add more groupings if further detail is required to understand the data and to identify trends and patterns. Otherwise, you may be adding unnecessary groupings and thus making the data overwhelming with too many details.

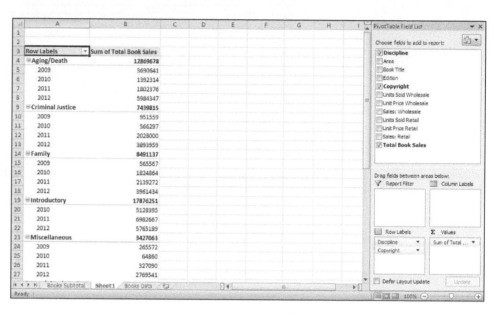

**FIGURE 16** PivotTable with Two Row Labels ➤

If you no longer want a field in a PivotTable, remove it. To remove a field from the PivotTable, do one of the following:

- Click the field name in the *Drag fields between areas below* section, and then select Remove Field.
- Deselect the check box next to the field name in the *Choose fields to add to report* section.
- Click a field name in the *Drag fields between areas below* section, and then drag it outside the PivotTable Field List.

## Rearrange Fields in a PivotTable

You can rearrange or reposition existing fields in a PivotTable to improve readability. For example, you might want more columns than rows, so you can switch the fields in the Row Labels and Column Labels areas in the PivotTable Field List. To move a field from one area to another, drag the field from one area to another area in the *Drag fields between areas below* section. You can also change the location or hierarchy of the fields by clicking the field arrow and selecting a Move option. Table 3 explains the Move options.

| TABLE 3 | Move Options |
| --- | --- |
| **Option** | **Moves the Field ...** |
| **Move Up** | Up one position in the hierarchy within the same area |
| **Move Down** | Down one position in the hierarchy within the same area |
| **Move to Beginning** | To the beginning of all fields in the same area |
| **Move to End** | To the end of all fields in the same area |
| **Move to Report Filter** | To the end of the Report Filter area of the PivotTable |
| **Move to Row Labels** | To the end of the Row Labels area of the PivotTable |
| **Move to Column Labels** | To the end of the Column Labels area of the PivotTable |
| **Move to Values** | To the end of the Values area of the PivotTable |

## Refresh a PivotTable

Although PivotTables are powerful, they do not update automatically if you make any changes to the underlying data in the data source. For example, if you change a sales value or delete a row, the PivotTable does not reflect the changed data. Unfortunately, this causes PivotTable summary statistics to be outdated with inaccurate results. If you change the data source, you must update the PivotTable yourself. To do this, click in the PivotTable to display the PivotTable Tools. Click the Options tab, and then click Refresh in the Data group to refresh the current PivotTable only. If you click the Refresh arrow, you can select to refresh either the current PivotTable or all PivotTables.

If you want to ensure your PivotTable is up to date when you open the workbook, click the PivotTable Tools Options tab, and then click Options in the PivotTable group. In the PivotTable Options dialog box, click the Data tab, select *Refresh data when opening the file*, and then click OK.

# HANDS-ON EXERCISES

## 2 PivotTable Basics

After exhausting the possibilities of outlines and subtotals, you want to create a PivotTable to analyze the sociology book sales. You realize you can see the data from different perspectives, enabling you to have a stronger understanding of the sales by various categories.

**Skills covered:** Create a PivotTable • Add Labels and Values • Rearrange Fields • Change the Value Field Settings • Change Data and Refresh the PivotTable

---

**CREATE A PIVOTTABLE**

Because you want to keep the subtotals you created in the Books Subtotal worksheet, you will create a PivotTable from the Books Data worksheet. Refer to Figures 12, 13, and 17 as you complete Step 1.

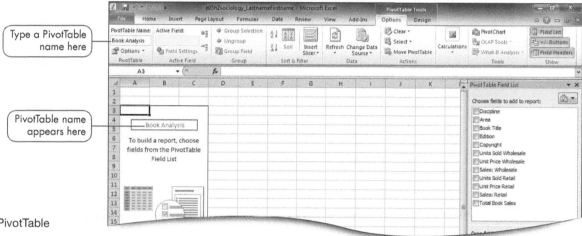

Type a PivotTable name here

PivotTable name appears here

**FIGURE 17** PivotTable Name ➤

a. Open *e05h1sociology_LastnameFirstname* if you closed it at the end of Hands-On Exercise 1, and then save it as **e05h2sociology_LastnameFirstname**, changing *h1* to *h2*.

b. Click the **Books Data worksheet tab**.

Excel does not let you create a PivotTable using subtotaled data. To preserve the subtotals you created in Hands-On Exercise 1, you will use the dataset in the Books Data worksheet.

c. Click anywhere in the list of sales data, click the **Insert tab**, and then click **PivotTable** in the Tables group.

The Create PivotTable dialog box opens (see Figure 12).

d. Verify that *Select a table or range* is selected and that the Table/Range is 'Books Data'!$A$4:$L$90.

The Table/Range is the range containing the dataset for which you wish to build a PivotTable.

e. Verify that *New Worksheet* is selected, and then click **OK**.

Excel inserts a new Sheet1 worksheet with the PivotTable placeholder on the left side and the PivotTable Field List on the right side (see Figure 13). The default name is PivotTable1.

f. Click in the **PivotTable Name box** in the PivotTable group, type **Book Analysis**, and then press **Enter**.

> **TROUBLESHOOTING:** If the PivotTable group is collapsed, click the PivotTable arrow to display the PivotTable Name box.

Unlike range names that must not contain spaces, you can use spaces in PivotTable names. You renamed the PivotTable to have a more descriptive name (see Figure 17).

g. Rename Sheet1 **PivotTable**. Save the workbook.

## STEP 2 ▶ ADD LABELS AND VALUES

Now that you have a PivotTable placeholder, you are ready to build it by adding values and row labels to start organizing the book sales. You want to compare sales combinations by discipline, copyright year, and edition. Refer to Figure 18 as you complete Step 2.

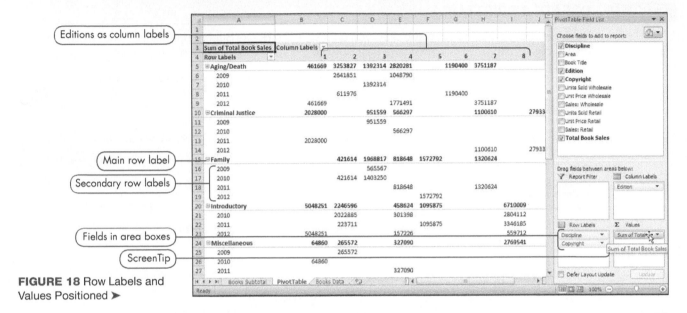

**FIGURE 18** Row Labels and Values Positioned ▶

a. Click the **Discipline check box** in the *Choose fields to add to report* section in the **PivotTable Field List**.

Excel displays the Discipline field in the Row Labels area in the PivotTable Field List because this field contains text. The first column of the PivotTable contains one label for each discipline name from the original dataset. You can also drag fields to the areas instead of clicking the check boxes. Your publishing company organizes sociology books into nine disciplines.

b. Click the **Total Book Sales check box** in the *Choose fields to add to report* section.

Excel adds the Total Book Sales field to the Values area in the PivotTable Field List because this field contains numerical data. The PivotTable calculates and displays the total book sales for each discipline as a second column within the PivotTable.

c. Drag the **Edition field** to the Column Labels area in the PivotTable Field List.

Excel displays the total book sales by a combination of discipline and edition. This enables you to compare sales of current editions within each discipline. Blanks appear in the PivotTable when a discipline does not have a specific edition. For example, the Family discipline does not have any first-edition books currently being published.

d. Drag the **Copyright field** to be below the Discipline field in the Row Labels area. Save the workbook.

You further subdivided the total book sales to compare the combination of discipline, copyright years, and editions.

Subtotals, PivotTables, and PivotCharts

**STEP 3** ## REARRANGE FIELDS

Although it is informative to compare sales by edition, you think that the PivotTable contains too much detail, so you will remove the Edition field. After you remove the field from the PivotTable, you will rearrange other fields to help simplify this PivotTable. Refer to Figure 19 as you complete Step 3.

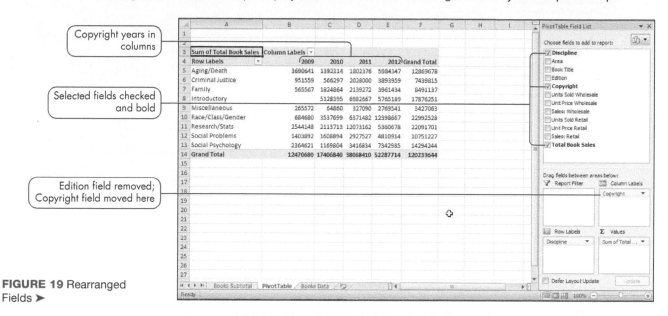

Copyright years in columns

Selected fields checked and bold

Edition field removed; Copyright field moved here

**FIGURE 19** Rearranged Fields ➤

a. Click the **Edition arrow** in the Column Labels area.

Excel displays a menu of options to apply to this field.

b. Select **Remove Field** on the menu.

You removed the Edition field from the PivotTable. Instead of several sales columns, Excel consolidates the sales into one sales column. Although you find it helpful to have sales breakdowns by copyright year, you think the PivotTable will be easier to read if you move the Copyright field to the Column Labels area now.

c. Drag the **Copyright field** from the Row Labels area to the Column Labels area. Save the workbook.

This arrangement consolidates the data better. Instead of repeating the copyright years for each discipline, the copyright years are listed only once each at the top of the sales columns.

After selecting the PivotTable fields, you want to improve the appearance of the sociology textbook PivotTable. You need to format the values for Accounting Number Format, and you want to replace the generic Row Labels description with a label that indicates the sociology disciplines. Refer to Figure 20 as you complete Step 4.

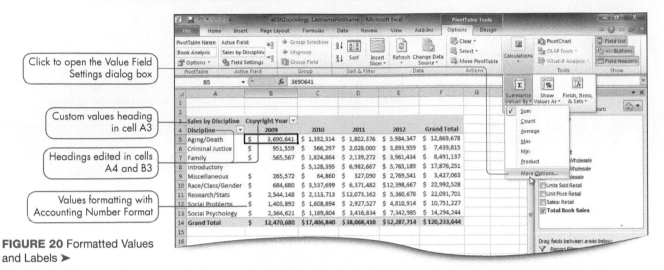

**FIGURE 20** Formatted Values and Labels ➤

a. Click **Calculations** in the Calculations group, and then click **Summarize Values By** in the Calculations group on the Options tab.

b. Select **More Options**.

The Value Field Settings dialog box opens so that you can format the field (see Figure 15).

c. Type **Sales by Discipline** in the **Custom Name box**.

You will leave Sum as the selected calculation type in the *Summarize value field by* section. You can enter a descriptive label directly in cell A3, and the label will display in the Value Field Settings dialog box.

d. Click **Number Format**.

Excel opens a Format Cells dialog box with only one tab: the Number tab.

e. Click **Accounting** in the **Category list**, click the **Decimal places spin arrow** twice to display **0**, click **OK** in the Format Cells dialog box, and then click **OK** in the Value Field Settings dialog box.

You formatted the values with Accounting Number Format with no decimal places, and the heading *Sales by Discipline* appears in cell A3.

f. Click **cell A4**, type **Discipline**, and then press **Enter**.

You replaced the generic *Row Labels* heading with *Discipline* to describe the contents of the first column. Although you can create custom names for values, you cannot create custom names for row and column labels. However, you can edit the headings directly in the cells.

g. Click **cell B3**, type **Copyright Year**, and then press **Enter**.

h. Center the copyright years and headings in the **range B4:F4**. Save the workbook.

**CHANGE DATA AND REFRESH THE PIVOTTABLE**

After consulting with the Accounting Department, you realize that the retail prices are incorrect. The unit retail prices are based on a percentage of the wholesale price. The retail unit price is 30% more than the wholesale unit price, but it should be 25%. You need to edit the input cell in the original worksheet and refresh the PivotTable to see the corrected results. Refer to Figure 21 as you complete Step 5.

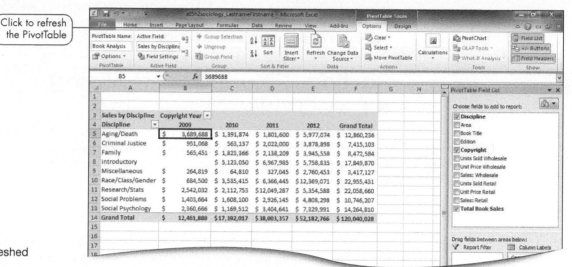

**FIGURE 21** Refreshed Values ➤

Click to refresh the PivotTable

a. Click the **Books Data worksheet tab**.

You need to locate and change the retail price percentage.

b. Click **cell J1**, the cell that contains the current retail price rate.

c. Type **125%** and press **Enter**. Save the workbook to update the formula results on the Books Data worksheet.

> **TROUBLESHOOTING:** If the formula results in the Unit Price Retail, Sales: Retail, and Total Book Sales columns do not change after you edit the data in step c, the workbook may be set for manual calculation. To ensure that formulas update automatically, click the File tab, click Options, click Formulas, click Automatic as the Workbook Calculation setting, and then click OK.

d. Click the **PivotTable worksheet tab**.

Notice that the PivotTable aggregate values did not change. The grand total is $120,233,644. You must refresh the PivotTable.

e. Click the **Options tab**, and then click **Refresh** in the Data group.

Excel updates the PivotTable values based on the changes to the Books Data worksheet sales data.

f. Save the workbook. Keep the workbook onscreen if you plan to continue with Hands-On Exercise 3. If not, close the workbook and exit Excel.

# PivotTable Options

As you have experienced, PivotTables consolidate and aggregate large amounts of data to facilitate data analysis. Although a basic PivotTable enables data analysis, you can customize the PivotTable for more in-depth analysis. In the previous section, you used the Options tab to change the PivotTable name, display the Value Field Settings dialog box, and refresh the PivotTable. However, the Options tab contains more ways for you to customize your PivotTable. For example, you can arrange and filter groups, display or hide particular groups temporarily, and add subtotals.

In this section, you will learn how to sort and filter data in a PivotTable. In addition, you will create a calculated field and display subtotals.

## Sorting, Filtering, and Slicing a PivotTable

Excel arranges PivotTable data alphabetically by the row label text. However, you can sort the data to arrange them in a different sequence. In addition, you can filter out data to focus on particular results. Both processes are similar to how you sort and filter tables and worksheet data. PivotTables include additional filtering capability.

### Sort a PivotTable

You might want to arrange the data in a different order. For example, you might want to arrange the data from the highest value to the lowest value in one of the aggregate columns. To rearrange data in a PivotTable, click any cell in the column that you wish to sort, and then click Sort Smallest to Largest (Sort A to Z for text) or Sort Largest to Smallest (Sort Z to A for text) in the Sort & Filter group. For more specialized sorting, click Sort to display the Sort By Value dialog box (see Figure 22) or the Sort dialog box (see Figure 23). These dialog boxes enable you to perform a manual sort, such as sorting data in a particular sequence.

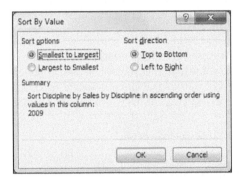

**FIGURE 22** Sort By Value Dialog Box ➤

**FIGURE 23** Sort (Discipline) Dialog Box ➤

Subtotals, PivotTables, and PivotCharts

The Sort By Value or Sort dialog box enables you to select a sort option and a sort direction. The dialog box options are slightly different, depending on what you click before you click Sort in the Sort & Filter group. If you click in a row label or column label first, the title bar displays the name of the field in parentheses, such as Sort (Discipline).

## Add Report and Group Filters

Although PivotTables consolidate data from the original data source into groups, the PivotTable might still be more detailed than you want. You can engage filters to show only a subset of the PivotTable. You can apply two types of filters: report filters and group filters. The *Drag fields between areas below* section of the PivotTable Field List contains a Report Filter area. You can drag a field to this area when you want to be able to engage a filter based on a particular field. For example, you might want to filter the PivotTable to show only aggregates for first-edition books. When you drag a field to the Report Filter area, Excel displays the field name in cell A1 with a filter arrow in cell B1. To set the filter, click the filter arrow, and then select the value to filter the data. To filter by multiple items, such as aggregates for first- and second-edition books, click the Selected Multiple Items check box, and then click the items you want to select. Only a subset of the data that meet those conditions appears in the PivotTable; Excel hides the unselected items. Figure 24 shows the filter list with the *Select Multiple Items* check box selected. When you select this check box, you can then select multiple items, such as 1, 4, 7, and 8. The filter list also enables you to enter a search condition to limit the list to items that meet your condition, which is helpful when you have a large list of items.

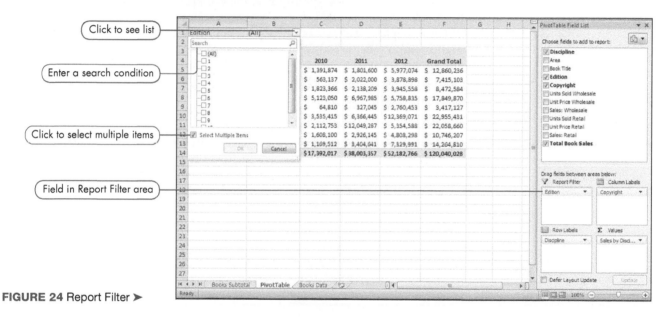

**FIGURE 24** Report Filter ➤

Cell B1 displays (All) when no filter is enabled, the value if one filter is enabled, or (Multiple Items) if more than one item is selected. To remove the filter entirely, remove it from the Report Filter area. To remove the filter temporarily, click the filter arrow in cell B1, select (All), and then click OK.

You can apply additional filters based on the row and column label groupings. For example, you can apply date filters to display summary statistics for data occurring within a particular time frame, or apply filters for values within a designated range. To apply group filters, click the Row Labels or Column Labels arrow in the PivotTable, and then specify the settings for the filter (see Figure 25). Excel calculates the summary statistics based on the filtered data rather than the complete dataset.

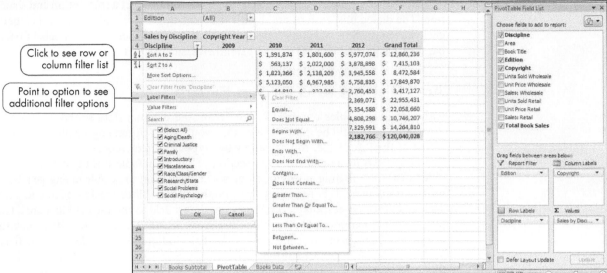

Click to see row or column filter list

Point to option to see additional filter options

**FIGURE 25** Label Filtering ➤

## Collapse and Expand Items

Multiple row labels add more depth to a PivotTable, but the results can be overwhelming. Perhaps you want to focus on one or two categories, but you do not want to engage a report or group filter just to see some specific data. You can hide or collapse subcategories within the PivotTable, which maintains the primary row categories but hides the subcategory details. For example, if the PivotTable contains both Discipline and Copyright row labels, you might want to collapse copyright years for some disciplines. The collapse and expand buttons should display to the left of the row labels. If they do not, click +/- Buttons in the Show group on the Options tab. This command is a toggle: click +/- Buttons again to hide the expand and collapse buttons.

To hide the subcategories for a particular category, click the collapse button (-) on the left side of the specific category you wish to collapse. Excel hides the subcategories for that particular category and shows only the aggregated totals for the category. Continue collapsing other categories as needed to focus on a particular category's details. When you want to expand the subcategories again, click the expand button (+) on the left side of the category labels. Figure 26 shows that the secondary row labels (i.e., the copyright years) for the first six disciplines are collapsed. The copyright years are expanded for the remaining disciplines.

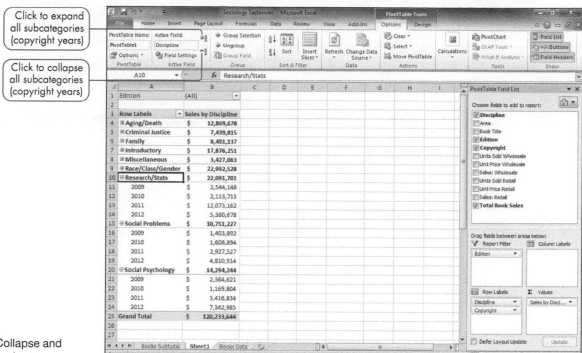

Click to expand all subcategories (copyright years)

Click to collapse all subcategories (copyright years)

**FIGURE 26** Collapse and Expand Categories ➤

---

**TIP** Collapse and Expand All

You can collapse all categories at one time by clicking Collapse Entire Field in the Active Field group on the Options tab. To expand all categories at one time, click Expand Entire Field. This approach is faster than collapsing or expanding each category individually.

## Insert Slicers

A **slicer** is a window listing all items in a field and enables efficient filtering.

In Excel 2010, you can insert a *slicer*, a small window containing one button for each unique item in a field so that you can filter the PivotTable quickly. This new feature is appropriate when distributing PivotTables to people who have limited experience in using PivotTables. Slicers are graphical and easy to use. To insert a slicer, do the following:

1. Click the Options tab.
2. Click the top half of Insert Slicer in the Sort & Filter group to display the Insert Slicers dialog box (see Figure 27).
3. Click one or more field check boxes to display one or more slicers, and then click OK.

**FIGURE 27** Insert Slicers Dialog Box ➤

Excel inserts slicers into the worksheet. You can drag the slicers to move them onscreen to see the PivotTable better. To use a slicer to filter data, click the desired condition within the filter. Excel highlights the item to make it clear how you filtered the PivotTable. For example, in Figure 28, no filter has been enabled for the Edition field, whereas the Discipline field is filtered by Research/Stats. To remove a filter, click Remove Filter in the top-right corner of the slicer window.

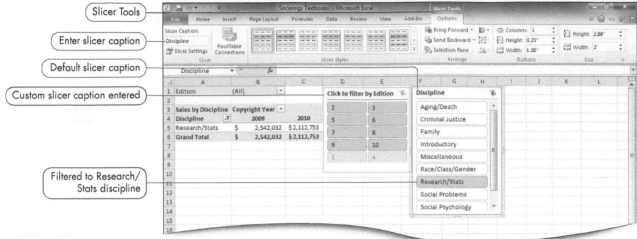

Slicer Tools

Enter slicer caption

Default slicer caption

Custom slicer caption entered

Filtered to Research/ Stats discipline

**FIGURE 28** Slicers ➤

When you select a slicer, the Slicer Tools appear, displaying the Options tab. You can customize the slicer by changing its caption. In Figure 28, the left slicer's caption displays an instruction to the user, whereas the right slicer's caption displays the default field name. Table 4 lists and describes the commands on the Slicer Tools Options tab.

| TABLE 4   Slicer Tools Commands | |
|---|---|
| **Group** | **Commands** |
| **Slicer** | Enables you to change the slicer caption, display the Slicer Settings dialog box for further customization, and manage the PivotTable connected to the slicer. In Figure 28, the Edition slicer has been sorted in ascending order. The light blue items 1 and 4 do not apply to the Research/Stats discipline. |
| **Slicer Styles** | Applies a style to the slicer by specifying the color of the filtered item in the slicer. For example, the default active filters appear in blue, and unavailable items appear in light blue. |
| **Arrange** | Specifies the placement in relation to other groups, such as placing a slicer on top of other slicers. |
| **Buttons** | Defines how many columns are displayed in the slicer and the height and width of each button inside the slicer. For example, the Edition slicer contains two columns, and the Discipline slicer contains one column in Figure 28. |
| **Size** | Sets the height and width of the slicer window. For example, the Discipline slicer's height is 2.89" in Figure 28. |

# Creating a Calculated Field

A **calculated field** is a user-defined field that performs a calculation based on other fields in a PivotTable.

In addition to selecting different summary functions, you can create a calculated field. Similar to a calculated field in Access, a *calculated field* is a user-defined field that does not exist in the original dataset. It derives its values based on performing calculations on other original dataset values. For example, you can create a calculated field that converts totals to percentages for easier relative comparison among categories, or you might want to set a goal of 10% increase in units sold for the upcoming year. You can create a calculated field that determines how many units that would be.

To create a calculated field, select a cell within the PivotTable, click the PivotTable Tools Options tab, click Calculations in the Calculations group, and then click Fields, Items, & Sets. Then select Calculated Field to display the Insert Calculated Field dialog box (see Figure 29).

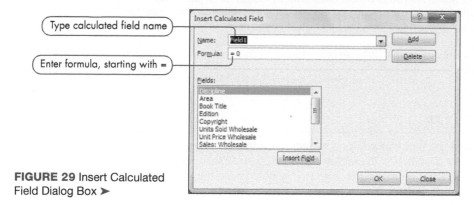

**FIGURE 29** Insert Calculated Field Dialog Box ➤

You should enter a descriptive column heading for the calculated field in the Name box. Then build a formula similar to how you build regular formulas, starting with the equal sign (=). Instead of using cell references, insert the field names and other operands. For example ='Total Book Sales'*.1 calculates a 10% royalty amount on the total book sales. Click OK after building the calculated field to insert the calculated field column in the PivotTable. If needed, format the numerical values in the calculated field column the same way you formatted other values in the PivotTable.

In addition to creating calculated fields, you can apply built-in custom calculations that display relationships between values in rows and columns in the PivotTable. For example, you can show each value as a percentage of the grand total or each value's percentage of the row total. To display values in relation to others, click Show Values As in the Calculations group (see command in Figure 20), and then select from the menu (see Figure 30).

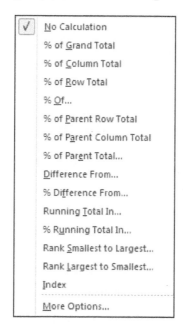

**FIGURE 30** Show Values As Menu ➤

## 3 PivotTable Options

The PivotTable you created has been beneficial for you to review sales data by discipline for each copyright year. In addition, you have used the PivotTable to compare grand total sales among disciplines and grand totals by copyright year. Now you want to extend your analysis. You will calculate author royalties from the sales and impose filters to focus your attention on each analysis.

**Skills covered:** Set a Report Filter • Set Group Filters • Collapse and Expand Items • Insert and Format a Slicer • Show Values as Calculations • Create a Calculated Field

---

STEP 1
### SET A REPORT FILTER

The level of success of the first two editions especially determines the likelihood of approving subsequent revisions and editions. To display aggregated sales for these editions, you need to set a report filter to remove the other editions from being included in the calculated sales data. Refer to Figure 31 as you complete Step 1.

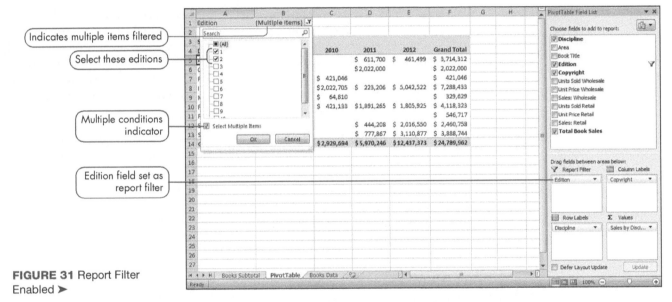

**FIGURE 31** Report Filter Enabled ➤

a. Open *e05h2sociology_LastnameFirstname* if you closed it at the end of Hands-On Exercise 2, and then save it as **e05h3sociology_LastnameFirstname**, changing *h2* to *h3*.

> **TROUBLESHOOTING:** Click in the PivotTable to display the PivotTable Field List, if necessary.

b. Drag the **Edition field** from the *Choose fields to add to report* section to the Report Filter area.

You can now filter the PivotTable based on the Edition field. Cell A1 displays the field name, and cell B1 displays (All) and the filter arrow.

c. Click the **Edition filter arrow** in **cell B1**, and then click the **Select Multiple Items check box**.

The list displays a check box for each item.

d. Click the **(All) check box** to deselect it.

e. Click the **1** and **2 check boxes**, and then click **OK**. Save the workbook.

The summary statistics reflect sales data for only first- and second-edition publications.

You have been reviewing the first- and second-edition sales data. You want to enable additional filters to review books published in the past two years only to see how well these books are selling. Once you do that, you will further filter data for select disciplines to share with the disciplines' editors. Refer to Figure 32 as you complete Step 2.

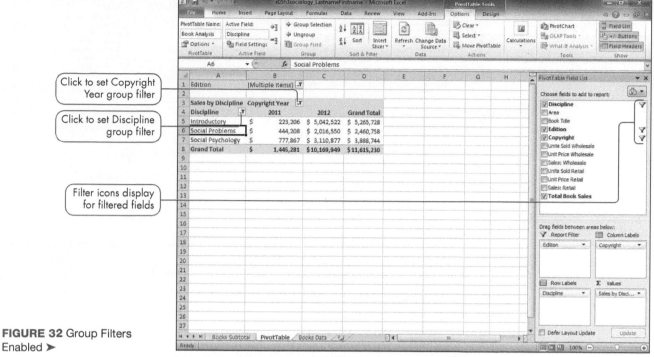

**FIGURE 32** Group Filters Enabled ➤

a. Click the **Copyright Year filter arrow** in **cell B3**.

You can select individual years, label filters, or value filters.

b. Point to **Label Filters**, and then select **Greater Than Or Equal To**.

The Label Filter (Copyright) dialog box opens.

c. Type **2011** and click **OK**.

Excel filters out data for years that do not meet the condition you set.

d. Click the **Discipline filter arrow**, and then click the **(Select All) check box** to deselect it.

e. Click the **Introductory**, **Social Problems**, and **Social Psychology check boxes**.

f. Click **OK**. Save the workbook.

As you review the sales data for the combination years and three disciplines, you want to identify textbooks that fit these conditions. You need to add the Book Title field to the PivotTable. After adding that field, you collapse and expand categories as you review the data. Refer to Figure 33 as you complete Step 3.

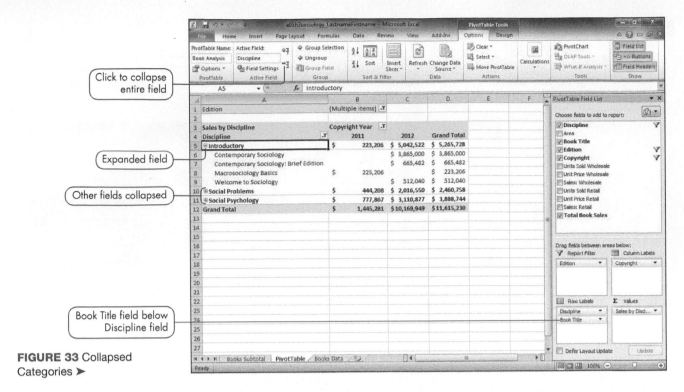

**FIGURE 33** Collapsed
Categories ➤

a. Add the **Book Title field** below the Discipline field in the Row Labels area.

Excel indents the titles below their respective disciplines. The disciplines are bold to stand out as the main row labels.

b. Click any book title in the Discipline column.

c. Click **Collapse Entire Field** in the Active Field group on the Options tab.

> **TROUBLESHOOTING:** If the Active Field group is collapsed on the Options tab, click the Active Field arrow, and then click Collapse Entire Field.

You collapsed the row labels to display the disciplines only.

d. Click the **Introductory expand button**. Save the workbook.

You expanded the Introductory discipline to display the titles within this discipline. The other disciplines are still collapsed, hiding the individual book titles.

## STEP 4 ➤ INSERT AND FORMAT A SLICER

You might distribute the workbook to colleagues who are not as skilled in Excel as you are. To help them set their own filters, you insert slicers. Refer to Figure 34 as you complete Step 4.

Subtotals, PivotTables, and PivotCharts

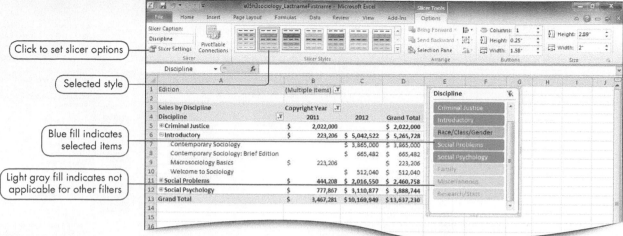

**FIGURE 34** Slicers ➤

a. Click **Insert Slicer** in the Sort & Filter group on the Options tab.

   The Insert Slicers dialog box opens, listing each field name.

b. Click **Discipline**, and then click **OK**.

   Excel inserts the Discipline slicer in the worksheet. The currently filtered disciplines (Social Psychology, Social Problems, and Introductory) display with a blue fill color. Research/Stats, Miscellaneous, and Family appear in gray because these disciplines are not applicable with the other filters in place—edition or copyright year.

c. Press and hold **Ctrl** as you click **Criminal Justice** in the Discipline slicer.

   The Criminal Justice discipline data display in the PivotTable.

d. Position the pointer on the border of the slicer, and then drag it to the right side of the PivotTable.

   You moved the slicer so that it does not cover up data in the PivotTable.

e. Click the **More button** in the Slicer Styles group on the Options tab, and then click **Slicer Style Dark 1**.

   Slicer Style Dark 1 applies a dark blue fill color for selected disciplines, dark gray and black font for available but not currently selected disciplines, and light gray fill with medium gray font for non-applicable disciplines.

f. Click **Slicer Settings** in the Slicer group.

   The Slicer Settings dialog box opens.

g. Click **Ascending (A to Z)** in the *Item Sorting and Filtering* section, if necessary, and then click **OK**. Save the workbook.

## STEP 5 ▶ SHOW VALUES AS CALCULATIONS

You want to see what copyright year generated the largest sales for each discipline, which discipline contributes the largest percentage of the total sociology sales, and which introductory book has the largest sales contribution within that discipline. Refer to Figure 35 as you complete Step 5.

Click to specify how to show values

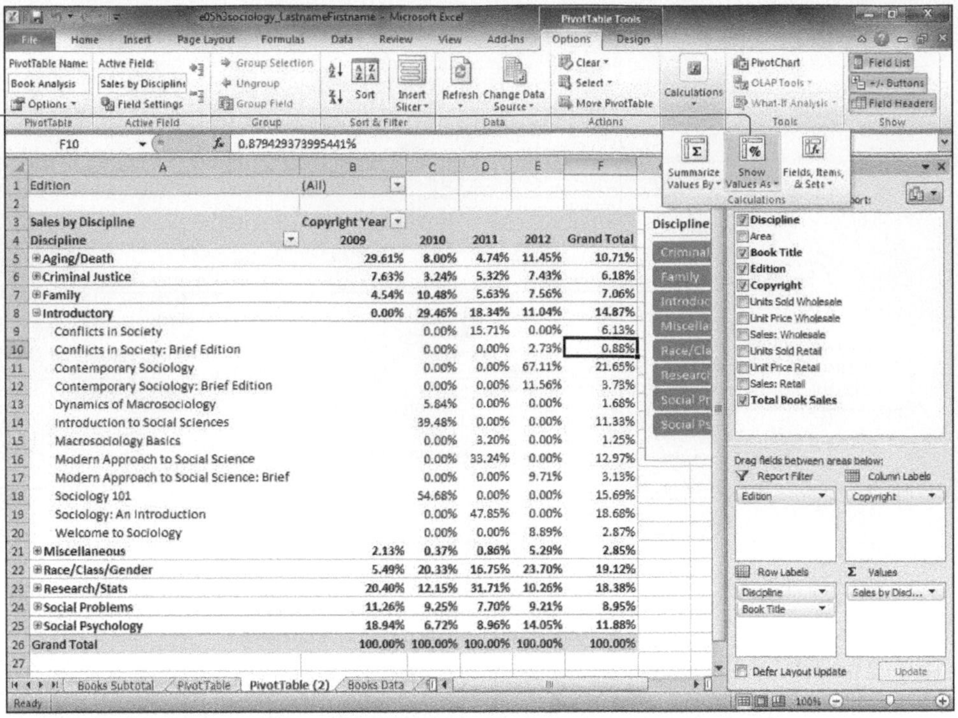

**FIGURE 35** Percentage of Parent Row ➤

a. Right-click the **PivotTable worksheet tab**, select **Move or Copy**, click **Books Data** in the **Before sheet list**, click the **Create a copy check box**, and then click **OK**.

You copied the PivotTable worksheet to maintain the previous tasks you completed as evidence. You will work with the PivotTable (2) worksheet, which is the active worksheet.

b. Click the **Edition filter** in cell B1, click the **(All) check box**, and then click **OK** to clear the Edition filter. Click the **Discipline filter** in cell A4, and then select **Clear Filter From "Discipline"**. Click the **Copyright Year filter** in cell B3, and then select **Clear Filter From "Copyright"**.

> **TROUBLESHOOTING:** If a slicer obstructs your view of PivotTable data, drag the slicer to the right of the PivotTable.

c. Click within any dollar amount in the PivotTable, click the **Options tab**, click **Calculations** in the Calculations group, click **Show Values As**, and then select **% of Row Total**.

Excel displays the yearly values as percentages of the grand total amount for each discipline. The 2012 Aging/Death books produce the largest percentage of sales (compared to other years) in most disciplines. However, the 2011 books earned greater sales compared to other sales for other years within both the Introductory and Research/Stats disciplines.

d. Click **Calculations** in the Calculations group, click **Show Values As**, and then select **% of Grand Total**.

Each discipline's yearly value displays as a percentage of the total sales. Which discipline and for what copyright year produces the highest percentage of total sales? Answer: 2012 Race/Class/Gender with 10.30%, followed closely by the 2011 Research/Stats with 10.04%. In general, the Race/Class/Gender discipline contributed the highest percentage of the total sales with 19.12%.

e. Click **Calculations** in the Calculations group, click **Show Values As**, and then select **% of Parent Row Total**. Save the workbook.

Within the Introductory discipline, each book's grand total is displayed as a percentage of total Introductory sales. Which two books contribute the highest sales? Answer: *Contemporary Sociology* with 21.65% and *Sociology: An Introduction* with 18.68%. Which

Subtotals, PivotTables, and PivotCharts

book contributes the least to the Introductory discipline? Answer: *Conflicts in Society: Brief Edition* with only 0.88% (see Figure 35).

## STEP 6 ▸ CREATE A CALCULATED FIELD

In addition to analyzing sales, you want to calculate the amount of the sales returned to the authors as royalties. The royalty rate is stored in cell J2 in the Books Data worksheet. However, you cannot use range names or cell references in calculated PivotTable fields. Refer to Figure 36 as you complete Step 6.

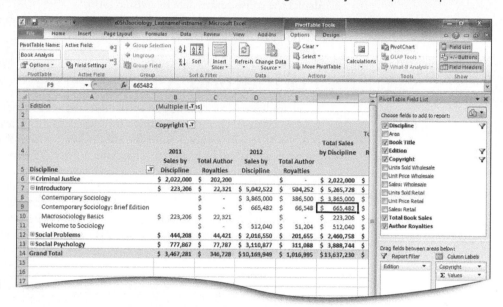

**FIGURE 36** Calculated Field in a PivotTable ➤

a. Click the **PivotTable worksheet tab**.

b. Click the **Options tab**, click **Calculations** in the Calculations group, click **Fields, Items, & Sets**, and then select **Calculated Field**.

The Insert Calculated Field dialog box opens.

c. Type **Author Royalties** in the **Name box**.

d. Scroll down the **Fields list**, click **Total Book Sales**, and then click **Insert Field**.

Excel starts to build the formula, which is currently ='Total Book Sales'.

e. Type **\*.1** at the end of the **Formula box**, and then click **OK**.

Excel adds Sum of Author Royalties calculated field columns, one for each copyright year category. It calculates the authors' royalties as 10% of the total sales for each copyright year.

f. Right-click the **Sum of Author Royalties heading** in **cell C5**, select **Value Field Settings**, type **Total Author Royalties** in the **Custom Name box**, and then click **OK**.

g. Wrap text for headings, adjust row height, adjust column widths, and center column headings. Move the slicer to the right of the PivotTable, if necessary.

h. Save the workbook. Keep the workbook onscreen if you plan to continue with Hands-On Exercise 4. If not, close the workbook and exit Excel.

# PivotTable Design and PivotCharts

Now that you know how to create and modify the structure of a PivotTable, you can focus on the overall appearance and format of the PivotTable. The PivotTable Tools Design tab enables you to control the position of grouped calculations and the PivotTable style. In addition to finalizing the PivotTable's appearance, you might want to create a PivotChart to depict the consolidated data in a visual form.

In this section, you will apply a different style and change the layout of a PivotTable. In addition, you will create and format a PivotChart.

## Formatting a PivotTable

Excel applies basic formatting to PivotTables. For example, it formats primary row labels in bold to distinguish those categories from the subcategories. In addition, the subtotals are bold to offset these values from the subcategory values. You can enhance the appearance even further by applying a PivotTable style. A PivotTable style controls the bolding, font colors, shading colors, and border lines. To change the style, click the PivotTable Tools Design tab, and then click the More button in the PivotTable Styles group to display the PivotTable Styles gallery as shown in Figure 37. A gallery of styles displays so that you can select the most appropriate style that accentuates the data in your PivotTable. As you move the pointer over the gallery, Excel shows how that style will affect the PivotTable. Click a style to apply that style to the PivotTable.

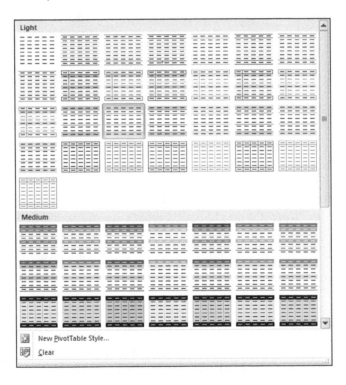

**FIGURE 37** PivotTable Styles ➤

After you apply a style, you can select which areas of the PivotTable are affected by the style. Select check boxes in the PivotTable Style Options group to apply formats to row headers, column headers, banded rows, and banded columns.

By default, the values area consolidates data by showing subtotals for each category. You can customize the location of subtotals by clicking Subtotals in the Layout group on the Design tab. For example, when the PivotTable is large, displaying the subtotals at the top of the group draws attention to the totals and enables you to scroll to view all of the supporting data if necessary. Table 5 describes the Subtotals options.

Subtotals, PivotTables, and PivotCharts

| TABLE 5 | PivotTable Subtotals Options |
|---------|------------------------------|
| **Option** | **Description** |
| **Do Not Show Subtotals** | Removes subtotals for each category but retains the category names and displays aggregated values for the subcategories. |
| **Show all Subtotals at Bottom of Group** | Displays category subtotals below the last subcategory value within each category. Subtotal labels and values appear in bold. |
| **Show all Subtotals at Top of Group** | Displays category subtotals at the top of the list on the same row as the category labels. This approach takes up fewer rows than Show all Subtotals at Bottom of Group. |
| **Include Filtered Items in Totals** | Includes values for filtered items in the total rows and columns. |

Figure 38 shows a PivotTable with subtotals at the bottom of each discipline. The PivotTable is formatted with Pivot Style Medium 9.

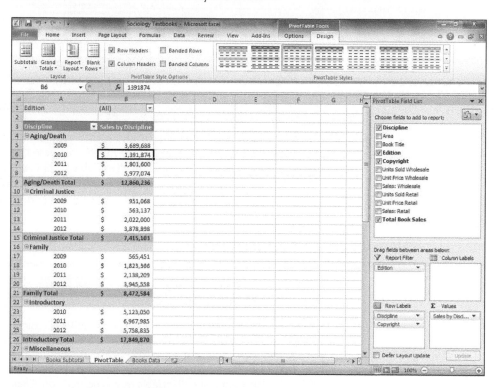

**FIGURE 38** PivotTable Subtotals ➤

# Creating a PivotChart

As you recall, charts help your audience understand the data better than merely presenting the data in a spreadsheet. Although PivotTables help reduce the amount of data to analyze, PivotTables can overwhelm people. You can aid people's comprehension of the aggregated data by creating a PivotChart. A ***PivotChart*** is an interactive graphical representation of the data in a PivotTable. A PivotChart enables you to present the consolidated data visually.

A **PivotChart** is a graphical representation of data in a PivotTable.

A PivotChart is associated with a PivotTable. When you change the position of a field in either the PivotTable or the PivotChart, the corresponding object changes as well. To create a PivotChart, click inside the PivotTable, click the Options tab, and then click PivotChart in the Tools group. Excel creates a PivotChart based on the current PivotTable settings—row labels, column labels, values, and filters. The PivotChart area contains elements that enable you to set report and axis field filters. The Row Labels area changes to Axis Fields, and the Column Labels area changes to Legend Fields when you select the PivotChart (see Figure 39).

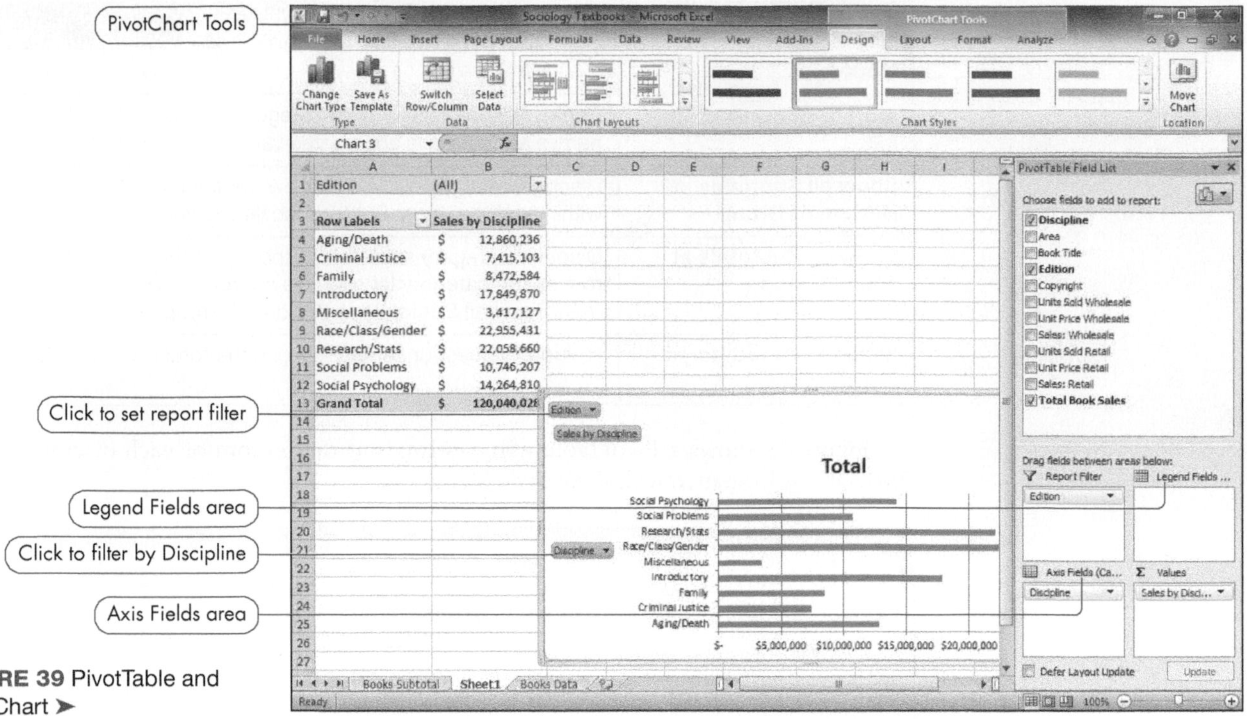
PivotChart Tools
Click to set report filter
Legend Fields area
Click to filter by Discipline
Axis Fields area
Total

**FIGURE 39** PivotTable and PivotChart ➤

The default chart may appear cluttered if you have too many details displayed in the PivotTable. Although Excel creates the PivotChart based on the current PivotTable settings, you can change the settings using the PivotTable Field List. Click the Report Filter arrow, and then select values to filter the chart and table. Click the Axis Field arrows to sort or filter the categories and subcategories in rows. Click the Legend Fields (Series) to sort or filter the chart representation based on the values. Any changes you make to the PivotChart also affect the corresponding PivotTable. For example, if you apply a report filter to the PivotChart, Excel also filters the PivotTable.

### TIP Creating a PivotTable and PivotChart

You can streamline the process and create the PivotTable and PivotChart at the same time. From within the original data source, click the Insert tab, click the PivotTable arrow (bottom half) in the Tables group, and then select PivotChart. The Create PivotTable with PivotChart dialog box opens (similar to the Create PivotTable dialog box). Select the desired options, and then click OK. Then create the PivotTable as you normally do. Excel builds the PivotChart as you go.

When you create a PivotChart or you select an existing PivotChart, Excel displays the PivotChart Tools Design, Layout, Format, and Analyze contextual tabs. The first three tabs enable you to customize the PivotChart similar to how you customize a regular chart. The last tab is specific to PivotCharts. Table 6 briefly explains these tabs.

| TABLE 6 | PivotChart Tools Tabs |
|---------|------------------------|
| **Tab** | **Functionality** |
| **Design** | Changes the chart type, selects the underlying data, selects a chart layout, applies a different chart style, and moves the chart to another location. |
| **Layout** | Selects chart elements to format, inserts objects inside the chart, displays and positions chart labels, formats the chart axes, formats the background area, and inserts analysis items, such as a Trendline. |
| **Format** | Selects chart elements to format, formats shape styles, applies WordArt styles, arranges chart elements, and sets the height and width of the chart. |
| **Analyze** | Selects the active PivotTable field, expands or collapses entire field groups, refreshes the PivotChart, and shows or hides the PivotTable Field List. |

Although you have most of the same functionality, such as chart types, for PivotCharts as you do for charts, you should use basic charts, such as column, bar, line, and pie. PivotCharts look too cluttered when you select some of the other chart types.

If you no longer need a PivotChart, you can delete it. Select the chart, and then press Delete. Deleting the PivotChart does not delete the associated PivotTable.

# 4 PivotTable Design and PivotCharts

You want to format the PivotTable to make it easier for you to analyze the sales data. In addition, you want to create a PivotChart to depict sales data.

**Skills covered:** Apply a PivotTable Style • Create a PivotChart • Change and Enhance a PivotChart

---

## STEP 1 ▶ APPLY A PIVOTTABLE STYLE

To enhance the readability of the sociology textbook PivotTable, you will apply a style. Refer to Figure 40 as you complete Step 1.

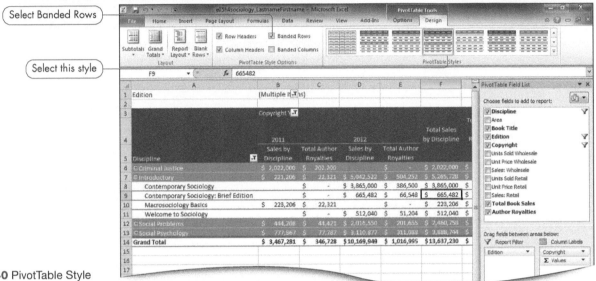

**FIGURE 40** PivotTable Style Applied ➤

a. Open *e05h3sociology_LastnameFirstname* if you closed it at the end of Hands-On Exercise 3, and then save it as **e05h4sociology_LastnameFirstname**, changing *h3* to *h4*.

b. Make sure the PivotTable worksheet is active and that the active cell is within the PivotTable, click the **Design tab**, and then click the **More button** in the PivotTable Styles group.

The PivotTable Style gallery displays styles that you can apply.

c. Click **Pivot Style Medium 3**.

d. Click the **Banded Rows check box** in the PivotTable Style Options group. Save the workbook.

---

## STEP 2 ▶ CREATE A PIVOTCHART

You want to create a PivotChart to depict the sales data by discipline. You know that you can create a PivotChart from a PivotTable; however, you want to preserve the filtered PivotTable. Therefore, you will create a new PivotTable and PivotChart. Refer to Figure 41 as you complete Step 2.

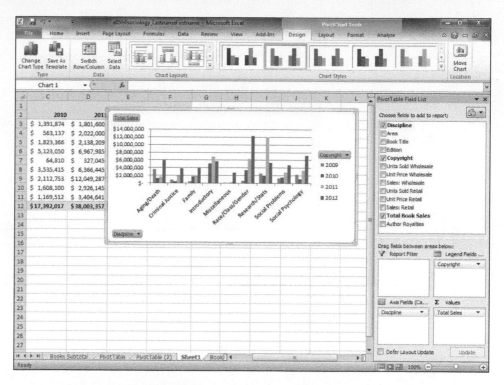

**FIGURE 41** PivotChart ➤

a. Click the **Books Data worksheet tab**, and then click inside the sales data.

b. Click the **Insert tab**, click the **PivotTable arrow** in the Tables group, and then select **PivotChart**.

The Create PivotTable with PivotChart dialog box opens, displaying the range of the PivotTable.

c. Click **OK**.

Excel displays a PivotTable placeholder, a PivotChart placeholder, and the PivotTable Field List. The PivotTable Field List contains a Legend Fields area, which typically represents columns, and an Axis Fields area, which typically represents row labels.

d. Drag the **Discipline field** to the Axis Fields area.

e. Drag the **Total Book Sales field** to the Values area.

f. Drag the **Copyright field** to the Legend Fields area.

The PivotTable appears on the left side of the worksheet, and the PivotChart appears on the right side. The row labels from the PivotTable appear along the horizontal category axis, and column heights represent the respective total sales for each discipline.

g. Click the **Sum of Total arrow** in the Values area, and then select **Value Field Settings**. Type **Total Sales** in the **Custom Name box**.

h. Click **Number Format**, select **Accounting** in the **Category list**, click the **Decimal places spin arrow** to display **0**, and then click **OK**. Click **OK** in the Value Field Settings dialog box, and then save the workbook.

**STEP 3**  ## CHANGE AND ENHANCE A PIVOTCHART

You want to modify the chart by changing it to a bar chart, which will make it easier for you to read the discipline labels. You will further improve the chart by including a more descriptive chart title. Refer to Figure 42 as you complete Step 3.

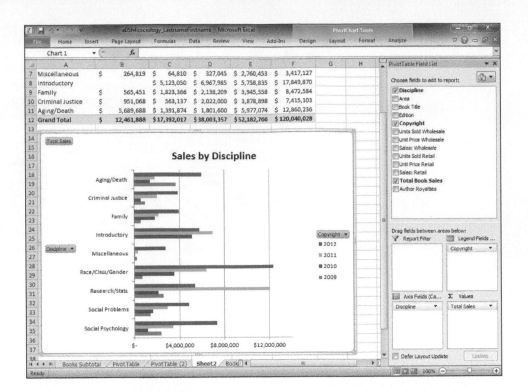

**FIGURE 42** Modified PivotChart ➤

a. Make sure the PivotChart is selected, and then click the **Design tab**, if necessary.

The Design tab contains options to change the chart type and apply chart layouts and styles.

b. Click **Change Chart Type** in the Type group on the Design tab, click **Bar** in the Change Chart Type dialog box, and then click **OK**.

You changed the type from a column to a bar chart. The category labels are easier to read on the vertical axis.

c. Click the **Layout tab**, click **Chart Title** in the Labels group, and then select **Above Chart**.

d. Type **Sales by Discipline** and press **Enter**.

e. Click the chart boundary, click the **Format tab**, type **5** in the **Shape Height box**, type **7** in the **Shape Width box**, and then press **Enter**.

You enlarged the chart. You notice the discipline labels appear in reverse alphabetical order because Excel arranges the labels from the axis point upward. You need to sort the PivotTable to alphabetize the category labels in the PivotChart.

f. Scroll to the left. Click **cell A4** or any cell in the **Row Labels column**, click the **Options tab**, and then click **Sort Z to A** in the Sort & Filter group.

Within the PivotTable, the discipline labels appear in reverse alphabetical order with Social Psychology first and Aging/Death last. Within the PivotChart, the discipline labels appear in alphabetical order because the lowest values always appear closest to the intersection of the vertical and horizontal axis and increase up the axis.

g. Drag the PivotChart so that the top-left corner is in **cell A14**. Scroll down to see the chart.

h. Save and close the workbook, and submit based on your instructor's directions.

# CHAPTER OBJECTIVES REVIEW

After reading this chapter, you have accomplished the following objectives:

1. **Group and ungroup data.** You can group related data by creating an outline. If the data contain columns of formulas based on other columns and/or row subtotals, use the auto outline process to create an outline based on the data structure. You can then collapse and expand the outline as you review the data. If you no longer need grouped data, select and ungroup the data again.

2. **Subtotal data.** The Subtotal dialog box enables you to insert subtotals, such as sums or averages, based on sorted data. This feature detects changes between categories arranged in rows to insert the subtotal rows. You can apply subtotals to one or more columns of data. In addition, you can add a second-level subtotal for further groups within the main group. To clear the subtotals, display the Subtotal dialog box, and then click Remove All.

3. **Create a PivotTable.** An alternative to using the Subtotal feature is to create a PivotTable, an organized structure of aggregated data by combinations of categories. The benefit of a PivotTable is that you can pivot or rotate the data by rearranging the fields from rows, columns, values, and report filters. Excel displays the aggregated values based on the arrangement you select. The PivotTable does not alter the arrangement of the original dataset.

4. **Change the values field.** After laying out the PivotTable, you can select the function used to calculate the summary statistics. The default is a sum for values or a count for text fields. You can also apply number formatting, such as Accounting Number Format, and specify a custom column heading.

5. **Modify a PivotTable.** As you analyze your data, you can add, remove, or rearrange fields to get a different perspective of the

PivotTable. If the original data change, you must click Refresh to update the PivotTable.

6. **Sort, filter, and slice a PivotTable.** You can sort data in a PivotTable for text labels, values, or dates. In addition, you can apply two types of filters: a report filter to set the overall conditions for aggregating data, and a group filter to filter out data based on a row or column category. You can even collapse and expand categories in the PivotTable, similar to collapsing or expanding categories in an outline. In addition, you can insert slices, which are little field windows containing buttons for unique values. You can click the buttons to filter the PivotTable.

7. **Create a calculated field.** A calculated field is a user-defined field based on other fields. This field does not exist in the original dataset. You can use basic arithmetic operations, but you cannot use cell references or range names in the calculated field syntax. You can also use built-in calculations, such as showing values as a percentage of the grand total.

8. **Format a PivotTable.** The PivotTable Tools Design tab enables you to improve the appearance of a PivotTable by applying a PivotTable style. The style controls the fill color, bolding, and other formatting aspects of data in the PivotTable.

9. **Create a PivotChart.** You can create a PivotChart from a PivotTable or at the same time you create a PivotTable. The PivotChart is similar to creating a regular chart, except it is based on the categories and structure of the PivotTable, not the original dataset. You can customize a PivotChart with the same methods you use to customize a regular chart. If you change fields or sort in either the PivotTable or the PivotChart, Excel automatically adjusts the corresponding pivot object.

# KEY TERMS

Calculated field
Data mining
Grouping

Outline
PivotChart

PivotTable
Slicer

1. A worksheet contains data for businesses that are sponsoring this year's Arts Festival. The worksheet contains these columns in this sequence: Business Name, Address, City, State, and Donation Amount. Data are sorted by State and then by City. What is the default *At a change in* setting within the Subtotal dialog box, and what would be a more appropriate setting?

   (a) Business Name (default field), Donation Amount (correct field)

   (b) Business Name (default field), State (correct field)

   (c) Donation Amount (default field), Address (correct field)

   (d) Address (default field), Donation Amount (correct field)

2. You created an outline for a dataset. What does the + button indicate to the left of a row heading?

   (a) You can add a new row at that location only.

   (b) One or more columns are hidden.

   (c) You can click it to collapse the details of that category.

   (d) You can click it to expand the details of that category.

3. A worksheet contains a PivotTable placeholder and the PivotTable Field List. Where do you drag the State field if you want a list of each state in the first column of the PivotTable?

   (a) Report Filter area

   (b) Column Labels area

   (c) Row Labels area

   (d) Values area

4. You just created a slicer for the State field in a PivotTable. Which of the following does not characterize the initial slicer?

   (a) The slicer buttons are set to filter out all records.

   (b) The slicer caption is State.

   (c) The slicer contains one column of state names or abbreviations.

   (d) The slicer may display on top of the PivotTable data.

5. You created a PivotTable and made some changes to values in the original dataset from which the PivotTable was created. How does this affect the PivotTable?

   (a) The PivotTable updates automatically when you make changes to the dataset.

   (b) You must create a new PivotTable if you want updated results in a PivotTable.

   (c) Click the Data tab, and then click Update to update the PivotTable to reflect changes you made in the dataset.

   (d) Click Refresh in the Data group on the Options tab to update the PivotTable.

6. You created a PivotTable to summarize salaries by department. What is the default summary statistic for the salaries in the PivotTable?

   (a) Average

   (b) Sum

   (c) Count

   (d) Max

7. What settings should you select for a PivotTable if you want to apply a different color scheme and display different fill colors for main category rows and horizontal lines within the PivotTable?

   (a) Banded Rows and Banded Columns check boxes

   (b) Banded Columns check box and a different PivotTable style

   (c) Banded Rows check box and a different PivotTable style

   (d) A different PivotTable style only

8. Which PivotTable calculated field is correctly constructed to calculate a 20% tip on a meal at a restaurant?

   (a) =Meal Cost * 20%

   (b) ='Meal Cost'*.2

   (c) ="Meal Cost"*.2

   (d) =B5*1.2

9. You have created a PivotChart showing sales by quarter by sales rep. Before presenting it to management, you notice the name of a rep who has since been fired. How do you remove this rep from the chart without deleting the data?

   (a) Filter the Sales Rep field in the PivotChart and deselect the employee's check box.

   (b) Make the employee's data points and axis titles invisible.

   (c) You can't delete the rep from the chart without first deleting the data.

   (d) Hide that rep's row(s) in the underlying list, which automatically removes that rep from the chart.

10. Currently, the House Types field is in the Row Labels area, the Real Estate Agent field is in the Column Labels area, and Sum of List Prices is in the Values area. How can you modify the PivotTable to display the agent names as subcategories within the house types in the first column?

    (a) Drag the Real Estate Agent field from the Column Labels area, and then drop it above the House Types field in the Row Labels area.

    (b) Drag the House Types field from the Row Labels area, and then drop it below the Real Estate Agent field in the Column Labels area.

    (c) Drag the House Types field from the Row Labels area to the Report Filter area, and then drag the Real Estate Agent field from the Column Labels area to the Row Labels area.

    (d) Drag the Real Estate Agent field from the Column Labels area, and then drop it below the House Types field in the Row Labels area.

# PRACTICE EXERCISES

## 1 The Men's Store

You work at The Men's Store, a department store that caters to businessmen in the Cheyenne, Wyoming, metropolitan area. You need to analyze a year's worth of transactions to determine which salesperson had the highest overall sales, and which salesperson had the best sales in the Dress Shirts and Ties category. You will use the Subtotal feature and outline the list of transactions for the year. This exercise follows the same set of skills as used in Hands-On Exercise 1 in the chapter. Refer to Figure 43 as you complete this exercise.

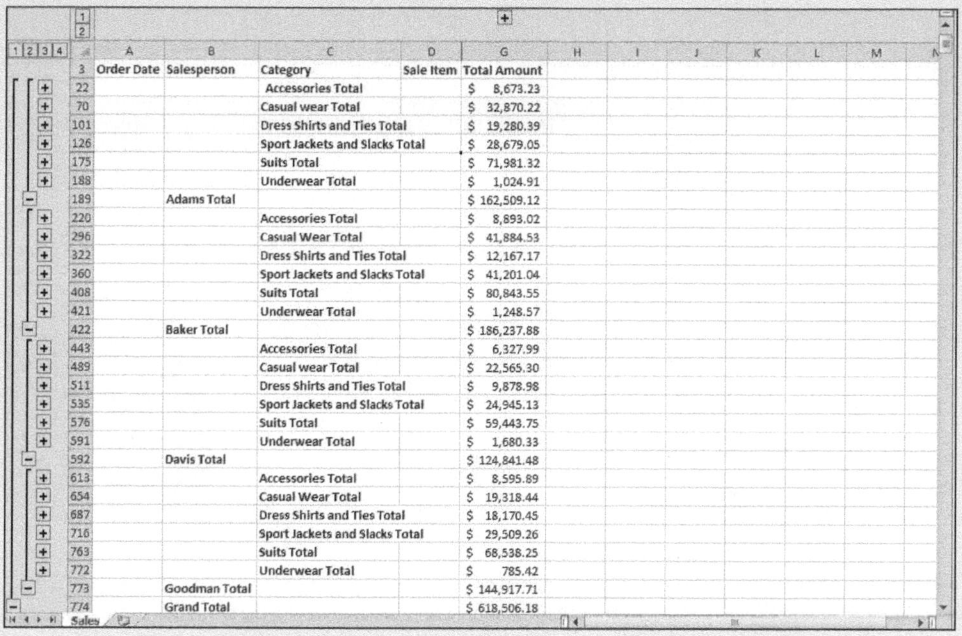

| | A | B | C | D | G |
|---|---|---|---|---|---|
| 3 | Order Date | Salesperson | Category | Sale Item | Total Amount |
| 22 | | | Accessories Total | | $ 8,673.23 |
| 70 | | | Casual wear Total | | $ 32,870.22 |
| 101 | | | Dress Shirts and Ties Total | | $ 19,280.39 |
| 126 | | | Sport Jackets and Slacks Total | | $ 28,679.05 |
| 175 | | | Suits Total | | $ 71,981.32 |
| 188 | | | Underwear Total | | $ 1,024.91 |
| 189 | | Adams Total | | | $ 162,509.12 |
| 220 | | | Accessories Total | | $ 8,893.02 |
| 296 | | | Casual Wear Total | | $ 41,884.53 |
| 322 | | | Dress Shirts and Ties Total | | $ 12,167.17 |
| 360 | | | Sport Jackets and Slacks Total | | $ 41,201.04 |
| 408 | | | Suits Total | | $ 80,843.55 |
| 421 | | | Underwear Total | | $ 1,248.57 |
| 422 | | Baker Total | | | $ 186,237.88 |
| 443 | | | Accessories Total | | $ 6,327.99 |
| 489 | | | Casual wear Total | | $ 22,565.30 |
| 511 | | | Dress Shirts and Ties Total | | $ 9,878.98 |
| 535 | | | Sport Jackets and Slacks Total | | $ 24,945.13 |
| 576 | | | Suits Total | | $ 59,443.75 |
| 591 | | | Underwear Total | | $ 1,680.33 |
| 592 | | Davis Total | | | $ 124,841.48 |
| 613 | | | Accessories Total | | $ 8,595.89 |
| 654 | | | Casual Wear Total | | $ 19,318.44 |
| 687 | | | Dress Shirts and Ties Total | | $ 18,170.45 |
| 716 | | | Sport Jackets and Slacks Total | | $ 29,509.26 |
| 763 | | | Suits Total | | $ 68,538.25 |
| 772 | | | Underwear Total | | $ 785.42 |
| 773 | | Goodman Total | | | $ 144,917.71 |
| 774 | | Grand Total | | | $ 618,506.18 |

**FIGURE 43** Men's Store Subtotals ➤

a. Open *e05p1menstore*, and then save it as **e05p1menstore_LastnameFirstname.**

b. Sort the list by salesperson and then by category within salesperson.

c. Click the **Data tab**, and then click **Subtotal** in the Outline group. Do the following in the Subtotal dialog box:
   - Click the **At each change in arrow**, and then select **Salesperson.**
   - Click the **Order Amount check box** and the **Sales Tax check box** in the **Add subtotal to list.** Keep the *Total Amount* check box selected.
   - Click **OK.**

d. Add a nested subtotal by category by doing the following:
   - Click **Subtotal** in the Outline group.
   - Click the **At each change in arrow**, and then select **Category.**
   - Keep the *Order Total, Sales Tax,* and *Total Amount* check boxes selected.
   - Click the **Replace current subtotals check box** to deselect it.
   - Click **OK.**

e. Click **2** to collapse the list to see the salesperson subtotals. Who had the highest order totals for the year? Who had the lowest order totals for the year?

f. Click **3** to expand the list to see category subtotals for each salesperson. Who had the highest dress shirts and tie sales for the year? Is this the same person who had the overall highest order totals for the year?

g. Click the **Group arrow** in the Outline group on the Data tab, and then select **Auto Outline.** Click **OK** when prompted to modify the existing outline. Click the **collapse button** above column G to collapse the columns.

h. Create a footer with your name on the left side, the date code in the center, and the file name code on the right side.

i. Save and close the workbook, and submit based on your instructor's directions.

## 2 Azteca Mexican Restaurant

Your college friend Antonio Martinez owns a successful Mexican restaurant in Amarillo, Texas. He tracks daily revenue for the lunch and dinner hours but needs your assistance to consolidate data for the entire year. Specifically, he wants to compare quarterly totals by weekday, and he wants to take a closer look at the fourth-quarter revenue. You will build two PivotTables and PivotCharts to help Antonio analyze the revenue. Your first task is to use VLOOKUP functions to convert dates to weekdays and quarters to help prepare the data for the analysis. This exercise follows the same set of skills as used in Hands-On Exercises 2, 3, and 4 in the chapter. Refer to Figures 44 and 45 as you complete this exercise.

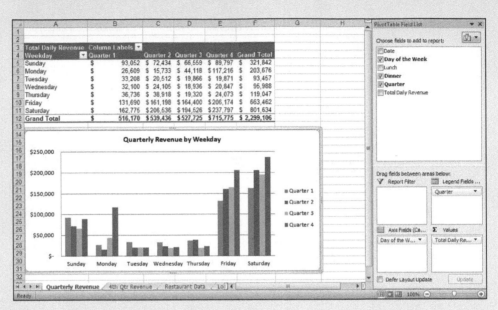

**FIGURE 44** Quarterly Revenue PivotTable and PivotChart ➤

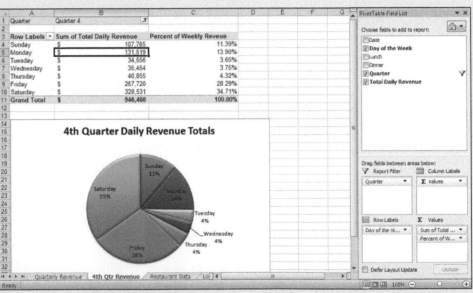

**FIGURE 45** Fourth-Quarter Revenue PivotTable and PivotChart ➤

a. Open *e05p2azteca*, and then save it as **e05p2azteca_LastnameFirstname**. Click the **Lookup Tables worksheet tab** to see the two lookup tables. The first table looks up a value to return a day of the week, such as 2 for Monday. The second table looks up a value within a breakpoint, identified by month numbers, and returns which quarter the month is in. For example, the fifth month (5) returns Quarter 2.

Subtotals, PivotTables, and PivotCharts

b. Create two formulas to calculate missing values by doing the following:
   - Click the **Restaurant Data worksheet tab**, and then click in **cell B2**. Insert a VLOOKUP function that looks up the date (A2) against the lookup table that is range-named **DayTable** and returns the day of the week. Use a nested WEEKDAY function to convert the date to a numerical day of the week. The function should look like this: =VLOOKUP(WEEKDAY(A2),DayTable,2). Copy the formula down the column. Save the workbook, if needed, to update the copied formulas.
   - Click **cell E2**. Insert a VLOOKUP function that looks up the date (A2) against the lookup table that is range-named **Quarters** and returns the quarter of the year for that date. Use a nested MONTH function to convert the date to a numerical month. Adapt the above VLOOKUP syntax for this calculation. Copy the formula down the column. Save the workbook, if needed, to update the copied formulas.

c. Click in the list. Click the **Insert tab**, click **PivotTable** in the Tables group, and then click **OK**. Create the PivotTable with these specifications:
   - Click the **Day of the Week check box** in the **PivotTable Field List** to add it to the Row Labels area.
   - Click the **Lunch** and **Dinner check boxes** to add these fields to the **Values area**.

d. Modify the PivotTable by doing the following:
   - Drag the **Quarter field** and drop it above the Values field in the Column Labels area.
   - Click the **Sum of Lunch arrow** in the Values area, and then select **Remove Field**.
   - Click **cell A4**, type **Weekday**, and then press **Enter**.
   - Click the **Design tab**, click the **More button** in the PivotTable Styles group, and then click **Pivot Style Medium 10**.

e. Format the values by doing the following:
   - Click **cell B5**, click the **Options tab**, click **Calculations** in the Calculations group, click **Summarize Values By**, and then select **More Options**.
   - Type **Total Daily Revenue** in the **Custom Name box**.
   - Click **Number Format**, click **Accounting**, click the **Decimal places spin arrow** to display **0**, click **OK** in the Format Cells dialog box, and then click **OK** in the Value Field Settings dialog box.

f. Create a PivotChart from the PivotTable by doing the following.
   - Click **PivotChart** in the Tools group, and then click **OK** in the Insert Chart dialog box to create a default column chart.
   - Click **Layout 1** in the Chart Layouts group.
   - Click the **Chart Title placeholder**, type **Quarterly Revenue by Weekday**, and then press **Enter**. Change the chart title font size to **12**.
   - Move the chart so that the top-left corner starts in **cell A14**. Resize the chart to extend through **cell G31**.
   - Click the **Analyze tab**, and then click **Field Buttons** to hide the buttons within the chart area.

g. Click the **Restaurant Data worksheet tab**. Adapt step c to create another PivotTable on another new worksheet. Then do the following:
   - Click the **Day of the Week check box** to add it to the Row Labels area.
   - Drag the **Quarter field** to the Report Filter area.

h. Create a calculated field to find the total daily revenue by doing the following:
   - Click **Calculations** in the Calculations group, click **Fields, Items, & Sets**, and then select **Calculated Field**.
   - Type **Total Daily Revenue** in the **Name box**.
   - Click **Lunch** in the **Fields list**, and then click **Insert Field**.
   - Type **+** and double-click **Dinner** to build the calculated field: =Lunch+Dinner. Click **OK**.
   - Format the calculated field with **Accounting Number Format** with zero decimal places, if necessary.

i. Click the **Quarter filter arrow** in **cell B1**, click **Quarter 4**, and then click **OK** to filter the results to show only the fourth-quarter revenue.

j. Drag another **Total Daily Revenue field** from the *Choose fields to add to report* list to the Values area below the existing Sum of Total. Click the second **Sum of Total arrow** in the Values area, select **Value Field Settings**, type **Percent of Weekly Revenue**, and then click **OK**. Click in the **Percent of Weekly Revenue column** in the PivotTable, click **Calculations** in the Calculations group on the Options tab, click **Show Values As**, and then select **% of Column Total**. The values in the Percent of Weekly Revenue column are formatted with Percent Style with two decimal places.

k. Create a PivotChart from the PivotTable by doing the following:
   - Click **PivotChart** in the Tools group. Click **Pie**, and then click **OK** to create a pie chart.
   - Click **Layout 1** in the Chart Layouts group.

- Click the **Chart Title placeholder**, type **4th Quarter Daily Revenue Totals**, and then press **Enter**. Change the chart title font size to **12**.
- Move the chart so that the top-left corner starts in **cell A14**. Resize the chart to extend through **cell D33**.
- Click the **More button** in the Chart Styles group on the PivotChart Tools Design tab, and then click **Style 26** (second style on the fourth row).

l.  Click the **Analyze tab**, and then click **Field Buttons** to hide the buttons within the chart area.

m. Rename the Sheet1 worksheet **Quarterly Revenue**. Rename Sheet2 **4th Qtr Revenue**. Create a footer with your name on the left side, the sheet name code in the center, and the file name code on the right side on each worksheet.

n.  Save and close the workbook, and submit based on your instructor's directions.

## 3  Spa Experts

As a manager at Spa Experts, you must analyze monthly sales data by hot tub manufacturer, sales representatives, and payment types. Because you want the assistant managers to analyze data as well, you will insert and format PivotTable slicers for them to use. This exercise follows the same set of skills as used in Hands-On Exercise 3 in the chapter. Refer to Figure 46 as you complete this exercise.

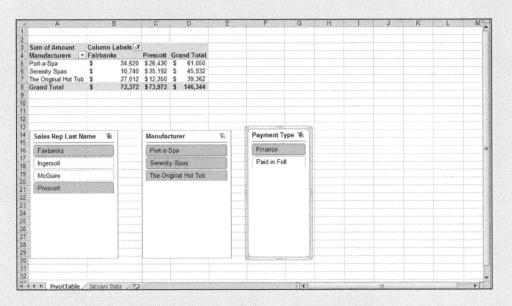

**FIGURE 46** PivotTable Slicers ➤

a.  Open *e05p3expert*, and then save it as **e05p3expert_LastnameFirstname**.

b.  Click inside the PivotTable, if necessary, and then click the **Options tab**.

c.  Click **Insert Slicer** in the Sort & Filter group. Click the **Sales Rep Last Name**, **Manufacturer**, and **Payment Type check boxes**. Click **OK**.

d.  Drag the **Sales Rep Last Name slicer** to cell A14, drag the **Manufacturer slicer** to cell C14, and then drag the **Payment Type slicer** to **cell F14**.

e.  Click **Finance** in the Payment Type slicer to filter the PivotTable.

f.  Click **Fairbanks** in the Sales Rep Last Name slicer, hold down **Ctrl**, and then click **Prescott** in the Sales Rep Last Name slicer.

g.  Click the border of the Payment Type slicer, and then click **Slicer Style Light 6** in the Slicer Styles group on the Options tab. Repeat this process for the other two slicers.

h.  Click the **Payment Type slicer**, click the **Options tab** if necessary, type **1.39** in the **Width box** in the Buttons group, and then press **Enter**.

i.  Create a footer with your name on the left side, the sheet name code in the center, and the file name code on the right side on each worksheet.

j.  Save and close the workbook, and submit based on your instructor's directions.

# MID-LEVEL EXERCISES

## 1  Mountain View Realty

You are a real estate analyst who works for Mountain View Realty in the North Utah County area. You have consolidated a list of houses sold during the past few months and need to start analyzing the data. For a simple analysis, you will outline the data and use the Subtotal feature. Then you will create a PivotTable to give you a way to perform more in-depth analysis.

a. Open *e05m1realestate*, and then save it as **e05m1realestate_LastnameFirstname**.

b. Make sure you are on the Sales Subtotals worksheet. Insert a column between the Selling Price and Listing Date columns. Enter the heading **% of Asking Price**, and then double-click between the column G and H headings to increase the column width. Insert a formula in **cell G2** to calculate the selling price percentage of the asking price, format it with **Percent Style** with one decimal place, and then copy the formula down the column.

c. Enter the heading **Days on Market** on the right side of the last column, and then double-click between the column J and K headings to increase the column width. Calculate the number of days between the listing date and sale date. Copy the formula down the column.

d. Sort the list by city, selling agent, and listing date.

e. Use the Subtotal feature to calculate the average selling price, % of asking price, and days on market by city.

f. Apply an automatic outline to the columns. Collapse the outline to hide the listing and sale dates. Click the appropriate button to display the grand average and city average rows only. Format the average days on market to zero decimal places. Apply wrap text, 10.00 column width, and increased row height to cells G1 and J1. Set a print area for the **range C1:J88**.

g. Click the **Sales Data worksheet** (an identical dataset without subtotals), and then create a PivotTable on a new worksheet. Name the new worksheet **PivotTable**.

h. Display the cities in the first row of the PivotTable, selling agents in the first column, and asking and selling prices in additional columns.

i. Modify the PivotTable by displaying averages rather than sums with **Accounting Number Format** with zero decimal places. Pivot the data by placing the cities in columns and the selling agents in rows.

j. Add a group filter to display only Alpine and Cedar Hills.

k. Adjust column widths, wrap text as needed, insert a bottom border line below the city names, and then add a more descriptive label for the first column and any other columns that need more descriptive labels. Adjust row heights so that column labels fully display.

l. Go back to the Sales Data worksheet. You realize that a selling price is incorrect. Change the selling price for Number 40 from *$140,000* to **$1,400,000**. Refresh the PivotTable.

m. Create a footer with your name on the left side, the sheet name code in the center, and the file name code on the right side for the Sales Subtotals and the PivotTable worksheets. Adjust the margins and scaling to fit on one page.

n. Save and close the workbook, and submit based on your instructor's directions.

## 2  Fiesta® Collection

Your Aunt Laura has been collecting Fiesta dinnerware, a popular brand from The Homer Laughlin China Company, since it was reintroduced in 1986. Her collection has grown, and she enlisted you to help her maintain a list. So far, you and Aunt Laura entered data by color, item number, and item. Previously, you helped her research current replacement costs from Homer Laughlin's Web site (www.fiestafactorydirect.com), Replacements, Ltd. (www.replacements.com), and eBay (www.ebay.com); however, you believe the retired colors may be worth more now. Laura is especially interested in the values of retired colors so that she can provide this information for her insurance agent. You will build a PivotTable and PivotChart to help her with the analysis.

a. Open *e05m2fiesta*, and then save it as **e05m2fiesta_LastnameFirstname**.

b. Create a PivotTable on a new worksheet, and then name the worksheet **Retired Colors**.

c. Display the colors as row headings and the sum of the replacement values.

d. Add a report filter to display aggregates for retired colors only. Note that current colors do not have a retirement date.

e. Apply the **Pivot Style Medium 12** to the PivotTable.

f. Add a calculated field named **Updated Values** that determines values based on a 15% increase over the replacement values. Do not add a new column to the original list; add it as a calculated field column in the PivotTable.

g. Format the values with **Accounting Number Format** with two decimal places. Create custom headings: **Replacement** and **Updated**. Change *Row Labels* in **cell A3** to **Retired Colors**. Adjust the column widths appropriately and center the column labels.

h. Create a PivotChart from the PivotTable, and then change the chart to a bar chart. Make the following changes to the PivotChart:
   - Move the chart below the PivotTable and adjust its size.
   - Format the value axis to show whole values without decimal places.
   - Sort the PivotChart data so that the most valuable color appears at the top and the least valuable color appears at the bottom of the bar chart. You need to explore how to perform the sort. Determine if you can do this from the PivotChart or if you have to sort the PivotTable.
   - Apply the **Layout 1 chart layout**, and then enter an appropriate chart title. Hide the field buttons in the PivotChart.

i. Create a copy of the Retired Colors worksheet. On the duplicate worksheet, remove the Replacement Values field, display the Updated Values as a percentage of the total, and then sort the percentages with the largest first. Change the chart to a pie chart, apply **Layout 1**, and then move the chart to its own sheet named **Retired Colors Chart**. Change the title to **Updated Replacement Values for Retired Colors**. Optional: Change the pie slice colors to match the Fiesta color names.

j. Create a footer with your name on the left side, the sheet name code in the center, and the file name code on the right side on all worksheets except the Inventory worksheet. Adjust the margins and scaling to fit on one page.

k. Save and close the workbook, and submit based on your instructor's directions.

<hr>

## 3  The Villages of Michigan

You work for The Villages of Michigan, an assisted living center business, at their Detroit location. Because Baby Boomers born between 1946 and 1964 are approaching your target age group for residency, you downloaded free data from the U.S. Census Bureau to analyze population trends. You need to conduct some preliminary assessment along with age profiling. Additionally, you also want to determine what states presently have higher populations of retired people, age 60 and older. You will create subtotals, PivotTables, and PivotCharts to answer these questions.

a. Open *e05m3census*, and then save it as **e05m3census_LastnameFirstname**.

b. Use the Data Subtotals worksheet to create population subtotals for males and females by state. Collapse the outline to show only subtotals. Widen the Male and Female columns as needed.

c. Use the Data worksheet to create a PivotTable in a new worksheet named **Age Profile PivotTable**, and then do the following:
   - Name the PivotTable **M-F by Age Group**.
   - Display age groups to identify each row, and then display male and female population totals per age group.
   - Format the values with **Number style** showing the comma separator with no decimal places. Create custom names for the two value columns.
   - Add another Male field and another Female field after their respective totals. Show these values as percentages of their respective columns. Create custom names for these two columns.
   - Use the Move option to move Under 5 years and 5 to 9 years to their respective locations at the top of the age groups. Replace *Row Labels* with a descriptive column heading. Note what 10-year age group has the highest population. Keep in mind that this is census data from the year 2000. What does this mean in terms of your business plan?
   - Enable the **Banded Columns option**, and then apply **Pivot Style Light 21**.
   - Wrap column headings, and then adjust column widths as needed.

d. Copy the Age Profile PivotTable worksheet. Position the Age Profile PivotTable (2) worksheet to the immediate right of the Age Profile PivotTable worksheet. Use the (2) worksheet to remove all four value columns, display the total number of people per age group, create a custom column heading, and format the values.

e. Create a PivotChart, move it to a new sheet named **Age Group PivotChart**, change the chart to a bar chart, remove the legend, and then add an appropriate chart title. Sort the related PivotTable so that the category axis in the PivotChart displays the age groups in ascending order vertically. Hide the field buttons on the PivotChart, if needed.

f. Use the Data worksheet to create another PivotTable in a new worksheet named **Age by State**, and then do the following:
- Name the PivotTable **Age by State**.
- Display states to identify each row, age groups to identify columns, and total population values. Enter a descriptive heading to replace the *Row Labels* heading.
- Format the values with **Number style** showing the comma separator with no decimal places. Adjust value column widths to **8.43″**, wrap text, and then right-align the headings.
- Insert a two-column **Age Range slicer**, apply **Slicer Style Light 2**, and then use the slicer to filter out age ranges below 60 years.

g. Create a State slicer on the Age Profile PivotTable worksheet. Move the slicer to the immediate right of the PivotTable. Display two columns of buttons, set a **4.5″** height, and then set a **4″** width. Apply **Slicer Style Dark 6**, and then enter **Click a state to filter the list** as the slicer caption. Select **Massachusetts** in the slicer.

h. Arrange the worksheet tabs in this order: Data Subtotals, Data, Age Profile PivotTable, Age Profile PivotTable (2), Age Group PivotChart, and Age by State.

i. Create a footer with your name on the left side, the sheet name code in the center, and the file name code on the right side on each worksheet.

j. Save and close the workbook, and submit based on your instructor's directions.

You are an analyst for an art gallery that is an authorized Greenwich Workshop® fine art dealer (www.greenwichworkshop.com). Customers in your area are especially fond of James C. Christensen's art. You prepared a list of artwork: art, type, edition size, release date, issue price, and estimated current market value. Studying the data will help you discuss trends with art collectors in assessing the value of different pieces. You need to organize the data using an outline, subtotals, PivotTables, and PivotCharts to aid you in your analysis.

## Sort, Subtotal, and Outline Data

You need to organize the workbook containing the list of art in a way that facilitates using the Subtotal feature. Then you will further outline the list so that you can collapse and expand groups.

a. Open *e05c1fineart*, and then save it as **e05c1fineart_LastnameFirstname.**

b. Click the **Subtotals worksheet**. Sort the data by type, and then further sort it by the name of the art, both in alphabetical order.

c. Use the Subtotal feature to identify the highest issue price, estimated market value, and percent increase.

d. Add an automatic outline, and then select and group the first and last name columns.

e. Collapse the names and collapse columns created by the automatic outline.

f. Study the list to see the highest percent increase in each type.

## Create a PivotTable

Although creating an outline and subtotaling data are helpful for an initial analysis of the artwork values, you believe you can learn more by creating a PivotTable. You will add initial fields and then add or remove fields to gain a better perspective on the artwork.

a. Click the **Christensen worksheet**, and then create a PivotTable from the data.

b. Use the Type, Release Date, and Issue Price fields, enabling Excel to determine where the fields go.

c. Remove the release date. Add the Est. Value field.

## Format the PivotTable

Calculating averages will help you see what the average values and percent increases are within each art type. In addition, you need to format the values and provide clear, descriptive headings in the PivotTable.

a. Modify the Sum of Price to determine the average issue price and average estimated market value by type.

b. Insert a calculated field to determine percent change in values by type.

c. Format the three columns of values appropriately, using whole numbers for dollar values and two decimal places for percentages.

d. Edit the custom names for the values columns. Apply these formats to the three values column headings: wrap text, center horizontally, increased row height, and adjusted column widths.

e. Enter appropriate labels for the first column and the grand total label.

## Filter the PivotTable and Apply a Style

You want to focus on average values for sold-out art because these pieces typically increase in value on the secondary market. In addition, you want to narrow the list to particular types. After filtering the data, you will apply a style.

a. Set a report filter to display only sold-out art.

b. Set a group filter to *omit* Hand Colored Print, Limited Edition Hand Colored Print, Open Edition Print, and Poster types.

c. Apply **Pivot Style Medium 5**.

d. Display banded columns and banded rows.

## Create a PivotChart

To help interpret the consolidated values of the art, you want to create a PivotChart. You realize that displaying both monetary values and percentages on the same chart is like mixing apples and oranges. If you modify the PivotChart, you will change the PivotTable; therefore, you will create a PivotChart from the original data source.

a. Use the Christensen worksheet to create a PivotChart.

b. Use the Type, Issue Price, and Est. Value fields. Find the average issue price and average estimated value.

c. Set report and group filters as you did for the first PivotTable.

d. Apply formatting as you did for the first PivotTable.

e. Change the chart type to **Bar**.

f. Move the PivotChart below the PivotTable, resize the PivotChart, and then hide the field buttons in the PivotChart.

g. Insert an appropriate chart title reflecting the contents and the report filter. Reduce the font size for the chart title to be more appropriate for the chart data.

h. Set the upper limit of the value axis to **2000**, if needed.

i. Sort the PivotTable in such a way that its effect on the PivotChart is to display the category labels alphabetically

j.  Change *Row Labels* in **cell A3** to a descriptive column label, and then enter **Overall Averages** in **cell A12**.

### Finalizing Your Workbook

You need to finalize your workbook.

a.  Rename the first PivotTable worksheet **PivotTable**.

b.  Rename the second PivotTable/PivotChart worksheet **PivotChart**.

c.  Adjust the margins so that the PivotTable and PivotChart data fit on one page.

d.  Select landscape orientation, and then adjust the top and bottom margins for the Subtotals worksheet.

e.  Create a footer on all four worksheets with your name, the sheet name code, and the file name code.

f.  Save and close the workbook, and submit based on your instructor's directions.

## Springfield Auto Rentals

**GENERAL CASE**

You work for Springfield Auto Rentals, which rents different classes of vehicles for both personal and business use. You track each transaction, including rental dates. Now you need to analyze the data. Open *e05b1autorent*, and then save it as **e05b1autorent_LastnameFirstname**. Use the Transactions1 worksheet to subtotal the total rental cost with the data arranged by car size, auto ID, and date rented. Add a second-level subtotal of total rental cost based on auto ID. Add an automatic outline to outline the columns. Use the Transactions2 worksheet to create a PivotTable arranged by car size and rental cost, separated by usage (business and personal). Only display results for account payments. Format the values, create custom headings, and then adjust column widths. Apply an appropriate Pivot Style with a similar fill color to that in the Transactions2 worksheet headings. Rename Sheet2 **PivotTable**. Copy the PivotTable worksheet. On the PivotTable (2) worksheet, display the car size values as percentages within each rental type. For example, the compact car rentals account for 7.48% of total business rentals. On the original PivotTable worksheet, create a PivotChart from the PivotTable, using a column chart. Move and size the chart accordingly, insert an appropriate chart title, format the value axis without decimal places, and then apply a different chart style. Hide the field buttons in the PivotChart. Insert and customize slicers for the Payment Type and Car Size fields. Adjust the height and width appropriately for the slicers. Apply scaling, margins, and page breaks on the Transactions1 worksheet. Create a footer with your name, the sheet name code, and the file name code for the Transactions1, PivotTable, and PivotTable (2) worksheets. Save and close the workbook, and submit based on your instructor's directions.

## Facebook® – A Social Networking Phenomenon

**RESEARCH CASE**

Facebook has experienced phenomenal growth since its creation in 2004. For a brief overview of its history, see http://www.checkfacebook.com. What is it that has made Facebook a huge success story, starting a decade after many of the other Web company startups? To understand how people use Facebook, look at its applications. Start a new Excel workbook, and then save it as **e05b2facebook_LastnameFirstname**. Go to http://statistics.allfacebook.com and use this site to build a worksheet that lists at least 250 application leaders for 10 categories, two of which must be Business and Just For Fun. Include data for these columns: Category, Name, Daily Average Use (DAU), Monthly Average Use (MAU), and Daily Growth. Format the data and headings appropriately. Name this worksheet **Application Leaders**.

Copy the worksheet, and then name the duplicate worksheet **Category Subtotals**. Subtotal the data, and then organize the categories from largest to smallest according to monthly active users. Show only category subtotals and the grand total. Use the Application Leaders data to create a PivotTable in a new worksheet named **Positive Growth Applications**. Show the applications with DAU with a custom name of **Daily Active Users** and Daily Growth with a custom name of **Daily Growth Rate**. Apply a filter to the Applications rows to show only positive Daily Active Users. Organize the data from the highest daily active users.

Create a similar PivotTable in a new worksheet named **Applications with 4x Growth**, but display only the Daily Growth rate for applications, and then create a report filter to show rates higher than 4x growth. Insert and customize a slicer for the Category field. Add a horizontal bar PivotChart to the worksheet with no legend and the chart title **High Growth Applications**. Move the PivotChart below the PivotTable, size it appropriately, and then hide the field buttons. Change *Row Labels* to descriptive labels in each PivotTable. Adjust margins and column widths on each sheet to optimize future printing. Create a footer with your name, the sheet name code, and the file name code on each worksheet. Save and close the workbook, and submit based on your instructor's directions.

## Innovative Game Studio

**DISASTER RECOVERY**

You work as an assistant to Terry Park, the producer for a video game studio in Phoenix, Arizona. The company produces games for the PlayStation®, Xbox®, and Wii™ consoles. The producer tracks salaries and performance for everyone on a particular team, which consists of artists, animators, programmers, etc. Terry tried to create a PivotTable to organize the data by department and then by title within department. He also wants to display total salaries by these categories and filter the data to show aggregates for team members who earned only Excellent and Good performance ratings. In addition, he wants to see what the percentages of total salaries for each job title are of each department's budget. For example, the total salary for Senior Artists is $263,300. That represents 50.27% of the Art Department's salary budget for Excellent and Good rated employees. However, the percentages are **not** displayed correctly. Terry called you in to correct his PivotTable. Open *e05b3games*, and then save it as **e05b3games_LastnameFirstname**. Identify the errors, and then make a list of these errors starting on row 41 in the PivotTable worksheet. Correct the errors, and then improve the format, including a medium Pivot Style, throughout the PivotTable. Create a footer with your name, the sheet name code, and the file name code. Save and close the workbook, and submit based on your instructor's directions.

# EXCEL
# WHAT-IF ANALYSIS
## Using Decision-Making Tools

Watch the
**Set-up Video**
for this
Case Study!

## CASE STUDY | Personal Finance: Buying a Car

You need a new car. After doing some preliminary research on prices, you developed a spreadsheet to help you calculate your monthly payment, total amount to repay a car loan, and the total amount of interest you will pay. You want a car that costs $25,000 including taxes, title, and other fees. You plan to take $5,000 out of your savings account for a down payment. You are currently investigating automobile loan interest rates at various banks and credit unions. You realize that you may need to find a less expensive car and/or change your down payment. Although you can change input values to see how different values affect the monthly payment, you want to be able to see the comparisons at the same time. In addition, you want to look at your annual monthly budget to review the impact of purchasing a new car on your income and expenses.

You will use Excel to help you analyze the variables that affect the car payment, total amount to repay the loan, and the total interest paid. To help you make a decision, you will use several tools, each with specific purposes, benefits, and restrictions. With these tools, you will have a better understanding of how a car payment will affect your overall budget.

## OBJECTIVES AFTER YOU READ THIS CHAPTER, YOU WILL BE ABLE TO:

1. Create a one-variable data table
2. Create a two-variable data table
3. Identify an input value with Goal Seek
4. Use Scenario Manager
5. Generate scenario summary reports
6. Load the Solver Add-In
7. Optimize results with Solver

From Excel Chapter 6 of *Exploring Microsoft Office 2010 Excel Comprehensive*, First Edition, Robert T. Grauer, Mary Anne Poatsy, Keith Mulbery. Copyright © 2011 by Pearson Education, Inc. Published by Pearson Prentice Hall, Inc. All rights reserved.

# One- and Two-Variable Data Tables

**What-if analysis** is the process of changing variables to observe how changes affect calculated results.

**A variable** is a value that you can change to see how that change affects other values.

> ... what-if analysis tools are just that—tools.... You must use these tools wisely to help you analyze data and interpret data.

You are now ready to explore Excel's powerful what-if analysis tools. ***What-if analysis*** enables you to experiment with different variables or assumptions so that you can observe and compare how these changes affect a related outcome. A ***variable*** is an input value that can change to other values to affect the results of a situation. People in almost every industry perform some type of what-if analysis to make educated decisions. For example, business people perform what-if analysis to see the impact that producing different quantities of a product will have on revenue. Remember that these what-if analysis tools are just that—tools. They do not provide the definitive, perfect solution to a problem. You must use these tools wisely to help you analyze data and interpret data, but you or another human must make ultimate decisions based on the data.

In this section, you will learn how to create one- and two-variable data tables to perform what-if analysis. You will design the data tables, insert formulas, and complete the data tables to compare the results for different values of the variables.

## Creating a One-Variable Data Table

A **one-variable data table** is a data analysis tool that provides various results based on changing one variable.

A ***one-variable data table*** is a structured range that contains different values for *one variable* to compare how these values affect one or more calculated results. For example, you can use a one-variable data table to compare monthly payments on a car. As you recall, monthly payments are based on the interest rate, number of payment periods, and the amount of the loan. Holding the number of payment periods and loan amount constant, you can compare how different values of the interest rate (the one variable), such as 5%, 5.5%, 6%, 6.5%, and 7.0%, affect the calculated results: monthly payment, total amount to repay the loan, and total interest paid.

When setting up a one-variable data table, you must decide which one variable you want to use. After you decide on an input variable, then you select one or more formulas that depend on that input variable for calculations.

### Set Up the Substitution Values

A **substitution value** replaces the original value of a variable in a data table.

Your first step is to decide which one variable, such as the interest rate, to manipulate. Then you need to specify the substitution values. A ***substitution value*** is a value that replaces the original input value of the variable in a data table. For example, the original interest rate is 4.5%, but you might want to substitute 5%, 5.5%, 6%, 6.5%, and 7% to see how changing the interest rate affects the calculations.

Locate a range to the right or below the regular worksheet data to create the one-variable data table. Leave at least one blank row and one blank column between the dataset and the data table. Enter the substitution values down one column or across in one row. With one variable and several results, a vertical orientation for the substitution values is recommended because people often look up a value in the first column of a table and then read across to see corresponding values.

You can enter the substitution values yourself or use the Series dialog box to help complete a series of values. To use the Series dialog box, do the following:

1. Type the first value (such as 5%) in the starting cell (cell D4), and keep that cell as the active cell.
2. Click the Home tab, click Fill in the Editing group, and then select Series to open the Series dialog box (see Figure 1).
3. Click Rows to place the series of substitution values in a row, or click Columns to place the series of substitution values down a column.

4. Enter the value increment in the *Step value* box, and enter the ending value for the series in the *Stop value* box. For example, if you want to create a list of incremental interest rates, such as 5%, 5.5%, and 6% up to 9%, then enter 0.5% in the *Step value* box and 9% in the *Stop value* box.

5. Click OK. Excel fills in a series of values as shown in Figure 1. You may need to format the percentages to show one or more decimal places, if desired.

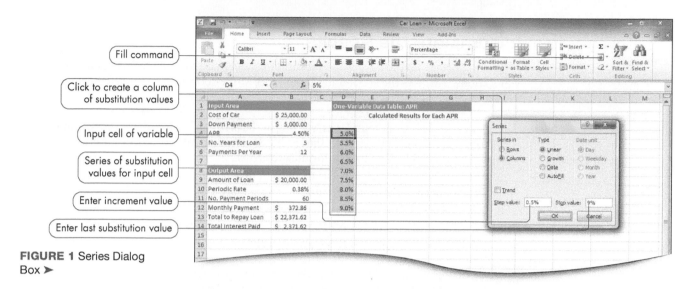

**FIGURE 1** Series Dialog Box ➤

> **TIP** Auto Fill a Series of Substitution Values
>
> Instead of using the Series dialog box, you can use Auto Fill to complete a series of substitution values. To do this, enter the first two substitution values (such as 5% and 5.5%). Select the cells containing these two values, and then drag the fill handle down until the ScreenTip displays the last substitution value you want. Excel sets the increment pattern based on the difference between the first two values.

## Add Formulas to the Data Table

After you enter the substitution values in either a column or row, you need to add one or more formulas that relate mathematically to the variable for which you are using substitution values. Although you can create formulas directly in the data table, referencing cells containing existing formulas outside the data table is preferable because you usually create a spreadsheet complete with formulas before you create a data table. Because the formulas often are already created, you can save time and reduce errors by referencing the original formula. For example, to reference the original monthly payment formula, type =B12. Within the data table range, the formula references must be entered in a specific location based on the location of your substitution values (see Table 1).

| TABLE 1 Locations for Formula References | | |
|---|---|---|
| **Location of Substitution Values** | **Enter the First Formula Reference** | **Enter Additional Formula References** |
| **Vertically in a Column** | On the row above and one column to the right of the first substitution value | To the right of the first formula reference |
| **Horizontally in a Row** | On the row below and one column to the left of the first substitution value | Below the first formula reference |

One- and Two-Variable Data Tables • Excel 2010

339

For example, assume you want to compare the effect of different interest rates on the monthly payment, the total amount repaid, and the total interest paid. You need to set up three columns to show the calculated results. The first formula reference for monthly payment goes in cell E3. To compare the effects of substitution values on other results, the second formula reference for total repaid goes in cell F3, and the third formula reference for total interest paid goes in cell G3. Be sure the cells you reference contain formulas, not actual values.

## Complete the Results

It is important that you enter the substitution values and formula references in the correct locations. This sets the left and top boundaries of the soon-to-be-completed data table. To complete the one-variable data table, do the following:

1. Select the data table boundaries, starting in the blank cell in the top-left corner of the data table. Drag down to select the last blank cell at the intersection of the last substitution value and the last formula reference.
2. Click the Data tab, click What-If Analysis in the Data Tools group, and then select Data Table to open the Data Table dialog box (see Figure 2).
3. Enter the cell reference of the cell containing the original variable for which you are substituting values. If you listed the substitution values in a row, enter the original variable cell reference in the *Row input cell* box. If you listed the substitution values in a column, enter the original variable cell reference in the *Column input cell* box. In Figure 2, for example, you would enter cell $B$4—the original interest rate variable—in the *Column input cell* box because you entered the substitution interest rates in a column. The cell reference is absolute so that Excel always refers to the original input cell as it performs calculations in the data table.
4. Click OK.

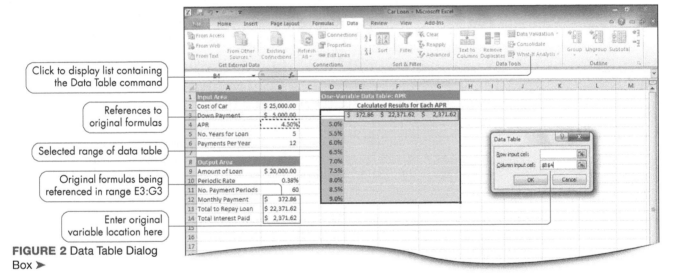

**FIGURE 2** Data Table Dialog Box ➤

When you create the one-variable data table, Excel uses these substitution values individually to replace the original variable's value and then uses the substitution values in the formulas to produce the results in the body of the data table. In Figure 3, the data table shows the substitution values of different interest rates, whereas the formulas produce the monthly payments (column E), total payments (column F), and total interest paid (column G) for the respective interest rates.

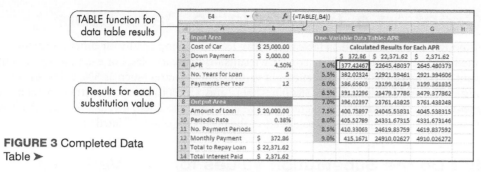

TABLE function for data table results

Results for each substitution value

**FIGURE 3** Completed Data Table ➤

## Format the Data Table

After creating the data table, you should format the values. In this case, you format the monetary values with Accounting Number Format. Sometimes, one of the substitution values is identical to the original variable's value, which produces the same results as the formula reference results on the first row of the table (row 3 in Figure 3) that contains the formulas used in the data table. You cannot delete that row because Excel needs those formulas to display results within the table. However, you can apply a custom number format to disguise the formula references as column labels.

1. Click in the cell containing a formula reference in the data table.
2. Click the Number Dialog Box Launcher in the Number group on the Home tab to open the Format Cells dialog box with the Number tab active.
3. Click Custom in the Category list, scroll up in the Type list, and then select General in the list.
4. Select General in the Type box above the Type list, and then type what you want to appear as a column heading. Enter the text within quotation marks, such as "Payment" (see Figure 4), and then click OK.

You can then apply bold and centering to the column headings. If you see pound signs, the column is too narrow to display the text, indicating you need to wrap the text or expand the column width. Although you are using a custom number format that displays text, Excel remembers that the actual contents are values derived from formulas.

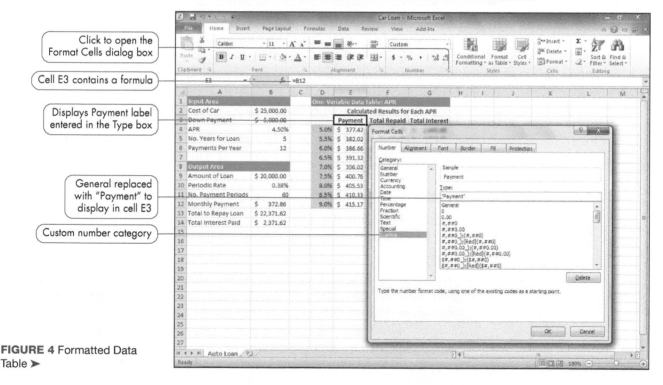

Click to open the Format Cells dialog box

Cell E3 contains a formula

Displays Payment label entered in the Type box

General replaced with "Payment" to display in cell E3

Custom number category

**FIGURE 4** Formatted Data Table ➤

# Creating a Two-Variable Data Table

Although a one-variable data table is effective for comparing results for different values for one variable, you might want to compare results for two variables. For example, you might want to compare the combined effects of various interest rates (such as 5%, 5.5%, and 6%) and different down payments ($5,000, $7,500, and $10,000) on the monthly payment. A *two-variable data table* is a structured range that contains different values for *two variables* to compare how these differing values affect the results for one calculated value.

A **two-variable data table** is a data analysis tool that provides results based on changing two variables.

## Set Up the Substitution Values for Two Variables

Create the two-variable data table separate from regular worksheet data, similar to how you did this for a one-variable data table. For a two-variable data table, you use the top row for one variable's substitution values and the first column for the other variable's substitution values. After deciding where to place the variables, enter the substitution values in the row and column in a similar manner as you did for a one-variable data table. Figure 5 shows substitution interest rates in the first column (range D4:D12) and substitution down payments in the first row (range E3:G3).

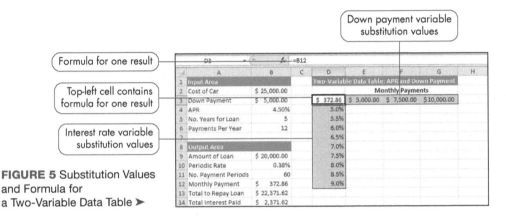

**FIGURE 5** Substitution Values and Formula for a Two-Variable Data Table ➤

## Add a Formula to the Data Table

The two-variable data table enables you to use two variables, but you are restricted to only one result instead of multiple results. With the one-variable data table, you could compare multiple results: monthly payment, total to repay the loan, and total interest paid. However, for the two-variable data table, decide which result you want to focus on based on the two variables. In the case of a car loan, you might want to focus on comparing the effects that changes in interest rates and down payments have on different monthly payments. Enter the formula or reference to the original formula in the blank cell in the top-left corner. For example, enter the cell reference for the monthly payment (=B12) in cell D3 in Figure 5.

## Complete the Two-Variable Data Table

After entering the substitution values and the reference to one formula result, you are ready to complete the table to see the results. To complete the two-variable data table, do the following:

1. Select the data table boundaries, starting in the top-left corner of the data table. Drag down and to the right to select the last blank cell at the intersection of the last substitution value for both the column and the row.
2. Click the Data tab, click What-If Analysis in the Data Tools group, and then select Data Table. The Data Table dialog box opens.

3. Enter the cell that contains the original value for the substitution values in the first row in the *Row input cell* box. Enter the cell that contains the original value for the substitution values in the first column in the *Column input cell* box. For example, the original horizontal (down payment) variable value is stored in cell B3, and the original vertical (APR) variable value is stored in cell B4.

4. Click OK.

After you complete the data table, you should format the results by applying a custom number format to the formula cell to appear as a heading and adding a merged heading above the row substitution values (see Figure 6).

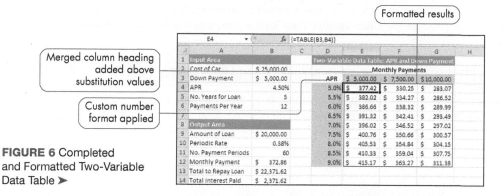

**FIGURE 6** Completed and Formatted Two-Variable Data Table ➤

**TIP** TABLE Array Function

If you click a result in the one-variable data table and look at the Formula Bar, you see {=TABLE(,B4)}. Excel uses the TABLE array function to produce multiple results based on the column input cell B4. The formula for the two-variable data table is {=TABLE(B3,B4)}, which uses cell B3 as the row input cell and B4 as the column input cell. Use Excel Help to learn more about the TABLE function and arrays.

# HANDS-ON EXERCISES

## 1 One- and Two-Variable Data Tables

As you consider different options for a new car purchase, you want to use data tables to compare how different interest rates and down payments will affect your monthly payment. You decide to create both one- and two-variable data tables to analyze the results.

**Skills covered:** Enter Substitution Values for a One-Variable Data Table • Enter Formulas and Complete the Data Table • Format the One-Variable Data Table • Set Up the Structure for a Two-Variable Data Table • Complete the Two-Variable Data Table

---

### STEP 1 ▶ ENTER SUBSTITUTION VALUES FOR A ONE-VARIABLE DATA TABLE

You want to compare monthly payments, total amounts to repay a loan, and total interest you will pay based on several interest rates—the variable. The interest rates range from 4% to 6% in 0.25% increments. Your first step is to enter a series of substitution values for the interest rate. Refer to Figure 7 as you complete Step 1.

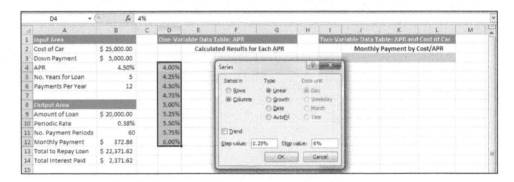

**FIGURE 7** Substitution Values ▶

a. Open the *e06h1carloan* workbook and save it as **e06h1carloan_LastnameFirstname**.

> **TROUBLESHOOTING:** If you make any major mistakes in this exercise, you can close the file, open *e06h1carloan* again, and start this exercise over.

b. Click **cell D4**, type **4%**, and then press **Ctrl+Enter**.

   Cell D4 is the first cell containing a substitution value. Make sure cell D4 is still the active cell.

c. Click **Fill** in the Editing group on the Home tab, and then select **Series**.

   The Series dialog box opens.

d. Click **Columns**.

   You changed the *Series in* option to Columns because you want the series of substitution values listed vertically in column D.

e. Delete the existing value in the **Step value box**, and then type **0.25%**.

f. Type **6%** in the **Stop value box**, and then click **OK**.

   Excel fills in the series of values; however, you need to increase the number of decimal points to see the full percentages.

> **TROUBLESHOOTING:** If you forget to type the decimal point and/or percent sign, the series will be incorrect. If this happens, click Undo and repeat steps c-f.

g. Select the **range D4:D12**, and then click **Increase Decimal** twice in the Number group. Save the workbook.

STEP 2 ## ENTER FORMULAS AND COMPLETE THE DATA TABLE

You need to enter references to the monthly payment, total amount to repay the loan, and total interest formulas. Then you will complete the table to compare the results for different interest rates ranging from 4% to 6%. Refer to Figure 8 as you complete Step 2.

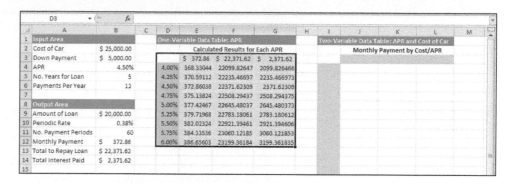

**FIGURE 8** Completed Data Table ➤

a. Click **cell E3**, type **=B12**, and then press ⟶.

You entered a reference to the original monthly payment formula. When the results of cell B12 change, they are reflected in cell E3.

b. Type **=B13** and press ⟶.

You entered a reference to the original total amount to repay the loan.

c. Type **=B14** and press **Enter**.

You entered a reference to the original total interest paid.

d. Select the **range D3:G12**.

You select the entire range of the data table, starting in the blank cell in the top-left corner. Note that you did not select the titles or headings in cells D1:G2.

e. Click the **Data tab**, click **What-If Analysis** in the Data Tools group, and then select **Data Table**.

f. Click in the **Column input cell box**, click **cell B4**, and then click **OK**. Save the workbook.

Because the substitution values are in a column, you reference cell B4 in the *Column input* box. Excel inserts the TABLE array function in the empty result cells and substitutes the values in range D4:D12 individually for the original APR to calculate the respective monthly payments, total amounts, and total interest payments. The higher the APR, the higher the monthly payment, total amount to repay the loan, and total interest.

STEP 3 ## FORMAT THE ONE-VARIABLE DATA TABLE

You want to format the results to show dollar signs and to display rounded values to the nearest penny. In addition, you want to add column headings to provide more detail to the data table. Because those formulas must remain on the first row, you will add custom formats to the cells to appear as column headings. Refer to Figure 9 as you complete Step 3.

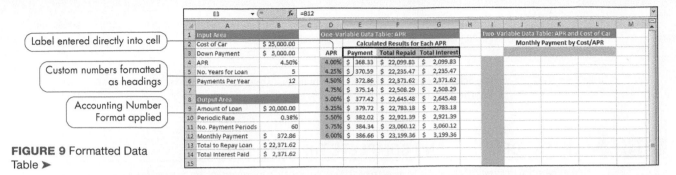

**FIGURE 9** Formatted Data Table ➤

**Label entered directly into cell**

**Custom numbers formatted as headings**

**Accounting Number Format applied**

a. Select the **range E4:G12**, click the **Home tab**, and then click **Accounting Number Format** in the Number group.

The values look more professional now that you formatted them.

b. Click **cell D3**, type **APR**, and then press ➡.

Because cell D3 was empty, you can type the label directly in the cell without adding a custom format. Cell E3 should be the active cell.

c. Click the **Number Dialog Box Launcher** in the Number group.

d. Select **Custom** in the **Category list**, scroll up through the **Type list**, and then select **General** in the list.

e. Select **General** in the **Type box**, type **"Payment"**, and then click **OK**.

The formula result $372.86 now appears as *Payment* in cell E3.

f. Repeat and adapt steps c through e to enter the following custom number formats: **"Total Repaid"** for **cell F3**, and **"Total Interest"** for **cell G3**.

> **TROUBLESHOOTING:** If you forget the quotation marks, the cell contents will contain a mix of numbers and characters. If this happens, open the Format Cells dialog box again, and then edit the contents of the Type box to display the text surrounded by quotation marks.

g. Center and bold the **range E3:G3**. Save the workbook.

## STEP 4 ▶ SET UP THE STRUCTURE FOR A TWO-VARIABLE DATA TABLE

Now you want to focus on how a combination of interest rates and different car costs will affect just the monthly payment. The interest rates range from 4% to 6% at 1/8% increments with car costs of $20,000, $25,000, and $30,000. Refer to Figure 10 as you complete Step 4.

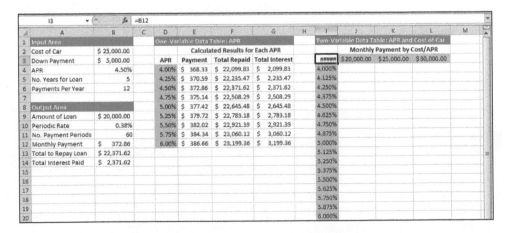

**FIGURE 10** Substitution Values ➤

a. Enter **20000, 25000,** and **30000** in the **range J3:L3.** Format these values with **Accounting Number Format.**

b. Click **cell I4,** type **4%,** and then press **Ctrl+Enter.**

c. Click **Fill** in the Editing group, select **Series,** and then click **Columns.**

d. Replace the existing value in the **Step value box** with **0.125%,** type **6%** in the **Stop value box,** and then click **OK.**

e. Format the **range I4:I20** with **Percent Style** with three decimal places.

f. Click **cell I3,** type **=B12,** and then press **Ctrl+Enter.** Save the workbook.

You inserted the reference to the formula in the top-left cell of the two-variable data table. The cell displays pound signs, indicating the column is too narrow to display the value; you will apply a custom number format in Step 5.

## STEP 5 COMPLETE THE TWO-VARIABLE DATA TABLE

You need to complete the data table, format the monthly payment results, and apply a custom number format to the cell containing the formula reference so that it displays the text APR. Refer to Figure 11 as you complete Step 5.

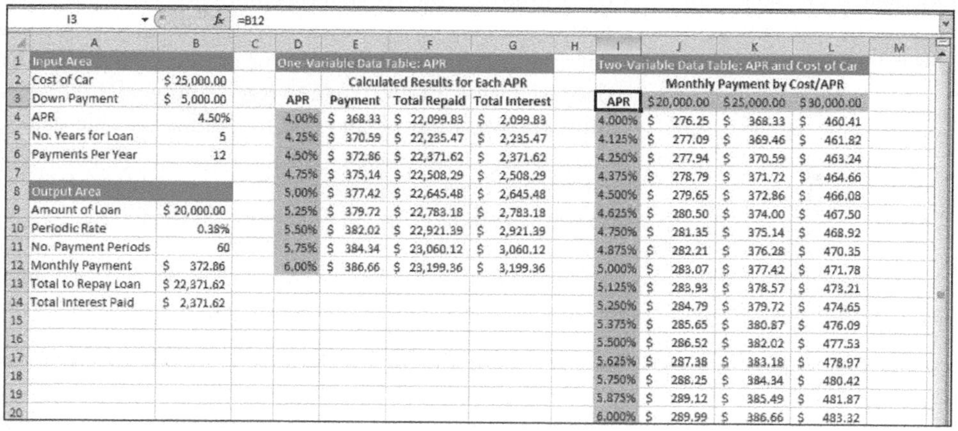

I3 =B12

| | A | B |
|---|---|---|
| 1 | Input Area | |
| 2 | Cost of Car | $ 25,000.00 |
| 3 | Down Payment | $ 5,000.00 |
| 4 | APR | 4.50% |
| 5 | No. Years for Loan | 5 |
| 6 | Payments Per Year | 12 |
| 7 | | |
| 8 | Output Area | |
| 9 | Amount of Loan | $ 20,000.00 |
| 10 | Periodic Rate | 0.38% |
| 11 | No. Payment Periods | 60 |
| 12 | Monthly Payment | $ 372.86 |
| 13 | Total to Repay Loan | $ 22,371.62 |
| 14 | Total Interest Paid | $ 2,371.62 |

| One-Variable Data Table: APR | | | |
|---|---|---|---|
| | Calculated Results for Each APR | | |
| APR | Payment | Total Repaid | Total Interest |
| 4.00% | $ 368.33 | $ 22,099.83 | $ 2,099.83 |
| 4.25% | $ 370.59 | $ 22,235.47 | $ 2,235.47 |
| 4.50% | $ 372.86 | $ 22,371.62 | $ 2,371.62 |
| 4.75% | $ 375.14 | $ 22,508.29 | $ 2,508.29 |
| 5.00% | $ 377.42 | $ 22,645.48 | $ 2,645.48 |
| 5.25% | $ 379.72 | $ 22,783.18 | $ 2,783.18 |
| 5.50% | $ 382.02 | $ 22,921.39 | $ 2,921.39 |
| 5.75% | $ 384.34 | $ 23,060.12 | $ 3,060.12 |
| 6.00% | $ 386.66 | $ 23,199.36 | $ 3,199.36 |

| Two-Variable Data Table: APR and Cost of Car | | | |
|---|---|---|---|
| | Monthly Payment by Cost/APR | | |
| APR | $20,000.00 | $25,000.00 | $30,000.00 |
| 4.000% | $ 276.25 | $ 368.33 | $ 460.41 |
| 4.125% | $ 277.09 | $ 369.46 | $ 461.82 |
| 4.250% | $ 277.94 | $ 370.59 | $ 463.24 |
| 4.375% | $ 278.79 | $ 371.72 | $ 464.66 |
| 4.500% | $ 279.65 | $ 372.86 | $ 466.08 |
| 4.625% | $ 280.50 | $ 374.00 | $ 467.50 |
| 4.750% | $ 281.35 | $ 375.14 | $ 468.92 |
| 4.875% | $ 282.21 | $ 376.28 | $ 470.35 |
| 5.000% | $ 283.07 | $ 377.42 | $ 471.78 |
| 5.125% | $ 283.93 | $ 378.57 | $ 473.21 |
| 5.250% | $ 284.79 | $ 379.72 | $ 474.65 |
| 5.375% | $ 285.65 | $ 380.87 | $ 476.09 |
| 5.500% | $ 286.52 | $ 382.02 | $ 477.53 |
| 5.625% | $ 287.38 | $ 383.18 | $ 478.97 |
| 5.750% | $ 288.25 | $ 384.34 | $ 480.42 |
| 5.875% | $ 289.12 | $ 385.49 | $ 481.87 |
| 6.000% | $ 289.99 | $ 386.66 | $ 483.32 |

**FIGURE 11** Completed Two-Variable Data Table ➤

a. Select the **range I3:L20.**

b. Click the **Data tab,** click **What-If Analysis** in the Data Tools group, and then select **Data Table.**

c. Click **cell B2** to enter that cell reference in the **Row input cell box.**

Because you entered the car cost substitution values in the top row of the data table, you entered the reference to the cell containing the original cost of car variable in the Row input cell box.

d. Click in the **Column input cell box,** click **cell B4,** and then click **OK.**

Because you entered the interest rate substitution values in the left column of the data table, you entered the reference to the cell containing the original APR variable in the Column input cell box.

e. Click **cell I3,** and then apply a custom number format to display *APR.* Center and bold the contents in **cell I3.**

f. Save the workbook. Keep the workbook onscreen if you plan to continue with Hands-On Exercise 2. If not, close the workbook and exit Excel.

# Goal Seek and Scenario Manager

Although data tables are useful for particular situations to compare effects of different values for one or two variables, other what-if analysis tools are better suited for other situations.

> ... you might need to review two or more variables and their effects on two or more results....

For example, you might want to do a what-if analysis to determine what grade you need to earn on your final exam to earn an A in the class. The process requires identifying the lowest score needed to reach your goal. You do not need to create a data table to show side-by-side comparisons. At other times, you might need to review two or more variables and their effects on two or more results, which is beyond the purpose of data tables.

In this section, you will learn when and how to use both Goal Seek and Scenario Manager to assist you in making decisions. These tools enable you to perform what-if analysis to make forecasts or predictions involving quantifiable data.

## Identifying an Input Value with Goal Seek

**Goal Seek** is a tool that identifies the necessary input value to obtain a desired goal.

Suppose the most you can afford for a monthly payment on a car loan is $300. How can you determine the down payment amount needed to meet that monthly payment? *Goal Seek* is a tool that enables you to specify a desired result from a formula ($300 monthly payment), without knowing what input value achieves that goal. Goal Seek works backward to identify the exact value for a variable to reach your goal. In this case, you can use Goal Seek to determine the maximum loan amount. Unlike variable data tables, Goal Seek uses the original worksheet data to change an input instead of displaying various combinations in a separate table. Goal Seek manipulates only one variable and one result; it does not produce a list of values to compare. To use Goal Seek, do the following:

1. Click What-If Analysis in the Data Tools group on the Data tab.
2. Select Goal Seek to open the Goal Seek dialog box.
3. Enter the cell reference for the cell to be optimized in the *Set cell* box. This cell must contain a formula, such as the monthly payment.
4. Enter the result you want to achieve (such as the $300 goal) in the *To value* box.
5. Enter the cell reference that contains the variable to adjust (such as the down payment) in the *By changing cell* box as shown in Figure 12. This cell must be a value, not a formula, which has a mathematical relationship with the cell containing the formula or goal. Then click OK.

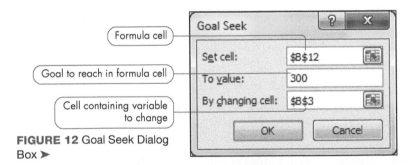

**FIGURE 12** Goal Seek Dialog Box ➤

Excel varies the input value until the desired result is achieved, if possible, and displays the Goal Seek Status dialog box. Click OK to accept the target value and change the value of the input cell you entered in Step 5 to achieve the goal you specified in Steps 3 and 4. Click Cancel to keep the original input cell value instead of changing it. If Excel cannot determine a solution given the input cell and the desired results, it displays a message box.

# Using Scenario Manager

A **scenario** is a set of values that represent a possible situation.

You may want to compare several variables and their combined effects on multiple calculated results. This type of analysis involves identifying and setting up *scenarios*, which are detailed sets of values that represent different possible situations. Business managers often create a best-case scenario, worst-case scenario, and most likely scenario to compare outcomes. For example, a best-case scenario could reflect an increase in units sold and lower production costs. A worst-case scenario could reflect fewer units sold and higher production costs.

Business managers often create a best-case scenario, worst-case scenario, and most likely scenario to compare outcomes.

**Scenario Manager** enables you to define and manage scenarios to compare how they affect results.

*Scenario Manager* is a what-if analysis tool that enables you to define and manage up to 32 scenarios to compare their effects on calculated results. You can perform more sophisticated what-if analyses with Scenario Manager than with data tables with the increased number of variables and results. The Scenario Manager dialog box (see Figure 13) enables you to create, edit, and delete scenario names. Each scenario represents different sets of what-if conditions to assess the outcome of spreadsheet models. Each scenario is stored under its own name and defines cells whose values change from scenario to scenario.

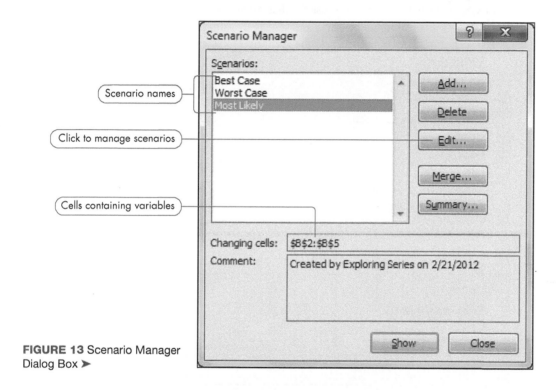

**FIGURE 13** Scenario Manager Dialog Box ➤

> **TIP** Scenarios on Different Worksheets
>
> When you create scenarios, Excel maintains those scenarios on the worksheet that was active when you created them. You can create scenarios for each worksheet in a workbook. The Scenario Manager dialog box displays only those scenarios you have created on the active worksheet.

## Create and Edit Scenarios

Before you start the Scenario Manager, identify cells that contain the variables you want to change or manipulate. For example, in evaluating car loans, you might want to manipulate the values for these variables: cost, down payment, interest rate, and the duration of the loan.

You enter the cell references for these variables as the changing cells because you change the values to compare the results. After identifying the variables you want to change, identify one or more cells containing formulas that generate results you want to compare. To create a scenario, do the following:

1. Click What-If Analysis in the Data Tools group on the Data tab.
2. Select Scenario Manager to open the Scenario Manager dialog box.
3. Click Add to open the Add Scenario dialog box (see Figure 14).
4. Enter a meaningful name in the *Scenario name* box.
5. Enter the input cells for the scenarios in the *Changing cells* box. These are the cells containing variable values that Scenario Manager will adjust or change. The changing cells should be identical cell references across all scenarios.
6. Click in the Comment box. Excel enters the name of the person who created the scenarios in the Comment box; however, you can change the name and enter additional descriptions and rationales for the scenarios.
7. Click OK to open the Scenario Values dialog box (see Figure 15), which lists the changing cell references that you specified in the previous dialog box. In each respective box, type the value you want to use for that particular scenario.
8. Click Add to add another scenario and specify its values. After you enter values for the last scenario, click OK to return to the Scenario Manager dialog box.

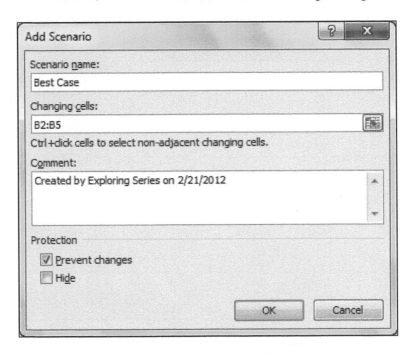

**FIGURE 14** Add Scenario Dialog Box ➤

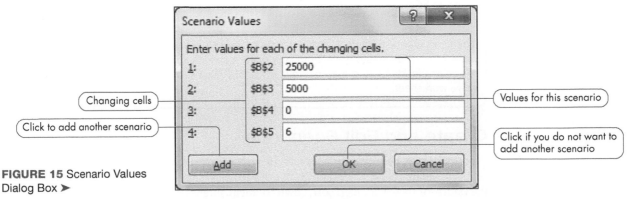

**FIGURE 15** Scenario Values Dialog Box ➤

What-If Analysis

350

If you need to modify the parameters of a scenario, such as the name or input values, open the Scenario Manager dialog box, select the scenario you want to modify in the Scenarios list, and then click Edit. The Edit Scenario dialog box opens so that you can change the values. Click OK after making the necessary changes.

If you have scenarios in several worksheets or workbooks, you can combine them. Click Merge in the Scenario Manager dialog box to open the Merge Scenarios dialog box. Select the workbook and worksheet, and then click OK. Use Help to learn more about merging scenarios.

## View Scenarios

After you create the scenarios, you can view each of them. To view your scenarios, click What-If Analysis in the Data Tools group on the Data tab, select Scenario Manager, select the name of the scenario you want to view in the Scenarios list, and then click Show. Excel places the defined values in the respective changing cells and displays the results.

# Generating Scenario Summary Reports

A **scenario summary report** is a worksheet that contains the scenario results.

Although you can view the defined values and their results individually, you will probably want to compare all scenarios in a table. A ***scenario summary report*** is an organized structured table of the scenarios, their input values, and their respective results. The summary report appears in the form of a worksheet outline and enables you to compare the results based on different values specified by the respective scenarios. Excel can produce two types of reports: scenario summary and scenario PivotTable report.

To create a scenario summary report, do the following:

1. Open the Scenario Manager dialog box.
2. Click Summary to open the Scenario Summary dialog box (see Figure 16).
3. Click *Scenario summary* or click *Scenario PivotTable report*. Enter the reference for the cell(s) whose values change in the scenarios in the *Result cells* box. Drag to select a range of adjacent results cells, or press Ctrl as you click cells in nonadjacent ranges. For example, in Figure 16, the result cells are monthly payment (B12) and total interest (B14).
4. Click OK. Excel creates the scenario summary on a new worksheet (see Figure 17).

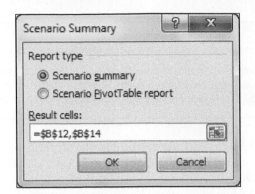

**FIGURE 16** Scenario
Summary Dialog Box ➤

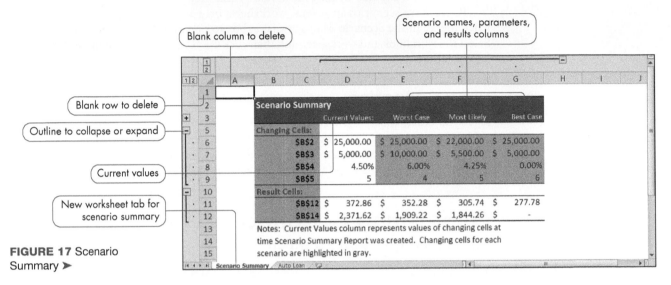

**FIGURE 17** Scenario
Summary ➤

The summary contains a column listing the changing and result cell references, current values and results, and a column of values and results for each defined scenario. This organized structure helps you compare the results as you analyze the scenarios. You should modify the structure and format the data. Typically, you should do the following:

- Delete the blank row 1 and the blank column A.
- Delete the Current Values column if it duplicates a defined scenario or if you do not want that data.
- Replace cell reference labels with descriptive labels in the first column.
- Delete the explanatory paragraph below the table and replace it with a narrative analysis relevant to the data.

# HANDS-ON EXERCISES

## 2 Goal Seek and Scenario Manager

You want to use Goal Seek and Scenario Manager to perform additional what-if analyses with your car loan data.

**Skills covered:** Use Goal Seek • Create a Scenario • Create Additional Scenarios • Generate and Format a Summary Report

---

**STEP 1**  USE GOAL SEEK

Given the current interest rate with a five-year loan and your planned down payment, you want to identify the most that you can afford on a car to keep your monthly payments at $300. You will use Goal Seek to work backward from your goal to identify the car cost. Refer to Figure 18 as you complete Step 1.

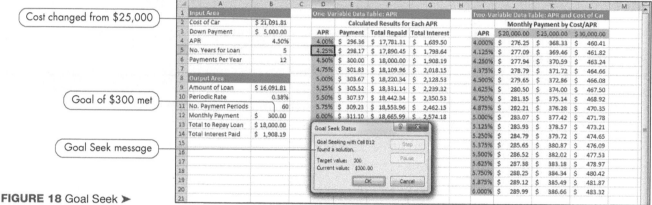

**FIGURE 18** Goal Seek ➤

a. Open the *e06h1carloan_LastnameFirstname* workbook and save it as **e06h2carloan_LastNameFirstname**, replacing *h1* with *h2*.

b. Click the **Data tab**.

c. Click **What-If Analysis** in the Data Tools group, and then select **Goal Seek**.

The Goal Seek dialog box opens.

d. Click **cell B12** to enter the cell reference in the **Set cell box**.

You indicated which cell contains the formula that produces the goal.

e. Click in the **To value box**, and then type **300**.

You want the monthly payment to be $300.

f. Click in the **By changing cell box**, and then click **cell B2**, the cell containing the cost of the car.

Cell B2 is the cell whose value will be determined using the Goal Seek analysis tool.

g. Click **OK**.

The Goal Seek Status dialog box opens, indicating that it reached the target monthly payment goal of $300.

h. Click **OK** to accept the solution and to close the Goal Seek Status dialog box. Save the workbook.

To achieve a $300 monthly car payment, you need to purchase a car that costs $21,091.81 instead of the original $25,000 car, assuming the other variables (down payment, interest rate, and term of loan) stay the same.

Hands-On Exercises • Excel 2010

353

**CREATE A SCENARIO**

You want to use Scenario Manager to explore different scenarios. Your first scenario is a best-case scenario with these parameters: $25,000 car, $5,000 down payment, special no-interest financing for 6 years. Refer to Figure 19 as you complete Step 2.

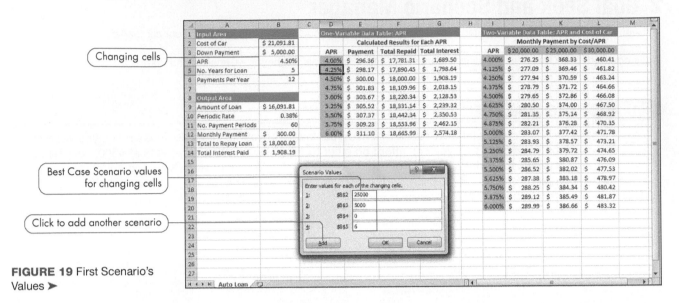

**FIGURE 19** First Scenario's Values ➤

a. Click the **Data tab**, if necessary, click **What-If Analysis** in the Data Tools group, and then select **Scenario Manager**.

The Scenario Manager dialog box opens.

b. Click **Add**.

The Add Scenario dialog box opens so that you can assign a scenario name and select the changing cells.

c. Select any content in the **Scenario name box**, and then type **Best-Case Scenario**.

d. Delete existing contents in the **Changing cells box**, and then select the **range B2:B5**.

Excel enters this range in the Changing cells box.

e. Edit the **Comment box**, if needed, to display your name and the date the scenario is created, such as *Created by Keith Mulbery on 7/14/2012*, and then click **OK**.

The Scenario Values dialog box opens so that you can enter the parameters for the scenario.

f. Type **25000** in the **$B$2 box**, and then press **Tab** twice to accept the current $5,000 down payment.

You entered 25000 as the cost of the car.

g. Type **0** in the **$B$4 box**, press **Tab**, and then type **6** in the **$B$5 box**.

h. Click **OK**, and then click **Close**. Save the workbook.

While you could have kept the Scenario Values dialog box open to continue to the next step, you closed it so that you could save the workbook.

What-If Analysis

**CREATE ADDITIONAL SCENARIOS**

You need to add two more scenarios: a worst-case scenario and a most likely scenario. In the worst-case scenario, you assume you will have to settle for a higher down payment, higher interest rate, and a shorter loan period. In the most likely scenario, you will enter values that are between those in the other two scenarios.

**a.** Click **What-If Analysis** in the Data Tools group, and then select **Scenario Manager**.

**b.** Click **Add**, type **Worst-Case Scenario**, and then click **OK**.

The Changing cells box displays $B$2:$B$5, the range you selected for the first scenario.

**c.** Type the following values in the respective changing cells boxes:

| Changing Cell Box | Value |
|---|---|
| $B$2 | 25000 |
| $B$3 | 8000 |
| $B$4 | 6% |
| $B$5 | 3 |

For the cell $B$4 box, you can enter the value as a percentage (6%) or as a decimal equivalent (0.06).

**d.** Click **Add**.

**e.** Type **Most-Likely Scenario** and click **OK** in the Add Scenario dialog box.

**f.** Type the following values in the respective changing cells boxes:

| Changing Cell Box | Value |
|---|---|
| $B$2 | 22500 |
| $B$3 | 6500 |
| $B$4 | 4.25% |
| $B$5 | 5 |

**g.** Click **OK**.

The Scenario Manager dialog box lists the three scenarios you created.

> **TROUBLESHOOTING:** If you believe you made any data entry errors, or if you want to double-check your values, select a scenario, and then click Edit. You can then change values in the Edit Scenario dialog box, and then click OK.

**h.** Click **Close** to close the Scenario Manager dialog box. Save the workbook.

**GENERATE AND FORMAT A SUMMARY REPORT**

You want to generate a scenario summary report to compare the three car loan scenarios you created. Refer to Figures 17 and 20 as you complete Step 4.

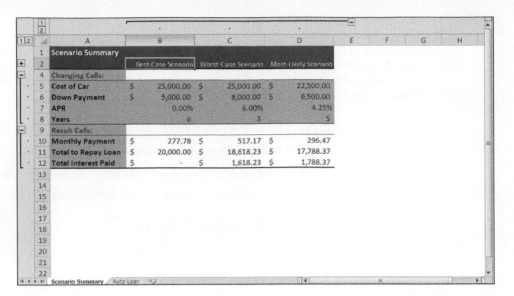

**FIGURE 20** Scenario Summary ➤

a. Click **What-If Analysis** in the Data Tools group, and then select **Scenario Manager**.

b. Click **Summary**.

Excel may select a range within a data table.

c. Select the **range B12:B14** to enter it in the **Result cells box**, and then click **OK**.

Excel generates the summary on a new worksheet named Scenario Summary. The results are similar to Figure 17 except your summary also includes $B$13 results. You need to make a few deletions and add descriptive labels.

d. Delete the following:
   - Column A
   - Row 1
   - Current Values column
   - Notes in the **range A13:A15**

e. Enter descriptive labels in the following cells:
   - **Cost of Car** in **cell A5**
   - **Down Payment** in **cell A6**
   - **APR** in **cell A7**
   - **Years** in **cell A8**
   - **Monthly Payment** in **cell A10**
   - **Total to Repay Loan** in **cell A11**
   - **Total Interest Paid** in **cell A12**

The labels describe data contained in each row. Now you can delete column B, which displays the cell references.

f. Delete column B, and then increase the width of column A.

The Best-Case Scenario provides the lowest monthly payment.

g. Save the workbook. Keep the workbook onscreen if you plan to continue with Hands-On Exercise 3. If not, close the workbook and exit Excel.

**TIP** Scenario Worksheets

Each time you generate a summary, Excel inserts another Scenario Summary worksheet. You can delete a summary worksheet if you no longer need the data.

What-If Analysis

# Solver

**Solver** is an add-in application that manipulates variables based on constraints to find the optimal solution to a problem.

*Solver* is an add-in application that searches for the best or optimum solution to a problem by manipulating the values for several variables within restrictions that you impose. You can use Solver to find the highest, lowest, or exact value for one particular result by adjusting values for selected variables. Solver is one of the most sophisticated what-if analysis tools, and people use Solver in a variety of situations and industries. For example, a cellular phone manufacturing facility can use Solver to maximize the number of phones made or minimize the number of labor hours required while conforming to other production specifications. A financial planner might use Solver to help a family adjust its expenses to stay within its monthly income earned.

> Solver is one of the most sophisticated what-if analysis tools, and people use Solver in a variety of situations and industries.

In this section, you will learn how to load the Solver add-in. Then you will use Solver to set a target, select changing cells, and create constraints.

## Loading the Solver Add-In

Solver is an add-in, which is an application that provides specialized functionality for Excel users. Because other companies create the add-ins, they are not active by default. You must load the Solver add-in before you can use it. To load Solver, do the following:

1. Click the File tab, and then select Options.
2. Click Add-Ins to see a list of active and inactive add-in applications. The Active Application Add-ins list displays currently enabled add-ins, and the Inactive Application Add-ins list displays add-ins that are not currently enabled.
3. Click the Manage arrow, select Excel Add-ins, and then click Go to open the Add-Ins dialog box (see Figure 21).
4. Click the Solver Add-in check box in the Add-Ins available list, and then click OK.

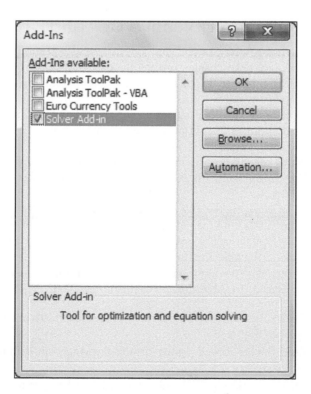

**FIGURE 21** Add-Ins Dialog Box ➤

When you load Solver, Excel displays Solver in the Analysis group on the Data tab (see Figure 22), where it remains until you remove the Solver add-in. However, if you are in a campus computer lab that resets software settings when you log off, you will have to load Solver again each time you log into the lab's network.

Solver command

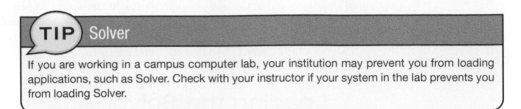

**FIGURE 22** Solver on Data Tab ➤

> **TIP** Solver
>
> If you are working in a campus computer lab, your institution may prevent you from loading applications, such as Solver. Check with your instructor if your system in the lab prevents you from loading Solver.

# Optimizing Results with Solver

Solver may be the best what-if analysis tool to solve complex problems. You can use it for complex equation solving and for constrained optimization where a set of constraints is specified and you want the outcome to be minimized or maximized. With Solver, you are able to change the values of several variables at once to achieve the desired result. For example, a business analyst might want to use Solver to maximize profits by changing selected variables while adhering to required limitations. Or, a fulfillment company might want to determine the lowest shipping costs to transfer merchandise from a distribution center to retail stores.

## Identify the Objective Cell and Changing Cells

Before using Solver, review your spreadsheet as you specify the goal, identify one or more variables that can change to reach the desired goal, and determine the limitations of the model. You will use these data to specify three parameters in Solver: objective cell, changing cells, and constraints.

The objective cell is the cell that contains the formula-based value that you want to maximize, minimize, or set to a value in Solver.

The **objective cell** specifies the cell that contains a formula that produces a value that you want to optimize (that is, maximize, minimize, or set to a value) by manipulating values of one or more variables. The formula in the objective cell relates directly or indirectly to the changing cells and constraints. Using the car loan case study as an example, the objective cell is B14 (the cell containing the total interest paid formula), and your goal is to minimize the total interest.

A changing variable cell is a cell containing a variable whose value changes until Solver optimizes the value in the objective cell.

The **changing variable cells** are the cells containing variables whose values change within the constraints until the objective cell reaches its optimum value. The changing variable cells typically contain values, not formulas, but these cells have a mathematical relationship to the formula in the objective. In the car loan example, the changing variable cells are B3 (down payment), B4 (APR), and B5 (number of years). You can select up to 200 changing cells.

To specify the objective and changing cells, do the following:

1. Click Solver in the Analysis group on the Data tab to open the Solver Parameters dialog box (see Figure 23).
2. Enter the cell containing the formula for which you want to optimize its value in the Set Objective box.
3. Click an option in the To section to specify what type of value you need to find for the target cell. Click Max to maximize the value, Min to find the lowest value, or Value Of, and then specify the value in the Value Of box.

4. Enter the cell references that contain variables in the By Changing Variable Cells box. These are the variables that you want to change to reach the objective.

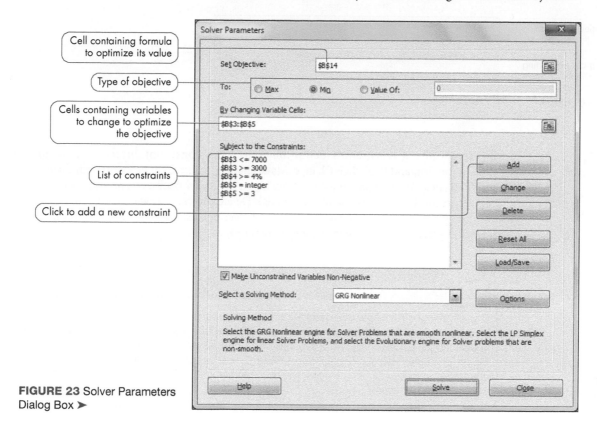

**FIGURE 23** Solver Parameters Dialog Box ➤

## Define the Constraints

A **constraint** is a limitation that imposes restrictions on Solver.

The *constraints* specify the restrictions or limitations imposed on a spreadsheet model as Solver determines the optimum value for the objective cell. Rules govern every business model, based on historical requirements, physical limitations, and other decisions. Probably the most challenging process is identifying all legitimate limitations. You may identify limitations through conversations with your supervisor, by reading policy statements, gathering information in meetings, and so on. Even after you enter data into Solver and run a report, you may gain knowledge of other limitations that you must build into the model. Using the car loan example, a constraint might be that the down payment must be between $3,000 and $7,000.

To add constraints to the Solver, do the following inside the Solver Parameters dialog box:

1. Click Add to the right of the Subject to the Constraints list to open the Add Constraint dialog box.
2. Enter the cell reference, the operator to test the cell references, and the constraint the cell needs to match (see Figure 24). The cell reference contains a variable whose value you want to constrain or restrict to a particular value or range. The operator defines the relationship between the variable and the constraint. For example, cell B3 (the down payment) is restricted to being less than or equal to $7,000. Solver will not allow the cost to be higher than this value.
3. Click OK to add the constraint and return to the Solver Parameters dialog box, or click Add to add the constraint and create another constraint.

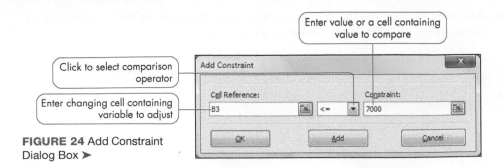

**FIGURE 24** Add Constraint Dialog Box ➤

To modify a constraint's definition, select the constraint in the Subject to the Constraints list, and then click Change. Make changes in the Change Constraint dialog box, and then click OK to update the definition. If you no longer need a constraint, select it in the Subject to the Constraints list, and then click Delete. Be careful when using Delete; Solver does not prompt you to confirm the deletion. Solver deletes the selected constraint immediately, and you cannot restore the deleted constraint.

> ### TIP Integer Constraint
>
> One of the constraint operators is int. This constraint requires the changing variable cell to be an integer, or whole number. For example, a manufacturing plant does not produce partial units such as 135.62 units, and a department store does not sell 18.32 shirts. To ensure that Solver produces realistic results, you should create integer constraints for these types of quantities. In Figure 23, the constraint $B$5 = integer limits the number of years for the loan to be a whole number.

> ### TIP Greater-Than-Zero Constraint
>
> Another often-overlooked constraint is the requirement that the value of a variable cell be greater than or equal to zero. Physically, it makes no sense to produce a negative number of products in any category. Mathematically, however, a negative value in a changing variable cell may produce a higher value for the objective cell. By default, the *Make Unconstrained Variables Non-Negative* check box is selected to ensure variable values are greater than or equal to zero. If you want to allow the lower end of a variable's value to be a negative value, you can create a constraint such as B2>=–100. That constraint takes priority over the Make Unconstrained Variables Non-Negative check box.

## Create a Solver Report

After defining the objective, changing variable cells, and constraints, select a solving method. Solver uses the selected solving method to determine which type of algorithms it executes to reach the objective. The Solver add-in for Excel 2010 contains these solving methods: GRG Nonlinear, Simplex LP, and Evolutionary. Look up *Solver* in Help to link to a specific set of descriptions on www.solver.com. For the purposes of this chapter, accept the default option, GRG Nonlinear.

You are now ready to use Solver to find a solution to the problem. Solver uses an iterative process of using different combinations of values in the changing variable cells to identify the optimum value for the objective cell. It starts with the current values and adjusts those values in accordance with the constraints. Once it finds the best solution, given the parameters you set, it identifies the values for the changing variable cells and shows you the objective value. If Solver cannot determine an optimum value, it does not enable you to generate summary reports. To solve the problem, do the following:

1. Click Solve in the Solver Parameters dialog box. When Solver completes the iterative process, the Solver Results dialog box appears (see Figure 25). If it finds a solution, the Reports list displays available report types. If Solver cannot reach an optimal solution, no reports are available. Solutions are unattainable if a logic error exists or if the constraints do not allow sufficient elasticity to achieve a result. For example, a constraint between 10 and 11 does not allow sufficient flexibility, or a constraint greater than 20 but also less than 10 is illogical. If this happens, check each constraint for range constraints or errors in logic.

2. Click Keep Solver Solution to keep the changed objective and variable values, or click Restore Original Values to return to the original values in the worksheet. If you keep the changed values, Excel makes those changes to the actual worksheet. Do this if you are comfortable with those changes. If you want to maintain the original values, you should restore the original values.

3. Select a report from the Reports list. Generating a report is appropriate to see what changes Solver made while preserving the original values in the worksheet from Step 2.

4. Click OK to generate the summary on a separate worksheet.

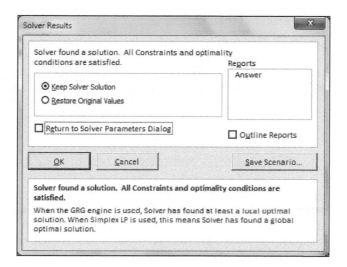

**FIGURE 25** Solver Results Dialog Box ➤

Solver creates a new worksheet for the Solver summary report containing four major sections (see Figure 26). The first section displays information about the Solver report. Specifically, it displays the report type, file name and worksheet containing the dataset, date and time the report was generated, Solver Engine details, and Solver Options that were set at the time the report was generated.

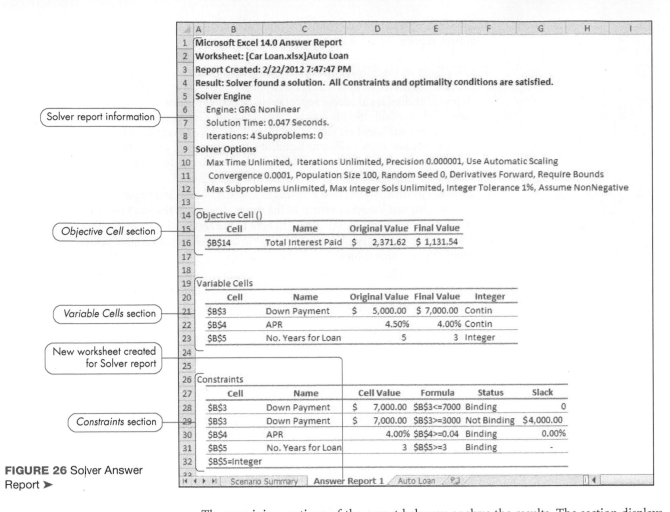

Solver report information

Objective Cell section

Variable Cells section

New worksheet created for Solver report

Constraints section

**FIGURE 26** Solver Answer Report ➤

A **binding constraint** is one that Solver enforces to reach the target value.

A **nonbinding constraint** is one that does not restrict the target value that Solver finds.

The remaining sections of the report help you analyze the results. The section displays the Objective Cell information. Specifically, this section shows the original and final objective cell values. For example, using the original worksheet values, the original total interest paid in cell B14 was $2,371.62. The final minimized total interest paid is $1,131.54.

The third section displays the Variable Cells. Specifically, it displays the cell references, the variable cell names, original values, and final values. For example, the original down payment was $5,000, and the final value is $7,000.

The final section lists the Constraints. Specifically, it displays the cell reference, description, new cell value, formula, status, and slack for each defined constraint. In this case, the down payment slack ($4,000) is the difference between the lower constraint ($3,000) and the final value ($7,000). The Status column indicates Binding or Not Binding. A ***binding constraint*** is a rule that Solver has to enforce to reach the objective value. That is, the value hits the maximum allowable value for a less-than-or-equal-to, minimum allowable value for a greater-than-or-equal-to, equal to, or int constraint. For example, $B$3<=7000 is a binding constraint. That is, the down payment was raised to its maximum limit of $7,000 to identify the optimal least amount of total interest paid. If this constraint had not been set, Solver could have identified a higher down payment to obtain a lower value for the objective cell. A ***nonbinding constraint*** is one that does not restrict the target value that Solver finds. For example, $B$3>=3000 is nonbinding. Solver did not have to stop at a lowest down payment of $3,000 to reach the optimal total interest paid value.

If you change any of the Solver parameters—objective cell, changing variable cells, or constraints—you need to generate another report. Solver does not update the report automatically. Each time you generate a report, Solver creates another new worksheet with names like Answer Report 1, Answer Report 2, etc. Delete any reports you no longer need to minimize the file size of your workbook.

## Configure Solver

You can closely monitor the trial solutions prior to reaching the final solution. Solver is a mathematical modeling operation, and you can determine solutions using the associated mathematics. However, stepping through Solver enables you to view the steps Solver performs. To step through trial solutions, do the following:

1. Click Options in the Solver Parameters dialog box to open the Options dialog box.
2. Select the Show Iteration Results check box to see the values of each trial solution, and then click OK.
3. Click Solve in the Solver Parameters dialog box.
4. When the Show Trial Solution dialog box appears, either:
   - Click Stop to stop the process and open the Solver Results dialog box, or
   - Click Continue to continue the process and display the next trial solution.

You can also use the Options dialog box to customize Solver further. Because Solver uses an iterative approach, you can specify the number of iterations to try, how much time to take to solve the problem, and how precise the answer should be (i.e., accuracy to what number of decimal places), among other settings.

## Save and Restore a Solver Model

When you use Solver, Excel keeps track of your settings and saves only the most recent Solver settings. In some cases, you may want to save the parameters of a model so that you can apply them again in the future. Saving a Solver model is helpful if the original data source might change and you want to compare results by generating multiple Solver answer reports. When you save a Solver model, you save the objective value, the changing variable cells, and the constraints.

Saving a Solver model places the information in a small block of cells on a worksheet. The number of cells required to save the Solver model is dependent on the number of constraints in the model. To save Solver settings, do the following:

1. Click Load/Save in the Solver Parameters dialog box.
2. Click in the worksheet where the first cell is to be placed. Make sure the worksheet has sufficient empty cells so the Solver information does not overwrite Excel data.
3. Click Save to return to the Solver Parameters dialog box.

If you want to use an existing Solver model with new or updated data, you must return to a previous Solver model. When you want to use a Solver model that you saved, do the following:

1. Click Load/Save in the Solver Parameters dialog box.
2. Select the worksheet cells that contain the Solver data. You must select all cells with the Solver data.
3. Click Load to load the model's values and return to the Solver Parameter dialog box.

## 3 Solver

Although using Goal Seek and Scenario Manager were helpful in further analyzing your car purchase, you want to ensure the spreadsheet model imposes constraints on the situation. Therefore, you will continue your analysis by using Solver.

**Skills covered:** Load the Solver Add-In • Set the Objective and Variable Cells • Define the Constraints • Generate a Report

---

### STEP 1 ▶ LOAD THE SOLVER ADD-IN

Before you can use Solver to analyze your car loan model, you need to load Solver. If Solver is already loaded, skip Step 1 and start with Step 2. Refer to Figure 27 as you complete Step 1.

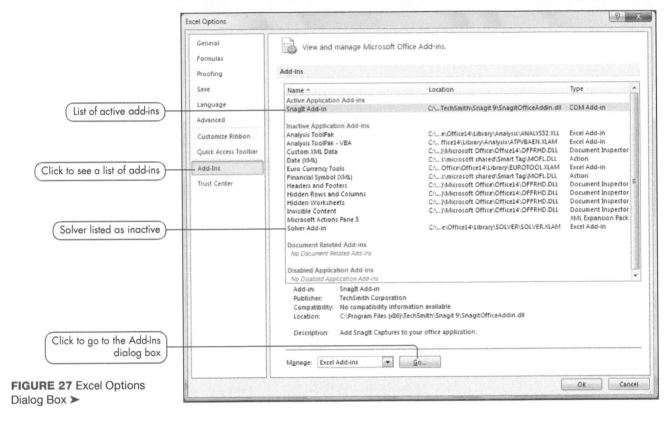

**FIGURE 27** Excel Options Dialog Box ➤

a. Click the **File tab,** and then click **Options.**

   The Excel Options dialog box opens so that you can customize Excel settings.

b. Click **Add-Ins** on the left side of the Excel Options dialog box.

   The Excel Options dialog box displays a list of active and inactive application add-ins.

c. Check to see where Solver is listed. If Solver is listed in the Active Application Add-ins list, click **OK,** and then skip step d. If Solver is listed in the Inactive Application Add-ins list, click the **Manage arrow,** select **Excel Add-ins** if necessary, and then click **Go.**

   The Add-Ins dialog box opens, containing a list of available add-in applications.

d. Click the **Solver Add-in check box** in the **Add-Ins available list,** and then click **OK.**

What-If Analysis

Before using Solver, you want to reset the variables to their original values. After entering the original variable values again, you will specify the monthly payment cell as the objective cell and the cost of car, down payment, APR, and number of years for the loan as the changing variable cells. Refer to Figure 28 as you complete Step 2.

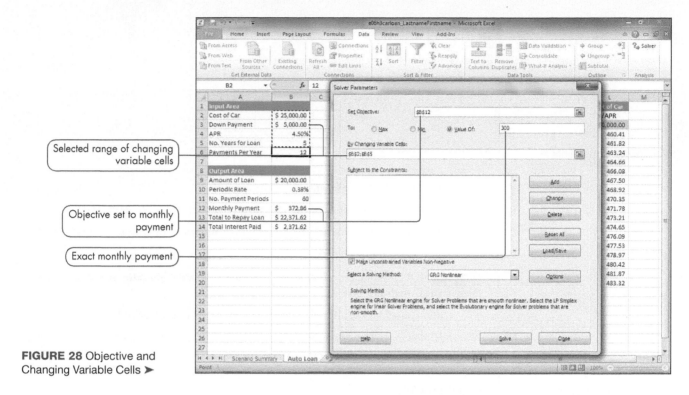

**FIGURE 28** Objective and Changing Variable Cells ➤

a. Open the *e06h2carloan_LastnameFirstname* workbook and save it as **e06h3carloan_LastNameFirstname**, replacing *h2* with *h3*.

b. Click the **Auto Loan worksheet tab**, and then enter **25000** in **cell B2** and **5000** in **cell B3**.

   Now that you reset the values to your original spreadsheet model, you are ready to use Solver.

c. Click the **Data tab**, and then click **Solver** in the Analysis group.

   The Solver Parameters dialog box opens so that you can define the objective and changing variable cells.

d. Click **cell B12** to enter it in the **Set Objective box**.

   You set the objective cell as the monthly payment.

e. Click **Value Of**, and then type **300** in the **Value Of box**.

   You specified that you want an exact $300 monthly car payment.

f. Click in the **By Changing Variable Cells box**, and then select the **range B2:B5**. Click **Close**, and then save the workbook.

> **TROUBLESHOOTING:** Be careful to select the correct range. If you accidentally select cell B6, Solver might produce inaccurate results.

## STEP 3 ▶ DEFINE THE CONSTRAINTS

You need to define the constraints: $20,000 to $30,000 cost, $5,000 to $7,500 down payment, 4% to 6% APR, and 4- to 6-year loan. In addition, you need to set an integer constraint for the years so that Solver does not produce a fractional year, such as 5.71. Refer to Figure 29 as you complete Step 3.

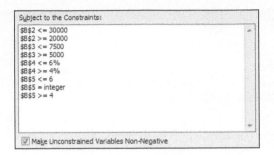

Subject to the Constraints:

```
$B$2 <= 30000
$B$2 >= 20000
$B$3 <= 7500
$B$3 >= 5000
$B$4 <= 6%
$B$4 >= 4%
$B$5 <= 6
$B$5 = integer
$B$5 >= 4
```

☑ Make Unconstrained Variables Non-Negative

**FIGURE 29** Constraints ▶

a. Click **Solver** in the Analysis group, and then click **Add**.

The Add Constraint dialog box opens so that you can define the first constraint.

b. Click **cell B2**, make sure <= is selected, click in the **Constraint box**, and then type **30000**.

You defined a constraint that the total car cost cannot exceed $30,000.

c. Click **Add** to define another constraint. Click **cell B2**, click the **operator arrow**, select >=, click in the **Constraint box**, and then type **20000**.

The second constraint specifies that the car cost must be at least $20,000.

d. Add the following constraints in a similar manner. After you enter the last constraint, click **OK** in the Add Constraint dialog box.

- B3<=7500
- B3>=5000
- B4<=6%
- B4>=4%
- B5<=6
- B5>=4
- B5 int

> **TROUBLESHOOTING:** Click Add to complete the current constraint and open an Add Constraint dialog box to enter another constraint. Click OK in the Add Constraint dialog box only when you have completed the last constraint and want to return to the Solver Parameters dialog box to solve the problem.

e. Check the constraints carefully against those shown in Figure 29 and step d. Click **Close**, and then save the workbook.

## STEP 4 ▶ GENERATE A REPORT

Now that you have completed the parameters for restricting the result based on the cost of the car, the down payment, the APR, and the number of years for the loan, you are ready to generate a Solver report. Refer to Figure 30 as you complete Step 4.

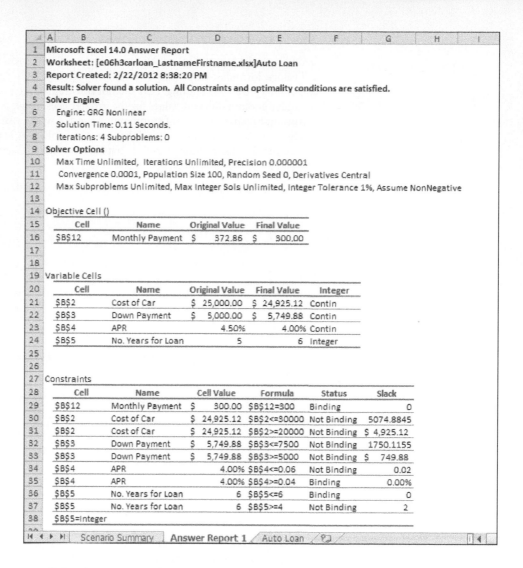

| | A | B | C | D | E | F | G | H | I |
|---|---|---|---|---|---|---|---|---|---|
| 1 | Microsoft Excel 14.0 Answer Report | | | | | | | | |
| 2 | Worksheet: [e06h3carloan_LastnameFirstname.xlsx]Auto Loan | | | | | | | | |
| 3 | Report Created: 2/22/2012 8:38:20 PM | | | | | | | | |
| 4 | Result: Solver found a solution. All Constraints and optimality conditions are satisfied. | | | | | | | | |
| 5 | Solver Engine | | | | | | | | |
| 6 | Engine: GRG Nonlinear | | | | | | | | |
| 7 | Solution Time: 0.11 Seconds. | | | | | | | | |
| 8 | Iterations: 4 Subproblems: 0 | | | | | | | | |
| 9 | Solver Options | | | | | | | | |
| 10 | Max Time Unlimited, Iterations Unlimited, Precision 0.000001 | | | | | | | | |
| 11 | Convergence 0.0001, Population Size 100, Random Seed 0, Derivatives Central | | | | | | | | |
| 12 | Max Subproblems Unlimited, Max Integer Sols Unlimited, Integer Tolerance 1%, Assume NonNegative | | | | | | | | |
| 13 | | | | | | | | | |
| 14 | Objective Cell () | | | | | | | | |

**Objective Cell ()**

| Cell | Name | Original Value | Final Value |
|---|---|---|---|
| $B$12 | Monthly Payment | $ 372.86 | $ 300.00 |

**Variable Cells**

| Cell | Name | Original Value | Final Value | Integer |
|---|---|---|---|---|
| $B$2 | Cost of Car | $ 25,000.00 | $ 24,925.12 | Contin |
| $B$3 | Down Payment | $ 5,000.00 | $ 5,749.88 | Contin |
| $B$4 | APR | 4.50% | 4.00% | Contin |
| $B$5 | No. Years for Loan | 5 | 6 | Integer |

**Constraints**

| Cell | Name | Cell Value | Formula | Status | Slack |
|---|---|---|---|---|---|
| $B$12 | Monthly Payment | $ 300.00 | $B$12=300 | Binding | 0 |
| $B$2 | Cost of Car | $ 24,925.12 | $B$2<=30000 | Not Binding | 5074.8845 |
| $B$2 | Cost of Car | $ 24,925.12 | $B$2>=20000 | Not Binding | $ 4,925.12 |
| $B$3 | Down Payment | $ 5,749.88 | $B$3<=7500 | Not Binding | 1750.1155 |
| $B$3 | Down Payment | $ 5,749.88 | $B$3>=5000 | Not Binding | $ 749.88 |
| $B$4 | APR | 4.00% | $B$4<=0.06 | Not Binding | 0.02 |
| $B$4 | APR | 4.00% | $B$4>=0.04 | Binding | 0.00% |
| $B$5 | No. Years for Loan | 6 | $B$5<=6 | Binding | 0 |
| $B$5 | No. Years for Loan | 6 | $B$5>=4 | Not Binding | 2 |
| $B$5=Integer | | | | | |

Scenario Summary  /  Answer Report 1  /  Auto Loan  /

**FIGURE 30** Solver Answer Report ➤

a. Click **Solver** in the Analysis group, and then click **Solve**.

The Solver Results dialog box opens. If you look at the worksheet data, the new values appear in the changing cells, and the $300 target monthly payment appears in cell B12.

b. Select **Answer** in the **Reports list**, and then click **OK**.

Solver generates a report and displays it in a new worksheet named Answer Report 1.

> **TROUBLESHOOTING:** If you see the error message, *Solver: An unexpected internal error occurred, or available memory was exhausted*, close Solver, click Undo, remove Solver as an add-in, save and close the workbook, open the workbook again, and enable the Solver add-in again. Then click Solver in the Analysis group, click Solve, select Answer Report, and then click OK.

c. Click the **Answer Report 1 worksheet tab**.

Solver adjusts the values in the changing cells B2:B5 to obtain the exact value of $300 for the objective cell B12. The report shows the previous and final values of the objective and variable cells. *Your final values may vary slightly from those shown in the figure.*

**d.** Scroll down through the worksheet to see the constraints.

In addition, the report displays the constraints—cell references, descriptive labels, current cell values, formulas, status (binding/not binding), and slack. Although not specified, integer constraints are always binding. Had you not constrained the years to a whole number, Solver might have found different values for the variable cells. However, you need to enforce that constraint because the term of automobile loans is a whole year. The 4% APR constraint is binding, meaning that Solver found the lowest possible APR to produce its answer. Finally, the six-year limit is binding, meaning that Solver could not use a larger number of years for the loan to derive its answer.

**e.** Save and close the workbook, and submit based on your instructor's directions.

# CHAPTER OBJECTIVES REVIEW

After reading this chapter, you have accomplished the following objectives:

1. **Create a one-variable data table.** A one-variable data table enables you to compare different values for one variable to compare their effects on one or more results. A one-variable data table is designed with the substitution values listed in the left column or first row. Enter references to formulas in the first row or left column, whichever does not have the substitution values. After creating the one-variable data table, format the results and create custom number formats to disguise the formula references as column or row headings.

2. **Create a two-variable data table.** A two-variable data table enables you to compare results for two variables at the same time but for only one result. The substitution values for one variable are listed down the left column, and the substitution values for the other variable are listed in the first row. The top-left cell must contain a reference to the original formula result. After you complete the two-variable data table, you need to format the result cells, apply a custom number format to disguise the formula cell, and apply other formatting to enhance the table.

3. **Identify an input value with Goal Seek.** Use Goal Seek to work backward with a problem when you know what you want for the end result but you do not know the value of a variable to achieve that goal. If you accept the results, Excel enters the identified input value directly in the variable cell.

4. **Use Scenario Manager.** Use Scenario Manager to create a set of scenarios, each with multiple variables. Scenarios are saved to the active worksheet so that you can create different scenarios on different worksheets. The Scenario Manager dialog box enables you to add, delete, and change scenarios. For each scenario, you specify a name, the changing cells, and the values for those changing cells.

5. **Generate scenario summary reports.** After you create the scenarios with specific values, you can generate a summary report. Excel creates the summary report in a structured format on a new worksheet and displays the values for the changing cells and their effects on the results cells so that you can compare the results easily. You can delete the blank row, blank column, and current values column. In addition, you can replace the cell references with descriptive labels for the row headings.

6. **Load the Solver Add-In.** Solver is an add-in program for Excel. That is, Solver is not loaded by default. When you enable Solver, Excel places Solver in the Analysis group on the Data tab. Solver remains on the Data tab unless you remove the program, or if you are in a computer lab that resets software settings when you log off.

7. **Optimize results with Solver.** Solver is an optimization technique that enables you to maximize or minimize the value of an objective function, such as profit or cost. To define a Solver model, you specify the objective cell (the formula cell that you want to optimize), changing variable cells (cells that are related to the objective cell and change until the objective value is reached), and constraints (limitations that constrain cell values to particular values or ranges). Solver uses an iterative process to use different values for variable cells until it finds the optimum objective value within the constraints you set. The answer report displays the final objective and variable cells values. In addition, the report specifies whether constraints are binding or nonbinding. A binding constraint is one that is enforced and restricts the objective value from being higher or lower. A nonbinding constraint is one that does not restrict the objective's final value.

# KEY TERMS

Binding constraint
Changing variable cell
Constraint
Goal Seek
Nonbinding constraint
Objective cell
One-variable data table
Scenario
Scenario Manager
Scenario summary report
Solver
Substitution value
Two-variable data table
Variable
What-if analysis

1. In the Solver Parameters dialog box, the _____ cell must always contain a formula.

   (a) changing variable

   (b) constraint

   (c) objective

   (d) result

2. When using the Goal Seek command, how many input variables can you change at a time?

   (a) 1

   (b) 2

   (c) 3

   (d) All of them, if necessary

3. How do you know if Solver is already loaded on your computer?

   (a) The Solver command displays on the Formulas tab and in the Solver Options dialog box.

   (b) The Solver command displays on the Add-Ins tab and in the Inactive Application Add-ins list in the Excel Options dialog box.

   (c) The Solver command displays on the Data Tools tab and in the Scenario Manager dialog box.

   (d) The Solver command displays on the Data tab and in the Active Application Add-ins list in the Excel Options dialog box.

4. You want to display tip amounts using multiple combinations of customer totals (such as $10, $15, and $20) and tip percentages (such as 15%, 17.5%, and 20%). What what-if analysis should you use?

   (a) One-variable data table

   (b) Two-variable data table

   (c) Goal Seek

   (d) Solver

5. As a college student, you created a worksheet to enter your test, assignment, and class project scores where each category average is weighted differently on your final grade. You want to conduct a what-if analysis to investigate nine different situations in which you do really well in one category, average in another category, and below average in the third category. Which tool would help you analyze and compare all nine situations and their individual effects on your final grade at the same time?

   (a) One-variable data table

   (b) Two-variable data table

   (c) Solver

   (d) Scenario Manager

6. A one-variable data table enables you to identify ___ variable(s) and ___ result(s).

   (a) one, unlimited

   (b) one, one

   (c) one, two

   (d) two, one

7. After you generate a Scenario Summary report, you should delete all of the following except:

   (a) Row 1.

   (b) Column A.

   (c) The *Changing Cells* section.

   (d) The Cell references column.

8. Which dialog box enables you to specify the result cells for a scenario summary report?

   (a) Scenario Summary

   (b) Scenario Values

   (c) Add Scenario

   (d) Solver Options

9. Which two tools have the ability to change actual values in the original dataset?

   (a) Goal Seek and Scenario Manager

   (b) Goal Seek and Solver

   (c) Data Tables and Scenario Manager

   (d) Solver and Data Tables

10. Which statement is not correct about a two-variable data table?

    (a) You must specify the row input cell and the column input cell from the original dataset.

    (b) The top-left corner must contain the formula for the result.

    (c) The data table can produce two types of results for the combination of two variables.

    (d) To avoid showing a formula result that builds the table, you can apply a custom number format to the cell to make it appear as a label.

## 1 Annual Bonuses

You manage a software development company in Portland. Employees earn an annual bonus that ranges from 0.5–5% of their gross salary. You are required by law to withhold applicable income taxes. To minimize employee disappointment from knowing what their qualified bonus is versus seeing the bonus on their paychecks, you developed a model that you can distribute to employees to help them predict their net bonus amount. You want to create a one-variable data table to list various bonus rates and their effects on the gross bonus, taxes withheld, and net bonus. Then you want to create a two-variable data table that compares combinations of various bonus rates and sample gross salaries to show net bonuses. This exercise follows the same set of skills as used in Hands-On Exercise 1 in the chapter. Refer to Figure 31 as you complete this exercise.

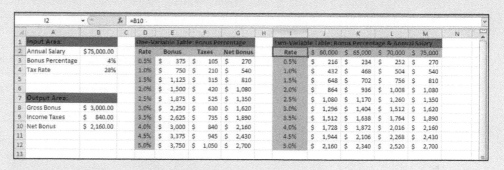

**FIGURE 31** Bonus Variable Data Tables ➤

a. Open *e06p1bonus* and save it as **e06p1bonus_LastnameFirstname**.

b. Click **cell D3**, and then do the following to enter a series of substitution values for the bonus percentage:
  - Type **0.5%** and press **Ctrl+Enter** to keep **cell D3** active.
  - Click **Fill** in the Editing group on the Home tab, and then select **Series**.
  - Click **Columns** in the *Series in* section, type **0.5%** in the **Step value box**, type **5%** in the **Stop value box**, and then click **OK**.

c. Enter the references to formulas in the following cells:
  - **Cell E2: =B8**
  - **Cell F2: =B9**
  - **Cell G2: =B10**

d. Complete the one-variable data table by doing the following:
  - Select the **range D2:G12**.
  - Click the **Data tab**, click **What-If Analysis** in the Data Tools group, and then select **Data Table**.
  - Click in the **Column input cell box**, click **cell B3**, and then click **OK**.
  - Select the **range E3:G12**, click the **Home tab**, and then apply **Accounting Number Format** with zero decimal places.

e. Create column headings for the data table by doing the following:
  - Type **Rate** in **cell D2**.
  - Click **cell E2**, and then click the **Number Dialog Box Launcher** in the Number group.
  - Click **Custom** in the **Category list**, scroll up in the **Type list**, and then select **General**.
  - Select **General** in the Type box, type **"Bonus"**, and then click **OK**.
  - Adapt the above steps to create a custom number format to display *Taxes* in **cell F2** and *Net Bonus* in **cell G2**.
  - Center and bold the **range D2:G2**.

f. Set up the variables for the two-variable data table by copying the **range D3:D12** and pasting it in the **range I3:I12**. Enter **60000** in **cell J2**, and then use the Series dialog box to fill the row data to **75000** in steps of **5000**.

g. Enter **=B10** in **cell I2**.

h. Complete the two-variable data table by doing the following:
  - Select the **range I2:M12**.
  - Click the **Data tab**, click **What-If Analysis** in the Data Tools group, and then select **Data Table**.

- Click **cell B2** to enter that reference in the **Row input cell box**.
- Click in the **Column input cell box**, click **cell B3**, and then click **OK**.
- Select the **range J3:M12**, and then apply **Accounting Number Format** with zero decimal places.
- Create a custom number format to display *Rate* in **cell I2**. Bold and center data in this cell.

i. Select **landscape orientation**, and then set **0.4"** left and right margins.

j. Create a footer with your name on the left side, the date code in the center, and the file name code on the right side.

k. Save and close the workbook, and submit based on your instructor's directions.

## 2  Health Supplements

Your friend Pierre Fatoel started an online business selling health supplements. Currently, he has one product—protein shake powder. Although he has an online business from his home, local customers often make cash purchases. His budget must account for fixed expenses, such as monthly Web hosting fees and standard credit card equipment fees. In addition, he accounts for variable costs including cost of goods sold and credit card processing fees. You will use Goal Seek to determine how many bags of protein powder he must sell to earn a net profit of $7,500. Then you will use Scenario Manager to evaluate several possible situations. This exercise follows the same set of skills as used in Hands-On Exercise 2 in the chapter. Refer to Figure 32 as you complete this exercise.

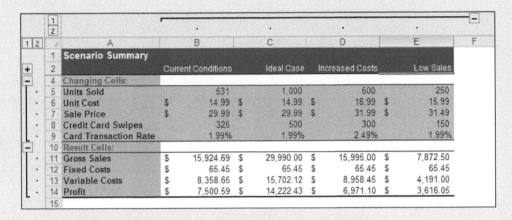

**FIGURE 32** Scenario Summary ➤

a. Open *e06p2protein* and save it as **e06p2protein_LastnameFirstname**.

b. Enter the following formulas:
- **Cell B14: =B15*B7** to calculate the projected credit card sales amount of the total sales
- **Cell B23: =B4*B5** to calculate the cost of goods sold, which is the product of the units sold and unit cost
- **Cell B24: =(B9*B14)+(B8*B10)** to calculate credit card processing fees, which are currently 1.99% of credit card amounts and 35 cents per transaction
- **Cell B28: =B15-B20-B25** to calculate the net profit

c. Click the **Data tab**, click **What-If Analysis** in the Data Tools group, and then select **Goal Seek**.

d. Complete the Goal Seek by doing the following:
- Click **cell B28** to add the cell reference to the **Set cell box**.
- Click in the **To value box**, and then type **7500**.
- Click in the **By changing cell box**, and then click **cell B4**.
- Click **OK** in the Goal Seek dialog box, and then click **OK** in the Goal Seek Status dialog box. How many bags of protein drink powder must Pierre sell to reach his net profit goal of $7,500? Answer: 531.

e. Click **What-If Analysis** in the Data Tools group, and then select **Scenario Manager**.

f. Create the first scenario by doing the following:
- Click **Add**, and then type **Current Conditions** in the **Scenario name box**.
- Click in the **Changing cells box**, select the **range B4:B6**, and then press and hold **Ctrl** while you select the **range B8:B9**.

- Click in the **Comment box**, and then edit it to reflect your name, such as *Created by Keith Mulbery on 7/21/2012*, and then click **OK**.
- Type **531** in the **$B$4 box**, leave the other current values intact, and then click **Add**.

g. Create the following three scenarios, clicking either **Add** or **OK** as indicated:

| Scenario Name | Ideal Case | Increased Costs | Low Sales |
|---|---|---|---|
| $B$4 | 1000 | 500 | 250 |
| $B$5 | 14.99 | 16.99 | 15.99 |
| $B$6 | 29.99 | 31.99 | 31.49 |
| $B$8 | 500 | 300 | 150 |
| $B$9 | 1.99% | 2.49% | 1.99% |
| Button | Add | Add | OK |

h. Click **Summary**, select and delete the suggested range in the **Result cells box**, press and hold **Ctrl** as you click **cells B15, B20, B25**, and **B28** to enter these cells, and then click **OK**.

i. Make these changes to the summary on the Scenario Summary worksheet:
- Delete the blank column A, the Current Values column, the blank row 1, and the notes in the **range A15:A17**.
- Click in **cell A5**, type **Units Sold**, and then press **Enter**.
- Enter **Unit Cost, Sale Price, Credit Card Swipes**, and **Card Transaction Rate** in the **range A6:A9**.
- Enter **Gross Sales, Fixed Costs, Variable Costs**, and **Profit** in the **range A11:A14**.
- Increase the width of column A to display the labels.
- Delete column B containing the cell references because these references would have no meaning if you distribute only the scenario summary worksheet to others.

j. Create a footer with your name on the left side, the sheet name code in the center, and the file name code on the right side for both worksheets.

k. Save and close the workbook, and submit based on your instructor's directions.

## 3   Worldwide Fitness Center Advertising

The marketing director at the Worldwide Fitness Center has a $125,000 weekly advertising budget. She wants to establish a presence in both magazines and television and requires a minimum of 4 magazine ads and 10 television ads each week. Each magazine ad costs $10,000 and is seen by 1 million readers. Each television commercial costs $5,000 and is seen by 250,000 viewers. The director wants to know how many ads of each type should be placed to reach at least 10 million customers at minimum cost. You will use Solver to achieve the goal of minimizing costs. Note that you cannot purchase a fractional part of an ad. After running Solver, you will relax a constraint because the integer constraint presents an infeasible solution. This exercise follows the same set of skills as used in Hands-On Exercise 3 in the chapter. Refer to Figure 33 as you complete this exercise.

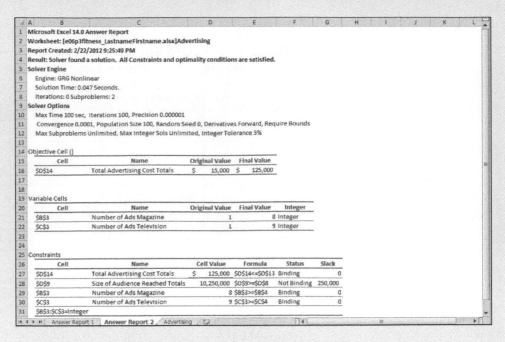

| | A | B | C | D | E | F | G | H | I | J | K | L |
|---|---|---|---|---|---|---|---|---|---|---|---|---|
| 1 | Microsoft Excel 14.0 Answer Report | | | | | | | | | | | |
| 2 | Worksheet: [e06p3fitness_LastnameFirstname.xlsx]Advertising | | | | | | | | | | | |
| 3 | Report Created: 2/22/2012 9:25:49 PM | | | | | | | | | | | |
| 4 | Result: Solver found a solution.  All Constraints and optimality conditions are satisfied. | | | | | | | | | | | |
| 5 | Solver Engine | | | | | | | | | | | |
| 6 | Engine: GRG Nonlinear | | | | | | | | | | | |
| 7 | Solution Time: 0.047 Seconds. | | | | | | | | | | | |
| 8 | Iterations: 0 Subproblems: 2 | | | | | | | | | | | |
| 9 | Solver Options | | | | | | | | | | | |
| 10 | Max Time 100 sec,  Iterations 100, Precision 0.000001 | | | | | | | | | | | |
| 11 | Convergence 0.0001, Population Size 100, Random Seed 0, Derivatives Forward, Require Bounds | | | | | | | | | | | |
| 12 | Max Subproblems Unlimited, Max Integer Sols Unlimited, Integer Tolerance 5% | | | | | | | | | | | |
| 13 | | | | | | | | | | | | |
| 14 | Objective Cell () | | | | | | | | | | | |
| 15 | Cell | Name | | Original Value | Final Value | | | | | | | |
| 16 | $D$14 | Total Advertising Cost Totals | | $ 15,000 | $ 125,000 | | | | | | | |
| 17 | | | | | | | | | | | | |
| 18 | | | | | | | | | | | | |
| 19 | Variable Cells | | | | | | | | | | | |
| 20 | Cell | Name | | Original Value | Final Value | Integer | | | | | | |
| 21 | $B$3 | Number of Ads Magazine | | 1 | 8 | Integer | | | | | | |
| 22 | $C$3 | Number of Ads Television | | 1 | 9 | Integer | | | | | | |
| 23 | | | | | | | | | | | | |
| 24 | | | | | | | | | | | | |
| 25 | Constraints | | | | | | | | | | | |
| 26 | Cell | Name | | Cell Value | Formula | Status | Slack | | | | | |
| 27 | $D$14 | Total Advertising Cost Totals | | $ 125,000 | $D$14<=$D$13 | Binding | 0 | | | | | |
| 28 | $D$9 | Size of Audience Reached Totals | | 10,250,000 | $D$9>=$D$8 | Not Binding | 250,000 | | | | | |
| 29 | $B$3 | Number of Ads Magazine | | 8 | $B$3>=$B$4 | Binding | 0 | | | | | |
| 30 | $C$3 | Number of Ads Television | | 9 | $C$3>=$C$4 | Binding | 0 | | | | | |
| 31 | $B$3:$C$3=Integer | | | | | | | | | | | |

**FIGURE 33** Worldwide Fitness Centers ➤

a. Open *e06p3fitness* and save it as **e06p3fitness_LastnameFirstname**.

b. Enter the formulas to calculate the size of audience reached and total advertising cost:
   - Click **cell D9**, and then enter **=B3*B7+C3*C7** to calculate the total audience size reached by summing the product of the number of ads by their respective audience sizes.
   - Click **cell D14**, and then enter **=B3*B12+C3*C12** to calculate the total advertising cost by summing the product of the number of ads by their respective cost per ad type.

c. Load Solver, if needed, by doing the following. If Solver is already loaded, skip this step and go to step d.
   - Click the **File tab**, and then select **Options**.
   - Click **Add-Ins** to see a list of active and inactive add-in applications.
   - Click the **Manage arrow**, select **Excel Add-ins**, and then click **Go**.
   - Click **Solver Add-in** in the **Add-Ins available list**, and then click **OK**.

d. Set the objective, enter changing variable cells, and enter the constraints:
   - Click the **Data tab**, and then click **Solver** in the Analysis group.
   - Click **cell D14** to enter it in the **Set Objective box**, and then click **Min**.
   - Click in the **By Changing Variable Cells box**, and then select the **range B3:C3**.
   - Click **Add** to open the Add Constraint dialog box.
   - Click **cell B3** to enter it in the **Cell Reference box**, click the **operator arrow**, select >=, and then click **cell B4** to enter it in the **Constraint box**.
   - Click **Add**, and then define the following three constraints:

| Constraint to Enter: | Click to Complete: |
|---|---|
| C3 >= C4 | Add |
| D9 >= D8 | Add |
| D14 <= D13 | OK |

e. Click **Solve**, verify that *Keep Solver Solution* is selected, select **Answer** in the **Reports list**, and then click **OK**. Click the **Answer Report 1 worksheet tab** to see the report. The final advertising cost was minimized at the constraint of $125,000, but the report indicates that 7.5 magazine ads must be placed. Because you cannot purchase one-half of an ad, you must add an integer constraint.

f. Impose an integer constraint:
   - Click the **Advertising worksheet tab**, type **1** in **cell B3**, type **1** in **cell C3** to reset the original variable cell values, and then type **9** in **cell C4**.
   - Click **Solver** in the Analysis group.
   - Click **Add** to add a constraint.

What-If Analysis

- Select **cells B3:C3**, click the **operator arrow**, select **int**, and then click **OK**.
- Click **Options** to open the Options dialog box, deselect the **Ignore Integer Constraints check box**, and then click **OK**. (When the Ignore Integer Constraints check box is selected, Solver ignores all integer constraints you create.)

g. Click **Solve**, click **Answer** in the **Reports list**, and then click **OK**. Click the **Answer Report 2 worksheet tab** to see the report. Look at the final results and study the constraints to see which ones are binding.

h. Create a footer with your name on the left side, the sheet name code in the center, and the file name code on the right side for all three worksheets. Select the option to fit each worksheet to one printed page.

i. Save and close the workbook, and submit based on your instructor's directions.

## 1 Housing Construction Cost Variables

Your friends, Elijah and Valerie Foglesong, want to build their dream house. They identified tentative costs, but they cannot afford the $414,717 estimated cost. You will use Goal Seek to determine an estimate of the total finished square footage they can afford. To help provide more flexibility in their decision making, you will create a data table listing various finished square footages and their effects on the base house cost and total cost. Finally, you will create another data table showing combinations of square footages and lot prices to identify total costs. Although a builder's overall house design specifies the square footage, the Foglesongs can use your data tables to help guide them in their decision.

a. Open *e06m1house* and save it as **e06m1house_LastnameFirstname**.
b. Use **Goal Seek** to determine the total finished square footage to meet the total cost goal of $350,000.
c. Enter a series of total square footages starting from 1,800 to 3,600 in 200 increments in the **range D6:D15**. Apply **Blue font** and **Comma Style** with zero decimal places to the series. Enter references to the base cost and total cost in the appropriate cells on row 5.
d. Complete the data table using the appropriate input cell. Apply custom number formats to give appropriate descriptions to the second and third columns. Apply these formats to the headings: bold, center, and **Blue font**.
e. Identify the square footage, base price, and total cost that come closest to their goal. Apply **Blue, Accent 1, Lighter 40% fill color** to those cells in the data table.
f. Copy the square footage substitution values to the **range H6:H15**, and then remove the fill color. Enter these lot price substitution values in the **range I5:K5: 90000, 96000**, and **102675**. Format these values with **Accounting Number Format** with zero decimal places and **Blue font**.
g. Enter the reference to the total cost formula in the appropriate location for the second data table. Complete the data table using the appropriate input cells. Apply a custom number format to the reference to the formula cell. Apply bold and **Blue font color** to that cell. Apply **Blue, Accent 1, Lighter 40% fill color** to the total price in each column that comes closest to their goal.
h. Format all results with **Accounting Number Format** with zero decimal places.
i. Create a footer with your name on the left side, the sheet name code in the center, and the file name code on the right side. Adjust the orientation, margins, and scaling to fit on one page.
j. Save and close the workbook, and submit based on your instructor's directions.

## 2 Grade Scenarios

You are taking a government class at your college. Your grade is based on assignments, two midterm tests, a final exam, and participation. You want to see what your final grade might be if you are strong on one or two areas and average or above average in other categories. You set up a basic spreadsheet with the category names, possible category points, and weighted averages. You need to insert a VLOOKUP function to identify the correct letter grade from a lookup table. To compare various scenarios of where your strengths might lie, you will use Scenario Manager.

a. Open *e06m2grades* and save it as **e06m2grades_LastnameFirstname**.
b. Insert a VLOOKUP function in **cell D7** to return the correct letter grade. The lookup table, appropriately named as a range called grades, is located on the Letter Grade worksheet.
c. Apply range names to the cells in the **range B2:B5** by using their respective labels in column A. Apply range names to **cells D6** and **D7**, individually.

d. Create the following scenarios to compare different strengths:

| Test Strength | Assign Part Strength | Final Exam Strength | Assign Midterm Strength |
|---|---|---|---|
| 85 | 100 | 75 | 95 |
| 95 | 75 | 80 | 90 |
| 95 | 75 | 95 | 85 |
| 75 | 100 | 80 | 75 |

e. Create a summary report with the total points and letter grade as results. Delete extraneous rows and columns as specified in the *Generating Scenario Summary Reports* section. Wrap the headings, and then set the column widths to **10** for the last four columns. Apply other formatting as needed. Compose two sentences below the summary: one sentence to address the best scenario and one sentence to address the worst scenario.

f. Generate a Scenario PivotTable report from the Points worksheet. Use the total points as the results. Remove the report filter, apply appropriate column headings, and display values to two decimal places.

g. Create a footer with your name on the left side, the sheet name code in the center, and the file name code on the right side of the Scenario Summary 1 and Scenario PivotTable 1 worksheets.

h. Save and close the workbook, and submit based on your instructor's directions.

## 3  Ringold Hospital Expansion Project

You are the chief financial officer at Ringold County Hospital, a small rural hospital in Mount Ayr, Iowa. With the closure of nearby hospitals, your hospital is planning an expansion to handle the increased demand. Given a budget of $750,000, you must determine the number of private and double rooms and the number of beds to add along with the number of each product to order. All beds need an overbed table and television. The hospital needs to add at least 10 private rooms, with the rest of the new rooms for double occupancy. At least half of the beds need rails, at least a quarter of the beds need a patient lift, at least 60% of the beds need a patient monitor, and at least 20% of the beds need a vital sign monitor. The hospital needs one blood pressure device for at least every five beds and one therapeutic ultrasound device for at least every 20 beds. The hospital needs at least 50 beds to meet the increased demand. Your staff started a worksheet that contains cost inputs.

a. Open *e06m3hospital* and save it as **e06m3hospital_LastnameFirstname**.

b. Load the Solver add-in if it is not already loaded.

c. Enter formulas to calculate the product totals and the total private and double room costs.

d. Enter other input values provided in the above information.

e. Create the Solver model to set an objective to calculate the minimum total cost possible using the units to order and the number of private and double rooms as the changing cells.

f. Set the following constraints:
- Total cost to be within budget
- Number of beds, overbed tables, and televisions match the total beds
- Appropriate unit orders for rails, patient lifts, patient monitors, vital sign monitors, and ultrasound devices based on their respective percentage of total beds
- Number of private rooms to meet the requirements
- Number of total beds needed
- Integer constraints as needed

g. Open the Options dialog box, and make sure integer constraints are not ignored.

h. Run Solver and keep the results. If Solver cannot find a solution, make sure the *Keep Solver Solution* check box is selected, and then click **OK**. Run Solver again, and then create an answer report.

i. Create a footer with your name on the left side, the sheet name code in the center, and the file name code on the right side on each worksheet. Adjust the scaling to fit on one page.

j. Save and close the workbook, and submit based on your instructor's directions.

You are on the budget committee for the formal Valentine's Day Ball at your university. The ball includes dinner and dancing. Your committee prepared a tentative budget outlining income and expenses. The primary sources of income are contributions from student organizations and ticket prices. Expenses include the actual cost of the dinner, facilities, parking, and other costs at a luxurious hotel in the city. Your goal is to balance the income and expenses, decide on the most appropriate ticket price per student, and ensure your budget falls within the limitations you must work with.

## Goal Seek

Currently, the estimated budget has a deficit. The fastest way to try to reconcile the income and expenses is to use Goal Seek. The goal is to break even, that is, to have a zero balance. Your instinct is to adjust the ticket price per person to reach the goal.

a. Open *e06c1dance* and save it as **e06c1dance_ LastnameFirstname**.

b. Use **Goal Seek** to achieve a $0 balance by changing the ticket price per person.

c. Enter the value of the ticket price per person variable in the Q&A worksheet.

## One-Variable Data Table

You believe that between 200 and 500 students will attend. Because the ticket revenue, chair setup, catering cost, and valet parking expenses are dependent on the number of students, you decide to create a one-variable data table to compare the budget effects based on different numbers of students attending.

a. Start in **cell E3**. Complete the series of substitution values ranging from 200 to 500 at increments of 20 students vertically down column E.

b. Enter references to the total revenue, total expenses, and balance formulas in the correct location for a one-variable data table.

c. Complete the one-variable data table, and then format the results with **Accounting Number Format** with two decimal places.

d. Apply custom number formats to make the formula references appear as descriptive column headings. Format the headings and substitution values.

e. Answer questions 2 through 4 on the Q&A worksheet. Save the workbook.

## Two-Variable Data Table

The break-even point for the one-variable data table is identical to the current model because all other variables are held constant. You want to compare the balances of different combinations of attendees and ticket prices per person using a two-variable data table.

a. Copy the number of attendees substitution values from the one-variable data table, and then paste the values starting in **cell E22**.

b. Type **$50** in **cell F21**. Complete the series of substitution values from **$50** to **$100** at **$10** increments.

c. Enter the reference to the balance formula in the correct location for a two-variable data table.

d. Complete the two-variable data table, and then format the results with **Accounting Number Format** with two decimal places.

e. Apply a fill color to the cells closest to break-even without creating a deficit.

f. Apply a custom number format to make the formula reference appear as a descriptive column heading. Format the headings and substitution values.

g. Answer questions 5 and 6 on the Q&A worksheet. Question 6 requires three combinations to list. Save the workbook.

## Scenario Manager

You negotiated different cost per meal and ballroom rental rates based on 500, 400, 300, or 200 attendees. You estimated tentative ticket prices per attendee. To help you decide the target number of attendees, you need to use Scenario Manager.

a. Create a scenario named **500 Attend**, using the number of attendees, meal cost per person, ticket price per person, and ballroom rental variables as the changing cells. Enter these values for the scenario: **500, 15.95, 75**, and **12500**.

b. Create a second scenario named **400 Attend**, using the same changing cells. Enter these values for the scenario: **400, 17.95, 85**, and **12500**.

c. Create a third scenario named **300 Attend**, using the same changing cells. Enter these values for the scenario: **300, 19.95, 90**, and **11995**.

d. Create a fourth scenario named **200 Attend**, using the same changing cells. Enter these values for the scenario: **200, 22.95, 95**, and **11995**.

e. Generate a scenario summary report using the total revenue, total expenses, and balance as the results.

f. Clean up the summary as discussed in the chapter.

g. Answer questions 7 through 9 on the Q&A worksheet. Save the workbook.

## Use Solver

You realize a perfect break-even point may be unrealistic, but you will donate any positive balance to charity. For this analysis, you will use Solver to keep the expenses constant while changing the number of attendees and ticket price per person.

a. Load the Solver add-in if it is not already loaded.

b. Set the objective to calculate the highest balance possible.

c. Use the number of attendees and the ticket price per person as changing variable cells.

d. Look at the *Limitations* section of the spreadsheet model.

e. Set a constraint for the number of attendees.

f. Set constraints for the ticket price per person.

g. Set an appropriate integer constraint.

h. Set a constraint that ensures the valet parking expense is less than or equal to the product of the number of parking stalls and the valet price per vehicle.

i. Solve the problem, but keep the original values in the Budget worksheet. Generate the Answer Report. If you get an internal memory error message, remove Solver as an add-in, close the workbook, open the workbook, add Solver in again, and finish using Solver.

j. Answer questions 10 through 13 on the Q&A worksheet. Apply **landscape orientation** to the Q&A worksheet. Save the workbook.

k. Create a footer on all four worksheets with your name on the left side, the sheet name code in the center, and the file name code on the right side.

l. Save and close the workbook, and submit based on your instructor's directions.

# BEYOND THE CLASSROOM

### Art Gallery

GENERAL CASE

Your sister runs an art gallery where she teaches art classes. Her clients pay monthly dues and can take as many classes as they want. Her gallery is losing money, and she asked you to help identify how she can become profitable. Open *e06b1gallery* and save it as **e06b1gallery_LastnameFirstname**. Your first step is to perform a simple what-if analysis using Goal Seek in which you set a target profit of $15,000 by changing the membership dues. Next, construct a one-variable data table using dues ranging from $50 to $70 at $2 increments and show results for the revenues and income. Then create a two-variable data table using the same dues substitution values and memberships ranging from 2,500 to 3,100 at 200 increments to show results for income. Format the tables (including substitution values, results, and headings) appropriately. Apply a fill color to the result cells closest to the break-even point without creating a deficit. Select landscape orientation, adjust the margins, and then adjust the column widths. Create a footer with your name, the sheet name code, and the file name code. Save and close the workbook, and submit based on your instructor's directions.

### Too Cold to Snow

RESEARCH CASE

Have you ever wondered whether it could be too cold to snow? Actually, it is much more likely to snow if the temperature is close to freezing than if it is much below. The reason is because the air gets too dry to snow. As the air gets colder, it holds less water vapor for making snow. This explains why Nashville, Tennessee, typically gets more snowfall each year than frigid Barrow, Alaska! Because snow in northern Alaska does not melt as quickly as snow in Nashville, the area appears to get more snow. You are a high school science teacher, preparing a lesson on the effect of temperature and water vapor on snowfall. The dew point is the temperature at which water vapor condenses and forms into liquid or frozen precipitation, and the wet bulb temperature is the lowest temperature that can be reached by the evaporation of water only. Typically, the greater the difference between wet bulb and air temperature, the drier the air. Because drier air is less likely to produce snow, you will use the wet bulb temperature to approximate the dryness of the air and the potential for snow. Use the Internet to find the temperature and dew point of Nashville on January 6 of the current year and develop an estimate of the wet bulb temperature.

Open *e06b2snow* and save it as **e06b2snow_LastnameFirstname**. Use Scenario Manager to create a Most Likely and Least Likely projection of wet bulb temperature for Nashville. The Most Likely statistics are those that you identified for January 6. The Least Likely statistics are a temperature of 18° and a dew point of 5°. Wet bulb temperature is calculated by subtracting dew point from temperature and dividing the result by 3. Edit the summary as specified in the *Generating Scenario Summary Reports* section in the chapter. Insert a text box and write an analysis about your results. Create a footer with your name, the sheet name code, and the file name code. Save and close the workbook, and submit based on your instructor's directions.

### Mining Company

DISASTER RECOVERY

You work for an investment corporation that is considering purchasing a coal mine. One of your colleagues developed a spreadsheet model and started a what-if analysis using Solver. Unfortunately, Solver is unable to solve the problem given the parameters entered. You need to identify and correct the errors, and then generate an answer report. Open *e06b3mining* and save it as **e06b3mining_LastnameFirstname**. Make sure that Solver is loaded. If not, load the Solver add-in. The objective is to maximize the rate of return by the end of the fifth year. The investment firm is considering paying between $20 and $25 million for the mine with an anticipated 1 to 1.5 million tons sold in the first year. Research indicates the price per ton to be between $12.35 and $14.50 initially. The price per ton increase should range from 0.5% to 1.25%. Before you run the Solver report, change the number of iterations to 1500 in the Solver Options dialog box. Insert notes to describe the parameter errors, correct the errors, and run a Solver answer report. Create a footer with your name, the sheet name code, and the file name code on the report. Adjust the left and right margins on the Answer Report 1 worksheet so that the data can print on one page. Deselect the options that print gridlines and headings on the Forecast worksheet. Save and close the workbook, and submit based on your instructor's directions.

## ACCESS

# INTRODUCTION TO ACCESS

## Finding Your Way Through a Database

### CASE STUDY | Managing a Business in the Global Economy

Watch the Set-up Video for this Case Study!

Northwind Traders* is an international gourmet food distributor that imports and exports specialty foods from around the world. Northwind's products include meats, seafood, dairy products, beverages, and produce. Keeping track of customers, vendors, orders, and inventory is no small task. The owners of Northwind have just purchased an order-processing database created with Microsoft Office Access 2010 to help manage their customers, suppliers, products, and orders.

Because the owners do not have time to operate the new database, you have been hired to learn, use, and manage the database. The Northwind owners are willing to provide training about their business and on Access. They expect the learning process to take about three months. After three months, your job will be to support the order-processing team as well as to provide detail and summary reports to the sales force as needed. Your new job at Northwind Traders will be a challenge! It is also an opportunity to make a great contribution to a global company. Are you up to the task?

*Northwind Traders was created by the Microsoft Access Team and is shipped with Access as a sample database you can use to learn about Access. The names of companies, products, people, characters, and/or data are fictitious. The practice database you will use is a modified version of Northwind Traders.

### OBJECTIVES   AFTER YOU READ THIS CHAPTER, YOU WILL BE ABLE TO:

1. Navigate among the objects in an Access database
2. Understand the difference between working in storage and memory
3. Practice good database file management
4. Back up, compact, and repair Access files
5. Create filters
6. Sort table data on one or more fields
7. Know when to use Access or Excel to manage data
8. Use the Relationships window
9. Understand relational power

From Access Chapter 1 of *Exploring Microsoft Office 2010 Volume 1*, First Edition, Robert T. Grauer, Mary Anne Poatsy, Keith Mulbery, Michelle Hulett, Cynthia Krebs, Keith Mast. Copyright © 2011 by Pearson Education, Inc. Published by Pearson Prentice Hall, Inc. All rights reserved.

# Databases Are Everywhere!

If you use the Internet, you use databases often. When you shop online or check your bank statement, you are connecting to a database. Even when you type a search phrase into Google and click Search, you are using Google's massive database with all of its stored Web page references and keywords. Look for something on eBay, and you are searching eBay's database to find a product on which you might want to bid. Need a new pair of shoes? Log on to the Columbia Web site (see Figure 1), and find the right pair in your style, your size, and your price range. All this information is stored in its products database.

> If you use the Internet, you use databases often.

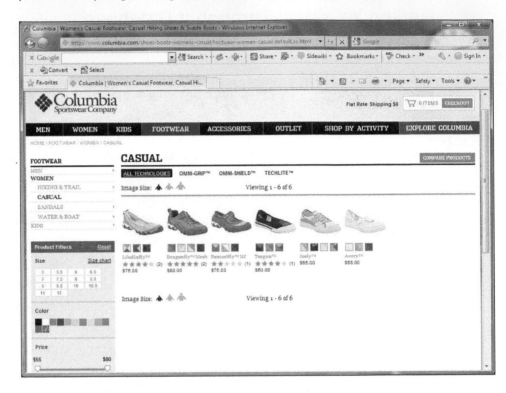

**FIGURE 1** Columbia Web Site ➤

You are exposed to other databases on a regular basis outside of Internet shopping. For example, your community college or university uses a database to store the registration data. When you registered for this course, your data was entered into a database. The database probably told you the number of available seats but not the names of the other students who enrolled in the class. In addition, social networking Web sites such as Facebook and LinkedIn are storing data on large database servers.

Organizations rely on data to conduct daily operations, regardless of whether the organization exists as a profit or not-for-profit environment. Organizations maintain data about their customers, employees, orders, volunteers, activities, and facilities. Every keystroke and mouse click creates data about the organization that needs to be stored, organized, and available for analysis. Access is a valuable decision-making tool that many organizations are using or want to use.

In this section, you will explore Access database objects and work with table views. You will also learn the difference between working in storage and working in memory, and you will learn how changes to database objects are saved. Finally, you will practice good database maintenance techniques by backing up, compacting, and repairing databases.

# Navigating Among the Objects in an Access Database

An **object** in an Access database is a main component that is created and used to make the database function.

A **field** is the smallest data element contained in a table. Examples of fields are first name, last name, address, and phone number.

A **record** is a complete set of all of the data elements (fields) about one person, place, event, or concept.

A **table**, the foundation of every database, is a collection of related records.

A **database** consists of one or more tables to store data, one or more forms to enter data into the tables, and one or more reports to output the table data as organized information.

The *objects* in an Access database are the main components that are created and used to make the database function. The four main object types are tables, queries, forms, and reports. Two other object types, macros and modules, are used less frequently. Throughout this chapter, you will learn how to use each type of object.

To understand how an Access database works and how to use Access effectively, you should first learn the terms of the key object—the table. A *field* is the smallest data element contained in a table. Fields define the type of data that is collected, for example, text, numeric, or date. Examples of fields are first name, last name, address, and phone number. A field may be required or optional. For example, a person's last name may be required, but a fax number may be optional. A *record* is a complete set of all of the data elements (fields) about one person, place, event, or concept. For example, your first name, last name, student ID, phone number, and e-mail address constitute your record in your instructor's class roster. A *table*, the foundation of every database, is a collection of related records. For example, all the students in your class would be entered into the Class Roster table during registration.

A *database* consists of one or more tables to store data, one or more forms to enter data into the tables, and one or more reports to output the table data as organized information. The main functions of a database are to collect data, to store data logically, to manipulate data to make it more useful, and to output the data to the screen and printed reports. Databases also export data to files so the files can be imported by other databases or other information-processing systems.

---

**TIP** Data Versus Information

*Data* and *information* are two terms that are often used interchangeably. However, when it comes to databases, the two terms mean different things. *Data* is what is entered into the tables of the database. *Information* is the finished product that is produced by the database in a query or in a printed report. Data is converted to information by selecting, calculating, sorting, or summarizing records. Decisions in an organization are usually based on information produced by a database, rather than raw data.

---

## Examine the Access Interface

Figure 2 shows the Access Interface for the Northwind Traders database, which was introduced in the Case Study at the beginning of this chapter. The top section, known as the Ribbon, remains the same no matter which database is open. Below the Ribbon, you find all the objects that are needed to make the current database function; these objects are stored in the Navigation Pane (on the left). To the right of the Navigation Pane, the currently open objects are displayed and are delimited with tabs. The title bar at the top of the window contains the name of the application (Microsoft Access), the name of the currently loaded database (Northwind), and the file format (Access 2007) of the loaded database. Because Access 2010 does not have a new file format, you will see Access 2007 in the title bar throughout this textbook. The Minimize, Maximize (or Restore), and Close icons can be found on the right of the title bar. The tab below the Ribbon shows that the Employees table is currently open. When more than one object is open at a time, one tab will be shown for each open object. Click on a tab to view or modify that object independently of the other objects.

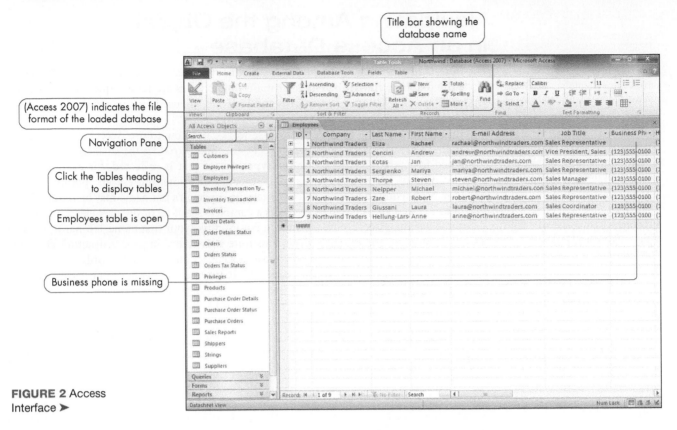

Title bar showing the database name

(Access 2007) indicates the file format of the loaded database

Navigation Pane

Click the Tables heading to display tables

Employees table is open

Business phone is missing

**FIGURE 2** Access Interface ➤

The **Navigation Pane** organizes and lists the database objects in an Access database.

Figure 2 shows that the Northwind database contains 20 tables: Customers, Employee Privileges, Employees, etc. Each table contains multiple records. The Employees table is currently open and shows nine records for the nine employees who work for the company. The Employees table contains 18 fields (or attributes) about each employee, including the employee's Last Name, First Name, E-Mail Address, Job Title, and so on. Occasionally, a field does not contain a value for a particular record. One of the employees, Rachael Eliza, did not provide a business phone. The value of that field is missing. Access shows a blank cell when data is missing.

The Suppliers table holds a record for each vendor from whom the firm purchases products; the Orders table holds one record for each order. The real power of Access is derived from a database with multiple tables and the relationships that connect the tables.

The *Navigation Pane* organizes and lists the database objects in an Access database. As stated earlier, six types of objects—tables, queries, forms, reports, macros, and modules—can exist in a database. Most databases contain multiple tables, queries, forms, and reports. Tables store the data, forms enable users to enter information into the tables, reports enable users to display data in an organized format, and queries enable users to ask questions about the data. In Figure 2, the Tables group shows all the table objects; the other objects are hidden until you click a group heading to expand the group and display the objects. Click a visible group name to hide the group. To change the way objects are displayed within a group, right-click the group, and select from a list of options. For example, you can right-click the Queries category, point to View By, and then click Details to see when each query was created.

The Access Ribbon contains the icons that help you perform the database functions to maintain a database. These commands are described in detail on the following Reference page. You do not need to memorize every icon, group, and tab; however, it will be helpful to refer to this page as you are learning Access.

# REFERENCE    Access Ribbon

| Tab and Groups | Description |
|---|---|
| **File** | The File tab leads to the Backstage view, which gives you access to a variety of database tools such as Compact and Repair, Back Up Database, and Print. |
| **Home**<br>Views<br>Clipboard<br>Sort & Filter<br>Records<br>Find<br>Text Formatting | The default Access tab. Contains basic editing functions, such as cut and paste, filtering, find and replace, and most formatting actions. |
| **Create**<br>Templates<br>Tables<br>Queries<br>Forms<br>Reports<br>Macros & Code | This tab contains all the create tools, such as create Tables, create Forms, create Reports, and create Queries. |
| **External Data**<br>Import & Link<br>Export<br>Collect Data<br>Web Linked Lists | This tab contains all of the operations to facilitate data import and export. |
| **Database Tools**<br>Tools<br>Macro<br>Relationships<br>Analyze<br>Move Data<br>Add-Ins | This tab enables you to use the more advanced features of Access. Set relationships between tables, analyze a table or query, and migrate your data to SQL Server or SharePoint. |

## Work with Table Views

The **Datasheet view** is where you add, edit, and delete the records of a table.

The **Design view** is where you create tables, add and delete fields, and modify field properties.

Access provides two different ways to view a table: the Datasheet view and the Design view. The *Datasheet view* is a grid containing columns (fields) and rows (records), similar to an Excel spreadsheet. You can view, add, edit, and delete records in the Datasheet view. The *Design view* is used to create and modify a table's design by specifying the fields it will contain, the fields' data types, and their associated properties. Data types define the type of data that will be stored in a field, such as currency, numeric, text, etc. For example, if you need to store the pay rate of an employee, you would enter the field name Pay Rate and select the data type currency. The field properties define the characteristics of the fields in more detail. For example, for the field Pay Rate, you could set a field property that requires Pay Rate to be less than $25 (a higher rate would trigger a manager's approval). To accomplish this, you would set the validation rule to <25 to prevent users from entering a pay rate higher than $25.

Figure 3 shows the Design view for the Customers table. In the top portion, each row contains the field names, the data type, and an optional description for each field in the table. In the bottom portion, the Field Properties pane contains the properties (details) for each field. Click on a field, and the field properties will be displayed in the bottom portion of the Design view window.

Figure 4 shows the Datasheet view for the Customers table. The top row in the table contains the field names. Each additional row contains a record (the data for a specific customer). Each column represents a field (one attribute about a customer). Every record in the table represents a different customer; all records contain the same fields.

Databases Are Everywhere! • Access 2010

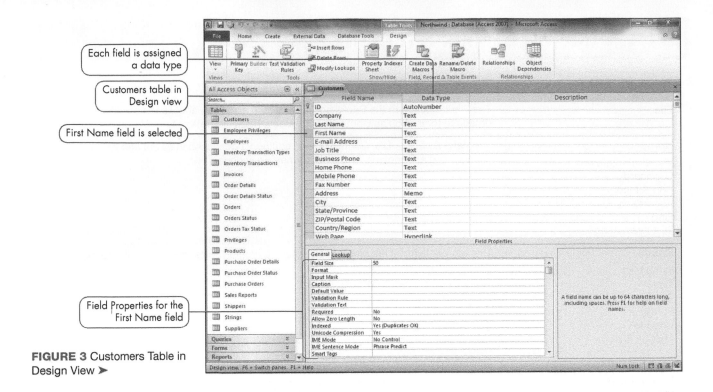

Each field is assigned a data type

Customers table in Design view

First Name field is selected

Field Properties for the First Name field

**FIGURE 3** Customers Table in Design View ➤

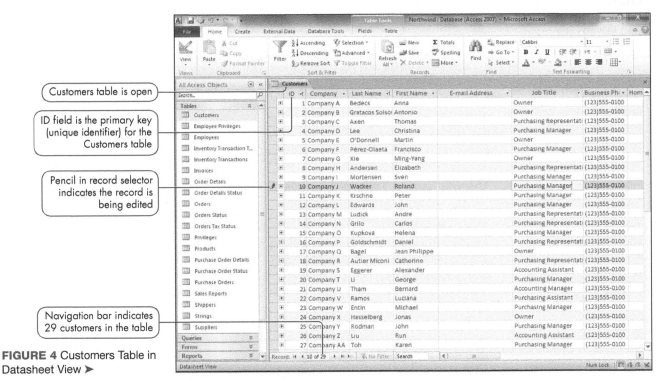

Customers table is open

ID field is the primary key (unique identifier) for the Customers table

Pencil in record selector indicates the record is being edited

Navigation bar indicates 29 customers in the table

**FIGURE 4** Customers Table in Datasheet View ➤

The **primary key** is the field (or combination of fields) that uniquely identifies each record in a table.

The *primary key* is the field (or combination of fields) that uniquely identifies each record in a table. The ID field is the primary key in the Customers table; it ensures that each record in the table can be distinguished from every other record. It also helps prevent the occurrence of duplicate records. Primary key fields may be numbers, letters, or a combination of both. In this case, the primary key is an autonumber (a number that is generated by Access and is incremented each time a record is added). Another example of a primary key is Social Security Number, which is often used in an employee table.

Introduction to Access

386

The navigation bar at the bottom of Figure 4 shows that the Customers table has 29 records and that record number 10 is the current record. The vertical scroll bar on the right side of the window only appears when the table contains more records than can appear in the window at one time. Similarly, the horizontal scroll bar at the bottom of the window only appears when the table contains more fields than can appear in the window at one time.

The pencil symbol to the left of Record 10 indicates that the data in that record is being edited and that changes have not yet been saved. The pencil symbol disappears when you move to another record. It is important to understand that Access saves data automatically as soon as you move from one record to another. This may seem counter-intuitive at first, since Word and Excel do not save changes and additions automatically. With Word and Excel, you must click the Save icon in order to save your work (or set auto-save to save automatically in the background).

Figure 5 shows the navigation buttons that you use to move through the records in a table, query, or form. The buttons enable you to go to the first record, the previous record, the next record, or the last record. The button with the asterisk is used to add a new (blank) record. You can also type a number directly into the current record cell, and Access will take you to that record. Finally, the navigation bar enables you to locate a record based on a single word. Type a word in the search cell box, and Access will locate the first record that contains the word.

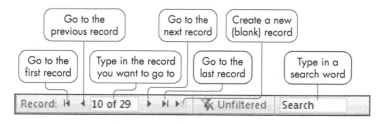

**FIGURE 5** Navigation Buttons ➤

No system, no matter how sophisticated, can produce valid output from invalid input. Access database systems are built to anticipate data entry errors. These systems contain table validation rules created to prevent invalid data entry. Two types of validation rules exist: those built into Access and those a developer creates specifically for a database. For example, Access will automatically prevent you from adding a new record with the same primary key as an existing record. Access does not allow you to enter text or numeric data into a date field. A database developer can add validation rules, such as requiring a person's last name or requiring an employee's social security number. A developer can also limit the length of data, such as only enabling five digits for a zip code or two characters for a state abbreviation.

## Use Forms, Queries, and Reports

As previously indicated, an Access database is made up of different types of objects together with the tables and the data they contain. The tables are the heart of any database because they contain the *actual* data. The other objects in a database—such as forms, queries, and reports—are based on one or more underlying tables. Figure 6 displays a form based on the Customers table shown earlier.

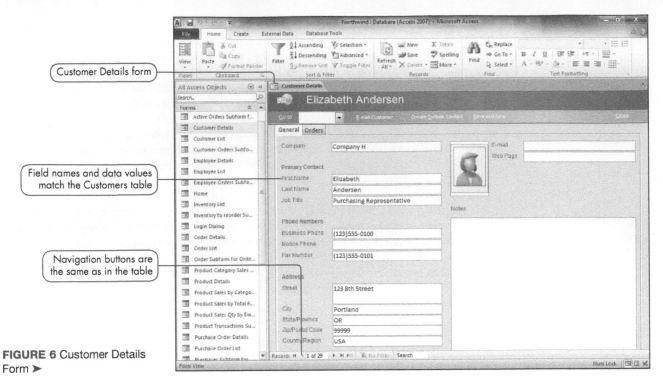

Customer Details form

Field names and data values match the Customers table

Navigation buttons are the same as in the table

**FIGURE 6** Customer Details Form ➤

---

A **form** is an object that enables you to enter, modify, or delete table data.

A **query** is a question that you ask about the data in the tables of your database.

A **criterion** (**criteria**, pl) is a number, a text phrase, or an expression used to filter the records in a table.

A **form** is an object that enables you to enter, modify, or delete table data. A form enables you to manipulate data in the same manner that you would in a table's Datasheet view. The difference is that you can create a form that will limit the user to viewing only one record at a time. This helps the user to focus on the data being entered or modified and also provides more reliable data entry. A form may also contain command buttons that enable you to add a new record, print a record, or close the form. The status bar and navigation buttons at the bottom of the form are similar to those that appear at the bottom of a table. As an Access user, you will add, delete, and edit records in Form view. As the Access designer, you will create and edit the form structure in Design view.

A **query** is a question that you ask about the data in the tables of your database. The answer is shown in the query results. A query can be used to display only records that meet a certain criterion and only the fields that are required. Figure 7 shows the query design for the question "Which products does Northwind purchase from Supplier A?" The Products table contains records for many vendors, but the records shown in Figure 8 are only the products that were supplied by Supplier A. If you want to know the details about a specific supplier (such as Supplier A), you set the criterion in the query to specify which supplier you need to know about.

A **criterion** (**criteria**, pl) is a number, a text phrase, or an expression used to filter the records in a table. If you need the names of all the suppliers in New York, you can set the supplier's state criterion to *New York*. The results would yield only those suppliers from New York. Query results are in Datasheet view and are similar in appearance to the underlying table, except that the query contains selected records and/or selected fields for those records. The query also may list the records in a different sequence from that of the table.

You also can use a query to add new records and modify existing records. If you open a query and notice an error in an address field, you can edit the record directly in the query results. When you edit a value in a query, you are also updating the data in the underlying table. Editing in a query is efficient but should be used with caution to avoid inadvertently updating the tables. Queries may be opened in Datasheet view or Design view. You use the Datasheet view to examine the query output; you use the Design view to specify which fields to display and what criteria you want.

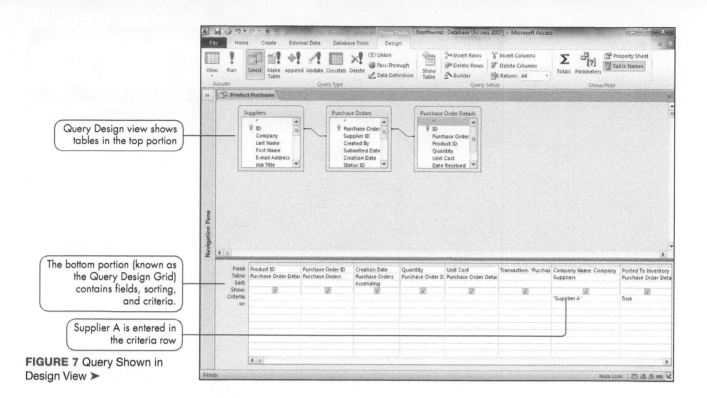

Query Design view shows tables in the top portion

The bottom portion (known as the Query Design Grid) contains fields, sorting, and criteria.

Supplier A is entered in the criteria row

**FIGURE 7** Query Shown in Design View ➤

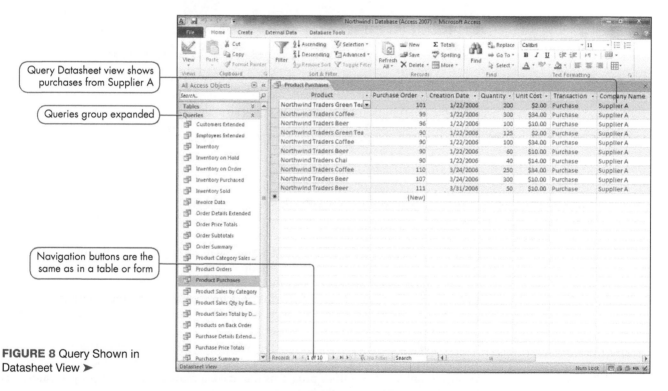

Query Datasheet view shows purchases from Supplier A

Queries group expanded

Navigation buttons are the same as in a table or form

**FIGURE 8** Query Shown in Datasheet View ➤

A **report** contains professional-looking formatted information from underlying tables or queries.

A *report* contains professional-looking formatted information from underlying tables or queries. Figure 9 displays a report that contains the same information as the query in Figure 8. Because the report information contains a more professional look than a query or table, you normally present database information using a report. Access provides different views for designing, modifying, and running reports. Most Access users use only the Print Preview, Layout, and Report views of a report.

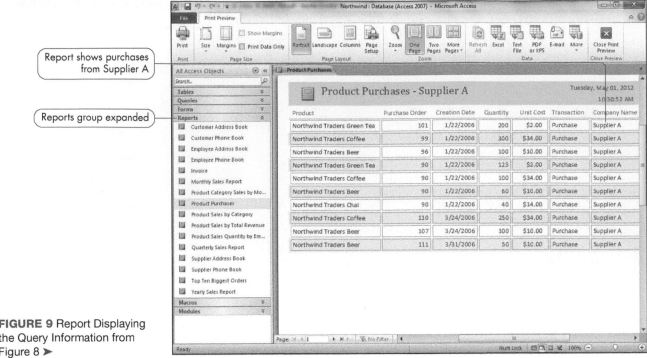

**FIGURE 9** Report Displaying the Query Information from Figure 8 ➤

# Understanding the Difference Between Working in Storage and Memory

Access is different from the other Microsoft Office applications. Word, Excel, and PowerPoint all work primarily from memory. In those applications, your work is not automatically saved to your hard drive unless you click the Save icon. This could be catastrophic if you are working on a large Word document and you forget to save it. If the power is lost, you may lose your document. Access, on the other hand, works primarily from storage. As you enter and update the data in an Access database, the changes are automatically saved to your hard drive. If a power failure occurs, you will only lose the changes from the record that you are currently editing. Another common characteristic among Word, Excel, and PowerPoint is that usually only one person uses a file at one time. Access is different. With an Access database file, several users can work in the same file at the same time.

When you make a change to a field's content in an Access table (for example, changing a customer's phone number), Access saves your changes as soon as you move the insertion point (or focus) to a different record. You do not need to click the Save icon. However, you are required to Save after you modify the design of a table, a query, a form, or a report. When you modify an object's design, such as the Customers form, and then close it, Access will prompt you with the message "Do you want to save changes to the design of form 'Customers'?" Click Yes to save your changes.

Also in Access, you can click Undo to reverse the most recent change (the phone number you just modified) to a single record immediately after making changes to that record. However, unlike other Office programs that enable multiple Undo steps, you cannot use Undo to reverse multiple edits in Access.

Multiple users, from different computers, can work on an Access database simultaneously. As long as two users do not attempt to change the same record at the same time, Access will enable two or more users to work on the same database file at the same time. One person can be adding records to the Customers table while another can be creating a query based on the Products table. Two users can even work on the same table as long as they are not working on the same record.

# Practicing Good Database File Management

Database files are similar to other files (spreadsheets, documents, and images) on your computer. They must be filed in an organized manner using folders and subfolders, they must be named appropriately, and they must be backed up in case of a computer failure. Access files require additional understanding and maintenance to avoid data loss.

Every time you open a student file, you will be directed to copy the file and to rename the copied file. As you are learning about Access databases, you will probably make mistakes. Since you'll be working from the copy, you can easily recover from one of these mistakes by reverting back to the original and starting over.

**Access speed** measures the time it takes for the storage device to make the file content available for use.

Access runs best from a local disk drive or network disk drive because those drives have sufficient access speed to support the software. *Access speed* measures the time it takes for the storage device to make the file content available for use. If your school provides you with storage space on the school's network, store your student files there. The advantage to using the network is that the network administration staff back up files regularly. If you have no storage on the school network, your next best storage option is a thumb drive, also known as a USB jump drive, a flash drive, a pen drive, or a stick drive.

# Backing Up, Compacting, and Repairing Access Files

**Compact and Repair** reduces the size of the database.

**Backup** creates a duplicate copy of the database.

Data is the lifeblood of any organization. Access provides two utilities to help protect the data within a database: *Compact and Repair* and *backup*. These two functions both help protect your data, but they each serve a different purpose. Compact and Repair reduces the size of the database. Backup creates a duplicate copy of the database.

## Compact and Repair a Database

All Access databases have a tendency to expand with everyday use. Entering data, creating queries, running reports, deleting objects, and adding indexes will all cause a database file to expand. This growth may increase storage requirements and may also impact database performance. In addition, databases that are compacted regularly are less likely to become corrupt—resulting in loss of data. Access provides a utility—Compact and Repair Database—in the Backstage view that addresses this issue. When you run the Compact and Repair utility, it creates a new database file behind the scenes and copies all the objects from the original database into the new one. As it copies the objects into the new file, Access will remove temporary objects and unclaimed space due to deleted objects, resulting in a smaller database file. Compact and Repair will also defragment a fragmented database file if needed. When the utility is finished copying the data, it deletes the original file and renames the new one with the same name as the original. This utility can also be used to repair a corrupt database. In most cases, only a small amount of data—the last record modified—will be lost during the repair process. You should compact your database every day.

## Back Up a Database

Imagine what would happen to a firm that loses the orders placed but not shipped, a charity that loses the list of donor contributions, or a hospital that loses the digital records of its patients. Fortunately, Access recognizes how critical backup procedures are to organizations and makes backing up the database files easy. You back up an Access file (and all of the objects inside) with just a few mouse clicks. To back up files, click the File tab, and then click Save & Publish from the list of options. From the list of Save & Publish options, double-click Back Up Database, and the Save As dialog box opens. You can designate the folder location and the file name for the backup copy of the database. Access provides a default file name that is the original file name followed by the current date. The default database type is accdb.

In the next Hands-On Exercise, you will work with the Northwind Traders database you read about in the Case Study at the beginning of the chapter. Northwind purchases food items from suppliers around the world and sells them to restaurants and specialty food shops. Northwind depends on the data stored in its Access database to process orders and make daily decisions.

# HANDS-ON EXERCISES

myitlab
HOE1 Training

## 1 Databases Are Everywhere!

In your new position with Northwind Traders, you need to spend time getting familiar with its Access database. You will open its database and add, edit, and delete records using both tables and forms. Finally, you will perform management duties by compacting and backing up the database file.

**Skills covered:** Open an Access File, Save the File with a New Name, and Work with the New File • Edit a Record • Navigate an Access Form and Add Records • Recognize the Connection Between Table and Form, Delete a Record • Compact, Repair, and Back Up the Database

---

### STEP 1 ▶ OPEN AN ACCESS FILE, SAVE THE FILE WITH A NEW NAME, AND WORK WITH THE NEW FILE

This exercise introduces you to the Northwind Traders database. You will use this database to practice working with database files. Refer to Figure 10 as you complete Step 1.

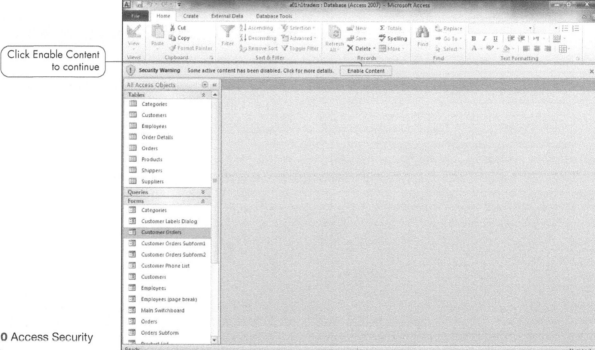

Click Enable Content to continue

**FIGURE 10** Access Security Warning ➤

 **FYI**

a. Open the database named *a01h1traders* in the folder location designated by your instructor.

b. Click the **File tab**, click **Save Database As**, and then locate the folder location designated by your instructor.

When you name solution files, use your last and first names. For example, as the Access author, I would name my database a01h1traders_MastKeith.

> **TROUBLESHOOTING:** If you make any major mistakes in this exercise, you can close the file, make another copy of *a01h1traders*, and then start this exercise over.

c. Type **a01h1traders_LastnameFirstname** as the new file name, and then click **Save** to create the new database.

This step creates the new Access database file. The Security Warning message bar may appear below the Ribbon, indicating that some database content is disabled.

d. Click **Enable Content** on the Security Warning message bar.

When you open an Access file from this book, you will need to enable the content. Several viruses and worms may be transmitted via Access files. You may be confident of the trustworthiness of the files in this book. However, if an Access file arrives as an attachment from an unsolicited e-mail message, you should not open it. Microsoft warns all users of Access that a potential threat exists every time a file is opened. Keep the database open for the rest of the exercise.

## STEP 2 ▶ EDIT A RECORD

You need to modify the data in the Northwind database since customers will change their address, phone numbers, and order data from time to time. Refer to Figure 11 as you complete Step 2.

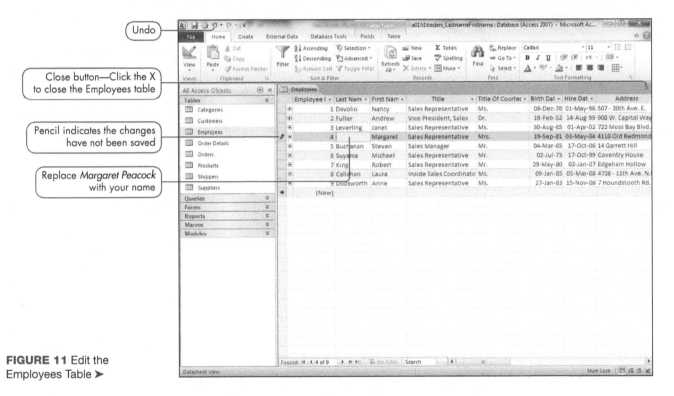

**FIGURE 11** Edit the Employees Table ➤

a. Click the **Tables group** in the Navigation Pane (if necessary) to expand the list of available tables.

The list of tables contained in the database file opens.

b. Double-click the **Employees table** to open it (see Figure 11).

c. Click on the **Last Name field** in the fourth row. Double-click **Peacock**; the entire name highlights. Type your last name to replace *Peacock*.

d. Press **Tab** to move to the next field in the fourth row. Replace *Margaret* with your first name, and then press **Tab**.

You have made changes to two fields in the same record (row); note the pencil symbol on the left side in the row selector box.

e. Click **Undo** in the Quick Access Toolbar.

Your first and last names reverts back to *Margaret Peacock* because you have not yet left the record.

f. Type your first and last names again to replace *Margaret Peacock*. Press **Tab**.

You should now be in the Title field and your title, *Sales Representative*, is selected. The pencil symbol still displays in the row selector.

g. Click anywhere in the third row where Janet Leverling's data is stored.

The pencil symbol disappears, indicating your changes have been saved.

h. Click the **Address field** in the first record, the one for Nancy Davolio. Select the entire address, and then type **4004 East Morningside Dr**. Click anywhere on Andrew Fuller's record.

i. Click **Undo**.

Nancy's address reverts back to *507 - 20th Ave. E*. However, the Undo command is now faded. You can no longer undo the change that you made replacing Margaret Peacock's name with your own.

j. Click the **Close button** (the X at the top of the table) to close the Employees table.

The Employees table closes. You are not prompted about saving your changes; they have already been saved for you because Access works in storage, not memory. If you reopen the Employees table, you will see your name in place of Margaret Peacock's name.

> **TROUBLESHOOTING:** If you click the Close (X) button on the title bar at the top right of the window and accidentally close the database, locate the file, and then double-click it to start again.

## STEP 3 ▶ NAVIGATE AN ACCESS FORM AND ADD RECORDS

You need to add new products to the Northwind database since the company will be adding a new line of products to the database. Refer to Figure 12 as you complete Step 3.

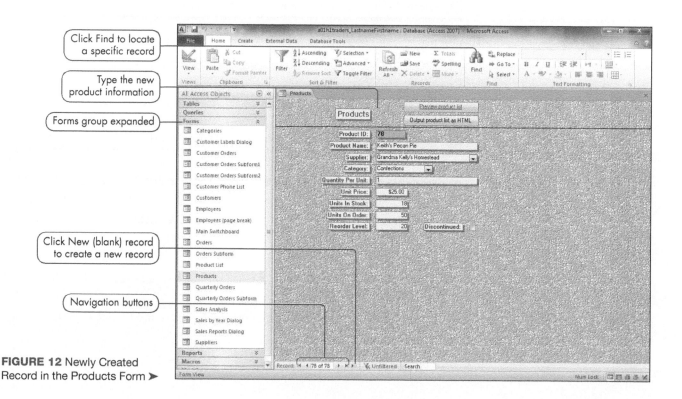

**FIGURE 12** Newly Created Record in the Products Form ➤

a. Click the **Tables group** in the Navigation Pane to collapse it.

The list of available tables collapses.

b. Click the **Forms group** in the Navigation Pane (if necessary) to expand the list of available forms.

c. Double-click the **Products form** to open it.

d. Use Figure 12 to locate the navigation buttons (arrows) at the bottom of the Access window. Practice moving from one record to the next. Click **Next record**, and then click **Last record**; click **Previous record**, and then **First record**.

e. Click **Find** in the Find group on the Home tab.

The Find command is an ideal way to search for specific records within a table, form, or query. You can search a single field or the entire record, match all or part of the selected field(s), move forward or back in a table, or specify a case-sensitive search. The Replace command can be used to substitute one value for another. Be careful when using the Replace All option for global replacement because unintended replacements are possible.

f. Type **Grandma** in the **Find What box**, click the **Match arrow**, and select **Any Part of Field**. Click **Find Next**.

You should see information about Grandma's Boysenberry Spread. Selecting the *any part of the field* option will return a match even if it is contained in the middle of a word.

g. Close the Find dialog box.

h. Click **New (blank) record** on the navigation bar.

i. Enter the following information for a new product. Press **Tab** to navigate through the form.

| Field Name | Value to Type |
| --- | --- |
| Product Name | *your name* **Pecan Pie** |
| Supplier | **Grandma Kelly's Homestead** (Note: click the arrow to select from the list of Suppliers) |
| Category | **Confections** (Click the arrow to select from the list of Categories) |
| Quantity Per Unit | 1 |
| Unit Price | 25.00 |
| Units in Stock | 18 |
| Units on Order | 50 |
| Reorder Level | 20 |
| Discontinued | **No** (the checkbox remains unchecked) |

As soon as you begin typing in the product name box, Access assigns a Product ID, in this case 78, to the record. The Product ID is used as the primary key in the Products table.

j. Click anywhere on the Pecan Pie record you just entered. Click the **File tab**, click **Print**, and then click **Print Preview**.

The first four records appear in the Print Preview.

k. Click **Last Page** in the navigation bar, and then click the previous page to show the new record you entered.

The beginning of the Pecan Pie record is now visible. The record continues on the next page.

l. Click **Close Print Preview** in the Close Preview group.

m. Close the Products form.

You need to understand how Access stores data. After you add the new products using a form, you verify that the products are also in the table. You also attempt to delete a record. Refer to Figure 13 as you complete Step 4.

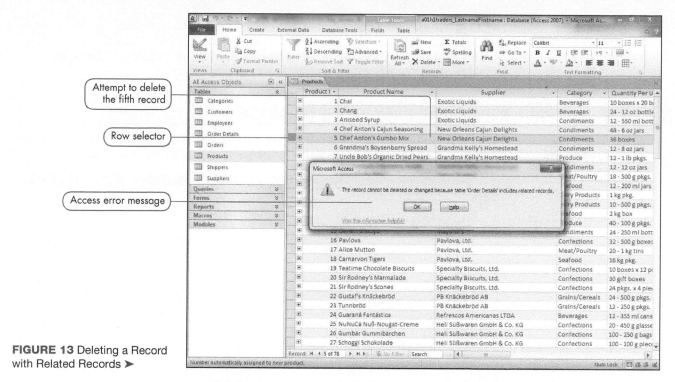

**FIGURE 13** Deleting a Record with Related Records ➤

a. Click the **Forms group** in the Navigation Pane to collapse it.

The list of available forms collapses.

b. Click the **Tables group** in the Navigation Pane to expand it.

The list of available tables is shown. You need to prove that the change you made to the Products form will appear in the Products table.

c. Double-click the **Products table** to open it.

d. Click **Last record** in the navigation bar.

The Pecan Pie record you entered in the Products form is listed as the last record in the Products table. The Products form was created from the Products table. Your newly created record, Pecan Pie, is stored in the Products table even though you added it in the form.

e. Navigate to the fifth record in the table, *Chef Anton's Gumbo Mix*.

f. Use the horizontal scroll bar to scroll right until you see the Discontinued field.

The check mark in the Discontinued check box tells you that this product has been discontinued.

g. Click the **row selector box** to the left of the fifth record.

The row highlights with a gold-colored border.

h. Click **Delete** in the Records group. Read the error message.

An error message appears. It tells you that you cannot delete this record because the table Order Details has related records. (Customers ordered this product in the past.) Even though the product is now discontinued and none of it is in stock, it cannot be deleted from the Products table because related records exist in the Order Details table.

i. Click **OK**.

**j.** Navigate to the last record. Click the **row selector box** to highlight the entire row.

**k.** Click **Delete** in the Records group. Read the warning.

A warning box appears. It tells you that this action cannot be undone. Although this product can be deleted because it was just entered and no orders were created for it, you do not want to delete the record.

**l.** Click **No**. You do not want to delete this record. Close the Products table.

> **TROUBLESHOOTING:** If you clicked Yes and deleted the record, return to Step 3i. Reenter the information for this record. You will need it later in the lesson.

## STEP 5 ▷ COMPACT, REPAIR, AND BACK UP THE DATABASE

You will protect the Northwind Traders database by using the two built-in Access utilities—Compact and Repair and Backup. Refer to Figure 14 as you complete Step 5.

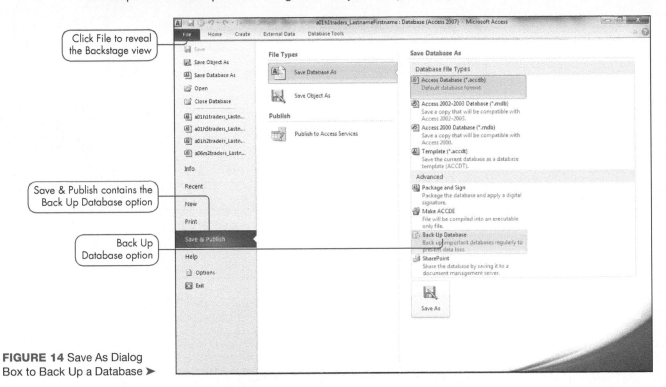

**FIGURE 14** Save As Dialog Box to Back Up a Database ➤

**a.** Click the **File tab**.

The File tab reveals the Backstage view, which gives you access to a variety of database tools: Compact and Repair, Back Up Database, and Print, to name a few.

**b.** Click **Compact & Repair Database**.

Databases tend to get larger as you use them. This feature acts as a defragmenter and eliminates wasted space. Before running this feature, close any open objects in the database.

**c.** Click the **File tab**, click **Save & Publish**, and then double-click **Back Up Database**.

The Save As dialog box opens. Verify the Save in folder is correct before saving. The backup utility assigns a default name by adding a date to your file name.

**d.** Click **Save** to accept the default backup file name with today's date.

You just created a backup of the database after completing Hands-On Exercise 1. The original database *a01h1traders_LastnameFirstname* remains onscreen.

**e.** Keep the database onscreen if you plan to continue with Hands-On Exercise 2. If not, close the database and exit Access.

Introduction to Access

# Filters, Sorts, and Access Versus Excel

Access provides you with many tools that you can use to identify and extract only the data needed at the moment. For example, you might need to know which suppliers are located in New Orleans or which customers have outstanding orders that were placed in the last seven days. You might use that information to identify possible disruptions to product deliveries or customers who may need a telephone call to let them know the status of their orders. Both Access and Excel contain powerful tools that enable you to extract the information you need and arrange it in a way that makes it easy to analyze. An important part of becoming a proficient Office user is learning how to use these tools to accomplish a task.

> Access provides you with many tools that you can use to identify and extract only the data needed at the moment.

In this section, you will learn how to isolate records in a table based on certain criteria. You will also examine the strengths of Access and Excel in more detail so you can better determine when to use which application to complete a given task.

## Creating Filters

In the first Hands-On Exercise, you added Pecan Pie to the Products table with a category of *Confections*, but you also saw many other products. Suppose you wanted a list of all of the products in the Confections category. To do this, you could open the Products table in Datasheet view and create a filter. A *filter* displays a subset of records based on specified criteria. A filter works with either a table's datasheet or a query's datasheet. You can use filters to analyze data quickly. Applying a filter does not delete any records; filters only *hide* records that do not match the criteria. Two types of filters are discussed in this section: Filter by Selection and Filter by Form. Filter by Selection selects only the records that match prese-lected single criteria, whereas Filter by Form offers a more versatile way to select a subset of records, including the use of comparison operators.

> A **filter** displays a subset of records based on specified criteria.

Figure 15 displays the Customers table with 29 records. The records in the table are displayed in sequence according to the CustomerID, which is also the primary key (the field or combination of fields that uniquely identifies a record). The navigation bar at the bottom indicates that the active record is the first row in the table. Many times you will only want to see a subset of the customer records—you can accomplish this using a filter. For example, suppose you want a list of all customers whose Job Title is *Owner*.

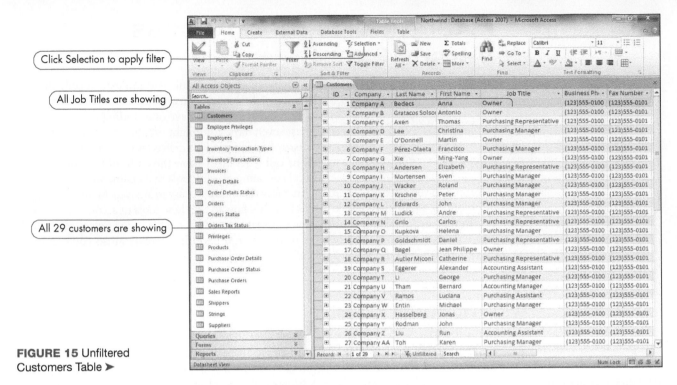

Click Selection to apply filter

All Job Titles are showing

All 29 customers are showing

FIGURE 15 Unfiltered
Customers Table ➤

Figure 16 displays a filtered view of the Customers table, showing records with Job Title of *Owner*. The navigation bar shows that this is a filtered list containing 6 records matching the criteria. (The Customers table still contains the original 29 records, but only 6 records are visible with the filter applied.)

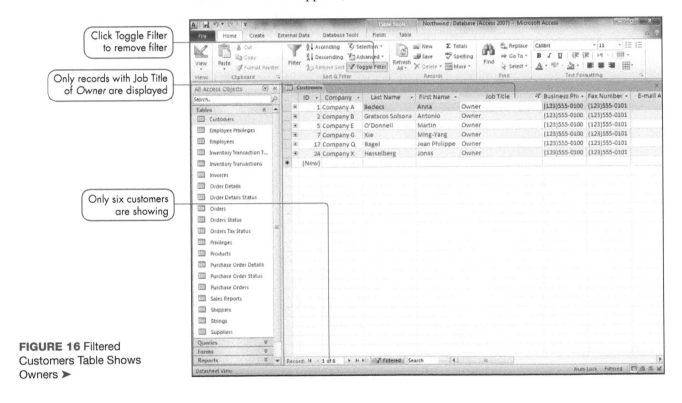

Click Toggle Filter to remove filter

Only records with Job Title of *Owner* are displayed

Only six customers are showing

FIGURE 16 Filtered
Customers Table Shows
Owners ➤

**Filter by Selection** displays only the records that match the selected criteria.

*Filter by Selection* displays only the records that match the selected criteria. The easiest way to implement a Filter by Selection is as follows:

1. Click in any field that contains the criterion on which you want to filter.
2. Click Filter by Selection in the Sort & Filter group.
3. Select Equals "criterion" from the list of options.

Only the records that match the selected criterion will be displayed.

Figure 17 illustrates another, more versatile, way to apply a filter, using Filter by Form. *Filter by Form* displays table records based on multiple criteria. Filter by Form enables the user to apply the logical operators AND and OR. For the AND operator, a record is included in the results if all the criteria are true; for the OR operator, a record is included if at least one criterion is true. Another advantage of the Filter by Form function is that you can use a comparison operator. A *comparison operator* is used to evaluate the relationship between two quantities to determine if they are equal or not equal; and, if they are not equal, a comparison operator determines which one is greater than the other. Comparison operator symbols include: equal (=), not equal (<>), greater than (>), less than (<), greater than or equal to (>=), and less than or equal to (<=). For example, you can use a comparison operator to select products with an inventory level greater than 30 (>30). Filter by Selection, on the other hand, requires you to specify criteria equal to an existing value. Figure 17 shows a Filter by Form designed to select Products with a reorder level of more than 10 units.

**Filter by Form** displays table records based on multiple criteria. Filter by Form enables the user to apply the logical operators AND and OR.

A **comparison operator** is used to evaluate the relationship between two quantities to determine if they are equal or not equal; and, if they are not equal, a comparison operator determines which one is greater than the other.

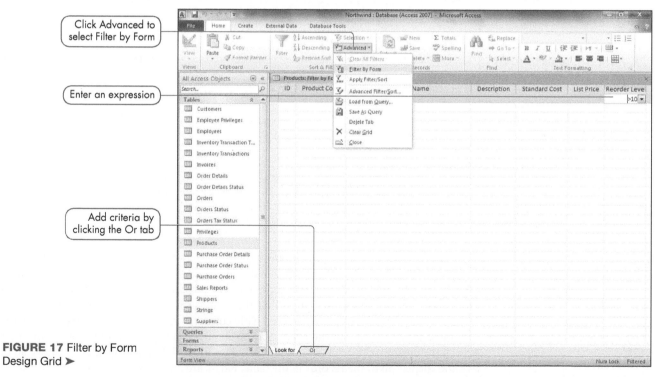

Click Advanced to select Filter by Form

Enter an expression

Add criteria by clicking the Or tab

**FIGURE 17** Filter by Form Design Grid ➤

To apply an OR comparison operator to a Filter by Form, click the Or tab at the bottom of the window. For example, you could add the criterion *Baked Goods & Mixes* to the category field, which would show all the Products with a reorder level of more than 10 units and all

Products in the Baked Goods & Mixes category. (This OR example is not shown in Figure 17.) Filters enable you to obtain information from a database quickly without creating a query or a report.

## Sorting Table Data on One or More Fields

A **sort** lists records in a specific sequence, such as ascending by last name or by ascending EmployeeID.

**Ascending** sorts a list of text data in alphabetical order or a numeric list in lowest to highest order.

**Descending** sorts a list of text data in reverse alphabetical order or a numeric list in highest to lowest order.

You can also change the order of the information by sorting by one or more fields. A **sort** lists records in a specific sequence, such as alphabetically by last name or by ascending EmployeeID.

To sort a table, do the following:

1. Click in the field that you want to use to sort the records.
2. Click Ascending or Descending in the Sort & Filter group.

**Ascending** sorts a list of text data in alphabetical order or a numeric list in lowest to highest order. **Descending** sorts a list of text data in reverse alphabetical order or a numeric list in highest to lowest order. Figure 18 shows the Customers table sorted in ascending order by state. You may apply both filters and sorts to tables or query results.

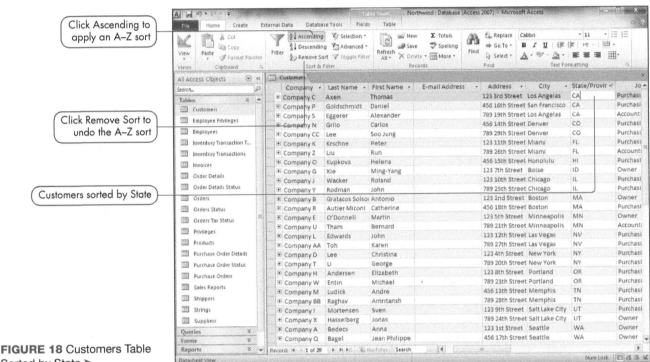

FIGURE 18 Customers Table Sorted by State ➤

The operations can be done in any order; that is, you can filter a table to show only selected records, and then sort the filtered table to display the records in a certain order. Conversely, you can sort a table first and then apply a filter. It does not matter which operation is performed first. You can also filter the table further by applying a second, third, or more criteria; for example, click in a Job Title cell containing *Owner*, and apply a Filter by Selection. Then click *WA* in the State column, and apply a second Filter by Selection to display all the customers from WA. You can also click Toggle Filter at any time to remove all filters and display all of the records in the table. Filters are a temporary method for examining table data. If you close the filtered table and then reopen it, the filter will be removed, and all of the records will be restored.

# Knowing When to Use Access or Excel to Manage Data

You are probably familiar with working in an Excel spreadsheet. You type the column headings, then enter the data, perhaps add a formula or two, then add totals to the bottom. Once the data has been entered, you can apply a filter, or sort the data, or start all over—similar to what we learned to do in Access with filters. It is true that you can accomplish many of the same tasks using either Excel or Access. In this section, you will learn how to decide whether to use Access or Excel. Although the two programs have much in common, they each have distinct advantages. How do you choose whether to use Access or Excel? The choice you make may ultimately depend on how well you know Access. Users who only know Excel are more likely to use a spreadsheet even if a database would be better. When database features are used in Excel, they are generally used on data that is in one table. When the data is better suited to be on two or more tables, then using Access is preferable. Learning how to use Access will be beneficial to you since it will enable you to work more efficiently with large groups of data. Ideally, the type of data and the type of functionality you require should determine which program will work best.

## Select the Software to Use

A contact list (e.g., name, address, phone number) created in Excel may serve your needs just fine at first. Each time you meet a new contact, you can add another row to the bottom of your worksheet, as shown in Figure 19. You can sort the list by last name for easier look-up of names. In Excel, you can easily move an entire column, insert a new column, or copy and paste data from one cell to another. This is the "ease of use" characteristic of Excel.

If you needed to expand the information in Excel, to keep track of each time you contacted someone on your contact list, for example, you may need an additional worksheet. This additional sheet would only list the contacts who you contacted and some information about the nature of the contact. Which contact was it? When was the contact made? Was it a phone contact or a face-to-face meeting? As you track these entries, your worksheet will contain a reference to the first worksheet using the Contact Name. As the quantity and complexity of the data increase, the need to organize your data logically also increases.

A **relationship** is a connection between two tables using a common field.

Access provides built-in tools to help organize data better than Excel. One tool that helps Access organize data is the ability to create relationships between tables. A *relationship* is a connection between two tables using a common field. The benefit of a relationship is to efficiently combine data from related tables for the purpose of creating queries, forms, and reports. Relationships are the reason why Access is referred to as a relational database. For example, assume you want to create a Contact Management Database. You would first create two tables to hold contact names and contact notes. You would then create a relationship between the Contact Name table and the Contact Notes table using ContactID as the common field. To create a Contacts Form or Query, you would take advantage of the two related tables.

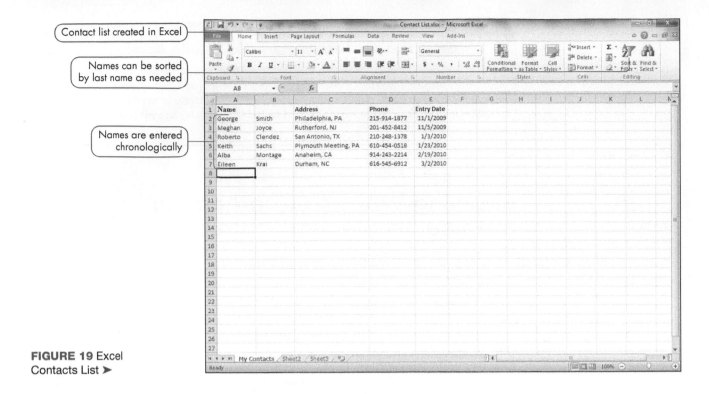

Contact list created in Excel

Names can be sorted by last name as needed

Names are entered chronologically

**FIGURE 19** Excel Contacts List ➤

## Use Access

You should use Access to manage data when you:

- Require multiple related tables to store your data.
- Have a large amount of data.
- Need to connect to and retrieve data from external databases, such as Microsoft SQL Server.
- Need to group, sort, and total data based on various parameters.
- Have an application that requires multiple users to connect to one data source at the same time.

## Use Excel

You should use Excel to manage data when you:

- Only need one worksheet to handle all of your data (i.e., you do not need multiple worksheets).
- Have mostly numeric data—for example, you need to maintain an expense statement.
- Require subtotals and totals in your worksheet.
- Want to primarily run a series of "what if" scenarios on your data.
- Need to create complex charts and/or graphs.

In the next Hands-On Exercise, you will create and apply filters, create comparison operator expressions using Filter by Form, and sort records in the Datasheet view of the Customers table.

# HANDS-ON EXERCISES

## 2 Filters, Sorts, and Access Versus Excel

The sales managers at Northwind Traders need quick answers to their questions about customer orders. You use the Access database to filter tables to answer most of these questions. Before printing your results, make sure you sort the records based on the managers' needs.

**Skills covered:** Use Filter by Selection with an Equal Condition • Use Filter by Selection with a Contains Condition • Use Filter by Form with a Comparison Operator • Sort a Table

### STEP 1 ▶ USE FILTER BY SELECTION WITH AN EQUAL CONDITION

As you continue to learn about the Northwind Traders database, you are expected to provide answers to questions about the customers and products. In this exercise, you use filters to find customers who live in London. Refer to Figure 20 as you complete Step 1.

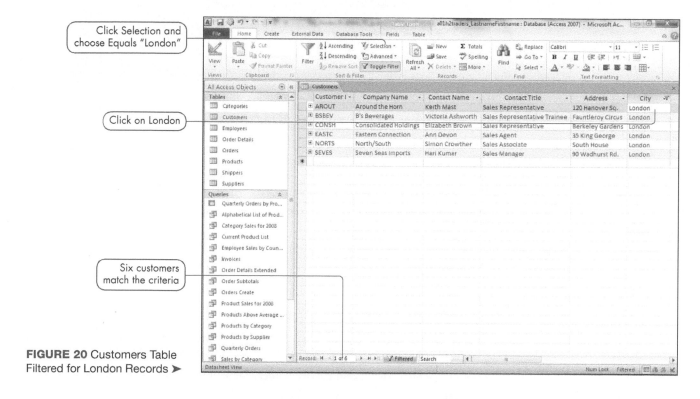

**FIGURE 20** Customers Table Filtered for London Records ➤

a. Open *a01h1traders_LastnameFirstname* if you closed it at the end of Hands-On Exercise 1. Click the **File tab**, click **Save Database As**, and then type **a01h2traders_LastnameFirstname**, changing *h1* to *h2*. Click **Save**.

> **TROUBLESHOOTING:** If you make any major mistakes in this exercise, you can delete the *a01h2traders_LastnameFirstname* file, repeat step a above, and then start the exercise over.

b. Open the Customers table, navigate to record four, and then replace *Thomas Hardy* with your name in the Contact Name field.

c. Scroll right until the City field is visible. The fourth record has a value of *London* in the City field. Click on the field to select it.

The word *London* has a gold-colored border around it to let you know that it is active.

d. Click **Selection** in the Sort & Filter group.

e. Choose **Equals "London"** from the menu.

Six records should be displayed.

f. Click **Toggle Filter** in the Sort & Filter group to remove the filter.

g. Click **Toggle Filter** again to reset the filter. Leave the Customers table open for the next step.

## STEP 2 ▸ USE FILTER BY SELECTION WITH A CONTAINS CONDITION

At times, you need to print information for the Northwind managers. In this exercise, you print your results. Refer to Figure 21 as you complete Step 2.

Click Selection and choose Contains "Sales Representative"

Select *Sales Representative*

Three customers match the criteria

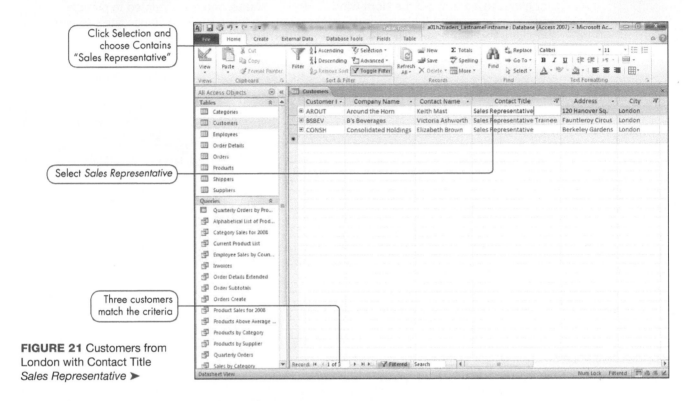

**FIGURE 21** Customers from London with Contact Title *Sales Representative* ➤

a. Click in any field in the Contact Title column that contains the value *Sales Representative*.

Sales Representative has a gold-colored border around it to let you know that it is activated.

b. Click **Selection** on the Sort & Filter group.

c. Click **Contains "Sales Representative"**.

You have applied a second layer of filtering to the customers in London. The second layer further restricts the display to only those customers who have the words *Sales Representative* contained in their titles.

d. Scroll left until you see your name. Compare your results to those shown in Figure 21.

e. Click **Toggle Filter** in the Sort & Filter group to remove the filters.

f. Close the Customers table. Click **No** if a dialog box asks if you want to save the design changes to the Customers table.

At Northwind Traders, you are asked to provide a list of records that do not match just one set of criteria. Use a Filter by Form to provide the information when two or more criteria are needed. Refer to Figure 22 as you complete Step 3.

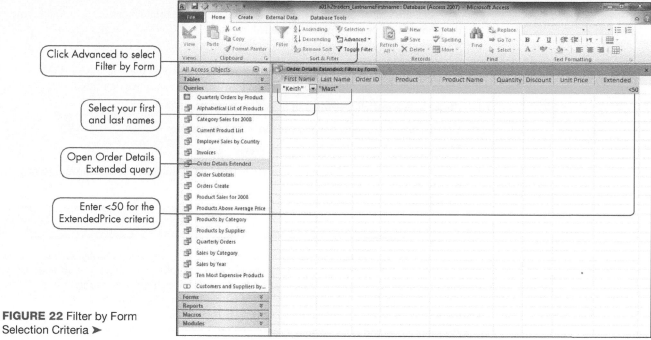

*Click Advanced to select Filter by Form*

*Select your first and last names*

*Open Order Details Extended query*

*Enter <50 for the ExtendedPrice criteria*

**FIGURE 22** Filter by Form Selection Criteria ➤

a. Click the **Tables group** in the Navigation Pane to collapse the listed tables.

b. Click the **Queries group** in the Navigation Pane to expand the lists of available queries.

c. Locate and double-click the **Order Details Extended query** to open it.

This query contains information about orders. It has fields containing information about the salesperson, the Order ID, the product name, the unit price, quantity ordered, the discount given, and an extended price. The extended price is a field used to total order information.

d. Click **Advanced** in the Sort & Filter group.

While you are applying a Filter by Form to a query, you can use the same process to apply a Filter by Form to a table.

e. Select **Filter by Form** from the list.

All of the records are now hidden, and you only see field names with an arrow in the first field. Click on the other fields, and an arrow appears.

f. Click in the first row under the First Name field.

An arrow appears at the right of the box.

g. Click the **First Name arrow**.

A list of all available first names appears. Your name should be on the list. Figure 22 shows Keith Mast, which replaced Margaret Peacock in Hands-On Exercise 1.

> **TROUBLESHOOTING:** If you do not see your name and you do see Margaret on the list, you probably skipped Steps 3c and 3d in Hands-On Exercise 1. Close the query without saving changes, turn back to the first Hands-On Exercise, and rework it, making sure not to omit any steps. Then you can return to this spot and work the remainder of this Hands-On Exercise.

h. Select your first name from the list.

i. Click in the first row under the Last Name field to reveal the arrow. Locate and select your last name by clicking it.

j. Scroll right until you see the Extended Price field. Click in the first row under the Extended Price field, and then type **<50**.

This will select all of the items that you ordered where the total was under $50. You ignore the arrow and type the expression needed.

k. Click **Toggle Filter** in the Sort & Filter group.

You have specified which records to include and have executed the filtering by clicking Toggle Filter. You should have 31 records that match the criteria you specified.

l. Click the **File tab**, click **Print**, and then click **Print Preview**.

You instructed Access to preview the filtered query results.

m. Click **Close Print Preview** in the Print Preview group.

n. Close the Order Details Extended query. Click **No** if a dialog box asks if you want to save your changes.

---

**TIP** Deleting Filter by Form Criterion

While working with Filter by Selection or Filter by Form, you may inadvertently save a filter. To view a saved filter, open the table or query that you suspect may have a saved filter. Click Advanced in the Sort & Filter group, and then click Filter by Form. If criteria appear in the form, then a filter has been saved. To delete a saved filter, click Advanced, and then click Clear All Filters. Close and save the table or query.

---

**STEP 4 ▶ SORT A TABLE**

Your boss at Northwind is happy with your work; however, he would like some of the information to appear in a different order. Sort the records in the Customers table using the boss's new criteria. Refer to Figure 23 as you complete Step 4.

FIGURE 23 Customers Table Sorted by Country and Then City ▶

a. Click the **Queries group** in the Navigation Pane to collapse the listed queries.

b. Click the **Tables group** in the Navigation Pane to expand the lists of available tables.

c. Locate and double-click the **Customers table** to open it.

This table contains information about customers. It is sorted in ascending order by the Customer ID field. Because this field contains text, the table is sorted in alphabetical order.

d. Click any value in the Customer ID field. Click **Descending** in the Sort & Filter group on the Home tab.

Sorting in descending order on a character field produces a reverse alphabetical order.

e. Scroll right until you can see both the Country and City fields.

If you close the Navigation Pane, locating the fields on the far right will be easier.

f. Click the **Country column heading**.

The entire column is selected.

g. Click the **Country column heading** again, and hold down the **left mouse button**.

A thick dark blue line displays on the left edge of the Country field column.

h. Check to make sure that you see the thick blue line. Drag the **Country field** to the left until the thick black line moves between the City and Region fields. Release the mouse and the Country field position moves to the right of the City field.

You moved the Country field next to the City field so you can easily sort the table based on both fields.

i. Click any city name in the City field, and then click **Ascending** in the Sort & Filter group.

j. Click any country name in the Country field, and then click **Ascending**.

The countries are sorted in alphabetical order. The cities within each country also are sorted alphabetically. For example, the customer in Graz, Austria, is listed before the customer in Salzburg, Austria.

k. Close the Customers table. Do not save the changes.

l. Click the **File tab**, and then click **Compact & Repair Database**.

m. Click the **File tab**, click **Save & Publish**, and then double-click **Back Up Database**. Accept *a01h2traders_LastnameFirstname_date* as the file name, and then click **Save**.

You just created a backup of the database after completing Hands-On Exercise 2. The *a01h2traders_LastnameFirstname* database remains onscreen.

n. Keep the database onscreen if you plan to continue with Hands-On Exercise 3. If not, close the database and exit Access.

# Relational Database

Access is known as a relational database management system (RDBMS).

Access is known as a **relational database management system** (RDBMS); using an RDBMS, you can manage groups of data (tables) and then set rules (relationships) between tables.

In the previous section, we compared Excel worksheets to Access relational databases. Access has the ability to create relationships between two tables, whereas Excel does not. Access is known as a ***relational database management system*** (RDBMS); using an RDBMS, you can manage groups of data (tables) and then set rules (relationships) between tables. When relational databases are designed properly, users can easily combine data from multiple tables to create queries, forms, and reports.

Good database design begins with grouping data into the correct tables. This practice, known as normalization, will take time to learn, but over time you will begin to understand the fundamentals. The design of a relational database management system is illustrated in Figure 24, which shows the table design of the Northwind Traders database. The tables have been created, the field names have been added, and the data types have been set. The diagram also shows the relationships that were created between tables using join lines. ***Join lines*** enable

**Join lines** enable you to create a relationship between two tables using a common field.

you to create a relationship between two tables using a common field. When relationships are established, three options are available to further dictate how Access will manage the relationship: Enforce referential integrity, Cascade update related fields, and Cascade delete related records. Later in this section, you will learn more about enforcing referential integrity. Using the enforce referential integrity option will help keep invalid data out of your database. Examples of invalid data include (1) entering an order for a customer that does not exist, (2) tagging a new product with a nonexistent category, and (3) entering a person's address with an invalid state abbreviation.

Figure 24 shows the join lines between related tables as a series of lines connecting the common fields. For example, the Suppliers table is joined to the Products table using the common field SupplierID.

When the database is set up properly, the users of the data can be confident that searching through the Customers table will produce accurate results about their order history or their outstanding invoices.

In this section, you will explore relationships between tables and learn about the power of relational data.

## Using the Relationships Window

A **foreign key** is a field in one table that is also the primary key of another table.

The relationships in a database are represented by the lines between the tables, as shown in Figure 24. Relationships are set in the Relationships window by the database developer after the tables have been created but before any sample data is entered. The most common method of connecting two tables is to connect the primary key from one table to the foreign key of another. A ***foreign key*** is a field in one table that is also the primary key of another table. For example, the SupplierID (primary key) in the Suppliers table is joined to the SupplierID (foreign key) in the Products table. As you learned before, the primary key is a field that uniquely identifies each record in a table.

To create a relationship between two tables, follow these guidelines:

1. Click Relationships in the Relationships group on the Database Tools tab.
2. Add the two tables that you want to join together to the Relationships window.
3. Drag the common field (e.g., SupplierID) from the primary table (e.g., Suppliers) onto the common field (e.g., SupplierID) of the related table (e.g., Products).
4. The data types of the common fields must be the same.
5. Check the Enforce Referential Integrity check box.
6. Close the Relationships window.

## Enforce Referential Integrity

**Enforce referential integrity** ensures that data cannot be entered into a related table unless it first exists in the primary table.

Enforce referential integrity is one of the three options you can select when setting a table relationship. When *enforce referential integrity* is checked, Access ensures that data cannot be entered into a related table unless it first exists in the primary table. For example, in Figure 24, you cannot enter an order into the Order table for a Customer with CustomerID 9308 if Customer 9308 has not been entered in the Customer table. This rule ensures the integrity of the data in the database and improves overall data accuracy. Referential integrity also prohibits users from deleting a record in one table if it has records in related tables (i.e., you cannot delete Customer 8819 if Customer 8819 has any orders).

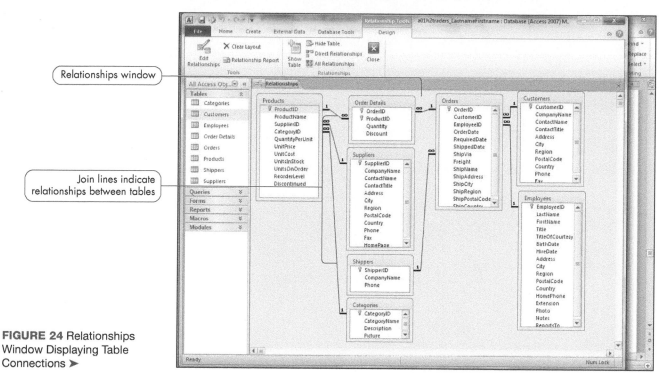

Relationships window

Join lines indicate relationships between tables

**FIGURE 24** Relationships Window Displaying Table Connections ➤

## Create Sample Data

When learning database skills, starting with a smaller set of sample data prior to entering all company records can be helpful.

When learning database skills, starting with a smaller set of sample data prior to entering all company records can be helpful. The same design principles apply regardless of the number of records. A small amount of data gives you the ability to check the tables and quickly see if your results are correct. Even though the data amounts are small, as you test the database tables and relationships, the results will prove useful as you work with larger data sets.

# Understanding Relational Power

In the previous section, you learned that you should use Access when you have relational data. Access derives power from multiple tables and the relationships between those tables. This type of database is illustrated in Figure 24. This diagram describes the database structure of the Northwind Traders company. If you examine some of the connections, you will see that the EmployeeID is a foreign key in the Orders table. That means you can produce a report displaying all orders for a customer and the employee name (from the Employees table) that entered the order. The Orders table is joined to the Order Details table where the OrderID is the common field. The Products table is joined to the Order Details table where ProductID is the common field. These table connections enable you to query (ask) the database for information stored in multiple tables. This feature gives the manager the ability to ask questions like "How many different beverages were shipped last week?" and "What was the total revenue generated from seafood orders last year?"

Suppose a customer called to complain that his orders were arriving late. Because the ShipperID is a foreign key field in the Orders table, you could query the database to find out which shipper delivered that customer's merchandise. Are the other orders also late? Does the firm need to reconsider its shipping options? The design of a relational database enables us to extract information from multiple tables in a single query or report.

In the next Hands-On Exercise, you will examine the Relationships window, create a filter in a query and a report, and remove a filter.

# HANDS-ON EXERCISES

## 3 Relational Database

You continue to use the Access database to filter tables and provide answers to the Northwind employees' questions. When the same question is repeated by several employees, you look for a way to save your filter by form specifications.

**Skills covered:** Use the Relationships Window • Filter a Query • Use Filter by Form with a Comparison Operator and Reapply a Saved Filter • Filter a Report • Remove a Filter

---

### STEP 1 ▶ USE THE RELATIONSHIPS WINDOW

In this exercise, you examine the relationships established in the Northwind Traders database to learn more about the overall design of the database. Refer to Figure 25 as you complete Step 1.

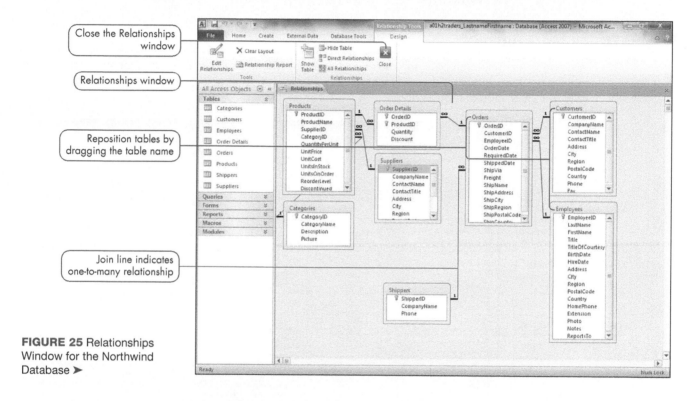

**FIGURE 25** Relationships Window for the Northwind Database ➤

**a.** Open *a01h2traders_LastnameFirstname* if you closed it at the end of Hands-On Exercise 2. Click the **File tab**, click **Save Database As**, and then type **a01h3traders_LastnameFirstname**, changing *h2* to *h3*. Click **Save**.

> **TROUBLESHOOTING:** If you make any major mistakes in this exercise, you can delete the *a01h3traders_LastnameFirstname* file, repeat step a above, and then start the exercise over.

**b.** Click the **Database Tools tab**, and then click **Relationships** in the Relationships group.

Examine the relationships that connect the various tables. For example, the Products table is connected to the Suppliers, Categories, and Order Details tables.

Hands-On Exercises • **Access 2010**

413

**c.** Click **Show Table** in the Relationships group on the Relationship Tools Design tab.

The Show Table dialog box opens. It tells you that eight tables are available in the database. If you look in the Relationships window, you will see that all eight tables are in the relationships diagram.

**d.** Click the **Queries tab** in the Show Table dialog box.

You could add all of the queries to the Relationships window. Things might become cluttered, but you could tell at a glance where the queries get their information.

**e.** Close the Show Table dialog box.

**f.** Click **All Access Objects** on the Navigation Pane.

**g.** Select **Tables and Related Views**.

You now see each table and all the queries, forms, and reports that are based on each table. If a query is created using more than one table, it appears multiple times in the Navigation Pane.

**h.** Close the Relationships window. Click **All Tables** on the Navigation Pane, and then select **Object Type**.

---

**STEP 2 ▶ FILTER A QUERY**

You notice a connection between tables and queries. Whenever you make a change in the query, the table is updated as well. Run a few tests on the Northwind database to confirm your findings. Refer to Figure 26 as you complete Step 2.

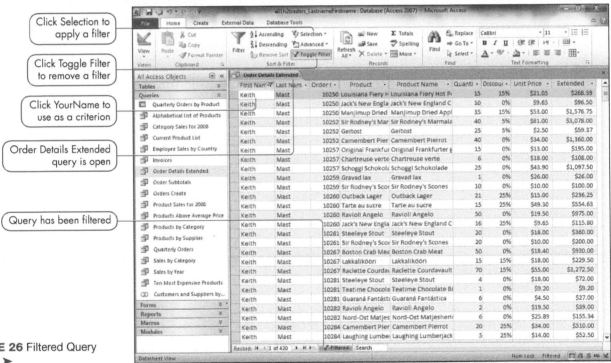

**FIGURE 26** Filtered Query Results ➤

**a.** Collapse the Tables group, and expand the Queries group, and then locate and double-click the **Order Details Extended query**.

**b.** Find an occurrence of your last name, and then click it to select it.

**c.** Click **Selection** in the Sort & Filter group. Select **Equals "YourName"** from the selection menu.

The query results are reduced to 420 records.

**d.** Click **Toggle Filter** in the Sort & Filter group to remove the filter.

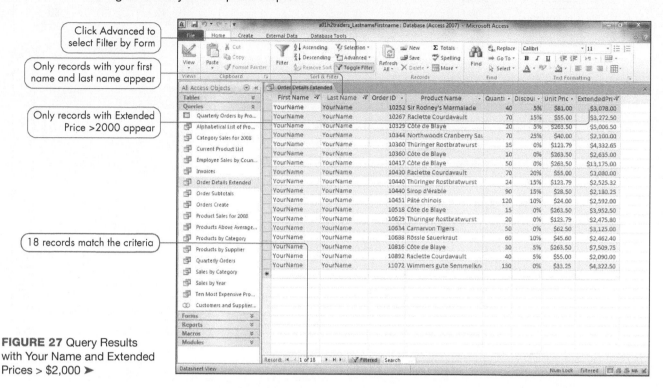

**STEP 3 ▶ USE FILTER BY FORM WITH A COMPARISON OPERATOR AND REAPPLY A SAVED FILTER**

Use Filter by Form to solve more complex questions about the Northwind data. After you retrieve the records, you save the Filter by Form specifications so you can reapply the filter later. Refer to Figure 27 as you complete Step 3.

Annotations on figure:
- Click Advanced to select Filter by Form
- Only records with your first name and last name appear
- Only records with Extended Price >2000 appear
- 18 records match the criteria

**FIGURE 27** Query Results with Your Name and Extended Prices > $2,000 ▶

a. Click **Advanced** in the Sort & Filter group.

b. Select **Filter By Form** from the list.

   Because Access will save the last filter you created, the Filter by Form design sheet opens with one criterion already filled in. Your name displays in the selection box under the Last Name field.

c. Scroll right (or press **Tab**) until the Extended Price field is visible. Click the first row in the Extended Price field.

d. Type **>2000**.

   The Extended Price field shows the purchased amount for each item ordered. If an item sold for $15 and a customer ordered 10, the Extended Price would display $150.

e. Click **Toggle Filter** in the Sort & Filter group. Examine the filtered results.

   Your comparison operator instruction, >2000, identified 18 items ordered where the extended price exceeded $2,000.

f. Close the Order Details Extended query by clicking the **Close button**. Answer **Yes** when asked *Do you want to save changes?*.

g. Open the Order Details Extended query again.

   The filter disengages when you close and reopen the object. However, the filter has been stored with the query. You may reapply the filter at any time by clicking the Toggle Filter command (until the next filter replaces the current one).

h. Click **Toggle Filter** in the Sort & Filter group.

i. Compare your results to Figure 27. If your results are correct, close and save the query.

Hands-On Exercises • Access 2010

415

You wonder if one report can serve several purposes. You discover that a report can be customized using the Filter by Selection feature. Refer to Figure 28 as you complete Step 4.

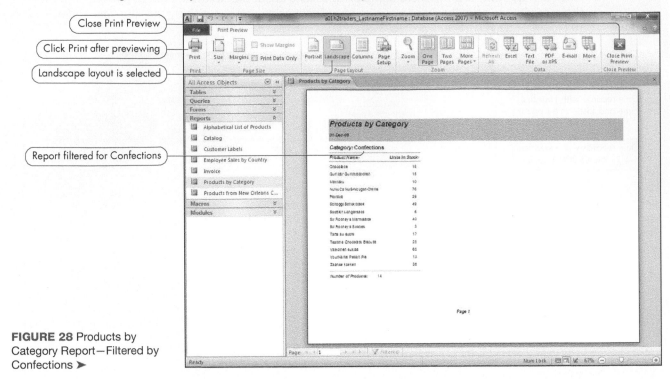

Close Print Preview

Click Print after previewing

Landscape layout is selected

Report filtered for Confections

**FIGURE 28** Products by Category Report—Filtered by Confections ➤

a. Click the **Queries group** in the Navigation Pane to collapse the listed queries, and then click the **Reports group** in the Navigation Pane to expand the list of available reports.

b. Open the Products by Category report located in the Reports group on the Navigation Pane. You may need to scroll down to locate it.

   The report should open in Print Preview with a gray title background highlighting the report title. The Print Preview displays the report exactly as it will print. This report was formatted to display in three columns.

> **TROUBLESHOOTING:** If you do not see the gray title background and three columns, you probably opened the wrong object. The database also contains a Product by Category query. It is the source for the Products by Category report. Make sure you open the report (shown with the green report icon) and not the query. Close the query and open the report.

c. Examine the Confections category products. You should see *Your Name Pecan Pie*.

   You created this product by entering data in a form in Hands-On Exercise 1. You later discovered that changes made to a form affect the related table. Now you see that other related objects also change when the source data changes.

d. Right-click the **Products by Category tab**, and then select **Report View** from the shortcut menu.

   The Report view displays the information a little differently. It no longer shows three columns. If you clicked the Print command while in Report view, the columns would print even though you do not see them. The Report view permits limited data interaction (for example, filtering).

e. Scroll down in the report until you see the title *Category: Confections*. Right-click the word *Confections* in the title. Select **Equals "Confections"** from the shortcut menu.

   The report now displays only *Confections*.

f. Right-click the **Products by Category tab**, and then select **Print Preview** from the shortcut menu.

   If you need to print a report, always view the report in Print Preview prior to printing.

g. Click **Close Print Preview** in the Close Preview group.

h. Save and close the report.

The next time the report opens in Report view, it will not be filtered. However, since the filter was saved, the filter can be reapplied by clicking Toggle Filter in the Sort & Filter group.

**STEP 5** ▶ REMOVE A FILTER

You notice that Access keeps asking you to save your changes when you close a table or query. You say "Yes" each time since you do not want to lose your data. Now you need to remove the filters that you saved. Refer to Figure 29 as you complete Step 5.

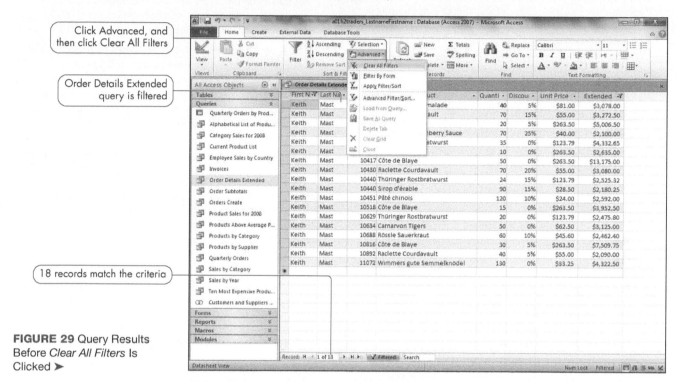

**FIGURE 29** Query Results Before *Clear All Filters* Is Clicked ▶

*Callouts in figure:*
- Click Advanced, and then click Clear All Filters
- Order Details Extended query is filtered
- 18 records match the criteria

a. Click the **Queries group** in the Navigation Pane to expand the list of available reports, then open the Order Details Extended query.

All 2,155 records should display in the query. You have unfiltered the data. However, the filter from the previous step still exists.

b. Click **Toggle Filter** in the Sort & Filter group.

You will see the same 18 filtered records that you created in Step 3.

c. Click **Advanced** in the Sort & Filter group, and then click **Clear All Filters**.

All 2,155 records are shown again.

d. Close the query. A dialog box opens asking if you want to save changes. Click **Yes**.

e. Open the Order Details Extended query.

f. Click **Advanced** in the Sort & Filter group.

g. Check to ensure the Clear All Filters option is dim, indicating there are no saved filters. Save and close the query.

h. Click the **File tab**, and then click **Compact & Repair Database**.

i. Click the **File tab**, and then click **Exit** (to exit Access).

j. Submit based on your instructor's directions.

After reading this chapter, you have accomplished the following objectives:

1. **Navigate among the objects in an Access database.** An Access database has six types of objects: tables, forms, queries, reports, macros, and modules. The Navigation Pane displays these objects and enables you to open an existing object or create new objects. You may arrange these by Object Type or by Tables and Related Views. The Tables and Related Views provides a listing of each table and all other objects in the database that use that table as a source. Thus, one query or report may appear several times, listed once under each table from which it derives information. Each table in the database is composed of records, and each record is in turn composed of fields. Every record in a given table has the same fields in the same order. The primary key is the field (or combination of fields) that makes every record in a table unique.

2. **Understand the difference between working in storage and memory.** Access automatically saves any changes in the current record as soon as you move to the next record or when you close the table. The Undo Current Record command reverses the changes to the previously saved record.

3. **Practice good database file management.** Because organizations depend on the data stored in databases, you need to implement good file management practices. For example, you need to develop an organized folder structure so you can easily save and retrieve your database files. You also need to develop a naming convention so it is easy to determine which file contains which data. As you learn new Access skills, it is recommended that you make a copy of the original database file and practice on the copy. This practice provides a recovery point in the event you make a fatal error.

4. **Back up, compact, and repair Access files.** Because using a database tends to increase the size of the file, you should always close any database objects and compact and repair the database prior to closing the file. Compact & Repair will reduce the size of the database by removing temporary objects and unclaimed space due to deleted objects. Adequate backup is essential when working with an Access database (or any other Office application). For increased security, a duplicate copy of the database can be created at the end of every session and stored externally (on a flash drive or an external hard drive).

5. **Create filters.** A filter is a set of criteria that is applied to a table to display a subset of the records in that table. Access lets you Filter by Selection or Filter by Form. The application of a filter does not remove the records from the table, but simply hides them temporarily from view.

6. **Sort table data on one or more fields.** The records in a table can be displayed in ascending or descending order by first selecting the appropriate column and clicking Ascending or Descending on the Home tab. The sort order will hold only if you save the table; otherwise the table will return to the original sort order when you close the table.

7. **Know when to use Access or Excel to manage data.** You should use Access to manage data when you require multiple related tables to store your data; have a large amount of data; need to connect to and retrieve data from external databases, such as Microsoft SQL Server; need to group, sort, and total data based on various parameters; and/or have an application that requires multiple users to connect to one data source at the same time. You should use Excel to manage data when you only need one worksheet to handle all of your data (i.e., you do not need multiple worksheets); have mostly numeric data—for example, if you need to maintain an expense statement; require subtotals and totals in your worksheet; want to primarily run a series of "what if" scenarios on your data; and/or need to create complex charts and/or graphs.

8. **Use the Relationships window.** Access enables you to create relationships between tables using the Relationships window. A *relationship* is a connection between two tables using a common field. The benefit of a relationship is to efficiently combine data from related tables for the purpose of creating queries, forms, and reports. Relationships are the reason why Access is referred to as a relational database.

9. **Understand relational power.** A relational database contains multiple tables and enables you to extract information from those tables in a single query. The related tables must be consistent with one another, a concept known as referential integrity. Once referential integrity is set, Access enforces data validation to protect the integrity of a database. No system, no matter how sophisticated, can produce valid output from invalid input. Changes made in one object can affect other related objects. Relationships are based on joining the primary key from one table to the foreign key of another table.

# KEY TERMS

Access speed

Backup

Compact and Repair

Comparison operator

Criterion

Database

Datasheet view

Design view

Enforce referential integrity

Field

Filter

Filter by Form

Filter by Selection

Foreign key

Form

Join lines

Navigation Pane

Object

Primary key

Query

Record

Relational database management system

Relationship

Report

Sort

Sort Ascending

Sort Descending

Table

1. Which sequence represents the hierarchy of terms, from smallest to largest?

   (a) Database, table, record, field

   (b) Field, record, table, database

   (c) Record, field, table, database

   (d) Field, record, database, table

2. You perform several edits in a table within an Access database. When should you execute the Save command?

   (a) Immediately after you add, edit, or delete a record

   (b) Each time you close a table or a query

   (c) Once at the end of a session

   (d) Records are saved automatically; the save command is not required.

3. You have opened an Access file. The left pane displays a table with forms, queries, and reports listed below a table name. Then another table and its objects display. You notice some of the object names are repeated under different tables. Why?

   (a) The Navigation Pane has been set to Object Type. The object names repeat because a query or report is frequently based on multiple tables.

   (b) The Navigation Pane has been set to Tables and Related Views. The object names repeat because a query or report is frequently based on multiple tables.

   (c) The Navigation Pane has been set to Most Recently Used View. The object names repeat because an object has been used frequently.

   (d) The database objects have been alphabetized.

4. Which of the following is not true of an Access database?

   (a) Every record in a table has the same fields as every other record.

   (b) Every table in a database contains the same number of records as every other table.

   (c) Text, Number, Autonumber, and Currency are valid data types.

   (d) Each table should contain a primary key; however, a primary key is not required.

5. Which of the following is true regarding the record selector box?

   (a) A pencil symbol indicates that the current record already has been saved.

   (b) An empty square indicates that the current record has not changed.

   (c) An asterisk indicates the first record in the table.

   (d) A gold border surrounds the active record.

6. You have finished an Access assignment and wish to turn it in to your instructor for evaluation. As you prepare to transfer the file, you discover that it has grown in size. It is now more than double the original size. You should:

   (a) Zip the database file prior to transmitting it to the instructor.

   (b) Turn it in; the size does not matter.

   (c) Compact and repair the database file prior to transmitting it to the instructor.

   (d) Delete extra tables or reports or fields to make the file smaller.

7. Which of the following will be accepted as valid during data entry?

   (a) Adding a record with a duplicate primary key

   (b) Entering text into a numeric field

   (c) Entering numbers into a text field

   (d) Omitting an entry in a required field

8. Which of the following conditions is available through Filter by Selection?

   (a) The AND condition

   (b) The OR condition

   (c) An Equals condition

   (d) A delete condition

9. You open an Access form and use it to update an address for customer Lee Fong. After closing the form, you later open a report that generates mailing labels. What will the address label for Lee Fong show?

   (a) The new address

   (b) The old address

   (c) The new address if you remembered to save the changes made to the form

   (d) The old address until you remember to update it in the report

10. You are looking at an Employees table in Datasheet view. You want the names sorted alphabetically by last name and then by first name—for example, Smith, Andrea is listed before Smith, William. To accomplish this, you must:

    (a) First sort ascending on first name and then on last name.

    (b) First sort descending on first name and then on last name.

    (c) First sort ascending on last name and then on first name.

    (d) First sort descending on last name and then on first name.

## 1 Member Rewards

The Prestige Hotel chain caters to upscale business travelers and provides state-of-the-art conference, meeting, and reception facilities. It prides itself on its international, four-star cuisine. Last year, it began a member rewards club to help the marketing department track the purchasing patterns of its most loyal customers. All of the hotel transactions are stored in the database. Your task is to update a customer record and identify the customers who had weddings in St. Paul. This exercise follows the same set of skills as used in Hands-On Exercise 1 in the chapter. Refer to Figure 30 as you complete this exercise.

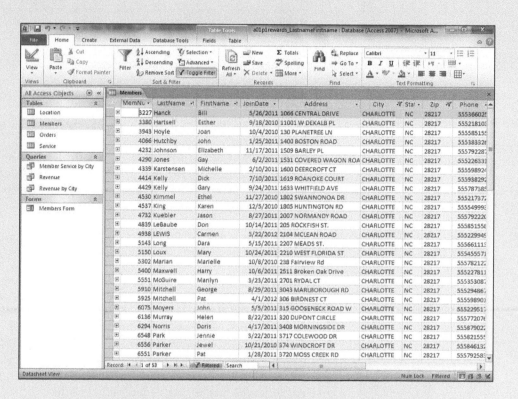

**FIGURE 30** Member Service by City—Filtered and Sorted ➤

a. Open the *a01p1rewards* file, and then save the database as **a01p1rewards_LastnameFirstname**.
b. Open the Members Form, and then click **New (blank) record** on the bottom navigation bar. (It has a yellow asterisk.)
c. Enter the information in the following table in the form. Press **Tab** to move to the next field.

| Field Name | Value |
|---|---|
| MemNumber | 4852 |
| LastName | your last name |
| FirstName | your first name |
| JoinDate | 7/30/2010 |
| Address | 124 West Elm, Apt 12 |

(*Continued*)

| Field Name | Value |
| --- | --- |
| City | your hometown |
| State | your state |
| Zip | your zip |
| Phone | **9995551234** |
| Email | your e-mail |
| OrderID | **9325** |
| ServiceDate | **8/1/2012** |
| ServiceID | **3** |
| NoInParty | **2** |
| Location | **20** |

d. Click the **Close (X) button** to close the form.

e. Double-click the **Members table** in the Navigation Pane. Use **Find** to verify your name is in the table.

f. In the Members table, find a record that displays *Charlotte* as the value in the City field. Click **Charlotte** to select that data value.

g. Click **Selection** in the Sort & Filter group on the Home tab. Select **Equals "Charlotte"**.

h. Find a record that displays *28217* as the value in the Zip field. Click **Zip** to select that data value.

i. Click **Selection** in the Sort & Filter Group, and then select **Equals "28217"**.

j. Right-click on any phone number field with a missing phone number, and then click **Does not Equal Blank**.

k. Click any value in the FirstName field. Click **Ascending** in the Sort & Filter group on the Home tab. Click any value in the LastName field. Click **Ascending** in the Sort & Filter group on the Home tab.

l. Click the **File tab**, click **Print**, and then click **Print Preview** to preview the sorted and filtered query.

m. Click **Close Print Preview** in the Close Preview group. Close the query (do not save when asked).

n. Click the **File tab**, and then click **Compact and Repair Database**.

o. Click the **File tab**, click **Save & Publish**, and then double-click **Back Up Database**.

p. Click **Save** to accept the default backup file name with today's date.

q. Click the **File tab**, and then click **Exit** (to exit Access).

r. Submit based on your instructor's directions.

## 2 Custom Coffee

The Custom Coffee Company provides coffee, tea, and snacks to offices in Miami. Custom Coffee also provides and maintains the equipment for brewing the beverages. The firm has a reputation for providing outstanding customer service. To improve customer service even further, the owner recently purchased an Access database to keep track of customers, orders, and products. This database will replace the Excel spreadsheets currently maintained by the office manager. The Excel spreadsheets are out of date and they do not allow for data validation while data is being entered. The company hired a temp to verify and enter all the Excel data into the Access database. This exercise follows the same set of skills as used in Hands-On Exercises 2 and 3 in the chapter. Refer to Figure 31 as you complete this exercise.

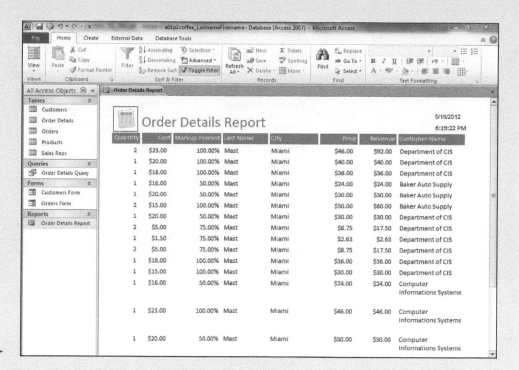

**FIGURE 31** Order Details Report Filtered for *YourName* ➤

a. Open the *a01p2coffee* file, and then save the database as **a01p2coffee_LastnameFirstname**.

b. Click the **Database Tools tab**, and then click **Relationships** in the Relationships group. Review the table relationships. Take note of the join line between the Customers and Orders Tables.

c. Click **Close** in the Relationships group.

d. Double-click the **Sales Reps table** in the Navigation Pane to open it. Replace *YourName* with your name in both the LastName and FirstName fields. Close the table by clicking the **Close (X) button** on the right side of the Sales Reps window.

e. Double-click the **Customers Form form** to open it. Click **New (blank) record** in the navigation bar at the bottom of the window. Add a new record by typing the following information; press **Tab** after each field.

| Customer Name: | *your name* **Company** |
|---|---|
| Contact: | your name |
| Email: | *your name@yahoo.com* |
| Address1: | 123 Main St |
| Address2: | Skip |
| City: | Miami |
| State: | FL |
| Zip Code: | 33133 |
| Phone: | (305) 555-1234 |
| Fax: | Skip |
| Service Start Date: | 1/17/2012 |
| Credit Rating: | A |
| Sales Rep ID: | 2 |

Notice the pencil in the top-left margin of the form window. This symbol indicates the new record has not been saved to storage. Press **Tab**. The pencil symbol disappears, and the new customer is automatically saved to the table.

f. Close the Customers Form form.

g. Double-click the **Orders Form form** to open it. Click **New (blank) record** in the navigation bar at the bottom of the window. Add a new record by typing the following information:

| | |
|---|---|
| **Customer ID:** | **15** (Access will convert it to *C0015*) |
| **Payment Type:** | **Cash** (select using the arrow) |
| **Comments:** | **Ship this order in 2 days** |
| **Product ID:** | **4** (Access will convert it to *P0004*) |
| **Quantity:** | **2** |

h. Add a second product using the following information:

| | |
|---|---|
| **Product ID:** | **6** (Access will convert it to *P0006*) |
| **Quantity:** | **1** |

i. Close the form (save changes if asked.)

j. Double-click the **Order Details Report** to open it in Report view. Right-click your name in the Last Name field, and then select **Equals "Your Name"** from the shortcut menu. Right-click **Miami** in the City field, and then select **Equals "Miami"** from the shortcut menu.

k. Click the **File tab**, click **Print**, and then click **Print Preview**.

l. Click **Close Print Preview** in the Close Preview group. Close the report.

m. Click the **File tab**, click **Info**, and then click **Compact and Repair Database**.

n. Click the **File tab**, click **Save & Publish**, and then double-click **Back Up Database**. Use the default backup file name.

o. Click the **File tab**, and then click **Exit** (to exit Access).

p. Submit based on your instructor's directions.

## 1 Real Estate

You are the senior partner in a large, independent real estate firm that specializes in home sales. Most of your time is spent supervising the agents who work for your firm. The firm has a database containing all of the information on the properties it has listed. You use the database to help evaluate the productivity of your team during weekly sales meetings you hold with each sales agent. Today, you are evaluating agent Angela Scott, who is responsible for the high-end properties at the firm. To prepare for your meeting, find all properties that are listed for over $1,000,000, and have four or more bedrooms. When you find these properties, sort the data by Subdivision then by list price in ascending order. Refer to Figure 32 as you complete this exercise.

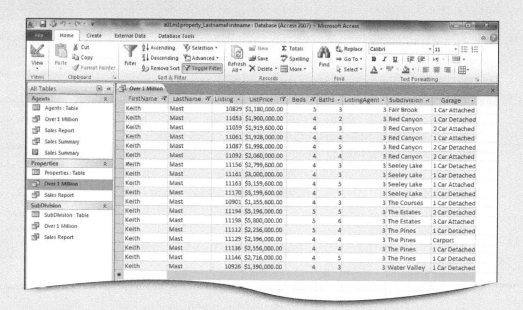

**FIGURE 32** Your Properties Listed for Over $1 Million ➤

a. Open the *a01m1property* file, and then save the database as **a01m1property_LastnameFirstname**.

b. Open the Agents table. Find and replace *YourName* with your name in the FirstName and LastName fields. Notice the pencil appears in the record selector box on the left while you type your name, then disappears once the record has been saved. Close the table.

c. Open the Over 1 Million query, and then create a filter by form on the data. Set the criteria to identify more than three bedrooms, a listing price over $1,000,000, and sales rep first and last names of your name.

d. Sort the filtered results by ascending **ListPrice** and by ascending **Subdivision**.

e. Save and close the query.

f. Compact and repair the database.

g. Back up the database. Use the default backup file name.

h. Exit Access.

i. Submit based on your instructor's directions.

The Association of Higher Education will host its National Conference on your campus next year. To facilitate the conference, the information technology department has replaced last year's Excel spreadsheets with an Access database containing information on the rooms, speakers, and sessions. Your assignment is to create a room itinerary that will list all of the sessions, dates, and times for each room. The list will be posted on the door of each room for the duration of the conference. Refer to Figure 33 as you complete this exercise.

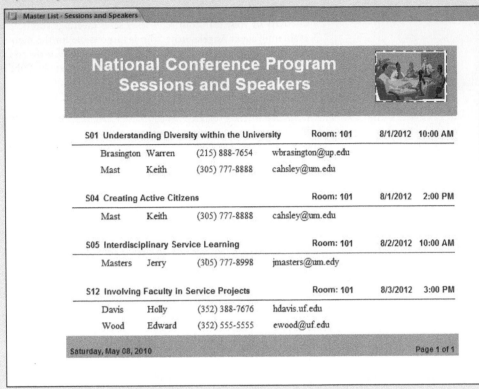

**FIGURE 33** Sessions and Speakers Report— Room 101 ➤

a. Open the *a01m2natconf* file, and then save the database as **a01m2natconf_LastnameFirstname**.

b. Open the Relationships window.

c. Review the objects in the database to see if any of the existing objects will provide the room itinerary information described above.

 **DISCOVER**

d. Open the SessionSpeaker table. Scroll to the first blank record at the bottom of the table, and then enter a new record using SpeakerID: **99** and SessionID: **09**. (Note: speaker 99 does not exist.) How does Access respond? Press **Esc.** Close the SessionSpeaker table. In the Relationships window, right-click on the join line between the Speakers table and SessionSpeaker table, and then click **Delete.** Click **Yes,** and then close the Relationships window. Open the SessionSpeaker table, and then enter the same record again. How does Access respond this time? Close the SessionSpeaker table. Open the Speakers table. Find and replace *YourName* with your name. Close the Speakers table.

e. Open the Speaker - Session Query query, and then apply a filter to identify the sessions where you or Holly Davis are the speakers. Use **Filter by Form** and the **Or tab.**

f. Sort the filtered results in ascending order by the RoomID field.

g. Save and close the query.

h. Open the Master List – Sessions and Speakers report in Report view.

i. Apply a filter that limits the report to sessions in Room 101 only.

j. Click the **File tab**, click **Print**, and then click **Print Preview.**

k. Click **Close Print Preview** in the Close Preview group.

l. Close the report.

m. Compact and repair the database.

n. Back up the database. Use the default backup file name.

o. Exit Access (and save the relationships layout when asked).

p. Submit based on your instructor's directions.

Your boss expressed a concern about the accuracy of the inventory reports in the bookstore. He needs you to open the inventory database, make modifications to some records, and determine if the changes you make carry through to the other objects in the database. You will make changes to a form and then verify those changes in a table, a query, and a report. When you have verified that the changes update automatically, you will compact and repair the database and make a backup of it.

## Database File Setup

You will open an original database file, and then save the database with a new name. Use the new database to replace an existing employee's name with your name, examine the table relationships, and then complete the remainder of this exercise.

a. Open the *a01c1books* file, and then save the database as **a01c1books_LastnameFirstname**.

b. Open the Maintain Authors form.

c. Navigate to Record 7, and then replace *YourName* with your name.

d. Add a new Title: **Technology in Action**. The ISBN is **0-13-148905-4**, the PubID is **PH**, the PublDate is **2006**, the Price is **$89.95** (just type 89.95, no $), and StockAmt is **95** units.

e. Move to any other record to save the new record. The pencil that appeared in the record selector box on the left while you were typing has now disappeared. Close the form.

f. Open the Maintain Authors form again, and then navigate to Record 7. The changes are there because Access works from storage, not memory. Close the form.

## Sort a Query and Apply a Filter by Selection

You need to reorder a detail query so that the results are sorted alphabetically by the publisher name.

a. Open the Publishers, Books, and Authors query.

b. Click in any record in the PubName column, and then sort the field in ascending order.

c. Check to make sure that three books list you as the author.

d. Click your name in the Author's Last Name field, and then filter the records to show only your books.

e. Close the query and save the changes.

## View a Report

You need to examine the *Publishers, Books, and Authors* report to determine if the changes you made in the Maintain Authors form appear in the report.

a. Open the Publishers, Books, and Authors report.

b. Check to make sure that the report shows three books listing you as the author.

c. Check the layout of the report in Print Preview.

d. Close the report.

## Filter a Table

You need to examine the Books table to determine if the changes you made in the Maintain Authors form carried through to the related table. You also will filter the table to display books published after 2006 with fewer than 100 copies in inventory.

a. Open the Books table.

b. Create a filter that will identify all books published after 2006 with fewer than 100 items in stock.

c. Apply the filter.

d. Preview the filtered table.

e. Close the table and save the changes.

## Compact and Repair a Database, Back Up a Database

Now that you are satisfied that any changes made to a form or query carry through to the table, you are ready to compact, repair, and back up your file.

a. Compact and repair your database.

b. Create a backup copy of your database, accept the default file name, and save it.

c. Exit Access.

d. Submit based on your instructor's directions.

## Applying Filters, Printing, and File Management

**GENERAL CASE**

The *a01b1bank* file contains data from a small bank. Open the *a01b1bank* file, and then save the database as **a01b1bank_LastnameFirstname**. Check the table relationships by opening the Relationships window, and then close the window. Use the skills from this chapter to perform several tasks. Open the Customer table, and sort the data in ascending order by LastName. Open the Branch table and make yourself the manager of the Western branch. Remove the Field1 field from the table design. Close the Branch table. Open the Branch Customers query and filter it to show only the accounts at the Campus branch with balances less than $2,000.00. Display the filtered query results in print preview. Close and save the query. Compact, repair, and back up your database, and then exit Access.

## Filtering a Report

**RESEARCH CASE**

Open the *a01b2nwind* file, and then save the database as **a01b2nwind_LastnameFirstname**. Open the Employees table and replace *YourName* with your first and last names. Before you can filter the Revenue report, you need to update the criterion in the underlying query to match the dates in the database. Right-click the Revenue query in the Navigation Pane, and then click Design View in the shortcut list. Scroll to the right until you see *Between #1/1/2007# And #3/31/2007#* in the OrderDate criteria row. Change the criterion to **Between #1/1/2012# And #3/31/2012#**. Save and close the query. Open the Revenue report. Use the tools that you have learned in this chapter to filter the report for only your sales of Confections. Close the report. Compact, repair, and back up your database, and then exit Access.

## Coffee Revenue Queries

**DISASTER RECOVERY**

A coworker called you into his office, explained that he was having difficulty with Access 2010, and asked you to look at his work. Open the *a01b3recover* file, and then save the database as **a01b3recover_LastnameFirstname**. Open the Relationships window, review the table relationships, and then close the window. Your coworker explains that the 2012 Product Introduction Report report is incorrect. It shows that Sazcick is the sales representative for Coulter Office Supplies and the Little, Joiner, & Jones customers, when in fact they are your customers. First, replace *YourName* in the Sales Reps table. Next, find the source of the error and correct it. Preview the corrected report. Compact, repair, and back up your database, and then exit Access.

## ACCESS

# RELATIONAL DATABASES AND QUERIES

## Designing Databases and Extracting Data

### CASE STUDY | Bank Auditor Uncovers Mishandled Funds

Watch the **Set-up Video** for this Case Study!

During a year-end review, a bank auditor uncovers mishandled funds at Commonwealth Federal Bank, in Wilmington, Delaware. In order to analyze the data in more detail, the auditor asks you to create an Access database so he can enter the compromised accounts, the associated customers, and the involved employees. Once the new database is created and all the data is entered, you will help the auditor answer questions by creating and running queries.

As you begin, you realize that some of the data is contained in Excel spreadsheets. After discussing this with the auditor, you decide importing this data directly into the new database would be best. Importing from Excel into Access is commonplace and should work well. Importing will also help avoid errors that are associated with data entry. Once the Excel data has been imported, you will use queries to determine which data does not belong in the database. Unaffected records will be deleted.

This chapter introduces the Bank database case study to present the basic principles of table and query design. You will use tables and forms to input data, and you will create queries and reports to extract information from the database in a useful and organized way. The value of that information depends entirely on the quality of the underlying data—the tables.

### OBJECTIVES    AFTER YOU READ THIS CHAPTER, YOU WILL BE ABLE TO:

1. Design data
2. Create tables
3. Understand table relationships
4. Share data with Excel
5. Establish table relationships
6. Create a single-table query

7. Specify criteria for different data types
8. Copy and run a query
9. Use the Query Wizard
10. Create a multi-table query
11. Modify a multi-table query

From Access Chapter 2 of *Exploring Microsoft Office 2010 Volume 1*, First Edition, Robert T. Grauer, Mary Anne Poatsy, Keith Mulbery, Michelle Hulett, Cynthia Krebs, Keith Mast. Copyright © 2011 by Pearson Education, Inc. Published by Pearson Prentice Hall, Inc. All rights reserved.

# Table Design, Properties, Views, and Wizards

Good database design begins with the tables. Tables provide the framework for all of the activities you perform in a database. If the framework is poorly designed, the rest of the database will be poorly designed as well. Whether you are experienced in designing tables or just learning how, the process should not be done haphazardly. You should follow a systematic approach when creating tables for a database. This process will take practice; however, over time you will begin to see the patterns and eventually see the similarities among all databases.

In this section, you will learn the principles of table design and the other essential guidelines used when creating tables. After developing and testing the table design on paper, you will implement that design in Access. The first step is to list all the tables you need for the database and then list all the fields in each table. When you create the tables in Access, you will refine them further by changing the properties of various fields. You will also be introduced to the concept of data validation. You want to make sure the data entered into the database is valid for the field and valid for the organization. Allowing invalid data into the tables will only cause problems later.

## Designing Data

Most likely you have a bank account and you know that your bank or credit union maintains data about you. Your bank has your name, address, phone number, and Social Security number. It also knows what accounts you have (checking, savings, money market), if you have a credit card with that bank, and what its balance is. Additionally, your bank keeps information about its branches. If you think about the data your bank maintains, you could make a list of the categories of data needed to store that information. These categories for the bank—customers, accounts, branches—become the tables in the bank's database. Previously, we defined a table as a collection of records. In this chapter, we expand on the definition—a *table* is a storage location in a database that holds related information. A table consists of records, and each record is made up of a number of fields. A bank's customer list is an example of a table: It contains a record for each bank customer, and each customer's details are contained in fields such as first and last name, street, city, state, and zip code. Figure 1 shows a customer table and two other tables found in a sample bank database.

A **table** is a storage location in a database that holds related information. A table consists of records, and each record is made up of a number of fields.

During the design process, it will help if you consider the output required for the database. Looking at the output will help determine the tables and fields needed to produce that output. Think of the specific fields you need in each table; list the fields under the correct table and assign each field a data type (such as text, number, or date) as well as its size (length) or format. The order of the fields within the table and the specific field names are not significant. What is important is that the tables contain all necessary fields so that the system can produce the required information.

```
┌─────────────────────────────────┐
│ Customers Table                 │
│ o  CustomerID                   │
│ o  FirstName                    │
│ o  LastName                     │
│ o  Street                       │
│ o  City                         │
│ o  State                        │
│ o  Zip                          │
│ o  Phone                        │
│                                 │
│ Accounts Table                  │
│ o  AccountID                    │
│ o  CustomerID                   │
│ o  BranchID                     │
│ o  OpenDate                     │
│                                 │
│ Branch Table                    │
│ o  BranchID                     │
│ o  Manager                      │
│ o  Location                     │
│ o  StartDate                    │
└─────────────────────────────────┘
```

**FIGURE 1** Tables and Fields in a Sample Bank Database ➤

Figure 1 shows the tables and fields needed in a sample bank database. After the tables have been identified, add the necessary fields using these six guidelines:

1. Include the necessary data.
2. Design for now and the future.
3. Store data in its smallest parts.
4. Add calculated fields to a table.
5. Design to accommodate date arithmetic.
6. Link tables using common fields.

## Include the Necessary Data

> ...ask yourself what information will be expected from the database, and then determine the data required to produce that information.

A good way to determine what data is necessary in the tables is to create a rough draft of the reports you will need and then to design tables that contain the fields necessary to create those reports. In other words, ask yourself what information will be expected from the system, and then determine the data required to produce that information. Consider, for example, the tables and fields in Figure 1. Is there required information that could not be generated from those tables?

- You can determine which branch a customer uses.
- You cannot, however, generate the monthly bank statement. In order to generate a customer bank statement (showing all deposits and withdrawals for the month), you would need to add an additional table—the Account Activity table.
- You can determine who manages a particular branch and which accounts are located there.
- You can determine how long a customer has banked with the branch because the date he or she opened the account is stored in the Accounts table.

If you discover a missing field, you can insert a row anywhere in the appropriate table and add the missing field. The databases found in a real bank are more complex, with more tables and more fields; however, the concepts illustrated here apply to both our sample bank database and to real bank databases.

## Design for Now and the Future

As the data requirements of an organization evolve over time, the information systems that hold the data must change as well. When designing a database, try to anticipate the future needs of the system, and then build in the flexibility to satisfy those demands. For example, when you add a text field, make sure that the number of characters allocated is sufficient to accommodate future expansion. On the other hand, if you include all the possible fields that anyone might ever need, you could drive up the cost of the database. Each additional field can increase the cost of the database, since it will require additional employee time to enter and maintain the data. The additional fields will also require more storage space, which you will need to calculate, especially when working with larger databases. Good database design must balance the data collection needs of the company with the cost associated with collection and storage.

> Good database design must balance the data collection needs of the company with the cost associated with collection and storage.

Suppose you are designing a database for a college. You would need to store each student's name, address, and phone number. You will need to store multiple phone numbers for most students—a cell phone number, a work number, and an emergency number. As a database designer, you will need to design the tables to accommodate multiple entries for similar data.

## Store Data in Its Smallest Parts

The table design in Figure 1 divides a customer's name into two fields (Firstname and Lastname) to reference each field individually. You might think it easier to use a single field consisting of both the first and last name, but that approach is too limiting. Consider a list of customers stored as a single field:

- Sue Grater
- Rick Grater
- Nancy Gallagher
- Harry Weigner
- Barb Shank
- Pete Shank

The first problem in this approach is the lack of flexibility: You could not easily create a salutation for a letter of the form *Dear Sue* or *Dear Ms. Gallagher* because the first and last names are not accessible individually.

A second difficulty is that the list of customers cannot be easily displayed in alphabetical order by last name because the last name begins in the middle of the field. The names could easily be alphabetized by first name because the first name is at the beginning of the field. However, the most common way to sort names is by the last name, which can be done more efficiently if the last name is stored as a separate field.

Think of how an address might be used. The city, state, and postal code should always be stored as separate fields. Any type of mass mailing requires you to sort on postal codes to take advantage of bulk mail. Other applications may require you to select records from a particular state or postal code, which can be done more efficiently if you store the data as separate fields. Often database users enter the postal code, and the database automatically retrieves the city and state information. You may need to direct a mailing only to a neighborhood or to a single street. The guideline is simple: Store data in its smallest parts.

## Add Calculated Fields to a Table

A **calculated field** produces a value from an expression or function that references one or more existing fields.

A *calculated field* produces a value from an expression or function that references one or more existing fields. Access 2010 enables you to store calculated fields in a table using the calculated data type. An example of a calculated field can be found in the bank database. Suppose the bank pays its customers 1.0% interest on the principal each month. A calculated field, such as Monthly Interest, could store the expression Principal x .01. The interest amount would then appear on the customer's monthly bank statement.

Previous versions of Access did not have the option of adding a calculated field to a table. Calculated fields were not available because they do not adhere to conventional database design principles. Database design principles avoid storing data that can be derived from other data. The Monthly Interest field mentioned above can be derived from the product of Principal x .01; therefore, you would not need to store the Monthly Interest value.

The new calculated field* can be very useful in certain circumstances, like a Monthly Interest field. Storing calculated data in a table enables you to add the data easily to queries, forms, and reports without the trouble of an additional calculation. Storing calculated data in a table may increase the size of the database slightly, but the benefits may outweigh this drawback.

## Design to Accommodate Date Arithmetic

Calculated fields are frequently created with numeric data, as the Monthly Interest field example above illustrates. You can also create calculated fields using date/time data. If you want to store the length of time a customer has been a customer, you would first create a field to hold the start date for each customer. Next, you would create a calculated field that contains an expression that subtracts the start date from today's date. The resulting calculation would store the number of days each customer has been a customer. Divide the results by 365 to convert days to years.

This same concept applies to bank accounts; a bank is likely to store the Open Date for each account in the Accounts table, as shown in Figure 1. Using this date, you can subtract the open date from today's date and calculate the number of days the account has been open. (Again, divide the results by 365 to convert to years.) If you open the Accounts table at least one day later, the results of the calculated field will be different.

A **constant** is an unchanging value, like a birth date.

A person's age is another example of a calculated field using date arithmetic—date of birth is subtracted from today's date and the results are divided by 365. It might seem easier to store a person's age rather than the birth date to avoid the calculation. But that would be a mistake because age changes over time and would need to be updated each time age changes. Storing the date of birth is much better since the data remains *constant*. You can use *date arithmetic* to subtract one date from another to find out the number of days, months, or years that have lapsed between them. You can also add or subtract a constant from a date.

**Date arithmetic** is the process of subtracting one date from another, or adding or subtracting a constant from a date.

## Link Tables Using Common Fields

As you create the tables and fields for the database, keep in mind that the tables will be joined in relationships using common fields. Draw a line between common fields to indicate the joins, as shown in Figure 2. These join lines will be created in Access when you learn to create table relationships later in the chapter. For now, you should name the common fields the same and make sure they have the same data type. For example, CustomerID in the Customers table will join to the CustomerID field in the Accounts table. CustomerID must have the same data type (in this case number/long integer) in both tables; otherwise, the join line will not be allowed.

**Data redundancy** is the unnecessary storing of duplicate data in two or more tables.

Avoid *data redundancy*, which is the unnecessary storing of duplicate data in two or more tables. You should avoid duplicate information in multiple tables in a database, because errors may result. Suppose the customer address data was stored in both the

*If you add a calculated field to a table in Access 2010, you will not be able to open the table using Access 2007.

Customers and Accounts tables. If a customer moved to a new address, a possible outcome would be that the address would be updated in only one of the two tables. The result would be unreliable data. Depending on which table served as the source for the output, either the new or the old address might be given to the person requesting the information. Storing the address in only one table is more reliable.

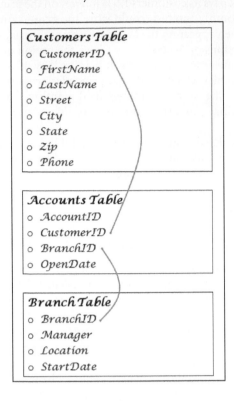

**FIGURE 2** Create Relationships Using Common Fields ➤

## Creating Tables

Before you can begin creating your tables, you must first create a new blank database and save it to a specific storage location. If you are creating tables in an existing database, you open the existing database and then create new tables or modify existing ones.

Access provides several ways to create a table. You can create a table by creating the fields in Design view (as shown in Figure 3) or by entering table data into a new row in Datasheet view, or you can import data from another database or application such as Excel. Regardless of how a table is first created, you can always modify it later to include a new field or to change an existing field.

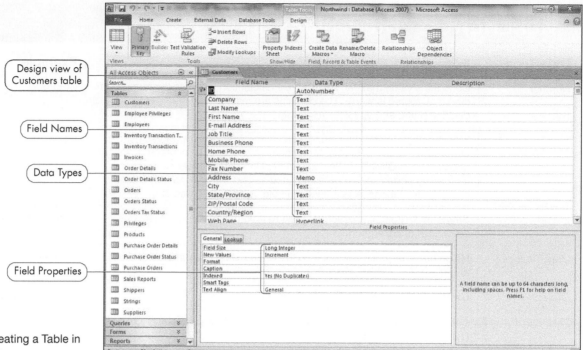

**FIGURE 3** Creating a Table in Design View ➤

Labels pointing to the figure:
- Design view of Customers table
- Field Names
- Data Types
- Field Properties

**CamelCase notation** uses no spaces in multi-word field names, but uses uppercase letters to distinguish the first letter of each new word.

The **data type** determines the type of data that can be entered and the operations that can be performed on that data.

The **AutoNumber** data type is a number that automatically increments each time a record is added.

Each field in a table has a field name to identify the data that it holds. The field name should be descriptive of the data and can be up to 64 characters in length, including letters, numbers, and spaces. Database developers use **CamelCase notation** for field names, object names, and filenames. Instead of spaces in multi-word field names, use uppercase letters to distinguish the first letter of each new word, for example, ProductCost or LastName. It is best to avoid spaces in field names, since spaces can cause problems when creating the other objects based on tables—such as queries, forms, and reports.

Every field also has a **data type** that determines the type of data that can be entered and the operations that can be performed on that data. Access recognizes 10 data types.

## Establish a Primary Key

As you learned earlier, the primary key is the field (or combination of fields) that uniquely identifies each record in a table. Access does not require that each table have a primary key. However, good database design usually includes a primary key in each table. You should select unique and infrequently changing data for the primary key. For example, a complete address (street, city, state, and postal code) may be unique but would not make a good primary key because it is subject to change when someone moves.

You probably would not use a person's name as the primary key, because several people could have the same name. A customer's account number, on the other hand, is unique and is a frequent choice for the primary key, as in the Customers table in this chapter. The primary key can be easily identified in many tables; for example, a PartNumber in a parts table, the ISBN in the book database of a bookstore, or a Student ID that uniquely identifies a student. When no primary key occurs naturally, you can create a primary key field with the AutoNumber data type. The **AutoNumber** data type is a number that automatically increments each time a record is added.

# REFERENCE   Data Types and Uses

| Data Type | Description | Example |
|---|---|---|
| Number | Contains a value that can be used in a calculation, such as the number of credits a course is worth. The contents are restricted to numbers, a decimal point, and a plus or minus sign. | Credits |
| Text | Stores alphanumeric data, such as a customer's name or address. It can contain alphabetic characters, numbers, and/or special characters (i.e., an apostrophe in O'Malley). Social Security Numbers, telephone numbers, and postal codes should be designated as text fields since they are not used in calculations. A text field can hold up to 255 characters. | Last name |
| Memo | Stores up to 65,536 characters; used to hold descriptive data (several sentences or paragraphs). | Notes or comments |
| Date/Time | Holds dates or times and enables the values to be used in date or time arithmetic. | 10/31/2012 |
| Currency | Used for fields that contain monetary values. | Account balance |
| Yes/No | Assumes one of two values, such as Yes or No, True or False, or On or Off (also known as a Boolean). | Dean's list |
| OLE | Contains an object created by another application. OLE objects include spreadsheets, pictures, sounds, or graphics. | One photo |
| AutoNumber | A special data type used to assign the next consecutive number each time you add a record. The value of an AutoNumber field is unique for each record in the file. | Customer ID |
| Hyperlink | Stores a Web address (URL) or the path to a folder or file. Hyperlink fields can be clicked to retrieve a Web page or to launch a file stored locally. | http://www.keithmast .com |
| Attachment | Used to store multiple images, spreadsheet files, Word documents, and other types of supported files. | An Excel workbook; a photo |
| Calculated | The results of an expression that references one or more existing fields. | [IntRate] + 0.25 |

In Figure 4, the book's ISBN is the natural primary key for the book table because no two book titles can have the same ISBN. This field uniquely identifies the records in the table. Figure 5 depicts the Speakers table, where no unique field can be identified from the data. When this happens, you can add the SpeakerID field with an AutoNumber data type. Access will automatically number each speaker record sequentially with a unique ID as each record is added.

| AuthorCode | Title | ISBN | PubID | PublDate | Price | StockAmt |
|---|---|---|---|---|---|---|
| 15 | Chasing the Dime | 0-316-15391-5 | LBC | 2002 | $51.75 | 400 |
| 13 | Blackhills Farm | 0-275-41199-7 | KN | 2002 | $18.87 | 528 |
| 13 | Blood and Gold | 0-679-45449-7 | KN | 2001 | $18.87 | 640 |
| 11 | Reaching for Glory | 0-684-80408-5 | SS | 2001 | $24.00 | 480 |
| 14 | From a Buick 8 | 0-743-21137-5 | SS | 2002 | $16.80 | 368 |
| 15 | City of Bones | 0-316-15405-9 | LBC | 2002 | $20.76 | 394 |
| 16 | Follow the Stars Home | 0-553-58102-3 | BB | 2000 | $6.99 | 496 |
| 14 | Hearts in Atlantis | 0-684-85351-5 | SS | 1999 | $28.00 | 528 |
| 12 | Personality Injuries | 0-742095692-X | FSG | 1999 | $27.00 | 403 |
| 15 | Darkness More than Midnight | 0-316-15407-5 | LBC | 2001 | $20.76 | 432 |
| 13 | Interview with the Vampire | 0-394-49821-6 | KN | 1976 | $19.57 | 371 |
| 16 | True Blue | 0-553-38398-0 | BB | 2002 | $7.50 | 492 |

ISBN provides a unique identifier

**FIGURE 4** Books Table with a Natural Primary Key ➤

**FIGURE 5** Speakers Table with an AutoNumber Primary Key ➤

SpeakerID (AutoNumber data type) is the primary key

Next record will be assigned SpeakerID 17

**FIGURE 5** Speakers Table with an AutoNumber Primary Key ➤

## Explore Foreign Key

A foreign key, as defined earlier, is a field in one table that is also the primary key of another table. The CustomerID is the primary key in the Customers table. It serves to uniquely identify each customer. It also appears as a foreign key in a related table. For example, the Accounts table contains the CustomerID field to establish which customer owns the account. A CustomerID can appear only once in the Customers table, but it may appear multiple times in the Accounts table (when viewed in Datasheet view) since one customer may own multiple accounts (checking, money market, home equity).

If you were asked to create an Access database for the speakers at a national conference, you would create a database with the tables Speakers and SessionSpeaker. You would add a primary key field to the Speakers table (SpeakerID) along with the speaker's First Name and Last Name; you would add two fields to the SessionSpeaker table (SpeakerID and SessionID). The SpeakerID in the SessionSpeaker table enables you to join the two tables in a relationship. The SpeakerID field in the SessionSpeaker table is an example of a foreign key. Figure 6 shows portions of the Speakers and SessionSpeaker tables.

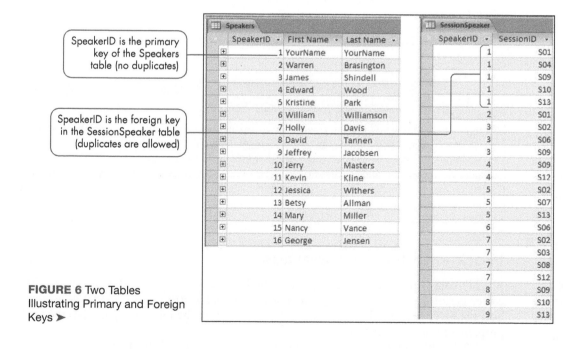

SpeakerID is the primary key of the Speakers table (no duplicates)

SpeakerID is the foreign key in the SessionSpeaker table (duplicates are allowed)

**FIGURE 6** Two Tables Illustrating Primary and Foreign Keys ➤

## Use Table Views

As defined earlier, users can work in Datasheet view to add, edit, and delete records. The Datasheet view of an Access table resembles an Excel spreadsheet and displays data in a grid format—rows represent records, and columns represent fields. Datasheet view indicates the current record using a gold border; you can select a record by clicking the record selector on the left side of each record, as shown in Figure 7. Use the new blank record (marked with an asterisk) at the end of the table to add a new record. Design view is used to create and modify the table structure by adding and editing fields and by setting the field properties.

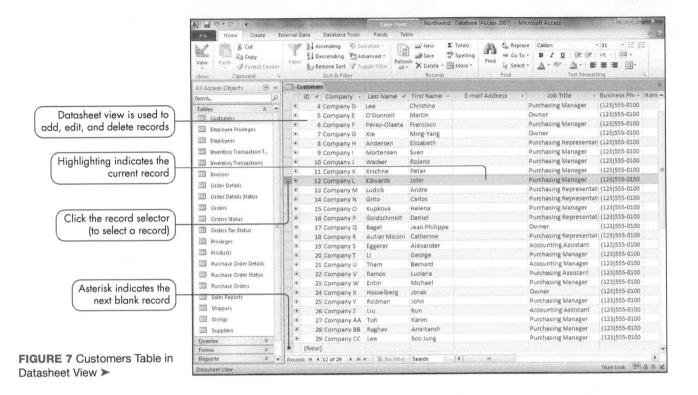

**FIGURE 7** Customers Table in Datasheet View ➤

> **TIP** Toggle Between Datasheet and Design Views
>
> To toggle from Datasheet view to Design view, click the Home tab, and then click View in the Views group. If you click the view arrow by accident, select the view you want from the menu. Or you can right-click on the table tab that appears above the datasheet and then choose Design View from the shortcut menu. To toggle back to Datasheet view, click View in the Views group, or right-click on the table tab again, and then choose Datasheet View from the shortcut menu.

## Work with Field Properties

A **field property** is a characteristic of a field that determines how the field looks and behaves.

A **text data type** can store either text or numerical characters.

A field's data type determines the type of data that can be entered and the operations that can be performed on that data. A *field property* is a characteristic of a field that determines how the field looks and behaves. (The reference table on the following page lists the field properties for a typical field.)

A field with a *text data type* can store either text or numerical characters. A text field can hold up to 255 characters; however, you can limit the characters by reducing the field size

A **number data type** can store only numerical data.

A **caption property** is used to create a more readable label that appears in the top row in Datasheet view and in forms and reports.

A **validation rule** prevents invalid data from being entered into the field.

property. For example, you would limit the State field to only two characters since all state abbreviations are two letters. A field with a ***number data type*** can store only numerical data. Set the Format field property to Integer to display the field contents as integers from –32768 to 32768. Set the Format field property to Long Integer for larger values.

You can use the ***caption property*** to create a more readable label that appears in the top row in Datasheet view and in forms and reports. For example, a field named ProductCostPerUnit could have the caption *Per Unit Product Cost*. The caption displays at the top of a table or query column in Datasheet view and when the field is used in a report or form. You must use the actual field name, ProductCostPerUnit, in any calculation.

Set the validation rule property to restrict data entry in a field to ensure the correct type of data is entered or that the data does not violate other enforced properties. The ***validation rule*** checks the data entered when the user exits the field. If the data entered violates the validation rule, an error message appears and prevents the invalid data from being entered into the field.

The field properties are set to default values according to the data type, but you can modify them if necessary. The property types are defined in the following Reference table.

In Hands-On Exercise 1, you will create a new database and enter data into a table. Then you will switch to the table's Design view to add additional fields and modify selected field properties of various fields within the table.

## REFERENCE   Access Table Property Types and Descriptions

| Property Type | Description |
| --- | --- |
| Field Size | Determines the maximum characters of a text field or the format of a number field. |
| Format | Changes the way a field is displayed or printed, but does not affect the stored value. |
| Input Mask | Simplifies data entry by providing literal characters that are typed for every entry, such as hyphens in a Social Security Number or slashes in a date. It also imposes data validation by ensuring that data entered conforms to the mask. |
| Caption | This enables an alternate name to be displayed other than the field name; alternate names appear in datasheets, forms, and reports. |
| Default Value | This option automatically enters a predetermined value for a field each time a new record is added to the table. For example, if most of your customers live in Los Angeles, you might consider setting the default value for the City to Los Angeles to save data entry time. |
| Validation Rule | Requires the data entered to conform to the specified rule. |
| Validation Text | Specifies the error message that is displayed when the validation rule is violated. |
| Required | Indicates that a value for this field must be entered. |
| Allow Zero Length | Enables text or memo strings of zero length. |
| Indexed | Increases the efficiency of a search on the designated field. |
| Expression | Used for calculated fields only. Enter the expression you want Access to evaluate and store. |
| Result Type | Used for calculated fields only. Enter the format for the calculated field results. |

# HANDS-ON EXERCISES

## 1 Table Design, Properties, Views, and Wizards

Assisting the bank auditor at Commonwealth Federal Bank as he investigates the mishandled funds will be a great opportunity for you to showcase your Access skills. Be sure to check your work each step of the way since your work will come under substantial scrutiny. Do a good job with this Access project and more opportunities might come your way, along with a promotion.

**Skills covered:** Create a New Database • Create a Table by Entering Data • Change the Primary Key, Modify Field Properties, and Delete a Field • Modify Table Fields in Design View • Create a New Field in Design View • Switch Between the Table Design and the Table Datasheet Views

---

### STEP 1 ▶ CREATE A NEW DATABASE

To start a new Access database project, you first need to create a new database. Use the Access interface to create a new file for the mishandled funds database. Refer to Figure 8 as you complete Step 1.

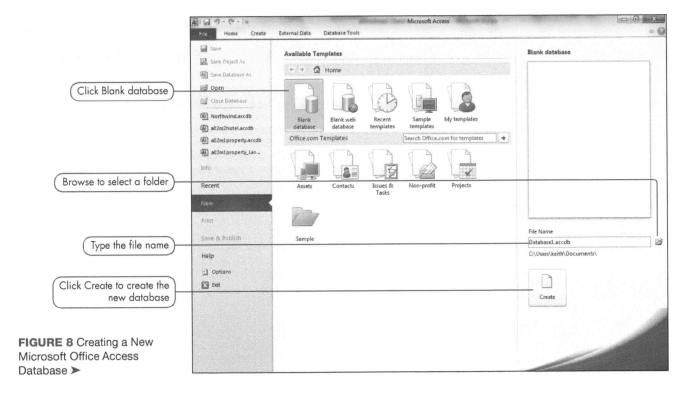

**FIGURE 8** Creating a New Microsoft Office Access Database ➤

a. Start Microsoft Access.

You will see the Backstage view with New selected by default.

b. Click **Blank database** in the Available Templates section of the Backstage view.

c. Type **a02h1bank_LastnameFirstname** into the **File Name box**.

d. Click **Browse**—the yellow folder icon—to find the folder location designated by your instructor, and then click **OK**.

e. Click **Create** to create the new database.

Access will create the new database named *a02h1bank_LastnameFirstname*, and a new table will automatically appear in Datasheet view.

> **TROUBLESHOOTING:** If you have a problem finding your file, use the Windows search tool to locate the file.

**STEP 2 ▶ CREATE A TABLE BY ENTERING DATA**

Create a new Branch table and enter the branch data as instructed. Only branches with suspicious data will be added. Refer to Figure 9 as you complete Step 2.

Save the table as Branch

Type the data directly into the datasheet

| ID | ▾ | Field1 | ▾ | Field2 | ▾ | Field3 | ▾ | Click to Add | ▾ |
|---|---|---|---|---|---|---|---|---|---|
| 1 | | B10 | | Mast | | Uptown | | | |
| 2 | | B20 | | Esposito | | Eastern | | | |
| 3 | | B30 | | Amoako | | Western | | | |
| 4 | | B40 | | Singh | | Southern | | | |
| 5 | | B50 | | YourLastName | | Campus | | | |
| * | | (New) | | | | | | | |

**FIGURE 9** Enter Data into the Branch Table in Datasheet View ➤

a.  Type **B10** in the second column, and then click **Click to Add**.

    The column heading becomes Field1 and Click to Add now appears as the third column.

b.  Type **Mast** in the third column, press **Tab**, and then type **Uptown** in the fourth column.

    You can advance to the next field by pressing Tab or move to the previous field by pressing Shift+Tab.

c.  Press **Tab** three times. Type **B20**, press **Tab**, type **Esposito**, press **Tab**, and then type **Eastern**.

d.  Enter the additional data for the new table as shown in Figure 9. Replace *YourLastName* with your last name.

e.  Click **Save** on the Quick Access Toolbar. Type **Branch** in the **Save As dialog box**, and then click **OK**.

    Entering data provides an easy way to create the table initially. You can now modify the table in Design view as described in the next several steps.

**STEP 3 ▶ CHANGE THE PRIMARY KEY, MODIFY FIELD PROPERTIES, AND DELETE A FIELD**

It is common to modify tables even after data has been entered; however, pay attention to the messages from Access after you make a design change. In this example, you will be modifying the Branch table field names to match the auditor's requirements. Refer to Figure 10 as you complete Step 3.

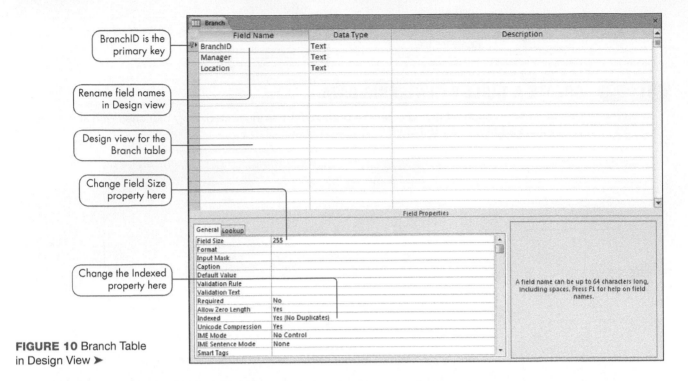

BranchID is the primary key

Rename field names in Design view

Design view for the Branch table

Change Field Size property here

Change the Indexed property here

**FIGURE 10** Branch Table in Design View ➤

a. Click **View** in the Views group to switch to the Design view of the Branch table.

The fields are named ID, Field1, Field2, and Field3, because they are the default names given to the fields when you create the table in Datasheet view. These field names are not descriptive of the data, so you need to change Field1, Field2, and Field3 to BranchID, Manager, and Location, respectively. You will also delete the ID field.

b. Click the **ID field** to select it. Click **Delete Rows** in the Tools group. Click **Yes** to both warning messages.

Access responds with a warning that you are about to permanently delete a field and a second warning that the field is the primary key. You delete the field since you will set a different field as the primary key.

c. Double-click the **Field1 field name** to select it, if necessary, and then type **BranchID**. Replace *Field2* with **Manager** and *Field3* with **Location**.

d. Click the **BranchID field**.

The cell field name now has an orange border as shown in Figure 10.

e. Click **Primary Key** in the Tools group.

You set BranchID as the primary key. The Indexed property in the *Field Properties* section at the bottom of the design window displays *Yes (No Duplicates)*.

f. Click **Save** to save the table.

**TIP** Shortcut Menu

You can right-click a row selector to display a shortcut menu to copy a field, set the primary key, and insert or delete rows. Use the shortcut menu to make these specific changes to the design of a table.

**MODIFY TABLE FIELDS IN DESIGN VIEW**

You need to modify the table design further to comply with the bank auditor's specifications. Be aware of messages from Access that indicate you may lose data. Refer to Figure 11 as you complete Step 4.

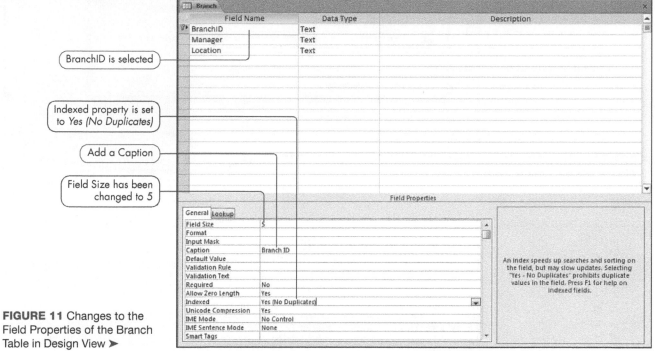

BranchID is selected

Indexed property is set to *Yes (No Duplicates)*

Add a Caption

Field Size has been changed to 5

**FIGURE 11** Changes to the Field Properties of the Branch Table in Design View ➤

a. Click the **BranchID field name** in the top section of the design window; modify the BranchID field properties in the bottom of the design window:

 • Click in the **Field Size property**, and then change *255* to **5**.

 • Click in the **Caption property**, and then type **Branch ID**. Make sure *Branch* and *ID* have a space between them.

 A caption provides a more descriptive field name. It will appear as the column heading in Datasheet view.

 • Check the Indexed property; confirm it is *Yes (No Duplicates)*.

b. Click the **Manager field name** at the top of the window; modify the following field properties:

 • Change the **Field Size property** from *255* to **30**.

 • Click in the **Caption property**, and then type **Manager's Name**.

c. Click the **Location field name**, and then modify the following field properties:

 • Change the **Field Size property** from *255* to **30**.

 • Click in the **Caption property**, and then type **Branch Location**.

**CREATE A NEW FIELD IN DESIGN VIEW**

You notify the auditor that a date field is missing in your new table. Modify the table and add the new field. The data can be entered at a later time. Refer to Figure 12 as you complete Step 5.

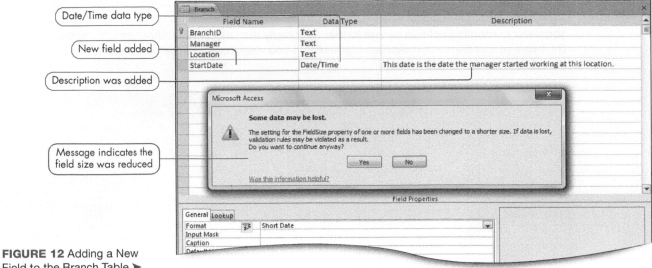

Date/Time data type

New field added

Description was added

Message indicates the field size was reduced

**FIGURE 12** Adding a New Field to the Branch Table ➤

a. Click in the first blank row below the Location field name, and then type **StartDate**.

You added a new field to the table.

b. Press **Tab** to move to the Data Type column. Click the **Data Type arrow**, and then select **Date/Time**.

**TIP** Keyboard Shortcut for Data Types

You also can type the first letter of the data type such as *d* for Date/Time, *t* for Text, or *n* for number. To use the keyboard shortcut, click on the field name, and then press Tab to advance to the Data Type column. Next, type the first letter of the data type.

c. Press **Tab** to move to the Description column, and then type **This is the date the manager started working at this location.**

d. Click in the **Format property**, click the arrow, and then select **Short Date** from the list of date formats.

e. Click in the **Caption property**, and then type **Manager's Start Date**.

f. Click **Save** on the Quick Access Toolbar to save the changes you made to the *a02h1bank_LastnameFirstname* database.

A warning dialog box opens to indicate that "Some data may be lost" since the size of the BranchID, Manager, and Location field properties were shortened. It asks if you want to continue anyway. Always read the Access warnings! In this case, you can click Yes to continue. You changed the size of the BranchID field from 255 to 5 in Step 4a.

g. Click **Yes** in the warning box.

As you work with the auditor, you will need to modify tables in the bank database from time to time. To modify the table, you will need to switch between Design view and Datasheet view. Refer to Figure 13 as you complete Step 6.

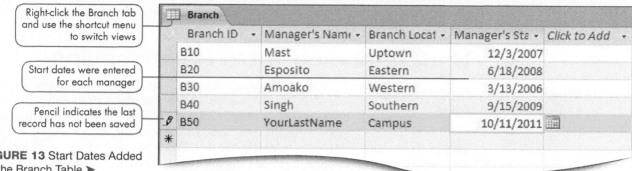

Right-click the Branch tab and use the shortcut menu to switch views

Start dates were entered for each manager

Pencil indicates the last record has not been saved

**FIGURE 13** Start Dates Added to the Branch Table ➤

a. Right-click the **Branch tab** shown in Figure 13, and then select **Datasheet View** from the shortcut menu. (To return to the Design view, right-click the tab again, and then select Design View.)

b. Click inside the **Manager's Start Date** in the first record, and then click the **Calendar**. Use the navigation arrows to find and select **December 3, 2007** from the calendar.

You can also enter the dates by typing them directly into the StartDate field.

c. Type directly in each field the Start Date for the rest of the managers as shown in Figure 13.

d. Click the **Close button** at the top-right corner of the datasheet, below the Ribbon.

> **TROUBLESHOOTING:** If you accidentally click the Close button on top of the Ribbon, you will exit out of Access completely. To start again, launch Access, click the File tab, click Recent, and then select the first database from the recent documents list.

e. Double-click the **Branch table** in the Navigation Pane to open the table. Check the start dates.

The start dates are still there even though you did not save your work in the previous step. Access saves the data to the hard drive as soon as you move off the current record (or close an object).

f. Click the **File tab**, click **Print**, and then click **Print Preview**.

Occasionally, users will print an Access table. However, database developers usually create reports to print table data.

g. Click **Close Print Preview**. Close the Branch table.

h. Click the **File tab**, and then click **Compact & Repair Database** (the top button).

i. Click the **File tab**, click **Save & Publish**, and then double-click **Back Up Database** in the right column. Accept *a02h1bank_LastnameFirstname_date* as the file name, and then click **Save**.

You created a backup of the database. The original database, *a02h1bank_LastnameFirstname*, remains open.

j. Keep the database onscreen if you plan to continue with Hands-On Exercise 2. If not, close the database and exit Access.

# Multiple Table Databases

In Figure 1, the sample bank database contains three tables—Customers, Accounts, and Branch. You already created one table, the Branch table, in the previous section using the Datasheet view. The two remaining tables will be created using a different method—importing data from Excel. In this section, you will learn how to import data from Excel, modify tables, create indexes, create relationships between tables, and enforce referential integrity.

## Understanding Table Relationships

> The benefit of a relationship is to efficiently combine data from related tables.

Relationships between tables are set in the Relationships window. In this window, join lines are created to establish relationships between two tables. As discussed earlier, the benefit of a relationship is to efficiently combine data from related tables for the purpose of creating queries, forms, and reports. For example, the join line between the CustomerID in the Accounts table and the CustomerID in the Customers table (see Figure 14) enables you to combine data from the Accounts and the Customers tables.

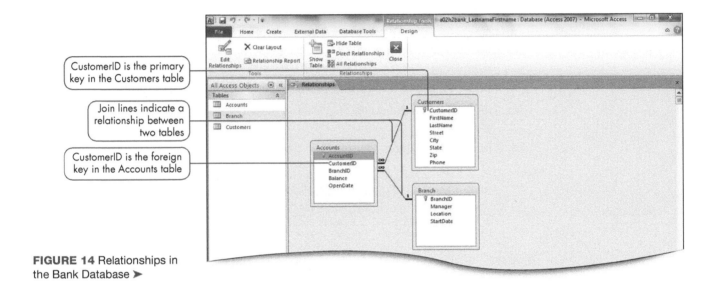

FIGURE 14 Relationships in the Bank Database ➤

The primary key of a table plays a significant role when setting relationships. You cannot join two tables unless a primary key has been set in the primary table. In our Bank database, the CustomerID has been set as the primary key in the Customers table. Therefore, a relationship can be set between the Customers table and the Accounts table. Similarly, the Branch table can be joined to the Accounts table since BranchID has been set as the primary key in the Branch table.

> Relationships between tables will almost always be set using primary and foreign keys.

The other side of the relationship join line is most often the foreign key of the related table. A foreign key is a field in one table that is also the primary key of another table. In the previous example, CustomerID in the Accounts table is a foreign key; BranchID in the Accounts table is a foreign key. Relationships between tables will almost always be set using primary and foreign keys.

## Establish Referential Integrity

When **referential integrity** is enforced, you cannot enter a foreign key value in a related table unless the primary key value exists in the primary table.

When you create a relationship in Access, the Edit Relationships dialog box appears, as shown in Figure 15. The first check box, Enforce Referential Integrity, should be checked in most cases. When *referential integrity* is enforced, you cannot enter a foreign key value in a related table unless the primary key value exists in the primary table. In the case of the Bank database, a customer's account information (which includes CustomerID) cannot be entered into the Accounts table unless the customer information is first entered into the Customers table. If you attempt to enter an account prior to entering the customer information, an error will appear, as shown in Figure 16. When referential integrity is enforced, you cannot delete a record in one table if it has related records in other tables.

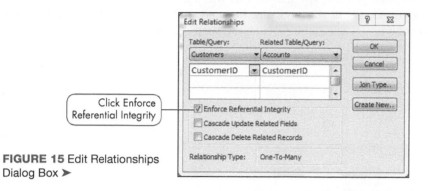

Click Enforce Referential Integrity

**FIGURE 15** Edit Relationships Dialog Box ➤

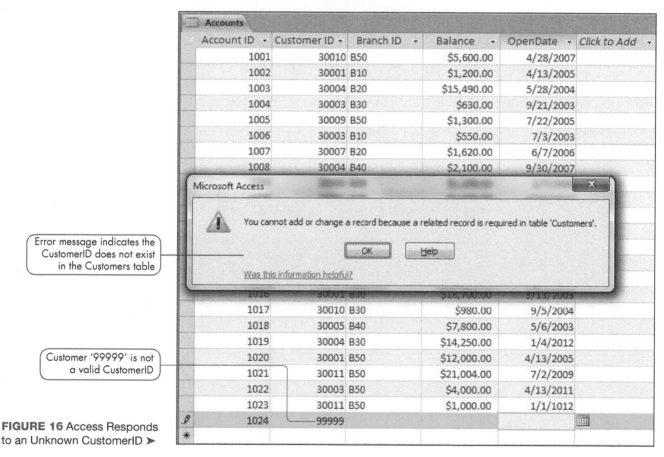

Error message indicates the CustomerID does not exist in the Customers table

Customer '99999' is not a valid CustomerID

**FIGURE 16** Access Responds to an Unknown CustomerID ➤

## Set Cascade Options

**Cascade Update Related Fields** is an option that directs Access to automatically update all foreign key values in a related table when the primary key value is modified in a primary table.

**Cascade Delete Related Records** is an option that directs Access to automatically delete all records in related tables that match the primary key that is deleted from a primary table.

When you create a relationship in Access and click the Enforce Referential Integrity checkbox, Access gives you two additional options—Cascade Update Related Fields and Cascade Delete Related Records. Check the *Cascade Update Related Fields* option so that when the primary key is modified in a primary table, Access will automatically update all foreign key values in a related table (see Figure 17). If a CustomerID is updated for some reason, all the CustomerID references in the Accounts table will automatically be updated.

Check the *Cascade Delete Related Records* option so that when the primary key is deleted in a primary table, Access will automatically delete all records in related tables that reference the primary key (see Figure 17). If one branch of a bank closes and its record is deleted from the Branch table, any account that was not transferred to a different branch would be deleted. Access will give a warning first and enable you to avoid the action. This may be a desired business rule, but it should be set with caution.

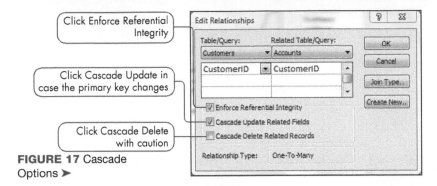

**FIGURE 17** Cascade Options ➤

## Retrieve Data Quickly with Indexing

The **indexed property** setting enables quick sorting in primary key order and quick retrieval based on the primary key.

When you set the primary key in Access, the *indexed property* is automatically set to *Yes (No Duplicates)*. The Indexed property setting enables quick sorting in primary key order and quick retrieval based on the primary key. For non-primary key fields, it may be beneficial to set the Indexed property to *Yes (Duplicates OK)*. Again, Access uses indexing to sort and retrieve data quickly based on the indexed field. As a general rule, indexed fields are usually foreign keys and are numeric.

# Sharing Data with Excel

Most companies store some type of data in Excel spreadsheets. Often the data stored in those spreadsheets can be more efficiently managed in an Access database. Fortunately, Access provides you with a wizard that guides you through the process of importing data from Excel. Access can also export data to Excel easily.

Figures 18 through 24 show the steps of the *Get External Data - Excel Spreadsheet* feature. Launch the feature by clicking the External Data tab and then clicking Excel in the Import & Link Group. Table 1 describes the four groups on the External Data tab. See Figure 18 to see the first step of the *Get External Data - Excel Spreadsheet* feature.

| TABLE 1 | Options on the External Data Tab |
|---|---|
| **Group** | **When Used** |
| **Import & Link** | To bring data into an Access database. The data sources include Excel, Access (other Access files), ODBC Database, Text File, XML File, and More. |
| **Export** | To send a portion of a database to other applications. You might use this to create a Mail Merge letter and envelopes in Word. You could create an Excel file for a coworker who is not using Access, or you could share your data over the Internet via a SharePoint List. |
| **Collect Data** | You could create an e-mail mail merge to send e-mails to your clients and then use Access to manage the clients' responses. |
| **Web Linked Lists** | Use these commands to interact with SharePoint lists on the Internet. If an Internet connection is unavailable, you can work offline and synchronize with SharePoint later. |

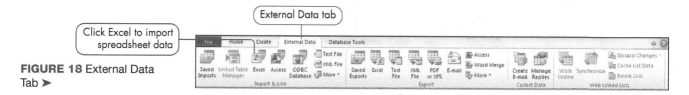

**FIGURE 18** External Data Tab ➤

Figure 19 shows the *Get External Data - Excel Spreadsheet* dialog box. This step enables you to locate the Excel file you want to import by clicking Browse. It asks you to choose among three options for the incoming data: Place it in a new table, append the data to an existing table, or create a link to the Excel source.

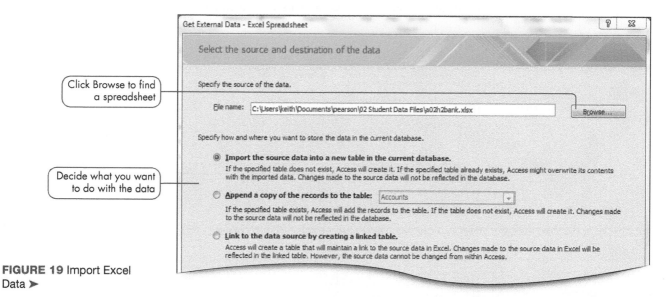

**FIGURE 19** Import Excel Data ➤

After you select an Excel workbook and accept the default option, import the source data into a new table in the current database, and then click OK. The Import Spreadsheet Wizard dialog box launches and displays a list of the worksheets in the specified workbook. The Customers worksheet is selected; click the Accounts worksheet, which will be imported first (see Figure 20). The bottom of the Import Spreadsheet Wizard dialog box displays a preview of the data stored in the specified worksheet.

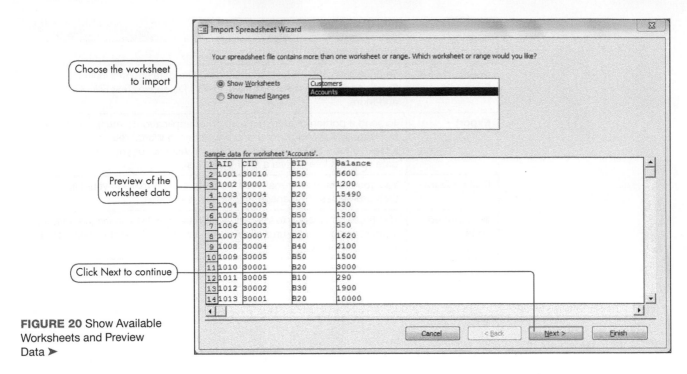

FIGURE 20 Show Available Worksheets and Preview Data ➤

Although a well-designed spreadsheet may include descriptive column headings, not all spreadsheets are ready to import. You may have to revise the spreadsheet before importing it. The second window of the Import Spreadsheet Wizard dialog box contains a check box that enables you to convert the first row of column headings to field names in Access (see Figure 21). If a column heading row exists in the spreadsheet, check the box. If no column headings exist, leave the check box unchecked, and the data will import using Field1, Field2, Field3, etc.

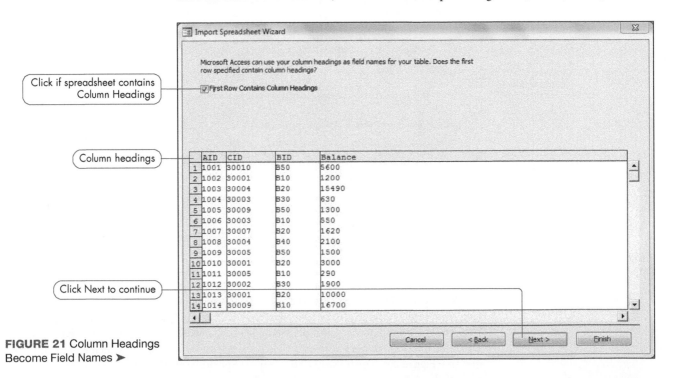

FIGURE 21 Column Headings Become Field Names ➤

The third window of the Import Spreadsheet Wizard dialog box enables you to specify field options (see Figure 22). The AID field is shown in this figure. Because it will become this table's primary key, you need to set the Indexed Property to *Yes (No Duplicates)*.

To modify the field options of the other fields, click the Field Name column heading, and then make the changes. Not all Access table properties are supported by the wizard. You will need to open the table in Design view after importing it to make additional field property changes.

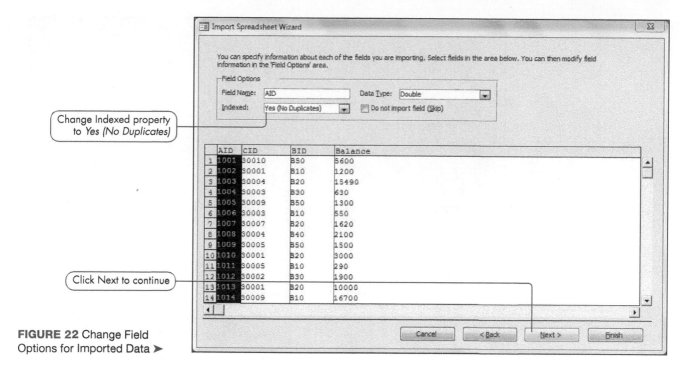

FIGURE 22 Change Field Options for Imported Data ➤

The fourth window of the Import Spreadsheet Wizard dialog box enables you to choose a primary key before the import takes place (see Figure 23). If the option *Let Access add primary key* is selected, Access will generate an AutoNumber field and designate it as the primary key. Otherwise, you can designate a field to be the primary key. In the import described in the figure, the Excel data has a unique identifier (AID) that will become the table's primary key.

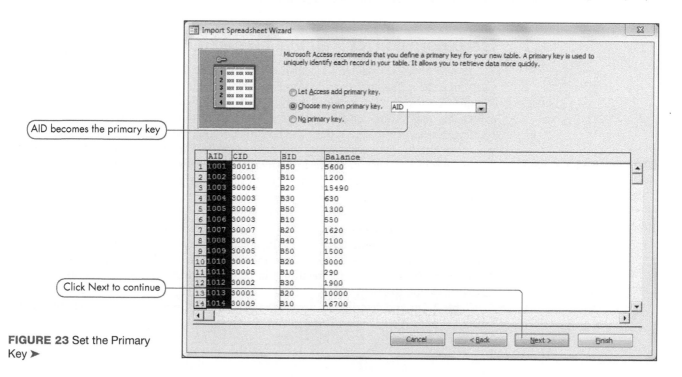

FIGURE 23 Set the Primary Key ➤

Use the final window of the Import Spreadsheet Wizard to name the Access table. If the worksheet in the Excel workbook was named, Access uses the worksheet name as the table name (see Figure 24).

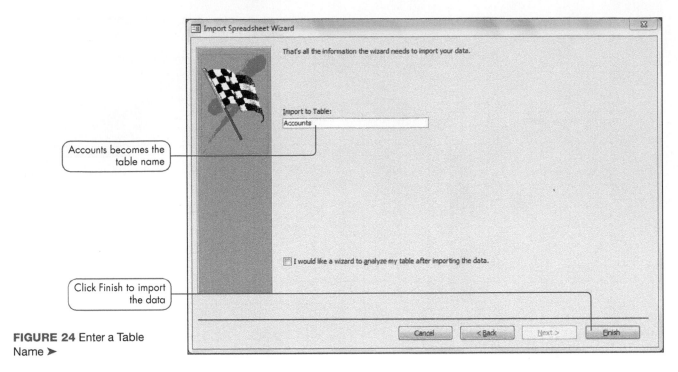

Accounts becomes the table name

Click Finish to import the data

**FIGURE 24** Enter a Table Name ➤

Finally, the Wizard will ask if you wish to save the import steps. If the same worksheet is imported from Excel to Access on a recurring basis, you could save the parameters and use them again. To save the import steps such as the indexing option and any new field names, click Saved Imports in the Import group. Saving the import steps will help you import the data the next time it is needed.

## Establishing Table Relationships

You should store like data items together in the same table. The customer data is stored in the Customers table. The Branch table stores data about the bank's branches, management, and location. The Accounts table stores data about account ownership and balances. You learned earlier that relationships enable you to combine data from related tables for the purpose of creating queries, forms, and reports. Access provides three different relationships for joining your data: one-to-one, one-to-many, and many-to-many. The most common type by far is the one-to-many relationship. A *one-to-many relationship* is established when the primary key value in the primary table can match many of the foreign key values in the related table. For example, a bank customer will be entered into the Customers table once and only once. The primary key value, which is also the customer's CustomerID number, might be 1585. That same customer could set up a checking, savings, and money market account. With each account, the CustomerID (1585) is required and therefore will occur three times in the Accounts table. The value appears once in the Customers table and three times in the Accounts table. Therefore, the relationship between Customers and Accounts would be described as one-to-many.

Table 2 lists and describes all three types of relationships you can create between Access tables.

A **one-to-many relationship** is established when the primary key value in the primary table can match many of the foreign key values in the related table.

| TABLE 2 | Relationship Types |
|---|---|
| **Relationship Name** | **Definition** |
| **One-to-Many** | This relationship is between a primary key in the first table and a foreign key in the second table. The first table must have only one occurrence of each value. For example, each customer must have a unique identification number in the Customers table, or each employee must have a unique EmployeeID in the Employee table. The foreign key field in the second table may have repeating values. For example, one customer may have many different account numbers, or one employee can perform many services. |
| **One-to-One** | Two different tables use the same primary key. Exactly one record exists in the second table for each record in the first table. Sometimes security reasons require a table to be split into two related tables. For example, anyone in the company can look in the Employee table and find the employee's office number, department assignment, or telephone extension. However, only a few people need to have access to the employee's salary, Social Security Number, performance review, or marital status. Both tables use the same unique identifier to identify each employee. |
| **Many-to-Many** | This is an artificially constructed relationship giving many matching records in each direction between tables. It requires construction of a third table called a junction table. For example, a database might have a table for employees and one for projects. Several employees might be assigned to one project, but one employee might also be assigned to many different projects. When Access connects to databases using Oracle or other software, you find this relationship type. |

## Establish a One-to-Many Relationship

Click the Database Tools tab, and then click Relationships in the Relationships group; the Relationships window opens (as shown in Figure 25). If this were an established database, this window would already contain tables and join lines indicating the relationships that were established in the database.

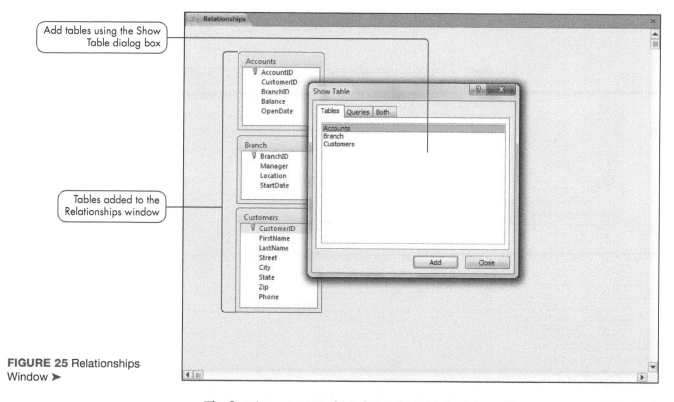

**FIGURE 25** Relationships Window ➤

The first time you open the Relationships window, you will not see any established relationships; you must first use the Show Table dialog box to add the required tables to the Relationships window. Select the tables you want to use to set relationships, and then add them to the Relationships window by clicking Add (as shown in Figure 25).

Where necessary, expand the table windows to display the complete list of field names shown in the table.

Establish the relationships by dragging the common field name from the primary table onto the common field name in the related table. (The common field name does not have to be an exact match, but the data type and field size must be the same.) When you release the mouse, the Edit Relationships dialog box opens (look back at Figure 15). Click Enforce Referential Integrity, and then click Create; Access checks the table data to ensure that the rules you are attempting to establish can be met. For example, in the bank database, if you attempt to enforce referential integrity between the Branch table and the Accounts table, Access will verify that one BranchID value exists in the Branch table for each BranchID value in the Accounts table. If one BranchID value (e.g., B80) in the Accounts table does not exist in the Branch table, Access cannot establish the relationship with referential integrity enforced. The data must be corrected prior to checking enforce referential integrity.

Figure 26 shows the Relationships window for the Bank database and all the relationships created using referential integrity. The join line between the CustomerID field in the Customers table and the CustomerID field in the Accounts table indicates that a one-to-many relationship has been set. You can rearrange the tables by dragging the tables by the title bar. You can switch the positions of the Branch and Accounts tables in the Relationships window without changing the relationship itself.

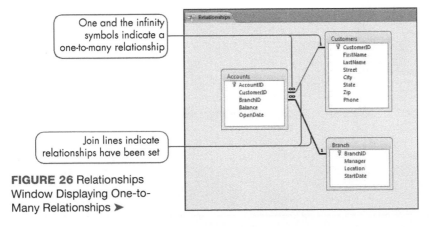

One and the infinity symbols indicate a one-to-many relationship

Join lines indicate relationships have been set

**FIGURE 26** Relationships Window Displaying One-to-Many Relationships ➤

In the following Hands-On Exercise, you will create two additional tables by importing data from Excel spreadsheets into the Bank database. You will establish and modify field properties. Then you will connect the newly imported data to the Branch table by establishing relationships between the tables.

Relational Databases and Queries

## 2 Multiple Table Databases

You created a new Bank database, and you created a new Branch table. Now you are ready to import Commonwealth Federal's customer and account data from Excel spreadsheets. Even though you believe the Excel data is formatted correctly, you decided to open the Excel spreadsheets before you import them into Access. Once you are satisfied the data is structured properly, you can begin the import process.

**Skills covered:** Import Excel Data into an Access Table • Import Additional Excel Data • Modify an Imported Table's Design • Add Data to an Imported Table • Establish Table Relationships • Test Referential Integrity

---

**STEP 1** ▸ **IMPORT EXCEL DATA INTO AN ACCESS TABLE**

You and the auditor have discovered several of Commonwealth's Excel spreadsheets that contain customer data. These files need to be analyzed, so you decide to import the Excel data into Access. Refer to Figure 27 as well as Figures 19 through 24 as you complete Step 1.

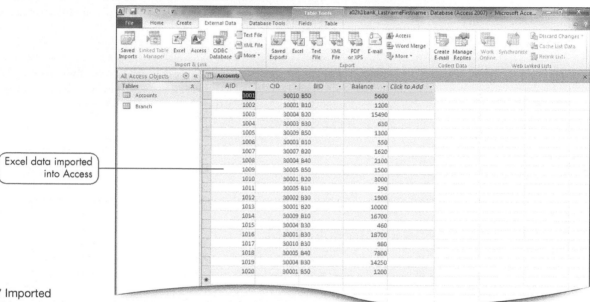

Excel data imported into Access

**FIGURE 27** Imported Accounts Table ➤

a. Open *a02h1bank_LastnameFirstname* if you closed it at the end of Hands-On Exercise 1. Click the **File tab**, click **Save Database As**, and then type **a02h2bank_LastnameFirstname**, changing *h1* to *h2*. Click **Save**.

b. Click the Enable Content button below the Ribbon to indicate you trust the contents of the database.

> **TROUBLESHOOTING:** Throughout the remainder of this chapter and textbook, click the Enable Content button whenever you are working with student files.

c. Click the **External Data tab**, and click **Excel** in the Import & Link group to launch the *Get External Data - Excel Spreadsheet* feature. Select the **Import the source data into a new table in the current database option**, if necessary, as shown in Figure 19.

d. Click **Browse**, and then go to the student data folder. Select the *a02h2bank* workbook. Click **Open**, and then click **OK** to open the Import Spreadsheet Wizard.

The top of the first window shows all of the worksheets in the workbook. This particular workbook contains only two worksheets: Customers and Accounts. The Customers worksheet is active, and a list of the data contained in the Customers worksheet displays in the Wizard.

e. Click **Accounts** (see Figure 20), and then click **Next**.

f. Ensure that the *First Row Contains Column Headings* check box is checked to tell Access that column headings exist in the Excel file (see Figure 21).

The field names, AID, CID, BID, and Balance, will import from Excel along with the data stored in the rows in the worksheet. The field names will be modified later in Access.

g. Click **Next**.

The AID (AccountID) will become the primary key in this table. It needs to be a unique identifier, so we must change the properties to no duplicates.

h. Ensure that *AID* is displayed in the Field Name box in Field Options. Then click the **Indexed arrow**, and then select **Yes** (**No Duplicates**), as shown in Figure 22. Click **Next**.

i. Click the **Choose my own primary key option** (see Figure 23). Make sure that the *AID* field is selected. Click **Next**.

The final screen of the Import Spreadsheet Wizard asks you to name your table. The name of the Excel worksheet was Accounts, and Access defaults to the worksheet name. It is an acceptable name (see Figure 24).

j. Click **Finish** to accept the Accounts table name.

A dialog box opens asking if you wish to save the steps of this import to use again. If this were sales data that was collected in Excel and updated to the database on a weekly basis, saving the import steps would save time. You do not need to save this example.

k. Click the **Close button**.

The new table displays in the Navigation Pane and resides in the Bank database.

l. Open the imported Accounts table in Datasheet view, and then compare it to Figure 27. Close the table.

## STEP 2 ▷ IMPORT ADDITIONAL EXCEL DATA

The first spreadsheet that you imported contained account information related to the mishandled funds. The auditor has asked you to import a second spreadsheet that contains customer account information. Follow the same process as you did in Step 1 as you answer each Import Wizard question. Refer to Figure 28 as well as Figures 19 through 24 as you complete Step 2.

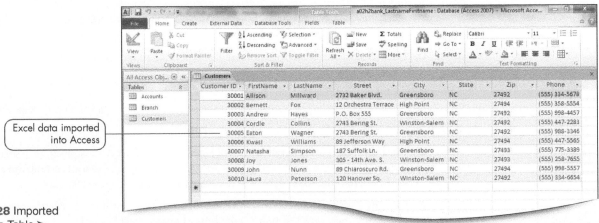

**FIGURE 28** Imported Customers Table ➤

a. Click the **External Data tab**, and then click **Excel** in the Import & Link group to launch the *Get External Data - Excel Spreadsheet* feature. Select the **Import the source data into a new table in the current database option**, if necessary.

b. Click **Browse**, and then go to the student data folder. Select the *a02h2bank* workbook. Click **Open**, and then click **OK** to open the Import Spreadsheet Wizard.

The Customers worksheet is active; you will import this worksheet.

c. Click **Next**.

d. Ensure that the *First Row Contains Column Headings* check box is checked to tell Access that column headings exist in the Excel file. Click **Next**.

The CID will become the primary key in this table. It needs to be a unique identifier, so you change the properties to no duplicates.

e. Ensure that *CID* is displayed in the Field Name box in Field Options. Click the **Indexed arrow**, and then select **Yes (No Duplicates)**. Click **Next**.

f. Click the **Choose my own primary key option**. Make sure that the *CID* field is selected. Click **Next**.

Access defaults to the table name Customers.

g. Click **Finish** to accept the Customers table name.

h. Click **Close** on the Save Import Steps dialog box.

The Navigation Pane contains three tables: Accounts, Branch, and Customers.

i. Open the imported Customers table in Datasheet view, and then compare it to Figure 28. Close the table.

## STEP 3 ▶ MODIFY AN IMPORTED TABLE'S DESIGN

The Excel worksheets became Access tables when you imported them into the Bank database. However, in order to answer all the auditor's questions (using queries), you need to modify the tables so that each field has the correct data type and field size. Refer to Figure 29 as you complete Step 3.

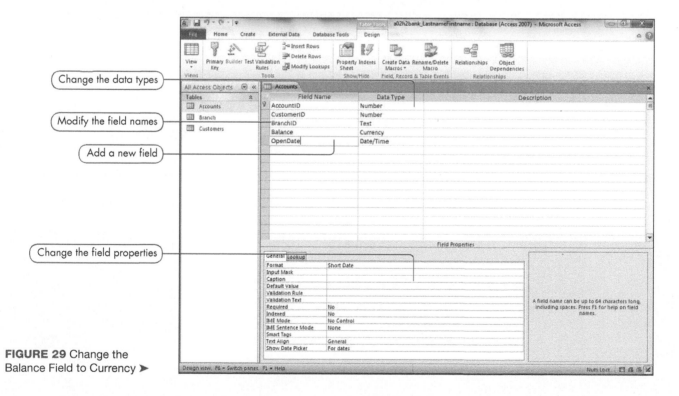

**FIGURE 29** Change the Balance Field to Currency ▶

a. Double-click the **Accounts table** in the Navigation Pane to open it in Datasheet view.

b. Click **View** in the Views group on the Home tab to switch to Design view.

c. Change the AID field name to **AccountID**.

d. Change the Field Size property to **Long Integer** in the Field Properties at the bottom of the design window.

   Long Integer ensures that there will be enough numbers as the number of accounts grow over time. Importing data from Excel saves typing, but modifications will usually be required.

e. Type **Account ID** in the **Caption property box** for the AccountID field. The caption contains a space between *Account* and *ID*.

f. Change the CID field name to **CustomerID**.

g. Change the Field Size property to **Long Integer** in the Field Properties at the bottom of the design window.

   You can select the Field Size option using the arrow, or you can type the first letter of the option you want. For example, type *l* for Long Integer or *s* for Single. Make sure the current option is completely selected before you type the letter.

h. Type **Customer ID** in the **Caption property box** for the CustomerID field. The caption contains a space between *Customer* and *ID*.

i. Click the **BID field**. Change the BID field name to **BranchID**.

j. Type **5** in the **Field Size property box** in the Field Properties.

k. Type **Branch ID** in the **Caption property box** for the Branch ID field.

l. Change the Data Type of the Balance field from *Number* to **Currency**.

m. Type a new field name, **OpenDate**, under the Balance field name. Assign data type **Date/Time**, and then add the **Short Date format** in the Field Properties.

n. Click **View** in the Views group to switch to Datasheet View. Read the messages, and then click **Yes** twice.

   In this case, it is OK to click Yes because the size of three fields was shortened. The new OpenDate field will store the date that each account was opened.

**o.** Add the OpenDate values as shown below:

| Account ID | OpenDate |
|---|---|
| 1001 | 4/28/2007 |
| 1002 | 4/13/2005 |
| 1003 | 5/28/2004 |
| 1004 | 9/21/2003 |
| 1005 | 7/22/2005 |
| 1006 | 7/3/2003 |
| 1007 | 6/7/2006 |
| 1008 | 9/30/2007 |
| 1009 | 2/7/2006 |
| 1010 | 3/18/2010 |
| 1011 | 10/16/2012 |
| 1012 | 3/14/2007 |
| 1013 | 5/15/2009 |
| 1014 | 9/17/2007 |
| 1015 | 4/4/2003 |
| 1016 | 3/13/2003 |
| 1017 | 9/5/2004 |
| 1018 | 5/6/2003 |
| 1019 | 1/4/2012 |
| 1020 | 4/13/2005 |

**p.** Right-click the **Customers table** in the Navigation Pane, and then select **Design View** from the shortcut menu. Change the CID field name to **CustomerID**. Change the Field Size property of the CustomerID field to **Long Integer**, and then add a caption, **Customer ID**. Take note of the intentional space between *Customer* and *ID*.

The Accounts table and the Customers table will be joined using the CustomerID field. Both fields must have the same data type.

**q.** Change the Field Size property to **20** for the FirstName, LastName, Street, and City fields. Change the Field Size for State to **2**.

**r.** Change the data type for Zip and Phone to **Text**. Change the Field size property to **15** for both fields. Remove the @ symbol from the Format property where it exists for all fields in the Customers table.

**s.** Click the **Phone field name**, and then click **Input Mask** in Field Properties. Click **Build** on the right side to launch the Input Mask Wizard. Click **Yes** to save the table, and then click **Yes** to the *some data may be lost* warning. Click **Finish** to apply the default phone number Input Mask.

The phone number input mask will enable users to enter 6105551212 and Access to display (610) 555-1212.

**t.** Click **Save** to save the design changes to the Customers table. Read the Warning Box, and then click **Yes**.

## STEP 4 ▶ ADD DATA TO AN IMPORTED TABLE

Now that you have created the Access tables, add data as directed by the auditor. You may also need to update and delete records if you and the auditor decide the information is no longer needed. Refer to Figure 30 as you complete Step 4.

Hands-On Exercises • Access 2010

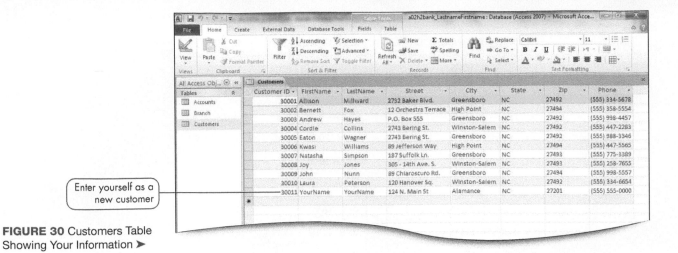

**FIGURE 30** Customers Table
Showing Your Information ➤

a. Click **View** in the Views group to display the Customers table in Datasheet view.

   The asterisk at the bottom of the table data in the row selector area is the indicator of a place to enter a new record.

b. Click the **Customer ID field** in the record after *30010*. Type **30011**. Fill in the rest of the data using your information as the customer. You may use a fictitious address and phone number.

c. Close the Customers table. Click the **Accounts table tab** if necessary.

d. Locate the new row indicator—the * in the row selector—and click in the **Account ID column**. Type **1021**. Type **30011** as the **Customer ID** and **B50** as the **Branch ID**. Type **21004** for the Balance field value. Type **7/2/2009** for the OpenDate.

e. Close the Accounts table; keep the database open.

---

**STEP 5 ▶ ESTABLISH TABLE RELATIONSHIPS**

The tables for the bank investigation have been designed. Now, you will need to establish connections between the tables. Look at the primary and foreign keys as a guide. Refer to Figure 31 as you complete Step 5.

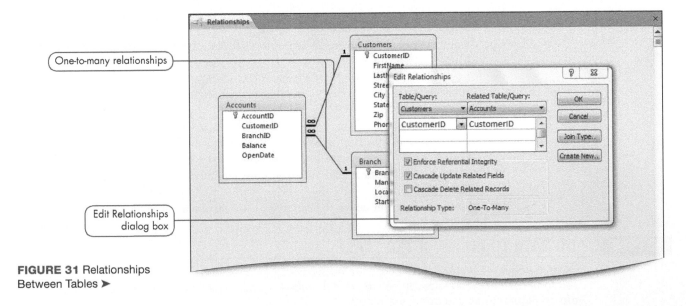

**FIGURE 31** Relationships
Between Tables ➤

Relational Databases and Queries

a.  Click the **Database Tools tab**, and then click **Relationships** in the Relationships group.

The Relationships window opens and the Show Table dialog box appears.

> **TROUBLESHOOTING:** If the Show Table dialog box does not open, click Show Table in the Relationships group on the Relationships Tools Design tab.

b.  Double-click each of the three tables displayed in the Show Table dialog box to add them to the Relationships window. (Alternatively, click a table, and then click Add.) Click **Close** in the Show Table dialog box.

> **TROUBLESHOOTING:** If you have a duplicate table, click the title bar of the duplicated table, and then press Delete.

c.  Resize the Customers table box so all the fields are visible. Arrange the tables as shown in Figure 31.

d.  Drag the **BranchID field** in the Branch table onto the BranchID field in the Accounts table. The Edit Relationships dialog box opens. Click the **Enforce Referential Integrity** and **Cascade Update Related Fields check boxes**. Click **Create**.

A black line displays, joining the two tables. It has a 1 on the end near the Branch table and an infinity symbol on the end next to the Accounts table. You have established a one-to-many relationship between the Branch and Accounts tables.

e.  Drag the **CustomerID field** in the Customers table onto the CustomerID field in the Accounts table. The Edit Relationships dialog box opens. Click the **Enforce Referential Integrity** and **Cascade Update Related Fields check boxes**. Click **Create**.

You have established a one-to-many relationship between the Customers and Accounts tables. A customer will have only a single CustomerID number. The same customer may have many different accounts: Savings, Checking, CDs, etc.

> **TROUBLESHOOTING:** If you get an error message when you click Create, verify the data types of the joined fields are the same. To check the data types from the Relationships window, right-click the title bar of a table, and then select Table Design from the shortcut menu. Modify the data type and field size of the join fields if necessary.

f.  Click **Save** on the Quick Access Toolbar to save the changes to the Relationships. Close the Relationships window.

## STEP 6 ▶ TEST REFERENTIAL INTEGRITY

The design of the bank database must be 100% correct; otherwise, data entry may be compromised. Even though you are confident that the table relationships are correct, you decide to test them by entering some invalid data. If the relationships are working, the invalid data will be rejected by Access. Refer to Figure 32 as you complete Step 6.

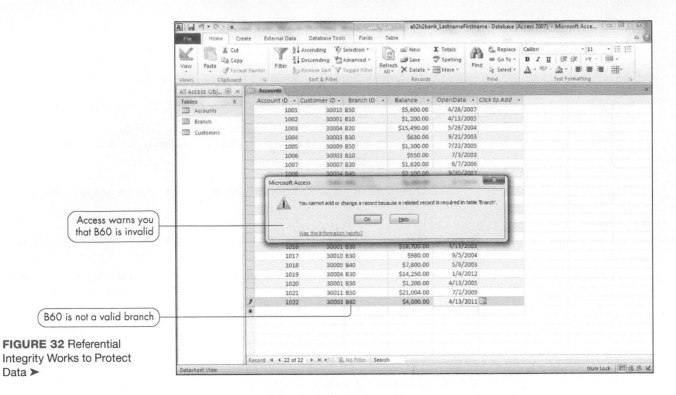

Access warns you that B60 is invalid

B60 is not a valid branch

**FIGURE 32** Referential Integrity Works to Protect Data ➤

a. Double-click the **Accounts table** to open it in Datasheet view.

b. Add a new record, pressing **Tab** after each field: Account ID: **1022**, Customer ID: **30003**, Branch ID: **B60**, Balance: **4000**, OpenDate: **4/13/2011**.

   A warning message is telling you that a related record in the Branch table is required since the Accounts table and the Branch table are connected by a relationship with enforce referential integrity checked.

c. Click **OK**. Double-click the **Branch table** in the Navigation Pane, and then examine the data in the BranchID field. Notice the Branch table has no B60 record. Close the Branch table.

d. Replace *B60* with **B50** in the new Accounts record, and then press **Tab** three times. As soon as the focus moves to the next record, the pencil symbol disappears and your data is saved.

   You successfully identified a BranchID that Access recognizes. Because referential integrity between the Accounts and Branch tables has been enforced, Access looks at each data entry item in a foreign key and matches it to a corresponding value in the table where it is the primary key. In Step 6b, you attempted to enter a nonexistent BranchID and were not allowed to make that error. In Step 6d, you entered a valid BranchID. Access examined the index for the BranchID in the Branch table and found a corresponding value for B50.

e. Close the Accounts table. Reopen the Accounts table; you will find that the record you just entered for 1022 has been saved. Close the table.

f. Close all open tables, if necessary.

g. Click the **File tab**, and then click **Compact & Repair Database**.

h. Click the **File tab**, click **Save & Publish**, and then double-click **Back Up Database**. Accept *a02h2bank_LastnameFirstname_date* as the file name, and then click **Save**.

   You just created a backup of the database. The *a02h2bank_LastnameFirstname* database remains open.

i. Keep the database onscreen if you plan to continue with Hands-On Exercise 3. If not, close the database and exit Access.

# Single-Table Queries

A **query** enables you to ask questions about the data stored in a database.

If you wanted to see which customers currently have an account with a balance over $5,000, you could find the answer by creating an Access query. A *query* enables you to ask questions about the data stored in a database. Since data is stored in tables in a database, you always begin a query by asking, "Which table holds the data I want?" For the question about account balances over $5,000, you would reference the Accounts table. In some cases, the data may be held in two or more tables. Multi-table queries will be covered later; for now, you will limit your study of queries to only one table.

If you want to invite customers in a certain zip code to the Grand Opening of a new branch, you could create a query based on the Customers table.

**Query Design view** enables you to create queries; the Design view is divided into two parts—the top portion displays the tables, and the bottom portion (known as the query design grid) displays the fields and the criteria.

You use the *Query Design view* to create queries; the Design view is divided into two parts—the top portion displays the tables, and the bottom portion (known as the query design grid) displays the fields and the criteria.

Using the Query Design view, you select only the fields you want arranged in the order that you want them. The design grid also enables you to sort the records based on one or more fields. You can also create calculated fields to display data based on expressions that use the fields in the underlying table. For example, you could calculate the monthly interest earned on each bank account.

In this section, you will use the Query Wizard and Query Design to create queries that display only data that you select.

## Creating a Single-Table Query

The **Simple Query Wizard** provides dialog boxes to guide you through the query design process.

You can create a single-table query in two ways—by using the Simple Query Wizard or by using the Query Design tool in the Queries group. Like all of the Microsoft wizards, the *Simple Query Wizard* provides dialog boxes to guide you through the query design process. The wizard is helpful for users who are not experienced with Access or with queries. More advanced users will usually use the Query Design tool to create queries. This method provides the most flexibility when creating queries (but without the prompting of the wizard). You can add criteria to a query while in the Query Design view, as compared to the wizard where you cannot add criteria while the wizard is running. After the query is created, you can switch to Design view and add criteria manually.

After you design a query (using either method), you can display the results of the query by switching to Datasheet view. A query's datasheet looks and acts like a table's datasheet, except that it is usually a subset of the records found in the entire table. The subset only shows the records that match the criteria that were added in the query design. The subset will usually contain different sorting of the records than the sorting in the underlying table. Datasheet view allows you to enter a new record, modify an existing record, or delete a record. Any changes made in Datasheet view are reflected in the underlying table.

> **TIP** Caution: Changes Made to Query Results Overwrite Table Data
>
> Be aware that query results display the actual records that are stored in the underlying table(s). On the one hand, being able to correct an error immediately while it is displayed in query results is an advantage. You save time by not having to close the query, open the table, find the error, fix it, and run the query again. However, you should use caution when editing records in query results since you might not expect to change the table data.

## Create a Single-Table Select Query

As stated above, more experienced users create queries using the Query Design tool. To begin click the Create tab, and then click Query Design in the Queries group. The Show Table dialog box appears automatically. Select the table that you need in your query, and then click Add to add the table to the top section of the query design, as shown in Figure 33. After the table has been added, close the Show Table dialog box and begin dragging the fields from the table to the query design grid. The grid holds the fields as well as the criteria (for filtering records) and the sorting options. Figure 34 shows the Design view of a sample query with four fields, with criteria set for one field, and sorting set on another field. After the query design is finished, click Run in the Results group to show the results in Datasheet view, as shown in Figure 35.

By default, when you create a query, you create a select query, which is the most common type of query. A *select query* displays only the records that match the criteria entered in Design view. A select query does not change the data. Other types of queries, known as action queries, can update, append, or delete records when they are run. Examples include Update Query, Append Query, and Make Table Query.

A **select query** displays only the records that match the criteria entered in Design view.

> ## TIP Examine the Records
>
> An experienced Access user always examines the records returned in the query results. Verify that the records in the query results match the criteria that you specified in Design view. As you add additional criteria, the number of records returned will usually decrease.

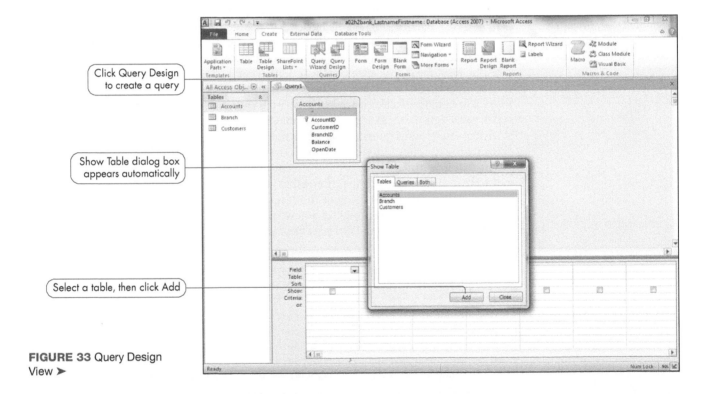

**FIGURE 33** Query Design View ➤

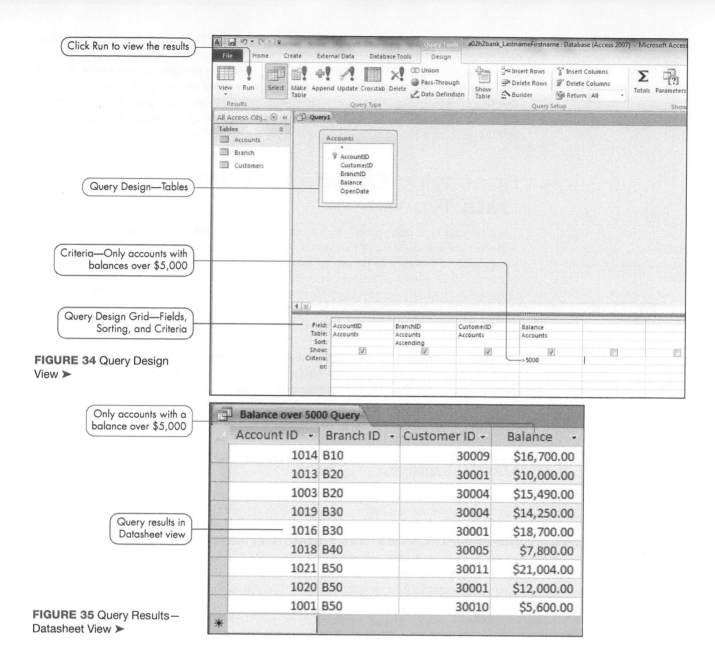

Click Run to view the results

Query Design—Tables

Criteria—Only accounts with balances over $5,000

Query Design Grid—Fields, Sorting, and Criteria

**FIGURE 34** Query Design View ➤

Only accounts with a balance over $5,000

Query results in Datasheet view

**Balance over 5000 Query**

| Account ID | Branch ID | Customer ID | Balance |
|---|---|---|---|
| 1014 | B10 | 30009 | $16,700.00 |
| 1013 | B20 | 30001 | $10,000.00 |
| 1003 | B20 | 30004 | $15,490.00 |
| 1019 | B30 | 30004 | $14,250.00 |
| 1016 | B30 | 30001 | $18,700.00 |
| 1018 | B40 | 30005 | $7,800.00 |
| 1021 | B50 | 30011 | $21,004.00 |
| 1020 | B50 | 30001 | $12,000.00 |
| 1001 | B50 | 30010 | $5,600.00 |

**FIGURE 35** Query Results— Datasheet View ➤

The **Field row** in the Query Design view displays the field name.

The **Table row** in the Query Design view displays the data source.

The **Sort row** in the Query Design view enables you to sort in ascending or descending order.

The **Show row** in the Query Design view controls whether the field will be displayed in the query results.

The **Criteria row** in the Query Design view determines which records will be selected.

# Use Query Design View

The Query Design view consists of two parts. The top portion contains tables with their respective field names. If a query contains more than one table, the join lines between tables will be displayed as they were created in the Relationships window.

The bottom portion (known as the query design grid) contains columns and rows. Each field in the query has its own column and contains multiple rows. The rows permit you to control the query results.

- The *Field row* in the Query Design view displays the field name.
- The *Table row* in the Query Design view displays the data source.
- The *Sort row* in the Query Design view enables you to sort in ascending or descending order.
- The *Show row* in the Query Design view controls whether the field will be displayed in the query results.
- The *Criteria row* in the Query Design view is used to set the rules that determine which records will be selected, such as customers with accounts greater than $5,000.

When you developed the tables, you toggled between the Design view and Datasheet view. Similarly, you will toggle between Design view and Datasheet view when you create queries. Use Design view to specify the criteria; you can use the results to answer a question or to make a decision about the organization. Use Datasheet view to see the results of your query. Each time you need to fine-tune the query, switch back to Design view, make a change, and then test the results in Datasheet view. After you are satisfied with the query results, you may want to save the query so it can become a permanent part of the database and can be used later.

# Specifying Criteria for Different Data Types

A **delimiter** is a special character that surrounds the criterion's value.

The field data type determines which delimiters are required for the criterion of a field. A *delimiter* is a special character that surrounds the criterion's value. You need to enter criteria for a text field enclosed in quotation marks. To find only the records of customers with accounts at the Campus branch, you would enter *Campus* as the criterion under the Location field. Access accepts values for text fields in the design grid with or without quotation marks; if you enter *Campus*, Access will add the quotes for you. You enter the criteria for a numeric field, currency, or AutoNumber as plain digits (no quotations). You can enter numeric criteria with or without a decimal point and with or without a minus sign. (Commas and dollar signs are not allowed.) When the criterion is in a date field, you enclose the criterion in pound signs, such as *#10/14/2012#*. Access accepts a date with or without the pound signs; if you enter 1/1/2012 without the pound signs, Access will add the pound signs when you move to another column in the design grid. The date value should be in the mm/dd/yyyy format. You enter criteria for a Yes/No field as *Yes* or *No*.

## Use Wildcards

A **wildcard** is a special character that can represent one or more characters in the criterion of a query.

Suppose you want to search for the last name of a customer but you are not sure how to spell the name; however, you know that his name starts with the letters Sm. You can specify the criteria in the LastName field as *Sm\**, which would display all last names that begin with *Sm*. The asterisk is known as a wildcard. *Wildcards* are special characters that can represent one or more characters in a text value. You enter wildcard characters in the Criteria row of a query. A question mark is a wildcard that stands for a single character in the same position as the question mark; for example, *H?ll* will return *Hall*, *Hill*, and *Hull*. The asterisk wildcard stands for any number of characters in the same position as the asterisk; for example, *S\*nd* will return *Sand*, *Stand*, and *StoryLand*. If you search the two-letter state code field using criterion Like *?C*, Access will return *DC*, *NC*, and *SC*. If you search the same field using criterion Like *\*C*, Access will return *DC*, *NC*, and *SC*. If you search the same field using criterion Like *C\**, Access will return *CA*, *CO*, and *CT*.

## Use Comparison Operators in Queries

A **comparison operator**, such as equal (=), not equal (<>), greater than (>), less than (<), greater than or equal to (>=), and less than or equal to (<=), can be used in the criteria of a query.

A *comparison operator*, such as equal (=), not equal (<>), greater than (>), less than (<), greater than or equal to (>=), and less than or equal to (<=), can be used in the criteria of a query. Comparison operators enable you to limit the query results to only those records that meet the criteria. For example, if you only want to see accounts that have a balance greater than $5,000, you would type >5000 in the criteria row. Table 3 shows more comparison operator examples as well as other sample expressions.

| TABLE 3 | Sample Query Criteria |
|---|---|
| **Expression** | **Example** |
| >10 | For a Price field, items with a price over $10.00. |
| <10 | For a Price field, items with a price under $10.00. |
| >=10 | For a Price field, items with a price of at least $10.00. |
| <=10 | For a Price field, items with a price of $10.00 or less. |
| =10 | For a Price field, items with a price of exactly $10.00. |
| <>10 | For a Price field, items with a price not equal to $10.00. |
| #2/2/2012# | For a field with a Date/Time data type, such as a ShippedDate field, orders shipped on February 2, 2012. |
| "Harry" | For a Text field, find the name Harry. |
| Date() | For an OrderDate field, orders for today's date. |
| Between #1/1/2012# and #3/31/2012# | For a specified interval between a start and end date, including the start and end dates. |

## Work with Null and Zero-Length Strings

**Null** is the term Access uses to describe a blank field.

Sometimes finding what is missing is an important part of making a decision. For example, if you need to know which orders have been completed but not shipped, you would ask for the orders with a missing ShipDate. Are there missing phone numbers or addresses for some of your customers? Ask for customers with a missing PhoneNumber. The term that Access uses for a blank field is *null*. Table 4 gives two illustrations of when to use the null criterion in a query.

| TABLE 4 | Establishing Null Criteria Expressions |
|---|---|
| **Expression** | **Example** |
| Is Null | For an Employee field in the Customers table when the customer has not been assigned a sales representative. |
| Is Not Null | For the ShipDate field; a value inserted indicates the order was shipped to the customer. |

## Understand Query Sort Order

The **query sort order** determines the order of records in the query's Datasheet view.

The *query sort order* determines the order of records in a query's Datasheet view. You can change the order of records by specifying the sort order in the Design view. The sort order is determined from left to right. The order of columns should be considered when first creating the query. For example, a query sorted by Lastname and then by Firstname must have those two fields in the correct order in the design grid. Change the order of the query fields in the design grid to change the sort order of the query results. To change the order of fields, select the column you want to move by clicking the column selector. Release the mouse, then click again and drag the selected field to its new location. To insert additional columns in the design grid, first select a column, and then click Insert Columns in the Query Setup group. The inserted column will insert to the left of the selected column.

## Establish AND, OR, and NOT Criteria

Recall the earlier question, "Which customers currently have an account with a balance over $5,000?" This question was answered by creating a query with a single criterion, as shown in Figure 34. At times, questions are more specific and require queries with multiple criteria. For example, you may need to know "Which customers from the Eastern branch currently have an account with a balance over $5,000?" To answer this question, you need to specify criteria in multiple fields. When the criteria are in the same row of the query design grid, Access interprets the instructions using the *AND logical operator*. This means that the query results will display only records that match *all* criteria. When the criteria are positioned in different rows of the design grid, Access interprets the instructions using the *OR logical operator*. The query results will display records that match any of the specified criteria. The *NOT logical operator* returns all records except the specified criteria. For example, "Not Eastern" would return all accounts except those opened at the Eastern branch.

Figure 36a shows a query with an AND logical operator. It will return all of the B20 branch accounts with balances over $5,000. (Both conditions must be met for the record to be included.) Figure 36b shows a query with an OR logical operator. It will return all of the B20 branch accounts regardless of balance plus all accounts at any branch with a balance over $5,000. (One condition must be met for a record to be included.) Figure 36c shows a query that uses the NOT logical operator. It will return all of the accounts—excluding the B20 branch—with a balance over $5,000. Figure 36d shows a query that combines AND and OR logical operators. The top row will return B20 branch accounts with a balance over $5,000, and the second row will return B30 branch accounts with a balance over $15,000.

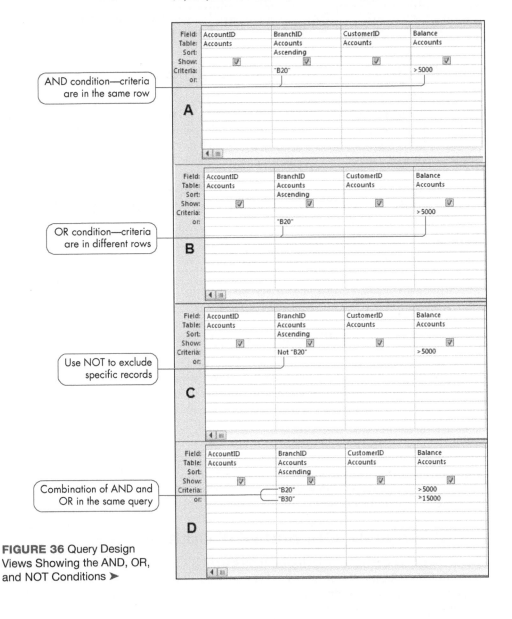

AND condition—criteria
are in the same row

OR condition—criteria
are in different rows

Use NOT to exclude
specific records

Combination of AND and
OR in the same query

**FIGURE 36** Query Design
Views Showing the AND, OR,
and NOT Conditions ➤

# Copying and Running a Query

After you create a query, you may want to create a duplicate copy to use as the basis for creating a similar query. Duplicating a query saves time when you need the same tables and fields but with slightly different criteria.

Several ways exist to run a query. One method is to locate the query in the Navigation Pane, and then double-click it. A similar method is to select the query, and then press Enter. Another way is to click Run in the Results group, when you are in Design view.

## Copy a Query

Sometimes you have a one-of-a-kind question about your data. You would create a query to answer this question and then delete the query. However, sometimes you need a series of queries where each query is similar to the first. For example, you need "Sales for This Month" in Houston, in Dallas, and in Chicago. In cases like this, you create a query for the first city and then save the query. Click Save As to save a copy of the query and name it for the second city. Change the criteria to match the second city. Repeat the process for the third city.

## Run a Query

After you create a query and save it, you can run it directly from the Design view. You run a query by clicking ***Run command*** (the red exclamation point) in the Results group. In the sample databases, the queries run quickly. For larger databases, query results may take several minutes to display. When you design queries in larger databases, include all necessary fields and tables, but do not include fields or tables that are not necessary to answer the question. You can also run a query from the Navigation Pane. Locate the query you want to run, and then double-click the query. The results will appear as a tab in the main window. (Note: This method is only recommended for select queries. This method is not recommended for action queries, which will be covered later.)

# Using the Query Wizard

You may create a query directly in Design view or by using the Query Wizard. Even if you initiate the query with a wizard, you will need to learn how to modify it in Design view. Often, copying an existing query and making slight modifications to its design is much faster than starting at the beginning with the wizard. You also will need to know how to add additional tables and fields to an existing query when conditions change. To launch the Query Wizard, click the Create tab, and then click Query Wizard in the Queries group (see Figure 37).

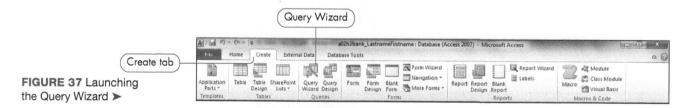

**FIGURE 37** Launching the Query Wizard ➤

Select the Simple Query Wizard in the Query Wizard dialog box, as shown in Figure 38.

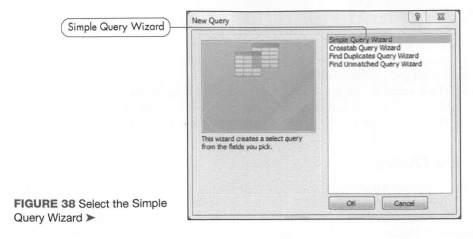

FIGURE 38 Select the Simple Query Wizard ➤

In the first step of the Simple Query Wizard dialog box, you specify the tables or queries and fields needed in your query. When you select a table from the Tables/Queries arrow, a list of the table's fields displays in the Available Fields list box. See Figures 39 and 40.

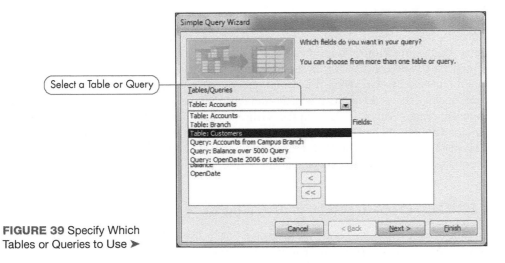

FIGURE 39 Specify Which Tables or Queries to Use ➤

Select the necessary fields, and then add them to the Selected Fields list box using the directional arrows shown in Figure 40.

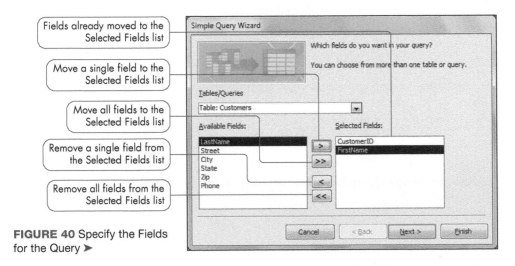

FIGURE 40 Specify the Fields for the Query ➤

In the next screen (shown in Figure 41), you choose between a detail and a summary query. The detail query shows every field of every record in the result. The summary query enables you to group data and view only summary records. For example, if you were interested in the total funds deposited at each of the bank branches, you would set the query to Summary, click Summary Options, and then click sum on the balance field. Access would then sum the balances of all accounts for each branch.

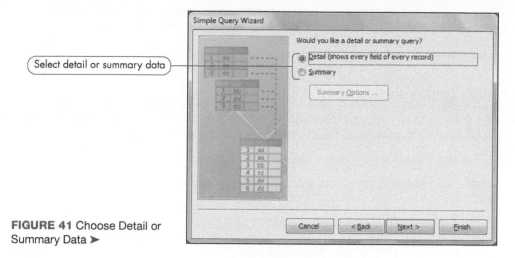

**FIGURE 41** Choose Detail or Summary Data ➤

The final dialog box of the Simple Query Wizard asks for the name of the query. Assign a descriptive name to your queries so that you know what each does by looking at the query name. See Figure 42.

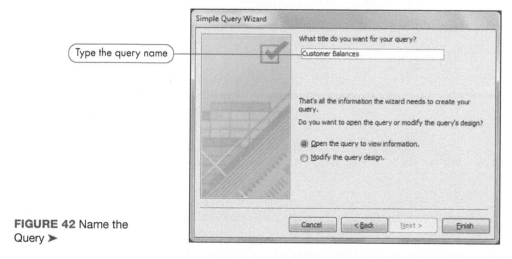

**FIGURE 42** Name the Query ➤

The next Hands-On Exercise enables you to create and run queries in order to find answers to questions you have about your data. You will use the Query Wizard to create a basic query and then modify the query in Design view by adding an additional field and by adding query criteria.

## 3 Single-Table Queries

The tables and table relationships have been created, and some data has been entered. Now, you need to begin the process of analyzing the bank data for the auditor. You will do so using queries. You decide to begin with the Accounts table.

**Skills covered:** Create a Query Using a Wizard • Specify Query Criteria and Sorting • Change Query Data

---

**STEP 1 ▸ CREATE A QUERY USING A WIZARD**

You decide to start with the Query Wizard, knowing you can always alter the design of the query later in Design view. You will show the results to the auditor using Datasheet view. Refer to Figure 43 as you complete Step 1.

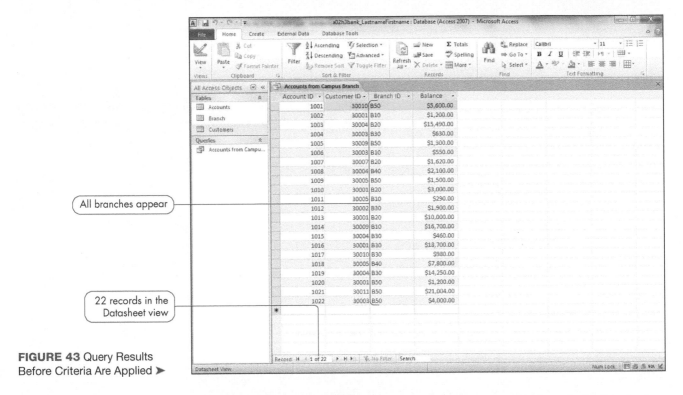

All branches appear

22 records in the Datasheet view

**FIGURE 43** Query Results Before Criteria Are Applied ➤

a. Open *a02h2bank_LastnameFirstname* if you closed it at the end of Hands-On Exercise 2. Click the **File tab**, click **Save Database As**, and then type **a02h3bank_LastnameFirstname**, changing *h2* to *h3*. Click **Save**.

b. Click the **Create tab**, and then click **Query Wizard** in the Queries group to launch the New Query wizard.

The New Query Wizard dialog box opens. Simple Query Wizard is selected by default.

c. Click **OK**.

d. Verify that **Table: Accounts** is selected.

e. Select **AccountID** from the **Available Fields list**, and then click >. Repeat the process with **CustomerID**, **BranchID**, and **Balance**. The four fields should now appear in the Selected Fields list box. Click **Next**.

f. Confirm **Detail** is selected, and then click **Next**.

g. Name the query **Accounts from Campus Branch**. Click **Finish**.

This query name describes the data in the query results. Your query should have four fields: AccountID, CustomerID, BranchID, and Balance.

## STEP 2 ▶ SPECIFY QUERY CRITERIA AND SORTING

The auditor indicated that the problem seems to be confined to the Campus branch. You use this knowledge to revise the query accordingly. Refer to Figure 44 as you complete Step 2.

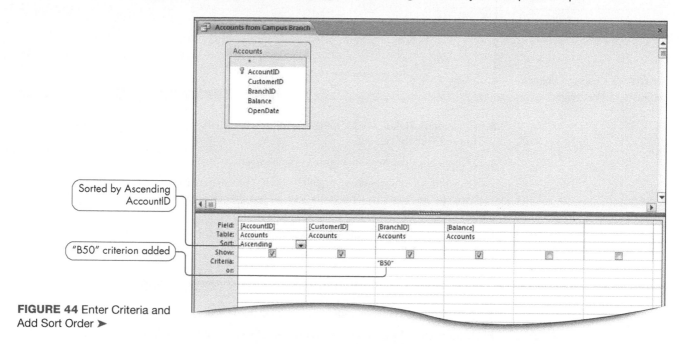

**FIGURE 44** Enter Criteria and Add Sort Order ▶

a. Click the **Home tab**, and then click **View** in the Views group to views the Accounts from Campus Branch query in Design view.

You have created the Campus Branch Customers query to view only those accounts at the Campus branch. However, other branch's accounts also display. You need to limit the query results to only the records of interest.

b. Click in the **Criteria row** (fifth row) in the **BranchID column**, and then type **B50**.

B50 is the BranchID for the Campus branch. Access queries are not case sensitive; therefore, b50 and B50 will produce the same results. Access adds quotation marks around text criteria.

c. Click in the **Sort row** (third row) in the **AccountID column**, and then choose **Ascending** from the list.

d. Click **Run** in the Results group.

You should see six records, all from Branch B50, in the query results.

e. Save the query.

When the query results are on the screen, the auditor notices that some of the data is incorrect, and one of the accounts is missing. From your experience with Access, you explain to the auditor that the data can be changed directly in a query rather than switching back to the table. Refer to Figure 45 as you complete Step 3.

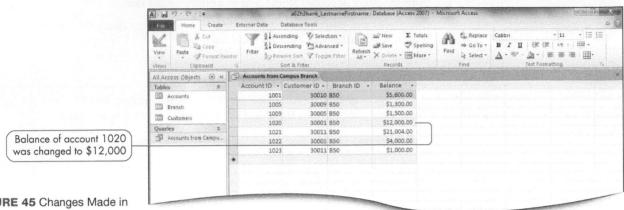

**Balance of account 1020 was changed to $12,000**

**FIGURE 45** Changes Made in the Query Datasheet ➤

a.  Click on the **Balance field** in the record for account *1020*. Change *$1,200* to **$12,000**. Press **Enter**. Close the query.

b.  Double-click the **Accounts table** in the Navigation Pane to open it.

Only one account shows a $12,000 balance. The Customer ID is 30001. The change you made in the Accounts table from the Campus Branch query datasheet automatically changed the data stored in the underlying table.

c.  Open the Customers table. Find the name of the customer whose CustomerID is *30001*. Close the Customers table.

Allison Millward's CustomerID number is 30001.

d.  Add a new record to the Accounts table. The Accounts table should be open. If not, open it now.

e.  Type **1023, 30011, B50, 1000**, and **1/4/2012** in the new record. Press **Tab**.

f.  Double-click the **Accounts from Campus Branch query** in the Navigation Pane.

Customer 30011 now shows two accounts: one with a balance of $21,004 and one with a balance of $1,000.

g.  Close the Accounts from Campus Branch query. Close the Accounts table.

h.  Click the **File tab**, and then click **Compact & Repair Database**.

i.  Click the **File tab**, click **Save & Publish**, and then double-click **Back Up Database**. Accept *a02h3bank_date* as the file name, and then click **Save**.

You just created a backup of the database. The *a02h3bank_LastnameFirstname* database remains open.

j.  Keep the database onscreen if you plan to continue with Hands-On Exercise 4. If not, close the database and exit Access.

# Multi-Table Queries

The sample bank database contains three tables: Customers, Accounts, and Branch. You learned how to connect the tables through relationships in order to store data efficiently and enforce consistent data entry. *Multi-table queries* contain two or more tables. They enable you to take advantage of the relationships that have been set in your database. When you need to extract information from a database with a query, most times you will need multiple tables to provide the answers you need.

A **multi-table query** contains two or more tables. It enables you to take advantage of the relationships that have been set in your database.

One table may contain the core information that you need. Another table may contain the related data that makes the query relevant to the users. For example, the Accounts table will list the balances of each account at the bank—the key financial information. However, the Accounts table does not list the contact information of the owner of the account. Therefore, the Customers table is needed to provide the additional information.

## Creating a Multi-Table Query

Creating a multi-table query is similar to creating a single-table query; however, choosing the right tables and managing the table relationships will require some additional skills. First, you should only include related tables in a multi-table query. *Related tables* are tables that are joined in a relationship using a common field. As a rule, related tables should already be established when you create a multi-table query. Using Figure 46 as a guide, creating a query with the Accounts and Branch tables would be acceptable, as would using Accounts and Customers tables, or Accounts, Branch, and Customers tables. All three scenarios include related tables. Creating a query with the Branch and Customers tables would not be acceptable, since these tables are *not* directly related.

**Related tables** are tables that are joined in a relationship using a common field.

> **TIP** Print the Relationship Report to Help Create a Multi-Table Query
>
> When creating a multi-table query, you should only include related tables. As a guide, you can print the Relationship Report in the Tools group on the Relationship Tools Design tab when the Relationships window is open. This report will help you determine which tables are related in your database.

In the previous example, you answered the question "Which customers from the Campus branch have an account with a balance over $5,000?" Figure 35 displays the datasheet results of the query. To make this report more useful, we can add the Branch Location (in place of the BranchID) and the Customer LastName (in place of the CustomerID). To make these changes we would need to add the Branch table and the Customers table to the query design.

## Add Additional Tables to a Query

As discussed earlier, you can modify a saved query using Design view for the query. If you wanted to change the Balance Over $5000 query, first open the query in Design view. To add additional tables to a query, open the Navigation Pane, and then drag tables directly into the top portion of the query design grid. For example, the Branch and Customers tables were added to the query as shown in Figure 46. The join lines between tables indicate that relationships were previously set in the Relationships window.

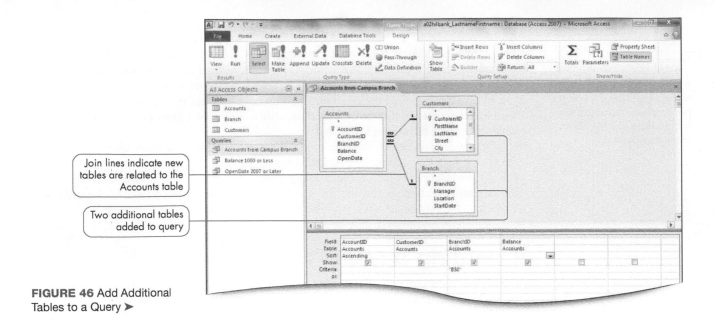

Join lines indicate new tables are related to the Accounts table

Two additional tables added to query

**FIGURE 46** Add Additional Tables to a Query ➤

## Get Answers Using a Multi-Table Query

You can get key information from your database using a multi-table query. For example, if you want to know how many orders each customer placed since the database was created, you would create a new query and add the Customers and Orders tables to the Query Design view. After you verify that the join lines are correct, add the CustomerID field from the Customers table and the OrderID field from the Order table to the query design grid. When you run the query, the results show duplicates in the CustomerID column because Customers place multiple orders.

To fix the duplicate CustomerID problem, return to the Query Design view, and then click Totals in the Show/Hide group. Both columns show the Group By option in the Total row. Change the total row of the OrderID field to Count, and then run the query again. This time the results show one row for each customer and the number of orders each customer placed since the database was created.

## Modifying a Multi-Table Query

To modify multi-table queries, you use the same techniques you learned for single-table queries. Add tables using the Show Table dialog box; remove tables by clicking the unwanted table and then pressing Delete. Add fields by double-clicking the field you want; remove fields by clicking the column selector and then pressing Delete. Join lines between related tables should appear automatically in a query if the relationships were previously established, as shown in Figure 46.

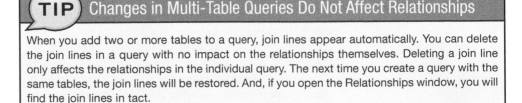

**TIP** Changes in Multi-Table Queries Do Not Affect Relationships

When you add two or more tables to a query, join lines appear automatically. You can delete the join lines in a query with no impact on the relationships themselves. Deleting a join line only affects the relationships in the individual query. The next time you create a query with the same tables, the join lines will be restored. And, if you open the Relationships window, you will find the join lines in tact.

# Add and Delete Fields in a Multi-Table Query

In Figure 46, three tables, as well as the join lines between the tables, now appear in the top pane of the Query Design view. All the fields from each of the tables are available to be used in the query design grid. Figure 47 shows that Location (from the Branch table) and LastName (from the Customers table) have been added to the design, and BranchID and CustomerID have been deleted. The BranchID was deleted from the query; therefore, the 'B50' criterion was removed as well. 'Campus' was added to the Location field's criteria row in order to extract the same results. Because criteria values are not case sensitive, typing 'campus' is the same as typing 'Campus', and both will return the same results. Run the query to see that the datasheet is more useful now that the Location and LastName fields have been added. The results are shown in Figure 48.

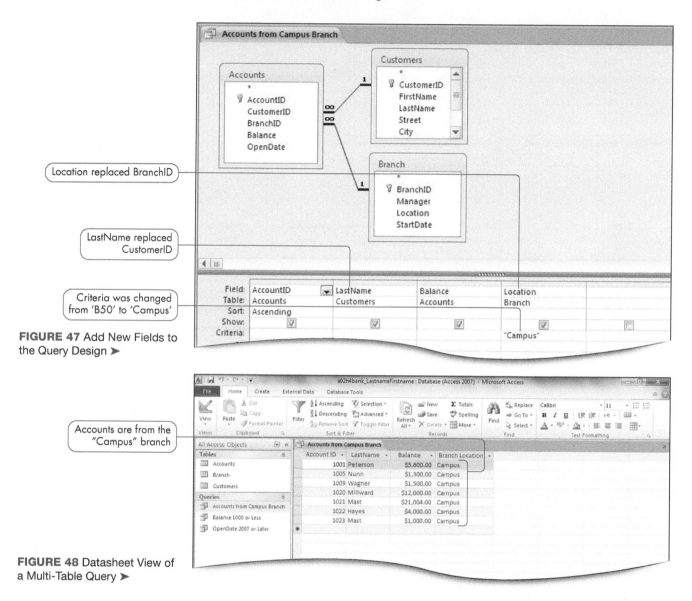

**FIGURE 47** Add New Fields to the Query Design ➤

**FIGURE 48** Datasheet View of a Multi-Table Query ➤

## Fix a Common Problem in a Multi-Table Query

In Figure 49, two tables are added to the query design, but no join line connects them. The results of the query will be unpredictable and larger (i.e., more records) than expected. The Customers table contains 11 records, and the Branch table contains 5 records. Since Access does not know how to interpret the unrelated tables, the results will show 55 records—every possible combination of customer and branch (11 × 5). See Figure 50.

To fix this problem, you can create join lines using the existing tables if the tables facilitate this. Or you can add an additional table that will provide a join between all three tables. In the Branch query, you can add the Accounts table, which will facilitate a join between the two existing tables, Customers and Branch. As soon as the third table is added to the query design, the join lines appear automatically, as shown in Figure 47.

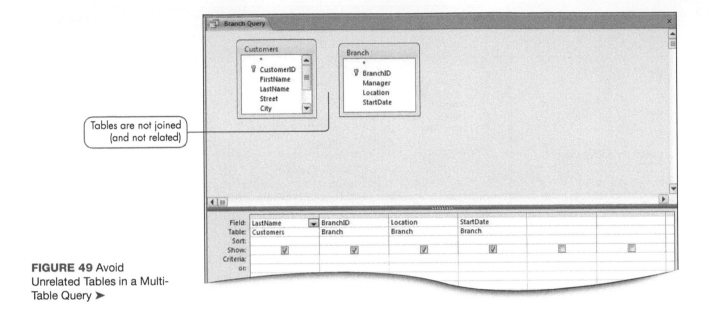

**FIGURE 49** Avoid Unrelated Tables in a Multi-Table Query ➤

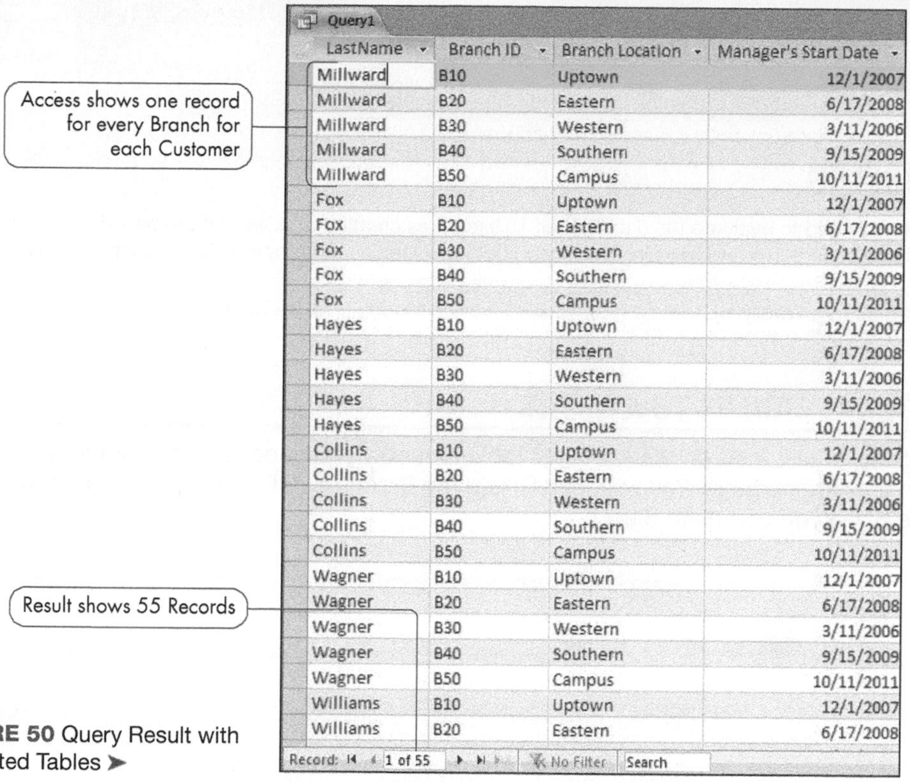

| LastName | Branch ID | Branch Location | Manager's Start Date |
|---|---|---|---|
| Millward | B10 | Uptown | 12/1/2007 |
| Millward | B20 | Eastern | 6/17/2008 |
| Millward | B30 | Western | 3/11/2006 |
| Millward | B40 | Southern | 9/15/2009 |
| Millward | B50 | Campus | 10/11/2011 |
| Fox | B10 | Uptown | 12/1/2007 |
| Fox | B20 | Eastern | 6/17/2008 |
| Fox | B30 | Western | 3/11/2006 |
| Fox | B40 | Southern | 9/15/2009 |
| Fox | B50 | Campus | 10/11/2011 |
| Hayes | B10 | Uptown | 12/1/2007 |
| Hayes | B20 | Eastern | 6/17/2008 |
| Hayes | B30 | Western | 3/11/2006 |
| Hayes | B40 | Southern | 9/15/2009 |
| Hayes | B50 | Campus | 10/11/2011 |
| Collins | B10 | Uptown | 12/1/2007 |
| Collins | B20 | Eastern | 6/17/2008 |
| Collins | B30 | Western | 3/11/2006 |
| Collins | B40 | Southern | 9/15/2009 |
| Collins | B50 | Campus | 10/11/2011 |
| Wagner | B10 | Uptown | 12/1/2007 |
| Wagner | B20 | Eastern | 6/17/2008 |
| Wagner | B30 | Western | 3/11/2006 |
| Wagner | B40 | Southern | 9/15/2009 |
| Wagner | B50 | Campus | 10/11/2011 |
| Williams | B10 | Uptown | 12/1/2007 |
| Williams | B20 | Eastern | 6/17/2008 |

Query1
Access shows one record for every Branch for each Customer
Result shows 55 Records
Record: 1 of 55
No Filter
Search

**FIGURE 50** Query Result with Unrelated Tables ➤

## Add a Join Line in a Multi-Table Query

Over time, your database will grow, and additional tables will be added. Occasionally, new tables are added to the database but not added to the Relationships window. When queries are created with the new tables, join lines will not be established. When this happens, you can create temporary join lines in the query design. These join lines will provide a temporary relationship between two tables and enable Access to interpret the query properly.

The process of creating a multi-table query works the same as creating a single-table query (covered previously in this chapter). In the Query Design view, you will add fields to the bottom portion (the query design grid), set the sorting, decide whether to show the fields, and add criteria as needed. You should take some precautions when working with multiple tables; these precautions will be discussed later.

## 4 Multi-Table Queries

Based on the auditor's request, you will need to evaluate the data further. This requires creating queries that are based on multiple tables, rather than a single table. You decide to open an existing query, add additional tables, and then save the query with a new name.

**Skills covered:** Add Additional Tables to a Query • Create a Multi-Table Query • Modify a Multi-Table Query

---

### STEP 1 › ADD ADDITIONAL TABLES TO A QUERY

The previous query was based on the Accounts table, but now you need to add information to the query that is in the Branch table. You will need to add the Branch and Customers tables to the query. Refer to Figure 51 as you complete Step 1.

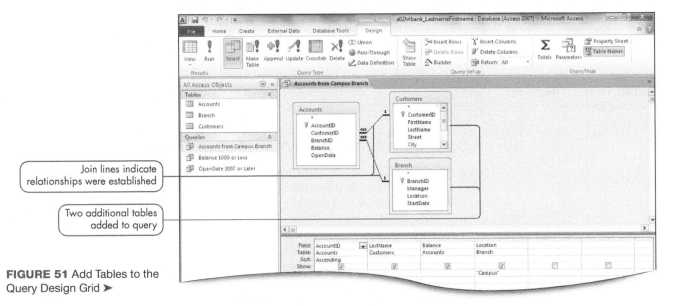

Join lines indicate relationships were established

Two additional tables added to query

**FIGURE 51** Add Tables to the Query Design Grid ➤

a. Open *a02h3bank_LastnameFirstname* if you closed it at the end of Hands-On Exercise 3. Click the **File tab**, click **Save Database As**, and then type **a02h4bank_LastnameFirstname**, changing *h3* to *h4*. Click **Save**.

b. Right-click the **Accounts from Campus Branch query** in the Navigation Pane, and then select **Design View** from the shortcut menu.

c. Drag the **Branch table** from the Navigation Pane to the top pane of the query design grid next to the Accounts table.

   A join line connects the Branch table to the Accounts table. The query inherits the join lines from the relationships created in the Relationships window.

d. Drag the **Location field** from the Branch table to the first empty column in the design grid.

   The Location field should be positioned to the right of the Balance column.

**e.** Click the **Show check box** under the BranchID field to clear the check box and hide this field in the results.

The BranchID field is no longer needed since the Location field provides the same information. Because you unchecked the BranchID show check box, the BranchID field will not appear the next time the query is opened.

**f.** Delete the **B50 criterion** in the BranchID field.

**g.** Type **Campus** as a criterion in the **Location field**, and then press **Enter**.

Access adds quotation marks around *Campus* for you; quotes are required for text criteria. You are substituting the Location criterion (*Campus*) in place of the BranchID criterion (B50).

**h.** Remove Ascending from the AccountID sort row. Click in the **Sort row** of the Balance field. Click the arrow, and then select **Descending** from the list.

The query will be sorted by descending balance order. The largest balance will be listed first, and the smallest will be last.

**i.** Click **Run** in the Results group.

Only Campus accounts should appear in the datasheet. Next, you will add the Customer LastName and criteria, and then delete CustomerID from the query.

**j.** Click **View** in the Views group to return to the Design view.

**k.** Drag the **Customers table** from the Navigation Pane to the top section of the query design grid.

The one-to-many relationship lines automatically connect the Customers table to the Accounts table (similar to step c above).

**l.** Drag the **LastName field** in the Customers table to the second column in the design grid.

The LastName field should be positioned to the right of the AccountID field.

**m.** Click the column selector in the CustomerID field to select it. Press **Delete**.

The CustomerID field is no longer needed in the results because we added the LastName field.

**n.** Click **Run** in the Results group.

**o.** Save and close the query.

---

**CREATE A MULTI-TABLE QUERY**

After discussing the query results with the auditor, you realize that another query is needed to show those customers with account balances of $1,000 or less. You create the query and view the results in Datasheet view. Refer to Figure 52 as you complete Step 2.

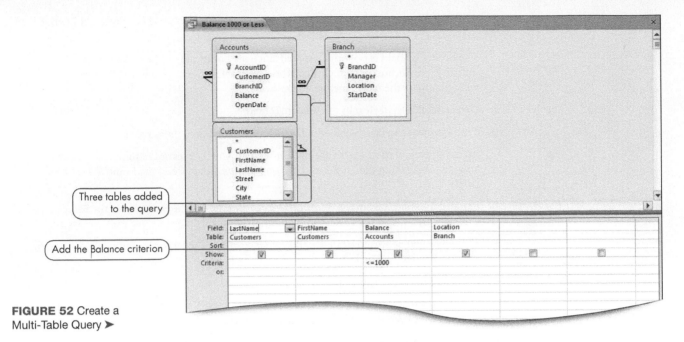

Three tables added to the query

Add the Balance criterion

**FIGURE 52** Create a Multi-Table Query ➤

a. Click the **Create tab**, and click **Query Design** in the Queries group.

b. Double-click each table name in the Show Table dialog box to add each one to the Query Design view. Click **Close** in the Show Table dialog box.

c. Double-click the following fields to add them to the design grid: **LastName**, **FirstName**, **Balance**, and **Location**.

d. Type **<=1000** in the **Criteria row** of the Balance column.

e. Click **Run** in the Results group to see the query results.

Six records appear in the query results.

f. Click **Save** on the Quick Access Toolbar, and then type **Balance 1000 or Less** as the Query Name in the **Save As dialog box**. Click **OK**.

## STEP 3 ▶ MODIFY A MULTI-TABLE QUERY

The auditor requests additional changes to the Balance 1000 or Less query you just created. You will modify the criteria to display the accounts that were opened after January 1, 2006, with balances of $2,000 or less. Refer to Figure 53 as you complete Step 3.

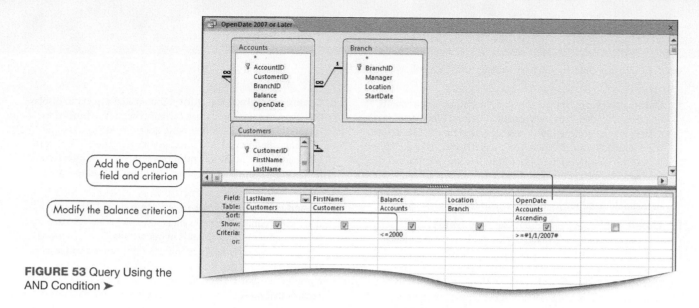

**FIGURE 53** Query Using the AND Condition ➤

Text annotations in figure:
- Add the OpenDate field and criterion
- Modify the Balance criterion

a. Click **View** in the Views group to switch the *Balance 1000 or Less* query to Design view.

b. Type **<=2000** in place of *<=1000* in the **Criteria row** of the Balance field.

c. Double-click the **OpenDate field** in the Accounts table in the top section of the Query Design view to add it to the first blank column in the design grid.

d. Type **>=1/1/2007** in the **Criteria row** of the OpenDate field to extract only accounts that have been opened since January 2007.

   After you type the expression and then move to a different column, Access will add the # symbols automatically.

e. Click **Run** in the Results group to display the results of the query.

   Three records appear in the query results.

f. Click the **File tab**, click **Save Object As**, and type **OpenDate 2007 or Later** as the query name. Click **OK**.

g. Click the **File tab** again to return to the database.

h. Click **View** in the Views group to return to the Design view of the query.

i. Click in the **Sort row** of the OpenDate field, and then select **Ascending**.

j. Click **Run** in the Results group to display the results of the query.

k. Save and Close the query.

l. Click the **File tab**, and then click **Compact & Repair Database**.

m. Click the **File tab**, click **Save & Publish**, and then double-click **Back Up Database**. Accept *a02h4bank_LastnameFirstname_date* as the file name, and then click **Save**.

   You just created a backup of the database. The *a02h4bank_LastnameFirstname* database remains open.

n. Click the **File tab**, and then click **Exit** (to exit Access).

o. Submit based on your instructor's directions.

After reading this chapter, you have accomplished the following objectives:

1. **Design data.** You should consider the output requirements of a database when creating the table structure. When developing a database, the designer must weigh the need for the data against the cost of collecting the data. You learned that design principles begin with identifying the tables of the database. You learned that storing the results of calculations in a table may assist you when creating queries, forms, and reports later. You also learned that data should be stored in its smallest parts.

2. **Create tables.** Access employs several ways to create a table. You can create a table by creating the fields in Design view or by entering table data into a new row in Datasheet view, or you can import data from another application such as Excel. You learned that each field needs a unique and descriptive name, and you were introduced to the CamelCase naming convention. Access accommodates many different types of data, including Text, Number, Date/Time, Yes/No, Memo, and others.

3. **Understand table relationships.** Relationships between tables are set in the Relationships window. In this window, join lines are created, and three options can be set: Enforce Referential Integrity, Cascade Update Related Fields, and Cascade Delete Related Records. When referential integrity is enforced, data cannot be entered into the related table unless it first exists in the primary table. Frequently, the primary key (unique identifier) from one table is entered as a foreign key in a related table. These two fields often become the basis of creating relationships between tables.

4. **Share data with Excel.** Microsoft Access can easily import and export data to (and from) Excel. You used the Import Wizard to import an Excel worksheet into an Access database table. The settings of the Import Wizard may be saved and reused when the import is cyclical.

5. **Establish table relationships.** You created relationship links between tables in the database and attempted to enter an invalid branch number in a related table. You discovered that the enforcement of referential integrity prevented you from creating an account in a nonexistent branch. The Cascade Update Related Fields option ensures that if the primary key is modified in one table, Access will automatically update all fields in related tables. Similarly, the Cascade Delete Related Records option ensures that if the primary key is deleted in one table, Access will automatically delete all records in related tables.

6. **Create a single-table query.** You created a query to display only those records that match certain criteria. You learned to add additional fields to an existing query, to add criteria, and to change the sort order of the query results. The primary sort field needs to be in the left-most position, with additional sort fields determined by their left-to-right positions in the query design grid.

7. **Specify criteria for different data types.** Different data types require different syntax. Date fields are enclosed in pound signs (#) and text fields in quotations ("). Numeric and currency fields require no delimiters. Additionally, you learned that logical operators, AND, OR, and NOT, help to answer complex questions. The AND logical operator returns only records that meet all criteria. The OR logical operator returns records meeting any of the specified criteria. The NOT logical operator returns all records except the specified criteria.

8. **Copy and run a query.** After specifying tables, fields, and conditions for one query, you can copy the query, rename it, and then modify the fields and criteria in the second query. Copying queries saves time since you do not have to select tables and fields again for queries that have a similar structure. To run a query during the design process, click Run in the Results group. To run a saved query, double-click the query name in the Navigation Pane.

9. **Use the Query Wizard.** An alternative way to create a select query is to use the Query Wizard. The wizard enables you to select tables and fields from lists. The last step of the wizard prompts you to save the query.

10. **Create a multi-table query.** Creating a multi-table query is similar to creating a single-table query; however, choosing the right tables and managing the table relationships requires some additional skills. You should only include related tables in a multi-table query. To add additional tables to a query, open the Navigation Pane, and then drag tables directly into the top section of the Query Design view.

11. **Modify a multi-table query.** To modify multi-table queries, you use the same techniques you used for single-table queries. Join lines between related tables should appear automatically in a query if the relationships were previously established. If join lines do not appear, the results will not be correct when you run the query. You can add temporary join lines from inside the query or set the Relationships permanently in the Relationships window.

# KEY TERMS

AND logical operator
AutoNumber
Calculated field
CamelCase notation
Caption property
Cascade Delete Related Records
Cascade Update Related Fields
Comparison operator
Constant
Criteria row
Data redundancy
Data type
Date arithmetic

Delimiter
Field property
Field row
Indexed property
Multi-table query
NOT logical operator
Null
Number data type
One-to-many relationship
OR logical operator
Query
Query Design view
Query sort order

Referential integrity
Related tables
Run command
Select query
Show row
Simple Query Wizard
Sort row
Table
Table row
Text data type
Validation rule
Wildcard

1. When entering, deleting, or editing table data:
   (a) The table must be in Design view.
   (b) The table must be in Datasheet view.
   (c) The table may be in either Datasheet or Design view.
   (d) Data may be entered only in a form.

2. Which of the following is true for the Query Wizard?
   (a) You can only select tables as the source.
   (b) No criteria can be added.
   (c) Fields from multiple tables are not allowed.
   (d) You do not need a summary.

3. Which of the following was not a suggested guideline for designing a table?
   (a) Include all necessary data.
   (b) Store data in its smallest parts.
   (c) Avoid calculated fields.
   (d) Link tables using common fields.

4. A query's specifications providing instructions about which records to include must be entered:
   (a) On the Show row of the query design grid.
   (b) On the Sort row of the query design grid.
   (c) On the Criteria row of the query design grid.
   (d) On the Table row of the query design grid.

5. An illustration of a one-to-many relationship would be:
   (a) A person changes his/her primary address.
   (b) A customer may have multiple orders.
   (c) A branch location has an internal BranchID code.
   (d) A balance field is totaled for all accounts for each person.

6. When adding criteria to the query design view:
   (a) The value you enter must be delimited by quotes (")(").
   (b) The value you enter must be delimited by pound signs (#).
   (c) The value you enter must be delimited by nothing ().
   (d) Access will add the correct delimiters for you ("),("), (#), or ().

7. Which of the following is true with respect to an individual's hire date and years of service?
   (a) Hire date should be a calculated field; years of service should be a stored field.
   (b) Hire date should be a stored field; years of service should be a calculated field.
   (c) Both should be stored fields.
   (d) Both should be calculated fields.

8. When importing data into Access, which of the following statements is true?
   (a) The Import Wizard only works for Excel files.
   (b) The wizard can be found on the Create tab.
   (c) You can assign a primary key while you are importing Excel data.
   (d) The wizard will import the data in one step after you select the file.

9. The main reason to enforce referential integrity in Access is to:
   (a) Limit the number of records in a table.
   (b) Keep invalid data from being entered into a table.
   (c) Make it possible to delete records.
   (d) Keep your database safe from unauthorized users.

10. It is more efficient to make a copy of an existing query, rather than create a new query, when which of the following is true?
    (a) The existing query contains only one table.
    (b) The existing query and the new query use the same tables and fields.
    (c) The existing query and the new query have the exact same criteria.
    (d) The original query is no longer being used.

## 1 Tom & Erin's Bookstore

Tom and Erin Mullaney own and operate a bookstore in Philadelphia, Pennsylvania. Erin asked you to help her create an Access database because of your experience in this class. You believe that you can help her by creating a database and then importing the Excel spreadsheets they use to store the publishers and the books that they sell. You determine that a third table—for authors—is also required. Your task is to design and populate the three tables, set the table relationships, and enforce referential integrity. If you have problems, reread the detailed directions presented in the chapter. This exercise follows the same set of skills as used in Hands-On Exercises 1 and 2 in the chapter. Refer to Figure 54 as you complete this exercise.

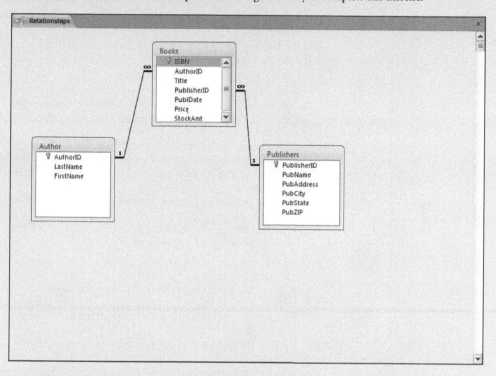

FIGURE 54 Access
Relationships Window ➤

a. Start Access, and then click **Blank Database** in the Available Templates section of the Backstage view. Click **Browse** to choose a folder location to store the database, type **a02p1books_LastnameFirstname** as the file name, click **OK**, and then click **Create** to create the new database.

b. Type **11** in the **Click to Add column**, and then click **Click to Add**. The field name becomes *Field1*, and *Click to Add* now appears as the third column. Type **Wayne** and press **Tab**. The process repeats for the fourth column; type **John** and then press **Tab** twice.

c. The cursor returns to the first column where *(New)* is selected. Press **Tab**. Type the rest of the data using the following table. This data will become the records of the Author table.

| ID | Field1 | Field2 | Field3 |
|-------|--------|--------|---------|
| 1 | 11 | Wayne | John |
| (New) | 12 | Allen | Keith |
| | 13 | Scott | Michael |
| | 14 | Carl | Richard |
| | 15 | Keen | Clara |
| | 16 | Swartz | Millie |
| | 17 | Allen | John |

d. Click **Save** on the Quick Access Toolbar. Type **Author** in the **Save As dialog box**, and then click **OK**.

e. Click **View** in the Views group to switch to the Design view of the Author table.

f. Select **Field1**—in the second row—in the top portion of the table design, and then type **AuthorID** to rename the field. In the *Field Properties* section in the lower portion of the table design, type **Author ID** in the **Caption property box**, and then verify that *Long Integer* appears for the Field Size property.

g. Select **Field2**, and then type **LastName** to rename the field. In the *Field Properties* section in the bottom portion of the table design, type **Author's Last Name** in the **Caption property box** and **20** as the field size.

h. Select **Field3**, and then type **FirstName** to rename the field. In the *Field Properties* section in the bottom portion of the table design, type **Author's First Name** as the caption, and then type **15** as the field size.

i. Click the **ID field row selector** (which shows the primary key) to select the row, and then click **Delete Rows** in the Tools group. Click **Yes** twice to confirm both messages.

j. Click the **AuthorID row selector**, and then click **Primary Key** in the Tools group to reset the primary key.

k. Click **Save** on the Quick Access Toolbar to save the design changes. Click **Yes** to the *Some data may be lost* message. Close the table.

l. Click the **External Data tab**, and then click **Excel** in the Import & Link group to launch the *Get External Data - Excel Spreadsheet* feature. Verify the *Import the source data into a new table in the current database* option is selected, click **Browse**, and then go to the student data folder. Select the *a02p1books* workbook, click **Open**, and then click **OK**. This workbook contains two worksheets. Follow these steps:
   - Select the **Publishers worksheet**, and then click **Next**.
   - Click the **First Row Contains Column Headings check box**, and then click **Next**.
   - Select the **PubID field**, click the **Indexed arrow**, select **Yes (No Duplicates)**, and then click **Next**.
   - Click the **Choose my own primary key arrow**, select **PubID**, if necessary, and then click **Next**.
   - Accept the name *Publishers* for the table name, click **Finish**, and then click the **Close button** without saving the import steps.

m. Repeat the Import Wizard to import the Books worksheet from the *a02p1books* workbook into the Access database. Follow these steps:
   - Select the **Books worksheet**, and then click **Next**.
   - Ensure the *First Row Contains Column Headings* check box is checked, and then click **Next**.
   - Click on the **ISBN column**, set the Indexed property box to **Yes (No Duplicates)**, and then click **Next**.
   - Click the **Choose my own primary key arrow**, select **ISBN** as the primary key field, and then click **Next**.
   - Accept the name *Books* as the table name. Click **Finish**, and then click the **Close button** without saving the import steps.

n. Right-click the **Books table** in the Navigation Pane, and then select **Design View**. Make the following changes:
   - Change the PubID field name to **PublisherID**.
   - Change the Caption property to **Publisher ID**.
   - Change the PublisherID Field Size property to **2**.
   - Click the **ISBN field** at the top, and then change the Field Size property to **13**.
   - Click the **Price field**, and then change the Price field Data Type to **Currency**.
   - Change the AuthorCode field name to **AuthorID**.
   - Change the AuthorID Field Size property to **Long Integer**.
   - Click the **ISBN field row selector** (which shows the primary key) to select the row, then release, press, and hold the mouse. Drag the row up to the first position.
   - Click **Save** on the Quick Access Toolbar to save the design changes to the Books table. Click **Yes** to the *Some data may be lost* warning.
   - Close the table.

o. Right-click the **Publishers table** in the Navigation Pane, and then select **Design View**. Make the following changes:
   - Change the PubID field name to **PublisherID**.
   - Change the PublisherID Field Size property to **2**.
   - Change the Caption property to **Publisher's ID**.
   - Change the Field Size property to **50** for the PubName and PubAddress fields.

- Change the Pub Address field name to **PubAddress** (remove the space).
- Change the PubCity Field Size property to **30**.
- Change the PubState Field Size property to **2**.
- Change the Pub ZIP field name to **PubZIP** (remove the space).
- Click **Save** on the Quick Access Toolbar to save the design changes to the Publishers table. Click **Yes** to the *Some data may be lost* warning. Close all open tables.

p. Click the **Database Tools tab**, and then click **Relationships** in the Relationships group. Click **Show Table** if necessary. Follow these steps:
  - Double-click each table name in the Show Table dialog box to add it to the Relationships window, and then close the Show Table dialog box.
  - Drag the **AuthorID field** from the Author table onto the AuthorID field in the Books table.
  - Click the **Enforce Referential Integrity** and **Cascade Update Related Fields check boxes** in the Edit Relationships dialog box. Click **Create** to create a one-to-many relationship between the Author and Books tables.
  - Drag the **PublisherID field** from the Publishers table onto the PublisherID field in the Books table.
  - Click the **Enforce Referential Integrity** and **Cascade Update Related Fields check boxes** in the Edit Relationships dialog box. Click **Create** to create a one-to-many relationship between the Publishers and Books tables.
  - Click **Save** on the Quick Access Toolbar to save the changes to the Relationships window.
  - Click **Relationship Report** in the Tools group on the Design tab.
  - Close the report; do not save it. Close the Relationships window.

q. Click the **File tab**, and then click **Compact & Repair Database**.

r. Click the **File tab**, click **Save & Publish**, and then double-click **Back Up Database**.

s. Click **Save** to accept the default backup file name with today's date.

t. Click the **File tab**, and then click **Exit** (to exit Access).

u. Submit based on your instructor's directions.

## 2   Davis Insurance Company

The Davis Insurance Company offers a full range of insurance services in four locations: Miami, Boston, Chicago, and Philadelphia. They store all of the firm's employee data in an Excel spreadsheet. This file contains employee name and address, job performance, salary, and title. The firm is converting from Excel to Access. A database file containing two of the tables already exists; your job is to import the employee data from Excel for the third table. Once imported, you will need to modify field properties and set new relationships. The owner of the company, Paul Davis, is concerned that some of the Philadelphia and Boston salaries may be below the guidelines published by the national office. He asks that you investigate the salaries of the two offices and create a separate query for each city. If you have problems, reread the detailed directions presented in the chapter. This exercise follows the same set of skills as used in Hands-On Exercises 2 and 3 in the chapter. Refer to Figure 55 as you complete this exercise.

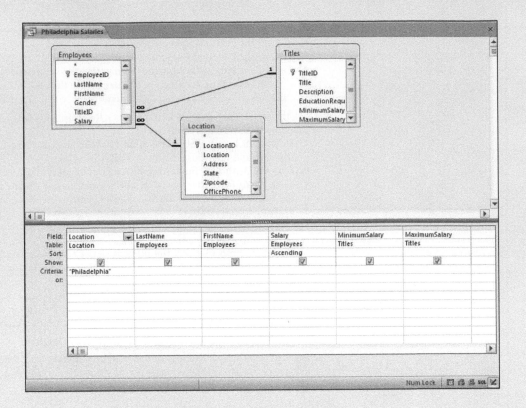

**FIGURE 55** Philadelphia Salaries Query ➤

a. Open *a02p2insurance*. Click the **File tab**, click **Save Database As**, and then type **a02p2insurance_LastnameFirstname**. Click **Save**. In the Navigation Pane, double-click to open the **Location** and **Titles tables**, and then look at the contents to become familiar with the field names and the type of information stored in each table. Note the number of Position titles. Close the tables.

b. Click the **External Data tab**, click **Excel** in the Import & Link group, and then follow these steps:
   - Click **Browse**, and then locate the *a02p2employees* workbook. Select it, click **Open**, and then click **OK**.
   - Select the **Employees worksheet**, and then click **Next**.
   - Click the **First Row Contains Column Headings check box**, and then click **Next**.
   - Click the **Indexed arrow** for the EmployeeID field, select **Yes (No Duplicates)**, and then click **Next**.
   - Click **Choose my own primary key arrow**, select the **EmployeeID** as the primary key, and click **Next**.
   - Accept the name *Employees* for the table name, click **Finish**, and then click **Close** without saving the import steps.

c. Double-click the **Employees table** in the Navigation Pane, click the **Home tab**, and then click **View** in the Views group to switch to the Design view of the Employees table. Make the following changes:
   - Click the **LocationID field**, and then change the Field Size property to **3**.
   - Change the Caption property to **Location ID**.
   - Click the **TitleID field**, and then change the Field Size property to **3**.
   - Change the Caption property to **Title ID**.
   - Change the Salary data type to **Currency**, select **General Number** in the Format property in field properties, and then press **Delete**.
   - Save the design changes. Click **Yes** to the *Some data may be lost* warning.

d. Click **View** in the Views group to view the Employees table in Datasheet view, and then examine the data. Click any record in the Title ID, and then click **Ascending** in the Sort & Filter group on the Home tab. Multiple employees are associated with the T01, T02, T03, and T04 titles.

e. Double-click the **Titles table** in the Navigation Pane to open it in Datasheet view. Notice the T04 title is not in the list.

f. Add a new record in the first blank record at the bottom of the Titles table. Using the following data:
   - Type **T04** in the **TitleID field**.
   - Type **Senior Account Rep** in the **Title field**.
   - Type **A marketing position requiring a technical background and at least three years of experience** in the **Description field**.
   - Type **Four year degree** in the **Education Requirements field**.
   - Type **45000** in the **Minimum Salary field**.
   - Type **75000** in the **Maximum Salary field**.

g. Close all tables. Click **No** if you are asked to save the table.

h. Click the **Database Tools tab**, and then click **Relationships** in the Relationships group. Click **Show Table** if necessary. Follow these steps:
   - Double-click each table name in the Show Table dialog box to add them to the Relationships window, and then close the Show Table dialog box.
   - Drag the **LocationID field** in the Location table onto the LocationID field in the Employees table.
   - Click the **Enforce Referential Integrity** and **Cascade Update Related Fields check boxes** in the Edit Relationships dialog box. Click **Create** to create a one-to-many relationship between the Location and Employees tables.
   - Drag the **TitleID field** in the Titles table onto the TitleID field in the Employees table.
   - Click the **Enforce Referential Integrity** and **Cascade Update Related Fields check boxes** in the Edit Relationships dialog box. Click **Create** to create a one-to-many relationship between the Titles and Employees tables.
   - Click **Save** on the Quick Access Toolbar to save the changes to the Relationships window.
   - Close the Relationships window.

i. Click the **Create tab**, and then click the **Query Wizard** in the Queries group. Follow these steps:
   - Select **Simple Query Wizard**, and then click **OK**.
   - Select **Table: Location** in the Tables/Queries box.
   - Double-click **Location** in the **Available Fields list** to move it to the Selected Fields list.
   - Select **Table: Employees** in the **Tables/Queries list**.
   - Double-click **LastName, FirstName**, and **Salary**.
   - Select **Table: Titles** in the **Tables/Queries list**.
   - Double-click **MinimumSalary** and **MaximumSalary**. Click **Next**.
   - Select the **Detail (shows every field of every record) option**, and then click **Next**.
   - Type **Philadelphia Salaries** as the query title, and then click **Finish**.

j. Click the **Home tab**, and then click **View** to switch to the Design view of the Philadelphia Salaries Query. In the **Criteria row** of the Location field, type **Philadelphia**. Click in the **Sort row** in the Salary field, and then select **Ascending**. Click **Run** in the Results group on the Design tab. Visually inspect the data to see if any of the Philadelphia employees have a salary less than the minimum or greater than the maximum when compared to the published salary range. These salaries will need to be updated later. Save and close the query.

k. Right-click on the **Philadelphia Salaries query** in the Navigation Pane, and then select **Copy**. Right-click a blank area in the Navigation Pane, and then select **Paste**. In the Paste As dialog box, type **Boston Salaries** for the query name. Click **OK**.

l. Right-click on the **Boston Salaries query** in the Navigation Pane, and then click **Design View**. In the Criteria row of the Location field, replace *Philadelphia* with **Boston**. Click **Run** in the Results group on the Design tab. Visually inspect the data to see if any of the Boston employees have a salary less than the minimum or greater than the maximum when compared to the published salary range. Save and close the query.

m. Click the **File tab**, and then click **Compact & Repair Database**.

n. Click the **File tab**, click **Save & Publish**, and then double-click **Back Up Database**.

o. Click **Save** to accept the default backup file name with today's date.

p. Click the **File tab**, and then click **Exit** (to exit Access).

q. Submit based on your instructor's directions.

## 1 Real Estate Firm

You are an intern in a large, independent real estate firm that specializes in home sales. A database contains all of the information on the properties marketed by your firm. Most real estate transactions involve two agents—one representing the seller (the listing agent) and the other the buyer (the selling agent). The firm owner has asked that you examine the records of recent listings (real estate is listed when the home owner signs a contract with an agent that offers the property for sale) and sort them by subdivision and the listing agent's name. The results need to include only the sold properties and be sorted by subdivision and the listing agent's last name. Refer to Figure 56 as you complete this exercise.

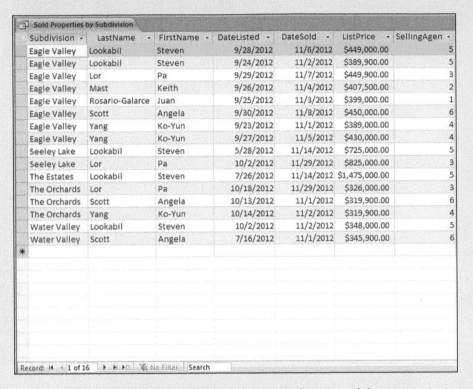

| Subdivision | LastName | FirstName | DateListed | DateSold | ListPrice | SellingAgen |
|---|---|---|---|---|---|---|
| Eagle Valley | Lookabil | Steven | 9/28/2012 | 11/6/2012 | $449,000.00 | 5 |
| Eagle Valley | Lookabil | Steven | 9/24/2012 | 11/2/2012 | $389,900.00 | 5 |
| Eagle Valley | Lor | Pa | 9/29/2012 | 11/7/2012 | $449,900.00 | 3 |
| Eagle Valley | Mast | Keith | 9/26/2012 | 11/4/2012 | $407,500.00 | 2 |
| Eagle Valley | Rosario-Galarce | Juan | 9/25/2012 | 11/3/2012 | $399,000.00 | 1 |
| Eagle Valley | Scott | Angela | 9/30/2012 | 11/8/2012 | $450,000.00 | 6 |
| Eagle Valley | Yang | Ko-Yun | 9/23/2012 | 11/1/2012 | $389,000.00 | 4 |
| Eagle Valley | Yang | Ko-Yun | 9/27/2012 | 11/5/2012 | $430,000.00 | 4 |
| Seeley Lake | Lookabil | Steven | 5/28/2012 | 11/14/2012 | $725,000.00 | 5 |
| Seeley Lake | Lor | Pa | 10/2/2012 | 11/29/2012 | $825,000.00 | 3 |
| The Estates | Lookabil | Steven | 7/26/2012 | 11/14/2012 | $1,475,000.00 | 5 |
| The Orchards | Lor | Pa | 10/18/2012 | 11/29/2012 | $326,000.00 | 3 |
| The Orchards | Scott | Angela | 10/13/2012 | 11/1/2012 | $319,900.00 | 6 |
| The Orchards | Yang | Ko-Yun | 10/14/2012 | 11/2/2012 | $319,900.00 | 4 |
| Water Valley | Lookabil | Steven | 10/2/2012 | 11/2/2012 | $348,000.00 | 5 |
| Water Valley | Scott | Angela | 7/16/2012 | 11/1/2012 | $345,900.00 | 6 |

**FIGURE 56** Sold Properties by Subdivision Query Results ➤

a. Open *a02m1property*. Click the **File tab**, click **Save Database As**, and then type **a02m1property_ LastnameFirstname**. Click **Save**. Open the Agents table. Find and replace Kia Hart's name with your name. Close the Agents table.

b. Open the SubDivision table in Design view, and then add the field **AssociationFee** with data type **Currency** to indicate the monthly fee for each subdivision. Save the table, switch to Datasheet view, and then enter in the AssociationFee field **95** for each subdivision without a pool and **125** for subdivisions with a pool. Close the table.

c. Open the Query Wizard, and then create a detail query using the Agents and Properties tables. Add the following fields: **LastName**, **FirstName**, **DateListed**, **DateSold**, **ListPrice**, **SellingAgent**, and **SubdivisionID**. Name the query **Sold Properties by Subdivision**. Run the query, and then examine the number of records.

d. In Design view, enter the appropriate criteria to exclude all of the records that contain properties from the Red Canyon Subdivision (SubdivisionID #7). Run the query, and then examine the number of records. It should be a smaller number than in step c.

e. Add the SubDivision table to the query design, and then drag the **Subdivision field** to the first column in the query design grid. Modify the SubdivisionID field so that the field does not show in the query results. Run the query, and then examine the results. The number of records should be the same as in step d; the first column will be different.

f. Sort the records by ascending Subdivision first, then by ascending LastName.

g. Add criteria that will limit the results to the properties sold after October 31, 2012. Run the query.

h. Save and close the query.

i. Compact and repair the database.

j. Make a backup copy of the database.

k. Close Access.

l. Submit based on your instructor's directions.

## 2  The Prestige Hotel

The Prestige Hotel chain caters to upscale business travelers and provides state-of-the-art conference, meeting, and reception facilities. It prides itself on its international, four-star cuisine. Last year, it began a member reward club to help the marketing department track the purchasing patterns of its most loyal customers. All of the hotel transactions are stored in the database. Your task is to help the managers of the Prestige Hotel in Denver and Chicago identify their customers who stayed in a room last year and who had three persons in their party. Refer to Figure 57 as you complete this exercise.

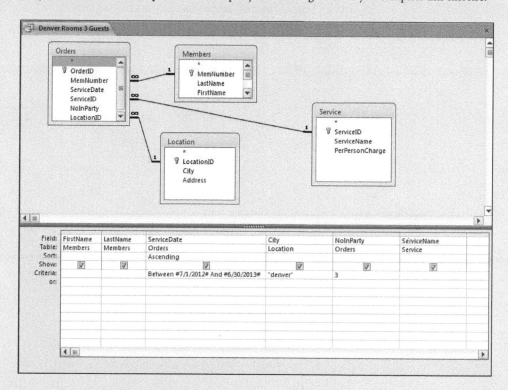

**FIGURE 57** Denver Rooms 3 Guests Query ➤

a. Open *a02m2hotel*. Click the **File tab**. click **Save Database As**, and then type **a02m2hotel_ LastnameFirstname**. Click **Save**. Review the data contained in the three tables. Specifically, look for the tables and fields containing the information you need: dates of stays in Denver suites, the members' names, and the numbers in the parties.

b. Import the Location data from the Excel file *a02m2location* into your database as a new table. Set the LocationID Indexed property to **Yes** (**No Duplicates**), and then set the data type to **Long Integer**. Select the **LocationID field** as the primary key. Name the table **Location**.

c. Open the Relationships window, and then create a relationship between the Location table and the Orders table using the LocationID field. Enforce referential integrity, and then select **Cascade Update Related Fields**. Set the other two relationships as shown in Figure 57. Save and close the Relationships window.

d. Open the Members table, and then find Bryan Gray's name. Replace his name with your own first and last name. Now find Nicole Lee's name, and then replace it with your name.

e. Create a query with fields ServiceDate, City, NoInParty, ServiceName, FirstName, and LastName. Set the criteria to limit the output to **denver**. Use the Between command to only show services from **7/1/2012** to **6/30/2013**. Set the Number in Party criterion to **3**. Sort the results in ascending order by the Service Date.

f. Run the query, and then examine the number of records in the status bar at the bottom of the query. It should display *154*. If your number of records is different, examine the criteria.

g. Change the order of the query fields so that they display as FirstName, LastName, ServiceDate, City, NoInParty, and ServiceName. Compare your results to Figure 57.

h. Save the query as **Denver Rooms 3 Guests**. Close the query, and then copy it and rename the new query **Chicago Rooms 3 Guests**. One of your colleagues in Chicago asked for your help in analyzing the guest data.

i. Open the Chicago Rooms 3 Guests query in Design view, and then change the criterion for denver to **chicago**. Run and save the changes.

j. Combine the two previous queries into a third query named **Denver and Chicago Rooms 3 Guests**. Use the criteria from the two individual queries to create a combination AND – OR condition. The records in the combined query should equal the sum of the records in the two individual queries.

k. Compact, repair, and back up the database file. Close the database.

l. Submit based on your instructor's directions.

The Morris Arboretum in Chestnut Hill, Pennsylvania, tracks its donors in Excel. They also use Excel to store a list of plants in stock. As donors contribute funds to the Arboretum, they can elect to receive a plant gift from the Arboretum. These plants are both rare plants and hard-to-find old favorites, and they are part of the annual appeal and membership drive to benefit the Arboretum's programs. The organization has grown, and the files are too large and inefficient to handle in Excel. Your task will be to begin the conversion of the files from Excel to Access.

## Create a New Database

You need to examine the data in the Excel worksheets to determine which fields will become the primary keys in each table and which fields will become the foreign keys. Primary and foreign keys are used to form the relationships between tables.

a. Locate the Excel workbook named *a02c1donors* and open it.

b. Locate the Excel workbook named *a02c1plants* and open it.

c. Examine the data in each worksheet and identify the column that will become the primary key in an Access table. Identify the foreign keys in each table.

d. Launch Access and create a new, blank database named **a02c1arbor_LastnameFirstname**.

## Create a New Table

Use the new blank table created automatically by Access to hold the donations as they are received from the donors. Switch to Design view, and then save the table as **Donations**. Add the remaining field names in Design view. Note: The data for this table will be added later in this exercise.

a. Change *ID* to **DonationID** with an **AutoNumber Data Type**.

b. Add **DonorID** (a foreign key) as **Number (Long Integer) Data Type**.

c. Add **PlantID** (a foreign key) as **Number (Long Integer) Data Type**.

d. Enter two additional fields with an appropriate data type and field properties. Hint: You need the date of donation and the amount of donation.

e. Verify the primary key is *DonationID*.

f. Save the table. Close the table.

## Import Data from Excel

You need to use the Import Spreadsheet Data Wizard twice to import a worksheet from each Excel workbook into Access. You need to select the worksheets, specify the primary keys, set the indexing option, and name the newly imported tables (see Figures 19 through 24).

a. Click the **Import Excel data command**.

b. Locate and select the *a02c1donors* workbook.

c. Set the DonorID field Indexed option to **Yes (No Duplicates)**.

d. Select **DonorID** as the primary key when prompted.

e. Accept the table name *Donors*.

f. Import the *a02c1plants* file, set the ID field as the primary key, and then change the indexing option to **Yes (No Duplicates)**.

g. Select the **ID** as the primary key when prompted.

h. Accept the table name *Plants*.

i. Open each table in Datasheet view to examine the data.

j. Change the ID field name in the Plants table to **PlantID**.

## Create Relationships

You need to create the relationships between the tables using the Relationships window. Identify the primary key fields in each table and connect them with their foreign key counterparts in related tables. Enforce referential integrity, and check the Cascade Update Related Fields option.

a. Open the Donors table, and then change the Field Size property for DonorID to **Long Integer** so it matches the Field Size property of DonorID in the Donations table.

b. Open the Plants table, and then change the Field Size property for PlantID to **Long Integer** so it matches the Field Size property for PlantID in the Donations table.

c. Close the open tables, and then open the Relationships window.

d. Add the three tables to the Relationships window using the Show Table dialog box. Close the Show Tables dialog box.

e. Drag the **DonorID field** in the Donors table onto the DonorID field in the Donations table. Enforce referential integrity, and then check the **Cascade Update Related Fields option**. Drag the **PlantID field** from the Plants table onto the PlantID field of the Donations table. Enforce referential integrity, and then check the **Cascade Update Related Fields option**.

f. Close the Relationships window and save your changes.

## Add Sample Data to the Donations Table

You need to add sample data to the Donations table. Add 20 records using the following guidelines:

a. Use any donor from the Donors table.

b. Enter the date of donation using dates from last month, this month, and next month.

c. Use any amount of donation.

d. Use any plant from the Plants table.

## Use the Query Wizard

Use the Query Wizard to create a query of all donations greater than $100 in the Donations table. Use the following guidelines:

a. Include the DonorID and AmountOfDonation fields.

b. Name the query **Donations Over 100**.

c. Add criteria to include only donations of more than $100.

d. Sort by descending AmountOfDonation.

## Create a Query in Design View

You need to create a query that identifies the people who have made a donation in the current month. The query should list the donor's full name, phone number, the amount of the donation, the date of the donation, and name of the plant they want. Sort the query by date of donation, then by donor last name and first name. This list will be given to the Arboretum staff so they can notify the donors that a plant is ready for pick up.

a. Click the **Create tab**, and then click **Query Design** in the Queries group.

b. Add the tables and fields necessary to produce the query as stated previously. Name the query **Plant Pickup List**.

c. Run and print the query from Datasheet view.

d. Compact, repair, and back up the file. Close the database.

e. Submit based on your instructor's directions.

# BEYOND THE CLASSROOM

## Employee Performance Review

**GENERAL CASE**

The *a02b1perform* file contains employee performance data for a large insurance agency. Open *a02b1perform*. Click the **File tab**, click **Save Database As**, and then type **a02b1perform_LastnameFirstname**. Click **Save**. Use the skills from this chapter to perform several tasks. Replace *yourname* in the Employees table with your name. The firm's employee policy states that an employee needs to maintain a performance rating of good or excellent to maintain employment. If an employee receives an average or poor performance rating, he or she receives a letter reminding him or her of this policy along with suggestions of how to improve. You are the manager of the Atlanta office. You need to identify the employees who need a letter of reprimand. You will prepare a query so that someone else can generate a form letter to the employees. You need to include fields in the query that contain the employees' first and last names, their position title, and their salary. You do not need to write the letter, only assemble the data that will later be merged into the letter. The query results need to be alphabetized by the employees' last names. As you work, consider the order that the fields will need to be used in the letter and order the query fields accordingly. Close the database. Check with your instructor and submit based on your instructor's directions.

## Database Administrator Position

**RESEARCH CASE**

You arrive at Secure Systems, Inc., for a database administrator position interview. After meeting the Human Resources coordinator, you are given a test to demonstrate your skills in Access. You are asked to create a database from scratch to keep track of all the candidates for the positions currently open at Secure Systems. Use these requirements:

a. Name the database **a02b2admin_LastnameFirstname**.

b. Create three tables: Candidates, JobOpenings, and Interviews.

c. Include a field to rank each candidate on a scale of 1 to 5 (5 is highest).

d. Set the table relationships.

e. Add 10 candidates—yourself and 9 other students in your class.

f. Add the Database Administrator job and four other sample jobs.

g. Add eight sample Interviews—four for the Database Administrator position and four others.

h. Create a query that lists all the Database Administrator interviews with a ranking of 4 or 5.

i. Add the last name and first name of the candidate to the query design. Sort by last name and first name. Run the query.

j. Close the database. Submit based on your instructor's directions.

## May Beverage Sales

**DISASTER RECOVERY**

A coworker called you into his office, explained that he was having difficulty with Access 2010, and asked you to look at his work. Open *a02b3traders*. Click the **File tab**, click **Save Database As**, and then type **a02b3traders_LastnameFirstname**. Click **Save**. It contains two queries, *May 2012 Orders of Beverages and Confections* and *2012 Beverage Sales by Ship Country*. The May 2012 Orders of Beverages and Confections query is supposed to have only information from May 2012. You find other dates included in the results. Change the criteria of ShippedDate to exclude the other dates. The 2012 Beverage Sales by Ship Country query returns no results. Check the criteria in all fields. Once the criteria are fixed, the records need to be ordered by ShipCountry. After you find and correct the error(s), close the database. Submit based on your instructor's directions.

# ACCESS

# CUSTOMIZE, ANALYZE, AND SUMMARIZE QUERY DATA

## Creating and Using Queries to Make Decisions

### CASE STUDY | Housing Slump Means Opportunity for College Students

Watch the **Set-up Video** for this Case Study!

Two students from Montgomery County Community College decided they would take advantage of the declining housing market. After taking several business courses at MCCC and a weekend seminar in real estate investing, Jeff Bryan and Bill Ryder were ready to test their skills in the marketplace. Jeff and Bill had a simple strategy—buy distressed properties at a significant discount, then resell the properties for a profit one year later when the market rebounds.

As they drove through the surrounding neighborhoods, if they noticed a For Sale sign in the yard, they would call the listing agent and ask for the key information such as the asking price, the number of bedrooms, square feet, and days on the market. Since they were just starting out, they decided to target houses that were priced at $100,000 or below and only houses that were on the market at least six months.

For the first two months, they gathered lots of information and began to get a feel for the houses and prices in the area. Some neighborhoods were definitely more distressed than others! But they still had not made any offers. The two MCCC investors realized they needed a more scientific approach to finding an investment property. Based on a tip from the real estate seminar, they decide to gather free lists of homes for sale and use that information to prequalify houses that meet their criteria. They have asked you to help them import the lists into Access. Once the data is in Access, Jeff, Bill, and you will be able to easily identify the qualifying properties.

This new database approach should help them become more successful and hopefully help them acquire their first investment property. And who knows, you might even become one of the partners.

---

### OBJECTIVES    AFTER YOU READ THIS CHAPTER, YOU WILL BE ABLE TO:

1. Understand the order of operations

2. Create a calculated field in a query

3. Create expressions with the Expression Builder

4. Use built-in functions in Access

5. Perform date arithmetic

6. Add aggregate functions to datasheets and queries

From Access Chapter 3 of *Exploring Microsoft Office 2010 Volume 1*, First Edition, Robert T. Grauer, Mary Anne Poatsy, Keith Mulbery, Michelle Hulett, Cynthia Krebs, Keith Mast. Copyright © 2011 by Pearson Education, Inc. Published by Pearson Prentice Hall, Inc. All rights reserved.

# Calculations, Expressions, and Functions

Previously, you learned that Access now allows calculated fields to be added to tables. In previous versions of Access, you could not add calculated fields to tables; you could only add calculated fields to queries, forms, and reports. In Access 2010, many situations exist where you will still need to add arithmetic calculations—using expressions and functions—to queries, forms, and reports.

For example, many Access developers prefer to create calculated fields in queries. Queries with calculated fields can then become the data source (or record source) for forms and reports. Calculated fields on a form cannot be edited the same way fields from a table can be edited. Calculated fields can only be displayed on a form. For example, if you store information about credit cards in a table, you would enter the bank (Chase), the credit card type (Visa), and the interest rate (9%). You would not enter the current amount due. That amount would be calculated and displayed on the form. You will recognize this restriction later when you create a form containing calculated fields.

In this section, you will learn about the order of operations and how to create a calculated field in a query.

## Understanding the Order of Operations

The *order of operations* determines the sequence by which operations are calculated in an expression. Evaluate expressions in parentheses first, then exponents, then multiplication and division, and, finally, addition and subtraction. Operations of equal value will be calculated from left to right. Table 1 shows some examples of the order of operations. You must have a solid understanding of these rules in order to create calculated fields in Access. Access, like Excel, uses the following symbols:

- Parentheses ( )
- Exponentiation ^
- Multiplication *
- Division /
- Addition +
- Subtraction −

| TABLE 1 | Examples of Order of Operations | |
|---|---|---|
| **Expression** | **Order to Perform Calculations** | **Output** |
| =2+3*3 | Multiply first, and then add. | 11 |
| =(2+3)*3 | Add the values inside the parentheses first, and then multiply. | 15 |
| =2+2^3 | Evaluate the exponent first, $2^3=2*2*2$ or 8. Then add. | 10 |
| =(2+2)^3 | Add the parenthetical values first (2+2=4), and then raise the result to the 3rd power. $4^3=4*4*4$. | 64 |
| =10/2+3 | Divide first, and then add. | 8 |
| =10/(2+3) | Add first to simplify the parenthetical expression, and then divide. | 2 |
| =10*2−3*2 | Multiply first, and then subtract. | 14 |

# Creating a Calculated Field in a Query

When creating a query, in addition to using fields from tables, you may also need to create a calculation based on the fields from one or more tables. For example, a table might contain the times when employees clock in and out of work. You could create a calculated field to calculate how many hours each employee worked by subtracting the ClockIn field from the ClockOut field. You create calculated fields in the Design view of a query. A formula used to calculate new fields from the values in existing fields is known as an *expression*. An expression can consist of a number of different elements to produce the desired output. The elements used in an expression may include the following:

An **expression** is a formula used to calculate new fields from the values in existing fields.

- Identifiers (the names of fields, controls, or properties)
- Arithmetic operators (e.g., *, /, +, or −)
- Functions (built-in functions like Date() or IIf())
- *Constants* (numbers such as 30 or .5)

A **constant** refers to a value that does not change.

You can use calculations to create a new value based on an existing field, verify data entered, set grouping levels in reports, or to help set query criteria.

## Build Expressions with Correct Syntax

Expressions are entered in the first row of the query design grid. You must follow the correct *syntax*—the set of rules that Access follows when evaluating expressions. You can create expressions to perform calculations using field names, constants, and functions. If you use a field name, such as Balance, in an expression, you must spell the field name correctly or Access will display an error. You should assign descriptive field names to the calculated fields. Access ignores spaces in calculations. An example of an expression with correct syntax is:

**Syntax** is the set of rules that Access follows when evaluating expressions.

MonthlyInterest: [Balance] * .035 / 12

In the above expression, if you omit the brackets [ ] around Balance, Access will add them for you. The arithmetic operators, the * symbol (multiply) and the / symbol (divide), first multiply the operands, [Balance] and .035, and then divide the result by 12. In calculated fields, the operands are usually a constant, a field name, or another calculated field. Figure 1 shows the NewBalance field which adds the [Balance] and the calculated field [MonthlyInterest]. This calculation will show the total amount owed.

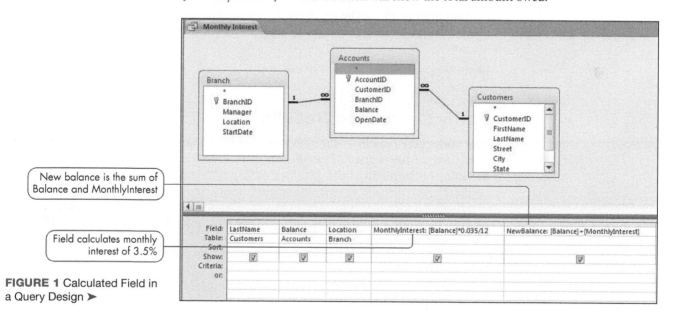

New balance is the sum of Balance and MonthlyInterest

Field calculates monthly interest of 3.5%

**FIGURE 1** Calculated Field in a Query Design ➤

The query contains a second calculated field named NewBalance. Its value is derived from the sum of the original balance plus the monthly interest amount. The query results, as shown in Figure 2, display a decimal number in the Interest column. The NewBalance column appears to be rounded to two decimal places since the output is in currency format. However, when you click in the NewBalance field, Access displays the extra digits that are stored behind the scenes.

| | LastName ▾ | Balance ▾ | Branch Locat ▾ | MonthlyInterest ▾ | NewBalance ▾ |
|---|---|---|---|---|---|
| | Peterson | $5,600.00 | Campus | 16.3333333333333 | $5,616.3333 |
| | Millward | $1,200.00 | Uptown | 3.5 | $1,203.50 |
| | Collins | $15,490.00 | Eastern | 45.1791666666667 | $15,535.18 |
| | Hayes | $630.00 | Western | 1.8375 | $631.84 |
| | Nunn | $1,300.00 | Campus | 3.79166666666667 | $1,303.79 |
| | Hayes | $550.00 | Uptown | 1.60416666666667 | $551.60 |
| | Simpson | $1,620.00 | Eastern | 4.725 | $1,624.73 |
| | Collins | $2,100.00 | Southern | 6.125 | $2,106.13 |
| | Wagner | $1,500.00 | Campus | 4.375 | $1,504.38 |
| | Millward | $3,000.00 | Eastern | 8.75 | $3,008.75 |
| | Wagner | $290.00 | Uptown | 0.845833333333333 | $290.85 |
| | Fox | $1,900.00 | Western | 5.54166666666667 | $1,905.54 |
| | Millward | $10,000.00 | Eastern | 29.1666666666667 | $10,029.17 |
| | Nunn | $16,700.00 | Uptown | 48.7083333333333 | $16,748.71 |
| | Collins | $460.00 | Western | 1.34166666666667 | $461.34 |
| | Millward | $18,700.00 | Western | 54.5416666666667 | $18,754.54 |
| | Peterson | $980.00 | Western | 2.85833333333333 | $982.86 |
| | Wagner | $7,800.00 | Southern | 22.75 | $7,822.75 |
| | Collins | $14,250.00 | Western | 41.5625 | $14,291.56 |
| | Millward | $12,000.00 | Campus | 35 | $12,035.00 |
| | YourName | $21,004.00 | Campus | 61.2616666666667 | $21,065.26 |
| | Hayes | $4,000.00 | Campus | 11.6666666666667 | $4,011.67 |
| | YourName | $1,000.00 | Campus | 2.91666666666667 | $1,002.92 |
| * | | | | | |

Callouts:
- NewBalance appears to be rounded to two digits (currency format)
- MonthlyInterest field shows a decimal number with many digits
- Click in the NewBalance field to reveal a decimal number with four digits

Record: ◄ ◄ 1 of 23 ► ►► ►* No Filter Search

**FIGURE 2** Results of Calculated Fields in a Query ➤

Another example of when to use a calculated field is calculating a price increase for a product or service. Suppose you need to calculate a 10% price increase on certain products you sell. You could name the calculated field NewPrice and use the expression (current price) + (current price × 10%). The first segment represents the current price and the second segment adds an additional 10%. The expression would be entered into the query design grid as follows:

NewPrice: [CurrentPrice] + [CurrentPrice] * .10

## Verify Calculated Results

After your query runs, look at the field values in the Datasheet view and also look at the calculated values. Ask yourself, "Does the data make sense?" Use a calculator to manually calculate some of the results in the calculated fields and compare the answers to the datasheet results. Another method to verify the results is to copy and paste all or part of the datasheet into Excel. Recreate the calculations in Excel and compare the answers to the query results in Access. The Access calculated field, the calculator, and the Excel calculations should all return identical results.

After verifying the calculated results, save the query for the next time you need to perform the same calculations.

**Resolve Rounding Problems**

In Figure 2, the Balance field contains numbers in currency format; the MonthlyInterest field contains decimal numbers with many digits. When you add the two numbers, the sum—shown in the NewBalance field—appears to be in currency format. However, if you click the NewBalance field, the actual number is a decimal with four digits. Decimal numbers can cause rounding problems when you total the column. To resolve this problem, the MonthlyInterest field must be rounded to two decimal places prior to totaling the column.

## Save a Query Containing Calculated Fields

As you already know, saving a query only saves the design of the query; saving does not save the data displayed in Datasheet view. While viewing the results of a query in Datasheet view, you can edit the data (and consequently update the data in the underlying table) providing the query is updatable. Calculated fields are the exception to this rule—calculated fields cannot be updated in Datasheet view. However, when the components of a calculated field are updated, the calculated field value will update automatically.

You can use a calculated field as input for other calculated fields. For example, calculate a 10% discount on an item (Calculation #1) and then calculate the sales tax on the discount price (Calculation #2).

In the first Hands-On Exercise, you will create calculated expressions, practice verification techniques, and recover from a common error.

**Avoid Spaces in Calculated Field Names**

Although you can use spaces in calculated field names, it is a good habit to not use spaces. For example, use NewPrice: [Price]*1.1 rather than New Price: [Price]*1.1. If you avoid spaces in calculated field names, it will be easier to reference these fields in other queries, related forms, and related reports.

## 1 Calculations, Expressions, and Functions

Using the data from the homes for sale lists that Jeff and Bill acquired, you are able to help them target properties that meet their criteria. As you examine the data, you discover other ways to analyze the properties. You create several queries and present your results to the two investors for their comments.

**Skills covered:** Create and Save a Query • Create a Calculated Field and Run the Query • Verify the Calculated Results • Recover from a Common Error

---

### STEP 1 ▶ CREATE AND SAVE A QUERY

You begin your analysis by creating a query using the Properties and Agents tables. The Properties table contains all the properties the investors will evaluate; the Agents table contains a list of real estate agents who represent the properties' sellers. In this exercise, add the fields you need and only show properties that have not been sold. Refer to Figure 3 as you complete Step 1.

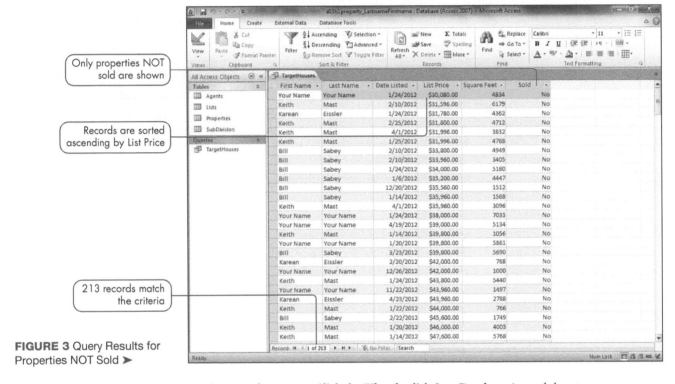

**FIGURE 3** Query Results for Properties NOT Sold ▶

a. Open *a03h1property*. Click the **File tab**, click **Save Database As**, and then type **a03h1property_LastnameFirstname**. Click **Save**.

> **TROUBLESHOOTING:** Throughout the remainder of this chapter and textbook, click Enable Content whenever you are working with student files.

> **TROUBLESHOOTING:** If you make any major mistakes while completing this Hands-On Exercise, you can delete the *a03h1property_LastnameFirstname* file, repeat step a above, and then start over.

**b.** Open the Agents table, and then replace *Angela Scott* with your name. Close the table.

**c.** Click the **Create tab**, and then click **Query Design** in the Queries group to start a new query.

The Show Table dialog box opens so you can specify the table(s) and/or queries to include in the query design.

**d.** Select the **Agents table**, and then click **Add**. Select the **Properties table**, and then click **Add**. Close the Show Table dialog box.

**e.** Double-click the **FirstName** and **LastName fields** in the Agents table to add them to the design grid.

**f.** Double-click the **DateListed, ListPrice, SqFeet**, and **Sold fields** in the Properties table to add them to the query design grid.

**g.** Click **Run** in the Results group to display the results in Datasheet view.

You should see 303 properties in the results.

**h.** Click **View** in the Views group to switch to Design view. Type **No** in the **Criteria row** of the Sold field.

**i.** Select **Ascending** from the Sort row of the ListPrice field.

**j.** Click **Run** to see the results.

You only want to see properties that were not sold. There should now be only 213 properties in the datasheet. Compare your results to those shown in Figure 3.

**k.** Save the query as **TargetHouses**.

---

**STEP 2 ▶ CREATE A CALCULATED FIELD AND RUN THE QUERY**

You need to create a calculated field to evaluate the relative value of all unsold properties on the market. To do this, you create a calculated field to analyze the sale price compared to the square footage of each property. Refer to Figure 4 as you complete Step 2.

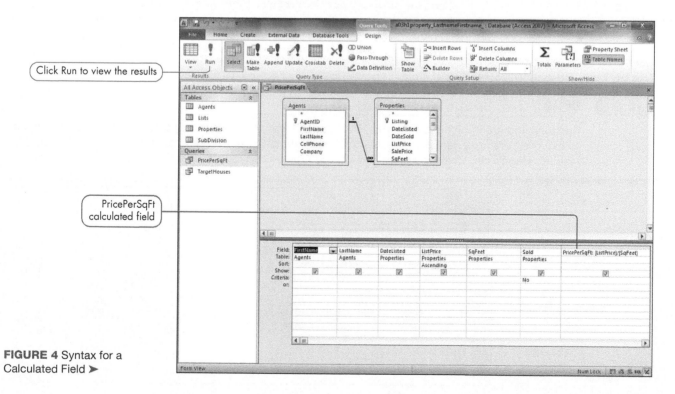

**FIGURE 4** Syntax for a Calculated Field ▶

**a.** Click **View** in the Views group to switch to Design view.

> **TROUBLESHOOTING:** If you accidentally click the View arrow, Access displays a list of options. Select the Design View option.

The TargetHouses query is based on two tables. The top portion of Query Design view displays the two tables, Agents and Properties, and the bottom portion (query design grid) displays the fields currently in the query.

**b.** Click the **File tab**, and then select **Save Object As**. Type **PricePerSqFt** in the **Save As dialog box**, and then click **OK**.

You made a copy of the TargetHouses query so you can add a calculated field to the new query but still preserve the original query.

**c.** Click the **File tab** to return to the query.

**d.** Scroll to the right until you see the first blank column in the query design grid.

**e.** Click in the top row of the first blank column, type **PricePerSqFt: ListPrice/SqFeet**, and then press **Enter**. Widen the PricePerSqFt column in order to see the entire expression.

Access inserts square brackets around the fields for you. The new field divides the values in the ListPrice field by the values in the SqFeet field. The : after *PricePerSqFt* is required.

**f.** Click **Run** in the Results group to view the results.

The new calculated field, PricePerSqFt, is displayed. Widen the PricePerSqFt column, if necessary, to see all the values.

**g.** Click **View** to switch back to Design view. Use Figure 4 to check your syntax. Click in the **PricePerSqFt calculated field cell**, and then click **Property Sheet** in the Show/Hide group.

The Property Sheet controls how the results of the calculated field will display in Datasheet view when you run the query.

**h.** Click the **Format property arrow**, and then select **Currency** from the list. Click in the **Caption box**, and then type **Price Per Sq Ft**. Close the Property Sheet.

**i.** Click **Run** to view your changes.

The calculated field values are formatted with Currency, and the column heading displays *Price Per Sq Ft* instead of *PricePerSqFt*.

## STEP 3 ▶ VERIFY THE CALCULATED RESULTS

Because you are in charge of the Access Database, you decide to verify your data prior to showing it to the investors. You use two methods to check your calculations: estimation and checking your results using Excel. Refer to Figure 5 as you complete Step 3.

| | A | B | C | D | E | F | G | H | I |
|---|---|---|---|---|---|---|---|---|---|
| 1 | First Name | Last Name | Date Listed | List Price | Square Feet | Sold | Price Per Sq Ft | | |
| 2 | Your Name | Your Name | 1/24/2012 | $30,080.00 | 4834 | FALSE | $6.22 | $6.22 | |
| 3 | Keith | Mast | 2/10/2012 | $31,596.00 | 6179 | FALSE | $5.11 | $5.11 | |
| 4 | Karean | Eissler | 1/24/2012 | $31,780.00 | 4362 | FALSE | $7.29 | $7.29 | |
| 5 | Keith | Mast | 2/25/2012 | $31,800.00 | 4712 | FALSE | $6.75 | $6.75 | |
| 6 | Keith | Mast | 4/1/2012 | $31,996.00 | 3832 | FALSE | $8.35 | $8.35 | |
| 7 | Keith | Mast | 1/25/2012 | $31,996.00 | 4768 | FALSE | $6.71 | $6.71 | |
| 8 | Bill | Sabey | 2/10/2012 | $33,800.00 | 4949 | FALSE | $6.83 | $6.83 | |
| 9 | Bill | Sabey | 2/10/2012 | $33,960.00 | 3405 | FALSE | $9.97 | $9.97 | |
| 10 | Bill | Sabey | 1/24/2012 | $34,000.00 | 5180 | FALSE | $6.56 | $6.56 | |
| 11 | Bill | Sabey | 1/6/2012 | $35,200.00 | 4447 | FALSE | $7.92 | $7.92 | |
| 12 | | | | | | | | | |
| 13 | | | | | | | | | |
| 14 | | | | | | | | | |

*Verified results in Excel*
*Calculated results from Access*
*First 10 rows of the Access query*

**FIGURE 5** Verify Calculated Results in Excel ▶

Customize, Analyze, and Summarize Query Data

a. Examine the Price Per Sq Ft column in the current query.

One of the ways to verify the accuracy of the calculated data is to ask yourself if the numbers make sense.

b. Locate the eighth record with *Bill Sabey* as the listing agent, an asking price of *$33,960*, and square footage of *3405*. Ask yourself if the calculated value of *$9.97* makes sense.

The sale price is $33,960 and the square footage is 3405. You can verify the calculated field easily by rounding the two numbers (to 34,000 and 3400) and then dividing the values in your head (34,000 div by 3400 = 10) to verify that the calculated value, $9.97 per sq ft, makes sense.

c. Launch Excel, and then switch to Access. Click the first row selector, and then drag through the first 10 records (the tenth record has a list price of *$35,200*). Click **Copy** in the Clipboard group on the **Home tab**.

You will also verify the calculation in the first 10 records by pasting the results in Excel.

d. Switch to Excel, and then click **cell A1** of the blank workbook. Click **Paste** in the Clipboard group on the Home tab.

The field captions appear in the first row, and the 10 records appear in the next 10 rows. The fields are located in columns A–G. The calculated field results are pasted in column G as values rather than as a formula.

> **TROUBLESHOOTING:** If you see pound signs (#####) in an Excel column, use the vertical lines between columns to increase the width.

e. Type =D2/E2 in **cell H2**, and then press **Enter**. Copy the formula from **cell H2** and paste it into **cells H3 to H11**.

The formula divides the list price by the square feet. Compare the results in columns G and H. The numbers should be the same. If the values differ, look at both the Excel and Access formulas. Determine which is correct, and then find and fix the error in the incorrect formula.

f. Close Excel without saving the workbook. Return to the Access database, and then click **Save** on the Quick Access Toolbar to save the design modifications made to the PricePerSqFt query.

> **TIP** Use Zoom (Shift+F2) to View Long Expressions
>
> To see the entire calculated field expression, click the field in Query Design view, and then press Shift+F2. A new window will appear to enable you to easily see and edit the entire contents of the cell. Access refers to this window as the Zoom dialog box, as shown in Figure 6.

**FIGURE 6** Use Zoom to See the Entire Calculated Field ➤

A few errors pop up as you test the new calculated fields. You check the spelling of the field names in the calculated field since that is a common mistake. Refer to Figure 7 as you complete Step 4.

Results are the same ($100) for every record

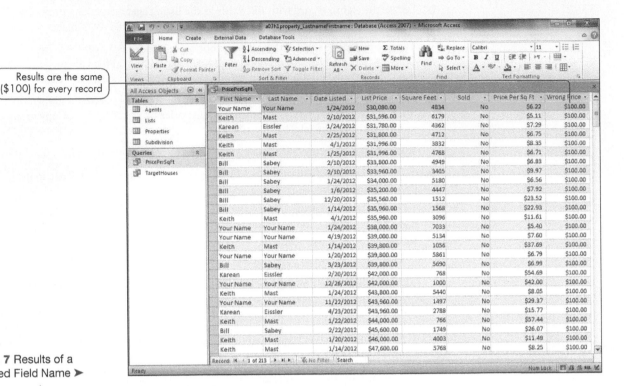

**FIGURE 7** Results of a Misspelled Field Name ➤

a. Click **View** in the Views group to switch to Design view. Scroll to the first blank column, and then click in the top row.

b. Type **WrongPricePerSqFt: xListPrice/xSqFeet**, and then press **Enter**. Widen the column to see the entire expression.

Be sure that you added the extra *x's* to the field names. You are intentionally misspelling the field names to see how Access will respond. Access inserts square brackets around the fields for you.

c. Click **Run** in the Results group.

You should see the Enter Parameter Value dialog box. The dialog box indicates that Access does not recognize xListPrice in the tables defined for this query in the first record. When Access does not recognize a field name, it will ask you to supply a value.

d. Type **100000** in the **first parameter box**. Press **Enter** or click **OK**.

Another Enter Parameter Value dialog box displays, asking that you supply a value for xSqFeet. Again, this error occurs because the tables defined for this query do not contain an xSqFeet field.

e. Type **1000** in the **second parameter box**, and then press **Enter**.

The query has the necessary information to run and returns the results in Datasheet view.

f. Scroll right and examine the results of the calculation for *WrongPricePerSqFt*.

All of the records show 100 because you entered the values 100000 and 1000, respectively, into the parameter boxes. The two values are treated as constants and give the same results for all the records.

g. Return to Design view and correct the errors in the WrongPricePerSqFt field by changing the formula to **WrongPricePerSqFt: [ListPrice]/[SqFeet]**.

Press Shift+F2 to view the calculated field and remove the *x* from the two field names.

Customize, Analyze, and Summarize Query Data

h.  Click in the **WrongPricePerSqFt calculated field**, click **Property Sheet**, and then change the Format property to **Currency**. Add the caption **Wrong Price Per Sq Ft**. Close the Property Sheet.

i.  Run and save the query.

    The calculated values in the last two columns should be the same.

j.  Close the query.

k.  Click the **File tab**, and then click **Compact & Repair Database**.

l.  Click the **File tab**, click **Save & Publish**, and then double-click **Back Up Database**. Accept *a03h1property_LastnameFirstname_date* as the file name, and then click **Save**.

    You just created a backup of the database you used to complete the first Hands-On Exercise. The *a03h1property_LastnameFirstname* database remains open.

m.  Keep the database onscreen if you plan to continue with Hands-On Exercise 2. If not, close the database and exit Access.

> **TIP** Learning from Your Mistakes
>
> Following step-by-step instructions is a good way to begin learning about Access. If you want to become proficient, however, you must learn how to recover from errors. As you work through the rest of the Hands-On Exercises in this book, follow the instructions as presented and save your work along the way. Then go back a few steps and make an intentional error just to see how Access responds. Read the error messages (if any) and learn from your mistakes.

# Expression Builder, Functions, and Date Arithmetic

In the last Hands-On Exercise, you calculated the price per square foot for real estate properties. That simple calculation helped you to evaluate all the properties on the investment list. You were able to type the expression manually.

When you encounter more complex expressions, you can use the *Expression Builder* tool to help you create more complicated expressions. When you create an expression in the field cell, you must increase the column width to see the entire expression. The Expression Builder's size enables you to easily see complex formulas and functions in their entirety.

In this section, you will learn how to create expressions using the Expression Builder. You also will learn how to use built-in functions. Finally, you will perform date arithmetic using the Expression Builder.

The **Expression Builder** is a tool to help you create more complicated expressions.

## Creating Expressions with the Expression Builder

Launch the Expression Builder while in the query design grid to assist you with creating a calculated field (or other expression). The Expression Builder helps you create expressions by supplying you with the fields, operators, and functions you need to create them. When you use the expression builder to help you create expressions, you can eliminate spelling errors in field names. Another advantage is with functions; functions require specific arguments in a specific order. When you insert a function using the Expression Builder, the builder gives you placeholders that tell you where each argument belongs.

Launch the Expression Builder while in the query design grid to assist you with creating a calculated field.

After you create an expression in the Expression Builder, click OK to close the Expression Builder window. The expression is then entered into the current cell in the query design grid. From the query design, click Run in the Results group to view the results (in Datasheet view). If the results are incorrect, return to Design view and click the cell that contains the calculated field. Next, launch the Expression Builder again and make any corrections to the expression.

You can also use the Expression Builder when working with controls in forms and reports. For example, if you need a calculated field in a form, you can launch the Expression Builder by clicking Build on the right side of the control source box in the Property Sheet. You can also use the Expression Builder to select a built-in function—for example, to calculate a payment on a loan. It will take some practice to master the Expression Builder; however, the effort will be well worth it as you learn to create more complication expressions.

### Launch the Expression Builder

To launch the Expression Builder, open a query in Design view and verify the Design tab is selected on the Ribbon. Click Builder in the Query Setup group and the Expression Builder launches, as shown in Figure 8. (You can also launch the Expression Builder by right-clicking the cell where you want the expression and selecting Build from the shortcut menu.) The top section of the Expression Builder dialog box contains a rectangular area (known as the *expression box*) where you create an expression. You can type your expression in the box manually, or you can use the Expression Elements, Expression Categories, and Expression Values in the bottom portion of the Expression Builder. Double-click an item in the *Expression Categories* or *Expression Values* section and it will automatically be added to the expression box.

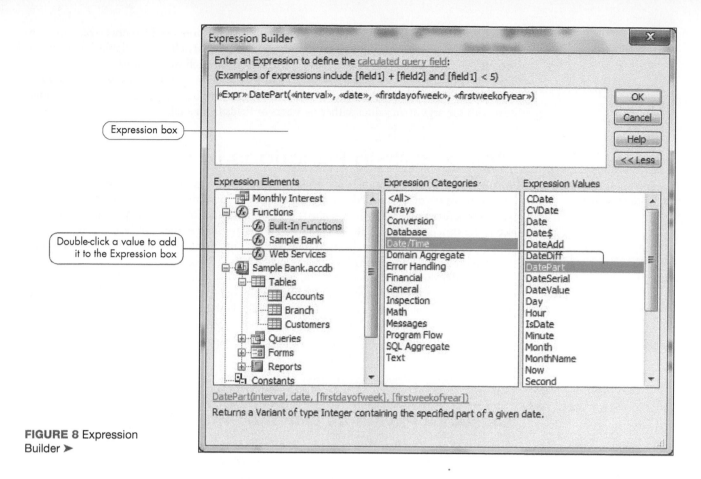

**FIGURE 8** Expression Builder ➤

## Create an Expression

The left column of the Expression Builder dialog box contains Expression Elements, which include the built-in functions, the tables and other objects from the current database, and common expressions. Select an item in this column; the middle column will show the list of options. For example, click a table in the left column and the fields from that table will appear in the middle column.

The middle column displays the Expression Categories based on the item selected in the Expression Elements box. For example, when the Built-in Functions item is selected in the Expression Elements box, the available built-in function categories are displayed in the Expression Categories box, such as the Date/Time category.

The right column displays the Expression Values, if any, for the categories that you selected in the Expression Categories box. For example, if you click Built-In Functions in the Expression Elements box, and then click Date/Time in the Expression Categories box, the Expression Values box lists all of the built-in functions in the Date/Time category, including DatePart.

You can create an expression by manually typing text in the expression box or by double-clicking the elements from the bottom section in the Expression Builder dialog box. For example, to create a calculated field using the fields in the tables, type the calculated field name, and then type a colon. Next, click the desired table listed in the *Expression Elements* section, and then double-click the field you want. Click the Operators item in the *Expression Elements* section, and then choose an operator (such as + or *) from the *Expression Categories* section (or just type the operator). The Expression Builder is flexible and will enable you to find what you need while still enabling you to modify the expression manually.

Calculated fields are relatively simple to create and most Access developers can create them without the Expression Builder. The main reason to use the builder for a calculated field is to eliminate spelling errors in field names. Using functions in Access almost always requires the Expression Builder since the syntax of functions can be difficult to remember.

When you double-click the Functions command in the Expression Elements box, and then click Built-In Functions, the Expression Categories box lists all the available functions in Access. The Expression Values box lists the functions in each of the categories. When you find the function you need, double-click it and the function appears in the expression box. You can see the <<placeholder text>> where the arguments belong; replace each placeholder text with the argument values, either numbers or fields from a table.

## Using Built-In Functions in Access

A function produces a result based on inputs known as arguments.

An argument is a variable or constant that is needed to produce the output for a function.

A *function* produces a result based on inputs known as arguments. An **argument** is a variable or constant that is needed to produce the output for a function. Once you identify what you need a function to do, you can check the Built-in Functions in the Expression Builder to see if the function exists. If it does, add the function to the expression box and replace the <<placeholder text>> with the argument values. Functions work the same in Access and Excel and other programming languages (such as Visual Basic).

Consider the Property database you used in the first Hands-On Exercise. If you wanted to group each home by the year it was listed, you could create a year listed field using the DatePart function. This function will help you calculate the year listed using the DateListed field as one of the arguments. The DatePart function requires one other argument—the date interval, which could be day, month, or year. The year listed calculated field would be entered into the query design grid as follows:

YearListed: DatePart("yyyy", [DateListed])

## Calculate Payments with the Pmt Function

The **Pmt function** calculates the monthly loan payment given the interest rate (monthly), term of the loan (in months), and the original value of the loan (the principal).

Figure 9 shows the *Pmt function*, which calculates the monthly loan payment given the interest rate (monthly), term of the loan (in months), and the original value of the loan (the principal). To use this function, you need to supply the five arguments as field names from underlying tables or as constants.

The first argument is the interest rate per period. Interest rates are usually stated as annual rates, so you will need to convert them to monthly rates by dividing by 12. The second argument is the number of periods. Because loan terms are usually stated in years, you will need to convert the period to months by multiplying by 12. The next argument is the present value—or principal—of the loan. It tells you how much each customer has borrowed. The last two arguments, future value and type (both optional), are usually 0 or blank. The future value shows the amount the borrower will owe after the last payment has been made. The type argument tells Access whether the payment is made at the beginning or the end of the period.

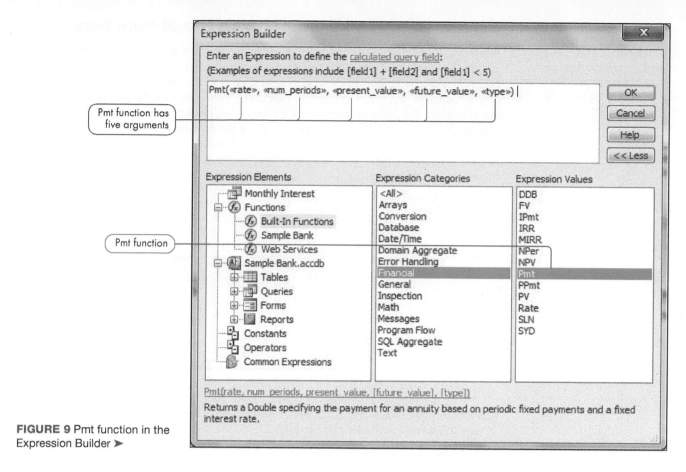

Pmt function has
five arguments

Pmt function

**FIGURE 9** Pmt function in the
Expression Builder ➤

The following example shows how to use the Pmt function to calculate the monthly payment on a $12,500 loan, at a 6.0% interest rate, with a four-year payback term. Table 2 describes the arguments for the Pmt function in more detail.

Function: Pmt(*rate, num_periods, present value, future value, type*)

Example: Pmt(0.06/12, 4*12, 12500)

| TABLE 2 | Arguments of the Pmt Function |
|---|---|
| **Part** | **Description** |
| () | Items inside the parentheses are arguments for the function. The arguments are separated by commas. Some arguments are optional; some arguments have a default value; in the Pmt function, the first three arguments are required and the last two are optional. |
| **rate** | Required. Expression or value specifying interest rate per period, usually monthly. A mortgage with an annual percentage rate of **6.0%** with monthly payments would have a rate entered as **0.06/12**. *The interest rate must match the period.* |
| **num_periods** | Required. Expression or integer value specifying total number of payment periods in the loan. For example, monthly payments on a four-year car loan give a total of 4 * 12 (or 48) payment periods. |
| **present_value** | Required. Expression or value specifying the present value of the money you borrow. If you borrow $12,500 for a car, the value would be 12500. |
| **future_value** | Optional. Expression or value specifying the future value after you've made the final payment. Most consumer loans have a future value of $0 after the final payment. However, if you want to save $50,000 over 18 years for your child's education, then 50000 is the future value. Zero is assumed if left blank. |
| **type** | Optional. Value (0 or 1) identifying when payments are due. Use 0 if payments are due at the end of the payment period (the default), or 1 if payments are due at the beginning of the period. Zero is assumed if left blank. |

# Create Conditional Output with the IIf Function

Another common function used in Access is the ***IIf function***, which evaluates an expression and displays one value when the expression is true and another value when the expression is false. The expression must evaluate as true or false only. For example, *balance >= 10000* or *City = "Sarasota"* are valid expressions. DateListed + *90* is not a valid expression for the IIf function since this expression will yield a date. Access evaluates the expression, determines whether it is true or false, then displays one value if the expression is true and another value if the expression is false. For example, if accounts with balances of $10,000 or more earn 3.5% interest, whereas accounts with balances below $10,000 earn only 1.5% interest, the following IIf function could be created:

Example: IIf (Balance >= 10000, .035, .015)

Function: IIf (expression, truepart, falsepart)

> **TIP** Using Comparison Operators
>
> To create an expression with a *greater than or equal to* comparison operator, type the two operators >=. To create an expression with a *less than or equal to* comparison operator, type the two operators <=. Both of these comparison operators require two operators and they must be typed in the correct order.

Suppose you want to display the phrase "New Listing" when a property has been on the market for 30 days, and "For Sale" when a property has been on the market for more than 30 days. Using the DateListed field and the Date() function, the calculated field would be:

PropertyStatus: IIf (Date() – [DateListed] <=30, "New Listing", "For Sale")

The expression Date() – [DateListed]<=30 evaluates each property and determines if the number of days on market is less than or equal to 30. When the expression is true, the function displays "New Listing." When the expression is false, the function displays "For Sale."

The IIf function can also evaluate text values. For example, to classify a list of customers based on whether they are in or out of the state of California, you could create the IIf function:

IIf([State]="CA", "CA", "Out of State")

> **TIP** Use a Nested IIf
>
> Experienced Access users sometimes need to create nested IIf functions. This happens when two conditions are not sufficient to evaluate an expression. For example, in the earlier example where a property was classified based on days on market, the function PropertyStatus: IIf(Date() – [DateListed]<=30,"New Listing","For Sale") was used. If a third status were needed for properties that were on the market for six months, the nested PropertyStatus: IIf(Date() – [DateListed]<=30,"New Listing", IIf(Date() – [DateListed]>=180,"Stagnant","For Sale")) would be used.

When you finish the expression, click OK to close the Expression Builder dialog box. If you are working in a query, nothing will happen until you run the query. Your newly calculated field displays in the Datasheet view of the query. If you are working in a form, switch to Form view to see the results of your expression. And if you are working in a report, click Print Preview to see the results.

**Use the Expression Builder to Create a Calculated Field**

1. Open the query in Design view.
2. Click in the top row of the first blank column.
3. Verify the Design tab is displayed.
4. Click Builder in the Query Setup group to launch the Expression Builder (or right-click in the blank column and select Build from the list).
5. Type the name of the calculated field followed by a colon (:).
6. If the expression requires a field from a table, select a table from the Expression Elements box, and then double-click field names as needed to add them to the expression.
7. Type an arithmetic operator (such as + or *), or click Operators in the Expression Elements box, and then double-click a symbol in the Expression Values box.
8. If the expression requires a function, double-click the Functions folder, click Built-In Functions to see the function categories displayed in the Expression Categories box, and then select the function category. From the Expression Values box, double-click the specific function needed, and then fill in the correct arguments.
9. Click OK to exit the Builder box and place the expression in the field cell.
10. Run the query.
11. Examine and verify the output.
12. Return to the Design view.
13. Modify the new expression if necessary.
14. Run the query.
15. Save the query.

## Performing Date Arithmetic

Working with dates in Access can be challenging, especially when performing date arithmetic. This can be even more problematic if your output will contain multiple formats for the United States, Europe, and Asia. Each has their own method of formatting dates. Fortunately, Access has some built-in functions to help work with dates and date arithmetic.

**Date formatting** affects the date's display without changing the actual underlying value in the table.

*Date formatting* affects the date's display without changing the actual underlying value in the table. All dates and times in Access are stored as the number of days that have elapsed since December 31, 1899. For example, January 1, 1900, is stored as 1, indicating one day after December 31, 1899. If the time were 9:00 PM on November 20, 2010, no matter how the date or time is formatted, Access stores it as 40502.875. The 40502 represents the number of days elapsed since December 31, 1899, and the .875 reflects the fraction of the 24-hour day that has passed at 9:00 PM. Because dates are stored by Access as sequential numbers, you can calculate the total numbers of hours worked in a week if you record the starting and ending times for each day. Using *date arithmetic* you can create expressions to calculate lapsed time, such as a person's age based on birth date or the number of days past due an invoice is based on the invoice date.

> All dates and times in Access are stored as the number of days that have elapsed since December 31, 1899.

Using **date arithmetic** you can create expressions to calculate lapsed time.

### Identify Partial Dates with the DatePart Function

Using a date function, you can isolate a portion of the date that is of interest to you. If your company increases the number of weeks of annual vacation from two weeks to three weeks after an employee has worked for five or more years, then the only part of the date of interest is the time lapsed in years. Access has a function, the *DatePart function*, to facilitate this. Table 3 shows the DatePart function parameters.

The **DatePart function** enables you to isolate a specific part of a date, such as the year.

Example: DatePart("yyyy", [Employees]![HireDate])

Function: DatePart(interval, date), firstdayofweek, firstweekofyear

Useful date functions are:

- Date—Inserts the current date into an expression.
- DatePart—Evaluates a date and returns only the portion of the date that is designated.
- DateDiff—Measures the amount of time elapsed between two dates. This is most often today's date as determined by the date function and a date stored in a field. For example, you might calculate the number of days a payment is past due by comparing today's date with the payment DueDate.

| TABLE 3 | Using the DatePart Function |
|---|---|
| **Function Portion** | **Explanation** |
| **DatePart** | An Access function that examines a date and returns a portion of the date. |
| **≪interval≫** | The first argument, the interval, describes the portion of the date that you wish to return. Use "yyyy" for years, "m" for month, or "d" for day. |
| **≪date≫** | The second argument, the date, tells Access where to find the Date/Time information. In this case, it is stored in the Employee table in a field named HireDate. |
| **≪firstdayofweek≫** | Optional. A constant that specifies the first day of the week. If not specified, Sunday is assumed. |
| **≪firstweekofyear≫** | Optional. A constant that specifies the first week of the year. If not specified, the first week is assumed to be the week in which January 1 occurs. |

After you practice using the DatePart function, the syntax for all date functions will become easier to understand. In the next Hands-On Exercise, you will copy and paste a query, use the Expression builder, and use functions.

# HANDS-ON EXERCISES

myitlab
HOE2 Training

## 2 Expression Builder, Functions, and Date Arithmetic

As you learn more about Access, you find it easier to answer Jeff and Bill's questions about the properties using queries. When they ask you to calculate the price per bedroom and the price per room for each property, you use the Expression Builder to make the task easier. You also add two additional fields that calculate the days on market and the estimated commission for each property.

**Skills covered:** Copy and Paste a Query Using a New Name • Use the Expression Builder to Modify a Field • Use the Expression Builder to Add a Field • Use Functions • Work with Date Arithmetic and Add Criteria

---

### STEP 1 ▶ COPY AND PASTE A QUERY USING A NEW NAME

You create a copy of the PricePerSqFt query from the previous Hands-On Exercise and paste it using a new name. You will add a few more calculated fields to the new query. Refer to Figure 10 as you complete Step 1.

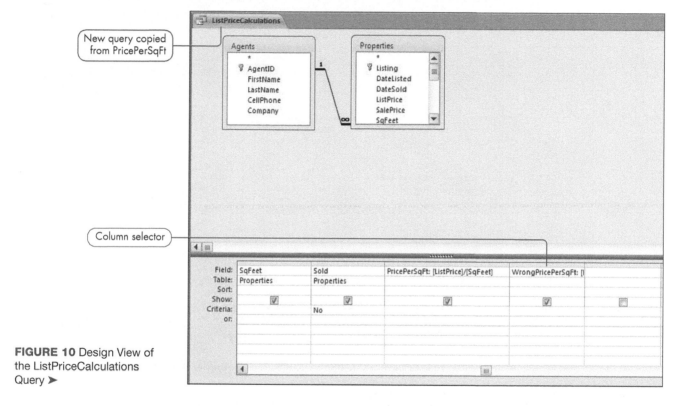

New query copied from PricePerSqFt

Column selector

**FIGURE 10** Design View of the ListPriceCalculations Query ➤

a. Open *a03h1property_LastnameFirstname* if you closed it at the end of Hands-On Exercise 1. Click the **File tab**, click **Save Database As**, and then type **a03h2property_LastnameFirstname**, changing *h1* to *h2*. Click **Save**.

b. Select the **PricePerSqFt query**, and then click **Copy** in the Clipboard group to copy the query.

c. Click **Paste**, and then type **ListPriceCalculations** as the query name. Click **OK**.

The new query is displayed in the Navigation Pane. The name of the query indicates that it contains calculations based on each property's list price.

d. Right-click **ListPriceCalculations**, and then choose **Design View** from the shortcut menu.

e. Delete the WrongPricePerSqFt field by clicking the column selector at the top of the column (as shown in Figure 10), and then pressing **Delete**.

The WrongPricePerSqFt field is not needed for this query.

f. Click **Run** to see the query results.

g. Click **View** to return to Design view. Save the query.

## STEP 2 USE THE EXPRESSION BUILDER TO MODIFY A FIELD

You need another calculation to help Jeff and Bill determine which houses to purchase. You will use the Expression Builder to modify an existing field. Refer to Figure 11 as you complete Step 2.

Price Per Bedroom calculated field

ListPriceCalculations

| First Name | Last Name | Date Listed | List Price | Square Feet | Sold | Price Per Bedroom |
|---|---|---|---|---|---|---|
| Your Name | Your Name | 1/24/2012 | $30,080.00 | 4834 | No | $7,520.00 |
| Keith | Mast | 2/10/2012 | $31,596.00 | 6179 | No | $7,899.00 |
| Karean | Eissler | 1/24/2012 | $31,780.00 | 4362 | No | $10,593.33 |
| Keith | Mast | 2/25/2012 | $31,800.00 | 4712 | No | $10,600.00 |
| Keith | Mast | 4/1/2012 | $31,996.00 | 3832 | No | $7,999.00 |
| Keith | Mast | 1/25/2012 | $31,996.00 | 4768 | No | $7,999.00 |
| Bill | Sabey | 2/10/2012 | $33,800.00 | 4949 | No | $8,450.00 |
| Bill | Sabey | 2/10/2012 | $33,960.00 | 3405 | No | $8,490.00 |
| Bill | Sabey | 1/24/2012 | $34,000.00 | 5180 | No | $8,500.00 |
| Bill | Sabey | 1/6/2012 | $35,200.00 | 4447 | No | $8,800.00 |
| Bill | Sabey | 12/20/2012 | $35,560.00 | 1512 | No | $11,853.33 |
| Bill | Sabey | 1/14/2012 | $35,960.00 | 1568 | No | $11,986.67 |
| Keith | Mast | 4/1/2012 | $35,960.00 | 3096 | No | $17,980.00 |
| Your Name | Your Name | 1/24/2012 | $38,000.00 | 7033 | No | $7,600.00 |
| Your Name | Your Name | 4/19/2012 | $39,000.00 | 5134 | No | $9,750.00 |
| Keith | Mast | 1/14/2012 | $39,800.00 | 1056 | No | $19,900.00 |
| Your Name | Your Name | 1/20/2012 | $39,800.00 | 5861 | No | $7,960.00 |
| Bill | Sabey | 3/23/2012 | $39,800.00 | 5690 | No | $9,950.00 |
| Karean | Eissler | 2/20/2012 | $42,000.00 | 768 | No | $21,000.00 |
| Your Name | Your Name | 12/26/2012 | $42,000.00 | 1000 | No | $21,000.00 |
| Keith | Mast | 1/24/2012 | $43,800.00 | 5440 | No | $10,950.00 |
| Your Name | Your Name | 11/22/2012 | $43,960.00 | 1497 | No | $14,653.33 |
| Karean | Eissler | 4/23/2012 | $43,960.00 | 2788 | No | $21,980.00 |
| Keith | Mast | 1/22/2012 | $44,000.00 | 766 | No | $22,000.00 |
| Bill | Sabey | 2/22/2012 | $45,600.00 | 1749 | No | $15,200.00 |
| Keith | Mast | 1/20/2012 | $46,000.00 | 4003 | No | $11,500.00 |
| Keith | Mast | 1/14/2012 | $47,600.00 | 5768 | No | $11,900.00 |

Record: 1 of 213 No Filter Search

**FIGURE 11** Calculated Field Created with the Expression Builder ➤

a. Click in the **PricePerSqFt column**, and then click **Builder** in the Query Setup group.

The Expression Builder dialog box opens.

b. Change the PricePerSqFt field name to **PricePerBR**.

c. Double-click the **[SqFeet] field** in the expression, and then press **Delete**.

d. Under Expression Elements, click the **plus sign** (+) next to the *a03h2property_LastnameFirstname* database in the Expression Elements box to expand the list. Click the (+) next to *Tables*, and then click the **Properties table**.

The fields from the Properties table are now listed in the middle column (Expression Categories).

e. Double-click the **Beds field** to add it to the expression box.

The expression now reads *PricePerBR: [ListPrice]/[Properties]![Beds].*

f.  Select the **[Properties]! prefix** in front of *Beds*, and then press **Delete**.

The expression now reads *PricePerBR: [ListPrice]/[Beds]*.

g.  Click **OK**, and then click **Run** to view the query results.

h.  Click **View** to switch to Design view, and then click the **PricePerBR field**. Click **Property Sheet** in the Show/Hide group, change the Format property to **Currency**, and then type **Price Per Bedroom** in the **Caption box**. Close the Property Sheet. Run the query and examine the changes.

i.  Click **View** in the Views group to switch back to Design view. Save the query.

---

**TIP** Switching Between Object Views

You can switch between object views quickly by clicking View or you can click the View arrow and select the desired view from the list. Another way to switch between views is to right-click the object tab, and then select the view from the shortcut menu. See Figure 12.

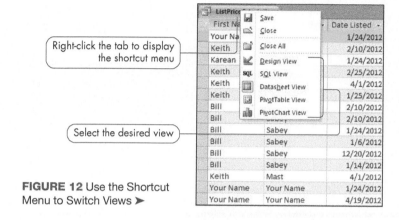

FIGURE 12 Use the Shortcut Menu to Switch Views ➤

---

**TIP** Expression Builder and Property Sheet

You can launch the Expression Builder by either clicking Builder in the Query Setup group on the Design tab or by right-clicking in the top row of the query design grid and selecting Build. Similarly, you can display the Property Sheet by clicking Property Sheet in the Show/Hide group on the Design tab or by right-clicking the top row of the query design grid and selecting Properties from the shortcut menu.

---

**STEP 3** USE THE EXPRESSION BUILDER TO ADD A FIELD

The MCCC investors ask you for another calculation—the list price per room. For this calculation, you will assume that each property has a kitchen, a living room, a dining room, and the listed bedrooms and bathrooms. Refer to Figure 13 as you complete Step 3.

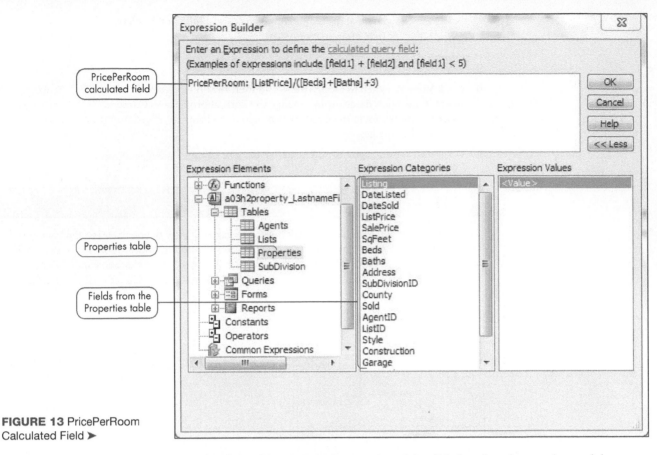

**FIGURE 13** PricePerRoom Calculated Field ➤

Labels pointing to the figure:
- PricePerRoom calculated field
- Properties table
- Fields from the Properties table

a. Select the entire **PricePerBR expression**, right-click the selected expression, and then select **Copy**.

b. Right-click in the next blank column, and then click **Paste**.

   You will edit the copy so that it reflects the price per room.

c. Click the new field, and then click **Builder** in the Query Setup group.

d. Add **parentheses** around the [Beds] portion of the formula. Type a **plus sign** (+) after *[Beds]*, inside the parentheses.

   The expression box should read *PricePerBR: [ListPrice]/([Beds]+)*.

e. Click the **plus sign** (+) next to the *a03h2property_LastnameFirstname* database in the Expression Elements box to expand the list. Click the **plus sign** (+) next to *Tables*, and then click the **Properties table**.

   The fields from the Properties table are now listed in the Expression Categories box.

f. Double-click the **Baths field** to add it to the expression box.

   The expression now reads *PricePerBR: [ListPrice]/([Beds]+[Properties]![Baths])*.

g. Type another plus sign after *[Baths]*, and then type **3**.

   The expression now reads *PricePerBR: [ListPrice]/([Beds]+[Properties]![Baths]+3)*.

h. Delete the [Properties]! portion of the expression.

i. Change the PricePerBR field name to **PricePerRoom**.

   The expression now reads *PricePerRoom: [ListPrice]/([Beds]+[Baths]+3)*.

j. Click **OK** to close the Expression Builder. Run the query. Widen the PricePerRoom column in order to see all the values.

k. Switch to **Design view**, click the **PricePerRoom field**, and then click **Property Sheet**.

l. Change the Format property to **Currency**, and then type **Price Per Room** in the **Caption box**. Close the Property Sheet.

m. Run the query and examine the query results.

n. Save the query, and then close the query.

Jeff and Bill feel like they are close to making an offer on a house. They would like to calculate the estimated mortgage payment for each house. You create this calculation using the Pmt function. Refer to Figures 14 and 15 as you complete Step 4.

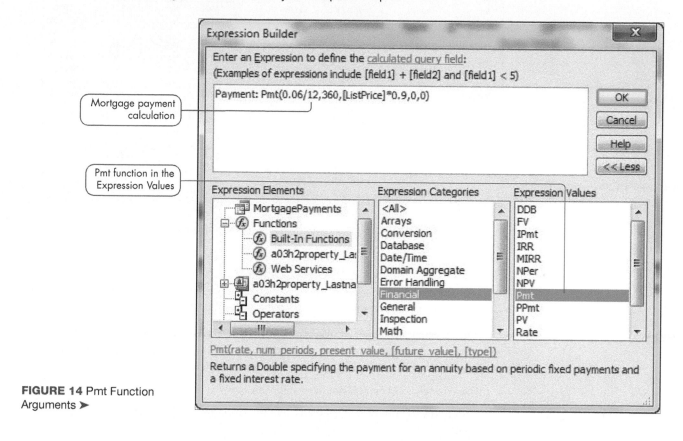

Mortgage payment calculation

Pmt function in the Expression Values

**FIGURE 14** Pmt Function Arguments ▶

**FIGURE 15** Payment Amounts for Each Property ➤

Mortgage payment calculation

| First Name | Last Name | Date Listed | List Price | Square Feet | Sold | Price Per Sq Ft | Payment |
|---|---|---|---|---|---|---|---|
| Your Name | Your Name | 1/24/2012 | $30,080.00 | 4834 | No | $6.22 | $162.31 |
| Keith | Mast | 2/10/2012 | $31,596.00 | 6179 | No | $5.11 | $170.49 |
| Karean | Eissler | 1/24/2012 | $31,780.00 | 4362 | No | $7.29 | $171.48 |
| Keith | Mast | 2/25/2012 | $31,800.00 | 4712 | No | $6.75 | $171.59 |
| Keith | Mast | 4/1/2012 | $31,996.00 | 3832 | No | $8.35 | $172.65 |
| Keith | Mast | 1/25/2012 | $31,996.00 | 4768 | No | $6.71 | $172.65 |
| Bill | Sabey | 2/10/2012 | $33,800.00 | 4949 | No | $6.83 | $182.38 |
| Bill | Sabey | 2/10/2012 | $33,960.00 | 3405 | No | $9.97 | $183.25 |
| Bill | Sabey | 1/24/2012 | $34,000.00 | 5180 | No | $6.56 | $183.46 |
| Bill | Sabey | 1/6/2012 | $35,200.00 | 4447 | No | $7.92 | $189.94 |
| Bill | Sabey | 12/20/2012 | $35,560.00 | 1512 | No | $23.52 | $191.88 |
| Keith | Mast | 4/1/2012 | $35,960.00 | 3096 | No | $11.61 | $194.04 |
| Bill | Sabey | 1/14/2012 | $35,960.00 | 1568 | No | $22.93 | $194.04 |
| Your Name | Your Name | 1/24/2012 | $38,000.00 | 7033 | No | $5.40 | $205.05 |
| Your Name | Your Name | 4/19/2012 | $39,000.00 | 5134 | No | $7.60 | $210.44 |
| Keith | Mast | 1/14/2012 | $39,800.00 | 1056 | No | $37.69 | $214.76 |
| Bill | Sabey | 3/23/2012 | $39,800.00 | 5690 | No | $6.99 | $214.76 |
| Your Name | Your Name | 1/20/2012 | $39,800.00 | 5861 | No | $6.79 | $214.76 |
| Your Name | Your Name | 12/26/2012 | $42,000.00 | 1000 | No | $42.00 | $226.63 |
| Karean | Eissler | 2/20/2012 | $42,000.00 | 768 | No | $54.69 | $226.63 |
| Keith | Mast | 1/24/2012 | $43,800.00 | 5440 | No | $8.05 | $236.34 |
| Your Name | Your Name | 11/22/2012 | $43,960.00 | 1497 | No | $29.37 | $237.21 |
| Karean | Eissler | 4/23/2012 | $43,960.00 | 2788 | No | $15.77 | $237.21 |
| Keith | Mast | 1/22/2012 | $44,000.00 | 766 | No | $57.44 | $237.42 |
| Bill | Sabey | 2/22/2012 | $45,600.00 | 1749 | No | $26.07 | $246.06 |
| Keith | Mast | 1/20/2012 | $46,000.00 | 4003 | No | $11.49 | $248.21 |
| Keith | Mast | 1/14/2012 | $47,600.00 | 5768 | No | $8.25 | $256.85 |

Record: 1 of 84 — No Filter — Search

a. Select the **PricePerSqFt query**, and then click **Copy** in the Clipboard group to copy the query.

b. Click **Paste**, and then type **MortgagePayments** as the query name. Click **OK**.

The new query is displayed in the Navigation Pane. The name of the query indicates that it contains calculations based on each property's list price.

c. Right-click **MortgagePayments**, and then choose **Design View** from the shortcut menu.

d. Delete the WrongPricePerSqFeet field by clicking the column selector at the top of the column (as shown in Figure 10), and then pressing **Delete**.

The WrongPricePerSqFt is not needed for this query.

e. Click in the top row of the first blank column. Click **Builder** in the Query Setup group to open the Expression Builder dialog box.

You will use the Pmt function to calculate an estimated house payment for each of the sold properties. You make the following assumptions: 90% of the sale price will be financed, a 30-year term, monthly payments, and a fixed 6.0% annual interest rate.

f. Double-click **Functions** in the Expression Elements box, and then click **Built-In Functions**.

g. Click the **Financial category** in the Expression Categories box.

h. Double-click the **Pmt function** in the Expression Values box. The expression box displays:

*Pmt(«rate», «num_periods», «present_value», «future_value», «type»)*

i. Type **Payment:** to the left of the Pmt function. The expression box now displays:

*Payment: Pmt(«rate», «num_periods», «present_value», «future_value», «type»)*

> **TROUBLESHOOTING:** If you forget to add the calculated field name to the left of the expression, Access will add *Expr1* to the front of your expression for you. You can edit the Expr1 name later, after the Expression Builder is closed.

j. Click each argument to select it, and then substitute the appropriate information. Make sure there is a comma between each argument.

| Argument | Replacement Value |
|---|---|
| <<rate>> | 0.06/12 |
| <<num_periods>> | 360 |
| <<present_value>> | [ListPrice] * 0.9 *(this represents 90% of the list price)* |
| <<future_value>> | 0 |
| <<due>> | 0 |

k. Examine Figure 14 to make sure that you have entered the correct arguments. Click **OK**. Run the query.

The Payment column shows ########. Widen the column and notice the payment amounts are negative numbers. You will edit the formula to change the negative payment values to positive.

l. Right-click the **MortgagePayments tab**, and then choose **Design View** from the shortcut menu. Right-click the **Payment field**, and then select **Build**. Add a **minus sign** (−) to the left of *[ListPrice]*.

The expression now reads *Payment: Pmt(0.06/12,360,−[ListPrice]*0.9,0,0)*.

m. Click **OK**. Open the **Property Sheet** for *Payment*, and then change the format to **Currency**. Close the Property Sheet.

The calculated field values should now appear as positive values formatted as currency, as shown in Figure 15.

n. Run and save the query.

## STEP 5 ▶ WORK WITH DATE ARITHMETIC AND ADD CRITERIA

You need to limit the query results to only houses on the market at least six months. The investors also want you to add the commission fee to the query since they are getting ready to make a purchase and this information will help them figure out their commission cost. Refer to Figure 16 as you complete Step 5.

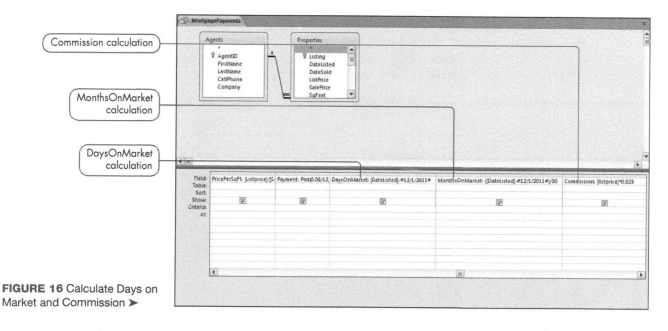

**FIGURE 16** Calculate Days on Market and Commission ➤

a. Click **View** to return to the Design view of the MortgagePayments query. Click in the top row of the first blank column. Press **Shift+F2** to open the Zoom dialog box.

You need to enter an expression to calculate the number of days that each property has been on the market.

b. Type **DaysOnMarket: [DateListed] – #12/1/2011#**.

This will display the number of days a house has been on the market since 12/1/2011.

c. Click **OK** to close the Zoom dialog box. Open the **Property Sheet**, and then add the Caption to **Days on Market**. Close the Property sheet.

d. Type **<=100000** in the **Criteria row** of the **ListPrice column**. Run the query. Save the query.

This expression will limit the query results to only houses with a list price of $100,000 or less. There should be 84 records.

e. Click **View** to switch to Design view. Click in the top row of the first blank column. Press **Shift+F2** to open the Zoom dialog box.

f. Type the formula **MonthsOnMarket: ([DateListed] – #12/1/2011#) / 30**.

The formula for MonthsOnMarket requires placing parentheses around *[DateListed] – #12/1/2011#* and then dividing the result by 30. This is an example of how to control the order of operations.

g. Click **OK** to close the Zoom dialog box. Open the Property Sheet, and then change the Format to **Fixed**, and the Caption to **Months on Market**. Close the Property Sheet dialog box. Run the query. Save the query.

h. Switch to Design view. Click in the top row of the first blank column to create another calculated field. Open the Zoom dialog box, and then type the formula **Commission: ListPrice * .025**. Click **OK** to close the Zoom dialog box.

The Commission field displays the projected commission for each house. The agent earns 2.5% of the sale price.

i. Right-click the **Commission field**, and then select **Properties**. Change the format to **Currency**, and then close the Property Sheet.

j. Run the query, examine the results, and then save the query. Close the query.

The values in the Commission field now display in Currency format.

k. Click the **File tab**, and then click **Compact & Repair Database**.

l. Click the **File tab**, click **Save & Publish**, and then double-click **Back Up Database**. Accept *a03h2property_LastnameFirstname_date* as the file name, and then click **Save**.

You just created a backup of the database you used to complete the second Hands-On Exercise. The *a03h2property_LastnameFirstname* database remains open.

m. Keep the database onscreen if you plan to continue with Hands-On Exercise 3. If not, close the database and exit Access.

# Aggregate Functions

An **aggregate function** performs calculations on an entire column of data and returns a single value.

Aggregate functions—such as Sum, Average, and Minimum—are used when you need to evaluate a group of record values rather than the individual records in a table or query.

Almost every company or organization that uses a database will require some type of aggregate data.

*Aggregate functions* perform calculations on an entire column of data and return a single value. Aggregate functions—such as Sum, Average, and Minimum—are used when you need to evaluate a group of record values rather than the individual records in a table or query.

Access refers to aggregate functions as Totals. In the Datasheet view of a query or table, click Totals in the Records group on the Home tab to add a Total row to the bottom of the datasheet. Each column can have its own aggregate function. Numeric fields are eligible for all of the functions, whereas text fields are only eligible for the count function.

When you create a query in Design view, click Totals in the Show/Hide group to change it to a totals query. The Total row now appears and you can select from the list of aggregate functions (e.g., Sum, Avg, Min).

The Datasheet view of a query or table displays individual records; users can edit these records, enter a new record, or delete a record in Datasheet view. However, when you work within a totals query in Datasheet view, no updates are allowed. A user cannot add, update, or delete records that have been totaled.

A car dealer's monthly inventory report is a good example of a report that might contain aggregate information. The cars would be grouped by model, and then by options package and color. At the end of the report, a summary page would list the count of cars in each model for quick reference by the sales reps. In the property database, aggregate information could be grouped by county or by subdivision. For example, the average home price per county could be presented in a query or a report. This would give prospective buyers a good idea of home prices in their target counties. Almost every company or organization that uses a database will require some type of aggregate data.

A list of common aggregate functions is shown in Table 4.

## TABLE 4  Aggregate Functions

| Function | Description | Use with Data Type(s) |
|---|---|---|
| Average | Calculates the average value for a column. The function ignores null values. | Number, Currency, Date/Time |
| Count | Counts the number of items in a column. The function ignores null values. | All data types except a column of multivalued lists. |
| Maximum | Returns the item with the highest value. For text data, the highest value is 'Z.' The function ignores null values. | Number, Currency, Date/Time, Text |
| Minimum | Returns the item with the lowest value. For text data, the lowest value is 'a.' The function ignores null values. | Number, Currency, Date/Time, Text |
| Standard Deviation | Measures how widely values are dispersed from an average value. | Number, Currency |
| Sum | Adds the items in a column. Works only on numeric and currency data. | Number, Currency |
| Variance | Measures the statistical variance of all values in the column. | Number |

In this section, you will learn how to create and work with aggregate functions. Specifically, you will learn how to use the Total row and create a totals query.

## Adding Aggregate Functions to Datasheets and Queries

Aggregate functions are most commonly used in tables, queries, and reports. Occasionally, aggregate functions are also added to the form footer section of forms. Aggregate data helps users evaluate the values in a single record as compared to the average of all the records.

If you are considering buying a property in Bucks county for $150,000 and the average price of a property in Bucks county is $450,000, you know you are getting a good deal (or buying a bad property).

Access provides two methods of adding aggregate functions to a query—a *Total row* displayed as the last row in the Datasheet view of a table or query and a totals query created in query Design view.

The first method enables you to add a Total row to the Datasheet view. This method is quick and easy and has the advantage of showing the total information while still showing the individual records. Adding a Total row to a query or table can be accomplished by most users (even those who are not familiar with designing a query).

The second method requires you to add a Total row in the Query Design view. This method has the advantage of enabling you to group your data by categories. For example, you can use the Count function to show the number of houses sold in each county in each subdivision. You could also use the Average function to show the average sale price for houses sold in each subdivision.

Once the totals data are assembled, you can use them to make decisions. Who is the leading salesperson? Which subdivisions are selling the most houses? This method requires the user to understand how to alter the design of a query.

Access also permits aggregates in reports. The Report Wizard gives users a choice to show all detail records or summary-only statistics. Select summary only to see aggregate data. You will learn to use both methods of creating aggregate data.

A **Total row** displays as the last row in the Datasheet view of a table or query and provides a number of aggregate functions.

## Add a Total Row in a Query or Table

Figure 17 shows the Total row added to the Datasheet view of a query. Using the balance column as illustrated, you can choose any of the aggregate functions that apply to numeric fields. To begin, click Totals in the Records group on the Home tab. The Total row is added at the bottom of the datasheet, below the new record row of the query or table. In the Total row, you can select one of the aggregate functions by clicking in the cell and then clicking the arrow. The list of aggregate functions includes Sum, Average, Count, and others.

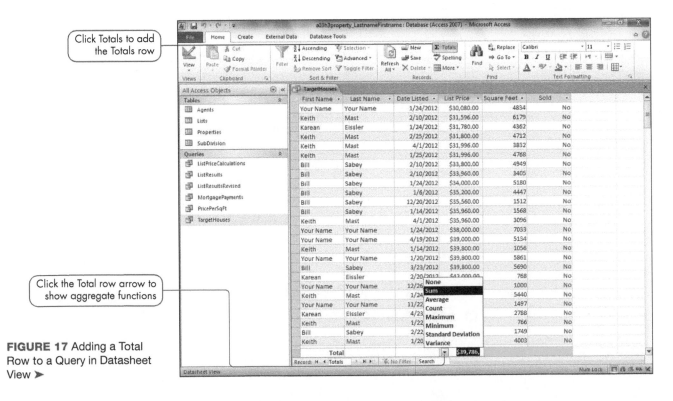

Click Totals to add the Totals row

Click the Total row arrow to show aggregate functions

**FIGURE 17** Adding a Total Row to a Query in Datasheet View ➤

Customize, Analyze, and Summarize Query Data

## Create a Totals Query

A **totals query** contains an additional row in the design grid and is used to display only aggregate data when the query is run.

A **totals query** contains an additional row in the query design grid and is used to display only aggregate data when the query is run. This is in contrast to using the Total row in a datasheet which shows both the detail records and the summary (as described in the previous section). The first column of a totals query will usually be a grouping field; the Total row will contain the Group function. The second and subsequent columns will usually contain the Count, Sum, or Avg function. Problems can arise when too many columns are included in a totals query; a typical totals query contains only two to five columns. Figure 18 shows the Design view of a totals query with three columns.

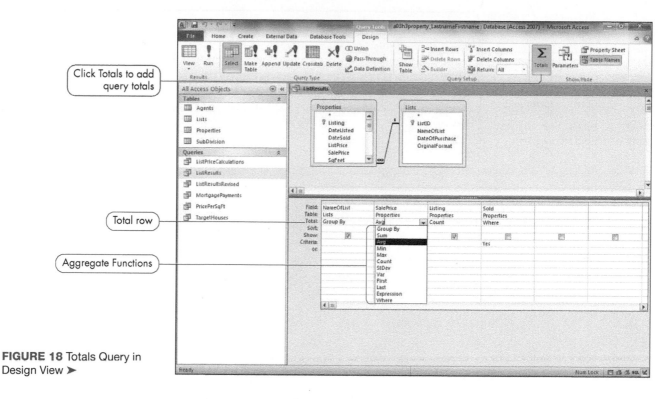

**FIGURE 18** Totals Query in Design View ➤

Figure 18 groups the properties by county and then shows the count of houses and the average price in each county. You could add the Subdivision field to the second column of this query—to create a group within a group. The data will now be grouped by county and then by subdivision within each county. In order to show the subdivision field, you must add the Subdivision table to the query design. Figure 19 shows the results of the Housing Info by County by Subdivision totals query.

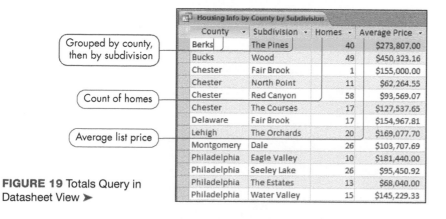

**FIGURE 19** Totals Query in Datasheet View ➤

# TIP  A Totals Query Helps Evaluate a Database

If you were asked to evaluate a database that contains home sales information, you could quickly determine which agents sold houses by creating a totals query with two tables and three fields. From the Properties and Agents tables, you would add the LastName field, the Listing field, and the Sold field. Click Totals in the Show/Hide group. Accept Group By in column one; change column two to Count, and change column three to Where. Add Yes to the Criteria row of column three. The results of this query would show which agents sold homes, as shown in Figure 20.

Reps who sold homes

Number of homes sold

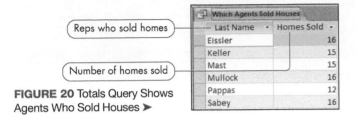

**FIGURE 20** Totals Query Shows Agents Who Sold Houses ➤

## 3 Aggregate Functions

The investors decide it would be helpful to analyze the property lists they purchased. Some of the lists do not have homes that match their target criteria. The investors will either need to purchase new lists or alter their criteria. You create several totals queries to evaluate the property lists.

**Skills covered:** Add a Total Row to Datasheet View • Create a Totals Query Based on a Select Query • Add a Calculated Field to a Totals Query

---

### STEP 1 ▶ ADD A TOTAL ROW TO DATASHEET VIEW

You begin your property list analysis by creating a Total row in the Datasheet view of the MortgagePayments query. This will give you a variety of aggregate information for each column. Refer to Figure 21 as you complete Step 1.

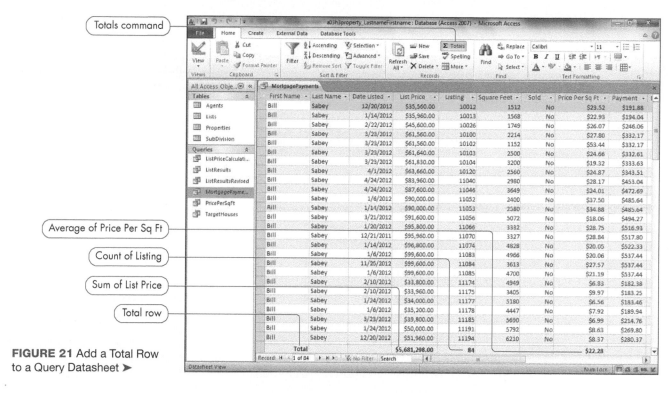

**FIGURE 21** Add a Total Row to a Query Datasheet ➤

a. Open *a03h2property_LastnameFirstname* if you closed it at the end of Hands-On Exercise 2. Click the **File tab**, click **Save Database As**, and then type **a03h3property_LastnameFirstname**, changing *h2* to *h3*. Click **Save**.

b. Right-click the **MortgagePayments query** in the Navigation Pane, and then select **Design View** from the shortcut menu. Drag the **Listing field** from the Properties table to the fifth column.

The Listing field is now in the fifth column and the other columns shift to the right.

c. Click **View** to switch to Datasheet view. Click **Totals** in the Records group on the Home tab to show the Total row.

The Total row is now displayed as the last row of the query results. Click Totals again to hide the Total row, then one more time to show it.

d. Click in the cell that intersects the Total row and the List Price column.

e. Click the arrow, and then select **Sum** to display the total of all the properties that have not sold. Widen the List Price column if you can't see the entire total value.

The total list price of all properties is $5,681,298.00.

f. Click the arrow in the Total row in the Listing column, and then select **Count** from the list.

The count of properties in this datasheet is 84.

g. Click in the Total row in the Price Per Sq Ft column. Click the arrow, and then select **Average** to display the average price per square foot.

h. Save and close the query.

## STEP 2 ▶ CREATE A TOTALS QUERY BASED ON A SELECT QUERY

You create a totals query to help Jeff and Bill evaluate the properties in groups. Refer to Figure 22 as you complete Step 2.

**FIGURE 22** Results of a Totals Query ▶

a. Click the **Create tab**, and then click **Query Design** in the Queries group.

You create a new query in Query Design; the Show Table dialog box opens.

b. Add the Properties table and the Lists table from the Show Table dialog box. Close the Show Table dialog box.

c. Add the NameOfList field from the Lists table and the SalePrice and Sold fields from the Properties table to the query design grid.

d. Click **Totals** in the Show/Hide Group to show the Total row.

e. Change the Total row to **Avg** in the SalePrice column.

f. Change the Total row to **Where** in the Sold column. Type **Yes** in the **Criteria row**.

This criterion will limit the results to sold houses only.

g. Click in the **SalePrice field**, and then click **Property Sheet** in the Show/Hide group. Change the SalePrice format to **Currency**. Close the Property Sheet. Run the query.

The query results indicate that the MLS list is the only source that is under the investor's target of $100,000 or less. They decide to continue using Realtor.com and Trulia even though the average price is over $100,000. The other sources will no longer be used.

Customize, Analyze, and Summarize Query Data

**h.** Click **View** to switch to Design View. Add the Listing field from the Properties table to the fourth column in the design grid. Change the Total row for *Listing* to **Count**. Run the query.

The query results now show the number of properties sold in each source, in addition to the average sale price. This will help determine which sources have been more effective.

**i.** Click **View** to return to the Design view of the query. Change the caption of the Listing column to **Number Sold**. Run the query, and then widen the columns as shown in Figure 22.

**j.** Save the query as **ListResults**. Keep the query open for the next step.

## STEP 3 ▶ ADD A CALCULATED FIELD TO A TOTALS QUERY

The totals query helped group the houses into categories. However, the groups contain all the properties, even the ones that do not match the investor's criteria. You need to create a new query with the investor's criteria included. Refer to Figure 23 as you complete Step 3.

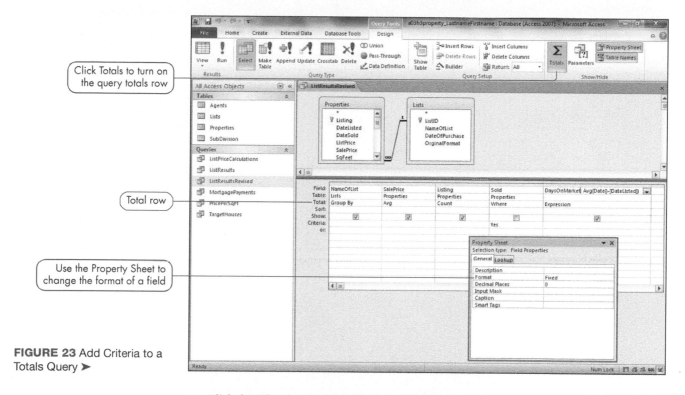

**FIGURE 23** Add Criteria to a Totals Query ➤

**a.** Click the **File tab**, and then click **Save Object As**. Save the query as **ListResultsRevised**. Click the **File tab** to return to the query.

**b.** Click **Totals** in the Records group, and then add **Sum** to the Number Sold column.

The total number of houses sold is 90.

**c.** Click **View** in the Views group to switch to Design view. In the first blank column, type **DaysOnMarket: [DateListed]** − **#12/1/2011#** to create a new calculated field. Change the Total row to **Avg**.

**d.** Right-click the **DaysOnMarket field**, and then select **Properties** from the shortcut menu. Change the Format property to **Fixed**. Close the Property Sheet.

**e.** Run the ListResultsRevised query, and then examine the DaysOnMarket.

**f.** Save and close the query.

g. Click the **File tab**, and then click **Compact & Repair Database**.

h. Click the **File tab**, click **Save & Publish**, and then double-click **Back Up Database**. Accept *a03h3property_LastnameFirstname_date* as the file name, and then click **Save**.

You just created a backup of the database you used to complete the third Hands-On Exercise. The *a03h3property_LastnameFirstname* database remains open.

i. Click the **File tab**, and then click **Exit** (to exit Access).

j. Submit based on your instructor's directions.

# CHAPTER OBJECTIVES REVIEW

After reading this chapter, you have accomplished the following objectives:

1. **Understand the order of operations.** The order of operations determines the sequence by which operations are calculated in an expression. Evaluate expressions in parentheses first, then exponents, then multiplication and division, and, finally, addition and subtraction. Operations of equal value will be calculated from left to right. A solid understanding of these rules will enable you to easily create calculated fields in Access.

2. **Create a calculated field in a query.** When creating a query, you may need to create a calculation based on the fields from one or more tables. Add a calculated field in the Design view of a query to the first blank column or by inserting a blank column where needed. A formula used to calculate new fields from the values in existing fields is known as an *expression*. An expression can consist of a number of fields, operators (such as $*$, $/$, $+$, or $-$), functions (such as IIf), and constants (numbers). When creating a calculated field, you must follow proper syntax—the set of rules that Access follows when evaluating an expression.

3. **Create expressions with the Expression Builder.** Launch the Expression Builder while in the query design grid to assist you with creating a calculated field (or other expression). The Expression Builder helps you create expressions by supplying you with the fields, operators, and functions you need to create them. When you use the Expression Builder to help you create expressions, you can eliminate spelling errors in field names. Another advantage is with functions; functions require specific arguments in a specific order. When you insert

a function using the Expression Builder, the builder gives you placeholders that tell you where each argument belongs.

4. **Use built-in functions in Access.** A function produces a result based on variable inputs known as *arguments*. Once you identify what you need a function to do, you can open the Built-In Functions folder in the Expression Builder to see if the function exists. If it does, add the function to the expression box and supply the required arguments. Functions work the same in Access and Excel.

5. **Perform date arithmetic.** All dates and times in Access are stored as the number of days that have elapsed since December 31, 1899. Working with dates in Access can be challenging, especially when performing date arithmetic. Fortunately, Access has some built-in functions to help work with dates and date arithmetic. Sample functions include DateDiff (), DateAdd(), Date(), and Now(). These functions help perform arithmetic on date fields.

6. **Add aggregate functions to datasheets and queries.** Aggregate functions perform calculations on an entire column of data and return a single value. Aggregate functions—such as Sum, Average, and Minimum—are used when you need to evaluate a group of records rather than the individual records in a table or query. Access refers to aggregate functions as Totals. In the Datasheet view of a query or table, click Totals to add a Total row to the bottom of the datasheet. When you create a query in Design view, click Totals to show the Total row.

# KEY TERMS

| | | |
|---|---|---|
| Aggregate function | DatePart function | Order of operations |
| Argument | Expression | Pmt function |
| Constant | Expression Builder | Syntax |
| Date arithmetic | Function | Total row |
| Date formatting | IIf function | Totals query |

1. Which of the following correctly identifies the rules for the order of operations?

    (a) Exponentiation, parentheses, addition, subtraction, multiplication, division

    (b) Parentheses, exponentiation, addition, subtraction, multiplication, division

    (c) Parentheses, exponentiation, multiplication, division, addition, subtraction

    (d) Addition, subtraction, multiplication, division, exponentiation, parentheses

2. What is the result of the following expression?

    $(3 * 5) + 7 - 2 - 6 * 2$

    (a) 12

    (b) 7

    (c) 28

    (d) 8

3. The Builder command that opens the Expression Builder is found in the:

    (a) Manage group on the Databases Tools tab.

    (b) Query Setup group on the Design tab.

    (c) Database Management group on the Design tab.

    (d) Design group on the Query Setup tab.

4. Which function enables you to insert today's date into an expression?

    (a) Date()

    (b) DatePart()

    (c) Now()

    (d) DateDiff()

5. You correctly calculated a value for the OrderAmount using an expression. Now you need to use the newly calculated value in another expression calculating sales tax. The most efficient method is to:

    (a) Run and save the query to make OrderAmount available as input to subsequent expressions.

    (b) Create a new query based on the query containing the calculated Order amount, and then calculate the sales tax in the new query.

    (c) Close the Access file, saving the changes when asked; reopen the file and reopen the query; calculate the sales tax.

    (d) Create a backup of the database, open the backup and the query, then calculate the sales tax.

6. If state law requires that a restaurant's wait staff be at least 21 to serve alcohol and you have a database that stores each

employee's birth date in the Employee table, which of the following is the proper syntax to identify the employees' year of birth?

    (a) Age:DatePart("yyyy",[Employee]![BirthDate])

    (b) Age=DatePart("yyyy",[Employee]![BirthDate])

    (c) Age:DatePart("yyyy",[BirthDate]![ Employee])

    (d) Age=DatePart("yyyy",[BirthDate]![ Employee])

7. Which statement about a totals query is true?

    (a) A totals query is created in Datasheet view.

    (b) A totals query may contain several grouping fields but only one aggregate field.

    (c) A totals query is limited to only two fields, one grouping field, and one aggregate field.

    (d) A totals query may contain several grouping fields and several aggregate fields.

8. After creating a calculated field, you run the query and a parameter dialog box appears on your screen. How do you respond to the Parameter dialog box?

    (a) Click OK to make the parameter box go away.

    (b) Read the field name specified in the parameter box, and then look for a possible typing error in the calculated expression.

    (c) Type numbers in the parameter box, and then click OK.

    (d) Close the query without saving changes. Re-open it and try running the query again.

9. An updatable query contains student names. You run the query and while in Datasheet view, you notice a spelling error on one of the student's names. You correct the error in Datasheet view. Which statement is true?

    (a) The name is correctly spelled in this query but will be misspelled in the table and all other queries based on the table.

    (b) The name is correctly spelled in the table and in all queries based on the table.

    (c) The name is correctly spelled in this query and any other queries, but will remain misspelled in the table.

    (d) You cannot edit data in a query.

10. Which of the following is not true about the Total row in the query design grid?

    (a) The Total row enables you to apply aggregate functions to the fields.

    (b) The Total row can apply to fields stored in different tables.

    (c) The Total row is located between the Table and Sort rows.

    (d) The Total row can only be applied to numeric fields.

# PRACTICE EXERCISES

The Comfort Insurance Agency is a mid-sized company with offices located across the country. Each employee receives a performance review annually. The review determines employee eligibility for salary increases and the annual performance bonus. The employee data are stored in an Access database, which is used by the human resources department to monitor and maintain employee records. Your task is to calculate the salary increase for each employee; you will also calculate each employee's performance bonus for employees who have been employed at least one year. This exercise follows the same set of skills as used in Hands-On Exercises 1 and 2 in the chapter. Refer to Figure 24 as you complete this exercise.

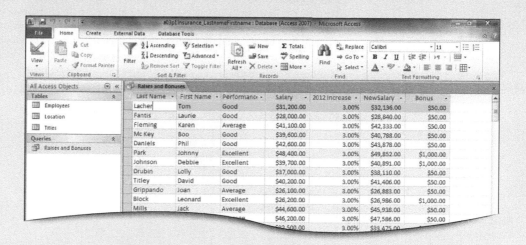

**FIGURE 24** Raises and Bonuses ➤

a. Open *a03p1insurance*. Click the **File tab**, click **Save Database As**, and then type **a03p1insurance_ LastnameFirstname**. Click **Save**.

b. Click the **Database Tools tab**, and then click **Relationships** in the Relationships group. Examine the table structure, relationships, and fields. Once you are familiar with the database, close the Relationships window.

c. Click the **Create tab**, and then click **Query Design** in the Queries group to start a new query. The Show Table dialog box opens. Add the Employees and Titles tables. Close the Show Table dialog box.

d. Add the **LastName**, **FirstName**, **Performance**, and **Salary fields** to the query. From the Titles table, add the **2012Increase field** to the query.

e. Click the top row of the first blank column in the query design grid, and then type **NewSalary:[Salary]\*[2012Increase]+[Salary]** to create a calculated field.

f. Click **Run** in the Results group to run the query. (If you receive the Enter Parameter Value dialog box, check your expression carefully for spelling errors.) Look at the output in the Datasheet view. Verify that your answers are correct. Notice that the fourth column heading displays *2012 Increase*. This is the caption for the 2012Increase field in the Titles table that was carried over to the query. When a caption exists for a field in the table Design view, the caption also displays in the Query Datasheet view instead of the field name in the query.

g. Click **View** in the Views group to switch back to Design view. Open the Property Sheet, click in the **NewSalary calculated field**, and then change the format to **Currency**. Type **New Salary** in the **Caption box**. Close the Property Sheet.

h. Save the query as **Raises and Bonuses**.

i. Click the top row of the first blank column, and then click **Builder** in the Query Setup group. In the Expression Elements box, double-click the folder for **Functions**. Select the **Built-In Functions folder**. Scroll down the Expression Values box to locate the IIf function. Double-click **IIf** to insert the function.

j. Click **<<expression>>**, and then replace it with **Performance = "Excellent"**. Click **<<truepart>>**, and then replace it with **1000**. Click **<<falsepart>>**, and then replace it with **50**.

k. Type **Bonus:** to the left of *IIf*, as the calculated field name. Click **OK**.

l. Change the format of the Bonus field to **Currency** in the Property Sheet.

m. Run the query. Save and close the query.

n. Click the **File tab**, and then click **Compact and Repair Database**.

o. Click the **File tab**, click **Save & Publish**, and then double-click **Back Up Database**. Click **Save** to accept the default backup file name.

p. Click the **File tab**, and then click **Exit** (to exit Access).

q. Submit based on your instructor's directions.

## 2  Northwind Traders

Northwind Traders maintains a database to store all of its product and inventory information, customer information, and sales information. You are the marketing manager of Northwind Traders and use this database to monitor sales trends. You need to determine the revenue from each order filled in the last year, and to summarize the revenue figures by product category. This exercise follows the same set of skills as used in Hands-On Exercises 2 and 3 in the chapter. Refer to Figure 25 as you complete this exercise.

**FIGURE 25** Revenue by Category ➤

| Revenue by Category | | |
| --- | --- | --- |
| Category Name ▾ | Total Revenue ▾ | Average Discount ▾ |
| Beverages | $25,109.20 | 5.74% |
| Condiments | $11,148.23 | 6.96% |
| Confections | $18,018.21 | 4.00% |
| Dairy Products | $24,288.60 | 6.62% |
| Grains/Cereals | $9,539.75 | 3.46% |
| Meat/Poultry | $11,474.25 | 5.63% |
| Produce | $10,637.46 | 2.69% |
| Seafood | $11,302.55 | 5.74% |

a. Open *a03p2traders*. Click the **File tab**, click **Save Database As**, and then type **a03p2traders_LastnameFirstname**. Click **Save**.

b. Click the **Database Tools tab**, and then click **Relationships** in the Relationships group. Examine the tables, fields, and relationships. After you are familiar with the database, close the Relationships window.

c. Click the **Create tab**, and then click **Query Design** in the Queries group to start a new query. The Show Table dialog box opens.

d. Add the Orders, Order Details, Products, and Categories tables. Close the Show Table dialog box.

e. Add the following fields to the query design grid:
   - OrderDate from the Orders table
   - Quantity and Discount from the Order Details table
   - UnitPrice and ProductCost from the Products table
   - CategoryName from the Categories table

f. Save the query as **Revenue**.

g. Type **>=1/1/2012 and <=3/31/2012** into the **Criteria row** of the OrderDate column (to limit the results to orders placed in the first Qtr of 2012).

h. Click the top row of the first blank column, and then click **Builder** in the Query Setup group. Type **Revenue:UnitPrice * (1-Discount) * Quantity**. Click **OK**.

i. Click **Property Sheet** in the Show/Hide group, and then change the format of the Revenue field to **Currency**. Close the Property Sheet dialog box.

j. Click **Run** to run the query. Use a calculator to check several records to verify the revenue calculation is correct. Save the query, and then close it.

k. Click the **Create tab**, and then click **Query Design** in the Queries group. Click the **Queries tab** in the Show Table dialog box. Double-click the **Revenue query** to add it to the design grid. Click **Close** in the Show Table dialog box.

l. Double-click the **CategoryName**, **Revenue**, and **Discount fields** in the Revenue query to add them to the design grid. Run the query.

m. Switch to Design View, and then click **Totals** in the Show/Hide group on the Design tab. The Total row will display. Change the Revenue Total row to **Sum**, and then change the Discount Total row to **Avg**.

n. Click **Property Sheet** in the Show/Hide group. Change the Revenue format to **Currency** and the Discount format to **Percent**.

o. Run the query. Verify the results. Notice that the second and third column headings are *SumOfRevenue* and *AvgOfDiscount*, respectively, to indicate the functions used on those fields. Save the query as **Revenue by Category**.

p. Click **View** in the Views group to switch to Design view. Change the Revenue field caption to **Total Revenue** and the Discount field caption to **Average Discount**. Save the query, and then run the query to see the captions. Close the query.

q. Click the **File tab**, and then click **Compact & Repair Database**.

r. Click the **File tab**, click **Save & Publish**, and then double-click **Back Up Database**. Use the default backup file name.

s. Click the **File tab**, and then click **Exit** (to exit Access).

t. Submit based on your instructor's directions.

## 1  The National Bank

You are the manager of the loan department of the National Bank. You need to monitor the total indebtedness of each customer to help them manage their debt load. Several customers may have multiple loans—a mortgage, a car loan, and a home equity loan. Your task is to use the Pmt function to calculate the loan payments for each loan and then to summarize the loans by customer. Refer to Figure 26 as you complete this exercise.

| Last Name | Total Payment |
|---|---|
| Collins | $3,318.36 |
| Fox | $7,274.63 |
| Greene | $3,798.04 |
| Hayes | $717.03 |
| Jones | $4,403.31 |
| Peterson | $956.21 |
| Simpson | $1,122.13 |
| Wagner | $2,529.52 |
| Williams | $3,462.30 |
| Your name | $4,152.81 |
| Total | $31,734.32 |

**FIGURE 26** Payment Summary ➤

a.  Open *a03m1bank*. Click the **File tab**, click **Save Database As**, and then type **a03m1bank_LastnameFirstname**. Click **Save**.

b.  Open the Customers table. Replace *Megan Royes* with your name. Close the table.

c.  Create a query that will calculate the payments for each loan. Add the following fields: LastName, Amount, InterestRate, Term, and Type from the Customers and Loans tables. Save the query as **Loan Payments**.

d.  Create a calculated field for the loan payment of each loan. Remember to divide the annual interest rate by 12 and multiply the loan's term by 12. Include a **minus sign** (–) in front of the loan amount in the expression so the result returns a positive value.

e.  Run the query. In the Datasheet view, add a Total row. Use it to calculate the average interest rate and the sum for the payment. Save and close the query.

f.  Create a totals query based on the Loan Payments query. Add the LastName and Payment fields to the design grid. Group by the LastName field, and then sum the Payment field.

g.  Format the Payment field as **Currency**, and then add the caption **Total Payment**.

h.  Run the query. Add a Total row to the Datasheet view that will sum the Total Payments. Save this query as **Payment Summary**.

i.  Compact the database. Back up the database. Exit Access.

j.  Submit based on your instructor's directions.

## 2  Investment Properties

You are in charge of LGS Investment's database, which contains all of the information on the properties your firm has listed and sold. Your task is to determine the length of time each property was on the market before it sold. You also need to calculate the sales commission from each property sold. Two agents will receive commission on each transaction: the listing agent and the selling agent. You also need to summarize the sales data by employee and calculate the average number of days each employee's sales were on the market prior to selling and the total commission earned by the employees. Refer to Figure 27 as you complete this exercise.

Customize, Analyze, and Summarize Query Data

**FIGURE 27** Sales
Summary ➤

| Sales Summary | | | | |
|---|---|---|---|---|
| Subdivision | Avg Days On Mkt | Sale Price | Listing Comm | Sell Comm |
| The Orchards | 22.8 | $1,288,000.00 | $45,080.00 | $32,200.00 |
| Fair Brook | 24.8 | $1,053,900.00 | $36,886.50 | $26,347.50 |
| Eagle Valley | 39.0 | $4,012,000.00 | $140,420.00 | $100,300.00 |
| Wood | 47.9 | $1,428,650.00 | $50,002.75 | $35,716.25 |
| Red Canyon | 52.0 | $3,790,000.00 | $132,650.00 | $94,750.00 |
| Total | | $11,572,550.00 | $405,039.25 | $289,313.75 |

a. Open *a03m2homes*. Click the **File tab**, click **Save Database As**, and then type **a03m2homes_LastnameFirstname**. Click **Save**.

b. Open the Agents table, and then replace *David Royes* with your name. Close the table.

c. Create a new query, add the necessary tables, and then add the following fields: LastName, DateListed, DateSold, SalePrice, SellingAgent, ListingAgent, and Subdivision. Type **Is Not Null** into the criterion row of the DateSold field. Save the query as **Sales Report**. Format the SalePrice field as **Currency**.

d. Using the Expression Builder, create the DaysOnMarket calculated field by subtracting DateListed from DateSold. This will calculate the number of days each sold property was on the market when it sold. Add an appropriate caption.

e. Calculate the commissions for the selling and listing agents using two calculated fields. The listing commission rate is **3.5%** and the selling commission rate is **2.5%**. Name the newly created fields **ListComm** and **SellComm**. These fields contain similar expressions. They need to be named differently so that the proper agent—the listing agent or the selling agent—gets paid. Add captions and format the fields as **Currency**.

f. Save the query after you verify that your calculations are correct. In Datasheet view, add the Total row. Calculate the Average number of days on the market and the sum for the SalePrice and the two commission fields. Save and close the query.

g. Create a totals query based on the Sales Report query. Group by LastName, and then show the average of the DaysOnMarket. Show the sum of SalePrice, ListComm, and SellComm. Format the fields as **Currency**, and then add appropriate captions. Run the query. Adjust column widths.

h. Add a Total row to the Datasheet view that will sum the sale price and commission fields. Save the query as **Sales Summary**.

i. Format the average of the Days on Market fields as fixed, one decimal place. (Note: if you do not see the Decimal Places property in the Property Sheet, switch to Datasheet view, then switch back to Design view.) Format the remaining numeric fields as **Currency**. Run the query.

**DISCOVER**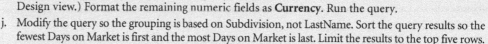

j. Modify the query so the grouping is based on Subdivision, not LastName. Sort the query results so the fewest Days on Market is first and the most Days on Market is last. Limit the results to the top five rows.

k. Compact the database. Back up the database. Exit Access.

l. Submit based on your instructor's directions.

Northwind Traders, an international gourmet food distributor, is concerned about shipping delays over the last six months. Review the orders over the past six months and identify any order that was not shipped within 30 days. Each customer that falls within that time frame will be called to inquire about any problems the delay may have caused. In addition, an order summary and an order summary by country will be created.

## Database File Setup

Open the food database, use Save As to make a copy of the database, and then use the new database to complete this capstone exercise. You will replace an existing employee's name with your name.

a. Locate and open *a03c1food*.

b. Click the **File tab**, click **Save Database As**, and then type **a03c1food_LastnameFirstname**.

c. Click **Save**.

d. Open the Employees table.

e. Replace *Rachael Eliza* with your name. Close the table.

## DaysToShip Query

You need to create a query to calculate the number of days between the date an order was placed and the date the order was shipped for each order. As you create the query, run the query at several intervals so you can verify that the data looks correct. The result of your work will be a list of orders that took more than three weeks to ship. The salespeople will be calling each customer to see if there was any problem with their order.

a. Create a query using Query Design. Include the fields CompanyName, ContactName, ContactTitle, Phone, OrderID, LastName, OrderDate, and ShippedDate. Use the Relationships window to determine which tables you need before you begin.

b. Run the query, and then examine the records. Save the query as **Shipping Efficiency**.

c. Add a calculated field named **DaysToShip** to calculate the number of days taken to fill each order. (*Hint*: The expression will include the OrderDate and the ShippedDate; the results will not contain negative numbers.)

d. Run the query, and then examine the results. Does the data in the DaysToShip field look accurate? Save the query.

e. Add criteria to limit the query results to include any order that took more than 30 days to ship.

f. Add the ProductID and Quantity fields to the Shipping Efficiency query. Sort the query by ascending OrderID. When the sales reps contact these customers, these two fields will provide useful information about the orders.

g. Switch to Datasheet view to view the final results. This list will be distributed to the sales reps so they can contact the customers. In Design view, add the **Sales Rep caption** to the LastName field.

h. Save and close the query.

## Order Summary Query

You need to create an Order Summary that will show the total amount of each order in one column and the total discount amount in another column. This query will require four tables: Orders, Order Details, Products, and Customers. Query to determine if employees are following the employee discount policy. You will group the data by employee name, count the orders, show the total dollars, and show the total discount amount. You will then determine which employees are following the company guidelines.

a. Create a query using Query Design and add the four tables above plus the Products table. Add the fields OrderID and OrderDate. Click **Totals** in the Show/Hide Group; the Total row for both fields should be Group By.

b. In the third column, add a calculated field: **ExtendedAmount: Quantity*UnitPrice**. Format the calculated field as Currency. This calculation will calculate the total amount for each order. Change the Total row to **Sum**.

c. In the fourth column, add a calculated field: **DiscountAmount: Quantity*UnitPrice*Discount**. Format the calculated field as **Currency**. This will calculate the total discount for each order. Change the Total row to **Sum**.

d. Run the query. Save the query as **Order Summary**. Return to Design view.

e. Enter the expression **Between 1/1/2012 And 12/31/2012** in the criteria of OrderDate. Change the Total row to **Where**. This expression will display only orders that were created in 2012.

f. Run the query and view the results. Save the query.

g. Add the **Total Dollars caption** to the ExtendedAmount field and add the **Discount Amt caption** to the DiscountAmount field.

h. Run the query. Save and close the query.

## Order Summary by Country Query

You need to create one additional query based on the Order Summary query you created in the previous step. This new query will enable you to analyze the orders by country.

a. Select the **Order Summary query**, and then use **Save Object As** to create a new query named **Order Summary by Country**.

b. In Design view of the new query, replace the OrderID field with the Country field.

c. Run the query, and then examine the summary records; there should be 21 countries listed.

d. In Design view, change the sort order so that the country with the highest Total Dollars is first, and the country with the lowest Total Dollars is last.

e. Run the query and verify the results.

f. Save and close the query, and then close the database and exit Access.

g. Submit based on your instructor's directions.

# BEYOND THE CLASSROOM

## Vacation Time for Bank Employees

GENERAL CASE

The *a03b1vacation* file contains data from a local bank. Open *a03b1vacation*. Click the File tab, click Save Database As, and then type **a03b1vacation_LastnameFirstname**. Click Save. Replace *Your Name* in the Customers table and the Branch table with your name. Use the skills from this chapter to perform several tasks. The bank's employee handbook states that a manager can take two weeks of vacation each year for the first three years of service, and three weeks of vacation after three years of employment. The Branch table stores the start date of each manager.

Create a query to determine how many years each manager has worked for the bank.

- Add a new field to calculate the number of weeks of vacation each manager is eligible to take.
- Use a nested IIf function to change the weeks of vacation to zero for any employee with a start date later than today.
- Change the format of each field to the appropriate type, and then add appropriate captions for the calculated fields.
- Save the query as **Vacation**.

Create another query to summarize each customer's account balances.

- List the customer's last name, first name, and a total of all account balances.
- Format the query results, and then add appropriate captions.
- Add the grand total of all accounts to the Datasheet view.
- Save the query as **Customer Balances**.

Close the query, and then close the database. Submit based on your instructor's directions.

## Combining Name Fields

RESEARCH CASE

This chapter introduced you to expressions. Use a search engine to search for information using the phrase *Combine text values by using an expression*. Open *a03b2combine*. Click the File tab, click Save Database As, and then type **a03b2combine_LastnameFirstname**. Click Save. Using the information from the Internet, create an expression to combine the last and first name fields into one field that displays "last name, first name." (Make sure you include a comma and a space after the last name.) You will use the Customers table in your query with LastName and FirstName. Once you successfully combine the fields in the query, alphabetize the list by last name, first name. Save the query as **Combined Names**. Close the query, and then close the database. Submit your work based on your instructor's directions.

## Coffee Revenue Queries

DISASTER RECOVERY

A co-worker called you into his office, explained that he was having difficulty with Access 2010, and then asked you to look at his work. Open *a03b3coffee*. Click the File tab, click Save Database As, and then type **a03b3coffee_LastnameFirstname**. Click Save. Replace *Your Name* in the Sales Reps table with your name. It contains two queries: Revenue and Revenue by City. The Revenue query calculates ProductRetailPrice (Cost + Cost * MarkupPercent) and NetRevenue ((ProductRetailPrice − Cost) * Quantity). You manually calculate the first row and discover both the ProductRetailPrice and NetRevenue fields are incorrect. Diagnose the error(s) in the two fields and correct them. After correcting the Revenue query, correct the Revenue by City query. Run both queries, and then add appropriate captions. Save and close both queries. Close the database and exit Access. Submit based on your instructor's directions.

Customize, Analyze, and Summarize Query Data

542

ACCESS

# CREATING AND USING PROFESSIONAL FORMS AND REPORTS

## Moving Beyond Tables and Queries

Watch the **Set-up Video** for this Case Study!

### CASE STUDY | Coffee Shop Starts New Business

For over 10 years, the Santiago Coffee Shop was an ordinary coffee shop selling retail coffee, tea, and pastries to its loyal customers in Bucks County. Then, in 2005, owner Alex Santiago decided to use his knowledge of the coffee industry to sell coffee products to businesses in his area. This new venture grew quickly and soon became 25% of his annual revenue. Realizing that this new business would need more of his time each day, he decided to create an Access database to help track his customer, product, and order information.

With the help of a student from Bucks County Community College, he created tables for customers, products, sales reps, and orders. He is currently using these tables as his primary method of entering and retrieving information.

Alex wants to have one of his employees, Tonya, manage the database. But he does not want her to work in the tables; he wants her to work with forms. Alex heard that forms have an advantage over tables because they can be designed to show one record at a time—this will reduce data entry errors. Alex would also like to create several reports for his own benefit so he can stay on top of the business by reviewing the reports each week.

You have been hired to help Alex create the new forms and reports that he needs for his business. He will describe the forms and reports to you in detail and also provide written instructions. You will be expected to work independently to create the forms and reports. Remember to identify the data source for each new form and report.

## OBJECTIVES AFTER YOU READ THIS CHAPTER, YOU WILL BE ABLE TO:

1. Create forms using the form tools
2. Modify a form
3. Sort records in a form
4. Identify form sections
5. Revise forms using form views
6. Identify control types in forms

7. Create reports using report tools
8. Modify a report
9. Sort records in a report
10. Identify report sections
11. Revise reports using report views
12. Identify control types in reports

From Access Chapter 4 of *Exploring Microsoft Office 2010 Volume 1*, First Edition, Robert T. Grauer, Mary Anne Poatsy, Keith Mulbery, Michelle Hulett, Cynthia Krebs, Keith Mast. Copyright © 2011 by Pearson Education, Inc. Published by Pearson Prentice Hall, Inc. All rights reserved.

# Form Basics

A *form* is a database object that is used to add data into or edit data in a table. Most Access database applications use forms rather than tables for data entry and for looking up information. Three main reasons exist for using forms rather than tables for adding, updating, and deleting data. They are:

> A **form** is a database object that is used to add data into or edit data in a table.

You are less likely to edit the wrong record by mistake.
You can create a form that shows data from more than one table simultaneously.
You can create Access forms to match paper forms.

> You are less likely to edit the wrong record by mistake ... You can create a form that shows data from more than one table simultaneously ... You can create Access forms to match paper forms.

If you are adding data using a table with many columns, you could jump to the wrong record in the middle of a record accidentally. For example, you could enter the data for one record correctly for the first 10 fields but then jump to the row above and overwrite existing data for the remaining field values unintentionally. In this case, two records have incorrect or incomplete data. A form will not allow this type of error since most forms restrict entry to one record at a time.

Many forms require two tables as their record source. For example, you may want to view a customer's details (name, address, e-mail, phone, etc.) as well as all of the orders he or she has placed. This would require using data from both the Customers and the Orders tables in one form. Similarly, you may want to view the header information for an order while also viewing the detail line items for the order. This would require data from both the Orders and Order Details tables. Both of these examples enable a user to view two record sources at the same time and make changes—additions, edits, or deletions—to one or both sources of data.

Finally, when paper forms are used to collect information, it is a good idea to design the electronic forms to match the paper forms. This will make data entry more efficient and reliable. Access forms can be designed to emulate the paper documents already in use in an organization. This facilitates the simultaneous use of both paper forms and electronic data. Databases do not necessarily eliminate paper forms; they supplement and coexist with them.

In this section, you will learn the basics of form design. You will discover multiple methods to create and modify Access forms. And you will learn how to create calculated controls.

## Creating Forms Using the Form Tools

Access provides a variety of options for creating forms. One size does not fit all—some developers may prefer a stacked layout form, whereas others prefer the multiple items form. The multiple items form can be styled to match a company's standards, whereas the datasheet form is simple and requires very little maintenance. And let's not forget the users; they will have their opinions about the type of forms they want to use.

Access provides 16 different tools for creating forms. The Forms group, located on the Create tab, contains four of the most common form tools (Form, Form Design, Blank Form, and Form Wizard), a list of Navigation forms, and a list of More Forms, as shown in Figure 1. Navigation forms provides a list of six templates to create a user interface for a database; the More Forms command lists six additional form tools (Multiple Items, Datasheet, Split Form, and more). Select a table or query, click one of the tools, and Access will create an automatic form using the selected table or query. The most common of these tools, the *Form tool*, is used to create data entry forms for customers, employees, products, and other primary tables. A primary table has a single field as its primary key and represents the "one" side of a one-to-many relationship. Once the form is created, as shown in Figure 2, you can customize the form using the Layout or Design views. After the form is created, it should be tested by both the database designer and the end users.

> The **Form tool** is used to create data entry forms for customers, employees, products, and other primary tables.

**FIGURE 1** Forms Group ➤

A complete list of all the Form tools available in Access is found in the Form Tools Reference at the end of this section. Many of the tools will be covered in this chapter. Some will not be covered since they are not commonly used or because they are beyond the scope of this chapter (e.g., Form Design, Blank Form, Navigation forms, and Modal Dialog form). Use Microsoft Access Help to find more information about Form tools not covered in this chapter.

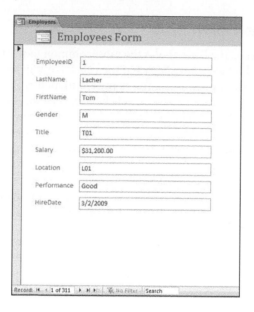

**FIGURE 2** Employees Form Created with the Form Tool ➤

Ideally, a form should simplify data entry. Creating a form is a collaborative process between the form designer and the form users. This process continues throughout the life of the form, because the data needs of an organization may change. Forms designed long ago to collect information for a new customer account may not have an e-mail field; the form would have to be modified to include an e-mail field. The form designer needs to strike a balance between collecting the information users need to do their jobs and cluttering the form with extraneous fields. The users of the data know what they need and usually offer good feedback about which fields should be on a form. By listening to their suggestions, your forms will function more effectively, the users' work will be easier, and your data will contain fewer data entry errors.

> Ideally, a form should simplify data entry.

## Identify a Record Source

**A record source** is the table or query that supplies the records for a form or report.

Before you create a form, you must identify the record source. A **record source** is the table or query that supplies the records for a form or report. Use a table if you want to include all the records from a single table. Use a query if you need to filter the records in a table, or if you need to combine records from two or more related tables.

**TIP** Record Source vs. Data Source

The term *record source* can be interchanged with the term *data source*. Both terms refer to the source of data for a form or a report. In this chapter, the term *record source* will be used exclusively. As stated earlier, a record source can refer to either a table or a query.

For example, if a sales rep wants to create a form that only displays customers from a single state—where his customers reside—he should base the form on a query. Or, if a parts manager needs to review only parts with a zero on-hand quantity, he could create a form based on a query that only includes records with on-hand equal to zero.

## Sketch the Form

It will help you to create the form in Access if you sketch the form first. A sketch may look similar to the form in Figure 2. After sketching the form, you will have a better idea of which form tool to use to create the form. After the form is created, use the sketch to determine which fields are required and what the order of fields should be.

## Use the Form Tool

A **stacked layout form** displays fields in a vertical column, and displays one record at a time.

A **tabular layout form** displays records horizontally, with label controls across the top and the data values in rows under the labels.

**Layout view** is used to modify the design of a form.

As noted earlier, the Form tool is the most common tool for creating forms. Select a table or query from the Navigation Pane, and then click Form in the Forms Group on the Create tab, and Access creates a new form. You may need to modify the form slightly, but you can create a stacked layout form in a just one click. A **stacked layout form** displays fields in a vertical column, and displays one record at a time, as shown in Figure 3. Multiple Items and Datasheet forms, in contrast to stacked layout forms, are examples of tabular layout forms. A **tabular layout form** displays records horizontally, with label controls across the top and the data values in rows under the labels. When a new form is created using the Form tool, Access opens the form in Layout view ready for customizing. You can generate forms for your database using the Form tool, and then use **Layout view** to modify the design of a form. Figure 3 shows the Employees form in Layout view.

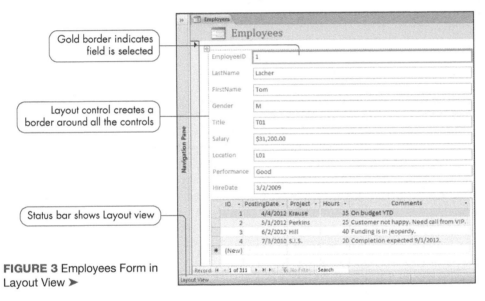

Gold border indicates field is selected

Layout control creates a border around all the controls

Status bar shows Layout view

**FIGURE 3** Employees Form in Layout View ➤

## Work with a Subform

When you use the Form tool to create a form, Access will analyze the table relationships you created in the database and automatically add a subform to the main form. A subform displays records with foreign key values that match the primary key value in the main form. For example, assume you have a database that contains the tables Employees and Project Time, and a relationship exists between the two tables based on the EmployeeID field. If you create a new form based on Employees, using the Form tool, Access will add a Project Time subform to the bottom of the main form (see Figure 3).

At times, you may want the subform as part of your form; other times, you may want to remove it. To remove a subform control from a form, switch to Design view, click the subform control, and then press Delete. The subform is deleted!

## Create a Split Form

A **split form** combines two views of the same record source—one section is displayed in a stacked layout and the other section is displayed in a tabular layout.

A *split form* combines two views of the same record source—one section is displayed in a stacked layout and the other section is displayed in a tabular layout. By default, the form view is positioned on the top and the datasheet view is displayed on the bottom; however, the orientation can be changed from horizontal to vertical in Layout view. If you select a record in the top half of the form, the same record will be selected in the bottom half of the form, and vice versa. For example, if you create a split form based on the Employees table, you can select an employee in the datasheet section and then see the employee's information in the *Form view* section (see Figure 4). If the selected employee is incorrect, click another employee in the datasheet section. The top and bottom halves are synchronized at all times.

To create a split form, first select a table or query in the Navigation Pane. Next, click the Create tab, click More Forms in the Forms group, and then select Split Form from the list of options. A new split form now appears. You can add, edit, or delete records in either section. The *splitter bar* divides the form into two halves. Users can adjust the splitter bar up or down unless the form designer disables this option.

The **splitter bar** divides the form into two halves.

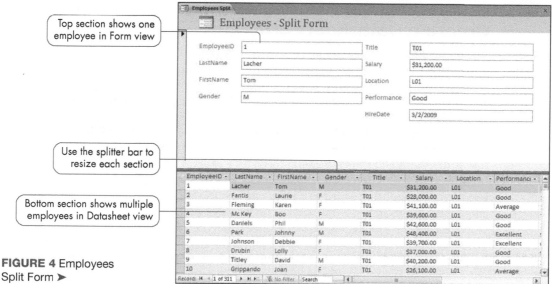

Top section shows one employee in Form view

Use the splitter bar to resize each section

Bottom section shows multiple employees in Datasheet view

**FIGURE 4** Employees Split Form ➤

## Create a Multiple Items Form

A **Multiple Items form** displays multiple records in a tabular layout similar to a table's Datasheet view.

A *Multiple Items form* displays multiple records in a tabular layout similar to a table's Datasheet view. However, a Multiple Items form gives you more customization options than a datasheet, such as the ability to add graphical elements, buttons, and other controls. Figure 5 shows a Multiple Items form created from the Employees table. Compare this Multiple Items form to the Employees Datasheet form shown in Figure 6. The color scheme applied to the Multiple Items form could not be applied to the Datasheet form since the Datasheet form is much more limited in design and control options. To create a Multiple Items form, first select a table or query from the Navigation Pane. Next, click the Create tab, click More Forms in the Forms group, and then select Multiple Items from the list of options.

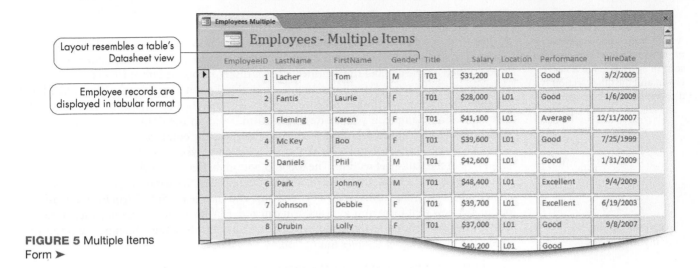

| | EmployeeID | LastName | FirstName | Gender | Title | Salary | Location | Performance | HireDate |
|---|---|---|---|---|---|---|---|---|---|
| ▶ | 1 | Lacher | Tom | M | T01 | $31,200 | L01 | Good | 3/2/2009 |
| | 2 | Fantis | Laurie | F | T01 | $28,000 | L01 | Good | 1/6/2009 |
| | 3 | Fleming | Karen | F | T01 | $41,100 | L01 | Average | 12/11/2007 |
| | 4 | Mc Key | Boo | F | T01 | $39,600 | L01 | Good | 7/25/1999 |
| | 5 | Daniels | Phil | M | T01 | $42,600 | L01 | Good | 1/31/2009 |
| | 6 | Park | Johnny | M | T01 | $48,400 | L01 | Excellent | 9/4/2009 |
| | 7 | Johnson | Debbie | F | T01 | $39,700 | L01 | Excellent | 6/19/2003 |
| | 8 | Drubin | Lolly | F | T01 | $37,000 | L01 | Good | 9/8/2007 |
| | | | | | | $40,200 | L01 | Good | |

**FIGURE 5** Multiple Items Form ➤

## Create a Datasheet Form

A **Datasheet form** is a replica of a table or query's Datasheet view except that it still retains some of the form properties.

A ***Datasheet form*** is a replica of a table or query's Datasheet view except that it still retains some of the form properties. A Datasheet form created from the Employees table is shown in Figure 6. To create a Datasheet form, first select a table or query from the Navigation Pane. Next, click the Create tab, click More Forms in the Forms group, and then select Datasheet from the list of options.

**Visual Basic for Applications (VBA)** is Microsoft's programming language that is built into all of the Office products.

A datasheet form, like all Access forms, can be customized to add additional functionality using ***Visual Basic for Applications (VBA)***. VBA is Microsoft's programming language that is built into all of the Office products. VBA enables an advanced Access user to customize forms and reports. Although a field's data type and field properties help prevent invalid data from being added to a table, you can use VBA to enforce more complex data entry rules. For example, if a data entry person were entering new products into the database, the cost of a product should not be more than the sale price. If that condition existed, the data entry form could alert the user using VBA.

Database designers can also use the Datasheet form to display data in a table-like format, but change the form properties to not allow a record to be deleted. This would protect the data from accidental damage while still providing the users with the familiar Datasheet view.

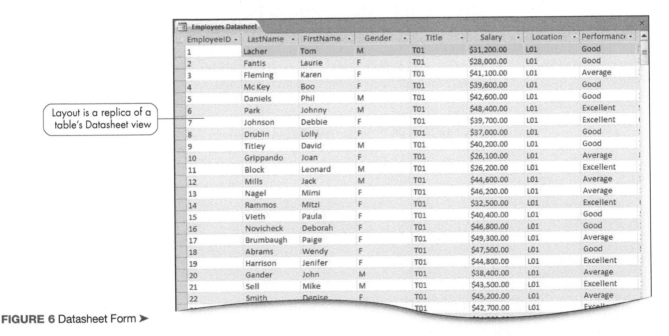

| EmployeeID ▾ | LastName ▾ | FirstName ▾ | Gender ▾ | Title ▾ | Salary ▾ | Location ▾ | Performanc ▾ |
|---|---|---|---|---|---|---|---|
| 1 | Lacher | Tom | M | T01 | $31,200.00 | L01 | Good |
| 2 | Fantis | Laurie | F | T01 | $28,000.00 | L01 | Good |
| 3 | Fleming | Karen | F | T01 | $41,100.00 | L01 | Average |
| 4 | Mc Key | Boo | F | T01 | $39,600.00 | L01 | Good |
| 5 | Daniels | Phil | M | T01 | $42,600.00 | L01 | Good |
| 6 | Park | Johnny | M | T01 | $48,400.00 | L01 | Excellent |
| 7 | Johnson | Debbie | F | T01 | $39,700.00 | L01 | Excellent |
| 8 | Drubin | Lolly | F | T01 | $37,000.00 | L01 | Good |
| 9 | Titley | David | M | T01 | $40,200.00 | L01 | Good |
| 10 | Grippando | Joan | F | T01 | $26,100.00 | L01 | Average |
| 11 | Block | Leonard | M | T01 | $26,200.00 | L01 | Excellent |
| 12 | Mills | Jack | M | T01 | $44,600.00 | L01 | Average |
| 13 | Nagel | Mimi | F | T01 | $46,200.00 | L01 | Average |
| 14 | Rammos | Mitzi | F | T01 | $32,500.00 | L01 | Excellent |
| 15 | Vieth | Paula | F | T01 | $40,400.00 | L01 | Good |
| 16 | Novicheck | Deborah | F | T01 | $46,800.00 | L01 | Good |
| 17 | Brumbaugh | Paige | F | T01 | $49,300.00 | L01 | Average |
| 18 | Abrams | Wendy | F | T01 | $47,500.00 | L01 | Good |
| 19 | Harrison | Jenifer | F | T01 | $44,800.00 | L01 | Excellent |
| 20 | Gander | John | M | T01 | $38,400.00 | L01 | Average |
| 21 | Sell | Mike | M | T01 | $43,500.00 | L01 | Excellent |
| 22 | Smith | Denise | F | T01 | $45,200.00 | L01 | Average |
| | | | | T01 | $42,700.00 | L01 | Excell |

Layout is a replica of a table's Datasheet view

**FIGURE 6** Datasheet Form ➤

Creating and Using Professional Forms and Reports

## Create Forms Using the Other Form Tools

The Form Design tool and the Blank Form tools can be used to create a form manually. Click one of these tools and Access will open a completely blank form. Click Add Existing Fields, on the Design tab, in the Tools group and add the necessary fields.

The Navigation option in the Forms group enables you to create user interface forms that have the look and feel of a Web-based form, and enable users to open and close the objects of a database. These forms are also useful for setting up an Access database on the Internet. For more information about Navigation forms, visit www.microsoft.com.

PivotTables and PivotCharts can also be converted to forms by selecting PivotChart or PivotTable in the More Forms option in the Forms group. After you create a PivotTable form or a PivotChart form, use the Layout view and Design view to customize the form.

The Modal Dialog Form tool can be used to create a dialog box. This feature is useful when you need to gather information from the user before working with another object. Dialog boxes are common in all Microsoft Office applications; creating a custom dialog box in Access can be useful when you need to collect information from the user.

## REFERENCE   Form Tools

| Form Tool | Location | Use |
|---|---|---|
| Form | Create tab, Forms group | Creates a form with a stacked layout displaying all of the fields in the record source. |
| Form Design | Create tab, Forms group | Create a new blank form in Design view. |
| Blank Form | Create tab, Forms group | Create a new blank form in Layout view. |
| Form Wizard | Create tab, Forms group | Answer a series of questions and Access will create a custom form for you. |
| Navigation | Create tab, Forms group, Navigation button | Create user interface forms that can also be used on the Internet. |
| Split Form | Create tab, Forms group, More Forms button | Creates a two-part form with a stacked layout in one section and a tabular layout in the other. |
| Multiple Items | Create tab, Forms group, More Forms button | Creates a tabular layout form that includes all of the fields from the record source. |
| Datasheet | Create tab, Forms group, More Forms button | Creates a form that resembles the datasheet of a table or query. |
| PivotTable | Create tab, Forms group, More Forms button | The PivotTable form tool enables you to present data from a table or query using a multi-dimensional table format. |
| PivotChart | Create tab, Forms group, More Forms button | The PivotChart form tool enables you to present data from a table or query using a multi-dimensional chart format. |
| Modal Dialog | Create tab, Forms group, More Forms button | Creates a custom dialog box that forces the user to respond before working with another object. |

## Modifying a Form

After a form is generated by a Form tool, you will usually need to modify it. The most common form changes are add a field, remove a field, change the order of fields, change the width of a field, and modify label text. These changes, as well as adding a theme, can be made in a form's Layout view. Advanced changes, such as adding a calculated field or adding VBA code, can be made in a form's Design view.

## Add a Field to a Form

To add a field to a form with a stacked layout, open the form in Layout view. Click Add Existing Fields in the Tools group on the Design tab to reveal the available fields from the form's record source. Drag the new field to the precise location on the form, using the orange line as a guide for the position of the new field. The other fields will automatically adjust to make room for the new field.

To add a field to a form with a tabular layout, follow the same steps for adding a field to a stacked layout form. The only difference is the orange line will appear vertically to help determine the insertion point of the new field.

## Work with a Form Layout Control

A **layout control** provides guides to help keep controls aligned horizontally and vertically, and give your form a uniform appearance.

Whenever you use one of the form tools to create a new form, Access will add a layout control to help align the fields. In general, form layout controls can help you create and modify forms. A *layout control* provides guides to help keep controls aligned horizontally and vertically, and give your form a uniform appearance. However, there are times when a layout control is too restrictive and will keep you from positioning controls where you want them. In this case, you can remove the layout control and position the controls manually on the grid.

To remove a form layout control, switch to Design view, and then click anywhere inside the control you want to remove. On the Arrange tab, click Select Layout in the Rows & Columns group. (You can also click the Layout Selector, the small square with a cross inside, to select the layout.) Click Remove Layout in the Table group and the layout control is gone. All of the other controls are still on the form, but the rectangle binding them together is gone.

You can add a layout control to a form by first selecting all the controls you want to keep together. Then, click Stacked or Tabular in the Table group and the layout control appears.

## Delete a Field from a Form

To delete a field in Layout view, click the text box control of the field to be deleted and note the orange border around the control. With the orange border showing, press Delete. The field's text box and label are both removed from the form and a space remains where the field used to be. Click the space, and then press Delete again, and the other fields will automatically adjust to close the gap around the deleted field.

## Adjust Column Widths in a Form

When column widths are adjusted in a form with a stacked layout, all columns will increase and decrease together. Therefore, it is best to make sure that field columns are wide enough to accommodate the widest value in the table. For example, if a form contains first name, last name, address, city, state, ZIP, phone, and e-mail address, you will need to make sure the longest address and the longest e-mail address are completely visible (since those fields are likely to contain the longest data values).

To decrease column widths in a form with a stacked layout, open the form in Layout view. Click the text box control of the first field—usually on the right—to select it. Move the mouse over the right border of the field until the mouse pointer turns into a double arrow, then drag the right edge to the left until you arrive at the desired width. All the fields change as you change the width of the first field. Drag the same edge to the right to increase the width.

## Add a Theme to a Form

An **Office Theme** is a defined set of colors, fonts, and graphics that can be applied to a form.

You can apply an Office Theme to a form in order to give the form a more professional finish. An *Office Theme* is a defined set of colors, fonts, and graphics that can be applied to a form. Click the Themes picker in the Themes group on the Design tab, select a theme from the Themes Gallery, and Access will apply the theme to your form. You can apply a theme to a single form or to all the forms in your database that share a common theme. Applying the same theme to all forms will provide a consistent look to your database; most users prefer a consistent theme when using Access forms. The same Office Themes found in Access are also available in Excel, Word, and PowerPoint. Therefore, you can achieve a uniformed look across all Office applications.

# Sorting Records in a Form

When a form is created using a Form tool, the sort order of the records in the form is dependent on the sort order of the record source—a table or a query. Tables are usually sorted by the primary key, whereas queries can be sorted in a variety of ways.

## Change the Sorting in a Form

To modify the sort order of a form, open the form in Form view, and then select the field you want to use for sorting. Next, click Ascending in the Sort & Filter group on the Home tab and the records will immediately be reordered based on the selected field.

You can also modify the sort order of a form by modifying the underlying query's sort order. The method enables you to create a more advanced sort order, based on multiple fields. To begin, switch to Design view, and then open the Property Sheet. Select the form by clicking the arrow under Selection type at the top of the Property Sheet, and then clicking Form. Next, locate the Record Source property on the Data tab, click in the property box, and then click Build to the right of the property box. Answer Yes to the message that appears. Access opens the underlying query in Design view. Add the sorting you want, close the query, and save the query when prompted. You will also need to save the form.

## Remove Sorting in a Form

To remove the sort order in a form, switch to Form view, and then click Remove Sort in the Sort & Filter group on the Home tab. If the form's sort order was modified, clicking this command will reset the form to the original order.

## 1 Form Basics

It is your first day on the job at Santiago Coffee Shop. After talking with Alex about his data entry needs, you decide to create several sample forms with different formats. You will show each form to Alex to get his feedback and see if he has a preference. Remember to select the correct record source prior to creating each new form.

**Skills covered:** Use the Form Tool and Adjust Column Widths in a Form • Create a Split Form • Create a Multiple Items Form • Create a Datasheet Form and Delete a Field from a Form • Add a Field to a Form • Change the Sorting in a Form and Remove Sorting in a Form

---

### STEP 1 ▶ USE THE FORM TOOL AND ADJUST COLUMN WIDTHS IN A FORM

Use the Form tool to create an Access form to help Alex manage his customers. This form will enable Tonya to add, edit, and delete records more efficiently than working with tables. Refer to Figure 7 as you complete Step 1.

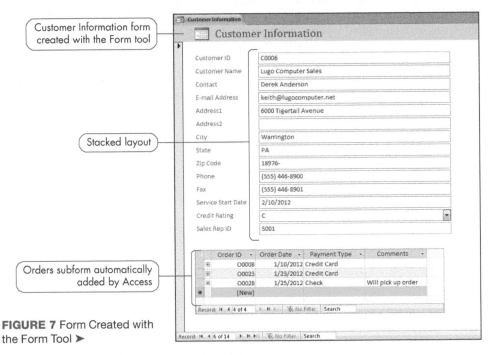

**FIGURE 7** Form Created with the Form Tool ▶

a. Open *a04h1coffee*. Click the **File tab**, click **Save Database As**, and then type **a04h1coffee_LastnameFirstname**. Click Save.

> **TROUBLESHOOTING:** Throughout the remainder of this chapter and textbook, click Enable Content whenever you are working with student files.

> **TROUBLESHOOTING:** If you make any major mistakes in this exercise, you can close the file, repeat step a above, and then start over.

b. Click the **Customers table** in the Navigation Pane. Click the **Create tab**, and then click **Form** in the Forms group.

Access creates a new form with two record sources—Customers (with stacked layout, on top) and Orders (with tabular layout, below). Access found a one-to-many relationship between the Customers and Orders tables. The form opens in Layout view.

Creating and Using Professional Forms and Reports

552

**c.** Click the top text box containing *C0001*. The text box is outlined with an orange border. Move the mouse to the right edge of the orange border until the mouse pointer changes to a double-headed arrow. Drag the right edge to the left until the text box is approximately 50% of its original size.

All the text boxes and the subform at the bottom adjust in size when you adjust the top text box. This is a characteristic of Layout view—enabling you to easily modify all controls at once.

> **TROUBLESHOOTING:** You may need to maximize the Access window, or close the Navigation Pane, if the right edge of the text box is not visible.

**d.** Click the Arrange tab, and then click **Select Layout** in the Rows & Columns group.

All the controls are now selected.

> **TROUBLESHOOTING:** Click any control in the top part of the form before you click Select layout.

**e.** On the Arrange tab, click **Control Padding** in the Position group. Select **Narrow** from the list of choices.

The space between the controls is reduced.

**f.** Click **Save** in the Quick Access Toolbar, and then type **Customer Information** as the form name in the **Save As dialog box**. Click **OK**.

**g.** Click the **Home tab**, and then click **View** in the Views group to switch to Form view, the view that most users will see. Advance to the sixth customer, *Lugo Computer Sales*, using the **Navigation bar** at the bottom of the form.

> **TROUBLESHOOTING:** Two Navigation bars exist, one for the main form and one for the subform. Make sure you use the bottom one that shows 14 records.

**h.** Double-click the **Customers table** in the Navigation Pane.

Two tabs now appear in the main window. You will compare the table data and the form data while you make changes to both.

**i.** Verify the sixth record of the Customers table is *Lugo Computer Sales*, which corresponds to the sixth record in the Customer Information form. Click the tabs to switch between the table and the form.

**j.** Click the **Customer Information tab**, and then replace *Derek Anderson*, the contact for Lugo Computer Sales, with your name. Advance to the next record to save the changes. Click the **Customers tab** to see that the contact name changed in the table as well.

The contact field and the other fields on the Customer Information form are bound controls. Changing the data in the form automatically changes the data in the underlying table.

> **TROUBLESHOOTING:** If the change to Derek Anderson does not appear in the Customers table, check the Customer Information form to see if the pencil appears in the left margin. If it does, save the record by advancing to the next customer, and then recheck to see if the name has changed.

**k.** Replace your name with **Derek Anderson**. Save the record by clicking on the record below *Lugo Computer Sales*. Click the **Customer Information tab**, and then find the sixth record. You should see the change you just made—Derek is back!

**l.** Switch to Layout view. Click the **Customers title** at the top of the form to select it, and then click again and change the title to **Customer Information**.

The Customer Information title, a label control, is an example of an unbound control; an unbound control does not have a connection to an underlying table.

**m.** Click **Save** in the Quick Access Toolbar to save the changes to the form's title. Close the form and the table.

> **TROUBLESHOOTING:** If you make a mistake that you cannot easily recover from, consider deleting the form and starting over. The Form tool makes it easy to start over again.

---

**STEP 2** ▶ **CREATE A SPLIT FORM**

Use the Split Form tool to create a different form to show to Tonya. She may prefer to use a split form to add, edit, and delete records rather than the Customer Information form that you created in the previous step. Refer to Figure 8 as you complete Step 2.

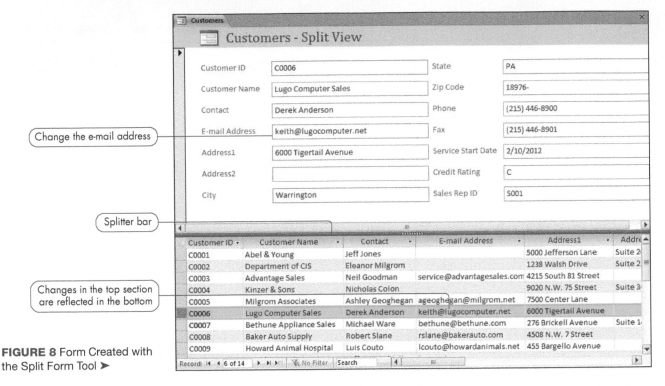

**FIGURE 8** Form Created with the Split Form Tool ➤

**a.** Verify the Customers table is selected in the Navigation Pane. Click the **Create tab**, click **More Forms** in the Forms group, and then select **Split Form** from the list.

Access creates a new form with a split view, one view in stacked layout and one view in tabular layout.

**b.** Switch to Form view. In the bottom portion of the split form, click **Lugo Computer Sales**, the sixth record. Notice the top portion now displays the information for Lugo Computer Sales.

**c.** Change *service@lugocomputer.net* to *yourname*@**lugocomputer.net** in the top portion of the form.

The bottom portion reflects your change when you move to another field or advance to another record.

**d.** Click another record, and then click back on **Lugo Computer Sales**.

The pencil disappears from the record selector box and the changes are saved to the table.

**e.** Click anywhere on the Coulter Office Supplies customer in the bottom portion of the form (record 14).

The top portion shows all the information for this customer.

f. Modify the Contact, E-mail Address, and Address1 information in the top portion of the form, by typing **xyz** at the end of each cell. Save your changes by clicking anywhere in the bottom portion of the window.

   Notice the xyz characters appear in the bottom portion of the form.

g. Remove the xyz's from the Coulter Office Supplies record in the top section.

h. Switch to Layout view. Click the **Customers title** at the top of the form to select it, and then click **Customers** again and change the title to **Customers - Split View**.

i. Click **Save** on the Quick Access Toolbar, and then type **Customers - Split View** in the **Form Name box**. Click **OK**.

j. Move your mouse over the splitter bar, the border between the top and bottom portions of the window. When the pointer shape changes to a double-headed arrow, drag the splitter bar up until it almost touches the Sales Rep ID field.

k. Close the form and save the changes when prompted.

## STEP 3 ▸ CREATE A MULTIPLE ITEMS FORM

You decide to use the Multiple Items tool to create a form for Alex to manage his products. Because of its tabular format, it will enable Alex and Tonya to view multiple records at one time. Refer to Figure 9 as you complete Step 3.

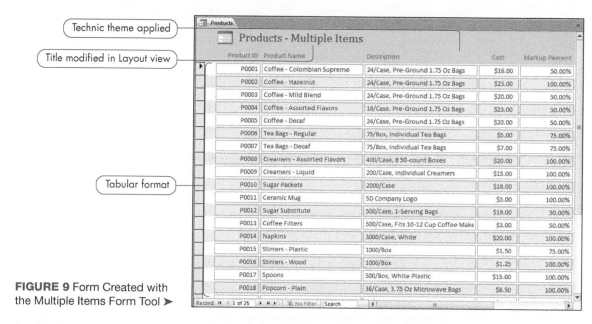

**FIGURE 9** Form Created with the Multiple Items Form Tool ➤

a. Click the **Products table** in the Navigation Pane. Click the **Create tab**, click **More Forms** in the Forms group, and then select **Multiple Items** from the list.

   Access creates a new multiple items form based on the Products table. The form resembles the datasheet of a table—both have a tabular layout.

b. Click **cell P0001**. Move the mouse over the bottom edge of cell P0001 until the pointer shape changes to a two-headed arrow. Drag the bottom edge up to reduce the height of the rows by 50%.

   Changing the height of one row affects the height of all the rows.

c. Click the **Products title** at the top of the form to select it, and then click again on **Products** and change the title to **Products - Multiple Items**.

**d.** Click the **Themes arrow** in the Themes group on the Design tab. Right-click the **Technic Theme** (near the bottom of the gallery), and then choose **Apply Theme to This Object Only**.

Hover over a theme and its name will display as a ScreenTip. The Technic theme is applied to the Products - Multiple Items form.

**e.** Close and save the form as **Products - Multiple Items**.

**STEP 4** **CREATE A DATASHEET FORM AND DELETE A FIELD FROM A FORM**

You decide to use the Datasheet tool to create another form for Alex to manage his products. The Datasheet form is in tabular format and is similar to the Multiple Items form, but requires little or no maintenance, which Alex may like. Refer to Figure 10 as you complete Step 4.

Datasheet form based on the Products table

Field name modified

Datasheet form looks similar to Datasheet view

| Product ID | Product Name | Description | Refrig? | Brand | Year Introduce |
|---|---|---|---|---|---|
| P0001 | Coffee - Colombian Supreme | 24/Case, Pre-Ground 1.75 Oz Bags | ☐ | Discount | 2008 |
| P0002 | Coffee - Hazelnut | 24/Case, Pre-Ground 1.75 Oz Bags | ☐ | Premium | 2008 |
| P0003 | Coffee - Mild Blend | 24/Case, Pre-Ground 1.75 Oz Bags | ☐ | House | 2008 |
| P0004 | Coffee - Assorted Flavors | 18/Case. Pre-Ground 1.75 Oz Bags | ☐ | House | 2008 |
| P0005 | Coffee - Decaf | 24/Case, Pre-Ground 1.75 Oz Bags | ☐ | Discount | 2008 |
| P0006 | Tea Bags - Regular | 75/Box, Individual Tea Bags | ☐ | House | 2008 |
| P0007 | Tea Bags - Decaf | 75/Box, Individual Tea Bags | ☐ | House | 2008 |
| P0008 | Creamers - Assorted Flavors | 400/Case, 8 50-count Boxes | ☐ | Discount | 2008 |
| P0009 | Creamers - Liquid | 200/Case, Individual Creamers | ☑ | Premium | 2008 |
| P0010 | Sugar Packets | 2000/Case | ☐ | House | 2008 |
| P0011 | Ceramic Mug | SD Company Logo | ☐ | House | 2008 |
| P0012 | Sugar Substitute | 500/Case, 1-Serving Bags | ☐ | Discount | 2008 |
| P0013 | Coffee Filters | 500/Case, Fits 10-12 Cup Coffee Maker | ☐ | House | 2008 |
| P0014 | Napkins | 3000/Case, White | ☐ | House | 2008 |
| P0015 | Stirrers - Plastic | 1000/Box | ☐ | Discount | 2008 |
| P0016 | Stirrers - Wood | 1000/Box | ☐ | Discount | 2008 |
| P0017 | Spoons | 500/Box, White Plastic | ☐ | House | 2008 |
| P0018 | Popcorn - Plain | 36/Case, 3.75 Oz Microwave Bags | ☐ | House | 2008 |
| P0019 | Popcorn - Buttered | 36/Case, 3.75 Oz Microwave Bags | ☐ | House | 2008 |
| P0020 | Soup - Chicken | 50 Envelopes | ☐ | Premium | 2008 |
| P0021 | Soup - Variety Pak | 50 Envelopes | ☐ | Premium | 2008 |
| P0022 | Styrofoam Cups - 10 ounce | 1000/Case | ☐ | House | 2008 |
| P0023 | Styrofoam Cups - 12 ounce | 1000/Case | ☐ | House | 2008 |
| P0024 | Milk - 1 quart | Delivered Daily | ☑ | House | 2008 |
| P0025 | Milk - 1 pint | Delivered Daily | ☑ | House | 2008 |
| * (New) | | | ☐ | House | 2010 |

**FIGURE 10** Datasheet Form ➤

**a.** Verify the Products table is selected in the Navigation Pane. Click the **Create tab**, click **More Forms** in the Forms group, and then select **Datasheet**.

Access creates a new datasheet form based on the Products table. The Tabular form looks similar to the Products table and could be easily mistaken for a table.

**b.** Click **Save** in the Quick Access Toolbar, and then type **Products - Datasheet** in the **Form Name box**. Click **OK**.

**c.** Widen the Navigation Pane so all object names are visible. Right-click the **Products - Datasheet form** in the Navigation Pane, and then choose **Layout View** from the list of options.

> **TROUBLESHOOTING:** The View arrow does not contain the Layout view options.

**d.** Click anywhere in an empty area to deselect the controls.

**e.** Click the **Cost box**, the control on the right, to select it (you will see the orange border), and then press **Delete**. Click the blank space, and then press **Delete** to remove the blank space. Repeat the process to delete *MarkupPercent*.

You removed fields from the Products form and the other fields adjust to maintain an even distribution (after you remove the blank space).

f. Click the **Refrigeration Needed label** to select it. Change the label to the abbreviation **Refrig?**. Save the form, and then switch to Datasheet view.

g. Double-click the **Products table** in the Navigation Pane to open it.

The Products - Datasheet form and the Products table now appear different because the Cost and MarkupPercent fields were deleted from the form.

h. Close the Products Datasheet form and the Products table.

## STEP 5 ▶ ADD A FIELD TO A FORM

The form tools made it easy to create forms for Alex's company. But Alex decided he needs a Website field, so you need to modify the form. Refer to Figure 11 as you complete Step 5.

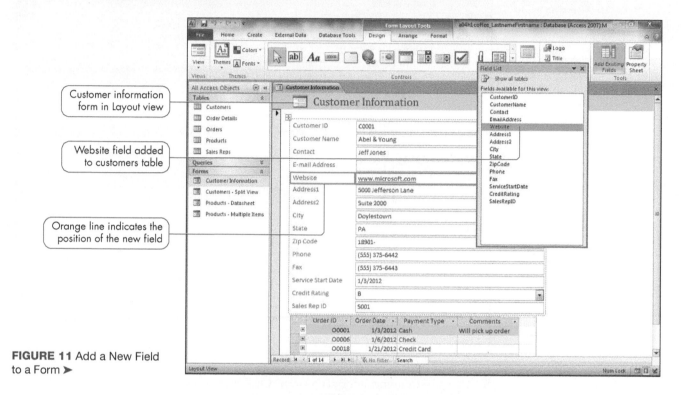

Customer information form in Layout view

Website field added to customers table

Orange line indicates the position of the new field

**FIGURE 11** Add a New Field to a Form ▶

a. Right-click the **Customers table** in the Navigation Pane, and then click **Design View**.

You will add the Website field to the Customers table.

b. Click the **Address1 field**, and then click **Insert Rows** in the Tools group.

A new row is inserted above the Address1 field.

c. Type **Website** in the blank **Field Name box**, and then choose **Hyperlink** as the Data Type.

d. Close and save the Customers table.

e. Right-click the **Customer Information form** in the Navigation Pane, and then click **Layout View**.

You will add the Website field to the Customer Information form.

f. Click **Add Existing Fields** in the Tools group to display the Field List pane (if necessary).

g. Drag the **Website field** from the Field List pane to the form, below the E-mail Address field, until an orange line displays between E-mail Address and Address1 and release the mouse.

Access shows an orange line to help you place the field in the correct location.

h. Switch to Form view. Press **Tab** until you reach the **Website field**, and then type **www.microsoft.com** into the field.

i. Press **Tab** until the focus reaches the Orders subform to verify the tab order is correct.

j. Close and save the Customer Information form.

## STEP 6 ▶ CHANGE THE SORTING IN A FORM AND REMOVE SORTING IN A FORM

Alex tested the Customer Information form and likes the way it is working. He asks you to change the sorting to make it easier to find customers with a similar Customer Name. Refer to Figure 12 as you complete Step 6.

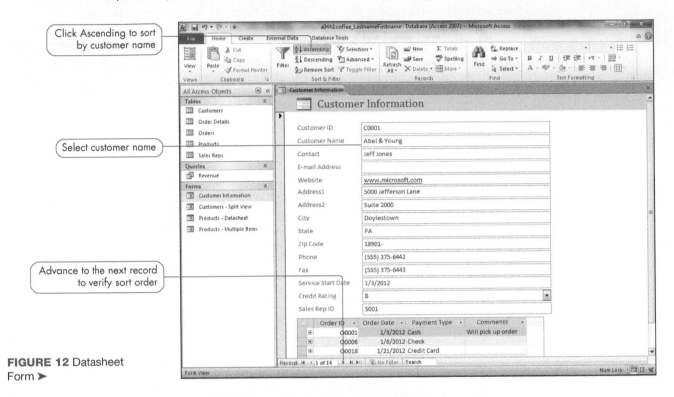

**FIGURE 12** Datasheet Form ▶

a. Open the Customer Information form. Click **Next record** in the Navigation bar at the bottom several times to advance through the records.

Take note that the customers are in Customer ID order.

b. Click **First record** in the Navigation bar to return to customer Abel & Young.

c. Click the **Customer Name field**, and then click **Ascending** in the Sort & Filter group.

d. Click **Next record** in the Navigation bar at the bottom to advance through the records.

The records are now in Customer Name order.

e. Close the Customer Information form.

f. Click the **File tab**, and then click **Compact & Repair Database**.

g. Keep the database onscreen if you plan to continue with Hands-On Exercise 2. If not, close the database and exit Access.

# Form Sections, Views, and Controls

As you work with the form tools to create and modify forms, you will often need to switch between the three form views in Access—Layout view, Form view, and Design view. Most of your design work will be done in Layout view; occasionally, you will switch to Design view to add a more advanced feature, such as a calculated field. Users of the form will only work in Form view. There should be no reason for a user to switch to Layout or Design view. Modifications to the form should be done by the designated form designer.

> ... you will often need to switch between the three form views in Access—Layout view, Form view, and Design view.

In this section, you will examine the different form sections. As you learn how to create forms, placing fields and labels in the right section will become second nature. You may have to use trial and error at first, switching between Form view and Layout view until the form is working correctly.

Controls are also covered in this section. You will learn the difference between bound and unbound controls. You will also learn how to add a calculated control.

## Identifying Form Sections

Access forms, by default, are divided into three sections that can be viewed when you display a form in Design view. Each section can be collapsed or expanded as needed, but only in Design view.

### Identify the Default Form Sections

Each form by default contains three main sections—*Form Header, Detail*, and *Form Footer*. These sections can vary depending on what type of form you create. Stacked layout forms will have different requirements than a tabular layout form. Form designers also have the option of removing certain sections from a form. Two additional sections—*Page Header* and *Page Footer*—are optional and can be added to a form as needed. These sections are visible in Design view and also during Print Preview and printing; however, page headers and footers are not visible in Form view or Layout view. Because these sections are less common in forms, they will not be explored further in this chapter. Use Microsoft Help for more information about the *Page Header* and *Page Footer* sections.

The **Form Header section**
displays at the top of each form.

The ***Form Header section*** displays at the top of each form. This section will usually contain the form title, a logo or other graphic, and the current date and time. Column headings (labels) will also be located in this section for Multiple Item forms.

The **Detail section** displays the records in the form's record source.

The ***Detail section*** displays the records in the form's record source. Stacked forms will display one label and one text box for each field placed in the *Detail* section. Navigation controls enable the user to advance to the next, last, previous, and first record. Multiple Item forms will display multiple records (text boxes) in the *Detail* section, as many as can fit onto one screen.

The **Form Footer section**
displays at the bottom of the form.

The ***Form Footer section*** displays at the bottom of the form. The Form Footer is commonly used to add totals for field values. For example, an invoice form would display the invoice subtotal, the shipping charges, the taxes, and the invoice total in the *Form Footer* section.

## Modify the Default Form Sections

In Figure 13, three light grey section bars mark the top boundary of each form section. The top bar denotes the top boundary of the Form Header; the middle bar designates the top of the *Detail* section; and the bottom bar shows the top boundary of the Form Footer. The grid-like area under the bars shows the amount of space allotted to each section. If you decide that the allotted space for a particular section is not needed, you can collapse that section fully so that the section bars are touching. In Figure 13, the form has no space allocated to the Form Footer. The section remains in the form's design but will not take up space in Form view. If you want to remove the *Form Footer* section from the form, right-click the Form Footer bar, and then click Form Header/Footer from the list. When you remove the Form Footer, the *Form Header* section will also be removed. This may cause a problem since the title of the form usually resides in the Form Header.

To expand or collapse the space between sections, move your mouse over the bottom bar, and when the mouse pointer changes to a double-headed arrow, click and drag to expand or collapse the section. If you expand or collapse the space allotment for one section, the overall height of the form will be affected.

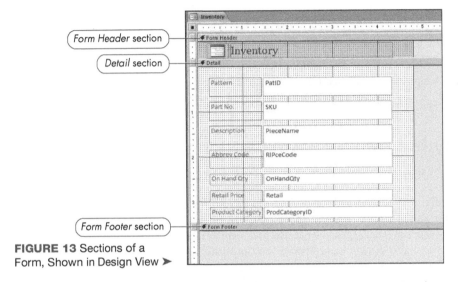

Form Header section

Detail section

Form Footer section

**FIGURE 13** Sections of a Form, Shown in Design View ➤

# Revising Forms Using Form Views

Access provides different views for a form, similar to the different views in tables and queries. Tables and queries have Design view and Datasheet view. Most forms have Layout view, Form view, and Design view. A Datasheet form has one additional view, the Datasheet view, but it does not have the Form view.

## Switch Between Form Views

A variety of methods for switching between form views exist: click View in the Views group, click the View arrow, right-click a form in the Navigation Pane, right-click the form tab, or click one of the small view icons in the status bar at the bottom right of the form. Perhaps the quickest method for switching between views is clicking View. This will toggle the form between Layout view and Form view. Click the View arrow or right-click the form tab to switch to Design view. Each view is described in the sections below.

## Edit Data in Form View

Use **Form view** to add, edit, and delete data in a form; the layout and design of the form cannot be changed in this view.

Use *Form view* to add, edit, and delete data in a form; the layout and design of the form cannot be changed in this view. Most users will only see Form view; if a form needs modification, the user will notify the database designer, who will make a change on the fly or during the next scheduled maintenance interval. Figure 14 shows a form in Form view. Users can print from this view by clicking the File tab and then selecting the Print option. However, printing from a form should be done with caution. A form with a stacked layout of 810 records could print as many as 810 pages (depending on how many records fit onto one page) unless you choose the Selected Record(s) option in the Print dialog box. The Selected Record(s) option will only print the current record or the number of records you selected.

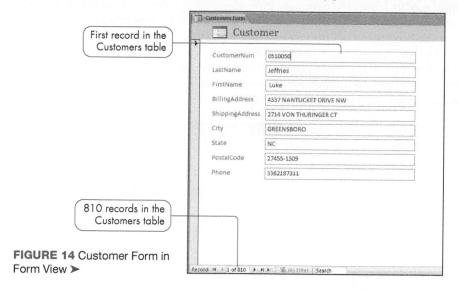

First record in the Customers table

810 records in the Customers table

**FIGURE 14** Customer Form in Form View ➤

## Alter a Form in Layout View

Use Layout view to alter the form design while still viewing the data. You use Layout view to add or delete fields in a form, modify field properties, change the column widths, and enhance a form by adding a color scheme or styling. While you are working in Layout view, you can see the data as it would appear in Form view, but you cannot edit the data in Layout view. Seeing the data in Layout view makes it easier to size controls, for example, to ensure the data is visible (see Figure 15). It is good practice to test a form in Form view after making changes in Layout view.

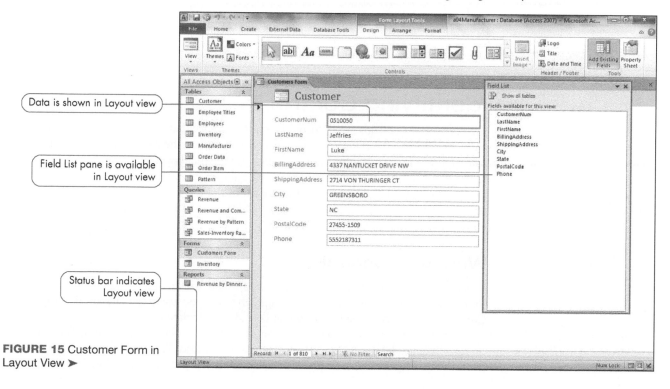

Data is shown in Layout view

Field List pane is available in Layout view

Status bar indicates Layout view

**FIGURE 15** Customer Form in Layout View ➤

## Perform Advanced Changes to a Form in Design View

Use **Design view** to perform advanced changes to a form's design.

Use **Design view** to perform advanced changes to a form's design. It provides you the most advanced method of editing an Access form. You can perform many of the same tasks in Design view as you can in Layout view—add and delete fields, change the field order, adjust field widths, modify labels, and customize form elements. But certain tasks cannot be done in Layout view, and Access displays a message telling you to use Design view. For example, changes to the form sections can only be made in Design view. After you finish making changes in Design view, it is best to switch to Form view to examine the results.

You need to experiment using both the Layout view and Design view to decide which view you prefer. Figure 16 displays the Customer form in Design view. The next section describes how to edit the finer details of a form.

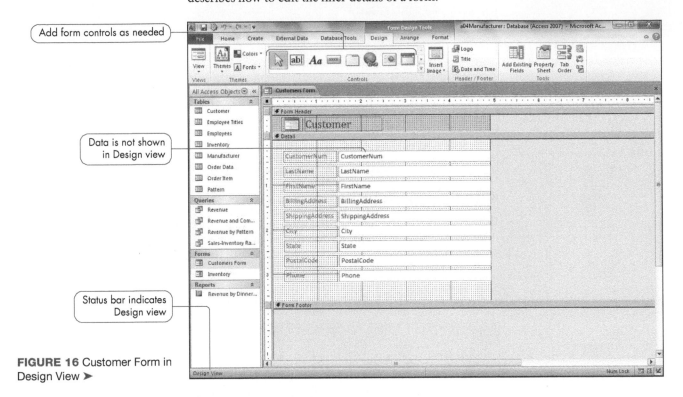

Add form controls as needed

Data is not shown in Design view

Status bar indicates Design view

**FIGURE 16** Customer Form in Design View ➤

# Identifying Control Types in Forms

A **text box control** displays the data found in a form's record source.

A **label control** is a literal word or phrase to describe the data.

If you examine the fields on the form in Figure 16, notice that each field has a label on the left and a text box on the right. The **text box control** displays the data found in a form's record source (the Customers table in this example) and the **label control** is a literal word or phrase to describe the data. The position of the label and the text box can be interchanged; however, in most cases, the label is positioned to the left of the text box in a stacked layout. Although the term *text box* might imply *text only*, a text box can also display numeric data, currency, and dates.

## Work with Controls

A **bound control** is a text box that is connected to a field in a table or query.

Label and Text Box objects are known as *controls*. They are among the many types of controls found in the Controls group on the Design tab when you are in the Design view of a form. Controls can be categorized as bound, unbound, or calculated.

A **bound control** is a text box that is connected to a field in a table or query. These controls display different data each time you switch to a new record. The most common way to add a bound control to a form is to drag a field from the Field List pane, and then drop it onto the form.

An **unbound control** is a label or other decorative design element, and is not connected to a source of data.

A **calculated control** contains an expression that generates a calculated result when displayed in Form view.

An ***unbound control*** is a label or other decorative design element, and is not connected to a source of data. These controls usually describe and decorate the data rather than display the data, and remain the same each time you switch to a new record. Unbound controls include labels, lines, borders, and images; they can be added to a form using the Controls group on the Design tab while in Design view. For example, a label that displays the title of the form is an unbound control.

A ***calculated control*** contains an expression that generates a calculated result when displayed in Form view. The expression can contain field names from the form's record source, constants, and functions. Use a text box, found in the Controls group, to create a calculated control.

Most forms include an unbound control (label) to describe each bound control (text box) on the form. In the form in Figure 17, each text box has a label describing it. As you add or delete fields from a form, be aware that many bound controls are connected to an unbound label. If you move the bound control, the label moves, too. Likewise, if you move the label, the bound control moves along with it. You can ungroup the controls and move them separately, but the default is that they are joined together.

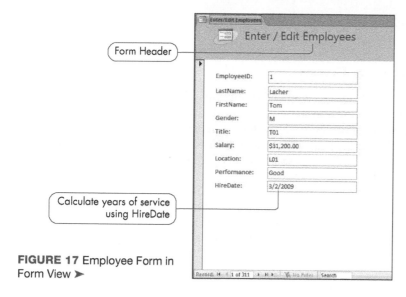

**FIGURE 17** Employee Form in Form View ➤

## Add a Calculated Control to a Form

Review the Enter/Edit Customers form in Figure 17 above. Users must manually calculate an employee's years of service using the HireDate field at the bottom of the form. Based on your knowledge of date arithmetic, you could calculate each employee's years of service using the expression:

= (Date( ) – HireDate) / 365

To add this expression to the form, you add a calculated field using a text box. Open the form in Design view, and then click Text Box in the Controls group on the Design tab. Place a text box at the desired location, and then enter the expression *=(Date() – HireDate)/365* into the control source property of the new text box. Format the control as needed. Figure 18 shows the Years of Service text box formatted as fixed with one decimal.

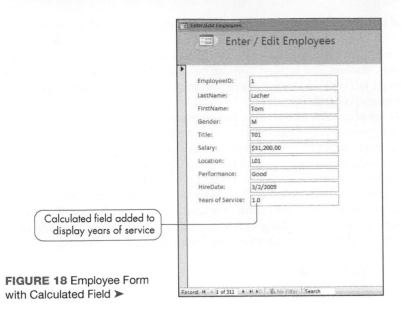

Calculated field added to display years of service

**FIGURE 18** Employee Form with Calculated Field ➤

## Add Styling to a Form

Modifying the font size of labels, changing the font color of labels, and adding a background color can enhance a form and also make it more usable. It is best to choose a familiar font family, such as Arial or Calibri, for both the form label controls and the text box controls. Apply bold to the labels in order to help the user distinguish labels from the text boxes. You should also consider left-aligning the labels to themselves and left-aligning the text box controls to themselves.

As illustrated in Figure 19, it is helpful to group like controls together and define the group visually by drawing a box around them using the Rectangle control. Similarly, separate the primary key field, such as the EmployeeID, from the rest of the form by providing a sufficient visual boundary. Also, the Years of Service field has been highlighted to help the user locate this information quickly.

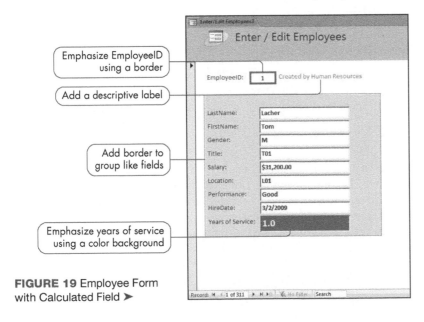

Emphasize EmployeeID using a border

Add a descriptive label

Add border to group like fields

Emphasize years of service using a color background

**FIGURE 19** Employee Form with Calculated Field ➤

## 2 Form Sections, Views, and Controls

You already created several forms for the Santiago Coffee Shop; however, Alex would like some additional forms. After the new forms are created, you use the different views to make changes and test the forms.

**Skills covered:** Understand the Main Form Sections and Alter a Form in Design View • Edit Data in Form View • Work with Controls • Add a Calculated Control to a Form • Add Styling to a Form

---

**STEP 1** ▶ **UNDERSTAND THE MAIN FORM SECTIONS AND ALTER A FORM IN DESIGN VIEW**

You have decided to use the Form tool to create a Revenue form. This form will enable Alex to track revenue for his company. You will use Design view to modify this form. Refer to Figure 20 as you complete Step 1.

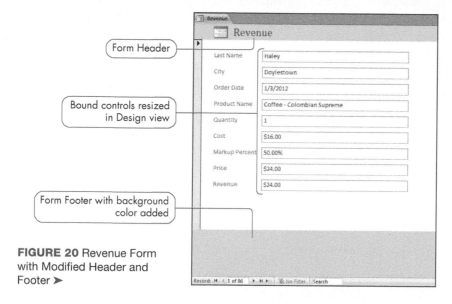

**FIGURE 20** Revenue Form with Modified Header and Footer ➤

a. Open *a04h1coffee_LastnameFirstname* if you closed it at the end of Hands-On Exercise 1. Click the **File tab**, click **Save Database As**, and then type **a04h2coffee_LastnameFirstname**, changing *h1* to *h2*. Click **Save**.

b. Select **Revenue query** in the Navigation Pane. Click the **Create tab**, and then click **Form** in the Forms group.

   Access creates a new form based on the Revenue query. The form opens in Layout view, ready to edit.

c. Place the mouse on the right edge of the Last Name control so the mouse pointer changes to a double-headed arrow. Drag to the left to size the control section to 50% of its original size.

   Access simultaneously reduces the size of all the controls.

d. Switch to Design view.

   Notice the three sections of the form—*Form Header*, *Detail*, and *Form Footer*.

e. Place the mouse on the bottom edge of the Form Footer bar so the mouse pointer changes to a double-headed arrow. Drag the bar down until the size of the *Form Footer* section is **1"**, using the vertical ruler.

**f.** Switch to Form view.

With a white background, it is difficult to tell where the *Form Footer* section begins and ends.

**g.** Switch to Design view. Click **Property Sheet** in the Tools group. Click the **Selection type arrow**, and select **FormFooter**.

**h.** In the Property Sheet, click the **Format tab**, click the **Back Color arrow**, and then select **Background Light Header** from the list. Close the Property Sheet, and then switch to Form view.

With the new background color, the Form Footer is now evident. You will add content to the footer in a later step.

**i.** Switch to Design view.

**j.** Place the mouse on the top edge of the Detail bar so the mouse pointer changes to a double-headed arrow. Drag the bar down until the *Form Header* section is **3/4"**.

**k.** Click **Save** in the Quick Access Toolbar and save the form as **Revenue**. Close the form.

## STEP 2 ▶ EDIT DATA IN FORM VIEW

You will use the Form tool to create an Access form to help Alex manage his products. This form will enable Tonya to make changes easily when product information changes. Refer to Figure 21 as you complete Step 2.

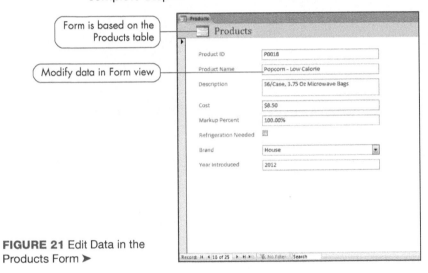

**FIGURE 21** Edit Data in the Products Form ➤

**a.** Select the **Products table** in the Navigation Pane. Click the **Create tab**, and then click **Form** in the Forms group.

Access creates a new form based on the Products table.

**b.** Click anywhere in the subform at the bottom of the window, click the Layout Selector, and then press **Delete** to delete the subform. Click **View** in the Views group to switch to Form view.

**c.** Click **Next Record** in the Navigation bar to advance to the third record in the Products form.

Use Next Record to advance through the records.

**d.** Click in the **Product Name box**, and then change *Coffee - Mild Blend* to **Coffee - Light**.

**e.** Click **Last Record** in the Navigation bar to advance to the last record in the Products form. Click **Previous Record** to locate record 23.

Use Last Record to advance to the last record.

**f.** Click in the **Product Name box**, and change *Styrofoam Cups - 12 ounce* to **Heavy Paper Cups - 12 ounce**.

g. Click in the **Current Record box** in the Navigation bar, type **12**, and then press **Enter** to go to the 12th record in the Products form.

Use the Current Record box to advance to a specific record.

h. Click in the **Product Name box**, and then change *Sugar Substitute* to **Splenda**.

i. Click in the **Search box** in the Navigation bar, and then type **pop** to locate any records with *pop* in any data value, in this case, record 18.

Use the Search box to find a record with a value you type.

j. Click in the **Product Name box**, and then change *Popcorn - Plain* to **Popcorn - Low Calorie**.

k. Click **Save** in the Quick Access Toolbar and save the form as **Products**. Close the form.

## STEP 3 ▶ WORK WITH CONTROLS

You make some enhancements to the Revenue form to increase its usability. Afterwards, Tonya and Alex test the form to determine if the changes are an improvement to the form. Refer to Figure 22 as you complete Step 3.

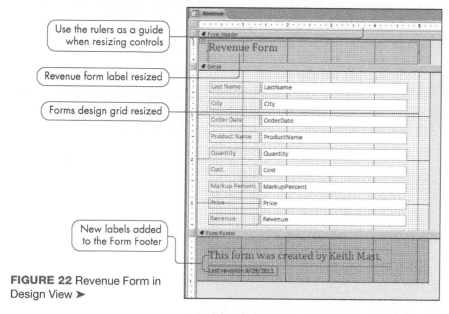

**FIGURE 22** Revenue Form in Design View ▶

a. Right-click the **Revenue form** in the Navigation Pane, and then click **Design View**.

b. Click the **Revenue label** in the Form Header, and then click it again to edit it. Change the label to **Revenue Form**.

c. Click the **Form Logo** to the left of the Revenue Form label, and then press **Delete** to delete the image.

d. Click **Label** in the Controls group, and then click in the **Form Footer** at the 1/4" mark from both the horizontal and vertical rulers to insert a text box. Type **This form was created by** *your name.*

e. Click the **Revenue Form label** in the Form Header, and then click **Format Painter** in the Clipboard group on the Home tab. Click the new label in the Form Footer to apply the same format. Click the label, and then drag the bottom-right sizing handle down and to the right so the entire text is visible.

f. Click **Label** in the Controls group on the Design tab, and then add a second label under the first label in the Form Footer at the 1/4" mark on the horizontal ruler. Type **Last revision** *today's date.* Accept the default font.

g. Click the **Form Header bar**, and then open the Property Sheet if necessary. Change the Height property to **.65**.

You can change the height of the Form Header by dragging it with the mouse or by modifying the Height property.

h. Click the **Revenue Form label** in the Form Header. Modify the following properties:
   - Change the Height property to **.5**.
   - Change the Width property to **4.75**. Close the Property Sheet.

i. Place the mouse on the right edge of the form's design grid so the mouse pointer changes to a double-headed arrow. Drag the grid to the left to change the form's width to **5.25"**.

Use the horizontal ruler to locate the 5.25" mark.

> **TROUBLESHOOTING:** If other Text box controls are too wide, reduce their width first, and then reduce the grid to 5.25".

j. Switch to Form view. Advance through the records using the Navigation bar at the bottom.

The controls in the Form Header and Form Footer do not change when you advance from one record to the next.

k. Click **Save** in the Quick Access Toolbar to save the changes to the form.

## STEP 4 ▶ ADD A CALCULATED CONTROL TO A FORM

After reviewing the changes you made to the Revenue form, Alex asks you to add a calculated control. The new control will show the total cost of each order. Refer to Figure 23 as you complete Step 4.

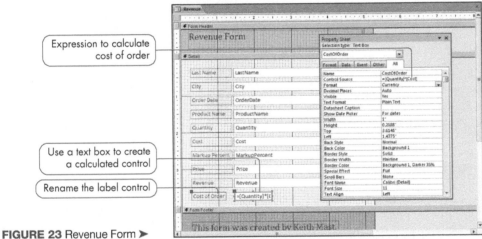

**FIGURE 23** Revenue Form ➤

a. Switch to Design view.

b. Position the mouse on the top edge of the Form Footer bar until the mouse pointer changes to the double-arrow resizing shape. Drag the **Form Footer bar** down to increase the *Detail* section to **4"**.

c. Click **Text Box** in the Controls group, and then click just below the **Revenue text box** (the white rectangle) at the bottom of the *Detail* section.

d. Click in the **text box**, and then type =**[Quantity]*[Cost]** in place of *Unbound*. Press **Enter**.

The expression you typed creates a calculated control that shows the total value of the current product.

e. Open the Property Sheet if necessary. Click the **All tab** in the Property Sheet, click in the **Name property box**, and then replace the existing text with **CostOfOrder**. Click the **Format property**, and then use the arrow to select **Currency** from the list of options.

Creating and Using Professional Forms and Reports

f. Switch to Form view. Advance through the records using the Navigation bar at the bottom.

As you advance from one record to the next, the cost of each order is displayed in the calculated control.

> TROUBLESHOOTING: If you see *#Name* in the calculated control, you have typed the expression incorrectly. Be sure you begin the expression with =.

g. Switch to Design view.

h. Click the label control for the new calculated control, and then replace the existing label caption with **Cost of Order**. Resize label control to fit new text, if necessary.

i. Click the calculated control, and then click the **Other tab** on the Property Sheet. Locate the Tab Stop property and change it to **No**.

j. Click **View** in the Views Group to switch to Form view. Press **Tab** to advance through the fields to test the tab stop change.

A calculated control does not require data entry. It is now skipped when Tab is pressed.

k. Save the form.

## STEP 5 ▶ ADD STYLING TO A FORM

The users of the Santiago Coffee Shop database have asked you to add some styling to the new form. You discuss their ideas with Alex, and then decide to apply the suggested styles. Refer to Figure 24 as you complete Step 5.

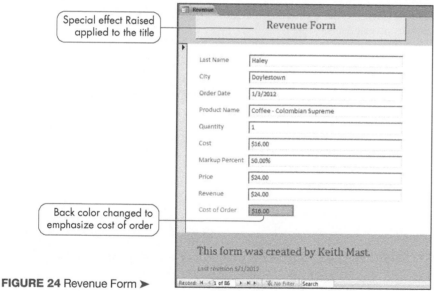

**FIGURE 24** Revenue Form ▶

a. Switch to Design view.

b. Open the Property Sheet (if necessary), and then click the **Revenue Form label**.

c. Click the **Back Color arrow** on the Property Sheet Format tab, and then choose **Access Theme 2**.

The background color of the title changes to a light blue.

d. Click the **Special Effect arrow** on the Property Sheet Format tab, and then choose **Raised**.

The title now appears raised.

e. Click **Center** in the Font group on the Format tab on the Ribbon.

The form title is now centered within the control box.

f. Click just above the LastName box on the blank grid space, and then drag the mouse through all the fields, except Cost of Order.

All the text box fields are now selected as indicated with an orange border, except the Cost of Order field.

g. Click the **Special Effect arrow** on the Property Sheet Format tab, and then choose **Sunken**.

The fields now appear sunken.

h. Click the **Cost of Order box control**, click the **Border Width arrow** in the Property Sheet Format tab, and then click **2 pt**. Close the Property Sheet.

The border of the calculated control increases.

i. Click **Background Color arrow** in the Font group on the Format tab, and then select **Light Gray 2** (Standard Colors, first column, third row).

The background color of the calculated control is now gray to set it apart from the bound data entry fields.

j. Click the **Cost of Order label control**, click the **Font Color arrow** in the Font group, and then select **Light Gray 4** (Standard Colors, first column, fifth row).

The font color of the calculated control is now gray to set it apart from the bound data entry fields.

k. Switch to Form view. Compare your results to Figure 24, and then close and save the form.

l. Click the **File tab**, and then click **Compact & Repair Database**.

m. Keep the database onscreen if you plan to continue with Hands-On Exercise 3. If not, close the database and exit Access.

# Report Basics

By now, you know how to plan a database, create a table, establish relationships between tables, enter data into tables, and extract data using queries. You generated output by printing table and query datasheets. You also learned how to create several types of data entry forms. These forms can also be used for inquiries about the data in a database. In this section, you will learn how to create professional reports using the report-writing tools in Access. A *report* is a printed document that displays information from a database in a format that provides meaningful information to its readers.

A **report** is a printed document that displays information from a database in a format that provides meaningful information to its readers.

Although you can print information from tables, queries, and forms, information printed from these database objects may not be in the best format. Most of the printed documents generated by Access will come from reports. Reports can be enhanced to help the reader understand and analyze the data. For example, if you print the Datasheet view from the Customers table, you will be able to locate the key information about each customer. However, using report tools, you can group the customers by sales rep, and then highlight the customers who have not placed an order in six months. This is an example of converting a list of customers into an effective business tool. To increase business, each sales rep could contact their customers who have not ordered in six months, and then review his or her findings with the sales manager. A sales report could be run each month to see if the strategy has helped produce any new business.

Most of the printed documents generated by Access will come from reports.

In this section, you will create reports in Access by first identifying a record source, then sketching the report, and finally choosing a Report tool. You will learn how to modify a report by adding and deleting fields, by resizing columns, and by adding a color scheme. You will also learn about the report sections, the report views, and controls on reports. After having worked through forms in the section above, you will discover that there are many similarities between forms and reports.

## Creating Reports Using Report Tools

Access provides five different report tools for creating reports. The report tools are found in the Reports group, as shown in Figure 25. Click one of these tools and Access will create an automatic report (or launch a wizard to guide you) using the table or query that is currently selected. The most common of the tools, the **Report tool**, is used to instantly create a tabular report based on the table or query currently selected. The Blank Report tool is used to create a new blank report so that you can insert fields and controls manually and design the report. The Report Design tool is used to create a new blank report in Design view. In Design view, you can make advanced design changes to reports, such as adding custom control types and working with report sections. The Report Wizard tool will ask a series of questions and help you create a report based on your answers. The Labels tool is used to create a page of labels using one of the preformatted templates provided by Access. After you create a report using one of the report tools, you can perform modifications in Layout view or Design view.

The **Report tool** is used to instantly create a tabular report based on the table or query currently selected.

**FIGURE 25** Report Tools in the Reports Group ➤

Before you create a report in Access, you should ask these questions:

- What is the purpose of the report?
- Who will use the report?
- Which tables are needed for the report?
- What fields, labels, and calculations need to be included?
- How will the report be distributed? Will users pull the information directly from Access or will they receive it through e-mail, fax, or the Internet?
- Will the results be converted to Word, Excel, HTML, or another format?

Sample reports include a telephone directory sorted by last name, a customer list grouped by sales rep, an employee list sorted by most years of service, a financial statement, a bar chart showing sales over the past 12 months, a shipping label, and a letter to customers reminding them about a past due payment.

## Identify the Record Source

The first step in planning your report is to identify the record source. You may use one or more tables, queries, or a combination of tables and queries as the report's record source. Sometimes, a single table contains all of the records you need for the report. Other times, you will need to incorporate several tables. When multiple tables are needed to create a report, you can add all the necessary tables into a single query, and then base the report on that query. (As stated earlier, multiple tables in a query must be related, as indicated with join lines. Tables with no join lines usually indicate an incorrect record source.)

Reports can also contain graphics as well as text and numeric data. For example, you can add a company logo, or a watermark to indicate the information is confidential or just a draft. After you identify the record source, you also need to specify which graphic images are needed (and the location of the images).

## Sketch the Report

In the *Forms* section, you learned that it is helpful to sketch an Access form before you launch Access. The same holds true for creating an Access report. Design the report and indicate the record source (table names or query name), the title, the format of the report (stacked or tabular), the fields, and the order of fields. It would also be helpful to indicate the grouping and totals needed for the report. Sketch the report first and you will be happier with the results. A sample sketch is shown in Figure 26.

| First Name | Last Name | Address | City | State | Zip Code | Phone Number | Specialization |
|---|---|---|---|---|---|---|---|
| Bonnie | Clinton | 10000 SW 59 Court | Coral Springs | FL | 33071 | (954) 777-8889 | Obstetrics |
| Warren | Brasington | 9470 SW 25 Street | Coral Springs | FL | 33071 | (954) 888-7654 | Hematology |
| James | Shindell | Avenue | Coral Springs | FL | 33070 | (954) 773-4343 | General Medicine |
| Edward | Wood | Avenue | Coral Springs | FL | 33072 | (954) 555-5555 | Cardiology |
| Michelle | Quintana | 3990 NW 3 Street | Coral Springs | FL | 33071 | (954) 888-1221 | Internal Medicine |
| Kristine | Park | 9290 NW 59 Steet | Coral Springs | FL | 33072 | (954) 777-1111 | Exercise Physiology |
| William | Williamson | 108 Los Pinos Place | Coral Springs | FL | 33071 | (954) 888-4554 | General Medicine |
| Holly | Davis | 8009 Riviera Drive | Coral Springs | FL | 33072 | (954) 388-7676 | Cardiology |
| Steven | Fisher | 444 SW 190 Street | Coral Springs | FL | 33070 | (954) 777-3333 | Internal Medicine |
| David | Tannen | 50 Main Street | Coral Springs | FL | 33171 | (954) 777-2211 | Hematology |
| Jeffrey | Jacobsen | 490 Bell Drive | Coral Springs | FL | 33070 | (954) 388-9999 | Internal Medicine |
| Patsy | Clark | 200 Harding Blvd | Coral Springs | FL | 33070 | (954) 777-1087 | Cardiology |
| Keith | Mast | 102 SCC | E. Norriton | PA | 19401 | (610) 555-1212 | General Medicine |

*Physicians Report - Draft*

**FIGURE 26** Sketch of the Physicians Report ➤

## Use the Report Tool

After you sketch the report, you can decide which report tool is appropriate to produce the desired report. Access provides several tools that you can use to create a report, as shown in Figure 27. Which one you select depends on the layout of the report, the record source, and the complexity of the report design.

The easiest way to create a report is with the Report tool. Select a table or query in the Navigation Pane, then click Report in the Reports group on the Create tab, and Access creates a tabular layout report instantly. A *tabular layout report* displays data horizontally across the page in a landscape view, as shown in Figure 27.

A **tabular layout report** displays data horizontally across the page in a landscape view.

A **stacked layout report** displays fields in a vertical column.

You can also create a *stacked layout report* in Access, although this type of report is less common. A stacked layout report displays fields in a vertical column. The number of records on one page depends on the number of fields in the record source. You can also force a new page at the start of each record.

Report created with the Report tool

Information is presented in tabular format

Physicians report could be grouped by specialization

| | Physicians | | | | | | | January 2012 |
|---|---|---|---|---|---|---|---|---|
| First Name | Last Name | Address | City | State | Zip Cod | Phone Number | Specialization |
| Bonnie | Clinton | 10000 SW 59 Court | Coral Springs | FL | 33071 | (954) 777-8889 | Obstetrics |
| Warren | Brasington | 9470 SW 25 Street | Coral Springs | FL | 33071 | (954) 888-7654 | Hematology |
| James | Shindell | 14088 Malaga Avenue | Coral Springs | FL | 33070 | (954) 773-4343 | General Medicine |
| Edward | Wood | 400 Roderigo Avenue | Coral Springs | FL | 33072 | (954) 555-5555 | Cardiology |
| Michelle | Quintana | 3990 NW 3 Street | Coral Springs | FL | 33071 | (954) 888-1221 | Internal Medicine |
| Kristine | Park | 9290 NW 59 Steet | Coral Springs | FL | 33072 | (954) 777-1111 | Exercise Physiology |
| William | Williamson | 108 Los Pinos Place | Coral Springs | FL | 33071 | (954) 888-4554 | General Medicine |
| Holly | Davis | 8009 Riviera Drive | Coral Springs | FL | 33072 | (954) 388-7676 | Cardiology |
| Steven | Fisher | 444 SW 190 Street | Coral Springs | FL | 33070 | (954) 777-3333 | Internal Medicine |
| David | Tannen | 50 Main Street | Coral Springs | FL | 33171 | (954) 777-2211 | Hematology |
| Jeffrey | Jacobsen | 490 Bell Drive | Coral Springs | FL | 33070 | (954) 388-9999 | Internal Medicine |
| Patsy | Clark | 200 Harding Blvd | Coral Springs | FL | 33070 | (954) 777-1087 | Cardiology |
| Keith | Mast | 102 SCC | E. Norriton | PA | 19401 | (610) 555-1212 | General Medicine |

**FIGURE 27** Tabular Report ➤

## Use the Report Wizard

The Report Wizard.... uses six dialog boxes to collect information about your report.

The **Report Wizard** asks you questions and then uses your answers to generate a report.

You can also create a professional report with the Report Wizard. The *Report Wizard* asks you questions and then uses your answers to generate a report. The wizard uses six dialog boxes to collect information about your report.

### Start the Report Wizard

After thinking through the structure, the layout, and the record source, you are ready to launch the Report Wizard. First, select the report's record source in the Navigation Pane, and then click Report Wizard in the Reports group on the Create tab. The wizard opens with the table or query (the record source) displayed in the first dialog box. Although you chose the record source before you started, the first dialog box enables you to select fields from additional tables or queries.

To demonstrate the Report Wizard, an Access database was created to track several health studies being conducted by a local physicians group. The studies are tracked using a StudyID code, S01, S02, S03, etc. The report that you need to create will list each volunteer alphabetically, grouped by study. See Figure 28 to review the fields in the Volunteers table—a key table in the Physicians database.

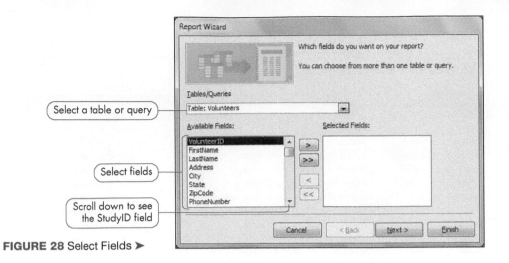

Select a table or query

Select fields

Scroll down to see
the StudyID field

**FIGURE 28** Select Fields ➤

## Add Grouping

The next dialog box asks, "Do you want to add any grouping levels?" As we learned earlier in this chapter, grouping lets you organize and summarize your data. You can also add totals (sum, count, average) at the end of a group. In the sample report, Access correctly predicts that you want the data grouped by the study field (as shown in Figure 29). If you did not want to group the report by the StudyID field, you could click the < button to remove the group in step two of the Report Wizard. After you remove the unwanted grouping, select the field you want to group by, and then click the > button to add the new group. If you need a second or third grouping level, add those field names in order. The order in which you select the groups dictates the order of display in the report.

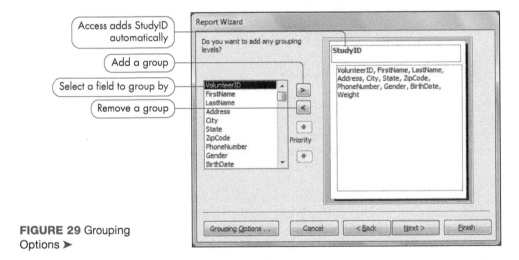

Access adds StudyID
automatically

Add a group

Select a field to group by

Remove a group

**FIGURE 29** Grouping
Options ➤

## Add Sorting and Summary Options

The next dialog box asks, "What sort order and summary information do you want for detail records?" The summary information option will only appear if there is a numeric field in the selected fields (see Figure 30). Click Summary Options if you want to add aggregate functions (e.g., sum, average, minimum, and maximum) and to specify whether you want to see detail records on the report or only the aggregate results. Click OK or Cancel to return to the Report Wizard (see Figure 31). For the sort options, specify which field you want to sort by first, then second, third, and fourth. For each field, choose ascending order and/or descending order.

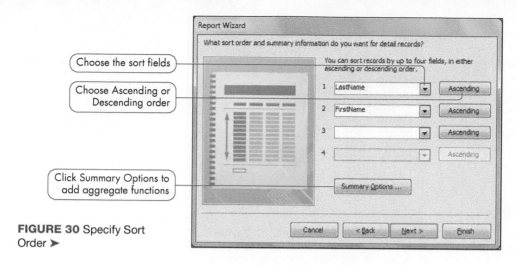

Choose the sort fields

Choose Ascending or Descending order

Click Summary Options to add aggregate functions

**FIGURE 30** Specify Sort Order ➤

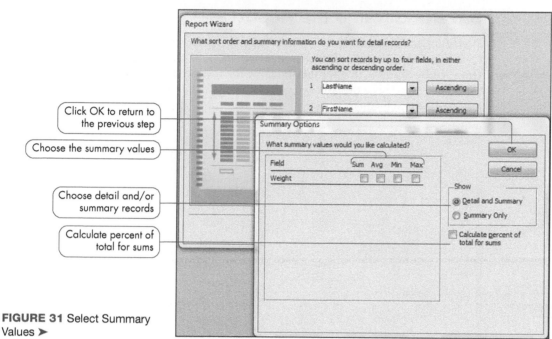

Click OK to return to the previous step

Choose the summary values

Choose detail and/or summary records

Calculate percent of total for sums

**FIGURE 31** Select Summary Values ➤

## Choose the Layout for the Report

The next dialog box will determine the report's appearance. First, you select the layout from three options—Stepped, Block, or Outline. Clicking an option will give you a general preview in the preview area. You can also select the orientation for the report, either Portrait or Landscape (see Figure 32). Select an appropriate format for the report.

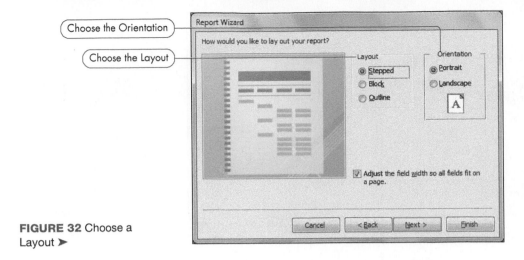

**FIGURE 32** Choose a
Layout ➤

## Save and Name the Report

Decide on an appropriate name for the report. Type a descriptive report name so you can
easily determine what information is in the report based on the title. For example, Volunteers
Grouped by Study is an appropriate name for the sample report created in this section
(see Figure 33). This is the last step in the Report Wizard; click Finish to see a preview of the
report, shown in Figure 34.

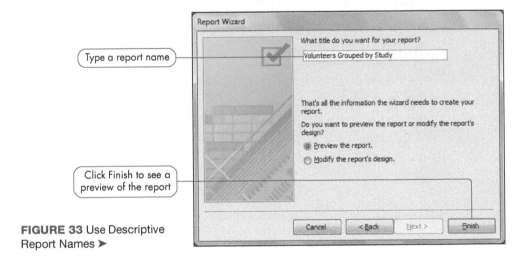

Type a report name

Click Finish to see a
preview of the report

**FIGURE 33** Use Descriptive
Report Names ➤

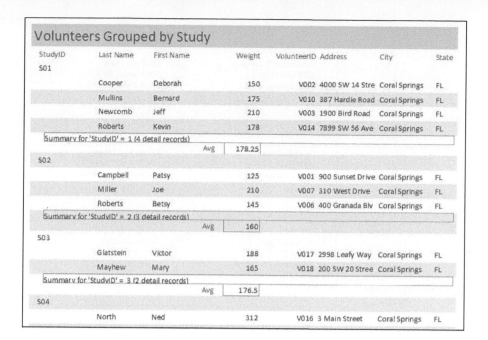

| StudyID | Last Name | First Name | Weight | VolunteerID | Address | City | State |
|---------|-----------|------------|--------|-------------|---------|------|-------|
| S01 | | | | | | | |
| | Cooper | Deborah | 150 | V002 | 4000 SW 14 Stre | Coral Springs | FL |
| | Mullins | Bernard | 175 | V010 | 387 Hardie Road | Coral Springs | FL |
| | Newcomb | Jeff | 210 | V003 | 1900 Bird Road | Coral Springs | FL |
| | Roberts | Kevin | 178 | V014 | 7899 SW 56 Ave | Coral Springs | FL |
| Summary for 'StudyID' = 1 (4 detail records) | | | | | | | |
| | | Avg | 178.25 | | | | |
| S02 | | | | | | | |
| | Campbell | Patsy | 125 | V001 | 900 Sunset Drive | Coral Springs | FL |
| | Miller | Joe | 210 | V007 | 310 West Drive | Coral Springs | FL |
| | Roberts | Betsy | 145 | V006 | 400 Granada Blv | Coral Springs | FL |
| Summary for 'StudyID' = 2 (3 detail records) | | | | | | | |
| | | Avg | 160 | | | | |
| S03 | | | | | | | |
| | Glatstein | Victor | 188 | V017 | 2998 Leafy Way | Coral Springs | FL |
| | Mayhew | Mary | 165 | V018 | 200 SW 20 Stree | Coral Springs | FL |
| Summary for 'StudyID' = 3 (2 detail records) | | | | | | | |
| | | Avg | 176.5 | | | | |
| S04 | | | | | | | |
| | North | Ned | 312 | V016 | 3 Main Street | Coral Springs | FL |

**FIGURE 34** Volunteers Grouped by Study Report ➤

# Use the Label Wizard

The **Label Wizard** enables you to easily create mailing labels, name tags, and other specialized tags.

A **mailing label** is a specialized report that comes preformatted to coordinate with name-brand labels, such as Avery.

The *Label Wizard* enables you to easily create mailing labels, name tags, and other specialized tags. A *mailing label* is a specialized report that comes preformatted to coordinate with name-brand labels, such as Avery. You then use the Label Wizard to create a label that fits the 5660 template. To begin, click Labels in the Reports group on the Create tab, and then select the manufacturer, the product number, and the label type. Next, choose the font type and size, and then add the fields to the label template, as shown in Figure 35. The Physicians Labels report is shown in Figure 36.

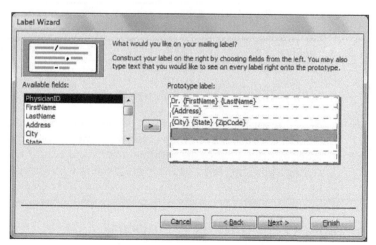

**FIGURE 35** Create a Mailing Label ➤

| Dr. Warren Brasington | Dr. Patsy Clark | Dr. Bonnie Clinton |
| 9470 SW 25 Street | 200 Harding Blvd | 10000 SW 59 Court |
| Coral Springs fl 33071 | Coral Springs fl 33070 | Coral Springs FL 33071 |
| | | |
| Dr. Holly Davis | Dr. Steven Fisher | Dr. Jeffrey Jacobsen |
| 8009 Riviera Drive | 444 SW 190 Street | 490 Bell Drive |
| Coral Springs FL 33072 | Coral Springs fl 33070 | Coral Springs fl 33070 |
| | | |
| Dr. Keith Mast | Dr. Kristine Park | Dr. Michelle Quintana |
| 102 SCC | 9290 NW 59 Steet | 3990 NW 3 Street |
| E. Norriton PA 19401 | Coral Springs fl 33072 | Coral Springs fl 33071 |

**FIGURE 36** Physicians Label Report ➤

Table 1 provides a summary of the five report tools and their usage.

| TABLE 1 Report Tools and Their Usage | |
|---|---|
| **Report Tool** | **Usage** |
| **Report** | Create a tabular report showing all of the fields in the record source. |
| **Report Design** | Create a new blank report in Design view. Add fields and controls manually. |
| **Blank Report** | Create a new blank report in Layout view. Add fields and controls manually. |
| **Report Wizard** | Answer a series of questions and Access will design a custom report for you. |
| **Labels** | Choose a preformatted label template and create a sheet of labels. |

# Modifying a Report

After a report is generated by one of the report tools, you will usually need to modify it. Similar to forms, the common changes to a report are add a field, remove a field, change the order of fields, change the width of a field, and modify the title. These changes, as well as adding a grouping level, are made in Layout view. Advanced changes, such as adding a calculated field or adding VBA code, can only be made in Design view.

## Add a Field to a Report

Adding a field to a report with a tabular layout is similar to adding a field to a form with a tabular layout. Right-click a report in the Navigation Pane, and then click Layout view. Next, click Add Existing Fields in the Tools group on the Design tab to reveal the available fields in the report's record source. Drag the new field to a precise location on the report, using the vertical orange line as a guide for the position of the new field, and release the mouse. The other fields will automatically adjust to make room for the new field.

The process of adding a field to a report with a stacked layout is the same as a tabular layout. The only difference is the orange line will appear horizontally.

## Delete a Field from a Report

To delete a field from the *Detail* section of a tabular report, first switch to the Layout view or Design view of the report. Next, click the text box of the field to be deleted and note the orange border around the field. With the orange border visible, press Delete. Repeat the process to delete the associated label from the Page Header. After the controls are deleted, click in the blank space, and then press Delete again. After the text box and label are removed from the report, the other fields automatically adjust to close the gap around the deleted field.

## Work with a Report Layout Control

Whenever you use one of the report tools to create a new report, Access will add a layout control to help align the fields. Layout controls in reports work the same as layout controls in forms. As discussed earlier in this chapter, the layout control provides guides to help keep controls aligned horizontally and vertically, and give your report a uniform appearance.

There are times when you may want to remove the layout control from a report in order to position the fields without aligning them to each other. If you want to remove the layout control from a report, switch to Design view, and then click anywhere inside the control you want to remove. On the Arrange tab, click Select Layout in the Rows & Columns group. Click Remove Layout in the Table group and the layout control is gone. All of the other controls are still on the report, but the rectangle binding them together is gone.

You can add a layout control to a report by first selecting all the controls you want to keep together. Then, click Stacked or Tabular in the Table group and the layout control appears.

## Adjust Column Widths in a Report

You can adjust the width of each column in a tabular report individually so that each column is wide enough to accommodate the widest value. For example, if a report contains first name, last name, address and city, and e-mail address, you will need to make sure the longest value in each field is completely visible. Scroll through the records to make sure this is the case.

To modify column widths in a tabular report, first switch to the Layout view or Design view of the report. Click the text box of the field you want to adjust. The field will have an orange border around it, indicating it is selected. Move the mouse to the right border of the selected field; when the mouse pointer turns to a double arrow, drag the edge to the right (to increase) or the left (to decrease) until you arrive at the desired width.

## Add a Theme to the Report

You can enhance the report's appearance by applying one of the themes provided by Access. To apply a theme, switch to Layout view, and then click Themes in the Themes group on the Design tab. Scroll through the themes until you find a theme you like; hover over one of the options to see a quick preview of the current report using the current theme. Right-click a theme, and then choose Apply Theme to This Object Only (as shown in Figure 37). You can also apply the theme to all matching objects.

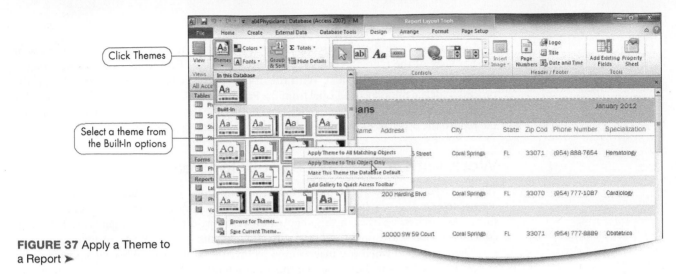

**FIGURE 37** Apply a Theme to a Report ➤

# Sorting Records in a Report

When a report is created using the Report tool, the sort order of the records in the report is initially dependent on the sort order of the record source—similar to the way records are sorted in a form. The primary key of the record source usually dictates the sort order. However, a report has an additional feature for sorting. While in Layout view or Design view, click Group & Sort in the Grouping & Totals group on the Design tab. The Group, Sort, and Total pane now appears at the bottom of the report. This section enables you to set the sort order for the report and override the sorting in the report's record source.

## Change the Sorting in a Report

While working in the Layout view of a report, click Group & Sort to display the *Group, Sort, and Total* section, as shown in Figure 38. To sort the records in a report by last name, click Add a sort and select LastName from the list. The report records will instantly sort by LastName in ascending order. Next, you can set a second sort by clicking Add a Sort again. For example, you could add the FirstName sort after the LastName sort, as shown in Figure 38.

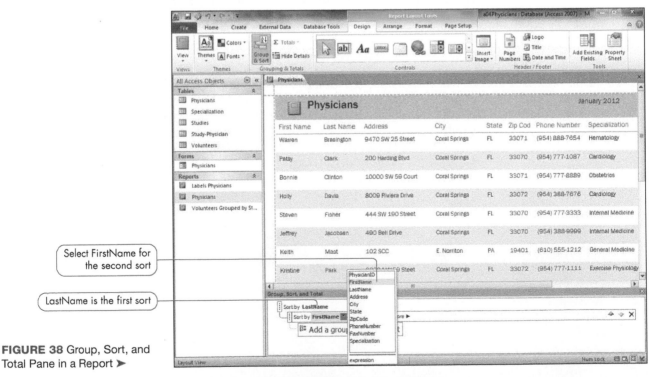

**FIGURE 38** Group, Sort, and Total Pane in a Report ➤

Creating and Using Professional Forms and Reports

## 3 Report Basics

You create a Products report using the Access Report tool to help Alex stay on top of the key data for his business. After Access creates the report, you modify the column widths so the entire report fits on one page (portrait or landscape, depending on the report). You also use the Report Wizard tool to create other reports for Alex.

**Skills covered:** Use the Report Tool • Add a Field to a Report • Delete a Field from a Report and Adjust Column Widths in a Report • Apply a Theme to the Report • Change the Sorting in a Report • Use the Report Wizard

---

**STEP 1** ▶ **USE THE REPORT TOOL**

You use the Report tool to create an Access report to help Alex manage his product information. This report is especially useful for determining which products he needs to order to fill upcoming orders. Refer to Figure 39 as you complete Step 1.

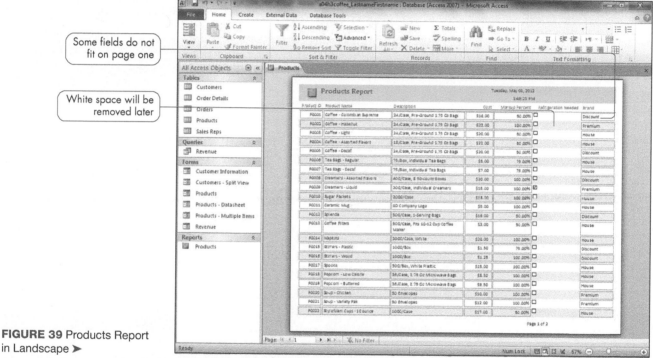

**FIGURE 39** Products Report in Landscape ➤

a. Open *a04h2coffee_LastnameFirstname* if you closed it at the end of Hands-On Exercise 2. Click the **File tab**, click **Save Database As**, and then type **a04h3coffee_LastnameFirstname**, changing *h2* to *h3*. Click **Save**.

b. Select the **Products table** in the Navigation Pane. Click the **Create tab**, and then click **Report** in the Reports group.

Access creates a new tabular layout report based on the Products table. The report opens in Layout view ready to edit.

c. Click the **Products title** at the top of the report to select it, and then click again on **Products** and change the title to **Products Report**.

d. Display the report in Print Preview.

The report is too wide for the page; you will change the orientation to Landscape.

e. Click **Close Print Preview**.

f. Click the **Page Setup tab**, and then click **Landscape** in the Page Layout group.

The report changes to Landscape orientation. Most of the columns now fit onto one page. You will make further revisions to the report later on so that it fits on one page.

g. Display the report in Print Preview.

h. Close and save the report as **Products**.

---

### STEP 2  ADD A FIELD TO A REPORT

The Products report you created for Santiago Coffee looks very good (according to Alex). However, Alex asks you to add a new field to the Products table and incorporate that into the Products report. Refer to Figure 40 as you complete Step 2.

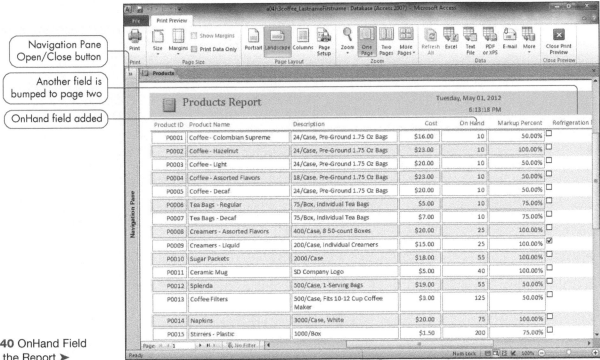

**FIGURE 40** OnHand Field Added to the Report ➤

a. Open the Products table, and then click **View** in the Views group to switch to Design view.

You need to add the OnHand field to the Products table.

b. Click the **MarkupPercent field**, and then click **Insert Rows** in the Tools group.

A new blank row appears above the MarkupPercent field.

c. Type **OnHand** in the **Field Name box**, and then select **Number** as the Data Type. In the Field Properties at the bottom, change the Field Size to **Integer**.

d. Save the table. Click **View** to change to Datasheet view.

The new OnHand column appears empty in each row. Next you will add sample data to the new field.

e. Type the following OnHand values starting at the top and continuing through the last row: **10, 10, 10, 10, 10, 10, 10, 25, 25, 55, 40, 55, 125, 75, 200, 200, 200, 75, 75, 42, 42, 175, 175, 22, 37.**

**f.** Close the Products table.

**g.** Open the Products report in Layout view.

**h.** Click the **Open/Close button** on the Navigation Pane to collapse the Navigation Pane so more of the report is visible. Close the Property sheet, if necessary.

**i.** Click **Add Existing Fields** in the Tools group on the Design tab. Drag the **OnHand field** from the Field List pane onto the Products report between the Cost and MarkupPercent fields. Close the Field List pane.

Because of the tabular layout control, Access adjusts all the columns to make room for the new OnHand field.

**j.** Insert a space in the OnHand label control in the Report Header so that it reads *On Hand*.

A space was added to make the heading more readable.

**k.** Display the report in Print Preview.

The report is still too wide for a single page. Next, you will modify the column widths.

**l.** Save the report.

**STEP 3** ⟩ **DELETE A FIELD FROM A REPORT AND ADJUST COLUMN WIDTHS IN A REPORT**

The Products report now contains the new OnHand value that Alex requested, but the report is too wide to print on one page. In this step, you delete unnecessary fields and read just the remaining column widths. Refer to Figure 41 as you complete Step 3.

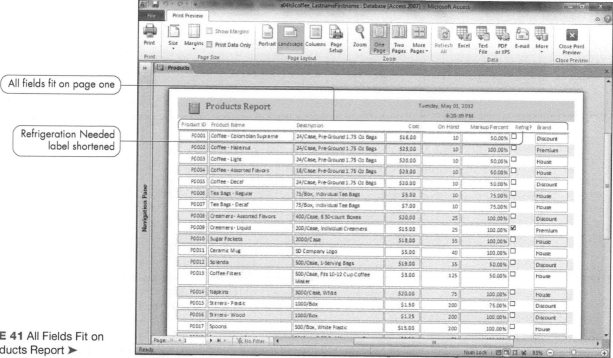

**FIGURE 41** All Fields Fit on the Products Report ➤

**a.** Click **Close Print Preview**.

**b.** Scroll to the right, right-click anywhere on the **Year Introduced column**, and then click **Select Entire Column** from the shortcut menu. Press **Delete** to remove the column.

The Year Introduced column is removed from the report.

**c.** Click the **ProductID column heading**, and then drag the right border to the left until the Product ID heading still fits, but any extra white space is removed.

d. Click the **Refrigeration Needed column heading**, and then rename the column **Refrig?**. Adjust the column width of the Refrig? column.

e. Adjust the width of the remaining columns until all fields fit on one page.

f. Display the report in Print Preview.

This report now fits nicely onto one landscape page.

g. Click **Close Print Preview**, and then save the report.

STEP 4 ▶ APPLY A THEME TO THE REPORT

The Products report now contains the new OnHand value and the report fits nicely onto one landscape page. You create two color schemes for Alex and ask him to select one of them. Refer to Figure 42 as you complete Step 4.

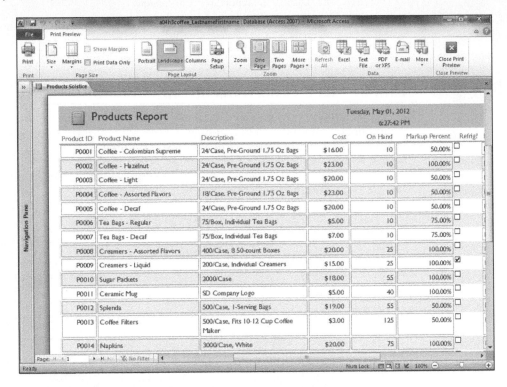

**FIGURE 42** Products Report with Solstice Theme ➤

a. Switch to Layout view, if necessary.

b. Click **Themes** in the Themes group on the Design tab.

The available predefined themes display.

c. Right-click a **Solstice theme** (second column, second row from bottom), and then choose **Apply Theme to This Object Only**. Display the report in Print Preview.

Access reformats the report using the Solstice theme.

d. Click **Close Print Preview**. Click the **File tab**, and then click **Save Object As**. Type **Products Solstice** as the report name, and then click **OK**. Click the **File tab** to return to the report.

You saved the report with one theme. Now, you will apply a second theme to the report and save it with a different name.

e. Switch to Layout view, and then click **Themes** in the Themes group to apply a different theme.

**f.** Right-click a **Module theme** (first column, seventh row), and then choose **Apply Theme to This Object Only**. Display the report in Print Preview.

Compare the Solstice theme to the Module theme.

**g.** Click **Close Print Preview**. Click the **File tab**, and then click **Save Object As**. Type **Products Module** as the report name, and then click **OK**. Click the **File tab** to return to the report.

**STEP 5** ▶ **CHANGE THE SORTING IN A REPORT**

Alex would like the Products Module report to be sorted by Product Name order (rather than ProductID order). You change the sort order and preview again to see the results. Refer to Figure 43 as you complete Step 5.

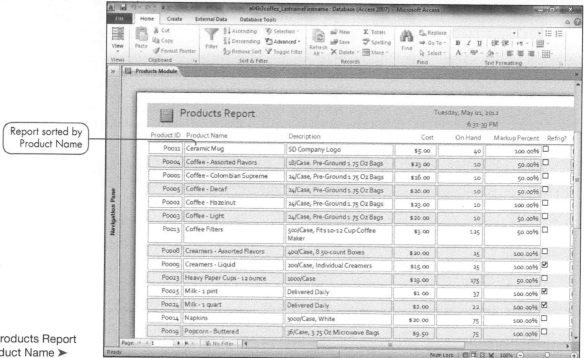

Report sorted by
Product Name

**FIGURE 43** Products Report Sorted by Product Name ➤

**a.** Verify the Products Module report is in Layout view.

**b.** Click **Group & Sort** in the Grouping & Totals group.

The Add a group and Add a sort options appear at the bottom of the report.

**c.** Click **Add a sort**.

A new Sort bar appears at the bottom of the report.

**d.** Select **ProductName** from the list.

The report is now sorted by ProductName.

**e.** Display the report in Print Preview.

**f.** Close Print Preview, and then save and close the report.

**STEP 6** ▶ **USE THE REPORT WIZARD**

You decide to create the Sales by City report for Santiago Coffee. After discussing the report parameters with Alex, you decide to use the Report Wizard. Refer to Figure 44 as you complete Step 6.

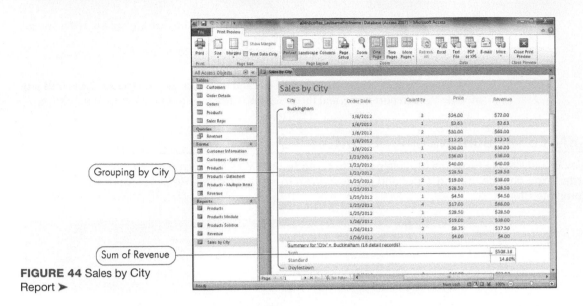

**FIGURE 44** Sales by City
Report ➤

*Grouping by City*

*Sum of Revenue*

a. Open the Navigation Pane, and then select the **Revenue query** in the Navigation Pane. Click the **Create tab**, and then click **Report Wizard** in the Reports group.

The Report Wizard launches.

b. Click the **>> button** to add all the fields to the selected Fields box. Click **Cost**, and then click the **< button** to remove the Cost field. Also remove the MarkupPercent, Lastname, and ProductName fields. Click **Next**.

c. Select **City**, and then click the **> button** to add grouping by city. Click **Next**.

d. Select **OrderDate** for the sort order. Click **Summary Options**.

e. Click **Sum** to summarize the Revenue field. Click the **Calculate percent of total for sums check box** to show the relationship between each group and the whole. Click **OK**.

f. Click **Next**. Click **Next** again to accept the default layout.

g. Type **Sales by City** for the title of the report. Click **Finish**.

The report is displayed in Print Preview mode. Some of the data values and labels cannot be seen. Next, you will adjust the controls.

h. Click **Close Print Preview**. In Layout view, adjust the controls so all the field values are visible, as shown in Figure 44. Widen the totals controls under the Revenue column. Click in the **Revenue total field**, open the Property Sheet, and then select the **Currency format**.

i. Display the report in Print Preview to verify your changes.

j. Close and save the report.

k. Click the **File tab**, and then click **Compact & Repair Database**.

l. Keep the database onscreen if you plan to continue with Hands-On Exercise 4. If not, close the database and exit Access.

Creating and Using Professional Forms and Reports

586

# Report Sections, Views, and Controls

You just created and modified reports in the previous section. In this section, you will learn about the various views you accessed while creating and modifying the reports. As you work with the report tools to create and modify reports, you will find the need to frequently switch between the four report views in Access—Layout view, Print Preview, Design view, and Report view. Most of your design work will be done in Layout view, but occasionally, you will need to switch to Design view to apply a more advanced feature, such as a calculated field. Users of the report will use Print Preview, Print, and occasionally Layout view. There should be no reason for a user to switch to Layout view or Design view. Modifications to the report should be done by the designated report designer.

To switch between the four views, click the View arrow in the Views group and select the desired view. Layout view and Print Preview are the most common views; Report view is useful for filtering a report based on a field value. You can also switch between views by right-clicking on the report tab or by right-clicking a report in the Navigation Pane. You can also click one of the small view icons in the bottom right of the Access window.

> Even though reports have more default sections than forms, working with report sections will be similar to working with form sections.

In this section, you will learn how to identify report sections. You learned about the form sections earlier in this chapter; you can apply that knowledge as you learn about the report sections. Even though reports have more default sections than forms, working with report sections will be similar to working with form sections.

Controls are also covered in this section. Again, the overlap between forms and reports will become evident (and be helpful).

## Identifying Report Sections

Access reports are divided into five main sections that can be viewed when you display a report in Design view. You need to become familiar with each section so you can manipulate reports to meet your needs.

### Identify the Default Report Sections

In the forms section, you learned that Access divides forms into three main sections. For reports, Access creates five main sections—*Report Header*, *Page Header*, *Detail*, *Page Footer*, and *Report Footer* as shown in Figure 45. When in Design view, you can collapse or expand each section as needed, and delete any header or footer section.

> The **Report Header section** prints once at the beginning of each report.

The ***Report Header section*** prints at the beginning of each report. This section will usually contain the report title, a logo or other graphic, and the date and time when the report was printed. You can remove this section by right-clicking on a section bar, and then clicking the Report Header/Footer option. Follow the same process to add the Report Header/Footer to a report. When you remove the Report Header, the Report Footer is also removed automatically.

> The **Page Header section** appears once at the top of each page.

The ***Page Header section*** appears at the top of each page. Use this section to add or edit column headings on the top of each page. The Page Header will usually contain a horizontal line to separate the column headings from the data values. You can remove this section by right-clicking on a section bar, and then clicking the Page Header/Footer option. Follow the same process to add the Report Header/Footer to a report. If you remove the Page Header, the Page Footer is also removed automatically.

The *Detail* section prints one line for each record in the report's record source. Fields that are connected to the report's record source are known as *bound controls*. The *Detail* section can be hidden, if necessary, by clicking Hide Details in the Grouping & Totals group on the Design tab. For reports that only require summarized data, you will want to hide the details. Access makes it easy for you to show or hide detail levels. Click Hide Details again to redisplay hidden details.

Although the *Detail* section cannot be removed from a report, you can hide it from Print Preview, Layout view, and Design view to show only the headers and footers. This is relevant when the output only requires the totals of each category and not the details that make up the category.

The **Page Footer section** appears once at the bottom of each page.

The ***Page Footer section*** appears at the bottom of each page. Use this section to show page numbers at the bottom of each page. Totals should not be added to this section since the results will produce an error. You can remove this section by right-clicking on a section bar, and then clicking the Page Header/Footer option. Follow the same process to add the Report Header/Footer to a report. If you remove the Page Footer, the Page Header is also removed automatically.

The **Report Footer section** prints once at the bottom of the report.

The ***Report Footer section*** prints one time at the bottom of the report. The Report Footer is commonly used for displaying the grand total of certain columns. You can also display the count of all records in the *Report Footer* section. You can remove this section by right-clicking on a section bar, and then clicking the Report Header/Footer option. Follow the same process to add the Report Header/Footer to a report. If you remove the Report Footer, the Report Header is also removed automatically.

In Figure 45, each gray section bar marks the top boundary of a report section. The top bar denotes the top boundary of the Report Header. The bottom bar displays the top boundary of the Report Footer. The grid-like area under the bars shows the space allotted to that section. Notice that the report has no space allocated to the Report Footer. If you decide that the allotted space for a particular section is not needed, you can collapse that section fully so that the section bars are touching. The section remains in the report's design but will not be visible on the Print Preview or the printed page.

Similar to form sections, you can expand or collapse the space between report sections by moving your mouse over the section bar. When the mouse pointer shape changes to a double-headed arrow, drag to expand or collapse the section. A grid-like area appears as your mouse drags down. If you expand or collapse the space allotment for one section, the other sections may also be affected.

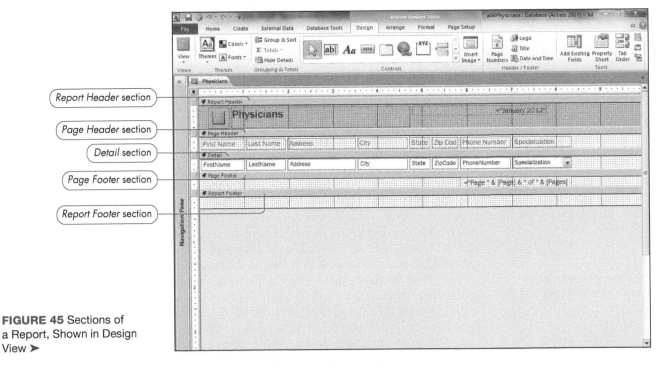

**FIGURE 45** Sections of a Report, Shown in Design View ➤

## Add a Group Header/Footer

In addition to the five main sections listed above, you can also add a custom *group header/footer* section to a report. For example, if you use the Report tool to create a report based on the Physicians table (as shown in Figure 46), you may want this report to be grouped by Specialization. It will be easier for users to locate a physician within a given specialization. Otherwise, you would have to search through the entire list to locate a doctor within a certain specialization.

To add a custom group to a report, open the report in Layout view, and then click Group & Sort in the Grouping & Totals group on the Design tab. The Group, Sort, and Total pane appears below the report. This section enables you to add a custom group. Click Add a Group, and then select the field that you want to group by. For a field to be a candidate for grouping, field values must repeat in the *Detail* section. For example, since specialization repeats in the *Detail* section, it could be used for grouping.

Once you establish the custom group, a **Group Header section** will appear just above the *Detail* section in Design view, along with the name of the field you are grouping. If you select the Specialization field as a custom group, the section will be named *Specialization Header*, as shown in Figure 46. Click Print Preview in the Views group to view the data in the report; each time the grouping field value changes, the group header will print with the new value. For example, in a physicians report with five specializations, grouped by Specialization, the group header will print five times, once for each specialization, with the physicians printed under each specialization.

A **Group Footer section** appears just below the *Detail* section in Design view, but only when you select this option in the Group, Sort, and Total pane. Locate the group header in question, and then click the More option on that group header bar; then click the *without a footer* arrow and select the *with a footer* option. The group footer is useful for totaling the data at the end of each group. If a group of physicians is part of a major practice, it would be good to know how many physicians are assigned to each specialization. The group footer could display the count of physicians for each specialization.

A **Group Header section**, when activated, will appear just above the *Detail* section in Design view, with the name of the field you are grouping.

The **Group Footer section**, when activated, will appear just below the *Detail* section in Design view, but only when you select this option in the Group, Sort, and Total pane.

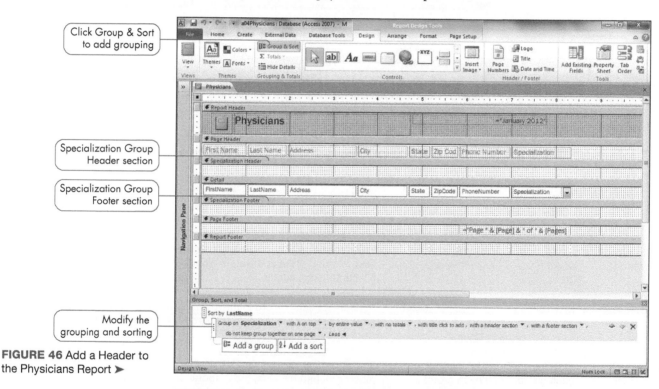

Click Group & Sort to add grouping

Specialization Group Header section

Specialization Group Footer section

Modify the grouping and sorting

**FIGURE 46** Add a Header to the Physicians Report ➤

## Add Totals to a Group Footer/Report Footer

Often, reports require totals at the group level and/or at the grand total level. For example, the Physicians Report might contain a count of physicians in each Specialization group, and again at the end of the report. Figure 47 shows a report with a total number of customers for each sales rep and the total number of customers at the end of the report.

To add totals to a report, first create the group section required for the totals. For example, add the Sales Rep group to a Customers report. Next, in Layout view, click the field that contains the data you want to total, click Totals in the Grouping & Totals group on the

Design tab, and then select the appropriate option. Access will add a total after each group and again at the end of the report.

You remove a total from a report in the same way you add a total. First, select the field that contains the total, click Totals in the Grouping & Totals group, and then uncheck the option you want to remove.

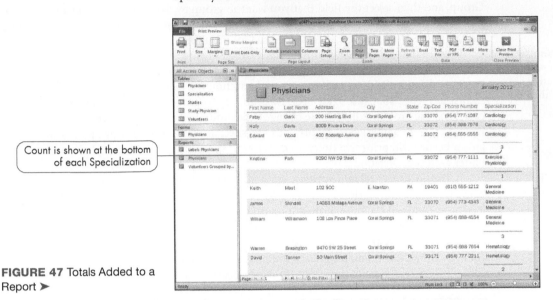

Count is shown at the bottom of each Specialization

**FIGURE 47** Totals Added to a Report ➤

See the reference table below for a summary of each report section.

# REFERENCE Report Sections

| Section | Location | Frequency | Usage | Default |
|---------|----------|-----------|-------|---------|
| Report Header | Top of the report | Once | Holds the report title, the organization's name, the company logo, and the run date & time. | On |
| Page Header | Top of each page | Once per page | Page Headers generally contain the column headings. In a multi-page report, the labels repeat at the top of each page to provide continuity. | On |
| Group Header | At the start of each new group | At the start of each group | Prints the value of each unique instance for a grouped field. A report grouped by state would print up to 50 unique state names. | Off |
| Detail | Middle | Once per record in the record source | Repeats for each record in the record source. If there were 500 records in the record source, the report would have 500 detail lines. | On |
| Group Footer | At the end of each group | At the end of each group | This section generally mirrors the group header. For a report grouped by state, group footer could be used to show a count of the records in each state. | Off |
| Page Footer | Bottom of each page | Once per page | The Page Footer is generally used to print page numbers on the report. | On |
| Report Footer | End of the report | Once | Use the Report Footer to print grand totals or other aggregate information for the records. | On |

# Revising Reports Using Report Views

Access provides different views for a report similar to the different views in tables, queries, and forms. Tables and queries have Design view and Datasheet view. Forms have Layout view, Form view, and Design view. Reports have Layout view, Print Preview, Design view, and Report view. To switch between certain views, click View in the Views group, or click the View arrow, and then select a view from the list. Each view is described in the sections below.

## Layout View

Use Layout view to alter the report design while still viewing the data. You should use Layout view to add or delete fields in the report, modify field properties, change the column widths, add grouping and sorting levels to a report, and to filter data by excluding certain records. Although Layout view appears similar to Print Preview, you will find sufficient variations between the two views, so that you will always need to verify the report in Print Preview to evaluate all the changes made in Layout view.

## Print Preview

**Print Preview** enables you to see exactly what the report will look like when it is printed.

*Print Preview* enables you to see exactly what the report will look like when it is printed. Most users prefer to use Print Preview prior to printing the report. This enables you to intercept errors in reports before you send the report to the printer. You cannot modify the design in this view; switch to Layout view or Design view to modify the design. By default, Print Preview will display all the pages in the report. Figure 47 shows an Access report in Print Preview.

## Design View

Design view displays the report's design without displaying the data. You can perform many of the same tasks in Design view as you can in Layout view—add and delete fields, add and remove sorting and grouping layers, rearrange columns, adjust column widths, and modify report elements. When a report is very long, Design view is useful because you can alter the design without needing to scroll through pages of data. However, after you make a change in Design view, it is best to switch to Layout view or Print Preview to examine the final output. You need to experiment using both the Layout view and Design view to decide which view you prefer. As with forms, some changes to reports can only be done in Design view. Figure 46 displays the Physicians report in Design view.

## Report View

**Report view** enables you to see what the printed report will look like in a continuous page layout.

*Report view* enables you to see what a printed report will look like in a continuous page layout. Because Report view is similar to Layout view, but not used as frequently, this view will not be discussed further in this chapter.

## Identifying Control Types in Reports

If you examine the fields in a report, such as the one in Figure 47, you will notice that each field has a label (heading) at the top with a column of data values under the heading. As you learned in the forms section earlier in this chapter, a text box displays the data found in the record source and a label is a literal word or phrase to describe the data. The heading in Figure 47 is a label, and the data values are displayed using a text box.

The label and text box controls are among the many types of controls found on the Controls group on the Design tab when you are in the Design view of a report. As discussed earlier in the forms section, controls can be categorized as bound, unbound, or calculated.

### Work with Controls

Bound controls are text boxes that are connected to a field in a table or a query. These controls display different data for each new record that is printed. To add a bound control to a report, switch to Layout view, and then drag a field from the Field List pane onto the report.

Unbound controls are labels and other decorative design elements. These controls usually describe and decorate the data rather than display the data. These controls remain the same each time a new record is printed. Unbound controls include labels, lines, borders, and images. Add an unbound control to a report using the Controls group on the Design tab in the Design view of a report.

Calculated controls contain an expression that generates a calculated result when displayed in Print Preview. The expression can contain field names from the report's record source, constants, or functions. Use a text box, found in the Controls group on the Design tab, while in Design view to create a calculated control.

### Add a Calculated Control to a Report

To add a calculated control to the report, switch to Design view, and then click Text Box in the Controls group on the Design tab. Place a text box at the desired location, then enter the expression to create the calculation. Format the control as needed.

In Hands-On Exercise 4, you will create a report, add sorting and grouping to refine the content, work with data aggregates, and add a new field to the report.

# HANDS-ON EXERCISES

myitlab
HOE4 Training

## 4 Report Sections, Views, and Controls

The reports you created for Alex are working nicely. Alex would like you to modify the layout of the new reports to make them more attractive. You suggest he add grouping to one of the reports.

**Skills covered:** Identify the Default Report Sections and Add a Group Header/Footer in Layout View • Add Totals to a Group Footer/Report Footer in Layout View • Work with Controls in Design View • Add a Calculated Control to a Report in Design View

---

**STEP 1** ▶ **IDENTIFY THE DEFAULT REPORT SECTIONS AND ADD A GROUP HEADER/FOOTER IN LAYOUT VIEW**

Alex asks you to make several changes to the Monthly Revenue by Salesperson report. First, you update the Sales Rep table with the latest information. Refer to Figure 48 as you complete Step 1.

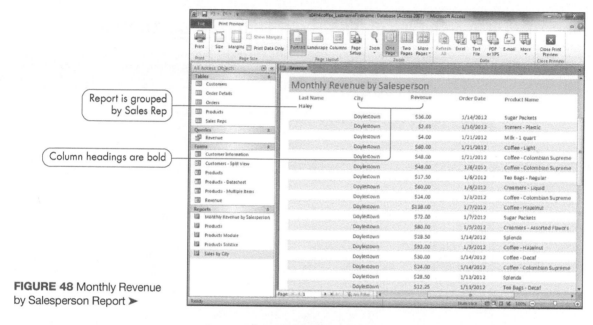

**FIGURE 48** Monthly Revenue by Salesperson Report ▶

a. Open *a04h3coffee_LastnameFirstname* if you closed it at the end of Hands-On Exercise 3. Click the **File tab**, click **Save Database As**, and then type **a04h4coffee_LastnameFirstname**, changing *h3* to *h4*. Click **Save**.

b. Open the Sales Reps table. Add your first name and last name to sales rep S0002. Leave the other fields as they are. Close the table.

c. Open the Customers table. For all the customers in the city of Buckingham, change the Sales Rep ID to **003**. The leading *S* appears automatically due to the Format property. Close the table.

d. Select the **Revenue query** in the Navigation Pane, click the **Create tab**, and then click **Report Wizard** in the Reports group.

e. Add the **LastName**, **City**, **Revenue**, **OrderDate**, and **ProductName fields** to the Selected Fields list. Click **Next** four times to accept the default settings. The wizard now asks "What title do you want for your report?" Type **Monthly Revenue by Salesperson**.

The completed report is displayed in Print Preview.

Hands-On Exercises • **Access 2010**

593

**f.** Close Print Preview, and then switch to Layout view.

Next, you will add the Last Name group.

**g.** Click **Group & Sort** in the Grouping and Sorting group. Click **Add a group**, and then select **LastName**. Close Group & Sort.

The report now contains the LastName group.

**h.** Select the **Last Name column heading**, and then click **Bold** in the Font group on the Format tab. Apply bold to the rest of the column headings.

**i.** Select the **Last Name column heading**, and then type **Sales Rep**.

**j.** Modify the report column widths so the column spacing is uniform (as shown in Figure 48).

**k.** Switch to Print Preview.

The report is now divided into Sales Rep groups.

**l.** Click **Close Print Preview**, and then save the report.

---

**STEP 2** ▶ ADD TOTALS TO A GROUP FOOTER/REPORT FOOTER IN LAYOUT VIEW

The Monthly Revenue by Salesperson report can be improved by adding a count of orders and a total of the revenue field. You suggest to Alex that the report show the totals at the bottom of each *Sales Rep* section. Refer to Figure 49 as you complete Step 2.

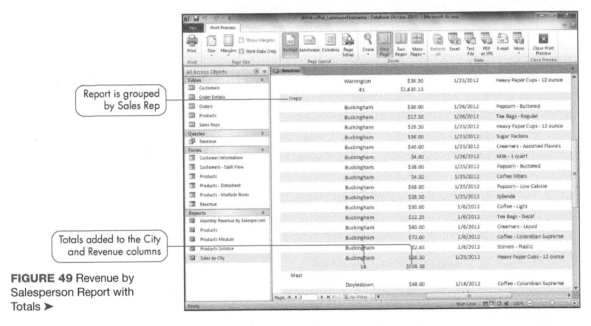

FIGURE 49 Revenue by Salesperson Report with Totals ▶

**a.** Verify the Monthly Revenue by Salesperson report is open in Layout view. Click the **Revenue field**, click **Totals** in the Grouping & Totals group, and then select **Sum** from the list.

A sum of revenue is now added to the group footer of each Sales Rep group.

b. Click the **View arrow** in the Views group, and then select **Print Preview**.

c. Advance to the next page to view the order count for each Sales Rep.

d. Click **Close Print Preview**, and then click the **City field**. Click **Totals** in the Grouping & Totals group, and then select **Count Records**.

e. Scroll down until the first totals control in the Revenue column is visible. Select the **totals calculated control box**, and then click **Property Sheet** in the Tools group. Click the **Format arrow** on the Format tab, and then choose **Currency** from the list.

The totals are now formatted for currency.

f. Scroll down to the bottom of the report, and then click the **grand total calculated control box** under the Revenue column. Click the **Format arrow** on the Format tab, and then choose **Currency** from the list. Close the Property Sheet.

The grand total is now formatted for currency.

g. Display the report in Print Preview. Advance through all the pages.

The total revenue is now added to the group footer of each Sales Rep group.

h. Click **Close Print Preview**, and then scroll to the bottom of the report.

The count of orders and the total revenue were automatically added to the Report Footer.

i. Switch to Design View.

In Design view, you can see the seven sections of the Monthly Revenue by Salesperson report. The data is no longer visible.

j. Save the report.

---

**STEP 3 ▶ WORK WITH CONTROLS IN DESIGN VIEW**

Alex asks you to add Santiago Coffee Shop at the top of the Monthly Revenue by Salesperson report. You add a new label to the report section and make a few other formatting enhancements. Refer to Figure 50 as you complete Step 3.

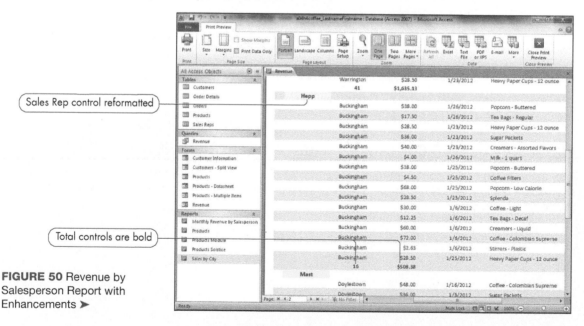

**Sales Rep control reformatted**

**Total controls are bold**

**FIGURE 50** Revenue by Salesperson Report with Enhancements ▶

a. Click the **Monthly Revenue by Salesperson label** in the Report Header. Press ↓ to move the label down 1/4" to make room for another label.

When you move the title down using $\downarrow$, the *Report Header* section grows automatically.

**b.** Click **Label** in the Controls group on the Design tab, and then click just above the *M* in the Monthly Revenue title.

The label control is ready for you to type a phrase.

**c.** Type **Santiago Coffee Shop** into the new label, and then press **Enter**.

An orange border indicates the label control is still selected.

**d.** Click the **Format tab**, and then use the **Font group commands** to modify the new label:

Font Size: **14**
Font Color: **Dark Blue, Text 2, Darker 25%** (fifth row, fourth column)
Style: **Italic**

**e.** Resize the new label using the bottom-right corner of the control box. Widen the box so the entire phrase is visible.

**f.** Click the **LastName text box** in the *LastName Header* section, and then modify the properties as follows:

Font Size: **12**
Font Color: **Dark Blue, Text 2** (first row, fourth column)
Style: **Bold**
Align: **Center**
Background Color: **Yellow**

**g.** Resize the **LastName text box** using the bottom-right corner of the control box. Widen the field so the entire last name is visible when you switch to Layout view.

**h.** Click the **Count control** in the LastName Footer, and then click **Center** in the Font group. Hold down **Shift**, and then click the **Revenue Sum control** in the LastName Footer.

Both controls are now selected.

**i.** Click **Bold** in the Font group.

**j.** Click the **Count control** in the Report Footer, hold down **Shift**, and then click the **Sum control** in the Report Footer.

Both controls are now selected.

**k.** Click **Bold** in the Font group. Click the **Background Color arrow**, and then select **Blue, Accent 1, Lighter 80%** (second row, fifth column in Theme Colors).

**l.** Display the report in Print Preview. Advance through all the pages to review your changes.

**m.** Click **Close Print Preview**, and then save the report.

## STEP 4 ▶ ADD A CALCULATED CONTROL TO A REPORT IN DESIGN VIEW

Alex asks you to add a comment to the report for all orders that are less than $10. You add a new expression using a text box control to display the word *minimum* if the order is under $10. Refer to Figure 51 as you complete Step 4.

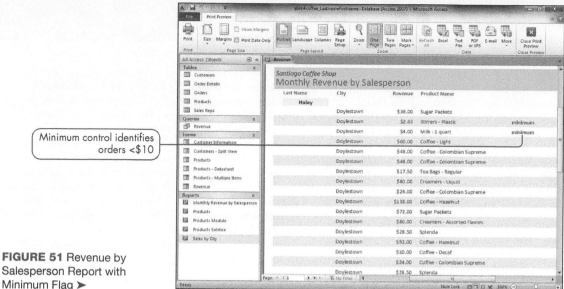

FIGURE 51 Revenue by Salesperson Report with Minimum Flag ➤

a. Switch to Design View if necessary. Click the **OrderDate box**, press **Delete**, and then delete the Order Date label. Drag the **Product Name box and label** to the **4 1/2"** mark on the horizontal ruler, moving the other labels and boxes, if necessary.

b. Click **Text Box** in the Controls group on the Design tab. Click in the **Detail section** to the right of the ProductName control.

   A new text box is created along with a label. The label overlaps the ProductName text box.

c. Click the new **Label control**, and then press **Delete**.

   The label control is deleted.

> **TROUBLESHOOTING:** If you delete the text box control, click Undo to restore the deleted control and delete only the Label control.

d. Click **Property Sheet** in the Tools group. Click the new text box, labeled *Unbound*, to select it.

e. Click the **All tab** in the Property Sheet pane. Type **MinimumOrder** in the **Name property box** and **="minimum"** in the **Control Source property box**. Change the Border Style property to **Transparent**.

f. Display the report in Print Preview.

   Minimum shows on all orders. You will now add an expression so that only orders less than $10 will show.

g. Click **Close Print Preview**. Verify the MinimumOrder control is selected.

h. Click the **Control Source**, and then press **Shift + F2** to expand the cell. Change the expression in the Control Source property to **=IIf(Revenue < 10, "minimum", "")**. Click **OK**.

   The second set of quote marks is an empty text string.

i. Display the report in Print Preview. Advance through all the pages to examine the minimum orders. Click **Close Print Preview**.

j. Click the **MinimumOrder control** in the *Detail* section, click **Bold** in the Font group on the Format tab, click the **Font Color arrow**, and then select **Red** under Standard Colors.

k. Display the report in Print Preview. Review the changes to the report, and then close and save the report.

l. Click the **File tab,** and then click **Compact & Repair Database**.

m. Exit Access.

n. Submit based on your instructor's directions.

After reading this chapter, you have accomplished the following objectives:

1. **Create forms using the form tools.** Access provides 16 different tools for creating forms. The form tools are found in the Forms group located on the Create tab, as shown in Figure 1. Click one of these tools and Access will create an automatic form using the table or query that is currently selected. The most common of these tools, the Form tool, is used to create stacked layout forms for customers, employees, products, and other primary tables. Once a form is created, you can customize the form using Layout and Design views.

2. **Modify a form.** After a form is generated by one of the form tools, you often need to modify it. Some common form changes are to add a field, remove a field, change the order of fields, change the width of a field, and modify label text. These changes, as well as adding a theme, can be made in a form's Layout view. Advanced changes, such as adding a calculated field or adding VBA code, can be made in a form's Design view.

3. **Sort records in a form.** When a form is created using a form tool, the sort order of the records in the form is dependent on the sort order of the record source. To modify the sort order of a form, open the form in Form view, and then select the field you want to use for sorting and click Ascending in the Sort & Filter group on the Home tab.

4. **Identify form sections.** Access forms, by default, are divided into three sections—Form Header, Detail, and Form Footer. These sections can vary depending on what type of form you create. Form designers also have the option of removing certain sections from a form. The *Form Header* section is displayed at the top of each form. This section will usually contain the form title, a logo or other graphic, and the date and time the report was printed. The *Detail* section displays the records in the form's record source. The *Form Footer* section is displayed at the bottom of the form. The Form Footer is commonly used to display totals for relevant field values.

5. **Revise forms using form views.** Access provides different views for a form, similar to the different views in tables and queries. Forms can be displayed in Layout view, Form view, and Design view. Use Layout view to alter the form design while still viewing the data. Use Design view to add or delete fields in a form, modify field properties, change the column widths, and enhance a form by adding a color scheme or styling.

   Most users will only see Form view; if a form needs modification, the user should notify the database designer. Use Design view to perform advanced changes to a form's design. It provides you the most advanced method of editing an Access form. You can perform many of the same tasks in Design view as you can in Layout view—add and delete fields, change the field order, adjust field widths, modify labels, and customize form elements.

6. **Identify control types in forms.** If you examine the elements on a form, you will notice that each field has a Label control box on the left and a Text Box control on the right. The text box displays the data found in the form's record source and

the label is a literal word or phrase to describe the data. Although text box might imply text only, numeric data, currency, and dates can also be displayed with a text box.

These two types of objects—Label and Text Box—are known as controls. They are among the many types of controls found in the Controls group on the Design tab when you are in Design view. Controls can be categorized as bound, unbound, or calculated. Bound controls are text boxes that are connected to a table or a query. Unbound controls are labels and other decorative design elements. These controls usually describe and decorate the data rather than display the data. Calculated controls contain an expression that generates a calculated result when displayed in Form view.

7. **Create reports using report tools**. Access provides five different report tools for creating reports. The report tools are found in the Reports group located on the Create tab, as shown in Figure 25. Click one of these tools and Access will create an automatic report using the table or query that is currently selected. The most common of the tools, the Report tool, is used to instantly create a tabular layout report based on the table or query currently selected. The Report Wizard will ask a series of questions and help you create the most appropriate report based on your answers. Use the Labels tool to create a page of labels using one of the preformatted templates provided by Access. After you create a report, you can perform modifications in Layout view and Design view.

8. **Modify a report**. After a report is generated by one of the report tools, you will usually need to modify it. The most common changes are to add a field, remove a field, change the order of fields, change the width of a field, and modify the title. These changes, as well as adding a grouping level, adding a sort order, and adding a theme, can be made in a report's Layout view or Design view. Advanced changes, such as adding a calculated field or adding VBA code, can be made in a report's Design view.

9. **Sort records in a report.** When a report is created using the Report tool, the sort order of the records in the report is initially dependent on the sort order of the record source. A report can be sorted while in Layout view or Design view by clicking Group & Sort in the Grouping & Totals group on the Design tab. The Group, Sort, and Total pane will appear at the bottom of the report. This section enables you to set the sort order for the report and override the sorting in the report's record source.

10. **Identify report sections.** Access reports are divided into five main sections, as shown in Figure 45. Each section can be collapsed or expanded as needed, but only in Design view. You can also remove any of the sections, except the *Detail* section, by right-clicking any section bar, and then clicking the *Header/Footer* section you wish to remove. The *Report Header* section prints once at the beginning of each report. The *Page Header* section appears once at the top of each page. The *Detail* section prints one line for each record in the report's record

source. The *Page Footer* section appears once at the bottom of each page. The *Report Footer* section prints once at the bottom of the report.

11. **Revise reports using report views.** Access provides different views for a report similar to the different views in tables, queries, and forms. Reports have Layout view, Print Preview, Design view, and Report view. To switch between views, click the View arrow in the Views group and select the Layout view or Design view. Use Layout view to alter the report design while still viewing the data. Print Preview enables you to see the closest approximation of what the report will look like when it is printed. Design view displays the report's layout without displaying the data. Report view enables you to see what the printed report will look like in a continuous page layout.

12. **Identify control types in reports.** If you examine the fields on a report, such as the one in Figure 47, you will notice that each field has a label (heading) at the top with a column of data values under the heading. A text box displays the data found in the record source and a label is a literal word or phrase to describe the data. The Label and Text Box controls are among the many types of controls found in the Controls group when you are in the Layout view or the Design view of a report. As discussed earlier, controls can be categorized as bound, unbound, or calculated. Bound controls are text boxes that are connected to a table or a query. Unbound controls are labels and other decorative design elements. Calculated controls contain an expression that generates a calculated result when displayed in Print Preview.

# KEY TERMS

Bound control
Calculated control
Datasheet form
Design view
Detail section
Form
Form Footer section
Form Header section
Form tool
Form view
Group Footer section
Group Header section
Label control

Label Wizard
Layout control
Layout view
Mailing label
Multiple Items form
Page Footer section
Page Header section
Print Preview
Record source
Report
Report Footer section
Report Header section
Report tool

Report view
Report Wizard
Split form
Splitter bar
Stacked layout form
Stacked layout report
Tabular layout form
Tabular layout report
Text box control
Unbound control
Visual Basic for Applications
   (VBA)

1. Which form tool does not place controls onto a form automatically?

   (a) Form Wizard
   (b) Form tool
   (c) Form Design tool
   (d) Datasheet tool

2. The Design view for a form enables you to do all of the following except:

   (a) Modify the form.
   (b) Add a new group.
   (c) View the data as it will be presented in the form.
   (d) Add a background color.

3. Which of the following guides you as you create a new report?

   (a) Report tool
   (b) Report Wizard
   (c) Blank Report tool
   (d) Report Design tool

4. Use the _____ to see exactly what the printed report will look like before printing.

   (a) Report tool
   (b) Report Wizard
   (c) Report view
   (d) Print Preview

5. The easiest way to modify control widths in a form is in:

   (a) Layout view.
   (b) Form view.
   (c) Design view.
   (d) Report view.

6. What happens if you click a text box control in Layout view, and then press Delete?

   (a) The control is deleted from the report, but the other controls do not adjust to the empty space.
   (b) Nothing; you cannot change fields in Layout view.
   (c) The record is deleted from the report and from the database.
   (d) An error message appears stating that you should not attempt to delete records in a report.

7. The mouse pointer shape changes to a _____ when you widen or narrow a column in Layout view.

   (a) single arrow
   (b) hand
   (c) two-headed arrow
   (d) four-headed arrow

8. Which of these is not a section in an Access form?

   (a) *Detail* section
   (b) *Group* section
   (c) *Form Header* section
   (d) *Form Footer* section

9. Which statement is true about controls?

   (a) Unbound controls are not used in reports.
   (b) Unbound controls are not used in the *Detail* section.
   (c) A calculated field is created with a text box control.
   (d) A form's title is usually created with the title control.

10. To organize your data in categories, you would use:

    (a) Sorting.
    (b) Grouping.
    (c) Queries.
    (d) Calculated fields.

You are working on a database that will track speakers for a national conference. The data entry person entered information in the Speakers table incorrectly. He entered the first half of a new record correctly, but then jumped to a different record and overwrote the existing information with incorrect data. When you discovered the error, it took you a long time to find the correct information and correct both records. You decide that a form would help your co-workers enter data more accurately and help eliminate these types of errors. You create a form that will help the office staff add new speakers and sessions to the database as plans are finalized. After creating the form, you will customize it to be more user-friendly. If you have problems, reread the detailed directions presented in the chapter. This exercise follows the same set of skills as used in Hands-On Exercises 1 and 2 in the chapter. Refer to Figure 52 as you complete this exercise.

**FIGURE 52** Sessions and Speakers Form in Form View ➤

a. Open *a04p1natconf*. Click the **File tab**, click **Save Database As**, and then type **a04p1natconf_LastnameFirstname**. Click **Save**.

b. Open the Speakers table, and then replace *Your_Name* with your name in the First Name and Last Name fields. Close the Speakers table.

c. Open the Sessions and Speakers query in Datasheet view, and then review the data.

d. Close the query; make sure it remains selected.

e. Click the **Create tab**, and then click **Form** in the Forms group to create a new form that opens in Layout view.

f. Click the **SpeakerID box**. Drag the right border of the first field to the left to shrink the column by 50%.

g. Right-click the **SessionID box**, and then select **Select Entire Row** from the list. Drag the **SessionID control** up to the first position.

h. Right-click the **SessionTitle box**, and then select **Select Entire Row** from the list. Drag the **SessionTitle** up to the second position.

i. Remove the stacked layout of the form as follows:
   - Switch to Design view.
   - Click the **SessionID label**.
   - Click **Select Layout** in the Rows & Columns group on the Arrange tab.
   - Click **Remove Layout** in the Table group.

j. Modify and reposition the controls as follows:
   - Switch to Layout view.
   - Click the **SessionID box**.
   - Drag the right border of the SessionID text box to the left to shrink the control to about 1/2" wide.
   - Click the **SessionTitle box**.
   - Drag the left border of the Understanding Diversity text box to the right to reduce the size of the control by 1/2".
   - Drag the **SessionTitle box** up and position it even with the SessionID control, as shown in Figure 52.
   - Rename the *SessionID* label as **Session:**
   - Delete the SessionTitle label.

k. Switch to Form view.

l. Click the **SessionID box**. Click **Ascending** in the Sort & Filter group. Click **Next Record** in the Navigation bar several times to verify the records are now ordered by SessionID.

m. Switch to Design view.

n. Add a message to the bottom of the form as follows:
   - Place the mouse on the bottom edge of the Form Footer bar so the mouse pointer changes to the double-arrow resizing shape. Drag the **Form Footer section** down to **2"**.
   - Click **Label** in the Controls group.
   - Click in the **Form Footer** on the 1" horizontal line, approximately 1/4" from the left edge.
   - Type **To register for a session, contact Steve Jones at sjones@yahoo.com**.
   - Compare the position of the new label to Figure 52.

o. Click **View** in the Views group to switch to Form view. Click **Next Record** in the Navigation bar to verify the new message appears on every record.

p. Save the form as **Sessions and Speakers**. Close the form and any other open objects.

q. Click the **File tab**, and then click **Compact & Repair Database**.

r. Close the database. Exit Access.

s. Submit based on your instructor's directions.

## 2 Comfort Insurance

The Human Resources department of the Comfort Insurance Agency has initiated its annual employee performance reviews. The reviews affect employee salary increases and bonuses. The employee data, along with forms and reports, are stored in an Access database. You need to prepare a report showing employee raises and bonuses by city. This exercise follows the same set of skills as used in Hands-On Exercises 1, 3, and 4 in the chapter. Refer to Figure 53 as you complete this exercise.

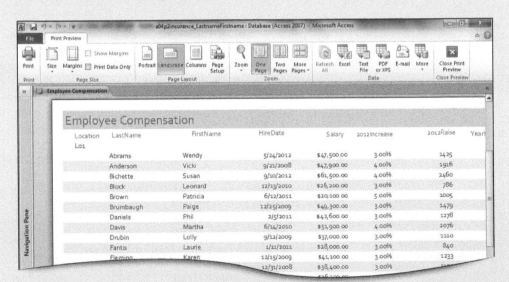

**FIGURE 53** Employee Compensation Report with Totals ➤

a. Open *a04p2insurance*. Click the **File tab**, click **Save Database As**, and then type **a04p2insurance_LastnameFirstname**. Click **Save**.

b. Select the **Locations table**. Click the **Create tab**, and then click **Form** in the Forms group to create a new form that opens in Layout view.

c. Click the **LocationID text box** containing *L01*. Move the mouse to the right edge of the orange border until the mouse pointer changes to a double-headed arrow. Drag the right edge to the left to reduce the size of the text box to approximately 50% of its original size.

d. Click the subform at the bottom of the form, and then click the **Layout Selector** (the small square with a four-headed arrow inside). Press **Delete** to delete the subform.

e. Click **Themes** in the Themes group on the Design tab. Right-click a **Solstice theme** (second column, second row from bottom), and then choose **Apply Theme to This Object Only**.

f. Save the form as **Locations**. Close the form.

g. Select the **Locations table**. Click the **Create tab**, and then click **Report** in the Reports group to create a new tabular layout report in Layout view.

h. Click the **Locations label**, and then drag the right border of the label to the left to reduce the size of the control to **50%**.

i. Repeat the sizing process with the Zipcode label and the OfficePhone label. Adjust the other columns if necessary until there are no controls on the right side of the vertical dashed line.

j. Display the report in Print Preview. Verify that the report is only one page wide. Close and save the report using the name **Locations**.

k. Select the **Employee Query**. Click the **Create tab**, and then click **Report Wizard** in the Reports group to launch the Report Wizard. Respond to the questions as follows:
   - Click (>>) to add all the fields to the Selected Fields box. Click **Next**.
   - Accept grouping by Location. Click **Next**.
   - Select **LastName** for the first sort order and **FirstName** for the second. Click **Summary Options**.
   - Click **Sum** for Salary, **Avg** for 2012Increase, and **Avg** for YearsWorked. Click **OK**. Click **Next**.
   - Accept the Stepped layout. Change Orientation to **Landscape**. Click **Next**.
   - Type **Employee Compensation** for the title of the report. Click **Finish**.
   - The Report is displayed in Print Preview mode. Some of the columns are too narrow. Next, you will adjust the columns and summary controls.

l. Click **Close Print Preview**. Switch to Layout view.

m. Adjust the column widths so that all the data values are showing. Some of the columns will need to be reduced and some will need to be widened. Change the YearsWorked label to **Years**. Use Figure 53 as a guide.

n. Adjust the Summary controls at the bottom of the first Location (L01) so all the values are visible. Adjust the Summary controls in the Report Footer so all the values are visible. Align all the Summary controls with their associated detail columns.

o. Open the Property Sheet. Click the **Avg Of YearsWorked control**, and then select **Fixed** for the Format property and **0** for the Decimal Places property.

p. Click **Themes** in the Themes group. Right-click the **Module theme** (first column, fourth row from bottom), and then choose **Apply Theme to This Object Only**.

q. Display the report in Print Preview. Close the Navigation Pane, and then verify that the report is still one page wide. Compare your report to Figure 53. Adjust column widths if necessary.

r. Save and close the Employee Compensation report.

s. Click the **File tab**, and then click **Compact & Repair Database**.

t. Close the database. Exit Access.

u. Submit based on your instructor's directions.

You are the general manager of a large hotel chain. You track revenue by categories: hotel rooms, conference rooms, and weddings. You need to create a report that shows which locations are earning the most revenue in each category. You also need to create a form that will enable you to enter and maintain member data for those guests who pay an annual fee in exchange for discounts and hotel privileges. Refer to Figure 54 as you complete this exercise.

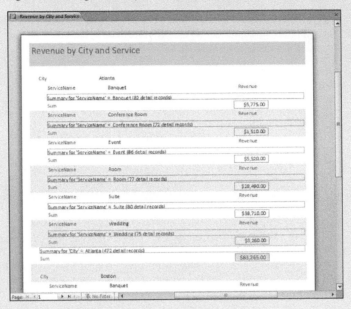

**FIGURE 54** Revenue by City and Service, Summary Only ➤

a. Open *a04m1rewards*. Click the **File tab**, click **Save Database As**, and then type **a04m1rewards_ LastnameFirstname**. Click **Save**.

b. Select the **Members table**, and then create a Multiple Items form. Save the form as **Maintain Members**.

c. Modify the form in Layout view as follows:
   • Reduce the row height by 50%.
   • Change the MemNumber label to **MemID**, and then reduce the MemNumber column width.
   • Adjust the column widths to eliminate extra white space.
   • Delete the form icon in the Form Header.

d. Switch to Design view, and then modify the form as follows:
   • Open the Property sheet, and then click the **Members title control** to change the Width property to **2.5"**.
   • Add the special effect **Raised** to the **Members title control**.
   • Increase the Form Footer to 1/2".
   • Add a new label control to the left side of the Form Footer.
   • Type **Form created by** *your name.*
   • Reduce the width of the form to **12"** (reduce the e-mail column width, if necessary).
   • Add today's date to the right side of the Form Header using the **Date and Time command** in the Header/Footer group.

e. Switch to Form view. Verify that the controls in the *Header* and *Footer* sections remain constant as you advance through the records. Close and save the form.

f. Select the **Revenue query**, and then create a report using the Report Wizard. Answer the wizard prompts as follows:
   • Include all fields.
   • Add grouping by City and by ServiceName.
   • Add a Sum to the Revenue field.
   • Check the **Summary Only option**.

- Choose **Outline Layout**.
- Name the report **Revenue by City and Service**.

g. Scroll through all the pages to check the layout of the report while in Print Preview mode.

h. Switch to Design view, and then delete the NoInParty and PerPersonCharge controls in the *Detail* and *ServiceName Header* sections. Drag the remaining controls in the *ServiceName Header* section to the top of the section. Reduce the height of the *ServiceName Header* section as shown in Figure 54.

i. Open the Property Sheet, and then use the Width property to change the width of the Revenue control in the *Detail* section to **1.0"**, the width of the Sum of Revenue control in the ServiceName Footer to **1.0"**, the width of the Sum of Revenue1control in the City Footer to **1.0"**, and the width of the Revenue Grand Total Sum control in the Report Footer to **1.0"**.

j. Click each of the revenue controls while holding down **Shift**, and then set the Format property of all the selected controls to **Currency**.

k. Change the font size, font color, and background color of the Sum of Revenue1 control in the City Footer so the control stands out from the other controls.

l. Apply a different style to the Grand Total Sum control in the Report Footer.

m. Close and save the report.

n. Compact and repair the database.

o. Close the database. Exit Access.

p. Submit based on your instructor's directions.

## 2 Philadelphia National Bank

You are the manager of the loan department at Philadelphia National Bank (PNB). PNB issues mortgages, car loans, and personal loans to its customers. The bank's database contains the records of all of the customer loans. You need to create a form to manage the customer list. You also need to create a report that summarizes the loan payments by month. Refer to Figure 55 as you complete this exercise.

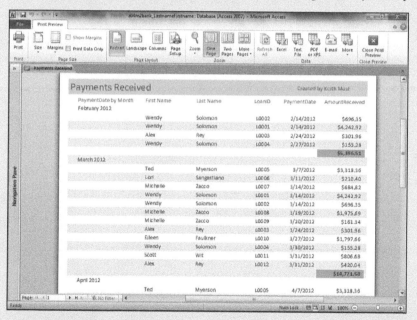

**FIGURE 55** Payments Received Report ▶

a. Open *a04m2bank*. Click the **File tab**, click **Save Database As**, and then type **a04m2bank_LastnameFirstname**. Click **Save**.

b. Create a form based on the Customers table. Access automatically adds the Loans subform to the bottom of the Customers form.

c. Close the form, but do not save it.

DISCOVER

d. Open the Relationships window, and then find the relationship between Customers and Loans (this relationship caused the subform to appear in step b). Double-click the join line, and then make a note of which check boxes are checked in the Edit Relationships dialog box. Close the dialog box. Right-click the join line, select **Delete**, and then click **Yes** to confirm deletion. Save the relationship changes. Create the Customers form again and notice the subform is not there. Save the form as **Customers**, and then close it. Restore the relationships.

e. Open the Customers form in Layout view. Reduce the size of the text box controls by 50%, and then close and save the form.

f. Select the **Payments Received query**, and then create a report using the Report Wizard. Include all fields, view data by Payments, add grouping by PaymentDate, skip the sorting step, accept the default layout, and name the report **Payments Received**.

g. Switch to Design view, and then add a label to the right side of the Report Header that says **Created by** *your name*. Switch to Layout view.

h. Click the **AmountReceived field**, and then click **Totals** in the Grouping & Totals group. Select **Sum** from the list of options.

i. Add a different style to the AccessTotalsAmountReceived control so it stands out from the other controls. Add a light gray box around the AccessTotalsAmountReceived1 control.

j. Close the Navigation Pane, preview the report, and then adjust column widths as needed. Close and save the report.

k. Compact and repair the database.

l. Close the database. Exit Access.

m. Submit based on your instructor's directions.

Your boss asked you to prepare a schedule for each speaker for the national conference being hosted next year on your campus. She wants to mail the schedules to the speakers so that they can provide feedback on the schedule prior to its publication. You assure her that you can accomplish this task with Access.

## Database File Setup

You need to copy an original database file, rename the copied file, and then open the copied database to complete this capstone exercise. After you open the copied database, you replace an existing employee's name with your name.

a. Open *a04c1natconf*.

b. Click the **File tab**, click **Save Database As**, and then type **a04c1natconf_LastnameFirstname**. Click **Save**.

c. Open the Speakers table.

d. Find and replace *Your_Name* with your name. Close the table.

## Create a Form

You need to create a form to add and update Speakers. Use the Form tool to create the form, and then modify the form as explained.

a. Select the **Speakers table** as the record source for the form.

b. Use the **Form tool** to create a new stacked form.

c. Change the title to **Enter/Edit Speakers**.

d. Reduce the width of the text box controls to **50%**.

e. Delete the Sessions subform.

f. Add a new label control in the Form Footer that says **Contact Elaine Carey if you have questions about Speakers**.

g. View the form and data in Form view. Sort the records by LastName. Locate your record.

h. Save the form as **Edit Speakers**. Close the form.

## Create a Report

You need to create a report based on the Speaker and Room Schedule query. You decide to use the Report Wizard to accomplish this task.

a. Select the **Speaker and Room Schedule query** as the record source for the report.

b. Activate the **Report Wizard** and use the following options as you go through the Wizard:
   • Select all of the available fields for the report.
   • View the data by Speakers.
   • Verify that LastName and FirstName will provide grouping levels.
   • Use **Date** as the primary sort field.
   • Accept the **Stepped** and **Portrait options**.
   • Name the report **Speaker Schedule**.
   • Switch to Layout view, and apply the **Module theme** to only this report.

c. Preview the report, and then adjust the column widths if necessary.

d. Close and save the report.

## Add an Additional Field

You realize the session times were not included in the query. You add the field to the query and then start over with the Report Wizard.

a. Open the Speaker and Room Schedule query in Design view.

b. Add the **StartingTime field** in the Sessions table to the design grid. Run the query.

c. Close and save the query.

d. Start the Report Wizard again and use the following options:
   • Select the **Speaker and Room Schedule query**.
   • Select all of the available fields for the report.
   • View the data by Speakers.
   • Use the **LastName, FirstName fields** as the primary grouping level.
   • Use **Date** as the primary sort field.
   • Use **StartingTime** as the secondary sort field.
   • Select the **Stepped** and **Portrait options**.
   • Name the report **Speaker Schedule Revised**.
   • Switch to Layout view, and then apply the **Trek theme** to only this report.

e. Adjust the column widths in Layout View so that all the data is visible.

f. Increase the width of the StartingTime label control in the *Page Header* section in Design view, so that the entire phrase is visible. Add a space to the column heading labels as needed.

g. Close and save the report. Compact the database.

h. Close the database. Exit Access.

i. Submit based on your instructor's directions.

# BEYOND THE CLASSROOM

### Inventory Value

GENERAL CASE

The owner of a bookstore asked for your help with her database. Her insurance company asked her to provide an inventory report listing the values of the books she has in stock. Open *a04b1books*. Click the File tab, click Save Database As, and then type **a04b1books_LastnameFirstname**. Click Save. Use the skills you learned in this chapter to create three stacked layout forms for Authors, Publishers, and Books. Delete any attached subforms. Next, create the inventory report that shows the inventory values for the books on hand. The database contains a query that you can use to create the report. Group the records by publisher name; alphabetize authors by last name and first name within groups. Name the report **Bookstore Inventory Value**. In Layout view, create a total value control for each publisher and create a grand total. Resize and reposition the total controls so they are visible and aligned with the correct column. Add Currency formatting where applicable, and then modify column headings as needed. Preview the report and verify that all the columns are correct, and then save and close the report. Compact and repair the database, and then close the database and close Access. Submit based on your instructor's directions.

### Create Mailing Labels

RESEARCH CASE

This chapter introduced you to Access reports. Use Access Help to search for mailing labels. Then put your new knowledge to the test. Open *a04b2arbor*. Click the File tab, click Save Database As, and then type **a04b2arbor_LastnameFirstname**. Click Save. It contains a query identifying volunteers who will be invited to this year's gala. Your challenge is to print the names and addresses as mailing labels in the format shown below. You already purchased Avery 5260 labels. Sort the labels by lastname, firstname. Name the report **Volunteer Invitation Labels**. After you create the labels, preview them and verify everything will fit onto the 5260 label template. Save and close the label report. Compact and repair the database, and then close the database and close Access. Submit based on your instructor's directions.

Label format:
Mr. (Dr., Ms., Mrs.,) John Doe, Jr.
Street Address
City, State Postal Code

### Real Estate Development Report

DISASTER RECOVERY

A co-worker is having difficulty with an Access report and asked you for your assistance. Open *a04b3property*. Click the File tab, click Save Database As, and then type **a04b3property_LastnameFirstname**. Click Save. The database contains the Sales Report query that was used to create the Sales by Agent report. The report is supposed to show each agent's total sales grouped by Subdivision. There should be totals for the sale price, the sales commissions, and the list price columns for each subdivision and each agent. The Percent of List should be averaged for each subdivision and each agent. Find and correct the errors. If you are unable to correct the errors, try creating the report again using the Report Wizard. Compact and repair the database, close the database, and then close Access. Submit based on your instructor's directions.

# Index